Business Communication

Building Critical Skills

Kitty O. Locker
The Ohio State University

Stephen Kyo Kaczmarek
Columbus State Community College

Kathryn Braun
Sheridan College

 **McGraw-Hill Ryerson**

Toronto Montréal Boston Burr Ridge, IL Dubuque, IA
Madison, WI New York San Francisco St. Louis Bangkok Bogotá
Caracas Kuala Lumpur Lisbon London Madrid Mexico City
Milan New Delhi Santiago Seoul Singapore Sydney Taipei

Dedication
For my husband, Bob Mills, with love.
—Kitty O. Locker

For my father, who always believes in me.
—Stephen Kyo Kaczmarek

For Frank and Tina
—Kathryn Braun

McGraw-Hill Higher Education

*A Division of The **McGraw-Hill** Companies*

BUSINESS COMMUNICATION
Building Critical Skills
First Canadian Edition

ISBN: 0-07-088058-1

1 2 3 4 5 6 7 8 9 10 TCP 0 9 8 7 6 5 4 3 2

Printed and bound in Canada

Statistics Canada information is used with the permission of the Minister of Industry, as Minister responsible for Statistics Canada. Information on the availability of the wide range of data from the Statistics Canada can be obtained from Statistics Canada's Regional Offices, its World Wide Web site at http://www.statcan.ca, and its toll-free access number 1-800-263-1136.

The Conference Board of Canada
Insights You Can Count On

The Conference Board of Canada's Employability Skills 2000+ are used with the permission of The Conference Board of Canada. Information about The Conference Board of Canada is available at http://www.conferenceboard.ca/

Care has been taken to trace ownership of copyright material contained in this text; however, the publisher will welcome any information that enables them to rectify any reference or credit for subsequent editions.

Vice President and Editorial Director: Pat Ferrier
Senior Sponsoring Editor: Veronica Visentin
Senior Developmental Editor: Lesley Mann
Marketing Manager: James Buchanan
Supervising Editor: Carrie Withers
Copy Editor: Karen Hunter
Production Coordinator: Emily Hickey
Composition: VISU*TronX*
Cover Design: Greg Devitt
Interior Design: Elise Lansdon/Greg Devitt
Art Direction: Dianna Little
Printer: Transcontinental Printing Group

Canadian Cataloguing in Publication Data

Locker, Kitty O.
    Business communication: building critical skills

1st Canadian ed.
Includes bibliographical references and index.
ISBN 0-07-088058-1

1. Business communication. 2. Business writing.
2. Communication in organizations. I. Braun, Kathryn, 1947-
II. Kaczmarek, Stephen Kyo III. Title.

HF5718.L63   2001   658.4'5   C2001-901532-1

Brief Contents

Unit Seven

Job Hunting 532

Contents

Unit **One**
Building Effective Messages   2

Module **1**

Module **2**

Module **3**

Module 11

Module 12

Module 13

Unit Four
Polishing Your Writing   298

Module 14

Editing for Grammar and Punctuation   298

Module 15

Choosing the Right Word   324

Module 16

Editing Sentences and Paragraphs   338

Unit Five
Interpersonal Communication 360

Unit Six

Research, Reports, and Visuals　430

Module 21

Module 22

Module 23

Contents

About the Authors

Kitty O. Locker is an Associate Professor of English at The Ohio State University, where she teaches courses in workplace discourse and research methods. She received her B.A. from DePauw University and her M.A. and Ph.D. from the University of Illinois at Urbana. She has also written *Business and Administrative Communication* (5th ed., Irwin/McGraw-Hill, 2000), *The Irwin Business Communication Handbook: Writing and Speaking in Business Classes* (1993), and co-edited *Conducting Research in Business Communication* (1988). Her consulting clients include URS Greiner, Abbott Laboratories, the Ohio Civil Service Employees Association, AT&T, and the American Medical Association. In 1994–95, she served as President of the Association for Business Communication (ABC). From 1997 to 2001, she edited ABC's *Journal of Business Communication*. She received ABC's Outstanding Researcher Award in 1992 and ABC's Meada Gibbs Outstanding Teacher Award in 1998.

Stephen Kyo Kaczmarek is on the faculty of Columbus State Community College. He teaches business and technical communication, composition, creative writing, journalism, public relations, freshman experience, and courses in film and literature he has designed. Steve received an M.A. in English and B.A.s in journalism and English from Ohio State. His consulting clients have included Nationwide Insurance, The Ohio Historical Society, The Ohio Association of Historical Societies and Museums, The Ohio Museums Association, United Energy Systems, The Thomas Moyer for Chief Justice of Ohio Campaign, and Van Meter and Associates. Prior to joining Columbus State, Steve managed staff development and information for the Franklin County, Ohio, Commissioners. He received an Award of Excellence from the National Association of County Information Officers. A movie buff, Steve has also appeared in educational videos and television commercials.

Kathryn Braun is a professor at Sheridan College and has taught interpersonal and business communications to postsecondary students in every discipline, including the arts, business, community and health services, computer studies, journalism, and public relations. She received her Honours B.A. from McMaster University and her Masters degree from the University of Toronto. Kathryn has published articles on communications and the media, authored a variety of multi-media education and distance education texts, and is the co-author of *The Report Writer's Manual*. Through her consulting business, communicore inc., Kathryn facilitates customized training in contemporary business communications for corporate and small business clients. Her areas of expertise include business language and culture, communication formats, international and non-verbal communications, negotiating and presentation skills. For more information, visit the communicore Web site at http://www.communicore.on.ca.

August 2001

Dear Reader:

Business Communication: Building Critical Skills encourages you to practice the thinking, writing, speaking, and listening skills considered crucial for success in the workplace.

As you read,

- Use the chapter features to guide your learning: 1) read the chapter-opening questions; 2) look for the answers to these questions; 3) Use the **Instant Replays** to test your memory of these concepts; 4) revisit the concepts in the **Review of Key Points** at the end of the module.

- Pay particular attention to terms in bold type; carefully review their definitions. Use the **rewind** and **fast forward** icons to go to discussion of terms.

- Carefully read the **Building a Critical Skill** boxes and practice these strategies both in assignments and on your own. These skills will serve you well for the rest of your life.

- Use items in the lists when you prepare your assignments or to review for tests.

- Use the examples, especially the paired examples of effective and ineffective communication, as models to help you draft and revise. Comments in red ink identify drafts in an example; comments in blue ink note revisions.

- Read the **Sites to See** and **FYI** boxes in the margins for resources on the Internet and facts about contemporary business communications.

The Conference Board of Canada
Insights You Can Count On

- Review the list of skills from the Conference Board of Canada's Employability Skills 2000+ to ensure you understand the knowledge, skills, and attitudes that will help you achieve your employment goals.

As you prepare an assignment,

- Review the PAIBOC questions in Module 1 and throughout the book. Some assignments have "Hints" to help probe the problem. Some of the longer assignments have preliminary assignments analyzing the audience or developing reader benefits or subject lines. Use these exercises to help you develop the various elements and sections of a larger document.

- If you're writing a letter or memo, read the sample problems in Modules 10, 11, and 12, together with their analyses and solutions, to explore how to apply the principles in this book to your own writing.

August 2001
Page 2

 • Use the **Polishing Your Prose** exercises to review grammar, punctuation and usage and to make your writing its best.

• Remember that most problems are open-ended, requiring original, critical thinking. Many of the problems are deliberately written in negative, ineffective language. You'll need to reword sentences, reorganize information, and think through the situation to produce the best possible solution to the business problem.

• Learn as much as you can about what's happening in business. The knowledge will not only help you develop reader benefits and provide examples but will also make you an even more impressive candidate in job interviews.

 • Visit the Online Learning Centre (http://www.mcgrawhill.ca/college/locker) to see how the resources presented there can help you. You will find updated articles, résumé and letter templates, links to job hunting Web sites, and much more.

Communication skills form the foundation for success in your personal and professional life, in both the new economy and the old. *Business Communication: Building Critical Skills* can help you identify and practice these skills.

Sincerely,

Kitty O. Locker
locker.1@osu.edu

Stephen Kyo Kaczmarek
kaz11111@hotmail.com

Kathryn Braun
communicore@accglobal.net

Business Communication
Building Critical Skills

August 2001

Dear Professor:

Business Communication: Building Critical Skills (BCS) makes business communications relevant to Canadian students. It accomplishes this objective while encouraging an interactive, experiential learning experience.

BCS's design and supplement package also makes it easy to integrate this text into your course. Its modular design is adaptable to five-, eight-, ten-, fifteen-, or twenty-week courses. Its video, new media tools, and supplements allow for easy integration with Internet courses.

Additional features that learners find useful are also here: contemporary anecdotes and examples, easy-to-follow lists, annotated sample documents, integrated coverage of national and international business communications, analyses of sample problems, and a wealth of in-class exercises and out-of-class assignments.

You'll find *BCS* a rich teaching resource because each module also provides:

- relevant experiences of Canadians who work in large, small, for-profit and not-for-profit businesses
- expert advice on every aspect of contemporary communications
- cross-referencing of the module's learning focus with the knowledge, skills and attitudes specified by the Conference Board of Canada's Employability Skills 2000+
- Up-to-date Web citations for students' national and international research

Other material that has been incorporated in response to your requests includes,

- **Module 3's** examination of Canadian business norms that we may often take for granted. This is just one example of how the text reflects the diversity of the Canadian workplace. This focus is maintained throughout the text's models, examples and assignments.
- **Module 19's** practical teamwork tips and techniques to guide group project management
- **Module 22's** research, analysis and documentation information useful for every discipline
- **Modules 26 to 30's** employability skills inform students throughout the job search process.

Each module of *BCS* contains several helpful features designed to help students understand and retain the contents under discussion. These features include:

The Conference Board of Canada
Insights You Can Count On

- Building Critical Skills boxes that describe work-world applications
- Polishing Your Prose boxes, featuring straightforward instructions to help students correct common writing errors, as well as exercises to test what they know
- Skills from the Conference Board of Canada's Employability Skills 2000+ that apply to the main module topics are set out at the end of each module
- FYI boxes that provide insights into current business communication practise

August 2001
Page 2

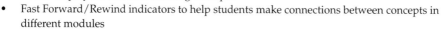

- Site to See boxes that invite students to use the Internet for timely information
- Instant Replays to reinforce learning concepts
- Fast Forward/Rewind indicators to help students make connections between concepts in different modules

BCS, First Canadian Edition, also includes a comprehensive package of supplements to help you and your students.

- An Instructor's Resource Manual (adapted for Canada by Kathryn Braun, the Canadian author of the text) with sample syllabi, an overview of each module, suggested lecture topics, in-class exercises, examples and transparency masters, discussion and quiz questions, and solutions to problems. (ISBN 0-07-088059x)
- A Test Bank featuring hundreds of questions for use in quizzes, midterms, and final examinations—with answers. The Test Bank is also available in a computerized format that allows you to create and edit your own tests. (ISBN 007-0880611; computerized test bank 007-088062x)
- CBC Video Cases, including seven brief (4-8 minutes each) segments from the CBC's renowned business affairs program *Venture*, and *Undercurrents*, its cutting-edge media show. Students will be entertained and impressed by these illustrations of real-life issues in Canadian business, focusing especially on interactive skills such as office etiquette and teamwork. Cases prepared by Susan Lieberman of Grant MacEwan College. (Available for online viewing via the Online Learning Centre)
- A video that includes segments on presentation skills, the job interview, and nonverbal messages. A brief instructor's manual to accompany this video is on the book's Online Learning Centre.
- Electronic Presentations in Microsoft® PowerPoint®, showing key figures from the text (and good and bad examples of PowerPoint design). Adapted for the first Canadian edition by Christine Frank of Georgian College. (ISBN 007-0890536)
- An Online Learning Centre with self-quizzes for students, e-learning sessions, Internet exercises, additional exercises, hyperlinks to all Web sites referenced in the textbook's Sites to See feature, online glossary, generic self-assessment activities, résumé and letter templates, career corner, links to professional resources, and sample letters, memos and emails. Instructors' resources include current articles and research in business communication, downloadable supplements, links to professional resources, and more. Content adapted by Christine Frank of Georgian College. (http://www.mcgrawhill.ca/college/locker)

We've done our best to provide you with comprehensive and easy-to-use teaching tools. Please tell us about your own success stories using *Business Communication: Building Critical Skills*, First Canadian Edition. We look forward to hearing from you!

Sincerely,

Kitty O. Locker
locker.1@osu.edu

Stephen Kyo Kaczmarek
kaz11111@hotmail.com

Kathryn Braun
communicore@accglobal.net

Acknowledgments

All writing is in some sense collaborative. This book in particular builds upon the ideas and advice of teachers, students, and researchers. The people who share their ideas in conferences and publications enrich not only this book but also business communications as a field.

People who contributed directly to the formation of the first Canadian edition include the following:

Vicky Day, Northern Alberta Institute of Technology
Raymond Desrosiers, Canadore College
Kendra Carmichael, Acadia University
Susan Lieberman, Grant MacEwan College
Andrea Lovering, Georgian College
Lynn Morrisey, Memorial University
Marion Ross, Georgian College
Heather Thompson, St. Mary's University
Panteli Tritchew, Kwantlen University College
Mary Clare Vautour, New Brunswick Community College—Moncton

Other important members of our team include everyone at McGraw-Hill Ryerson who contributed to the development of the book: Veronica Visentin, Senior Sponsoring Editor; Lesley Mann, Senior Development Editor; Karen Hunter, Copy Editor; Stephanie Hess and Carole Harfst, Editorial Coordinators; Carrie Withers, Supervising Editor; Emily Hickey, Production Coordinator; Nicla Dattolico, Production Supervisor; and Greg Devitt, Designer. The assistance and advice of Sarah Reed, Development Editor for the U.S. edition, was also much appreciated.

Finally, a special thank-you to Bernie Koenig, Fanshawe College, who prepared the vignettes at the start of each module, and to Janet Fear, Sheridan College, for her invaluable advice.

Kathryn Braun

Kathryn Braun
August 2001

Unit One

Building Effective Messages

Module 1
Introduction to Business Communication

Topics

- What is business communication?
- Will I really have to write?
- What is an effective message?
- How do I begin to analyze communications situations?

Review of Key Points

Learning Applications

Polishing Your Prose: Sentence Fragments

Learning Focus

After reading and applying the information in Module 1, you'll be able to demonstrate

Knowledge of

- Contemporary Canadian employability skills
- The forms, applications, and rewards of effective communication skills
- The purposes of communications
- The key communication questions

Skills to

- Reflect on your own current communication skills
- Establish realistic goals for building on those skills
- Analyze the purpose, audience, context, and form of your messages
- Identify and analyze communication situations

"Two things are important: using one's critical skills and having an insatiable curiosity."

"Communicators have the job of creating meaning from information for people who are too busy to be able to do it themselves, or who do not have the background. Communicators must be clear about what is said and who said it."

These are the words of Peter Snow, founder of the Syndicon Group, a communication consulting firm based outside London, Ontario. Clients range from non-profit organizations to large corporations such as Bayer where he publishes newsletters for both employees and customers. Peter describes this job as "asking questions that might be considered stupid of a chemist so I can explain to an engineer what he is doing."

Peter uses what he calls an interpersonal model of communications with a journalistic approach. Journalists are supposed to use analytical skills to find the truth. An interpersonal approach treats the communicator and the communicatee—the speaker and listener—as equals. "If an interpersonal approach is not used then knowledge becomes power and the communicator controls the situation. This is not true communication. This point holds true in newsletters, in communications between employers and employees and between teachers and students."

Peter is articulate and loves to talk about the communication process. He proves to be an excellent communicator—

not surprisingly, as Peter's Ph.D. dissertation from Queen's University was on the politics of interpersonal communication. After receiving his degree he taught in the graduate journalism program at the University of Western Ontario. In 1981 Peter founded the Syndicon Group as a place where communicators could pursue their own interests in a cooperative manner. Soon the demand for the services of the group forced him into working in the business full-time.

Peter's academic background in communication theory and journalism and his professional experience with the Syndicon Group lead him to emphasize that the effective communicator must overcome psychological and sociological barriers to communication. This is done not just by using one's critical and interpersonal skills, but by realizing that communication is not just words on a page. The format, the means of presentation, the visual aspects of the page, the body language of the speaker are all aspects of the communication process. It is not just what is said, but how it is said that counts.

When asked for his advice to communication students, Peter says, "Two things are important: using one's critical skills and having an insatiable curiosity. These lead to a commitment to lifelong learning." And, we hope, great communication skills.

 http://www.syndicon.on.ca/
Syndicon Group

All human activity requires communication. People communicate to dream about, plan, transform, and reflect on their lives. Working people communicate to develop, improve, and expand products and services; to establish and maintain meaningful relationships; to hire, train, orient, and motivate colleagues; to coordinate production, manufacturing, and delivery; to persuade customers to buy and to bill them for their purchases.

Many businesses and non-profit, community and government organizations offer information or services rather than tangible products; nonetheless, information and services are created, marketed, and delivered through communications. People communicate to express themselves, to get work done, to gain recognition, and to make meaning of their lives.

People communicate to **make meaning** in a variety of simple and complex ways. Communicating with words, for example, can be formal and informal:

- Speaking (face-to-face, on the phone, by voicemail)
- Active listening (paraphrasing, asking questions, giving feedback)
- Meeting (meal-time conversations, conferences, hall meetings)
- Reading (for information, knowledge, and pleasure)
- Writing (letters, email, memos, proposals, reports)

Non-verbal communication—older, more frequent and more pervasive than words—encompasses all other communication symbols, including:

- Facial expressions, gestures, posture, and personal adornment
- Use of time and space
- *How* we say what we say, or *paralanguage*: tone, inflection, rate and volume of speech, vocal interferences, pauses, and "uptalk" (a rising inflection at the end of a sentence)
- An individual's choice of seats in the classroom or at a meeting
- Organizational logos, use of colour, space, office design, pictures, and decor
- A culture's cityscape, including layout, building design, pedestrian, bicycle and handicapped access, greenery and parks, housing, and sidewalks

From the moment you were born (and some claim even before) your primary purpose has been to connect through communication. Even in your very first job you had to communicate. Whether operating your lemonade stand or waiting tables to pay your way through school, you've had to comprehend, conceptualize, and realize ideas; listen to, interpret, understand and convey instructions; ask questions, provide feedback and support others in solving problems; make telephone and in-person inquiries; negotiate with customers and co-workers; perhaps write sales letters and make formal presentations.

Indeed, both The Conference Board of Canada and The U.S. Secretary's Commission on Achieving Necessary Skills (SCANS) identify sophisticated communications skills as one of the keys to careers in the twenty-first century. (See page 17 for the complete text of The Conference Board of Canada's Employability Skills 2001+. The skills that are pertinent to each module of this book are included as a checklist at the end of each module.)

In his study *Education and Technological Revolution: The Role of the Social Sciences and the Humanities in the Knowledge-based Economy*, University of British Columbia economics professor Robert Allen finds that social sciences and humanities grads are the most sought after in today's knowledge-based economy. "Demand is increasing for those workers who can…understand the information generated by computer

Dell works to build enthusiasm. Talented people who are excited about what they do give companies a compettitive advantage. Here, managers dash to a meeting.

Thinking Creatively

Creative thinkers perceive the world imagina-tively. Because change is the only constant in to-day's workplace, the ability to bring a fresh per-spective to situations is essential for success. For example,

- Before Nortel Networks' reversal of fortune, the company's creative approach guaranteed a high employee retention rate. Nortel used a number of creative best practices to attract and keep staff—including providing travel prizes and spirituality rooms, each with a footbath, for employees of various religions in its Brampton, Ontario headquarters. Ranked first among Canada's 35 top employers in *Report on Business Magazine* and consulting firm Hewlett Associate's second annual survey, Nortel had an annual employee retention rate double that of the information technology industry average.

- Why not a "free" (advertisers pay) commuter paper? The *Metro's* successful North American launch in Philadelphia encouraged Swedish parent company Modern Times Group to provide subway papers to Canadian readers in Toronto, Vancouver, and Montreal. The *Toronto Sun* and the *Toronto Star* responded by producing their own free subway papers. Now Toronto, one of the most competitive newspaper markets in North America, can boast of five dailies!

- In 1991, Finnish student Linus Torvolds developed a computer operating system and posted the code online as an innovative response to the Microsoft monopoly. Today corporations including Corel, IBM, Dell Computer, and Red Hat Inc. are pursuing software applications initiatives based on the free, Linux open-source code.

Creative, right brain, or lateral thinking can be learned, like any skill, through application and practice. To increase your creativity, try brain-storming and mind-mapping techniques. (See Figure 1.1 for examples.) In particular, use the problem-solving model to learn how to analyze and identify problems in innovative ways.

IBM's tips for creativity are even more diverse:

- Have an argument
- Brainstorm with someone 10 years older and someone 10 years younger
- Clean your desk
- Come in early—enjoy the quiet
- Leave the office. Sit with just a pencil and a pad of paper. See what happens

Sources: "Newspaper wars flare up on subways," *The Globe and Mail*, July, 2000, B1, B5; "Destroying More Creatively" *Report on Business Magazine*, August 2000; visited Web site June 28, 2001, http://globeandmail.workopolis.com/servlet/News/robmag/20010126/RO02BES6; Liz Zack, "How IBM Gets Unstuck," *Fast Company*, October 1999, 104.

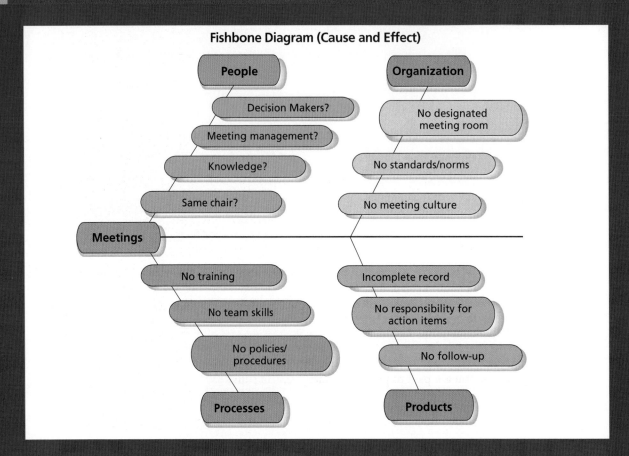

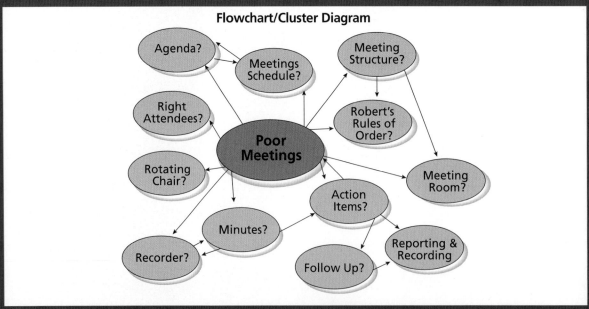

Figure 1.1
Problem-Solving Models Using "Poor Meetings" as an Example

systems, apply models to problems, deal effectively with customers and other members of a …team, speak and write clearly, and make informed and independent judgments."[1]

Moreover, good writers earn more. Linguist Stephen Reder has found that among people with two- or four-year degrees, workers in the top 20 percent of writing ability earn, on average, more than three times as much as workers whose writing falls into the worst 20 percent.[2]

Go to
http://www.sshrc.ca
The Social Sciences and Humanities Research Council (SSHRC) is Canada's primary granting council for social sciences and humanities research.

What is business communication?

Business communication focuses on making meaning to get the job done.

Every effective communication transaction must be tailored to its specific purpose and audience. But business communication demands even more rigorous conformity to audience expectations because "time is money": people resent spending their time interpreting or clarifying messages. Business messages are very different from the communication methods you learn in school.

Go to
http://www.conferenceboard.ca/nbec/pdf/esp2000.pdf
In a downloadable version of their Employability Skills 2000+ report, The Conference Board of Canada identifies communications as one of the key skills for work success.

Different Purposes

- In school, you speak and write to demonstrate that you have learned the course material. In business, people communicate to meet an organizational need or to go on record. No one will pay you to discuss or write something that he or she already knows. You are paid to produce, strategize, and summarize.

Different Audiences

- In school, your real audience is "an educated person", usually the teacher and the other students. If the teacher disagrees with your views, but you can support your them, you may still earn a good grade. It is the teacher's job to read your papers and he or she will read them even if they are boring.
- The audiences for business communication include people both inside and outside the organization (◀▶ Module 2). Real audiences read messages only if they seem important, relevant, and interesting. If the real audience doesn't read and understand the message, then it has failed.

Different Information

- The information contained in school writing may be new to you, but it is rarely new to your teacher. Information contained in business communication is, however, usually new to your reader. (If it isn't new, you will have to work to make it interesting.)

Different Organization

- Academic writing follows the traditional essay format: thesis, paragraphs of evidence, concluding paragraph. You're expected to pile on the proof, and teachers have a high degree of tolerance for lots of information.
- Business communication is organized to meet the psychological needs of the reader. The reader's first priority is to get the necessary information as quickly and easily as possible. In business you are rewarded for quality and conciseness. (◀▶ Modules 10–14).

Different Style

- The style for school writing is often formal. Big words, long sentences, and large paragraphs often earn marks.
- The style for business communication is friendly, not formal; small words, short sentences, and brief paragraphs establish your credibility and persuade the reader more readily to your point of view, as shown in Figure 1.2, below (◀▶ Modules 15 and 16).

Different Layout

- School writing often rewards long paragraphs. Papers are usually double-spaced, with no attention to visual design.
- Business people want to be able to skim documents for relevant information. Left justification, headings, bulleted lists, and single-spaced paragraphs with double-spacing between paragraphs help readers find information quickly (◀▶ Module 5).

Different Visuals

- Only a few academic courses require writing to contain anything other than words. Business writers are expected to choose the most effective way to convey information. Even a one-page memo may contain a table, graph, or other visual. You are expected to be able to use computer programs to create graphs, visuals, and slides for presentations (◀▶ Modules 5, 20, and 25).

Figure 1.2

Example of Typical Business Communication Style

Date:	September 28, 2001
To:	Lindsay Marshall
From:	Brandon Schraff
Subject:	Health and Safety Seminar

Thank you for arranging last week's health and safety seminar for plant personnel. You did a great job; feedback was most impressive and I've noticed that staff are applying what they have learned.

Lunch and Learn Ideas

For next month's lunch and learn, people suggested the following topics:

- Tips for time management

- Best management practices

- Email etiquette

- Negotiating strategies

Let me know your ideas, and let's talk after the management meeting next Thursday to decide on a topic.

Unless you have a fairy godmother, you'll need to know how to communicate.

Source: © The New Yorker Collection 1993 Warren Miller from cartoonbank.com.

What does business communication accomplish?

Communication makes business happen.

According to Canadian management guru Dr. Henry Mintzberg, managers have three basic jobs: to collect and convey information, to make decisions, and to promote interpersonal unity—that is, to make people want to work together to achieve organizational goals.[3] All of these jobs require communication in order to happen. Effective managers are able to use a wide variety of media and strategies to communicate. They know how to interpret comments from informal channels such as the company grapevine; they can speak effectively in small groups and in formal presentations; they write well.

Communication—oral, non-verbal, and written—goes to both internal and external audiences. **Internal audiences** (Figure 1.3 on page 10) are other people in the same organization: subordinates, superiors, peers. **External audiences** (Figure 1.4 also on page 10) are people outside the organization: customers, suppliers, unions, stockholders, potential employees, government agencies, the press, and the general public.

Figure 1.3
The Internal Audiences of the Sales Manager— West

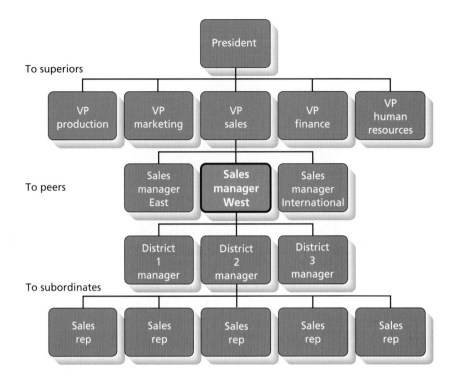

To superiors

To peers

To subordinates

President

VP production | VP marketing | VP sales | VP finance | VP human resources

Sales manager East | **Sales manager West** | Sales manager International

District 1 manager | District 2 manager | District 3 manager

Sales rep | Sales rep | Sales rep | Sales rep | Sales rep

Figure 1.4
The Corporation's External Audiences
Source: Daphne A. Jameson

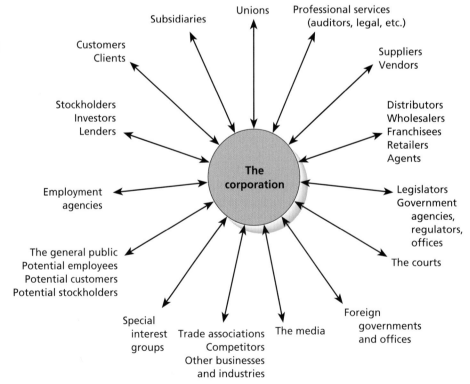

Subsidiaries

Unions

Professional services (auditors, legal, etc.)

Customers Clients

Suppliers Vendors

Stockholders Investors Lenders

Distributors Wholesalers Franchisees Retailers Agents

Employment agencies

The corporation

Legislators Government agencies, regulators, offices

The general public Potential employees Potential customers Potential stockholders

The courts

Special interest groups

Trade associations Competitors Other businesses and industries

The media

Foreign governments and offices

The Importance of Listening, Speaking, and Interpersonal Communication

Informal listening, speaking, and working in groups are just as important as writing formal documents and giving formal presentations. In every organization, you need to listen to others to find out what you're supposed to do, to learn the organization's values, and to establish and maintain supportive work relationships. Daily conversations about yesterday's game or about what's happening at work connect you to the **grapevine**, an informal source of company information. You may speak to small groups, inside or outside your organization.[4] Networking and working with others will be crucial to your success, because people prefer to do business with someone they know.

The Importance of Written Communication

People in organizations produce a large variety of documents to inform, request or persuade. When you **inform**, you explain or tell readers something. When you **request or persuade** you want the reader to act.

Your primary purpose, however, is to build goodwill with the reader—to create a positive image of you and your organization so that people will want to do business with you.

Most messages have multiple purposes:

- When answering a question, you're providing information, and you're also building goodwill by suggesting that you're competent since you know the correct answer.
- When responding to a customer's request for an invoice adjustment, whether your answer is yes or no, you want to build goodwill by suggesting that the reader's claim has been given careful consideration and that the decision is fair, businesslike, and justified.
- When preparing your résumé, you provide pertinent information to prove that you're qualified for the job. But your choices of layout, appearance, font type, and language can also emphasize your credibility enough to secure that all-important interview.

Will I really have to write?

Yes. A lot.

Claims that people can get by without writing are false.

Claim 1: Secretaries will do all my writing.
Reality: Technology has transformed organizational structures and reduced the need for support staff. Of the secretaries who remain, 71 percent are executive assistants whose duties are managerial, not clerical.[5]

Technological innovation requires workers to exhibit increasingly sophisticated listening, critical and creative thinking, writing, reading, and speaking skills.

Claim 2: I'll use form letters or templates when I need to write.
Reality: A **form letter** is a prewritten fill-in-the-blank letter designed to fit standard situations. But form letters cover only routine situations. The high-

FYI

A July 2000 study by Pitney Bowes Inc. reports that Canadian workers send and receive an average of 160 messages per day. "This includes an average of 33 daily email messages—up 7 percent from last year—on top of phone calls, voicemail, pager messages, faxes, regular mail, post-it notes, and old-fashioned telephone message slips."

Source: "Workers still struggle in 'e-mail hell'," *The Globe and Mail,* July 24, 2000, B7.

Internal and External Audiences

Internal audiences are other people in the same organization: subordinates, superiors, peers. **External audiences** are people outside the organization: customers, suppliers, unions, stockholders, potential employees, government agencies, the press, and the general public.

er you rise, the more frequently you'll face situations that aren't routine and that demand creative thinking and written solutions.

Claim 3: I'm being hired as an accountant, not a writer.

Reality: Almost every entry-level professional or managerial job requires you to write memos and email messages, and to work productively in small groups. People who do these things well are more likely to be promoted beyond the entry level. Moreover, since writing is such a high-level cognitive skill, people who have developed good writing abilities also tend to demonstrate superior reading and thinking skills. Superior communicators achieve more recognition and make more money.

Claim 4: I'll just pick up the phone.

Reality: Important phone calls require follow-up letters, memos, or email messages. People in organizations put things in writing to create a record, to make themselves visible, to convey complex data, to make things convenient for the reader, to save money, and to convey their own messages more effectively. "If it isn't in writing," says a manager at one company, "it didn't happen." Writing well is an essential way to make yourself visible and convey a favourable impression of you and your organization.

How much does correspondence cost?

$80 a page and even more if it doesn't work.

Go to http://www.crane. com/business/business-identity/

On this site you can find the current cost of correspondence and tips for building a business identity.

Writing costs money. In 1996, according to a study by the Dartnell Institute of Business, a 10-minute message cost between $13.60 and $20.52 U.S., depending on how it was produced.[6] Dartnell no longer calculates the cost, but it seems unlikely to have fallen. Most messages take more than 10 minutes to write. A consultant who surveyed employees in seven industries found that most of them spent 54 minutes planning, composing, and revising a one-page letter.[7] Her respondents, then, each spent over $84 U.S. at 1996 prices to create a one-page letter. One company in Minneapolis writes 3,000 original letters a day. If each of those letters can be written in less than an hour, it spends at least $252,000 U.S. a day just on outgoing correspondence.

In many organizations, all external documents must be approved before they go out. A document may **cycle** from writer to superior to writer to another superior to writer again three, four or even 11 times before it is finally approved. The cycling process increases the cost of correspondence.

Documents' Purposes

Business documents have three purposes: to inform, to request or persuade, and to build goodwill. Most documents have more than one purpose.

Longer documents can involve large teams of people and take months to write. An engineering firm that relies on military contracts for its business calculates that it spends $500,000 to put together an average proposal and $1 million to write a large proposal.[8]

And poor correspondence costs even more. When writing isn't clear, complete, and correct, you and your organization pay in wasted time, wasted effort, and lost goodwill.

Poor writing

- Takes more time to read and interpret
- Requires more time for revisions
- Confuses and irritates the reader
- Delays action while the reader requests more information or tries to figure out the meaning

People communicate to plan products and services; hire, train, and motivate workers; coordinate manufacturing and delivery; persuade customers to buy; and bill them for the sale.

Quite simply, ineffective messages get negative results. A reader who has to guess what the writer means may guess wrong. A reader who finds a letter or memo unconvincing or insulting won't do what the message asks.

Whatever the literal content of the words, every letter, memo, and report serves either to enhance or to damage the image the reader has of the writer. Poor messages damage business relationships. Good communication is worth every minute it takes and every penny it costs. In fact, in a survey conducted by the International Association of Business Communicators, CEOs said that communication yielded a 235 percent return on investment.[9]

FYI

Writing, scholars believe, was invented to record inventories of livestock and grain and to calculate taxes.

Source: Denise Schmandt-Besserat, "The Earliest Precursor of Writing," *Scientific American*, 238, no. 6 (1978): 50–59.

What makes an effective message?

Successful business correspondence builds goodwill by focussing on the reader.

An effective, reader-centred message meets five criteria:

- The message **is clear**: the writer chooses the facts—and the organization and language to convey those facts—that enable the reader to get the meaning the writer intended
- The message **is concise**: the writer conveys maximum meaning using as few words as possible
- The message **is comprehensive**: the style, organization, and visual impact of the message help the reader to read, understand, and act
- The message **is complete**: the reader has enough information to evaluate the message and act on it
- The message **is correct**: the information in the message is accurate and is free from errors in punctuation, spelling, grammar, word order, and sentence structure

Site *to* See

Go to http://www.grammarlady.com/

Call on *The Grammar Lady* for fast, free, easy, and painless answers to your grammar queries.

An effective message initiates or cements a positive relationship between the writer and the reader (◀▶ Modules 6–8).

The Benefits of Becoming a Better Writer

Good business writers are more productive and make more money! Better writing

- **Saves time** because well-written correspondence is easy to read and respond to
- **Saves money** because effective writing increases the number of requests that are answered positively and promptly on the first request and presents your

point of view—to other people in your organization; to clients, customers, and suppliers; to government agencies; to the public—more persuasively
- **Saves energy** because effective messages reduce the misunderstandings that occur when the reader has to supply missing or unclear information Moreover, good writing clarifies the issues so that disagreements can surface and be resolved more quickly
- **Builds goodwill** because as it projects a positive image of your organization and of the writer as a knowledgeable, intelligent, capable person

Instant Replay

Criteria for Effective Messages

Effective business and administrative writing is clear, concise, comprehensive, complete, and correct. The best messages save the reader's time and build goodwill.

Whether a message meets these criteria depends on **the interactions among the writer, the audience, the purposes of the message, and the situation**. No single set of words will work in all possible situations.

Site *to* **See**

Go to www1.fubu.com

Word-of-mouth rather than traditional advertising has fuelled FUBU's success.

How do I begin to analyze business communication situations?

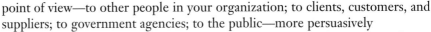

Excellent communicators use the six journalism questions or PAIBOC to analyze every communication situation.

Before you write, read, listen, or speak, you need to analyze and understand the situation for maximum efficacy. Ask yourself the following questions:

- **What's the point?** What information am I reading, imparting, or listening to, and why is it relevant?
- **What's my purpose?** What is the intended result? What do I want to have happen as a result of this communication? Do I want to inform or to confirm plans? Do I want to change attitudes and behaviours? Do I want to make a favourable impression? What do I really want as a result?
- **Who's my audience?** What are their wants and needs? What do they already know? What do they need to know to make a decision? What's in it for them?
- **Where will the communication happen?** Is the environment conducive to my intention? If I'm reading complicated material, where's the quietest place for me to be? If my message is confidential, where can I obtain maximum privacy?
- **When will the communication happen?** What time of day and what length of time have I chosen to deliver the message? When will the audience really be able to pay attention to my message? If I am reading difficult material, when am I most alert to absorb it? What is the optimum time of day for my team to meet for highest productivity?
- **What's the best way?** Formal channels—paper documents and presentations—require the most preparation but give you considerable control over the message. Email, phone calls, and office visits are considered less formal. Face-to-face conversations—informal and most personal—often work best for group decision-making, negotiating, and conflict resolution, but may require a written record for reference. Sometimes you may need more than one message, in more than one channel.

When faced with a communication situation, these questions analyze the "problem". You'll find that this analysis will generate fresh perspectives and enhance your solution strategies.

Use the PAIBOC acronym (Figure 1.5) to remember the key questions you need to answer for optimum communication results:

P   What are your **purposes** in writing or speaking?

What must this message do to solve the problem? What must it do to meet your own needs? What do you want your audience to do? To think or feel? List all your purposes, major and minor. Specify *exactly* what you want your reader to know or think or do. Specify *exactly* what kind of image of yourself and of your organization you want to project.

Even a simple message may have several related purposes: to announce a new policy, to make readers aware of the policy's provisions and requirements and to have them think that the policy is a good one, that the organization cares about its employees, and that you are a competent writer and manager.

A   Who is (are) your **audience(s)**? How are they going to feel about your message? What commonalties do they share? What's in the message that will appeal to them?

How much does your audience know about your topic? How will audience members respond to your message? Some characteristics of your readers will be irrelevant; focus on ones that matter *for this message*. Whenever you write to several people or to a group (like a memo to all employees), try to identify the economic, cultural, or situational differences that may affect how various subgroups respond to what you have to say.

I   What **information** must your message include?

Make a list of the points that must be included; check your draft to make sure you include them all. If you're not sure whether a particular fact must be included, ask your teacher or your boss.

To include information without emphasizing it, put it in the middle of a paragraph or document and present it as briefly as possible.

B   What reasons or reader **benefits** can you use to support your position?

Brainstorm to develop reasons for your decision, the logic behind your argument, and possible benefits to readers if they do as you ask. Reasons and reader benefits do not have to be monetary. Making the reader's job easier or more pleasant is a good reader benefit. In an informative or persuasive message, identify at least five reader benefits. In your message, use those that you can develop most easily and most effectively.

Be sure that the benefits are adapted to your reader. Many people do not identify closely with their companies; the fact that the company benefits from a policy will help the reader only if the saving or profit is passed directly on to the employees. That is rarely the case: Savings and profits are often eaten up by returns to stockholders, bonuses to executives, and investments in plants and equipment or in research and development.

Figure 1.5
PAIBOC Questions for Analysis

PAIBOC

Use the PAIBOC questions to analyze business communication problems:

P   What are your **purposes** in writing?

A   Who is (are) your **audience(s)**? How do members of your audience differ? What characteristics are relevant to this particular message?

I   What **information** must your message include?

B   What reasons or reader **benefits** can you use to support your position?

O   What **objection(s)** can you expect your reader(s) to have? What negative elements of your message must you de-emphasize or overcome?

C   How will the context affect reader response? Think about your relationship to the reader, morale in the organization, the economy, the time of year, and any special circumstances.

Instant Replay

Business communications needs to solve the organizational problem and to meet the psychological needs of the people involved.

O What **objections** can you expect your reader(s) to have? What negative elements of your message must you de-emphasize or overcome?

Some negative elements can only be de-emphasized. Others can be overcome. Be creative: is there any advantage associated with (even though not caused by) the negative? Can you rephrase or redefine the negative to make the reader see it differently?

C How will the **context** affect the reader's response? Think about your relationship to the reader, morale in the organization, the economy, the time of year, and any special circumstances.

Readers may like you or resent you. You may be younger or older than the people you're writing to. The organization may be prosperous or going through hard times; it may have just been reorganized or may be stable. All these different situations will affect what you say and how you say it. Consider the news, the economy, and the weather. Think about the general business and regulatory climate, especially as it affects the organization specified in the problem. Use the real world as much as possible. Think about interest rates, business conditions, and the economy. Is the industry in which the problem is set doing well? Is the government agency in which the problem is set enjoying general support? Think about the time of year. If it's fall when you write, is your business in a seasonal slowdown after a busy summer? Gearing up for the Christmas shopping rush? Or going along at a steady pace unaffected by seasons?
To answer these questions, draw on your experience, your courses, and your research. You may want to talk to other students, read newspapers and magazines, search the Internet and look at a company's annual report. You may want to phone a local businessperson to get information. For instance, if you need more information on reader benefits for a problem set in a bank, call a local banker to research services and loan rates.

Site *to* **See**

Go to
http://www.gmcanada.com/ssi/english/vehicles/saturn/saturn.html

Saturn's "no haggle" prices remove the obstacles to buying a car.

The remaining modules in this book will show you how to use the PAIBOC analysis to create business messages that meet your needs, the needs of the audience, and the needs of the organization.

Employability Skills 2000+

The Conference Board of Canada
Insights You Can Count On

The skills you need to enter, stay in, and progress in the world of work— whether you work on your own or as a part of a team.

These skills can also be applied and used beyond the workplace in a range of daily activities.

Fundamental Skills

The skills needed as a base for further development

You will be better prepared to progress in the world of work when you can:

Communicate
- read and understand information presented in a variety of forms (e.g., words, graphs, charts, diagrams)
- write and speak so others pay attention and understand
- listen and ask questions to understand and appreciate the points of view of others
- share information using a range of information and communications technologies (e.g., voice, email, computers)
- use relevant scientific, technological, and mathematical knowledge and skills to explain or clarify ideas

Manage Information
- locate, gather, and organize information using appropriate technology and information systems
- access, analyze, and apply knowledge and skills from various disciplines (e.g., the arts, languages, science, technology, mathematics, social sciences, and the humanities)

Use Numbers
- decide what needs to be measured or calculated
- observe and record data using appropriate methods, tools, and technology
- make estimates and verify calculations

Think & Solve Problems
- assess situations and identify problems
- seek different points of view and evaluate them based on facts
- recognize the human, interpersonal, technical, scientific, and mathematical dimensions of a problem
- identify the root cause of a problem
- be creative and innovative in exploring possible solutions
- readily use science, technology, and mathematics as ways to think, gain and share knowledge, solve problems, and make decisions
- evaluate solutions to make recommendations or decisions
- implement solutions
- check to see if a solution works, and act on opportunities for improvement

Personal Management Skills

The personal skills, attitudes, and behaviours that drive one's potential for growth

You will be able to offer yourself greater possibilities for achievement when you can:

Demonstrate Positive Attitudes & Behaviours
- feel good about yourself and be confident
- deal with people, problems, and situations with honesty, integrity, and personal ethics
- recognize your own and other people's good efforts
- take care of your personal health
- show interest, initiative, and effort

Be Responsible
- set goals and priorities balancing work and personal life
- plan and manage time, money, and other resources to achieve goals
- assess, weigh and manage risk
- be accountable for your actions and the actions of your group
- be socially responsible and contribute to your community

Be Adaptable
- work independently or as a part of a team
- carry out multiple tasks or projects
- be innovative and resourceful: identify and suggest alternative ways to achieve goals and get the job done
- be open and respond constructively to change
- learn from your mistakes and accept feedback
- cope with uncertainty

Learn Continuously
- be willing to continuously learn and grow
- assess personal strengths and areas for development
- set your own learning goals
- identify and access learning souces and opportunities
- plan for and achieve your learning goals

Work Safely
- be aware of personal and group health and safety practices and procedures, and act in accordance with these

Teamwork Skills

The skills and attributes needed to contribute productively

You will be better prepared to add value to the outcomes of a task, project, or team when you can:

Work with Others
- understand and work within the dynamics of a group
- ensure that a team's purpose and objectives are clear
- be flexible: respect, be open to and supportive of the thoughts, opinions, and contributions of others in a group
- recognize and respect people's diversity, individual differences, and perspectives
- accept and provide feedback in a constructive and considerate manner
- contribute to a team by sharing information and expertise
- lead or support when appropriate, motivating a group for high performance
- understand the role of conflict in a group to reach solutions
- manage and resolve conflict when appropriate

Participate in Projects & Tasks
- plan, design, or carry out a project or task from start to finish with well-defined objectives and outcomes
- develop a plan, seek feedback, test, revise, and implement
- work to agreed quality standards and specifications
- select and use appropriate tools and technology for a task or project
- adapt to changing requirements and information
- continuously monitor the success of a project or task and identify ways to improve

Review of Key Points

- Communication is an inherent need to make meaning. Successful communication involves a meaning exchange. Business communication focusses on making meaning for increased productivity.

- Organizations and the people in them achieve their goals through communications. The ability to write and speak well becomes increasingly important as you rise in an organization.

- People put things in writing to create a record, to convey complex data, to make things convenient for the reader, to save money, and to convey their own messages more effectively.

- **Internal documents** go to people inside the organization. **External documents** go to audiences outside: clients, customers, suppliers, stockholders, the government, the media, the general public.

- The three basic purposes of business and administrative communication are **to inform**, **to request or persuade**, **and to build goodwill**. Most messages have more than one purpose.

- A one-page message that took an hour to plan, write, and revise costs at least $84 U.S. in 1996. Poor writing costs even more since it wastes time, wastes efforts, and jeopardizes goodwill.

- Good business and administrative writing meets five basic criteria: **it's clear, concise, comprehensive, complete, and correct;** it **saves the reader's time;** and it **builds goodwill.**

- To evaluate a specific document, we must know the interactions among the writer, the reader(s), the purposes of the message, and the situation. No single set of words will work for all readers in all situations.

- To analyze business communication situations, ask the following questions:
  - What's the topic? What's the situation?
  - Why? What's the purpose? What do I want to have happen?
  - Who? Who is the audience? What are their needs and what's in it for them?
  - Where and when? What environment and time will optimize communication impact?
  - How? What's the best way to communicate? Should I send an email? Speak in person?

- Use the PAIBOC questions (refer to Figure 1.5, page 15) to analyze business communication problems:

  P   What are your **purposes** in writing?

  A   Who is (are) your **audience(s)**? How do members of your audience differ? What characteristics are relevant to this particular message?

  I   What **information** must your message include?

  B   What reasons or reader **benefits** can you use to support your position?

  O   What **objection(s)** can you expect your reader(s) to have? What negative elements of your message must you de-emphasize or overcome?

- A solution to a business communication problem must both solve the organizational problem and meet the needs of the writer or speaker, the organization, and the audience.

Learning Applications

Questions for Comprehension

1.1   What are the three basic purposes of business messages?

1.2   What are the five basic criteria for effective messages?

1.3   What does PAIBOC stand for?

Questions for Critical Thinking

1.4   Why do you need to understand the purposes, audience, and context for a message to know whether a specific set of words will work?

1.5   Why do writing and speaking become even more important as people rise in the organization?

1.6   If you're just looking for a low-level job, why is it still useful to be able to write and speak well?

1.7   Is the writing you've done for other classes more like "school" writing or business writing?

Questions for Building Skills

1.8   What skills have you read about in this module?

1.9   What skills are you practising in the assignments you're doing for this module?

1.10 How could you further develop the skills you're working on?

Exercises and Problems

1.11 Letters for Discussion—Landscape Plants

Your nursery sells plants, not only in your store but also by mail order. Today you've received a letter from Pat Sykes, complaining that the plants (in a $572 order) did not arrive in satisfactory condition. "All of them were dry and wilted. One came out by the roots when I took it out of the box. Please send me a replacement shipment immediately."

The following letters are possible approaches to answering this complaint. How well does each message meet the needs of the reader, the writer, and the organization? Is the message clear, complete, and correct? Does it save the reader's time? Does it build goodwill?

1.

> Dear Sir:
>
> I checked to see what could have caused the defective shipment you received. After ruling out problems in transit, I discovered that your order was packed by a new worker who didn't understand the need to water plants thoroughly before they are shipped. We have fired the worker, so you can be assured that this will not happen again.
>
> Although it will cost our company several hundred dollars, we will send you a replacement shipment.
>
> Let me know if the new shipment arrives safely. We trust that you will not complain again.

2.

> Dear Pat:
>
> Sorry we screwed up that order. Sending plants across country is a risky business. Some of them just can't take the strain. (Some days I can't take the strain myself!) We'll credit your account for $572.

3.

> Dear Mr. Smith:
>
> I'm sorry you aren't happy with your plants, but it isn't our fault. The box clearly says "Open and water immediately." If you had done that, the plants would have been fine. And anybody who is going to buy plants should know that a little care is needed. If you pull by the leaves, you will pull the roots out. Always lift by the stem! Since you don't know how to handle plants, I'm sending you a copy of our brochure, "How to Care for Your Plants." Please read it carefully so that you will know how to avoid disappointment in the future.
>
> We look forward to your future orders.

4.

> Dear Ms. Sikes:
>
> Your letter of the 5th has come to the attention of the undersigned.
>
> According to your letter, your invoice #47420 arrived in an unsatisfactory condition. Please be advised that it is our policy to make adjustments as per the Terms and Conditions listed on the reverse side of our Acknowledgment of Order. If you will read that document, you will find the following:
>
> ". . . if you intend to assert any claim against us on this account, you shall make an exception on your receipt to the carrier and shall, within 30 days after the receipt of any such goods, furnish us detailed written information as to any damage."
>
> Your letter of the 5th does not describe the alleged damage in sufficient detail. Furthermore, the delivery receipt contains no indication of any exception. If you expect to receive an adjustment, you must comply with our terms and see that the necessary documents reach the undersigned by the close of the business day on the 20th of the month.

5.

> Dear Pat Sikes:
>
> Next week you'll receive a replacement shipment of the perennials you ordered.
>
> Your plants were watered carefully before shipment and packed in specially designed cardboard containers. But if the weather is unusually warm, or if the truck is delayed, small root balls may dry out. Perhaps this happened with your plants. Plants with small root balls are easier to transplant, so they do better in your yard.
>
> The violas, digitalis, aquilegias, and hostas you ordered are long-blooming perennials that will get even prettier each year. Enjoy your garden!

1.12 Memos for Discussion—Announcing a Web Page

The Acme Corporation has just posted its first Web page. Ed Zeplin in Management Information Systems (MIS), who has created the page, wants employees to know about it.

The following memos are possible approaches. How well does each message meet the needs of the reader, the writer, and the organization? Is the message clear, complete, and correct? Does it save the reader's time? Does it build goodwill?

1.

Subject: It's Ready!

I am happy to tell you that my work is done. Two months ago the CEO finally agreed to fund a Web page for Acme, and now the work of designing and coding is done.

I wanted all of you to know about Acme's page. (Actually it's over 40 pages.) Now maybe the computerphobes out there will realize that you really do need to learn how to use this stuff. Sign up for the next training session! The job you save may be my own.

If you have questions, please do not hesitate to contact me.

L. Ed Zeplin, MIS

2.

Subject: Web Page

Check out the company Web page at

www.server.acme.com/homepage.html

3.

Subject: Visit Our Web Page

Our Web pages are finally operational. The 43 pages take 460 MB on the server and were created using Hot Metal, a program designed to support HTML creation. Though the graphics are sizeable and complex, interlacing and code specifying the pixel size serve to minimize download time. Standard HTML coding is enhanced with forms, Java animation, automatic counters, and tracking packages to ascertain who visits our site.

The site content was determined by conducting a survey of other corporate Web sites to become cognizant of the pages made available by our competitors and other companies. The address of our Web page is www.server.acme.com/homepage.html. It is believed that this site will support and enhance our marketing and advertising efforts, improving our outreach to desirable demographic and psychographic marketing groups.

L. Ed Zeplin, MIS

Voice: 713-555-2879; Fax: 713-555-2880; Email : zeplin.1@acme.com

"Only the wired life is worth living."—Anonymous

4.

> Subject: Web Page Shows Acme Products to the World, Offers Tips to Consumers, and Tells Prospective Employees about Job Possibilities
>
> Since last Friday, Acme's been on the World Wide Web. Check out the page at www.server.acme.com/homepage.html. You can't view the page if you don't have a computer.
>
> I have included pages on our products, tips for consumers, and job openings at Acme in the hope of making our page useful and interesting. Content is the number one thing that brings people back, but I've included some snazzy graphics, too.
>
> When I asked people for ideas for the company pages, almost nobody responded. But if seeing the page inspires you, let me know what else you'd like. I'll try to fit it into my busy schedule.
>
> So check it out. But don't spend too much time on the Web: you need to get your work done, too!
>
> L. Ed Zeplin, MIS
>
> zeplin.1@acme.com
>
> Today's Joke
>
> Fun Links

5.

> Subject: How to Access Acme's Web Page
>
> Tell your customers that Acme is now on the Web:
>
> www.server.acme.com/homepage.html
>
> Web pages offer another way for us to bring our story to the public. Our major competitors have Web pages; now we do, too. Our advertisements and packaging will feature our Web address. And people who check out our Web page can learn even more about our commitment to quality, protecting the environment, and meeting customer needs.
>
> If you'd like to learn more about how to use the Web or how to create Web pages for your unit, sign up for one of our workshops. For details and online registration, see www.server.acme.com/training.
>
> If you have comments on Acme's Web pages or suggestions for making them even better, just let me know.
>
> L. Ed Zeplin
>
> zeplin.1@acme.com

1.13 Discussing Strengths

Introduce yourself to a small group of other students. Identify three of your strengths that might interest an employer. These can be experience, knowledge, or personality traits (like enthusiasm).

1.14 Introducing Yourself to Your Instructor

Write a memo (at least 1¹/₂ pages long) introducing yourself to your instructor. Include the following topics:

- Background: Where did you grow up? What have you done in terms of school, extracurricular activities, jobs, and family life?
- Interests: What are you interested in? What do you like to do? What do you like to think about and talk about?
- Achievements: What achievements have given you the greatest personal satisfaction? List at least five. Include things that gave you a real sense of accomplishment and pride, whether or not they're the sort of thing you'd list on a résumé.

- Goals: What do you hope to accomplish this term? Where would you like to be professionally and personally five years from now?

Use a memo format with appropriate headings. (Your teacher will provide you with an overview of the memo format ◀▶ Module 9 for examples of memo format.) Use a conversational writing style; check your draft to polish the style and edit for mechanical and grammatical correctness. A good memo will enable your instructor to see you as an individual. Use specific details to make your memo vivid and interesting. Remember that one of your purposes is to interest your reader!

1.15 Describing Your Experiences in and Goals for Writing

Write a memo (at least 1¹/₂ pages long) to your instructor describing the experiences you've had writing and what you'd like to learn about writing during this course. Use any of the following questions to prompt you:

- What would you most like to learn in a writing course? What topics would motivate your interest in writing?
- What memories do you have of writing? What made writing fun or miserable in the past?
- What have you been taught about writing? List the topics, rules, and advice you remember.
- What kinds of writing have you done in school? How long have the papers been?
- How has your school writing been evaluated? Did the instructor mark or comment on mechanics and grammar? Style? Organization? Logic? Content? Audience analysis and adaptation? Have you received extended comments on your papers? Have instructors in different classes had the same standards, or have you changed aspects of your writing for different classes?

- What voluntary writing have you done— journals, poems, stories, essays? Has this writing been just for you, or has some of it been shared or published?
- Have you ever written on a job or in a student or volunteer organization? Have you ever input other people's writing? What have these experiences led you to think about real-world writing?
- What do you see as your current strengths and weaknesses in writing skills? What skills do you think you'll need in the future? What kinds of writing do you expect to do after you graduate?

Use complete memo format with appropriate headings. (Your teacher will provide you with an overview of the memo format ◀▶ Module 9 for examples of memo format.) Use a conventional writing style; edit your final draft for mechanical and grammatical correctness.

Polishing Your Prose

Sentence Fragments

A complete sentence has a subject and a verb. If either the subject or the verb is missing, the result is a sentence fragment.

> The job candidates.

> Passed seven rounds of interviews.

> And have taken three tests.

To fix the fragment, join it to other words to make a complete sentence.

> The job candidates passed seven rounds of interviews and have taken three tests.

Sentence fragments also occur when a clause has both a subject and a verb but is unable to stand by itself as a complete sentence.

> Although I read my email

> Because she had saved her work

> If he upgrades his computer

The words *although*, *because*, and *if* make the clause subordinate, which means the clause cannot stand alone. It must be joined to a main clause.

> Although I read my email, I did not respond to the draft of the proposal.

> Because she had saved her work, Paula was able to restore it after the crash.

> If he upgrades his computer, he will be able to use the new software.

Words that make clauses subordinate are

after	if
although, though	when, whenever
because, since	while, as
before, until	

Sometimes fragments are OK. For instance, fragments are used in résumés, advertisements, and some sales and fund-raising letters. However, fragments are inappropriate for most business documents. Because they are incomplete, they can confuse or mislead readers.

But the biggest problem with grammatical errors like sentence fragments is that readers sometimes assume that people who make errors are unprofessional or illiterate (◀▶ Module 14). Of course, using "incorrect" grammar has nothing to do with intelligence, but many people nevertheless use grammar as a yardstick. People who cannot measure up to that yardstick may be stuck in low-level jobs.

Exercises

Make the following sentence fragments into complete sentences.

1. Our retail sales division.
2. Fax the contract to the Legal Department for review.
3. Ms. Baumgardner began the meeting a few minutes late. Because the computer crashed.
4. Making our profit margin higher.
5. Although the car ran fine. We were late to the meeting because of traffic.
6. Our first attempt to make the document more readable.
7. Terrell announced a plan to introduce our latest computer model. To retail electronics stores.
8. But instead completed the report.
9. The Accounting Department.
10. Works well into the night.

Check your answers to the odd-numbered exercises on page 632.

Module 2
Adapting Your Message to Your Audience

Topics

- Why is audience analysis so important?
- What do I need to know about my audience?
- How do I use audience analysis?
- What if my audiences have different needs?
- How do I reach my audience(s)?

Review of Key Points

Learning Applications

Polishing Your Prose: Comma Splices

Learning Focus

After reading and applying the information in Module 2, you'll be able to demonstrate

Knowledge of

- The variables of the communication process
- The disparate audiences who may evaluate your business messages
- The importance of adapting your message to your audience
- Audience-analysis strategies

Skills to

- Reflect on your own personality characteristics
- Analyze your audience when composing messages
- Adapt the content, organization, and form of your messages to meet audience needs

"Using communications skills to solve engineering problems..."

"Technical information can be overwhelming. That's why the ability to clarify data so that a customer can understand it is vital to my job," says Sarah Marshall, who works as a Technical Service Specialist for NOVA Chemicals Corporation at the Technical Centre in Calgary, Alberta.

Sarah has a chemical engineering degree from McGill University and uses her engineering skills when dealing with the customers of NOVA Chemicals, a petrochemicals company whose major products are ethylene, polyethylene, styrene, and polystyrene. Polyethylene is a basic plastic that is used in such diverse consumer products as toys, pipes, garbage bags, and foam.

If customers have a technical problem with a polyethylene product manufactured by NOVA Chemicals, they contact Sarah. Her job is to resolve customer complaints as quickly as possible. NOVA Chemicals' customers are manufacturers, often with round-the-clock production, so a fast resolution is critical to their business.

The complaint resolution process Sarah works with requires clear communications and analytical problem solving. The first step is contacting the customer to define the problem. This is where Sarah's technical expertise comes in: she has to be able to understand what the manufacturer is saying, and the manufacturer has to understand what she is saying. Manufacturers often use a different vocabulary than do chemical engineers, so communications must be tailored to each specific audience. The process involves constant translation from technical language to basic language and back again. Sarah not only must know her product, but must develop a detailed understanding of how her product is used by NOVA Chemicals' customers.

Once the scope of the problem is understood, the complaint resolution will then involve testing the material at issue, to establish what the problem is. The process must "determine the root cause of the problem," says Sarah. Both NOVA Chemicals and the customer do not want the same problem to reoccur.

Because of this direct involvement with the process and the product, Sarah defines her job as "using engineering skills in a technical position, and using communications skills to solve engineering problems."

When asked for advice to people going into technical communications work, Sarah notes that "Different fields can use the same terms differently, and this can hinder the communication process. Instead of using technical jargon, use descriptions."

http://www.novachem.com/
NOVA Chemicals

Audience analysis is fundamental to the success of any message: to capture and hold audience attention, and to motivate readers and listeners, you must shape your message to meet the audience's goals, interests, and needs.

Who is my audience?

More people than you might think!

In an organizational setting, a message may have five separate audiences.[1]

1. The **initial audience** receives the message first and routes it to other audiences. Sometimes the initial audience also tells you to write the message.
2. The **primary audience** will act on the basis of your message. You must reach the decision-maker to fulfill your purposes.
3. The **secondary audience** may be asked to comment on your message or to implement your ideas after they've been approved. Secondary audiences can also include lawyers who may use your message—perhaps years later—as evidence of your organization's culture and practices.
4. A **gatekeeper** has the power to stop your message before it gets to the primary audience. The executive assistant who decides what personnel get to speak to the boss is a gatekeeper. Sometimes the supervisor who assigns the message is also the gatekeeper; however, sometimes the gatekeeper is higher in the organization. In some cases, gatekeepers exist outside the organization.
5. A **watchdog audience**, though it does not have the power to stop the message and will not act directly on it, has political, social, or economic power. The watchdog pays close attention to the transaction between you and the primary audience and may base future actions on its evaluation of your message.

As Figures 2.1 and 2.2 on page 29, show, one person or group can be part of two audiences. Frequently, a supervisor is both the initial audience and the gatekeeper. Sometimes the initial audience is also the primary audience who will act on the message.

Why is audience so important?

Successful messages anticipate and meet the audiences' needs.

Good business communication is audience-centred. Audience focus is central to both the communication process and message analysis (PAIBOC).

Audience and the Communication Process

Audience is central to understanding the communication process.

The following model of the communication process drastically simplifies what is perhaps the most complex of human activities. However, even a simplified model can give us a sense of the complexity of the process. And the model is useful in helping us see where and why miscommunication occurs. Figure 2.3 on page 30 illustrates the process that occurs when one person tries to communicate ideas to someone else.

FYI

Fanning the Flames

In our wired world, you can assume that everyone is your audience. Cerner Corporation CEO, Neal Patterson, sent an inflammatory email message to 400 company managers. The memo, which included threats of staff reductions and hiring freezes and used words like "sick", was leaked and posted on Yahoo for all the world to read. Patterson's company's stock market value plummeted.

Sources: Edward Wong, "Stinging office e-mail lights 'firestorm'" *The Globe and Mail*, Monday, April 9, 2001, B1; and "Patterson E-mail Sinks Cerner Stock", *Health Management Data*; visited Web site June 27, 2001. http://www.health datamanagement.com/html/StockStory.cfm?DID= 5237

Dawn is an account executive in an ad agency.

Her boss asks her to write a proposal for a marketing plan for a new product the agency's client is introducing. Her boss, who must approve the plan before it is submitted to the client, is both the **initial audience and the gatekeeper.**

Her **primary audience** is the executive committee of the client company, who will decide whether to adopt the plan.

The **secondary audience** includes the marketing staff of the client company, who will be asked for comments on the plan, as well as the artists, writers, and media buyers who will carry out details of the plan if it is adopted.

Figure 2.1

The Audiences for a Marketing Plan

Jim and Hiro work for a consulting think-tank.

Their company has been hired by a consortium of manufacturers of a consumer product to investigate how proposed federal regulations would affect manufacturing, safety, and cost. The consortium is both the consultants' **initial audience and a gatekeeper.** If the consortium doesn't like the report, it won't send the report to the federal government.

The federal government agency that regulates this consumer product is the **primary audience.** It will set new regulations, based in part (the manufacturers hope) on Jim and Hiro's report. Within this audience are economists, engineers, and policymakers.

Secondary audiences include the general public, other manufacturers of the product, and competitors and potential clients of the consulting company.

During the revision process, industry reviewers emerge as a **watchdog audience.** They read drafts of the report and comment on it. Although they have no direct power over this report, their goodwill is important for the consulting company's image—and its future contracts. Their comments are the ones that authors take most seriously as they revise their drafts.

Figure 2.2

The Audiences for a Consulting Report

Source: Based on Vincent J. Brown, "Facing Multiple Audiences in Engineering and R&D Writing: The Social Context of a Technical Report," *Journal of Technical Writing and Communication* 24, no. 1 (1994): 67–75.

Figure 2.3
A Model of Two-Person Communication with Feedback

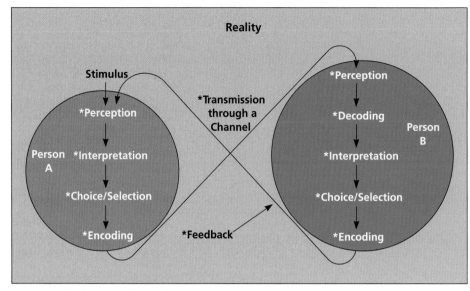

*Noise (and miscommunication) can occur here.

Instant Replay

Five Kinds of Audiences

Initial: Is first to receive the message; may assign message

Gatekeeper: Has the power to stop the message before it gets to primary audience

Primary: Decides whether to accept recommendations; acts

Secondary: Comments on message or implements recommendations

Watchdog: Has political, social, or economic power; may base future actions on its evaluation of your message

The process begins when Person A (let's call him Alex) **perceives** some stimulus. Here we are talking about literal perception: the ability to see, to hear, to taste, to smell, to touch. Next, Alex **interprets** what he has perceived. Is it important? Unusual? The next step is for Alex to **choose** or **select** the information he wishes to send to Person B (whom we'll call Barbara). Now Alex is ready to put his ideas into words. (Some people believe that we can think only in words and would, therefore, put this stage before interpretation and choice.) Words are not the only way to convey ideas; gestures, clothing, and pictures can carry meaning non-verbally. The stage of putting ideas into any of these symbols is called **encoding**. Then Alex must **transmit** the message to Barbara using some **channel**. Channels include memos, phone calls, meetings, billboards, TV ads, and email, to name just a few.

To receive the message, Barbara must first **perceive** it. Then she must **decode** it, that is, extract meaning from the symbols. Barbara then repeats the steps Alex has gone through: interpreting the information, choosing a response, and encoding it. The response Barbara sends to Alex is called **feedback**. Feedback may be direct and immediate or indirect and delayed; it may be verbal or non-verbal.

Noise can interfere with every aspect of the communication process. Noise may be physical or psychological. Physical noise could be a phone line with static, a lawn mower roaring outside a classroom, or handwriting that is hard to read. Psychological noise includes emotional, intellectual, or psychological dissonance: it could include disliking a speaker, being concerned about something other than the message, having preconceived notions about an issue, or harbouring deeply-felt prejudices about the message or the messenger.

Channel overload occurs when the channel cannot handle all the messages that are being sent. Two people may be speaking to you simultaneously, or a small business may have only two phone lines so no one else can get through when both lines are in use.

Information overload occurs when more messages are transmitted than the human receiver can handle. Information overload seems to be a constant modern complaint. Some receivers process information "first come, first served." Some may try to select the most important messages and ignore others. A third way is to depend on abstracts or summaries prepared by other people. None of these ways is completely satisfactory.

At every stage, both Alex and Barbara could misperceive, misinterpret, choose badly, encode poorly, or choose inappropriate channels. Miscommunication also frequently occurs because every individual makes meaning using different frames of reference. We always interpret messages in light of our personal experiences, our cultures and subcultures, and the point in history when we live.

Successful communication depends on identifying and establishing common ground between you and your audience. Choose information that your audience needs and will find interesting. Encode your message in words and other symbols the audience will understand. Transmit the message along a channel that your audience will attend to.

Correctly identifying your audience and then choosing audience-appropriate symbols (words, gestures, illustrations) guarantees a more accurate meaning transfer.

Audience and Business Messages

Consider the PAIBOC questions introduced in Module 1 (see Figure 1.5, page 15). Five of the six questions relate to **audience**:

P What are your **purposes** in writing?
Your purposes come from you and your organization. Your audience determines how you achieve those purposes.

A Who is (are) your **audience(s)**? What characteristics are relevant to this particular message?
These questions ask directly about your audience.

I What **information** must your message include?
The information you need to give depends on your audience. You need to add relevant facts when the topic is new to your audience. If your audience has heard something but may have forgotten it, protect readers' egos by saying "As you know," or putting the information in a subordinate clause: "Because we had delivery problems last quarter, ..."
If your audience is familiar with specific facts, concentrate more on clarifying new information.

B What audience-related reasons or reader **benefits** can you use to support your position?
Regardless of your own needs, a good reason or benefit depends on your audience's perception. For some audiences, personal experience counts as a good reason. Other audiences are more persuaded by scientific studies or by experts. For some people, saving money is a good benefit of growing vegetables. Other people may care more about avoiding chemicals, growing varieties that aren't available in grocery stores, or working outside in the fresh air than about costs or convenience. Module 8 ◀▶ gives more information on developing reader benefits.

Figure 2.4
PAIBOC Questions for Analysis

PAIBOC

Use the PAIBOC questions to analyze business communication problems:

P What are your **purposes** in writing?

A Who is (are) your **audience(s)**? How do members of your audience differ? What characteristics are relevant to this particular message?

I What **information** must your message include?

B What reasons or reader benefits can you use to support your position?

O What **objection(s)** can you expect your reader(s) to have? What negative elements of your message must you de-emphasize or overcome?

C How will the **context** affect reader response? Think about your relationship to the reader, morale in the organization, the economy, the time of year, and any special circumstances.

O   What **objection(s)** can you expect your reader(s) to have? What elements of your message will your audience perceive as negative? How can you arrange the message to overcome audience objections or de-emphasize negative elements?

Different audiences have different attitudes. One audience may object to a price increase. Another audience may expect price changes as routine but be bothered by time constraints. Module 12 on persuasion ◁▷ gives more information on overcoming objections

C   How will the **context** affect reader response? Think about your relationship to the reader, the reader's values and expectations, recent organizational history and current morale, the economy, the time of year, the place and time of day, and any special circumstances surrounding message exchange.

People, information, and organizations exist in a context. How well your audience knows you, how they feel about you and your organization, how well the economy is doing, even what's been in the news recently: all will influence the way they respond to your message.

What do I need to know about my audience(s)?

Everything that's relevant to what you're writing or talking about.

Almost everything about your audience is relevant to some message. But for any particular message, only a few facts about your audience will be relevant, and these will vary depending on each communication situation.

Figure 2.5

Identifying Key Audience Characteristics for Messages

Message/purpose	Audience	Relevant factors
Memo announcing that the company will reimburse employees for tuition if they take work-related college courses	All employees	1. Attitudes toward education (some people find courses fun; others may be intimidated) 2. Time available (some may be too busy) 3. Interest in being promoted or in getting cross-training 4. Attitude toward company (those committed to its success will be more interested in program)
Letter offering special financing on a new or used car	College students	1. Income 2. Expectations of future income (and ability to repay loan) 3. Interest in having a new car 4. Attitude toward cars offered by that dealership 5. Knowledge of interest rates 6. Access to other kinds of financing
Letter containing a meeting agenda and saying that you can bring your child along	Client	1. How well the client knows you 2. How much the client likes you 3. How important agenda items are to the client 4. How the client feels about children 5. Physical space for meeting (room for child to play)

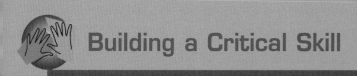

Understanding What Your Organization Wants

Michelle wondered whether her boss was sexist. Everyone else who had joined the organization when she had, had been promoted. Her boss never seemed to have anything good to say about her or her work.

Michelle didn't realize that, in her boss's eyes, she wasn't doing good work. Michelle was proud of her reports; she thought she was the best writer in the office. But her boss valued punctuality, and Michelle's reports were always late.

Just as every sport has rules about scoring, so, too, workplaces have rules about what "counts." Even in the same industry, different organizations and different supervisors may care about different things. One boss circles misspelled words and posts the offending message on a bulletin board for everyone to see. Other people are more tolerant of errors. One company values original ideas, while another workplace tells employees just to do what they're told. One supervisor likes technology and always buys the latest hardware and software; another is technophobic and has to be persuaded to get needed upgrades.

Succeeding in an organization depends first on understanding what "counts" at your organization. To find out what counts in your organization,

- Ask your boss, "What parts of my job are most important? What's the biggest thing I could do to improve my work?"
- Listen to the stories colleagues tell about people who have succeeded and those who have failed. When you see patterns, check for confirmation: "So his real problem was that he didn't socialize with co-workers?" This gives your colleagues a chance to provide feedback: "Well, it was more than never coming to happy hour. He didn't really seem to care about the company."
- Observe. See who is praised, who is promoted.

In general, you need to use empathy and critical-thinking tools. **Empathy** is the ability to put yourself in someone else's shoes, to feel with that person. Empathy requires being audience-centred because the audience is *not* just like you.

Critical thinking involves gathering as much information as you can about someone or something, and then making decisions based on that information.

You need to use your research and your knowledge about people and about organizations to predict likely responses.

Analyzing Individuals and Members of Groups

When you write or speak to people in your own organization and in other organizations you work closely with, you may be able to analyze your audience as individuals. You may already know your audience; it will usually be easy to get additional information by talking to members of your audience, talking to people who know your audience, and observing your audience.

In other organizational situations, however, you'll analyze your audience as members of a group: "taxpayers who must be notified that they owe more income tax," "customers living in the northeast end of the city," or "employees with small children."

FYI

Mining engineer Carlos Morales, a recent immigrant from Colombia, watches the Discovery Channel and *Blind Date* to learn the three kinds of North American English: street English, newspaper and magazine English, and technical English.

Source: Hamida Ghafour, "TV does double duty as English teacher," The *Toronto Star*, May 27, 2001, A1.

Pertinent audience information includes

- Knowledge about your topic
- Demographic factors, such as age, education, income, class, number of children, and so forth
- Attitudes, values, and beliefs
- Personality
- Past behaviour

Prior Knowledge

Even people in your own organization won't share all your knowledge. Salespeople in the automotive industry, for example, don't now the technical language of their service mechanics.

Most of the time, you won't know exactly what your audience knows. Moreover, even if you've told readers before, they may not remember the old information when they read the new message. Avoid lengthy, mind-numbing details in any case! If, however, you want to remind readers of **relevant facts** tactfully,

- Preface statements with "As you know," "As you may know," "As we've discussed," or a similar phrase
- Always spell out acronyms the first time you use them: "Employee Stock Ownership Plan (ESOP)"
- Provide brief definitions in the text: "the principal—the money you have invested—"
- Put information readers should know in a subordinate clause: "Because the renovation is behind schedule, . . . "

Demographic Factors

Demographic characteristics can be objectively quantified, or measured: age, gender, religion, education level, income, location, and so on.

Sometimes demographic information is irrelevant; sometimes it's important. Does age matter? Almost always, since people's perspectives and priorities change as they grow older. For example, if you were explaining a change in your company's pension plan, you'd expect older workers to pay much closer attention than younger workers would. And you would need to shape your explanation to appeal to that older audience.

Demographic data has certainly determined the sharp increase in small business start-ups devoted to personal services. For example, the North American concierge industry—providing services from housesitting to running errands—is thriving because it offers time to busy boomers.

Business and non-profit organizations get demographic data by surveying their customers, clients, and donors; by using Statistics Canada data; or by purchasing demographic data from marketing companies. For many messages, simply identifying subsets of your audience is enough. For example, a school board trying to win support for a tax increase knows that not everyone living in the district will have children in school. It isn't necessary to know the exact percentages to realize that successful messages will need to contain appeals not only to parents but also to those voters who won't directly benefit from the improvements that the tax increase will fund.

Go to
http://www.gotime
makers.com/about/
This Ottawa-based corporate concierge service provides personalized, home, and business support to time-starved corporations and individuals.

Go to
http://www.stat
can.ca
A wealth of demographic information is available at the Statistics Canada Web site.

Personality

Understanding and adapting to your primary audience's personality can also help make your message more effective.

Personality and learning style-assessment instruments can provide you with useful insights into your own and others' behaviours. One of the most common assessment tools is the **Myers-Briggs Type Indicator**®, which uses four dimensions to identify personality differences.[2]

1. **Introvert–extravert:** the source of one's energy. Introverts get their energy from within; extraverts are energized by interacting with other people.
2. **Sensing–intuitive:** how someone gathers information. Sensing types gather information step-by-step through their senses. Intuitive types see relationships among ideas.
3. **Thinking–feeling:** how someone makes decisions. Thinking types use objective logic to reach decisions. Feeling types make decisions that feel "right."
4. **Judging–perceiving:** the degree of certainty someone needs. Judging types like closure. Perceptive types like possibilities.

Figure 2.6 on page 36, shows how you can use this information to adapt a message to your audience.

Through reading, research, realistic self-assessment, and feedback from others, you can identify your own and others' personality characteristics.

You'll be most persuasive if you play to your audience's strengths. Indeed, many of the general principles of business communications reflect the types most common among managers. Putting the main point up front satisfies the needs of judging/driver types, and some 75 percent of managers are judging. Giving logical reasons satisfies the needs of the nearly 80 percent of managers who are thinking/analytical types.[3]

Values and Beliefs

Psychographic characteristics are qualitative rather than quantitative and include values, beliefs, goals, and lifestyles. For example, two families living next door to each other might have about the same income and each has two children. But one family might save every possible penny for college and retirement, taking inexpensive vacations and cooking meals at home rather than eating out. The other family might spend almost everything they make on clothes, cars, vacations, entertainment, and dinners out. One family might do most things together as a family, while in the other, members might spend most of their time on individual activities. The families might have different religious and political beliefs.

If you wanted to persuade each family to do the same thing, you'd need to use different reasons and reader benefits; you would have to overcome different objections. Knowing what your audience finds important allows you to organize information in a way that seems natural to your audience and to choose appeals that audience members will find persuasive.

Looking at values enables a company to identify customer segments. Taco Bell identified two groups of high-potential customers: penny pinchers, who visit Taco Bell frequently but don't spend much on a visit, and speed freaks, who are more interested in convenience than price. To attract these consumers, Taco Bell lowered prices on its core menu items and reengineered its production, cutting wait time by

Site to See

Go to
http://209.224.198.54/aptmbtiw.htm
http://www.personalitypage.com/

Here are two of many online quizzes you can use to determine your Myers-Briggs personality type.

Site to See

Go to
http://www.enel.ucalgary.ca/~goss/693/short/11.html#Social
http://www.ldpride.net/learningstyles.MI.htm

Here's information about social styles.

Site to See

Go to
http://erg.environics.net/surveys/3sc/

Take the Environics' social values online survey and find out which Canadian psychographic group you belong to.
http://erg.environics.net/surveys/techsurvey

This Environics online survey analyzes your technology adoption profile.

Figure 2.6

Using Myers-Briggs Types in Persuasive Messages

If your audience is	Use this strategy	Because
An introvert	Write a memo and let the reader think about your proposal before responding.	Introverts prefer to think before they speak. Written documents give them the time they need to think through a proposal carefully.
An extravert	Try out your idea orally, in an informal setting.	Extraverts like to think on their feet. They are energized by people; they'd rather talk than write.
A sensing type	Present your reasoning step-by-step. Get all your facts exactly right.	Sensing types usually reach conclusions step-by-step. They want to know why something is important, but they trust their own experience more than someone else's say-so. They're good at facts and expect others to be, too.
An intuitive type	Present the big picture first. Stress the innovative, creative aspects of your proposal.	Intuitive types like solving problems and being creative. They can be impatient with details.
A thinking type	Use logic, not emotion, to persuade. Show that your proposal is fair, even if some people may be hurt by it.	Thinking types make decisions based on logic and abstract principles. They are often uncomfortable with emotion.
A feeling type	Show that your proposal meets the emotional needs of people as well as the dollars-and-cents needs of the organization.	Feeling types are very aware of other people and their feelings. They are sympathetic and like harmony.
A perceiving type	Show that you've considered all the alternatives. Ask for a decision by a specific date.	Perceiving types want to be sure they've considered all the options. They may postpone coming to closure.
A judging type	Present your request quickly.	Judging types are comfortable making quick decisions. They like to come to closure so they can move on to something else.

Source: Based on Isabel Briggs Myers, "Effects of Each Preference in Work Situations," *Introduction to Type* (Palo Alto, CA: Consulting Pychologists Press, 1962, 1980).

71 percent. These changes tripled sales and—even with lower prices—raised profits $20 million.[4]

Eresearcher Mary Modahl's survey of 250,000 households found that online buying depends not on demographics such as age and postal area but on psychographics: the consumer's attitude toward technology along a continuum from "profoundly suspicious" to "eagerly accepting."[5] Canadians' attitudes toward technology have been charted by the Environics Research Group; see Site to See for an online survey to determine your technology adoption segment.

Ford Motor Company's ebusiness transformation strategy depends on direct contact with consumers. Ford has partnered with Teletech, the consumer-marketing firm, to identify consumer preferences and trends as part of its B2C brand value enhancement. The company also sponsors interactive automotive sections on teen Web sites in order to cultivate and build relationships with future car buyers.[6]

White Rose has traditionally been known for its gardening and craft products. But in response to the exploding home decorating market, the company is reinventing itself to compete with American big box stores that are moving into Canada. See http://whiterose.ca/

Past Behaviour

Human resource managers maintain that you can predict people's future actions based on their past behaviours; the more recent the behaviour, the more accurate the prediction.

For example, records of customer purchases showed U.S. retailer Fingerhut that customers who moved made large purchases of furniture and decorations. Fingerhut developed a "mover's catalogue" filled with products likely to appeal to this group—and saved money by not mailing other catalogues to this group right after they moved.

Analyzing People in Organizations

Audience reaction is also strongly influenced by the perceptions and expectations of the groups to which they belong. These groups or **discourse communities** include family, peers, professional associations, clubs, and the workplace—all communities with which your audience identifies.

A **discourse community** is a group of people who share assumptions about their particular culture and values: what to wear, how to behave, what topics to discuss and how to discuss them, what channels, formats, and styles to use, and what constitutes evidence. Each person is part of several discourse communities, which may or may not overlap.

Discourse Community

A **discourse community** is a group of people who share assumptions about what channels, formats, and styles to use, what topics to discuss and how to discuss them, and what constitutes evidence.

Some aspects of corporate culture may no longer serve an obvious purpose.

"I don't know how it started, either. All I know is that it's part of our corporate culture."
© The New Yorker Collection 1994 Mick Stevens from cartoonbank.com.

FYI

"You need to dress the part of where you want to be," according to Paul Capelli, vice president of CNBC.

Source: Rachel Emma Silverman, "Job candidates master the quick change," quoted from *The Wall Street Journal*, in *The Globe and Mail*, "Working Life," April 20, 2001, B9.

When analyzing an organization's discourse community, consider the following:

• What channels, formats, and styles are preferred for communication? How do people in the organization communicate? Do they write a paper memo, send email, or walk down the hall to talk to someone? How formal or informal are people expected to be—in their apparel, on the telephone, in meetings?

For example, "dress-down Fridays", an unquestioned part of the North American work culture, was revolutionary only five years ago. Silicon Valley's young, male, computer and Internet entrepreneurs redefined work time from 9 to 5 to 24-7, dressed accordingly, and in the process, transformed the "clothes-make-the-man" stereotype. Traditional businesspeople—even academics—co-opted casual Fridays fashion to emulate the youth, inventiveness, and style of the New Economy's new rich. However, since the dot.com bust of late 2000, early 2001, "casual dress" has re-emerged as the most appropriate work attire.

• What does the physical environment say about who and what is important? What departments and service areas are front and centre? What does the office space layout indicate about organizational values? How are people encouraged or discouraged to work together? Where is the reception area located? How are visitors welcomed? Where are the library, training rooms, gymnasium, and cafeteria located? How are they resourced? How are newcomers oriented?
• What do people talk about? What is not discussed?
• What kind of and how much evidence is needed to be convincing? Is personal experience convincing? Do people need to supply numbers and formal research to be credible?

Procter & Gamble's discourse community requires that recommendations be just one page. So writers create one-page memos—and then add as many pages of "attachments" as they need. In contrast, a Silicon Valley company expects recommendations to be presented as a PowerPoint slide showing a triangle with three words around it.

An **organization's culture** is expressed through its values, attitudes, and philosophies. Organizational or **corporate culture** reveals itself verbally in the organization's myths, stories, and heroes, and non-verbally in the allocation of space, money, and power (◀▶ Module 3).

The following questions will help you analyze an organization's culture:

- What are the organization's goals? Making money? Serving customers and clients? Advancing knowledge? Contributing to the community?
- What does the organization value? Diversity or homogeneity? Independence or being a team player? Creativity or following orders?
- How do people get ahead? Are rewards based on seniority, education, being well-liked, making technical discoveries, or serving customers? Are rewards available to only a few top people, or is everyone expected to succeed?
- How formal are behaviour, language, and dress?
- What behavioural expectations predominate? How do employees treat one another? Do employees speak in "I", "we" or "them and us" language? How do employees get organizational information?

Two companies in the same field may have very different cultures. FedEx sales representatives court large customers with frequent phone calls. UPS workers send a bid and let that speak for itself—an approach consistent with UPS's culture of humility and modesty.[7] Researcher Jennifer Chatman found that new hires who "fit" a company's culture were more likely to stay with the job, be more productive, and be more satisfied than those who did not fit the culture.[8]

Organizations are also comprised of subcultures. For example, manufacturing and marketing may represent different subcultures in the same organization: workers may dress differently and espouse different values. In a union environment, management and union representatives traditionally employ adversarial language to advance their own subculture's perspective while undermining the other's point-of-view.

You can learn about organizational culture by paying attention to communication clues and cues. For example, observe people and listen to their stories. Here are two of the stories Nike's leaders tell

Instant Replay

Organizational Culture

An **organization's culture** is its values, attitudes, and philosophies. Organizational culture (or **corporate culture**, as it is also called) is revealed verbally in the organization's myths, stories, and heroes and non-verbally in the allocation of space, money, and power.

Story	Lesson
Coach Bowerman (a company cofounder) decided his team needed better running shoes. So he went into his workshop and poured rubber into the family waffle iron to create a waffle sole.	Nike is committed to innovation.
Steve Prefontaine (a runner and another cofounder) worked to make running a professional sport and to get better-performing equipment.	Nike is committed to helping athletes.

You can also learn about a company's culture by looking at its Web site. Many companies try to describe their cultures, usually as part of the section on employment. Job candidates who research the company culture to identify how their skills match enjoy a significant advantage in the interview.

Conscious awareness of an organization's spoken and unspoken messages can provide you with important information on its values and norms.

How do I use audience analysis to reach my audience(s)?

> Use it to plan strategy, organization, style, document design, and visuals.

Take the time to analyze your audience; then adapt your strategy, style, and organizational pattern to your audience's needs.

For paper or electronic documents, you can also adapt the document's design and the photos or illustrations you choose. To realize optimum results, revise your message with your audience in mind.

Strategy

- Choose appeals and reader benefits that work for the specific audience (◀▶ Module 8)
- Use details and language that reflect your knowledge of and respect for the specific audience, the organizational culture, and the discourse community
- Make it easy for the audience to respond positively
- Include only necessary information
- Anticipate and overcome objections (◀▶ Modules 7, 11, and 13 will show you how to emphasize positive aspects, decide how much information to include, and overcome obstacles)

Organization

- Since most managers are intuitive/analytical or driver types, it's usually better to get to the point right away. The major exceptions are
  - When you must persuade a reluctant reader
  - When your audience would see the message as bad news and you want to break the news gradually
- Anticipate and meet the audience's expectations of format: make the organizational pattern clear to the audience. (◀▶ Modules 9, 23, and 24 show you how to use headings and overviews. Module 20 shows how to use overviews and signposts in oral presentations.)

Style

- Strive for clarity and accessibility: use easy-to-understand words, a mixture of sentence lengths, and short paragraphs with topic sentences (◀▶ Modules 15 and 16)
- Use natural, conversational, personable, tactful language: avoid negative, defensive, arrogant and "red-flag" words—*unfortunately, fundamentalist, liberal, crazy, incompetent, dishonest*—that may generate a negative reaction

Before their redesign, Olathe Lanes East and West looked alike. But East's customers bowl to relax while West's customers bowl to compete. Now a food court with soothing curves is the center of the East facility, with bowling lanes attached. At West, lanes still dominate, decorated with energetic triangles.

- Use the language(s) that appeals to your audience. In parts of Canada, including Québec and some areas of Manitoba and New Brunswick, bilingual messages in English and in French, with French first, are the norm
- Use conversational language

Document Design

- Use telegraphing: bulleted lists, headings, and a mix of paragraph lengths to create white space
- Choose the format, footnotes, and visuals expected by the organizational culture or the discourse community. (◀▶ Module 5 provides advice about effective document design.)

Photographs and Visuals

- Photos and visuals can make a document look more informal or more formal. Carefully consider the difference between cartoons and photos of "high art."
- Use bias-free photographs. Unintentional cultural, gender, religious, and economic assumptions can cost you goodwill, and, ultimately, a sale.
- Choose photographs and illustrations that project positive cultural meanings for your audience. Middle-Eastern readers, for example, find pictures of bare-legged and bare-armed women offensive and may also object to pictures of clean-shaven men.
- Do your research and audience analysis: some cultures (e.g., France, Japan) use evocative photographs that bear little direct relationship to the text. North American audiences expect photos to relate to the text.

Site to See

Go to
http://www.gdsourcing.com/works/conretailing.htm
Canadian Demographics

www.demographics.com
American Demographics

Both Web sites offer detailed analyses of major and niche groups.

What if my audiences have different needs?

Focus on gatekeepers and decision makers.

When the members of your audience share the same interests and the same level of knowledge, you can use these principles for individual readers or for members of

FYI

Over an 11-year period, companies with strong corporate cultures averaged 571 percent higher gains in operating earnings than those with weak corporate cultures.

Source: "Ladies and Gentlemen, Dust off Your Shelves," *Inc.,* July 1999, 98.

homogenous groups. But sometimes, different members of the audience have different needs.

When you're writing or speaking to pluralistic audiences, meet the needs of gatekeepers and primary audiences first.

Content and Choice of Details

- Always provide an overview—the introductory or topic sentence—for reader orientation
- In the body of the document, provide enough detail to prove your point

Organization

- Organize your message based on the primary audiences' attitudes toward it: give good news up front; provide the explanation before you deliver the bad news.
- Organize documents to make reading easy: provide a table of contents for documents over five pages in length, so that your readers can turn to the portions that interest them.
- Use headings as signposts: use headings to tell readers what they're about to read and to connect ideas throughout your document. This strategy reinforces your credibility through unity and coherence. If the primary audiences don't need details that other audiences will want, provide those details in attachments and/or appendices.

Level of Language

- Contemporary business communication uses conversational, semi-formal language. Use "I" and "you," and address your reader by name. Do research, however, to discover your reader's title preference (for example, Mr. Ms. etc.)
- When both internal and external audiences will read the document, use a slightly more formal style and the third person; avoid "I"
- Use a more formal style when you write to international audiences

Use of Technical Terms and Theory

- Know what your reader knows; then provide only the necessary information. Use technical terms if these will increase reader comprehension.
- Put background information and theory under separate headings. Then readers can use the headings to read or skip these sections, as their knowledge dictates.
- If primary audiences will have more knowledge than other audiences, provide a glossary of terms. Early in the document, let readers know that the glossary exists.

FYI

Bell Canada repair technicians wear voice-activated computers to convey immediate, real-time messages between customers and Bell's repair managers. The wireless relay of voice, data, and images saves troubleshooting time and money

Source: Danylo Hawaleshka, "Wearing your computer," *Maclean's,* March 5, 2001, 49.

How do I reach my audience(s)?

Effective messages make use of multiple channels

Since communication channels vary in

- transmission speed

- transmission accuracy
- cost
- efficiency and
- audience impact

your purpose, the audience, and the situation—**known as the communication context**—will all determine which and how many channels you choose.

A written message makes it easier to

- Present many specific details of a law, policy, or procedure
- Present extensive or complex financial data
- Minimize undesirable emotions

But writing requires much more time and intellectual effort than speaking face-to-face.

Messages on paper are more formal than email messages. Email messages are appropriate for routine messages to people you already know. Paper is usually better for someone to whom you're writing for the first time.

Speaking is easier and more efficient to

- Answer questions, resolve conflicts, and build consensus
- Use emotion to help persuade the audience
- Get immediate action or response
- Focus the audience's attention on specific points
- Modify a proposal that may not be acceptable in its original form

Scheduled meetings and oral presentations are more formal than phone calls or stopping someone in the hall.

Important messages should use more formal channels, whether they're oral or written. Oral and written messages have many similarities. In both, you should

- Adapt the message to the specific audience
- Show the audience members how they benefit from the idea, policy, service, or product (◀▶ Module 8)
- Overcome any objections the audience may have
- Use you-attitude and positive emphasis (◀▶ Modules 6 and 7)
- Use visuals to clarify or emphasize material (◀▶ Module 25)
- Specify exactly what the audience should do

Even when everyone in an organization has access to the same channels, different discourse communities often prefer different channels. When a university updated its employee benefits manual, the computer scientists and librarians wanted the information online. Faculty wanted to be able to read the information on paper. Maintenance workers and carpenters wanted to get answers on voicemail.[9]

The bigger your audience, the more complicated channel choice becomes, because few channels reach everyone in your target audience. When possible, use multiple channels. Also use multiple channels for very important messages. For example, talk to key players about a written document before the meeting where the document will be discussed.

Employability Skills 2000+ Checklist for Adapting Your Message to Your Audience

In this module, the key skills from The Conference Board of Canada's Employability Skills 2000+ are:

Communicate
✔ write and speak so others pay attention and understand
✔ listen and ask questions to understand and appreciate the points of view of others

Think & Solve Problems
✔ assess situations and identify problems
✔ seek different points of view and evaluate them based on facts

Demonstrate Positive Attitudes & Behaviours
✔ deal with people, problems, and situations with honesty, integrity, and personal ethics
✔ show interest, initiative, and effort

Be Adaptable
✔ be open and respond constructively to change
✔ cope with uncertainty

Learn Continuously
✔ be willing to continuously learn and grow
✔ assess personal strengths and areas for development
✔ identify and access learning sources and opportunities

Work with Others
✔ understand and work within the dynamics of a group
✔ be flexible: respect, be open to and supportive of the thoughts, opinions, and contributions of others in a group
✔ recognize and respect people's diversity, individual differences, and perspectives
✔ accept and provide feedback in a constructive and considerate manner

Review of Key Points

- The **primary audience** will make a decision or act on the basis of your message. The **secondary audience** may be asked by the primary audience to comment on your message or to implement your ideas after they've been approved. The **initial audience** routes the message to other audiences and may assign the message. A **gatekeeper** controls whether the message gets to the primary audience. A **watchdog audience** has political, social, or economic power and may base future actions on its evaluation of your message.

- A sender goes through the following steps: **perception, interpretation, choice** or **selection, encoding, transmitting** the message through a **channel**. The receiver perceives the message, **decodes** it, interprets it, chooses a response, encodes the response, and transmits it. The message transmitted to the original sender is called **feedback**. **Noise** is anything that interferes with communication; it can be both physical and psychological. Miscommunication can occur at every point in the communication process.

- **Channel overload** occurs when a channel cannot handle all the messages being sent. **Information overload** occurs when the receiver cannot process all the messages that arrive. Both kinds of overload require some sort of selection to determine which messages will be sent and which ones will be attended to.

- **Common sense** and **empathy** are crucial to good audience analysis.

- A **discourse community** is a group of people who share assumptions about what channels, formats, and styles to use, what topics to discuss and how to discuss them, and what constitutes evidence.

- An **organization's culture** is its values, attitudes, and philosophies. Organizational culture is revealed verbally in the organization's myths, stories, and heroes and non-verbally in the allocation of space, money, and power.

- When you write to multiple audiences, use the primary audience and the gatekeeper to determine level of detail, organization, level of formality, and use of technical terms and theory.

- You can adapt your message's strategy, organization, and style to meet the audience's needs. For paper or electronic documents, you can also adapt the document's design and the photos or illustrations you choose.

- The best channel for a message will depend on the audience, the sender's purposes, and the situation. Channel choice may be shaped by the organizational culture.

- When you communicate to a big audience or about an important topic, use **multiple channels**.

Learning Applications

Questions for Comprehension

2.1 What are the five kinds of audiences?

2.2 What are ways to analyze your audience?

2.3 What are three ways to adapt your message to your audience?

2.4 Why do internal audiences, especially your boss, sometimes feel more important than primary audiences outside your organization?

2.5 What are your options if your boss's criteria for a document are different than those of the primary audience?

2.6 Emphasizing the importance of audience, marketers frequently say, "The customer is in control." To what extent do you feel in control as a customer, a student, a citizen? What actions could you take to increase your control?

2.7 If you are employed, which aspects of your organization's culture match your own values? What kind of culture would you like to join when you are next on the job market?

Questions for Building Skills

2.8 What skills have you read about in this module?

2.9 What skills are you practising when doing the assignments for this module?

2.10 How could you further develop the skills you're working on?

Exercises and Problems

2.11 Identifying Audiences

In each of the following situations, label the audiences as initial, gatekeeper, primary, secondary, or watchdog.

1. Russell is seeking venture capital so that he can expand his business of offering soccer camps to youngsters. He's met an investment banker whose clients regularly hear presentations from business people seeking capital. The investment banker decides who will get a slot on the program, based on a comprehensive audit of each company's records and business plan.

2. Maria is marketing auto loans. She knows that many car buyers choose one of the financing options presented by the car dealership, so she wants to persuade dealers to include her company in the options they offer.

3. Paul works for the mayor's office in a big city. As part of a citywide cost-cutting measure, a panel has recommended requiring employees who work more than 40 hours in a week to take compensatory time off rather than be paid overtime. The only exceptions will be the Police and Fire Departments. The mayor asks Paul to prepare a proposal for the city council, which will vote on whether to implement the change. Before they vote, council members will hear from (1) citizens, who will have an opportunity to read the proposal and communicate their opinions to the city council; (2) mayors' offices in other cities, who may be asked about their experiences; (3) union representatives, who may be concerned about the reduction in income that will come if the proposal is implemented; (4) department heads, whose ability to schedule work might be limited if the proposal passes; and (5) panel members and good-government lobbying groups. Council members come up for reelection in six months.

2.12 Choosing a Channel to Reach a Specific Audience

Suppose that your business, government agency, or non-profit group has a product, service, or program targeted for each of the following audiences. What would be the best channel(s) to reach people in that group in your city? Would that channel reach all group members?

1. Renters
2. Sikh owners of small businesses
3. People who use wheelchairs
4. Teenagers who work part-time while attending school
5. Competitive athletes
6. Parents whose children play soccer
7. People willing to work part-time
8. Financial planners
9. Hunters

2.13 Introducing a Wellness Program

Assume your organization has decided to implement a wellness program that will give modest rebates to employees who adopt healthy practices (see Problem

10.17). As director of human resources, you explain the program and build support for it. Pick a specific organization that you know something about and answer the following questions about it.

1. What percent of employees currently (a) smoke? (b) drink heavily? (c) are overweight? (d) don't exercise? (e) have high blood pressure? or (f) high cholesterol?

2. Why don't people already follow healthy lifestyles?

3. Do company vending machines, cafeteria, or other facilities make it easy for employees to get low-fat snacks and meals?

4. How much exercise do people get on the job? What work-related injuries are most common?

5. What exactly do people do on the job? Will being healthier help them work more efficiently? Better deal with stress? Have more confidence in interacting with clients and customers?

6. What aspects of health and fitness would employees like to know more about? What topics might seem boring or "old hat"?

2.14 Persuading an Organization to Adopt Flextime

Flextime is a system that allows workers to set their own starting and stopping hours. Most companies require that some provision be made to cover the phones during normal business hours, even if doing so means that not all employees can have exactly the schedules they want.

Flextime is especially appealing to organizations that have a hard time keeping good employees or that cannot easily raise salaries. It also is appealing to companies with the philosophy of giving workers as much independence as possible. Flextime can make it difficult to schedule meetings or for employees working on the same project to have enough time together. In some organizations, flextime creates conflicts between workers who get the schedules they want and those who have to work traditional hours to cover the phones. Some firms are afraid that the quality of work may suffer if employees and supervisors aren't on the job at the same time. Record-keeping may be more complicated. Most employees like flextime.

Identify the major argument that you could use to persuade each of the following organizations to use flextime and the major objection you anticipate. Which of the organizations would be fairly easy to convince? Which would be harder to persuade?

1. A large, successful insurance company
2. A branch bank
3. A small catering service
4. The admissions office on your campus
5. A church, synagogue, temple, or mosque with a staff of two clergy, a director of music, two secretaries, and a custodian
6. A government agency

2.15 Analyzing the Other Students in Your College or University

Analyze the students in your college/university. (If your college or university is large, analyze the students in your program of study.) Is there a "typical" student? If all students are quite different, how are they different? Consider the following kinds of information in your analysis:

Demographic Data

Age (Average; high and low)

Gender (What proportion are men? What proportion are women?)

Race or ethnic background (What groups are represented? How many of each?)

Marital status

Number of children

Parents' income/personal or family income

Going to school full- or part-time

Outside jobs (What kinds? How many hours a week?)

Membership in campus organizations

Religious affiliations

Political preferences

Proportion going on for further education after graduation

Psychographics

What values, beliefs, goals, and lifestyles do students have? Which are common? Which are less common?

What's the relationship between the students' values and their choice of major or program?

What do students hope to gain from the classes they're taking? What motivates them to do their best work in classes?

Additional Information

What are students' attitudes toward current campus problems? Current political problems?

What is the job market like for students in your college or major? Will students find it easy to get jobs after graduation? How much will they be making? Where will they be working?

After you answer these questions, identify the factors that would be most relevant in each of the following situations:

1. You want to persuade students to participate in an internship program (see Problem 12.15)

2. You want to persuade students to join a campus organization (see Problem 12.6)

3. You want to find out if there are enough parking spaces on campus (see Problem 24.17)

4. You want to know whether the campus placement office is providing adequate services to students (see Problem 24.18)

5. You want to hire students to staff a business that you're starting

2.16 Analyzing People in Your Organization

1. Analyze your supervisor
   - Does he or she like short or long explanations?
   - Does he or she want to hear about all the problems in a unit or only the major ones?
   - How important are punctuality and deadlines?
   - How well informed about a project does he or she wish to be?
   - Is he or she more approachable in the morning or the afternoon?
   - What are your supervisor's major hassles?

2. Analyze other workers in your organization
   - Is work "just a job" or do most people really care about the organization's goals?
   - How do workers feel about clients or customers?

   - What are your co-workers' major hassles?

3. Analyze your customers or clients
   - What attitudes do they have toward the organization and its products or services?
   - What are their major hassles?
   - Do education, age, or other factors affect the way they read?

As Your Instructor Directs,

a. Write a memo to your instructor summarizing your analysis

b. Discuss your analysis with a small group of students

c. Present your analysis orally to the class

d. Combine your information with classmates' information to present a collaborative report comparing and contrasting your audiences at work

2.17 Analyzing a Discourse Community

Analyze the way one of your discourse communities uses language. Possible groups include

- Family
- Peers
- Work teams
- Sports teams
- Honour organizations and other service or social groups
- Churches, synagogues, temples, and mosques
- Geographic or ethnic group

Questions to ask include the following:

- What specialized terms might not be known to outsiders?
- What topics do members talk or write about? What topics are considered unimportant or improper?
- What channels do members use to convey messages?
- What forms of language do members use to build goodwill? To demonstrate competence or superiority?
- What strategies or kinds of proof are convincing to members?
- What formats, conventions, or rules do members expect messages to follow?

As Your Instructor Directs,

a. Share your results orally with a small group of students

b. Present your results in an oral presentation to the class

c. Present your results in a memo to your instructor

d. Share your results in an email message to the class

e. Share your results with a small group of students and write a joint memo reporting the similarities and differences you found

2.18 Analyzing Corporate Culture on the Web

Analyze three organizations' Web descriptions of their corporate cultures.

1. Do all three discuss the same aspects of corporate culture?

2. Are the statements about each organization's culture consistent with the rest of its Web pages? With what you know about each organization?

3. What aspects of each culture do you like best? What, if anything, do you not like? What questions do you have about the organizations' culture that the Web pages don't answer?

As Your Instructor Directs,

a. Share your results orally with a small group of students

b. Present your results in an oral presentation to the class

c. Present your results in a memo to your instructor

d. Share your results in an email message to the class

e. Share your results with a small group of students and write a joint memo reporting the similarities and differences you found

2.19 Analyzing an Organization's Culture

Interview several people about the culture of their organization. Possible organizations include

- Work teams
- Sports teams
- Honour organizations and other service or social groups
- Churches, synagogues, temples, and mosques
- Geographic or ethnic group
- Groups of friends

Questions to ask include those in this module and the following:

1. Tell me about someone in this organization you admire. Why is he or she successful?
2. Tell me about someone who failed in this organization. What did he or she do wrong?
3. What ceremonies and rituals does this organization have? Why are they important?
4. Why would someone join this group rather than a competitor?

As Your Instructor Directs,

a. Share your results orally with a small group of students
b. Present your results in an oral presentation to the class
c. Present your results in a memo to your instructor
d. Share your results in an email message to the class
e. Share your results with a small group of students and write a joint memo reporting the similarities and differences you found

Polishing Your Prose

Comma Splices

In filmmaking, editors splice, or connect, two segments of film with tape to create one segment. A comma splice occurs when writers try to create one sentence by connecting two sentences with only a comma.

Correct: We shipped the order on Tuesday. It arrived on Wednesday.

Incorrect: We shipped the order on Tuesday, it arrived on Wednesday. (comma splice)

Comma splices are almost always inappropriate in business communication. (Poetry and fiction sometimes use comma splices to speed up action or simulate dialect; some sales letters and advertisements use comma splices for the same effect, though not always successfully.)

Fix a comma splice in one of four ways:

1. If the ideas in the sentences are closely related, use a semicolon:

   We shipped the order on Tuesday; it arrived on Wednesday.

2. Add a coordinating conjunction (such as and, or, or but):

   We shipped the order on Tuesday, and it arrived on Wednesday.

3. Make the incorrect sentence into two correct ones:

   We shipped the order on Tuesday. It arrived on Wednesday.

4. Subordinate one of the clauses:

   Because we shipped the order on Tuesday, it arrived on Wednesday.

Exercises

Fix the comma splices in the following sentences.

1. The conference call came at 1 P.M., we took it immediately.

2. We interviewed two people for the accounting position, we made a job offer to one.

3. Janelle drafted her problem-solving report, she sent a copy to each of the committee members for review.

4. The director of purchasing went to our Main Street warehouse to inspect the inventory, Chuck called him later to ask how things went.

5. Katya called the hotel in Montréal for a reservation, the desk staff booked a room for her immediately.

6. Mr. Margulies gave an audiovisual presentation at our September sales meeting in Whistler, it went very well.

7. I'll have Tina call the main office, you ask Brian to set up an appointment for the four of us tomorrow.

8. Working weekends is tough, it's part of life in the business world today.

9. I like to make oral presentations, they're fun.

10. Sunil is our most experienced employee, he joined the department in 1992.

Check your answers to the odd-numbered exercises on page 632 at the back of the book.

Module 3
Communicating across Cultures

Topics

- What is "culture"?
- How does culture affect business communication?
- There are so many different cultures! How can I know enough to communicate?
- How can I make my documents bias-free?

Review of Key Points

Learning Applications

Polishing Your Prose: Using Idioms

Learning Focus

After reading and applying the information in Module 3, you'll be able to demonstrate

Knowledge of

- The components of "culture"
- Workplace diversity
- Some North American cultural norms
- The importance and variety of non-verbal communication symbols
- Bias-free language

Skills to

- Consider diversity as part of your audience analysis
- Apply your awareness of others' values to your spoken and written messages
- Use bias-free language and photos

"I want to communicate how Arctic people enjoy a way of life connected to the land and sea."

"Arctic visitors have a spirit for adventure that lures them to experience a different environment and a different culture," says Kristiina Alariaq, who, with her husband Timmun, operates Huit Huit tours on Cape Dorset at the western end of Baffin Island. "I designed and wrote the brochure personally because I wanted to give a realistic description to travellers of what they could experience in our part of the Arctic." Huit Huit, named after the command that dogsledders yell to their dogs, offers a variety of experiences from a four-day cultural experience in town to a week on the land, or any combination a client wants.

"Many visitors who come to Cape Dorset have a curiosity and an interest to learn about Inuit culture and art. I want to communicate how Arctic people enjoy a way of life connected to the land and sea," continues Kristiina.

The cultural experience involves visiting the world famous Cape Dorset Print Gallery, where limited edition prints are made from drawings of such famous artists as Kenojuak. If you are lucky, you can actually get to see the printmaking process. You can hire an interpreter and the Alariaqs will arrange a visit with one of these famous artists, as well as with town elders, who will share the memories of what it was like living in the old hunting camps before the Inuit were forced to move into towns.

Visitors will also experience the landscape, which is granite outcropping and, in the summer, filled with small but vibrant wildflowers. A sail on the Arctic Ocean will bring you to old ruins of an earlier Inuit culture, whose people lived in dugout homes before the climate changed. And after a long day on the land the visitor will return to the Alariaq home for a dinner of caribou or arctic char, thereby literally getting a real taste of the arctic.

When travelling to Cape Dorset you must be prepared. The weather is totally different from the south; not only is it colder, it is more unpredictable. It is not unheard of to be fogged in for days at a time. The Alariaqs provide lists of what visitors should bring, including proper cold weather clothing and sunglasses.

So as not to be dependent on the weather many people in Dorset shop by the year. At the beginning of August a huge ocean-going freighter pulls into the harbour. Because of the rock drop off there is no dock. People take a raft out to the freighter, unload their yearly supplies, bring them to beach, load their trucks with the supplies and take them home.

Because of the climate home construction is totally different. Water pipes cannot be built, so a big job in the community is driving the water truck that supplies fresh water to each home. Houses must be built off the ground so the permafrost won't damage them.

When asked for a final word, Kristiina said, "It is important to communicate to visitors that they will have guides who know this land and that they will be safe and well taken care of." And the visitor will return with a truly Canadian multicultural experience.

http://huithuit@capedorsettours.com
Huit Huit Tours

FYI

When exchanging business cards with Asian acquaintances, observe important cultural niceties. Chinese businesspeople, for example, expect you to hand over your card with the print facing them, accompanied by a slight bow. When you receive the card, study it carefully before putting it in your pocket.

Site *to* **See**

Go to
http://www.asian connections.com/ business/

Angi Ma Wong provides additional information on Asian business etiquette.

In today's global village, you will work with people whose cultural backgrounds differ from yours.

Culture refers to the beliefs, customs, and assumptions that determine perception and behaviour. For example, residents of small towns and rural areas have different notions of friendliness than do people from big cities. Montréalers and Cape Bretoners talk and dress differently, as do people who live in Vancouver, Regina, Halifax, and Toronto. The cultural icons that resonate for baby boomers mean little to members of Generation X and Y. And gender culture often creates conversational incongruence between men and women.

All human beings conform to a culturally predetermined reality. Part of Canadian cultural identity, for example, has been formed by our dual linguistic heritage and by the economic and military might of our southern neighbour. Geography, weather, population density, and natural resources also contribute to cultural reality. For example, the Canadian values of courtesy, community, and cooperation may have evolved as survival strategies in a vast, sparsely populated land. Perceptions about gender, age, and social class are culturally based, as are our ideas about race, ethnicity, religious practices, sexual orientation, physical appearance and ability, and regional and national characteristics.

Regardless of your own cultural biases, however, your organizational productivity and individual professional success depend on your ability to communicate sensitively and flexibly with others.

Because of new waves of immigration and increasing numbers of women and minorities joining the workforce, the last 15 years have seen a growing emphasis on Canadian workplace diversity. Workplace "diversity" implies recognition of the heterogeneous nature of the Canadian population. This recognition has been legally enshrined in the *Canadian Charter of Rights and Freedoms* (1982) and the *Official Languages Act* (1988).

Legally and economically, today's employers and employees must be aware of and sensitive to others' values, beliefs, and practices that are based on

- Gender
- Race and ethnicity
- Regional and national origin
- Social class
- Religion
- Age
- Sexual orientation
- Physical ability

Most urban Canadians already share a multicultural perspective. Part of the Canadian identity derives from our dual French and British cultural heritage. But now immigrants from Italy, Greece, India, Jamaica, Japan, Pakistan, Poland, the former Yugoslavia, and Hong Kong add their voices to the medley of French, English, and Canadian native languages. According to Statistics Canada, in 1971, 96.3 percent of the Canadian population had origins in Britain or Europe, and only

1.3 percent of the population was of Asiatic origin. Canada's most recent census indicated people of Asian origin comprise 36 percent of the population.[1] Moreover, people work in Japanese plants in Alliston, Cambridge, and Mississauga, Ontario; in Vancouver, British Columbia; in Sherbrooke, Quebec; and in Saskatoon, Saskatchewan.

And successful Canadian businesses must understand the importance of catering to their disparate audiences. For example, radio station CHIN in Toronto broadcasts in 32 languages.[2]

Furthermore, foreign trade is essential to the growth of both individual businesses and to a country's economy as a whole. Although the United States remains our primary trading partner, the *North American Free Trade Act* (NAFTA) and the economic interests of countries worldwide offer opportunities for Canadian businesses.

As many companies have discovered, valuing diversity is good economic as well as good social practice. A growing body of literature shows that ethnically diverse teams produce more and higher-quality ideas.[3] One problem with our awareness of difference, however, is that members of a dominant group can acknowledge difference but still expect everyone else to adapt to them, rather than making the effort to understand the preferred communication styles of other workers.

What is "culture"?

Our deepest beliefs.

Each of us grows up in a **culture** that provides patterns of acceptable behaviour and belief. We may not be aware of the most basic features of our own culture until we come into contact with people who do things differently. If we come from a culture where dogs are pets, that may seem "natural" until we learn that in other cultures, dogs, like chickens, are raised for food.

We can categorize cultures as high-context or low-context.

- In **high-context cultures**, most of the information is inferred from the context of a message; little is "spelled out." Japanese, Arabic, and Latin American cultures are high-context.
- In **low-context cultures**, context is less important; most information is explicitly spelled out. German, Scandinavian, and the dominant North American cultures are low-context.

As David Victor points out in Figure 3.1 on page 56, high- and low-context cultures value different kinds of communication and have different attitudes toward oral and written channels.[4] As Figure 3.1 shows, low-context cultures favour direct approaches and perceive indirectness as dishonest or manipulative. The written word is seen as more important than spoken agreements, so contracts are binding but promises may be broken. Details, logic, and time constraints matter. North American communication practices reflect these low-context preferences.

FYI

Extensive studies prove that cultivating fluency in two languages contributes to reading and learning success. Despite this research, however, no more than 20,000 English-speaking American students participate in "dual immersion" programs, compared to the 300,000 Canadian Anglophones in French immersion studies.

Source: James Crawford, "A nation divided by one language," in Learning English, *The Guardian Weekly*, February 2001, 3.

FYI

We're less policed (182 cops per 100,000 Canadians) than the U.S. (247 per 100,000) and England and Wales (233). We can also boast about our increase in female officers: the number of women officers has more than doubled over the last ten years. British Columbia has the largest proportion of female cops; the Atlantic provinces have the lowest.

Source: "That's Ms. Officer," *Maclean's*, December/January 2001, 18.

Figure 3.1
Views of Communication in High- and Low-Context Cultures

	High Context (Examples: Japan, United Arab Emirates)	Low Context (Examples: Germany, Canada, the United States)
Preferred communication strategy	Indirectness, politeness, ambiguity	Directness, confrontation, clarity
Reliance on words to communicate	Low	High
Reliance on non-verbal signs to communicate	High	Low
Importance of written word	Low	High
Agreements made in writing	Not binding	Binding
Agreements made orally	Binding	Not binding
Attention to detail	Low	High

Source: Adapted from David A. Victor, *International Business Communication* (New York: HarperCollins, 1992), 148, 153, 160.

How does culture affect business communication?

Cultural expectations and assumptions determine business interaction!

Culture influences every single aspect of business communication: how to show politeness and respect, how much information to give, how to motivate people, when, how much and how loudly to talk and laugh, how to organize a letter, even what size paper to use.

Communication is also influenced by the organizational culture and by personal culture, such as gender, race and ethnicity, social class, and so forth. As Figure 3.2 suggests, all of these intersect to determine what kind of communication is needed in a given situation. Sometimes one kind of culture may dominate another culture. For example, in a study of aerospace engineers in Europe, Asia, and the United States, researchers John Webb and Michael Keene found that the similarities of the professional discourse community (one kind of culture) outweighed differences in national cultures.[5]

Figure 3.2
National Culture, Organizational Culture, and Personal Culture Overlap

Values, Beliefs, and Practices

Values and beliefs, often unconscious, affect our response to people and situations. Most Canadians, for example, value "fairness." "You're not playing fair" is a sharp criticism calling for changed behaviour. In some countries, however, people expect certain groups to receive preferential treatment. Most North Americans accept competition and believe that it produces better performance. The Japanese, however, believe that competition leads to disharmony. U.S. business people believe that success is based on individual achievement and is open to anyone who excels. Canadians prefer cooperation to blatant competition. In England and in France,

Dealing with Discrimination

Although two-thirds of us believe that our treatment of visible minorities is better today than in 1975, many Canadians deal with discrimination daily. Native Canadians, Canadians of East Asian, Middle Eastern, and Asian background often face prejudice. In the Greater Toronto area, where visible minorities comprise over 50 percent of the population, blacks in particular have real concerns. And no ethnic group is more stigmatized than the Jamaican community. Three-quarters of Jamaicans polled believe that the media misrepresents the black community, and that the police treat them unfairly. And two-thirds believe that Canada Customs and the courts treat them inequitably.

Media Misrepresentation

Anthropology professor, Caribbean community and anti-racism expert Frances Henry agrees. Her study of racist discourse in the media demonstrated that one-third of the Toronto newspaper articles featuring Jamaicans focussed on "…crime, justice, deportation, immigration and social programs. Another 38.3 percent of articles …involved sports and entertainment." "Even when reporting about Jamaica, the stories are about crime in Jamaica, political tension, or police brutality," Henry says. "Where are the stories about the general vibrancy of Jamaican culture, the superb accomplishments of its people, its serious musicians, its excellent literature and poetry?" Henry found racism "…rampant in schools…. There have been a lot of good education initiatives, but they don't touch down into the day-to-day experiences in the classroom." According to Henry, only Vietnamese Canadians come close to receiving similarly negative media coverage.

Race, Class, or Cultural Discrimination?

Other black Canadians speak of different experiences. According to Ilias Abdurhman, who immigrated to Toronto from Ethiopia a decade ago, "Everything is 100 percent better here. I don't have any fear of being discriminated against. I'm not saying everything is perfect here, but overall, Toronto is a wonderful place." Barbadian-born business analyst David Grant offers a similar perspective, "I'm sure there are stereotypes but I don't let it be a problem…. My attitude is 'That's their problem.' I go about my business and try to be respectful of other people…. I believe in trying to get along with people without giving up your identity. I like my culture, but I truly believe in the corporate world, there are no differences…I love Toronto…." Moreover, Grant suggests that discrimination may be class- rather than race-based, "I think if you survey professional blacks and non-professionals, the answers would be dramatically different. It all depends on the people you associate with." Although Ontario provincial parliament member Alvin Curling, who was born in Jamaica, agrees that the media foster discriminatory attitudes, he believes that ignorance of cultural character strengths contributes to racist stereotypes, "It comes from a positive assertiveness of Jamaicans. If it's discrimination or a job opportunity, they will go after it in a very aggressive and assertive way."

Positive Cultural Identity Promotes Success

Many community leaders feel that increasing awareness of ethnic Canadians' cultural identities—and of their contribution to Canadians' pride in their pluralistic society—will change attitudes. Worrick Russell, head of the Caribbean and African Canadian Chamber of Commerce, asserts that this awareness is reflected in our education, legal, and social systems. Political involvement, he believes, will create the greatest attitudinal change, as such involvement did for previous waves of immigrants.

Meanwhile, school systems across the country are experimenting with educational choices that provide young people with a positive sense of their cultural identity. Edmonton's Amiskwaciy Academy public school, which opened in the fall of 2000, follows the provincial curriculum within the context of significant aboriginal cultural norms: "elders provide guidance through storytelling, sweat lodges, ghost dances, and other ceremonies." Amiskwaciy Academy is one of many alternative education choices—including parent-run charter schools, home schools, and private schools—that not only address a growing aboriginal student population, but also meet a specific "customer" need within the Edmonton public school system. Similarly, Toronto school board's parents, teachers, and trustees have fought successfully to retain its programs in international languages and black culture at 17 schools across the city. While students' continuity in their mother tongue is preserved, they learn about their cultural heritage and heroes. Language learning facilitates all learning, according to Jack Jedwab, executive director of the Association for Canadian Studies at the University of Québec, Montréal. Equally important, the success of these students will transform the Canadian cultural landscape.

Sources: Brian Bergman, "Edmonton experiments with a diversity of choice," *Maclean's*, May 14, 2001, 25; Catherine Dunphy, "'My boys have done well,'" The *Toronto Star*, May 27, 2001, A7; Elaine Carey, "Black pride, city prejudice: Discrimination lingers on—Racism remains a concern for 71% of those polled"; visited Web site June 27, 2001.
http://www.geocities.com/CapitolHill/2381/tobeblack1.html;I and Ashante Infantry, "You don't have to be black to suffer prejudice. You just have to sound black," visited Web site June 27, 2001. http://www.geocities.com/obarri.geo/tobeblack.html.

success is more obviously linked to social class. And in some countries, the law prohibits people of some castes or races from participating fully in society.

Many North Americans value individualism. Other countries rely on group consensus for decision making. In traditional classrooms, North American students are expected to complete assignments alone; if they receive too much help from anyone else, they're "cheating." In Japan, however, groups routinely work together to solve problems. In the dominant North American culture, quiet is a sign that people are working. In Latin American, Mediterranean, Middle Eastern and Asian countries, people talk to get the work done.[6]

Values and beliefs are influenced by religion. Christianity coexists with a view of the individual as proactive. In some Muslim and Asian countries, however, it is seen as presumptuous to predict the future by promising action by a certain date. Some Amish and Jewish communities live and work in strict adherence to traditional customs. The Puritan work ethic, embraced as a cultural value throughout the northeastern United States regardless of race or religion, legitimizes wealth by seeing it as a sign of divine favour. In other Christian cultures, a simpler lifestyle is considered to be closer to God.

These differences in values, beliefs, and practices lead to differences in the kinds of appeals that motivate people, as Figure 3.3 below illustrates.

Figure 3.3
Cultural Contrasts in Motivation

	North American	Japan	Arab Countries
Emotional appeal	Opportunity	Group participation; company success	Religion; nationalism; admiration
Recognition based on	Individual achievement	Group achievement	Individual status; status of class/society
Material rewards	Salary; bonus; profit sharing	Annual bonus; social services; fringe benefits	Gifts for self/family; salary
Threats	Loss of job	Loss of group membership	Demotion, loss of reputation
Values	Competition; risk taking; freedom	Group harmony; belonging	Reputation; family security; religion

Source: Adapted from Farid Elashmawi and Philip R. Harris, *Multicultural Management 2000: Essential Cultural Insights for Global Business Success* (Houston: Gulf, 1998), 169.

Non-verbal Communication

Non-verbal communication—communication that makes meaning without words—permeates every part of our lives. Facial expressions, gestures, our use of time and space—even our pauses and vocal intonations— all communicate pleasure or anger, friendliness or distance, power and status.

Non-verbal communication is older and more powerful than spoken language. And its symbols can be misinterpreted just as easily as can verbal symbols (words). For example, a young woman brought a new idea to her boss, who glared at her, brows together in a frown, as she explained her proposal. The stare and lowered brows symbolized anger to her, and she assumed that he was rejecting her idea. Several months later, she learned that her boss always "frowned" when he was concentrating. The facial expression she had interpreted as anger had been intended to convey thinking.

Misunderstandings are even more common in communication across cultures, since non-verbal signals are culturally defined. An Arab student assumed that his North American roommate disliked him intensely because the roommate sat around the room with his feet up on the furniture, soles toward the Arab roommate. Arab culture sees the foot in general and the sole in particular as unclean; showing the sole of the foot is an insult.[7]

As is true of any aspect of communication, knowledge is power: learning about non-verbal symbols gives you the information you need to project the image you want and makes you more conscious of the signals you are interpreting. Since experts claim that 93 percent of all our meaning making is based on non-verbal symbols, your awareness and correct interpretation of non-verbal communication is vital to your personal and professional development. Remember, however, always to check your perceptions before making assumptions about others' non-verbal signals.

Body Language

Posture and body movements connote self-concept, energy, and openness. North American **open body positions** include leaning forward with uncrossed arms and legs, with the arms away from the body. **Closed** or **defensive body positions** include leaning back, sometimes with both hands behind the head, arms and legs crossed or close together, or hands in pockets. As the labels imply, open positions suggest that people are accepting and open to new ideas. Closed positions suggest that people are physically or psychologically uncomfortable, that they are defending themselves and shutting other people out.

People who cross their arms or legs claim that they do so only because the position is more comfortable. Certainly crossing one's legs is one way to be more comfortable in a chair that is the wrong height. Canadian women used to be taught to adopt a "ladylike" posture: arms close to their bodies and knees and ankles together. But notice your own body the next time you're in a perfectly comfortable discussion with a good friend. You'll probably find that you naturally assume open body positions. The fact that so many people in organizational settings adopt closed positions may indicate that many people feel at least slightly uncomfortable in school and on the job.

People of eastern cultures value the ability to sit quietly. They may see the North American tendency to fidget and shift as an indication of a lack of mental or spiritual balance. Even Canadian interviewers and audiences usually respond negatively to

nervous gestures such as fidgeting with a tie or hair or jewellery, tapping a pencil, or swinging a foot.

Eye Contact

Canadians of European background see **eye contact** as a sign of honesty. But in many cultures, dropped eyes are a sign of appropriate deference to a superior. Puerto Rican children are taught not to meet the eyes of adults.[8] The Japanese are taught to look at the neck.[9] In Korea, prolonged eye contact is considered rude. The lower-ranking person is expected to look down first.[10] In Muslim countries, women and men are not supposed to have eye contact.

These differences can lead to miscommunication in the multicultural workplace. Supervisors may infer that from their eye contact that employees are being disrespectful, when, in fact, the employee is behaving appropriately according to the norms of his or her culture.

Gestures

Canadians sometimes assume that, if language fails, they can depend on gestures to communicate with non-English-speaking people. But Birdwhistell reported that "although we have been searching for 15 years [1950–65], we have found no gesture or body motion which has the same meaning in all societies."[11]

Gestures that mean approval in Canada may have very different meanings in other countries. The "thumbs up" sign that means "good work" or "go ahead" in Canada, the United States, and most of Western Europe is a vulgar insult in Greece. The circle formed with the thumb and first finger that means *OK* in Canada is obscene in Southern Italy and can mean "you're worth nothing" in France and Belgium.[12]

In the question period after a lecture, a man asked the speaker, a Puerto Rican professor, if shaking the hands up and down in front of the chest, as though shaking off water, was "a sign of mental retardation." The professor was horrified: in her culture, the gesture meant "excitement, intense thrill."[13] Studies have found that Spanish-speaking doctors rate the mental abilities of Latino patients much higher than do English-speaking doctors. The language barrier is surely part of the misevaluation by English-speaking doctors. Cultural differences in gestures may contribute to the misevaluation. Similarly, European Canadian supervisors in the workplace may underestimate the abilities of Filipinos because behaviours, vocal expressiveness, and gestures differ in the two cultures.

Space

Concepts of space are also culturally understood. **Personal space** is the distance someone wants between himself or herself and other people in ordinary, non-intimate interchanges. Observation and limited experimentation show that most North Americans, North Europeans, and Asians want a bigger personal space than do Latin Americans, French, Italians, and Arabs. People who are accustomed to lots of personal space and are forced to accept close contact on a crowded elevator or subway react in predictable and ritualistic ways: they stand stiffly and avoid eye contact with others.

Even within a culture, some people like more personal space than do others. One study found that men took more personal space than women did.[14] In many cultures, people who are of the same age and sex take less personal space than do mixed-age or mixed-sex groups. Latin Americans stand closer to people of the same sex than North Americans do, but North Americans stand closer to people of the opposite sex.[15]

Touch

Repeated studies prove that babies need to be touched to grow and thrive, and that older people are healthier both mentally and physically if they are touched. But some people are more comfortable with touch than others. Some people shake hands in greeting but otherwise don't like to be touched at all, except by family members or lovers. Other people, having grown up in families that touch a lot, hug as part of a greeting and touch even casual friends. Each kind of person may misinterpret the other. A person who dislikes touch may seem unfriendly to someone who's used to touching. A toucher may seem overly familiar to someone who dislikes touch.

Studies indicate that in North American culture, touch is interpreted as power: more powerful people touch less powerful people. When the toucher had higher status than the recipient, both men and women liked being touched.[16]

Most parts of North America allow opposite-sex couples to hold hands or walk arm-in-arm in public but frown on the same behaviour in same-sex couples. People in Asia, the Middle East, and South America have the opposite expectation: male friends or female friends can hold hands or walk arm-in-arm, but it is slightly shocking for an opposite-sex couple to touch in public. In Iran, even handshakes between men and women are seen as improper.[17]

People who don't know each other well may feel more comfortable with each other if a piece of furniture separates them. For example, in most Canadian interviews, a desk, which both perceive as part of the interviewer's space, separates the interviewer and the applicant. It's considered inappropriate for the applicant to place his/her property (notebook, purse) or to lean on the desk. In some situations, a group may work better sitting around a table than just sitting in a circle. In North America, a person sitting at the head of a table is generally assumed to be the group's leader. However, one experiment showed that when a woman sat at the head of a mixed-sex group, observers assumed that one of the men in the group was the leader.[18]

Spatial Arrangements

In North America, the size, placement, and privacy of one's office connote status. Large corner offices have the highest status. An individual office with a door that closes connotes more status than a desk in a common area. Japanese firms, however, see private offices as "inappropriate and inefficient," reports Robert Christopher. Only the very highest executives and directors have private offices in the traditional Japanese company, and even they will also have desks in the common areas.[19]

Japanese homes have much smaller rooms than most North American homes. The Japanese use less furniture and arrange it differently: a small table will be in the centre of the room. In cold weather, a heater is placed under the table; the table-cloth keeps the warm air around the legs and feet of everyone who sits at the table.

Site *to* **See**

Go to
http://www.parl.gc.ca/36/information/library/PRBpubs/bp453-e.htm
A 1997 study on Canadian linguistic and cultural diversity demonstrates that 31percent of Canadians are of neither British nor French descent.

http://www.diversitywatch.ryerson.ca
Stereotypical coverage of minorities in Canada is tracked by this Web site produced by the School of Journalism at Ryerson Polytechnic University.

A private office is a hotly contested sign of status in North American businesses but a privilege reserved for only the highest executives in Japan. This middle-level manager in Tokyo works in a common area alongside his co-workers.

Traditional Japanese may see Western rooms as "empty" since Western furniture lines the walls, leaving a large empty space in the middle of the room.[20]

Time

Canadian organizations—businesses, government, and schools—keep time by the calendar and the clock. Being "on time" is seen as a sign of dependability. Other cultures may keep time by the seasons and the moon, the sun, internal "body clocks," or a personal feeling that "the time is right."

Canadians who believe that "time is money" are often frustrated in negotiations with people who take a much more leisurely approach. Part of the miscommunication stems from this major perception difference: people in many other cultures want to take the time to establish a personal relationship before they decide whether to do business with each other.

Miscommunication occurs because various cultures perceive time differently. Many Canadians measure time in five-minute blocks. Someone who is five minutes late to an appointment or a job interview feels compelled to apologize. If the executive or interviewer is running half an hour late, the caller expects to be told about the likely delay upon arriving. Some people won't be able to wait that long and will need to reschedule their appointments. But in Latin American and other cultures, 15 minutes or half an hour may be the smallest block of time. To someone who mentally measures time in 15-minute blocks, being 45 minutes late is no worse than being 15 minutes late is to someone who is conscious of smaller units.

Edward T. Hall distinguishes between **monochronic** cultures, where one does only one important activity at a time, and **polychronic** cultures, where people do several things at once. Researchers see the United States as monochronic. When U.S. managers feel offended because a Latin American manager also sees other people during "their" appointments, the two kinds of time are in conflict. However, people who eat breakfast or use car phones while they drive are doing more than one thing at a time. In a few organizations, it is even acceptable to do other work during a meeting. Such "multi-tasking" may indicate that some North American companies are evolving from a monochronic culture to a somewhat polychronic culture.

According to some scholars, Europeans schedule fewer events in a comparable period of time than do North Americans. Perhaps as a result, Germans and German Swiss see North Americans as too time-conscious.[21]

Other Non-verbal Symbols

Many other symbols can carry non-verbal meanings: clothing, colours, age, and height, to name a few.

In Canada, certain styles and colours of clothing are considered more "professional" and more "credible." Certain clothes and fabrics—silk and linen, for example—carry non-verbal messages of success, prestige, and competence. In Japan, clothing denotes not only status but also occupational group. Private-school students wear

Site *to* See

Go to
http://www2.soc.
hawaii.edu/css/dept/
com/resources/inter
cultural/Hall.html

Begin your exploration of culture and communications with non-verbal communications expert E.T. Hall. *The Silent Language* (New York: Anchor Books, Doubleday, 1981); *The Hidden Dimension* (New York: Anchor Books, Doubleday, 1982); E.T. Hall and Mildred Hall, *Hidden Differences: Doing Business with the Japanese* (Yarmouth, ME: Intercultural Press, 1990).

uniforms. Company badges indicate rank within the organization. Workers wear different clothes when they are on strike than they do when they are working.[22]

Colours can also carry meanings in a culture. In Canada, mourners wear black to funerals, while brides wear white. In pre-Communist China and in some South American tribes, white is the colour of mourning. Purple flowers are given to the dead in Mexico.[23] In Korea, red ink is used to record deaths but never to write about living people.[24]

North American culture values youth. More and more individuals choose to colour their hair and have surgery to look as youthful as possible. In Japan, younger people defer to older people. North Americans attempting to negotiate in Japan are usually taken more seriously if at least one member of the team is noticeably grey-haired.

Height connotes status in many parts of the world. Executive offices are usually on the top floors; the underlings work below. Even being tall can help a person succeed. Studies have shown that employers are more willing to hire men over 1.85 metres tall than shorter men with the same credentials. Studies of real-world executives and graduates have shown that taller men make more money. In one study, every extra inch of height brought in an extra $600 a year.[25] But being too big can be a disadvantage. A tall, brawny football player complained that people found him intimidating off the field and assumed that he "had the brains of a Twinkie."

Oral Communication

Effective oral communication also requires cultural understanding. As Figure 3.4 shows, both purpose and content of business introductions differ across cultures.

Deborah Tannen uses the term **conversational style** to denote our conversational patterns and the meanings we give to them: the way we show interest, courtesy, social decorum.[26] Your answers to the following questions reveal your own conversational style:

- How long a pause tells you that it's your turn to speak?
- Do you see interruption as rude? Or do you say things while other people are still talking to show that you're interested and to encourage them to say more?
- Do you show interest by asking lots of questions? Or do you see questions as intrusive and wait for people to volunteer whatever they have to say?

Instant Replay

Two Views of Time

In **monochronic** cultures, one does only one important activity at a time. In **polychronic** cultures, people do several things at once.

Site to See

Go to http://www.enel.ucalgary.ca/~goss/693/short/11.html

This site provides information on how to assess your own and others' behavioural styles, in order to adapt to others' styles.

Figure 3.4
Cultural Contrasts in Business Introductions

	North America	Japan	Arab Countries
Purpose of introduction	Establish status and job identity; network	Establish position in group, build harmony	Establish personal rapport
Image of individual	Independent	Member of group	Part of rich culture
Information	Related to business	Related to company	Personal
Use of language	Informal, friendly; use first name	Little talking	Formal; expression of admiration
Values	Openness, directness, action	Harmony, respect, listening	Religious harmony, hospitality, emotional support

Source: Adapted from Farid Elashmawi and Philip R. Harris, *Multicultural Management 2000: Essential Cultural Insights for Global Business Success* (Houston: Gulf, 1998), 113.

One conversational style is not better or worse than another, but people with different conversational styles may feel uncomfortable without knowing why. A boss who speaks slowly may frustrate a subordinate who talks quickly. People who talk more slowly may feel shut out of a conversation with people who talk more quickly. Someone who has learned to make requests directly ("Please pass the salt") may be annoyed by someone who uses indirect requests ("This casserole needs some salt").

In the workplace, conflicts may arise because of differences in conversational style. Generation Xers often use a rising inflection on statements as well as questions. Xers see this style as gentler and more polite. But baby boomer bosses may see this speech pattern as hesitant, as if the speaker wants advice—which they then proceed to deliver.[27] Thomas Kochman claims that African Americans often use direct questions to criticize or accuse.[28] If Kochman is right, an African-American employee might see a question ("Will that report be ready Friday?") as a criticism of his or her progress. One supervisor might mean the question simply as a request for information. Another supervisor might use the question to mean, "I want that report Friday."

Daniel N. Maltz and Ruth A. Borker believe that differences in conversational style may be responsible for the miscommunication that sometimes occurs in male–female conversations. For example, researchers have found that women are much more likely to nod and to say *yes* or *mm hmm* than men are. Maltz and Borker hypothesize that to women, these symbols mean simply, "I'm listening; go on." Men, on the other hand, may decode these symbols as "I agree" or at least "I follow what you're saying so far." A man who receives nods and *mms* from a woman may feel that she is inconsistent and unpredictable if she then disagrees with him. A woman may feel that a man who doesn't provide any feedback isn't listening to her.[29]

Site *to* **See**

Go to
**http://georgetown.
edu/tannen**

Explore differences
in men's and
women's
communication
styles on the
*"General Audience
Publications"* Web
page of inter-gender
communications
expert Deborah
Tannen.

Understatement and Exaggeration

Closely related to conversational style is the issue of understatement and overstatement. The British have a reputation for understatement. Someone good enough to play at Wimbledon may say he or she "plays a little tennis." Or ask a Canadian how the meeting yesterday or last night's game went, and the answer will be "Not bad!" even if the event was a roaring success. On the other hand, many people in the United States exaggerate. A U.S. businessman negotiating with a German said, "I know it's impossible, but can we do it?" The German saw the statement as nonsensical: By definition, something that is impossible cannot be done at all. The American saw "impossible" as merely a strong way of saying "difficult" and assumed that with enough resources and commitment, the job could in fact be done.[30]

Compliments

The kinds of statements that people interpret as compliments and the socially correct way to respond to compliments also vary among cultures. The statement "You must be really tired" is a compliment in Japan since it recognizes the other person has worked hard. The correct response is "Thank you, but I'm OK." A Canadian who is complimented on giving a good oral presentation will probably say "Thank you." A Chinese or Japanese person, in contrast, will apologize: "No, it wasn't very good."[31]

Statements that seem complimentary in one context may be inappropriate in another. For example, businesswomen may feel uncomfortable if male colleagues or superiors compliment them on their appearance: the comments suggest that the women are being treated as visual decoration rather than as contributing workers.

Silence

Silence also has different meanings in different cultures and subcultures. North Americans have difficulty doing business in Japan because they do not realize that silence almost always means that the Japanese do not like the ideas. Muriel Saville-Troike reports that during a period of military tension, Greek traffic controllers responded with silence when Egyptian planes requested permission to land. The Greeks intended silence as a refusal; the Egyptians interpreted silence as consent. Several people were killed when the Greeks fired on the planes as they approached the runway.[32]

Matthews . . . We're getting another one of those strange "ah blaw es span yol" sounds

Source: THE FAR SIDE © 1985 EARWORKS, Inc. Used by permission.

Successful intercultural communicators attempt to understand the communication style the other group prefers.

Different understandings of silence can prolong problems with sexual harassment in the workplace. Women sometimes use silence to respond to comments they find offensive, hoping that silence will signal their lack of appreciation. But some men may think that silence means appreciation or at least neutrality.

Writing to International Audiences

Most cultures are more formal than ours. When you write to international audiences, use titles, not first names. Avoid contractions, slang, and sports metaphors.

The patterns of organization that work for Canadian audiences may need to be modified for international correspondence beyond the U.S. For most cultures, buffer negative messages (◀▶ Module 11) and make requests (◀▶ Module 12) more indirect. As Figure 3.5 on page 66 suggests, you may need to modify style, structure, and strategy when writing to international readers. Make a special effort to avoid phrases that your audience could interpret as arrogant or uncaring. Cultural mistakes made orally may float away on the air; those made in writing are permanently recorded.

Figure 3.5

Cultural Contrasts in Written Persuasive Documents

	North America	**Japan**	**Arab Countries**
Opening	Request action or get reader's attention	Offer thanks; apologize	Offer personal greetings
Way to persaude	Immediate gain or loss of opportunity	Waiting	Personal connections; future opportunity
Style	Short sentences	Modesty, minimize own standing	Elaborate expressions; many signatures
Closing	Specific request	Desire to maintain harmony	Future relationship, personal greeting
Values	Efficiency; directness, action	Politeness; indirectness; relationship	Status; continuation

Source: Adapted from Farid Elashmawi and Philip P. Harris, *Multicultural Management 2000: Essential Cultural Insights for Global Business Success* (Houston: Gulf, 1998), 139.

Go to
www.travlang.com
Learn languages for
international travel.

There are so many different cultures! How can I know enough to communicate?

Focus on being sensitive and flexible.

The first step in understanding people of another culture is to realize that they may do things very differently, and that they value their way as much as you do yours. Moreover, people within a single culture differ. The kinds of differences summarized in this module can turn into stereotypes, which can be just as damaging as ignorance. Don't try to memorize the material here as a rigid set of rules. Instead, use the examples to get a sense for the kinds of things that differ from one culture to another. Test these generalizations against your experience. When in doubt, ask.

If you work with people from other cultures or if you plan to travel to a specific country, read about that country or culture and learn a little of the language. Also talk to people. That's really the only way to learn whether someone is wearing black as a sign of mourning, as a fashion statement, or as a colour that slenderizes and doesn't show dirt.

As Brenda Arbeláez suggests, the successful international communicator is

- Aware that his or her preferred values and behaviours are influenced by culture and are not necessarily "right"
- Flexible and open to change
- Sensitive to verbal and non-verbal behaviour
- Aware of the values, beliefs, and practices in other cultures
- Sensitive to differences among individuals within a culture[33]

How can I make my documents bias-free?

Start by using nonsexist, nonracist, and nonagist language.

Bias-free language is language that does not discriminate against people on the basis of sex, physical condition, race, age, or any other category. Bias-free language is fair and friendly; it complies with the law. It includes all readers; it helps to sustain goodwill. When you produce newsletters or other documents with photos and illustrations, choose a sampling of the whole population, not just part of it.

Making Language Nonsexist

Nonsexist language treats both sexes neutrally. Check to be sure that your writing is free from sexism in four areas: words and phrases, job titles, pronouns, and courtesy titles. Courtesy titles are discussed in ◀▶ Module 9 on format. Words and phrases, job titles, and pronouns are discussed in this module.

Words and Phrases

If you find any of the terms in the first column in Figure 3.6 on page 68 in your writ-

Many developing countries have gone straight to cell phones, skipping the expensive step of laying cables. In Bangladesh, Laili Begum makes her first call on a cell phone. Many owners of cell phones have become entrepreneurs, allowing townspeople to make calls on their phones for a small fee. Now farmers can call to find out what prices are in the cities, so they aren't at the mercy of what middleman claim.

Source: "It Takes a Cell Phone," *The Wall Street Journal,* June 25, 1999, B1.

ing or your company's documents, replace them with terms from the second column.

Not every word containing *man* is sexist. For example, *manager* is not sexist. The word comes from the Latin *manus*, meaning *hand*; it has nothing to do with maleness.

Avoid terms that assume that everyone is married or is heterosexual.

Biased: You and your husband or wife are cordially invited to the dinner.
Better: You and your guest are cordially invited to the dinner.

Job Titles

Use neutral titles that imply that a person of either gender could hold the job. Many job titles are already neutral: *accountant, banker, doctor, engineer, inspector, manager, nurse, pilot, secretary, technician,* to name a few. Other titles reflect gender stereotypes and need to be changed. (See Figure 3.6 for specific examples.)

Pronouns

When you write about a specific person, use the appropriate gender pronouns:

In his speech, John Jones said that . . .
In her speech, Judy Jones said that . . .

Figure 3.6

Getting Rid of Sexist Terms and Phrases

Instead of	Use	Because
The girl at the front desk	The woman's name or job title: "Ms. Browning," "Rosa," "the receptionist"	Call female employees *women* just as you call male employees *men*. When you talk about a specific woman, use her name, just as you use a man's name to talk about a specific man.
The ladies on our staff	The women on our staff	Use parallel terms for males and females. Therefore, use *ladies* only if you refer to the males on your staff as *gentlemen*. Few businesses do, since social distinctions are rarely at issue.
Manpower Manhours Manning	Personnel Hours or worker hours, Staffing	The power in business today comes from both women and men. Use nonsexist alternatives.
Managers and their wives	Managers and their guests	Managers may be female; not everyone is married.
Businessman	A specific title: executive, accountant, department head, owner of a small business, men and women in business, business person	Gender-neutral title
Chairman	Chair, chairperson, moderator	Gender-neutral title
Foreman	Supervisor (from *Job Title Revisions*)	Gender-neutral title
Salesman	Salesperson, sales representative	Gender-neutral title
Waitress	Server	Gender-neutral title
Woman lawyer	Lawyer	Gender-neutral title. You would not describe a man as a "male lawyer".
Workman	Worker, employee. Or use a specific title: crane operator, bricklayer, etc.	Gender-neutral title

When you are not writing about a specific person, but about anyone who may be in a given job or position, traditional gender pronouns are sexist.

Sexist: a. Each supervisor must certify that the time sheet for his department is correct.

Sexist: b. When the nurse fills out the accident report form, she should send one copy to the Central Division Office.

Business writing uses four ways to eliminate sexist generic pronouns: use plurals, use second person *you*, revise the sentence to omit the pronoun, and use pronoun pairs. Whenever you have a choice of two or more ways to make a phrase or sentence nonsexist, choose the alternative that is the smoothest and least conspicuous.

The following examples use these methods to revise sentences *a* and *b* above.

1. Use plural nouns and pronouns.

Nonsexist: a. Supervisors must certify that the time sheets for their departments are correct.

Note: When you use plural nouns and pronouns, other words in the sentence may need to be made plural too. In the example above, plural supervisors have plural time sheets and departments.

Avoid mixing singular nouns and plural pronouns.

Nonsexist but   a. Each supervisor must certify that the time sheet for their
lacks agreement: department is correct.

Since *supervisor* is singular, it is incorrect to use the plural *they* to refer to it. The resulting lack of agreement is becoming acceptable orally but is not yet acceptable to many readers in writing. Instead, use one of the four grammatically correct ways to make the sentence nonsexist.

2. Use you.

Nonsexist: a. You must certify that the time sheet for your department is correct.

Nonsexist: b. When you fill out an accident report form, send one copy to the Central Division Office.

You is particularly good for instructions and statements of the responsibilities of someone in a given position. Using *you* also frequently shortens sentences, because you write "Send one copy" instead of "You should send one copy." It also makes your writing more direct.

3. Substitute an article (*a*, *an*, or *the*) for the pronoun, or revise the sentence so that the pronoun is unnecessary.

Nonsexist: a. The supervisor must certify that the time sheet for the department is correct.

Nonsexist: b. The nurse will
                  1. Fill out the accident report form.
                  2. Send one copy of the form to the Central Division Office.

4. When you must focus on the action of an individual, use pronoun pairs.

Nonsexist: a. The supervisor must certify that the time sheet for his or her department is correct.

Nonsexist: b. When the nurse fills out the accident report form, he or she should send one copy to the Central Division Office.

Making Language Nonracist and Nonagist

Language is **nonracist** and **nonagist** when it treats all races and ages fairly, avoiding negative stereotypes of any group. Use these guidelines to check for bias in documents you write or edit:

- **Give someone's race or age only if it is relevant to your story.** When you do mention these characteristics, give them for everyone in your story—not just the non-Caucasian, non-young-to-middle-aged adults you mention.

FYI

Statistics Canada reports that across Canada some 777,700 women own businesses. Women-led firms make up approximately one third of all businesses in Canada and provide almost one million jobs for Canadians. The number of women-owned businesses is increasing at twice the national average.

Source: "100 Top Women Entrepreneurs," *Chatelaine*, November 1999, p.72; Women Business Owners of Canada, http://www.wboc.ca/about_f.htm; visited Web site August 17, 2000.

Instant Replay

To eliminate sexist pronouns,

1. Use plurals
2. Use second person *you*
3. Revise the sentence to omit the pronoun
4. Use pronoun pairs

- **Refer to a group by the term it prefers. As preferences change, change your usage.** Sixty years ago, *Negro* was preferred as a more dignified term than *coloured* for North Americans of African origin. As times changed, *black* and *African American* replaced it in the United States. In Canada, *black* is generally preferred to *African Canadian*, which is more often used for recent immigrants from Africa and thus might not include, for example, black Canadians from Caribbean nations or black Canadians who came to Nova Scotia as Loyalists in the late 1700s.

  Asian is preferred to *Oriental*, which may be considered offensive.

  East Indian is frequently misused to include people of non-Indian origin, such as new Canadians from Pakistan, Sri Lanka, and Bangladesh. *South Asian* is more accurate, and Pakistani, Sri Lankan, and Bangladeshi are preferred.

  Eskimo is a negative label. A better term is *Inuit*, which means *the people*.

  Native Canadian is generally used to refer to Canada's aboriginal peoples: Indians, Inuit, and Métis. But usage will vary depending on the preference of the individual or group referred to. For example, some native people consider *Indian* offensive or at least a source of confusion with people from India, while others may find it acceptable and use it to describe themselves. Where possible, consider referring to the specific band or nation of the individual (for example, Métis, Mohawk, Cree, Haida).

  Older people and *mature customers* are more generally accepted terms than senior citizens or golden agers.

- **Avoid terms that suggest that competent people are unusual.** The statement "She is an intelligent Métis woman" suggests that the writer expects most Métis women to be stupid. "He is an asset to his race" suggests that excellence in the race is rare. "He is a spry 70-year-old" suggests that the writer is amazed that anyone that old can still move.

Talking about People with Disabilities and Diseases

A disability is a physical, mental, sensory, or emotional impairment that interferes with the major tasks of daily living. A March 2000 study identified 14.5 percent of the working-age Canadian population as disabled. The number of people with disabilities will rise as the population ages.[33]

- **People-first language** focusses on the person, not the condition. Use it instead of outdated adjectives used as nouns that imply that the condition defines the person.
- **Avoid negative terms, unless the audience prefers them.** You-attitude takes precedence over positive emphasis: use the term a group prefers. People who lost their hearing as infants, children, or young adults often prefer to be called *deaf*. But people who lose their hearing as older adults often prefer to be called *hard of hearing*, even when their hearing loss is just as great as someone who identifies as part of deaf culture.

Instead of	Use	Because
The mentally retarded	Developmentally delayed	The condition does not define the person or his or her potential.
The blind	People with vision impairments	
Cancer patients	People being treated for cancer	

Figure 3.7

Getting Rid of Terms and Phrases That Discriminate Against People with Disabilities

Just as people in a single ethnic group may prefer different labels based on generational or cultural divides, so differences exist within the disability community. Using the right term requires keeping up with changing preferences. If your target audience is smaller than the whole group, use the term preferred by that audience, even if the group as a whole prefers another term.

Some negative terms, however, are never appropriate. Negative terms such as *afflicted*, *suffering from*, and *struck down* also suggest an outdated view of any illness as a sign of divine punishment.

Choosing Bias-Free Photos and Illustrations

When you produce a document with photographs or illustrations, check the visuals for possible bias. Do they show people of both sexes and all races? Is there a sprinkling of various kinds of people (younger and older, people using wheelchairs, etc.)? It's OK to have individual pictures that have just one sex or one race; the photos as a whole do not need to show exactly 50 percent men and 50 percent women. But the general impression should suggest that diversity is welcome and normal.

Check relationships and authority figures as well as numbers. If all the men appear in business suits and the women in maids' uniforms, the pictures are sexist even if an equal number of men and women are pictured. If the only blacks and Filipinos pictured are factory workers, the photos support racism even when an equal number of people from each race are shown.

In the late 1990s, as Marilyn Dyrud has shown, only 22 percent of the images of humans in standard clip art files were women, and most of those showed women in traditional roles. An even smaller percent pictured members of minority groups.[34] Don't use biased clip art or stock photos: look for alternatives to the kind of clip art shown at right, or create your own bias-free illustrations.

Employability Skills 2000+ Checklist for Communicating Across Cultures

In this module, the key skills from The Conference Board of Canada's Employability Skills 2000+ are:

Communicate
- ✔ write and speak so others pay attention and understand
- ✔ listen and ask questions to understand and appreciate the points of view of others

Manage Information
- ✔ access, analyze, and apply knowledge and skills from various disciplines (e. g., the arts, languages, science, technology, mathematics, social sciences, and the humanities)

Think & Solve Problems
- ✔ assess situations and identify problems
- ✔ seek different points of view and evaluate them based on facts
- ✔ recognize the human, interpersonal, technical, scientific, and mathematical dimensions of a problem

Work with Others
- ✔ understand and work within the dynamics of a group
- ✔ be flexible: respect, be open to and supportive of the thoughts, opinions, and contributions of others in a group
- ✔ recognize and respect people's diversity, individual differences, and perspectives
- ✔ accept and provide feedback in a constructive and considerate manner
- ✔ contribute to a team by sharing information and expertise

Participate in Projects & Tasks
- ✔ adapt to changing requirements and information

Review of Key Points

- **Culture** provides patterns of acceptable behaviour and beliefs.
- In **high-context cultures**, most of the information is inferred from the context of a message; little is explicitly conveyed. In **low-context cultures**, context is less important; most information is explicitly spelled out.
- Non-verbal signals can be misinterpreted just as easily as can verbal symbols (words).
- No gesture has a universal meaning across all cultures. Gestures that signify approval in North America may be insults in other countries, and vice versa.

- **Personal space** is the distance someone wants between him or herself and other people in ordinary, non-intimate interchanges.

- North Americans who believe that "time is money" are often frustrated in negotiations with people who want to establish a personal relationship before they decide whether to do business with each other or who measure time in 15- or 30-minute increments rather than the 5-minute intervals North Americans are used to.

- In **monochronic** cultures, people do only one important activity at a time. Canada is classified as monochronic. In **polychronic** cultures, people do several things at once.

- **Conversational style** denotes our conversational patterns and the way we show interest, politeness, appropriateness.

- The successful intercultural communicator is
  - Aware that his or her preferred values and behaviours are influenced by culture and are not necessarily "right."
  - Flexible and open to change.
  - Sensitive to verbal and non-verbal behaviour.
  - Aware of the values, beliefs, and practices in other cultures.
  - Sensitive to differences among individuals within a culture.

- Traditional pronouns are sexist when they refer to a class of people, not to specific individuals. Four ways to make the sentence nonsexist are to use plurals, to use you, to revise the sentence to omit the pronoun, and to use pronoun pairs.

- Bias-free language is fair and friendly; it complies with the law. It includes all readers; it helps to sustain goodwill.

Learning Applications

Questions for Comprehension

3.1 What sources create diversity in the workplace?

3.2 What is intercultural competence?

3.3 What four methods make a sentence nonsexist?

Questions for Critical Thinking

3.4 It's sexist to always put the male pronoun first in pronoun pairs (e.g., *he/she* rather than *she/he* or *s/he*). Why do the authors of this book recommend that method? Which method do you prefer?

3.5 Suppose that you have an audience that is sexist, racist, or prejudiced in some other way. To what extent, if any, should you adapt to this aspect of your audience?

3.6 You can't possibly learn what every symbol means in every culture. How can you avoid offending the people you work with?

3.7 What other cultures are you most likely to work with? How could you learn about those cultures?

Questions for Building Skills

3.8   What skills have you read about in this module?

3.9   What skills are you practising in the assignments you're doing for this module?

3.10 How could you further develop the skills you're working on?

Exercises and Problems

3.11 Revising Sexist Job Titles

Suggest nonsexist alternatives for each of the following:

cleaning lady   mailman

alderman   night watchman

garbage man   repairman

male nurse   salesman

mail boy   waitress

3.12 Eliminating Biased Language

Explain the source of bias in each of the following and revise to remove the bias.

1. We recommend hiring Jim Renker and Elizabeth Shuman. Both were very successful summer interns. Jim drafted the report on using rap music in ads, and Elizabeth really improved the look of the office.

2. All sales associates and their wives are invited to the picnic.

3. Although he is blind, Mr. Morin is an excellent group leader.

4. Unlike many Caribbean Canadians, Yvonne has extensive experience designing Web pages.

5. Chris Gottlieb
   Pacific Perspectives
   6300 West 12th Avenue
   Vancouver, BC
   Gentlemen:

6. Enrique Torres is very intuitive for a man.

7. *Twenty-First-Century Parenting* shows you how to persuade your husband to do his share of child-care chores.

8. Mr. Paez, Mr. O'Connor, and Tonya will represent our office at the convention.

9. Sue Corcoran celebrates her 50th birthday today. Stop by her cubicle at noon to get a piece of cake and to help us sing "The Old Grey Mare Just Ain't What She Used to Be."

10. Because older customers tend to be really picky, we will need to give a lot of details in our ads.

3.13 Dealing with Discrimination

Despite Canada's reputation for tolerance, courtesy, and fair play, many of its citizens frequently experience discriminatory behaviour. Some believe that prejudice is systemic—that bias against visible minorities, women, people with disabilities, and seniors is built into our legal and judicial systems and demonstrated daily in our assumptions and attitudes. For example, customers frequently asked a young Canadian clerking in a grocery store what country he was from—although Alex speaks perfect English and is finishing his honours degree in sociology. Alex believes that the question comes from customers' assumptions that he must be an immigrant because he's Asian. In fact, he's fourth-generation Canadian.

Consider discrimination that you have experienced or witnessed at work, school or in your community. Write a full description of the experience, including details about how you responded. Next, using what you have learned in Modules 2 and 3, write a memo to your teacher with specific ideas about how to deal with such discrimination. Be sure to include a paragraph about your specific experience.

3.14 Identifying Sources of Miscommunication

In each of the following situations, identify one or more ways that cultural differences may be leading to miscommunication.

a. Alan is a Canadian sales representative in Mexico. He makes appointments and is careful to be on time. But the person he's calling on is frequently late. To save time, Alan tries to get right to business. But his hosts want to talk about sightseeing and his family. Even worse, his appointments are interrupted constantly, not only by business phone calls, but also by long conversations with other people and even the customers' children who come into the office. Alan's first progress report is very negative. He hasn't yet made a sale. Perhaps Mexico just isn't the right place to sell his company's products.

b. To help her company establish a presence in Japan, Susan wants to hire a local interpreter who can advise her on business customs. Kana Tomari has superb qualifications on paper. But when Susan tries to probe about her experience, Kana just says, "I will do my best. I will try very hard." She never gives details about any of the previous positions she's held. Susan begins to wonder if the résumé is inflated.

c. Stan wants to negotiate a joint venture with a Chinese company. He asks Tung-Sen Lee if the Chinese people have enough discretionary income to afford his product. Mr. Lee is silent for a time, and then says, "Your product is good. People in the West must like it." Stan smiles, pleased that Mr. Lee recognizes the quality of his product, and he gives Mr. Lee a contract to sign. Weeks later, Stan still hasn't heard anything. If China is going to be so inefficient, he wonders if he really should try to do business there.

d. Elspeth is very proud of her participatory management style. On assignment in India, she is careful not to give orders but to ask for suggestions. But people rarely suggest anything. Even a formal suggestion system doesn't work. And to make matters worse, she doesn't sense the respect and camaraderie of the plant she managed in Canada. Perhaps, she decides gloomily, people in India just aren't ready for a woman boss.

3.15 Advising a Hasty Subordinate

Three days ago, one of your subordinates forwarded to everyone in the office a bit of email humour he'd received from a friend. Titled "You know you're a Newfie when . . ." The message poked fun at Newfoundland speech, attitudes, and lifestyles. Today you get this message from your subordinate:

Subject: Should I Apologize?

I'm getting flamed left and right because of the Newfoundland message. I thought it was funny, but some people just can't take a joke. So far I've tried not to respond to the flames, figuring that would just make things worse. But now I'm wondering if I should apologize. What do you think?

Answer the message.

3.16 Responding to a Complaint

You're the director of corporate communications; your office produces the employee newsletter. Today you get this email message from Caroline Huber:

Subject: Complaint about Sexist Language

The article about the "Help Desk" says that Martina Luna and I "are the key customer service representatives 'manning' the desk." I don't MAN anything! I WORK.

Respond to Caroline. And send a message to your staff, reminding them to edit newsletter stories as well as external documents to replace biased language.

3.17 Asking about Travel Arrangements

The CEO is planning a trip to visit colleagues in another country (you pick the country). As executive assistant to the CEO of your organization, it's your job to make travel plans. At this stage, you don't know anything except dates and flights. (The CEO will arrive in the country at 7 A.M. local time on the 28th of next month, and stay for three days.) It's your job to find out what the plans are and communicate any of the CEO's requirements.

Write an email message to your contact.

Hints:

• Pick a business, non-profit organization, or government agency you know something about, making assumptions about the kinds of things its executive would want to do during an international visit.

• How much international travelling does your CEO do? Has he or she ever been to this country before? What questions will he or she want answered?

3.18 Sending a Draft to Japan

You've drafted instructions for a product that will be sold in Japan. Before the text is translated, you want to find out if the pictures will be clear. So you send an email to your Japanese counterpart, Takashi Haneda, asking for a response within a week.

Write an email message; assume that you will send the pictures as an attachment.

3.19 Creating a Web Page

Create a Web page for managers who must communicate across cultures.

Assume that this page can be accessed from the organization's intranet. Offer at least seven links. (More is better.) You may offer information as well as links to other pages with information. At the top of the page, offer an overview of what the page covers. At the bottom of the page, put the creation/update date and your name and email address.

As Your Instructor Directs,

a. Turn in two laser copies of your page(s). On another page, give the URLs for each link.

b. Turn in one laser copy of your page(s) and a disk with the HTML code and .gif files.

c. Write a memo to your instructor (1) identifying the audience for which the page is designed and explaining (2) the search strategies you used to find material on this topic, (3) why you chose the pages and information you've included, and (4) why you chose the layout and graphics you've used.

d. Post your memo in an email message to the class.

e. Present your page orally to the class.

Hints:

- Limit your page to just one culture or country.

- Try to cover as many topics as possible: history, politics, notable people, arts, conversational style, customs, and so forth. For a culture in another country, also include money, living accommodations, geography, transport, weather, business practices, and so forth.

- Chunk your links into small groups under headings.

- See ◀ ▶ Module 5 on Web page design.

3.20 Requesting Information about a Country

Use one or more of the following ways to get information about a country. Information you might focus on could include

- Business opportunities
- History and geography
- Principal exports and imports
- Dominant religions
- Holidays
- School system
- Political system

1. Visit Industry Canada's Strategis Web site for International Market Research and Country Commercial Guides at http://strategis.ic.gc.ca/SSG/bi18305e.html.

2. Check the country's trade office, if there is one in your city.

3. Interview someone from that country or someone who has lived there.

4. Read published materials about the country.

As Your Instructor Directs,

a. Share your findings orally with a small group of students

b. Summarize your findings in a memo to your instructor

c. Present your findings to the class

d. Email your findings to the class

e. Join with a group of classmates to write a group report on the country

3.21 Answering an Inquiry about Photos

You've just been named vice president for diversity, the first person in your organization to hold this position.

Today, you receive the following memo from Sheila Lathan, who edits the employee newsletter:

Subject: Photos in the Employee Newsletter

Please tell me what to do about photos in the monthly employee newsletter. I'm concerned that almost no single issue represents the diversity of employees we have here.

As you know, our layout allows two visuals each month. One of those is always the employee of the month (EM). In the last year, most of those have been male and all but two have been white. What makes it worse is that people want photos that make them look good. You may remember that Ron Olmos was the EM two months ago; in the photo he wanted me to use, you can't tell that he's in a wheelchair. Often the EM is the only photo; the other visual is often a graph of sales or something relating to quality.

Even if the second visual is another photo, it may not look balanced in terms of gender and race. After all, 62 percent of our employees are men, and 78 percent are white. Should the pictures try to represent those percentages? The leadership positions (both in management and in the union) are even more heavily male and white. Should we run pictures of people doing important things, and risk continuing the imbalance?

I guess I could use more visuals, but then there wouldn't be room for as many stories—and people really like to see their names in print. Plus, giving people information about company activities and sales is important to maintaining goodwill. A bigger newsletter would be one way to have more visuals and keep the content, but with the cost-cutting measures we're under, that doesn't look likely.

What should I do?

As Your Instructor Directs,

a. Work in a small group with other students to come up with a recommendation for Sheila

b. Write a memo responding to her

c. Write an article for the employee newsletter about the photo policy you recommend and how it relates to the company's concern for diversity

Polishing Your Prose

Using Idioms

Idioms are phrases that have specific meanings different from the meanings for each individual word.

Idiom	Meaning
Cut to the chase	Express your main point immediately
Read between the lines	Look for a hidden message

Like idioms, slang changes the definitions of words. *Bad*, a word that is negative, becomes positive when used in slang to denote something good or desirable. Dictionaries often are slow to adapt to slang, which changes constantly.

You need to understand a culture to make sense of its idioms. Because idioms usually violate the rules of standard edited English, they are particularly troublesome for people new to the language.

To learn idioms,

1. Study native speakers in person and on television. When possible, ask native speakers what unfamiliar words and phrases mean.

2. Underline unfamiliar passages in newspapers and magazines. Ask a friend or your instructor to explain their meaning.

3. Practice what you learn with a conversation partner.

Exercises

Explain what these 10 common idiomatic phrases mean in business.

1. Race the clock
2. From A to Z
3. Juggle a schedule
4. Catch a plane (or cab)
5. Punch the clock

6. Sign on the dotted line
7. Cold call a customer
8. In the black/in the red
9. Open up new markets
10. Slam the competition

Check your answers to the odd-numbered exercises on page 632.

Module 4

Planning, Writing, and Revising

Topics

- Does it matter what process I use?

- I don't have much time. How should I use it?

- What planning should I do before I begin writing or speaking?

- What is revision? How do I do it?

- Can a grammar checker do my editing for me?

- I spell check. Do I still need to proofread?

- How can I get better feedback?

- How can I overcome writer's block?

- Can I use form letters?

Review of Key Points

Learning Applications

Polishing Your Prose: Commas in Lists

Learning Focus

After reading and applying the information in Module 4, you'll be able to demonstrate

Knowledge of
- The writing process
- Composing, revising, and editing techniques

Skills to
- Plan your written and spoken messages
- Overcome writer's block
- Apply revision strategies
- Edit your own and others' writing

"What people don't realize is that writing is a strategic process which requires thoughtful planning to achieve one's goals," says Simone Graham, owner of Graham Communications Strategies, a consulting company that provides services in writing, editing, and project management. Simone further states that "any piece of writing must get the reader to focus on the client's goals."

Originally from Nova Scotia, Simone did a Bachelor of commerce at St. Mary's University in Halifax. She has an M.A. in journalism from the University of Western Ontario and has completed entrepreneurial training at the Small Business Centre in London.

Before forming her own company, Simone worked at Cuddy Foods, where she wrote and edited all internal and external publications. She also wrote for trade magazines and helped produce product information materials that were often used at trade shows. These days, Simone takes on jobs such as writing for and editing the alumni magazine for a community college as well as editing and rewriting materials for a variety of profit and non-profit enterprises.

In addition to being editor, her main writing job at the alumni magazine is to profile successful graduates of the college. Here she must work from a variety of sources such as student records, the person's own résumé, comments from employers and former fellow students and teachers, and personal interviews. Simone must take all this information and focus on the overall goal of the piece so she can create one cohesive story. In this way, Simone says, "editing and revising become part of the writing process." This last point is important because often Simone must use the same material for a different purpose, such as providing a profile of a graduate who is being nominated for some alumni award. Since the purpose is different, the story will be different.

Once Simone had to completely rewrite a volunteer handbook for a non-profit agency. The book was seven years old and couldn't just be updated as the agency had changed significantly. It had to be completely rewritten. In order to do this Simone asked herself the crucial question: "If we had to do this job today from scratch, what would be included?" Her revision of the book was guided by the needs of the current volunteers , giving them and any new volunteers the information they needed in a practical manner.

When asked for parting advice to editors and writers, Simone says, "The measure of success of any written piece is that it moves people towards a specific action, whether to donate to a fundraising drive, become more involved in a team project at work, better understand a complex concept, or even buy a product."

FYI

Writing is a developmental skill highly divergent from speech in its more sophisticated stages. Moreover, "writing aids thinking in ways that speech cannot perform. Writing is a medium where there is time to reflect, to re-think, to use language as a way of shaping thought."

Source: David Crystal, *The Cambridge Encyclopedia of Language* (Cambridge: Cambridge University Press, 1987), 255.

Skilled performances look easy and effortless. In reality, as every dancer, musician, and athlete knows, they're the product of hard work, hours of practice, attention to detail, and intense concentration. Like all skilled performances, writing rests on a base of work. Writers themselves agree that writing is like communicating in another language, with its own set of rules and requirements. Proficient writers also share two lifelong habits: they read and they write constantly.

Writers usually use eight activities to produce a finished piece: planning, information gathering, writing, assessing, getting feedback, revising, editing, and proofreading:

- **Planning** includes analyzing the problem, defining your purposes, and analyzing the audience; thinking of information, benefits, and objections; choosing a pattern of organization or making an outline; and so on.
- **Gathering** includes getting the information you need—from the message you're answering, from conversations with other, from reading books, magazines or newspapers, or from surfing the Web.
- **Writing** includes putting words on paper or on a screen and changing the words until they suit your purpose and the needs of your audience. Writing includes lists, fragmentary notes, stream-of-consciousness writing, and formal drafts.
- **Assessing** means rereading your work and measuring it against your goals and the requirements of the situation and audience. The best evaluation results from re-seeing your draft as if someone else had written it. Will your audience understand it? Is it complete? Convincing? Friendly?
- **Getting feedback** means asking someone else to read and respond to your work. You'll want your reader/appraiser to assess for clarity and completion: is your pattern of organization appropriate? Does a revision solve an earlier problem? Is the document free of mechanical errors?
- **Revising** means adding, deleting, substituting, and/or rearranging your work. It means changing your writing to reflect your own assessment and the feedback from your readers/appraisers. When you revise, you'll find that you may have to change single words or large sections of a document in order to create the meaning you want.
- **Editing** means checking the draft to see that it satisfies the requirements of standard English. Here you correct spelling and mechanical errors and check word choice and format. Unlike revision, which can produce major changes in meaning, editing focusses on the surface of writing.
- **Proofreading** means checking the final copy to see that it's free from typographical errors.

Note the following points about these eight activities:

- **Writers do not necessarily follow these processes in this order.** Some people gather information *after* writing a draft when they see that they need more specifics to achieve their purposes.
- **You may multitask throughout the process, moving constantly from one activity to start another.** Some writers plan a short section and write it, plan the next short section and write it, and so on through the document. Constantly assessing what is already written may cause a writer to do more planning or to change the original plan.

The most useful feedback evaluates the document in terms of purposes, audience, information, and context.

- **You may perform an activity several times, not just once.** For an important document, you might get feedback, revise, get more feedback, revise yet again, and so on. This work is part of the **recursive** nature of the writing process: many writers read what they've written to write more. Then they re-read what they've composed, change it, and write another paragraph or page. Then they re-read all over again, modifying what they've written, and compose another section. Competent writers perceive the process as perpetual: they understand that they can change anything until the work is "published". William Faulkner, who won the Nobel Prize in literature and is considered one of the greatest American writers, wrote revisions in the margins of his already published novels!
- **Most writers do not use all eight activities for all the documents they write.** You'll use more activities when you write a new kind of document, about a new subject, or to a new audience.

Does it matter what process I use?

The more you write—and read—the more aware you'll become of what processes work best for you, and the more your writing will improve.

Just as athletes can improve their game by studying videotapes and focussing on exactly how they kick a ball or spin during a jump, so writers improve their writing by studying their own processes. No single writing process works for all writers all of the time. However, expert writers seem to use different processes than novice writers.[1] Expert writers are more likely to

- Understand that the first draft will be revised
- Have clear goals focussing on purpose and audience
- Read daily
- Write regularly
- Have a large vocabulary
- Break big writing jobs into a series of steps
- Choose and use several different strategies

Site *to* **See**

Go to
http://phoenix.
marymount.edu/
~hosulliv/SITES503.
HTM

Use these business
communication
sites to explore
everything from
audience analysis to
writers' newsgroups.

Instant Replay

How Experts Write

Expert writers

- Understand that the first draft will be revised
- Have clear goals focussing on purpose and audience
- Read daily
- Write regularly
- Have a large vocabulary
- Break big writing jobs into a series of steps
- Choose and use several different strategies
- Use rules flexibly
- Wait to edit for mechanical errors until after the draft is complete

- Use rules flexibly
- Wait to edit for mechanical errors until after the draft is complete

Research shows that experts differ from novices in identifying and analyzing the initial problem more effectively, understanding the task more broadly and deeply, drawing from a wider repertoire of strategies, and seeing patterns more clearly. Experts actually composed more slowly than novices, perhaps because they rarely settled for work that was just "OK." Finally, experts were better at evaluating their own work.[2]

Thinking about the writing process and consciously adopting "expert" processes will help you become a better writer.

I don't have much time. How should I use it?

Save two-thirds of your time for planning and revising.

To get the best results from the time you have, spend only one-third of your time actually "writing." Spend at least one-third of your time analyzing the situation and your audience, gathering information, and organizing what you have to say. Spend another third evaluating what you've said, revising the draft(s) to meet your purposes and the needs of the audience and the organization, editing a late draft to remove any errors in grammar and mechanics, and proofreading the final typed copy.

When you first get an assignment, think about all the steps you'll need to go through so that you can plan your time for that project. Certainly two writers might need different amounts of time to produce the same quality document. But for any one writer, different projects have different lead times, as Figure 4.1 on page 85 shows.

What planning should I do before I begin writing or speaking?

As much as you can!

Spend at least one-third of your time planning and organizing before you begin to write. The better your ideas are when you start, the fewer drafts you'll need to produce a good document. Start by using the analysis questions from ◀▶ Module 1 to identify purpose and audience. Use the strategies described in Module 2 to analyze audience and in ◀▶ Module 8 to develop reader benefits. Gather information you can use for your document.

If ideas won't come, try the following techniques:

- **Brainstorm.** Write down all your ideas without judging them. Consciously try to get at least a dozen different ideas before you stop.
- **Freewrite.**[3] Make yourself write, without stopping, for 10 minutes or so, even if you must write "I will think of something soon." At the end of 10 minutes, read what you've written and identify the best point in the draft. Get a clean paper or screen and write for another 10 uninterrupted minutes. Read this draft, marking anything that's good and should be kept, and then write again for another 10 minutes. By the third session, you will probably produce several sections that are worth keeping—maybe even a complete draft that's ready to be revised.

Figure 4.1

Time Lines for Various Documents (your actual times may vary)

EMail message answering a simple question. Total time: 15 minutes

5 minutes	5 minutes	5 minutes
Read the question Gather any information necessary for reply Plan the message	Draft the message	Re-read the message Run the message through spell check Make small changes Send the message

EMail message answering a question that requires simple research. Total time: 2 hours

1 hour	30 minutes	30 minutes
Read the question Think about what is needed to reply Do research (on the Web, ask people, etc.) Analyze the information Plan the message	Draft the message and any attachments	Re-read the message Revise the message and attachments Run the message through spell check Send the message

Memo explaining a new policy. Total time: 6½ hours

90 minutes	60 minutes	90 minutes	30 minutes	90 minutes
Understand the policy Answer the PAIBOC questions (◄ ► Module 1) Think about document design Organize the message	Draft	Re-read draft Measure draft against PAIBOC questions and principles of business communication Revise draft	Ask for feedback	Revise draft based on feedback Run spell check Proof by eye Initial memo Duplicate and distribute document

Report recommending ways to improve customer service. Total time: 30 business days

6 days	1 day	2 days	9 days
Collect information about weaknesses in service Plan research to gather more information Get library sources; check the Web; plan survey or interview questions Write proposal to do research to find solution	Ask for feedback on proposal, research plan	Revise proposal	Conduct research Analyze data Create visuals for report Prepare appendices

5 days	1 day	5 days	1 day
Draft report Evelute draft against proposal and principles of business communication	Ask for feedback on recommendations, report design, and visuals	Revise report Revise visuals Plan oral presentation Edit document and visuals Run spell check Proof by eye Duplicate document	Submit report Present results orally

- **Cluster.**[4] Write your topic in the middle of the page and circle it. Write down the ideas the topic suggests, circling them, too. (The circles are designed to tap into the non-linear half of your brain.) When you've filled the page, look for patterns or repeated ideas. Use different coloured pens to group related ideas. Then use these ideas to develop reader benefits in a memo, questions for a survey, or content for the body of a report. Figure 4.2 presents the clusters that one writer created about business communication in Canada and France.
- **Talk to your audiences.** As communications analyst Rachel Spilka's research shows, talking to internal and external audiences helped writers involve readers in the planning process, understand the social and political relationships among readers, and negotiate conflicts orally rather than depending solely on the document. These writers were then able to think about content as well as

Figure 4.2
Clustering Helps Generate Ideas

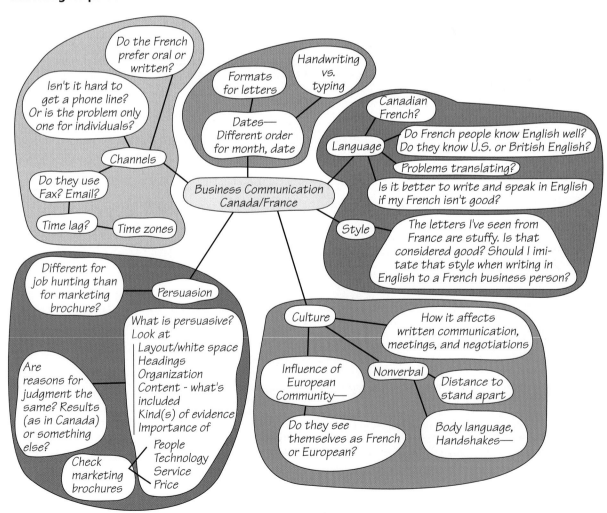

about organization and style, appeal to common grounds (such as reducing waste or increasing productivity) which several readers shared, and reduce the number of revisions needed before documents were approved.[5]

Thinking about the content, layout, or structure of your document can also give you ideas. For long documents, **write out the headings you'll use**. For anything that's shorter than five pages, less formal notes will probably work. You may want to jot down ideas that you can use as the basis for a draft. For an oral presentation, a meeting, or a document with lots of visuals, use your presentation software to create a **storyboard**, or make your own paper storyboard with a rectangle representing each page or unit. Draw a box with a visual for each main point. Below the box, write a short caption or label.

Letters and memos will go faster if you choose a basic organizational pattern before you start. ◁▶ Modules 11, 12, and 13 give detailed patterns of organization for the most common kinds of letters and memos. You may want to customize those patterns with a **planning guide**[6] to help you keep the "big picture" in mind as you write. Figure 4.3 shows planning guides developed for specific kinds of documents.

Site *to* **See**

Go to
http://www.visual
thesaurus.com/
Plumb Design's
Visual Thesaurus will
help you cluster
ideas on screen!

http://www.uwm.
edu/~spilka/
At Spilka's
"Technical Writing
Links" you can find
up-to-the-minute
information on
writing tips, tricks,
and techniques.

http://webreview.
com/pub/2000/03/
10/feature/index4.
html
Freelance writer
Josh Smith's "Ten
Steps to Effective
Web Writing"
demonstrate that,
regardless of the
medium, all good
writing uses the
same ground rules.

Figure 4.3

Customized Planning Guides for Specific Documents

Planning guide for a trip report • The Big Picture from the Company's Point of View: We Can Go Forward on the Project • Criteria/Goals • What We Did • Why We Know Enough to Go Forward	**Planning guide for a proposal** • Customer's Concern #1 Our Proposal/Answer • Customer's Concern #2 Our Proposal/Answer • Customer's Concern #3 Our Proposal/Answer
Planning guide for an email message • My Purpose • Points I Want to Make • Document(s) to Attach • Next Steps	**Planning guide for a credit rejection** • Reason • Refusal • Alternative (Layaway/Co-signer/Provide more information) • Goodwill Ending

Source: Email and proposal guides based on Fred Reynolds, "What Adult Work-World Writers Have Taught Me About Adult Work-World Writing," *Professional Writing in Context: Lessons from Teaching and Consulting in Worlds of Work* (Hillsdale, NJ: Lawrence Erlbaum Associates, 1995), 18, 20.

Figure 4.4
Checklist for Thorough Revision

Checklist for Thorough Revision

Content and Clarity

☐ Does your document meet the needs of the organization and of the reader—and make you look good?

☐ Have you given readers all the information they need to understand and act on your message?

☐ Have you organised your message for optimum positive audience impact? (◀ ▶ Modules 2 and 10)

☐ Is all the information accurate?

☐ Is each sentence clear? Is the message free from apparently contradictory statements?

☐ Are generalizations and benefits backed up with adequate supporting detail?

Organization and Layout

☐ Are transitions between ideas smooth? Do ideas within paragraphs flow smoothly?

☐ Does the design of the document make it easy for readers to find the information they need? Is the document visually inviting?

☐ Are the most important points emphasized?

☐ Are the first and last paragraphs effective?

Style and Tone

☐ Does the message build goodwill?

☐ Is the message easy to read?

☐ Is the message friendly and free from biased language?

What is revision? How do I do it?

Revision means "re-seeing" the document from the reader's point of view.

Good writers make their drafts better by judicious revising, editing, and proofreading.

- **Revising** means making changes that will better satisfy your purposes and your audience
- **Editing** means making surface-level changes that make the document grammatically correct
- **Proofreading** means checking to be sure the document is free from typographical errors

When you're writing to a new audience or solving a particularly difficult problem, plan to revise the draft at least three times. The first time, look for content and clarity. The second time, check the organization and layout. Finally, check style and tone, using the information in ◀ ▶ Modules 15 and 16. Figure 4.4 summarizes the questions you should ask.

Figure 4.5
Checklist for Light Revision

✓ **Checklist for Light Revision**

☐ Are the first and last paragraphs effective?
☐ Does the design of the document make it easy for readers to find the information they need?
☐ Have you told the reader what to do?

Often you'll get the best revision by setting aside your draft, getting a blank page or screen, and redrafting. This strategy takes advantage of the thinking you did on your first draft without locking you into the sentences in it.

As you revise, be sure to read the document through from start to finish. This is particularly important if you've composed in several sittings or if you've used text from other documents. Researchers have found that such documents tend to be well organized, but don't flow well.[7] You may need to add transitions (◀▶ Module 16), cut repetitive parts, or change words to create a uniform level of formality throughout the document.

If you're really in a time bind, do a light revision. The quality of the final document may not be as high as with a thorough revision, but even a light revision is better than skipping revision.

Can a grammar checker do my editing for me?

No. You have to decide whether to make each change.

Grammar checkers are good at finding missing halves. For example, if you open a parenthesis and never close it, a grammar checker will note that a second one is needed. Of course, you have to decide where it goes. In terms of other errors, all a grammar checker can do is to ask you about what you have done. A grammar checker can tell you that you've used a passive verb (◀▶ Module 16) and ask if you want to change it. But you have to decide whether the passive is justified. If it finds the word *well*, the grammar checker can tell you that *good* and *well* are sometimes confused. But **you** have to decide which word fits your meaning (◀▶ Module 15). You still need to know the rules so that you can decide which changes to make.

Check to be sure that the following are accurate:

- Sentence structure
- Subject-verb and noun-pronoun agreement
- Punctuation
- Word usage
- Spelling—including spelling of names
- Numbers

You need to know the rules of grammar and punctuation to edit. Most writers make a small number of errors over and over. If you know that you have trouble with dangling modifiers or subject-verb agreement, for example, specifically look

Instant
Replay

Revising, Editing, and Proofreading

Revising means making changes that will better satisfy your purposes and your audience

Editing means making surface-level changes that make the document grammatically correct

Proofreading means checking to be sure the document is free of typographical errors

Site *to* **See**

Go to
http://www.fpd.
finop.umn.edu/
groups/ppd/
documents/
information/
writing_tips.cfm

Gunning Fog Index
explanation and
online calculator are
provided at this Web
site

for them in your draft. Also look for any errors that especially bother your boss and correct them.

Grammar checkers frequently include an option for checking the **readability** of a selected passage. Microsoft Word's grammar check will indicate readability based on the Flesch-Kincaid Grade Level (corresponding to years of education required to comprehend the material) and a Flesch Reading Ease score (assessing the difficulty level based on the average number of words per sentence and the average number of syllables per word). Figure 4.6 sets out guidelines for interpreting these results.

Another popular measure for determining readability is the Gunning Fog Index, which is based on determining the number of words with more than three syllables ("foggy" words) in an average sentence. However, readability measures should be used with caution, as they do not reflect the needs and background of a particular audience that may be quite comfortable with familiar, multi-syllable words but have difficulty with unfamiliar short words.

Editing should always *follow* revision. There's no point in taking time to fix a grammatical error in a sentence that may be cut when you clarify your meaning or tighten your style. Some writers edit more accurately when they print out a copy of a document and edit the hard copy. But beware: laser printing makes a page look good but does nothing to correct errors.

I spell check. Do I still need to proofread?

Yes.

Proofread every document both with a spell checker and by eye to catch the errors a spell checker can't find.

Figure 4.6
Interpreting Flesch Readability Scores

Flesch Reading Ease	Difficulty	Flesch-Kincaid Grade Level	Example
0-29	Very Difficult	Post graduate	
30-49	Difficult	College	32: *Harvard Law Review* 40-50: standard score for insurance documents required by law in several US states
50-59	Fairly Difficult	High school	52: *Time*
60-69	Standard	8th to 9th grade	60: "plain English" (20 words per sentence, 1.5 syllables per word) 65: *Reader's Digest*
70-79	Fairly Easy	7th grade	
80-89	Easy	5th to 6th grade	
90-100	Very Easy	4th to 5th grade	

Source: Tom McArthur, ed., *The Oxford Companion to the English Language* (Oxford: Oxford University Press, 1992), 407.

Revising after Feedback

When you get feedback that you understand and agree with, make the change.
If you get feedback you don't understand, ask for clarification.

- Paraphrase: "So you're asking me to give more information?"
- Ask for more information: "Can you suggest a way to do that?"
- Test your inference: "Would it help if I did such and such?"

Sometimes you may get feedback you don't agree with.

- If it's an issue of grammatical correctness, check this book (sometimes even smart people get things wrong)
- If it's a matter of content, recognize that something about the draft isn't as good as it could be: *something* is leading the reader to respond negatively

- If the reader thinks a fact is wrong (and you know it's right), show where the fact came from "According to . . . ."
- If the reader suggests a change in wording you don't like, try another option
- If the reader seems to have misunderstood or misread, think about ways to make the meaning clearer

Your supervisor's comments on a draft can help you improve that document, help you write better drafts the next time, and teach you about the culture of your organization. Look for patterns in the feedback you receive. Are you asked to use more formal language, or to make the document more conversational? Does your boss want to see an overview before details? Does your company prefer information presented in bulleted lists rather than in paragraphs?

Proofreading is hard because writers tend to see what they know should be there rather than what really is there. Since it's always easier to proof something you haven't written, you may want to swap papers with a proofing buddy. (Be sure the person looks for typos, not for content.)

To proofread,

- Read once quickly for meaning to see that nothing has been left out.
- Read a second time, slowly. When you find an error, correct it and then *reread that line*. Readers tend to become less attentive after they find one error and may miss other errors close to the one they've spotted.
- To proofread a document you know well, read the lines backward or the pages out of order.

Always triple-check numbers, headings, the first and last paragraphs, and the reader's name.

How can I get better feedback?

Ask for the kind of feedback you need.

The process of drafting, getting feedback, revising, and getting more feedback is called **cycling**. Communications expert and author Dianna Booher reports that documents in her clients' firms cycled an average of 4.2 times before reaching the

Figure 4.7
Questions to Ask Readers

Questions to Ask Readers

Outline or Planning Draft
☐ Does the plan seem "on the right track"?
☐ What topics should be added? Should any be cut?
☐ Do you have any other general suggestions?

Revising Draft
☐ Does the message satisfy all its purposes?
☐ Is the message adapted to the audience(s)?
☐ Is the organization effective?
☐ What parts aren't clear?
☐ What ideas need further development?
☐ Do you have any other suggestions?

Polishing Draft
☐ Are there any problems with word choice or sentence structure?
☐ Did you find any inconsistencies?
☐ Did you find any typos?
☐ Is the document's design effective?

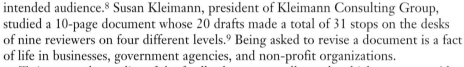

Instant Replay

How to Revise

When you're writing to a new audience or solving a particularly difficult problem, plan to revise the draft at least three times. The first time, look for content and clarity. The second time, check the organization and layout. Finally, check style and tone. Do all this **before** you edit and proofread.

intended audience.[8] Susan Kleimann, president of Kleimann Consulting Group, studied a 10-page document whose 20 drafts made a total of 31 stops on the desks of nine reviewers on four different levels.[9] Being asked to revise a document is a fact of life in businesses, government agencies, and non-profit organizations.

To improve the quality of the feedback you get, tell people which aspects you'd especially like comments about. For example, when you give a reader the outline or planning draft,[10] you might want to know whether the general approach is appropriate. After your second draft, you might want to know whether reader benefits are well developed. When you reach the polishing draft, you'll be ready for feedback on style and grammar. Figure 4.7 lists questions to ask.

It's easy to feel defensive when someone criticizes your work. If the feedback stings, put it aside until you can read it without feeling defensive. Even if you think that the reader has misunderstood what you were trying to say, the fact that the reader complained means the section could be improved. If the reader says "This isn't true" and you know that the statement is true, rephrasing the statement, giving more information or examples, or documenting the source might make the truth clear to the reader.

Can I use form letters?

Yes. But make sure they're good.

A **form letter** is a pre-written fill-in-the blank letter designed for routine situations. Some form letters have different paragraphs that can be inserted, depending on the situation. For example, a form letter admitting students to college might have additional paragraphs to be added for students receiving financial aid.

Boilerplate is language—sentences, paragraphs, even pages—from a previous document that a writer includes in a new document. In academic papers, material written by others must be quoted and documented. However, because businesses own the documents their employees write, old text may be included without attribution.

In some cases, boilerplate may have been written years ago. For example, many legal documents, including apartment leases and sales contracts, are almost completely boilerplated. In other cases, writers may use boilerplate they themselves have written. For example, a section from a proposal describing the background of the problem could also be used in the final report after the proposed work was completed. A section from a progress report describing what the writer had done could be used with only a few changes in the methods section of the final report.

Writers use form letters and boilerplate to save time and energy and to use language that has already been approved by the organization's legal staff. However, reusing old text creates two problems:[11]

- Using unrevised boilerplate can create a document with incompatible styles and tones
- Form letters and boilerplate can encourage writers to see situations and audiences as identical when, in fact, they differ

Before you use a form letter, make sure that it is well written and that it applies to the situation in which you are thinking of using it.

Before you incorporate old language in a new document,

- Check to see that the old section is well written
- Consciously look for differences between the two situations, audiences, or purposes that may require different content, organization, or wording
- Read through the whole document at a single sitting to be sure that style, tone, and level of detail are consistent in the old and new sections

How can I overcome writer's block?

Talk, participate, and practice.

According to psychologist Robert Boice, a combination of five actions works best to overcome writer's block:[12]

1. **Participate actively in the organization and the community.** The more you talk to people, the more you interact with some of your audiences, the more you learn about the company, its culture, and its context, the easier it will be to write—and the better your writing will be.
2. **Practice writing regularly.**
3. **Learn as many strategies as you can.** Good writers have a "bag of tricks" on which to draw ; they don't have to "reinvent the wheel" in each new situation. This book suggests many strategies and patterns. Try them; memorize them; make them your own.
4. **Talk positively to yourself.** "I can do this." "If I keep working, ideas will come." "It doesn't have to be wonderful; I can always make it better later."
5. **Talk about writing to other people.** Value the feedback you get from your manager. Talk to your manager about writing. Ask him or her to share particu-

larly good examples—from anyone in the organization. Find colleagues at your own level and talk about the writing you do. Do different managers value different qualities? What aspects of your own supervisor's preferences are individual and which are part of the discourse community of the organization? Talking to other people expands your repertoire of strategies and helps you understand the discourse community in which you write.

Employability Skills 2000+ Checklist for Planning, Writing, and Revising

In this module, the key skills from The Conference Board of Canada's Employability Skills 2000+ are:

Communicate
✔ write and speak so others pay attention and understand

Think & Solve Problems
✔ assess situations and indentify problems
✔ seek different points of view and evaluate them based on facts
✔ recognize the human, interpersonal, technical, scientific, and mathematical dimensions of a problem
✔ identify the root cause of a problem
✔ be creative and innovative in exploring possible solutions
✔ readily use science, technology, and mathematics as ways to think, gain and share knowledge, solve problems and make decisions
✔ evaluate solutions to make recommendations or decisions

Demonstrate Positive Attitudes & Behaviours
✔ show interest, initiative, and effort

Be Adaptable
✔ be innovate and resourceful: identify and suggest alternative ways to achieve goals and get the job done
✔ be open and respond constructively to change
✔ learn from your mistakes and accept feedback
✔ cope with uncertainity

Learn Continuously
✔ be willing to continuously learn and grow
✔ identify and access learning sources and opportunities

Review of Key Points

- Writing processes can include eight activities: planning, gathering, writing, assessing, getting feedback, revising, editing, and proofreading. **Revising** means changing the document to make it better satisfy the writer's purposes and the audience. **Editing** means making surface-level changes that make the document grammatically correct. **Proofreading** means checking to be sure the document is free from typographical errors.

- Processes that help writers write well include expecting to revise the first draft, writing regularly, modifying the initial task if it's too hard or too easy, having clear goals, knowing many different strategies, using rules as guidelines rather than as absolutes, and waiting to edit until after the draft is complete.

- To think of ideas, try brainstorming, **freewriting** (writing without stopping for 10 minutes or so), and **clustering** (brainstorming with circled words on a page).

- You can improve the quality of the feedback you get by telling people which aspects of a draft you'd like comments about. If a reader criticizes something, fix the problem. If you think the reader misunderstood you, try to figure out what caused the misunderstanding and revise the draft so that the reader can see what you meant.

- If the writing situation is new or difficult, plan to revise the draft at least three times. The first time, look for content and clarity. The second time, check the organization and layout. Finally, check style and tone.

- **Boilerplate** is language from a previous document that a writer includes in a new document. Using form letters and boilerplate can encourage writers to see as identical situations and audiences that, in fact, differ. Putting boilerplate into a new document can create incompatible styles and tones.

- To overcome writer's block,
  1. Participate actively in the organization and the community
  2. Follow a regimen. Practice writing regularly
  3. Learn and apply as many strategies as you can
  4. Talk positively to yourself
  5. Talk about writing to other people

Learning Applications

Questions for Comprehension

4.1   What processes do expert writers use?

4.2   How is revision different from editing? From proofreading?

4.3   What three aspects of a document does thorough revision cover?

Questions for Critical Thinking

4.4   Of the processes that expert writers use, which do you already use? How could you modify your process to incorporate at least one more on the list?

4.5   Of the people who have seen your writing, which one(s) have given you the most useful feedback? What makes it useful?

4.6 In which areas are you best at giving feedback to other people? How could you make your feedback even better?

4.7 Think about the form letters you have received. How do they make you feel? If they have flaws, how could they be improved?

Questions for Building Skills

4.8 What skills have you read about in this module?

4.9 What skills are you practising in the assignments you're doing for this module?

4.10 How could you further develop the skills you're working on?

Exercises and Problems

4.11 Interviewing Writers about Their Composing Processes

Interview someone who writes for a living about the composing process(es) he or she uses. Questions you could ask include the following:

- What kind of planning do you do before you write? Do you make lists? formal or informal outlines?
- When you need more information, where do you get it?
- How do you compose your drafts? Do you dictate? Draft with pen and paper? Compose on screen? How do you find uninterrupted time to compose?
- When you want advice about style, grammar, and spelling, what source(s) do you consult?
- Does your supervisor ever read your drafts and make suggestions?
- Do you ever work with other writers to produce a single document? Describe the process you use.

- Describe the process of creating a document where you felt the final document reflected your best work.
- Describe the process of creating a document which you found difficult or frustrating. What sorts of things make writing easier or harder for you?

As Your Instructor Directs,

a. Share your results orally with a small group of students

b. Present your results in an oral presentation to the class

c. Present your results in a memo to your instructor

d. Post an email message to the class discussing your results

e. Share your results with a small group of students and write a joint memo reporting the similarities and differences you found

4.12 Analyzing Your Own Writing Processes

Save your notes and drafts from several assignments so that you can answer the following questions:

- Which of the eight activities discussed in Module 4 do you use?
- How much time do you spend on each of the eight activities?
- What kinds of revisions do you make most often?

- Do you use different processes for different documents, or do you have one process that you use most of the time?
- Which practices of good writers do you follow?
- What parts of your process seem most successful? Are there any places in the process that could be improved? How?
- What relation do you see between the process(es) you use and the quality of the final document?

As Your Instructor Directs,

a. Discuss your process with a small group of other students.

b. Write a memo to your instructor analyzing in detail your process for composing one of the papers for this class.

c. Write a memo to your instructor analyzing your process during the term. What parts of your process(es) have stayed the same throughout the term? What parts have changed?

4.13 Checking Spell and Grammar Checkers

Each of the following paragraphs contains errors in grammar, spelling, and punctuation. Which errors does your spelling or grammar checker catch? Which errors does it miss? Does it flag as errors any words that are correct?

1. Answer to an Inquiry
   Enclosed are the tow copies you requested of our pamphlet, "Using the Internet to market Your products. The pamphlet walks you through the steps of planning the Home Page (The first page of the web cite, shows examples of other Web pages we have designed, and provide a questionnaire that you can use to analyze audience the audience and purposes.

2. Performance Appraisal
   Most staff accountants complete three audits a month. Ellen has completed 21 audits in this past six months she is our most productive staff accountant. Her technical skills our very good however some clients feel that she could be more tactful in suggesting ways that the clients accounting practices could be improved.

3. Brochure
   Are you finding that being your own boss crates it's own problems? Take the hassle out of working at home with a VoiceMail Answering System. Its almost as good as having your own secretary.

4. Presentation Slides

   How to Create a Web Résumé
   - Omit home address and phone number
   - Use other links only if they help an employer evaluate you
   - Be Professional
   - Carefully craft and proof read the phrase on the index apage

   How to Create a Scannable Résumé
   - Create a "plain vanilla" document
   - Use include a "Keywords" section Include personality traits as well as accomplishments
   - Be specific and quantifiable

Polishing Your Prose

Commas in Lists

Use commas in lists to separate items:

> At the office supply store, I bought pens, stationery, and three-ring binders.

Commas show distinctions between items in a list. Technically, the comma before the coordinating conjunction *and* is optional, but the additional comma always adds clarity. Use commas consistently throughout your document. Missing or improperly placed commas confuse readers:

> We bought the following items for the staff lounge: television cabinet computer desk refrigerator and microwave oven.

Does *television* describe *cabinet* or is it a separate item? Is *computer desk* one item? Or are *computer* and *desk* two separate things? Inserting commas makes the distinction clear:

> We bought the following items for the staff kitchen: television, cabinet, computer, desk, refrigerator, and microwave oven.

Semicolons replace commas in lists where the items themselves contain commas:

> Our company has plants in Moncton, New Brunswick; Red Deer, Manitoba; and Lethbridge, Alberta.

Exercises

Use commas to make these lists clearer.

1. Please send the "fruit of the month" in April May June and July.

2. At the weekly staff meeting we will be joined by Mr. Loomis Ms. Handelman Ms. Lang and Mr. Kim.

3. The special parts division is opening offices in Brampton Ontario Fredericton New Brunswick and Big Salmon Yukon.

4. Buy small medium and large paper clips at the office supply store.

5. I need to telephone Mary Frank and Paul to finish my report and mail copies of it to Ted Sam and Latanya.

6. Applicants should send copies of their résumés to Mr. Arthur Bramberger human resource director Ms. Tina Ramos vice president of marketing and Ms. Ellen Choi administrative assistant in marketing.

7. The weather affects our offices in Montréal New York City and Philadelphia.

8. Interns will be rotated through the receiving claims adjustment customer service and shipping departments.

9. Elizabeth Tyrone Mark and Sara presented the team's recommendations.

10. We are open until 9 P.M. on Mondays Wednesdays Fridays and Saturdays.

Check your answers to the odd-numbered exercises on page 632.

Module 5

Designing Documents, Slides, and Screens

Topics

- How should I design paper pages?
- How should I design presentation slides?
- How should I design Web pages?
- How should I assess my design?
- When should I think about design?

Review of Key Points

Learning Applications

Polishing Your Prose: Active and Passive Voice

Learning Focus

After reading and applying the information in Module 5, you'll be able to demonstrate

Knowledge of

- The impact of document appearance, layout, and design
- Essential design principles
- The relationship between readability and your credibility

Skills to

- Assess visual literacy
- Apply design principles to paper pages, presentation slides, and Web pages
- Use computers to increase document readability

"Using communications skills to solve engineering problems..."

"If Web-writing is in your future, you owe it to your readers to spend time on the Web yourself," says Katie FitzRandolph, communications director for the Ontario Public Service Employees Union. "You must figure out how to use the Web and to determine the things you like and the things you hate about the Web. Some of the things you will like, and hate, about Web sites deal with the structure of a site, its graphics, and its ease of navigation."

Katie has been in journalism all of her working life. She has a B.A. from the University of New Brunswick and a journalism degree from Carleton University. Before coming to OPSEU she spent fifteen years as a reporter/editor with such papers as *The Vancouver Times, Regina Leader-Post, Winnipeg Free Press,* and the *Ottawa Citizen.* She became a member of the Newspaper Guild while in Winnipeg, was president of the Ottawa local for four years, and has experience in negotiating collective agreements. At OPSEU Katie gets to use all of her communication skills and labour knowledge.

OPSEU has nearly 100,000 members spread through nearly 500 locals. In addition to working on the union's Web site, Katie is responsible for communicating with all members through the union's main print publications *Our Ontario* and *In Solidarity.* As well as editing and writing for these publications, she provides media relations and communications support for locals on strike or in tough negotiations. She also writes speeches for senior officials of the union and delivers educational programs on communications issues, the most interesting one being an annual three-day conference for editors of union newsletters.

When working on a Web site, Katie confirms, the most important things to remember are that writing is still writing and the rules for print also apply to Web sites. The first thing to think of is "who am I writing to?" and the second question is "what do they want and need?"

Katie says most people hit the site for specific information and that information has to be accessible. A "focus group" at the 2000 Canadian Association for Labour Media came up with the following suggestions: ditch all needless words; give short, focussed facts; use short paragraphs; think visual display; and think bullets.

One way to implement this approach is to underline key terms in a story so that by clicking on the specific word the reader can get the background information he or she wants without interrupting the flow of the story. A recent piece on bargaining begins like this:

"Bargaining begins with members, because it's the members who decide contract demands."

One can read the whole piece in one sitting, or one can get all the background information one needs or wants. The appeal of the site is maintained and all aspects of the reader's needs are met.

When asked to give advice to other Web page designers, Katie says, "To sum it up in a nutshell, writing for the Web is exactly like writing for print—except more so. Just because you can do something technically wizzy, doesn't mean you should. Only do so if you can come up with a darn good reason."

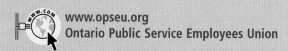

www.opseu.org
Ontario Public Service Employees Union

FYI

FedEx saved $400,000 a year by redesigning its ground-operations manuals. Before, employees could find the right answer only 53 percent of the time. Afterwards, their success rate was 80 percent, and they found answers 25 percent more quickly.

Source: Joseph Kimble, "Writing for Dollars, Writing to Please," *The Scribes Journal of Legal Writing,* 6 (1996–1997): 14–15.

A well-designed document looks inviting, friendly, and accessible. Good document design saves time and money, builds goodwill and reduces legal problems. Effective design also groups ideas visually, making the structure of the document more obvious and easier to read. Research shows that easy-to-read documents enhance your credibility and build an image of you as a professional, competent person.[1]

How should I design paper pages?

Use the following guidelines to create visually attractive documents:

- Use white space to separate and emphasize points
- Use headings to group points
- Limit the use of words set in all capital letters
- Use no more than two typefaces in a single document
- Decide whether to justify margins based on the situation and the audience

Use White Space

White space—the empty space on the page—emphasizes the material that it separates from the rest of the text. This emphasis makes the material easier to read. Creating white space is also known as "menu writing", because the visual design principle—brief text highlighted by space—is the same as you find on restaurant menus.

To create white space,

Instant **Replay**

Guidelines for Page Design

- Use white space to separate and emphasize points
- Use headings to group points
- Limit the use of words set in all capital letters
- Use no more than two typefaces in a single document
- Decide whether to justify margins based on the situation and the audience

- Use headings
- Use a mix of paragraph lengths (maximum six to seven typed lines)
- Use lists
- Use tabs or indents—not spacing—to align items vertically
- Use numbered lists when the number or sequence of items is exact
- Use **bullets** (large dots or squares like those in this list) when the number and sequence are equal

When you create a list, use parallelism: begin each item on the list with the same part of speech. If you begin your list with a verb, for example, begin every following item on the list with a verb. This parallel structure meets the reader's subconscious expectation. ***And meeting reader expectation is the most important aspect of business writing.***

Not Parallel: The following suggestions can help employers avoid bias in job interviews:

1. Base questions on the job description
2. Questioning techniques
3. Selection and training of interviewers

Parallel: The following suggestions can help employers avoid bias in job interviews:

1. Base questions on the job description
2. Ask the same questions of all applicants
3. Select and train interviewers carefully

Also parallel: Employers can avoid bias in job interviews by

1. Basing questions on the job description
2. Asking the same questions of all applicants
3. Selecting and training interviewers carefully

Figure 5.1 below shows an original typed document. In Figure 5.2 on page 104, the same document is improved by using shorter paragraphs, lists, and headings. These devices take space. When saving space is essential, it's better to cut the text and keep white space and headings.

Figure 5.1

A Document with Poor Visual Impact

Full capital letters make title hard to read

MONEY DEDUCTED FROM YOUR WAGES TO PAY CREDITORS

When you buy goods on credit, the store will sometimes ask you to sign a Wage Assignment form allowing it to deduct money from your wages if you do not pay your bill. When you buy on credit, you sign a contract agreeing to pay a certain amount each week or month until you have paid all you owe. The Wage Assignment Form is separate. It must contain the name of your present employer, your social insurance number, the amount of money loaned, the rate of interest, the date when payments are due, and your signature. The words "Wage Assignment" must be printed at the top of the form and also near the line for your signature. Even if you have signed a Wage Assignment agreement, Roysner will not withhold part of your wages unless all of the following conditions are met: 1. You have to be more than forty days late in payment of what you owe; 2. Roysner has to receive a correct statement of the amount you are in default and a copy of the Wage Assignment form; and 3. You and Roysner must receive a notice from the creditor at least twenty days in advance stating that the creditor plans to make a demand on your wages. This twenty-day notice gives you a chance to correct the problems yourself. If these conditions are all met, Roysner must withhold 15 percent of each paycheque until your bill is paid and give this money to your creditor.

Long para-graph is visually uninviting

If you think you are not late or that you do not owe the amount stated, you can argue against it by filing a legal document called a "defence." Once you file a defence, Roysner will not withhold any money from you. However, be sure you are right before you file a defence. If you are wrong, you have to pay not only what you owe but also all legal costs for both yourself and the creditor. If you are right, the creditor has to pay all these costs.

Important information is hard to find

Figure 5.2

A Document Revised to Improve Visual Impact

Money Deducted from Your Wages to Pay Creditors

First letter of each main word capitalized— Title split onto two lines

When you buy goods on credit, the store will sometimes ask you to sign a Wage Assignment form allowing it to deduct money from your wages if you do not pay your bill.

Have You Signed a Wage Assignment Form?

Headings divide document into chunks

When you buy on credit, you sign a contract agreeing to pay a certain amount each week or month until you have paid all you owe. The Wage Assignment Form is separate. It must contain

- The name of your present employer,
- Your social insurance number,
- The amount of insurance,
- The rate of interest,
- The date when payments are due, and
- Your signature.

List with bullets where order of items doesn't matter

The words "Wage Assignment" must be printed at the top of the form and also near the line for your signature.

When Would Money Be Deducted from Your Wages to Pay a Creditor?

Headings must be parallel. Here, all are questions.

Even if you have signed a Wage Assignment agreement, Roysner will not withhold part of your wages unless all of the following conditions are met:

1. You have to be more than 40 days late in payment of what you owe;

2. Roysner has to receive a correct statement of the amount you are in default and a copy of the Wage Assignment form; and

3. You and Roysner must receive a notice from the creditor at least 20 days in advance stating that the creditor plans to make a demand on your wages. This 20-day notice gives you a chance to correct the problem yourself.

White space between items emphasizes them

Numbered list where number, order of items matter

If these conditions are all met, Roysner must withhold fifteen percent (15 percent) of each paycheque until your bill is paid and give this money to your creditor.

What Should You Do if You Think the Wage Assignment Is Incorrect?

If you think you are not late or that you do not owe the amount stated, you can argue against it by filing a legal document called a "defence." Once you file a defence, Roysner will not withhold any money from you. However, be sure you are right before you file a defence. If you are wrong, you have to pay not only what you owe but also all legal costs for both yourself and the creditor. If you are right, the creditor has to pay all these costs.

Use Headings

Headings are words or short phrases that identify a complete idea and divide your letter, memo, or report into sections. Headings increase readability because they summarize what the reader is about to read and increase white space.

- Make headings specific
- Make each heading cover all the material until the next heading
- Keep headings at any one level parallel: all nouns, all complete sentences, or all questions

In a letter or memo, type main headings flush with the left-hand margin in bold. Capitalize the first letters of the first word and of other major words; use lowercase for all other letters. (See Figure 5.2 on page 104 for an example.) In single-spaced text, triple space between the previous text and the heading; double space between the heading and the text that follows.

In a report, you may need more levels of headings. ◄► Module 15 shows how to set up five levels of headings for reports.

Limit the Use of Words Set in All Capital Letters.

We recognize words by their shapes.[2] (See Figure 5.3.) Using capital letters, all words are rectangular; letters lose the descenders and ascenders that make reading go more quickly. Use full capitals sparingly. Instead, make text bold to emphasize it.

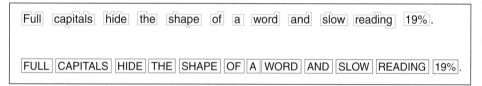

Figure 5.3
Full Capitals Hide the Shape of a Word

Use No More than Two Fonts in a Single Document.

Each font comes in several sizes and usually in several styles (bold, italic, etc.). Most computer fonts are **proportional**: wider letters (like *w*) take more space than narrow letters (like *i*). Times Roman, Palatino, Helvetica, Geneva, and Arial are proportional fonts. Fonts such as Courier and Prestige Elite, which were designed for typewriters and are still offered as computer fonts, are **fixed**. Every letter takes the same space, so that an *i* takes the same space as a *w*.

Serif fonts have little extensions, called serifs, from the main strokes. (In Figure 5.4 on page 106, look at the feet on the *t* in Times Roman and the little flicks on the ends of the top bar of the *t*.) Courier, Times Roman, Palatino, and Lucinda Calligraphy are serif fonts. *Serif fonts are easier to read* since the serifs help the eyes move from letter to letter. Helvetica, Geneva, and Arial are **sans serif** fonts since they lack serifs (*sans* is French for *without*). Sans serif fonts are good for titles, tables, and narrow columns.

In magnified text, sans serif fonts are easier to read; therefore, use sans serif fonts for your PowerPoint presentations.

Most business documents use just one font—usually Times Roman, Palatino, Helvetica, or Arial in 11- or 12-point. In a complex document, use bigger type for main headings and slightly smaller type for subheadings and text. If you combine two fonts in one document, choose one serif and one sans serif typeface.

Resist the temptation to use all the fonts on your computer.

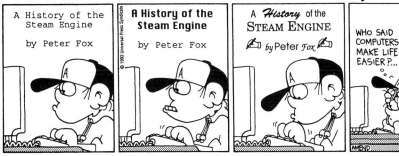

Decide Whether to Justify Margins Based on the Situation and the Audience.

Margins that are justified only on the left are sometimes called **ragged right margins**. Lines end in different places because words are of different lengths. The FYI and Instant Replay boxes use ragged right margins, which are most common in current business usage. However, computers allow you to use **full justification**, so that type on the both sides of the page is evenly lined up. This paragraph justifies margins.

Use ragged right margins when you

- Do not have proportional typefaces
- Want a less formal look
- Want to be able to revise an individual page without reprinting the whole document

Use justified margins when you

- Can use proportional typefaces
- Want a more formal look
- Use very short line lengths

Figure 5.4

Examples of Different Fonts

This sentence is set in 12-point Times Roman

This sentence is set in 12-point Arial

This sentence is set in 12-point New Courier

This sentence is set in 12-point Lucinda Calligraphy

This sentence is set in 12-point Broadway

This sentence is set in 12-point Technical

Using Computers to Create Good Design

Standard word processing programs such as WordPerfect and Word let you control how your page looks. Different versions of each program handle these commands differently. Look up the bolded terms below in a manual, a book about the program, or the online Help menu of your computer program to find out how to use each feature.

Letters and Memos

Choose a businesslike font in 11- or 12-point type. Times Roman, Palatino, Helvetica, and Arial are the most commonly used business fonts.

Use **bold** headings. Avoid having a heading all by itself at the bottom of the page. If you can't have at least one line of text under it, move the heading to the next page. You can check this by eye or set your program to avoid **widows** and **orphans**.

Use **tabs** or **indents** to line up the return address and signature blocks in modified block format (◀▶ Module 9), the To/From/Subject line section of a memo, or the items in a list.

Change your **tab settings** to create good visual impact. A setting at .6" works well for the Date/To/From/Subject line section of memos. Use .4" for paragraphs and .6" for the start of bulleted lists. For lists with 10 or more items, the setting will need to be a bit further to the right—about .65".

Choose the design for **bullets** under Insert or Format. Both WordPerfect and Word will create bulleted or numbered lists automatically. If you have lists with paragraphs, turn off the automatic bullets and create them with the bullets in Symbols. Use **indent** (not tab) to move the whole list in, not just a single line of it.

Use a **header** (in the Insert or View menu) with automatic **page numbering** (pull down Format to Page) for second and subsequent pages. That way, when you delete a paragraph or expand your reader benefits, you don't have to manually move the header. You can either **delay** the header till page 2 or create it on page 2. For best visual impact, make your header one point size smaller than the body type.

For a two-page document, change the top **margin** of the second page to .5" so the header is close to the top of the page.

Use the same side margins as your letterhead. If you aren't using letterhead, use 1" side margins.

On a two-page document, make sure the second page has at least 4 to 6 lines of text for letters and at least 10 lines of text for memos. If you have less, either (1) add details, (2) start the message further down on page one so that there is more text on page two or (3) make the text fit on just one page by (a) tightening your prose, (b) using full justification to save space, or (c) using less white space.

Word processing programs have a **quick correct** or **auto correct** feature that changes *hte* to *the*, (c) to ©, and so forth. Go into the Tools or Format menus to find these features and edit them so they make only the changes you want.

Hyphenation may be under Format or under Language in Tools.

Printing

To save paper, check **print preview** on the File menu. You'll be able to see how your document will look on the page and make minor layout changes before you print.

If you prepare your document on one computer and print it from another, be sure to open the document and check all of it before you print. Different printers may change margins slightly. Even the same size font may differ from printer to printer, so that a document that fit nicely on one page in 11-point on one computer may suddenly take up more room on a different one.

How should I design presentation slides?

Keep slides simple, relevant, and interesting.

As you design slides for PowerPoint and other presentation programs, keep these guidelines in mind

- Always use more pictures than text
- Contrast background and text: the rule is light on dark or dark on light
- Use a big font: 44- or 50-point for titles, 32-point for subheads, and 28-point for examples
- Use bullet-point phrases rather than complete sentences
- Use clear, concise language
- Keep the text to five lines and five words per line, maximum. When you have additional information, use two slides
- Customize your slides with the company logo, charts, and scanned-in photos and drawings
- Place illustrations at the top right of the slide, for a stronger and longer impression

Use clip art only if the art is really appropriate to your points and only if you are able to find nonsexist and nonracist images. (At the end of the 1990s, the clip art in major software programs was still biased; ◀▶ Module 4.)

Choose a consistent template, or background design, for the entire presentation. Make sure that the template is appropriate for your subject matter. For example, use a globe only if your topic is international business and palm trees only if you're talking about tropical vacations. One problem with PowerPoint is that the basic templates may seem repetitive to people who see lots of presentations made with the program. For a very important presentation, customize the basic template.

Choose a light background if the lights will be off during the presentation and a dark background if the lights will be on. Slides will be easier to read if you use high contrast between the words and background. See Figure 5.5 for examples of effective and ineffective colour combinations.

Figure 5.5
Effective and Ineffective Colours for Presentation Slides

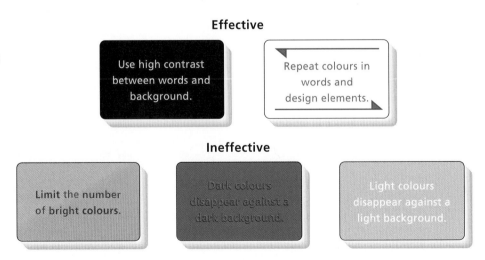

How should I design Web pages?

Pay attention to content, navigation, and the first screen.

Good Web pages have both good content and an interesting design.

Your opening screen is crucial. Jakob Nielsen claims that only 10 percent of users scroll beyond the first screen.[3] To make it more likely that visitors will scroll down, on the first screen

- Provide an introductory statement orienting the surfing reader to the organization
- Offer an overview of the content of your page, with links to take readers to the parts that interest them
- Put information that will be most interesting and useful to most readers

The rest of the page can contain information that only a limited number of readers will want. When a document reaches four pages or more, think about dividing it into several documents. Specialized information can go on another page, which readers can click on if they want it.

Make it clear what readers will get if they click on a link.

Ineffective phrasing: Employment. <u>Openings and skills levels are determined by each office.</u>

Better phrasing: Employment. Openings listed by <u>skills level</u> and by <u>location</u>.

Minimize the number of links readers have to click through to get to the information they want.

As you design pages,

- Use small graphics; keep animation to a minimum. Both graphics and animation take time to load, especially with a slow modem.
- Provide visual variety. Use indentations, bulleted or numbered lists, and headings.
- Unify multiple pages with a small banner, graphic, or label so surfers know who sponsors each page.
- On each page, provide a link to the home page, the name and email address of the person who maintains the page, and the date when the page was last revised.

How do I know whether my design works?

Test it

A design that looks pretty may or may not work for the audience. To know whether your design is functional, test it with your audience:

- Watch someone as he or she uses the document to do a task. Where does the reader pause, reread, or seem confused? How long does it take? Does the document enable the reader to complete the task accurately?
- Ask the reader to "think aloud" while completing the task, interrupt the reader at key points to ask what he or she is thinking, or ask the reader to describe the thought process after completing the document and the task. Exploring the reader's thought processes is important, since a reader may get the right

FYI

PowerPoint® Pros and Cons

Canadian-born psychology professor and writer Steven Pinker muses that ideas are multi-dimensional and when used appropriately, "PowerPoint makes the logical structure of an argument more transparent. Two channels sending the same information are better than one."

But Scott McNealy, CEO of Sun Microsystems, argues, "If I want to tell my forty-thousand employees to attack, the word 'attack' in ASCII is forty-eight bits. As a Microsoft Word document it's 90,112 bits. But put that same word in a PowerPoint slide and it becomes 458,048 bits. That's a pig through the python when you try to send it over the Net."

Source: Ian Parker, "Absolute PowerPoint: Can a software package edit our thoughts?" *The New Yorker* (May 28, 2001), 86.

Designing PowerPoint Slides

- Use a big font
- Use bullet-point phrases
- Make only three to five points on each slide
- Customize your slides

answer for the wrong reasons. Thus you can identify where and how the design needs work.

- Test the document with the people who are most likely to have trouble with it: very old or young readers, people with little education, people who read English as a second language.

When should I think about design?

At each stage of the writing process.

Because layout and design make the first impression on readers, document design is a vital component of persuasion. Indeed, you create the best documents when you think about design at each stage of your writing process(es):

- As you plan, think about your audience. Are they skilled readers? Are they busy? Will they read the document straight through or skip around in it? Design the document to meet readers' needs and expectations.
- As you write, incorporate lists and headings. Use visuals to convey numerical data clearly and forcefully.
- Get feedback from people who will be using your document. What parts of the document do they find hard to understand? What additional information do they need?
- As you revise, check your draft against the guidelines in this module.

Employability Skills 2000+ Checklist for Designing Documents, Slides, and Screens

In this module, the key skills from The Conference Board of Canada's Employability Skills 2000+ are:

Communicate

- ✔ listen and ask questions to understand and appreciate the points of view of others
- ✔ share information using a range of information and communication technologies (e.g., voice, email, computers)
- ✔ use relevant scientific, technological, and mathematical knowledge and skills to explain or clarify ideas

Think & Solve Problems

- ✔ seek different points of view and evaluate them based on facts
- ✔ recognize the human, interpersonal, technical, scientific, and mathematical dimensions of a problem
- ✔ be creative and innovative in exploring possible solutions

Work with Others

- ✔ recognize and respect people's diversity, individual differences, and perspectives

Review of Key Points

- An attractive document looks inviting, friendly, and easy to read. The visual grouping of ideas also makes the structure of the document more obvious so it is easier to read.
- Good document design can save time, money, and legal problems.
- To create visually attractive documents,
  - Use white space
  - Use headings
  - Limit the use of words set in all capital letters
  - Limit the number of typefaces in a single document
  - Decide whether to justify margins based on the situation and the audience
- As you design slides for PowerPoint and other presentation programs,
  - Use a big, sans serif font
  - Use bullet-point phrases
  - Make only three to five points on each slide
  - Customize your slides
- Good Web pages have both good content and an interesting design.
  - Orient the surfing reader to the organization
  - Offer an overview of the content of your page, with links to take readers to the parts that interest them

- Make it clear what readers will get if they click on a link
- Keep graphics small
- Provide visual variety
- Unify multiple pages with a small banner, graphic, or label
- On each page, provide a link to the home page, the name and email address of the person who maintains the page, and the date when the page was last revised
- To test a document, observe readers, ask them to "think aloud" while completing the task, interrupt them at key points to ask what they are thinking, or ask them to describe the thought process after completing the document and the task.
- The best documents are created when you think about design at each stage of the writing process.
  - As you plan, think about the needs of your audience
  - As you write, incorporate lists, headings, and visuals
  - Get feedback from people who will be using your document
  - As you revise, check your draft against the guidelines in this chapter

Learning Applications

Questions for Comprehension

5.1   How can you create white space?

5.2   How do you decide whether to use bullets or numbers in a list?

5.3   What are three criteria for good Web pages?

Questions for Critical Thinking

5.4   "Closed captions" for people with hearing impairments are almost always typed in full capital letters. Why is that a bad idea? Are there any advantages to using full capitals? What arguments could you use for changing the practice?

5.5   Suppose that, in one company, a worker says, "We don't need to worry about design. People pay a toll charge to call us, and we make a slight profit on each call. So if they have questions about the product, that's OK. If better design reduced the number of calls, we might actually lose money!" How would you persuade such a person that good document design is worth doing?

5.6   West Coast University College is preparing a brochure to persuade prospective students to consider taking classes. The school doesn't want to invest a lot of money in full-scale document testing. What free or almost-free things could it do to make the document as effective as possible?

5.7   Design choices may have ethical implications. Indicate whether you consider each of the following actions ethical, unethical, or a grey area. Which of the actions would you do? Which would you feel uncomfortable doing? Which would you refuse to do?

1.   Putting the advantages of a proposal in a bulleted list, while discussing the disadvantages in a paragraph

2.   Using a bigger type size so that a résumé visually fills a whole page

3.   Putting the services that are not covered by your health plan in full caps to make it less likely that people will read the page

Questions for Building Skills

5.8   What skills have you read about in this module?

5.9   What skills are you practising in the assignments you're doing for this module?

5.10   How could you further develop the skills you're working on?

Exercises and Problems

5.11 Evaluating Page Designs

Use the guidelines in Module 5 to evaluate each of the following page designs. What are their strong points? What could be improved?

Figure 5.7

Source: Diane Burns and S. Venit, "What's Wrong with This Paper," *PC Magazine* 6, no. 17 (October 13, 1987): 174–75.

5.12 Evaluating PowerPoint Slides

Evaluate the following drafts of PowerPoint slides.

- Is the background appropriate for the topic?
- Do the slides use words or phrases rather than complete sentences?
- Is the font big enough to read from a distance?
- Is the art relevant and appropriate?
- Is each slide free from errors?

a.

1

2

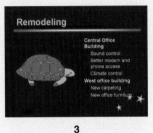

3

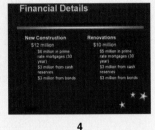

4

b.

1

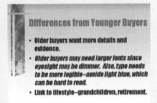

2

3

4

c.

Add Builds and Transitions.

- Let you direct audience's attention.
- Provide visual interest.
- Develop consistent "look."
  - Use same transition throughout.
  - Use build for a reason--not necessarily for every line.

Use Strong Visuals.

- Choose art that is
  - Relevant.
  - Bias-free.
  - Fresh to the audience.
  - Adapted to the company and the audience.

5.13 Using Headings

Reorganize the items in each of the following lists, using appropriate headings. Use bulleted or numbered lists as appropriate.

a. Rules and Procedures for a Tuition Reimbursement Plan

1. You are eligible to be reimbursed if you have been a full-time employee for at least three months

2. You must apply before the first class meeting

3. You must earn a "C" or better in the course

4. You must submit a copy of the approved application, an official grade report, and a receipt for tuition paid to be reimbursed

5. You can be reimbursed for courses related to your current position or another position in the company, or for courses that are part of a degree related to a current or possible job

6. Your supervisor must sign the application form

7. Courses may be at any appropriate level (high school, college, or graduate school)

b. Activities in Starting a New Business

- Getting a loan or venture capital
- Getting any necessary city or state licences
- Determining what you will make, do, or sell
- Identifying the market for your products or services
- Pricing your products or services
- Choosing a location
- Checking zoning laws which may affect the location
- Identifying government and university programs for small business development
- Figuring cash flow
- Ordering equipment and supplies
- Selling
- Advertising and marketing

5.14 Analyzing Documents

Collect several documents available to you as a worker, student, or consumer: letters and memos, newsletters, ads and flyers, reports. Use the guidelines in Module 5 to evaluate each of them.

As Your Instructor Directs,

a. Discuss the documents with a small group of classmates.

b. Write a memo to your instructor evaluating three or more of the documents. Include originals or photocopies of the documents you discuss as an appendix to your memo.

c. Write a memo to your supervisor recommending ways the organization can improve its documents.

d. In an oral presentation to the class, explain what makes one document good and another one weak. If possible, use transparencies so classmates can see the documents as you evaluate them.

5.15 Evaluating Web Pages

Compare three Web pages in the same category (for example, non-profit organizations, car companies, university departments, sports information). Which page(s) are most effective? Why? What would you change? Why?

As Your Instructor Directs,

a. Discuss the pages with a small group of classmates.

b. Write a memo to your instructor evaluating the pages. Include URLs of the pages in your memo.

c. In an oral presentation to the class, explain what makes one page good and another one weak. If possible, put the pages on screen so classmates can see the pages as you evaluate them.

d. Post your evaluation of the pages in an email message to the class. Include hot links to the pages you evaluate.

5.16 Analyzing a Document

Your municipal and provincial governments may offer internships and cooperative placements to post-secondary students. Research (visit, telephone, email, find someone who knows someone) the placement possibilities through your college/university co-op placement office, or contact the government department directly. Request a copy of the application or information documents for these positions. Write an analysis of the document's layout and page design.

5.17 Revising a Financial Aid Form

You've just joined the Financial Aid office at your school. The director gives you the accompanying form and asks you to redesign it.

"We need this form to see whether parents have other students in college besides the one requesting aid. Parents are supposed to list all family members that the parents support— themselves, the person here, any other kids in college, and any younger dependent kids.

"Half of these forms are filled out incorrectly. Most people just list the student going here; they leave out everyone else.

"If something is missing, the computer sends out a letter and a second copy of this form. The whole process starts over. Sometimes we send this form back two or three times before it's right. In the meantime, students' financial aid is delayed—maybe for months. Sometimes things are so late that they can't register for classes, or they have to pay tuition themselves and get reimbursed later.

"If so many people are filling out the form wrong, the form itself must be the problem. See what you can do with it. But keep it to a page."

As Your Instructor Directs,

a. Analyze the current form and identify its problems.

b. Revise the form. Add necessary information; reorder information; change the chart to make it easier to fill out.

Hints:

- Where are people supposed to send the form? What is the phone number of the financial aid office? Should they need to call the office if the form is clear?

- Does the definition of *half-time* apply to all students or just those taking courses beyond high school?

- Should capital or lower-case letters be used?

- Are the lines big enough to write in?

- What headings or subdivisions within the form would remind people to list all family members whom they support?

- How can you encourage people to return the form promptly?

Please complete the chart below by listing all family members for whom you (the parents) will provide more than half support during the academic year (July 1 through June 30). Include yourselves (the parents), the student, and your dependent children, even if they are not attending college.

EDUCATIONAL INFORMATION, 200_ - 200_						
FULL NAME OF FAMILY MEMBER	AGE	RELATIONSHIP OF FAMILY MEMBER TO STUDENT	NAME OF SCHOOL OR COLLEGE THIS SCHOOL YEAR	FULL-TIME	HALF-TIME* OR MORE	LESS THAN HALF-TIME
STUDENT APPLICANT						

*Half-time is defined as 6 credit hours or 12 clock hours a term.

When the information requested is received by our office, processing of your financial aid application will resume.

Please sign and mail this form to the above address as soon as possible. Your signature certifies that this information and the information on the FAF is true and complete to the best of your knowledge. If you have any questions, please contact a member of the need analysis staff.

_____   _____
Signature of Parent(s)   Date

Polishing Your Prose

Active and Passive Voice

Because it depicts the action, the verb is the most important word in the sentence. Verbs indicate who or what is doing the action through "voice". When whoever is acting is also the subject of the sentence, the verb is active; in the passive voice, the subject is acted upon by someone or something else.

Contemporary communication prefers verbs in the active voice, because the resulting sentence is clearer and shorter. When writers want to avoid or downplay delegating responsibility, they use the passive voice.

Active: The man bought grapes at the store.

Passive: The grapes were bought by the man at the store.

In the active voice, the subject—the man—is doing the action—bought. In the passive version, "The grapes" is the subject, yet it is the man, not the grapes, that is actually doing the action. It is harder for the reader to follow who or what did the action. In addition, it takes more words to convey the same idea.

To change a passive voice construction into the active voice, start by identifying who or what is doing the action. If no agent ("by _____") is present in the sentence, you will need to supply it. A passive verb is usually accompanied by a copula verb, such as *is*, *are*, or *were*. Rewrite the sentence by putting the actor in the role of subject and dropping the helping verb:

Passive: The plan was approved by our clients.

Active: Our clients approved the plan.

Passive: PowerPoint slides have been created.

Active: Susan created the PowerPoint slides.

Passive: It is desired that you back up your work daily.

Active: Back up your work daily.

In business communication, active voice is usually better. However, passives are better in three situations:

1. Use passives to emphasize the object receiving the action, not the agent.

   Your order was shipped November 15.

   The customer's order, not the shipping clerk, is important.

2. Use passives to provide coherence within a paragraph. A sentence is easier to read if "old" information comes at the beginning of a sentence. When you have been discussing a topic, use the word again as your subject even if that requires a passive verb.

   The bank made several risky loans in the late 1980s. These loans were written off as "uncollectible" in 1998.

   Using *loans* as the subject of the second sentence provides a link between the two sentences, making the paragraph as a whole easier to read.

3. Use passives to avoid assigning blame.

   The order was damaged during shipment.

   An active verb would require the writer to specify *who* damaged the order. The passive here is more tactful.

Exercises

Identify whether the passives in the following sentences are acceptable, or whether the verb should be changed to active.

1. The contract was signed by the vice president of finance.

2. New employees Ms. Taleroski, Mr. Franklin, and Ms. Holbreck were introduced at last week's staff meeting.

3. Two visitors are expected to arrive at headquarters tomorrow.

4. Outgoing correspondence was collected by the mailroom staff.

5. The proposal was turned in late.

Turn these passive voice constructions into active voice:

6. Correspondence was collected by the mailroom staff.

7. Phone calls were returned by the human resources administrator.

8. In April, budgets were amortized and files created for the project.

9. Phone calls need to be returned within 24 hours.

10. Packages are to be sent to the mailroom for delivery.

Check your answers to the odd-numbered exercises on page 632 at the back of the book.

CBC Video Case

Go to www.mcgrawhill.ca/college/locker for "Office Etiquette", an online CBC Video Case that explores how good manners aid communication between co-workers.

Unit Two

Creating Goodwill

Module 6
You-Attitude

Topics

- **How do I create you-attitude in my sentences?**
- **Does you-attitude mean using the word *you*?**
- **I've revised my sentences. Do I need to do anything else?**

Review of Key Points

Learning Applications

Polishing Your Prose: It's/Its

Learning Focus

After reading and applying the information in Module 6, you'll be able to demonstrate

Knowledge of

- The differences between writer-centred and reader-centred messages
- Elements of persuasive writing

Skills to

- Begin building goodwill
- Adapt your message to the audience
- Emphasize what the reader wants to know
- See another point of view

"Consistency, consistency, consistency..."

"You must focus on your client rather than on the product," says Robin Honey, founder and president of HONEY Design, Marketing and Communications. At one time the firm would have been called an advertising agency. Today it provides the package of design, marketing, and communications services listed in the firm's name. Robin's philosophy is that "each client requires specific expertise and talents. We combine the science of marketing with the art of creativity to produce outstanding results for our clients." The awards that line Robin's office testify to the success of this approach.

Robin is from London, Ontario, and originally set out to be a fine artist. But when she found she could not make a living in art, she looked for a field in which she could use her talents and discovered the Illustration and Design course at Sheridan College in Oakville, Ontario. In addition to the subject matter of the course, Robin was impressed with the high placement rate for its graduates.

When Robin returned to London she realized a niche existed for someone with the exact combination of talents she possessed. There were small agencies that worked with small clients and there were big agencies, but none in the middle. Many client firms were beginning to grow and needed something more than a one-person operation but could not afford a large agency. Today, twelve years later, HONEY has a staff of 10 and a list of clients from both the public and private sectors. It still services small businesses but also has international clients.

Robin describes the approach of her business as "client focussed." Rather than centring on a particular product,

HONEY focusses on marketing the brand, or the image of the company. The important point here is what Robin calls "Brand Synergy." This means that in any campaign, all aspects of the campaign must be consistent so that the target audience gets a clear message about what the company represents.

Two recent client campaigns that demonstrate this approach are for the University of Western Ontario and for a new ecommerce firm called ICINITI. For Western, Robin planned the fund raising campaign. First she designed a brochure. The form and content of the brochure were the basis for all media ads. The brochure was followed by a video and a Web site. The key aspect of the campaign was that all forms of communication were consistent in their message and their appearance. Brand identity was maintained and the content reflected the target audience.

The same factors went into the INCINITI campaign—with two differences. Robin had to work within existing brand identification and with a limited budget for the university. With ICINITI she began with a brand new company and with a large budget. But the focus was the same: maintain brand identity and make all communications consistent.

When asked for parting words of advice, Robin simply said, "Consistency, consistency, consistency. You must meet your clients' needs creatively and consistently."

 http://www.honey.on.ca/
Honey Design, Marketing &
Communications

You-attitude is a matter of understanding that effective communication acknowledges the needs of the audience. In fact, competent speakers and writers know that they can get what they want (make a sale, influence change, inform or persuade) only when they recognize and attempt to provide what their audience wants. **YOU-ATTITUDE** is a way of writing that

- Looks at things from the reader's point of view
- Respects the reader's intelligence
- Protects the reader's ego
- Emphasizes what the reader wants to know

In written messages, we can often create you-attitude by changing words. Sometimes, however, it's necessary to revise organization and content as well as style to create a reader-centred document.

How do I create you-attitude in my sentences?

Talk about the reader—except in negative situations.

To create you-attitude,

1. Talk about the reader, not about yourself.
2. Don't talk about feelings, except to congratulate or offer sympathy.
3. In positive situations, use *you* more often than *I*. Use **we** when it includes the reader.
4. Avoid "you" in negative situations.

1. Talk about the reader, not about yourself.

Readers want to know how they benefit or are affected. When you provide this information, you make your message more complete and more interesting.

Lacks you-attitude: I have negotiated an agreement with Apex Rent-a-Car that gives you a discount on rental cars.

You-attitude: As a SunLife employee, you can now get a 20 percent discount when you rent a car from Apex.

Any sentence that focusses on the writer's work or generosity lacks you-attitude, even if the sentence contains the word *you*. Instead of focussing on what you are doing for the reader, it's important to stress how the reader will benefit. To change the emphasis, you may need to change the structure of the sentence.

Lacks you-attitude: We are shipping your order of September 21 this afternoon.

You-attitude: The two dozen Umbra mini cans you ordered will be shipped this afternoon and should reach you by September 28.

Emphasize what the reader wants to know. The reader is less interested in when you shipped the order than in when it will arrive. Note that the phrase "should reach you by" leaves room for variations in delivery schedules. If you can't be exact, give your reader the information you do have: "UPS shipment from Burnaby to Regina normally takes three days." If you have absolutely no idea, give the reader

FYI

Does rudeness cost? Absolutely: 80 percent of people polled by North American etiquette companies felt that incivility in business had increased, and 58 percent claimed that, as a result, they'd take their business elsewhere, no matter the cost or inconvenience to do so.

Source: Lewena Bayer and Karen Mallett, "How rude! Your manners mean business"; visited Web site June 27, 2001. http://www.canoe.ca/LifewiseWorkEtiquette/eti_work14.html

Me-attitude can make you seem pompous and self-serving.

Source: MARVIN. Reprinted with special permission of King Features Syndicate.

the name of the carrier, so the reader knows whom to contact if the order doesn't arrive promptly.

2. Don't talk about others' feelings, except to congratulate or offer sympathy.

Lacks you-attitude: We are happy to extend you a credit line of $5,000.

You-attitude: You can now charge up to $5,000 on your Bank of Montreal card.

In most business situations, your feelings are irrelevant. The reader doesn't care whether you're happy, bored stiff at granting a routine application, or worried about granting so much to someone who barely qualifies. *All the reader cares about is the situation from his or her point of view.*

It *is* appropriate to talk about your own emotions in a message of congratulation or condolence.

You-attitude: Congratulations on your promotion to district manager! I was really pleased to read about it.

You-attitude: I was sorry to hear that your father died.

In internal memos, it may be appropriate to comment that a project has been gratifying or frustrating. In the letter of transmittal that accompanies a report, it is permissible to talk about your feelings about doing the work. But even other readers in your own organization are primarily interested in their own concerns, not in your feelings.

Don't talk about the reader's feelings, either. It can be offensive to have someone else tell us how we feel—especially if the writer is wrong.

Lacks you-attitude: You'll be happy to hear that Open Grip Walkway Channels meet Occupational Health and Safety requirements.

You-attitude: Open Grip Walkway Channels meet Occupational Health and Safety requirements.

Instant Replay

Definition of You-Attitude

You-attitude is a style of writing that

- Looks at things from the reader's point of view
- Respects the reader's intelligence
- Protects the reader's ego
- Emphasizes what the reader wants to know

Instant Replay

Four Ways to Create You-Attitude

1. Talk about the reader, not about yourself.

2. Don't talk about feelings, except to congratulate or offer sympathy.

3. In positive situations, use *you* more often than *I*. Use *we* when it includes the reader.

4. Avoid *you* in negative situations.

Maybe the reader expects that anything you sell would meet government regulations (Occupational Health and Safety, Canada's national centre for workplace safety, is a federal government agency). The reader may even be disappointed if he or she expected higher standards. Simply explain the situation or describe a product's features; don't predict the reader's response.

When you have good news for the reader, simply give the good news.

Lacks you-attitude: You'll be happy to hear that your scholarship has been renewed.

You-attitude: Congratulations! Your scholarship has been renewed.

3. In positive situations, use *you* more often than *I*. Use *we* when it includes the reader.

Talk about the reader, not you or your company.

Lacks you-attitude: We provide dental coverage to all employees.

You-attitude: You receive dental coverage as a full-time BCE employee.

Most readers are tolerant of the word *I* in email messages and memos. Edit external messages to ensure *I* is used rarely. *I* suggests that you're concerned about personal issues, not about the organization's problems, needs, and opportunities. *We* works well when it includes the reader. Avoid *we* if it excludes the reader (as it would in a letter to a customer or supplier, or as it might in a memo about what *we* in management want *you* to do).

4. Avoid *you* in negative situations.

To avoid blaming the reader, use an impersonal expression or a passive verb. Talk about the group to which the reader belongs so readers don't feel that they're singled out for bad news.

Lacks you-attitude: You failed to sign your cheque.

You-attitude (impersonal): Your cheque arrived without a signature.

You-attitude (passive) Your cheque was not signed.

Impersonal constructions omit people and talk only about things.
Passive verbs describe the action performed on something, without necessarily saying who did it. (◀▶ Module 5 for active and passive voice. ◀▶ Module 16 for a full discussion of passive verbs.)

In most cases, active verbs are better. But when your reader is at fault, passive verbs may be useful to avoid assigning blame.

Normally, writing is most lively when it's about people—and most interesting to readers when it's about them. When you have to report a mistake or bad news, however, you can protect the reader's ego by using an impersonal construction, one in which things, not people, do the acting.

Lacks you-attitude: You made no allowance for inflation in your estimate.

You-attitude (passive): No allowance for inflation has been made in this estimate.

Figure 6.1

A Letter Lacking You-Attitude

700 Upper Ottawa Street Hamilton ON L8T 3T6 (905) 555-4670 FAX: (905) 555-4672

December 11, 2002

Ms. Carol McFarland
Rollins Equipment Corporation
3105 Unity Drive
Mississauga, ON L5L 4L1

Not you-attitude

Dear Ms. McFarland   *Legalistic*

We are now ready to issue a cheque to Rollins Equipment in the amount of $14,207.02. To receive said cheque, you will deliver to me a release of the mechanic's liens in the amount of $14,207.02.   *Sounds dictatorial*

Focusses on negative   *Lacks you-attitude*

Before we can release the cheque, we must be satisfied that the release is in the proper form. We must insist that we be provided with a stamped original of the lien indicating the document number in the appropriate court where it is filed. Also, either the release must be executed by an officer of Rollins Equipment, or we must be provided with a letter from an officer of Rollins Equipment authorizing another individual to execute the release.   *Hard to read, remember*

Please contact the undersigned so that an appointment can be scheduled for this transaction.   *Jargon*

Sincerely

Kelly J. Pickett

Kelly J. Pickett

Figure 6.2

A Letter Revised to Improve You-Attitude

700 Upper Ottawa Street Hamilton ON L8T 3T6 (905) 555-4670   FAX: (905) 555-4672

December 11, 2002

Ms. Carol McFarland
Rollins Equipment Corporation
3105 Unity Drive
Mississauga, ON L5L 4L1

Dear Ms. McFarland

Let's clear up the lien in the Allen contract.

Starts with main point from the reader's point of view

Rollins will receive a cheque for $14,207.02 when you give us a release for the mechanic's lien of $14,207.02. To assure us that the release is in the proper form,

Focusses on what reader gets

1. Give us a stamped original of the lien indicating the document's court number, and

2. Either
    a. Have an officer of Rollins Equipment sign the release
        or
    b. Give us a letter from a Rollins officer authorizing someone else to sign the release.

List makes it easy to see that reader needs to do two things—and that the second can be done in two ways.

Please call me to tell me which way is best for you. *Emphasizes reader's choice*

Sincerely

Kelly J. Pickett

Kelly J. Pickett
Extension 5318   *Extension number makes it easy for reader to phone.*

Employability Skills 2000+ Checklist for You-Attitude

In this module, the key skills from The Conference Board of Canada's Employability Skills 2000+ are:

Communicate

✔ listen and ask questions to understand and appreciate the points of view of others

Think & Solve Problems

✔ seek different points of view and evaluate them based on facts
✔ recognize the human, interpersonal, technical, scientific, and mathematical dimensions of a problem
✔ be creative and innovative in exploring possible solutions

Be Responsible

✔ be accountable for your actions and the actions of your group

Work with Others

✔ be flexible: respect, be open to and supportive of the thoughts, opinions and contributions of others
✔ recognize and respect people's diversity, individual differences and perspectives

Review of Key Points

- You-attitude is a style of writing that
  - Looks at things from the reader's point of view
  - Respects the reader's intelligence
  - Protects the reader's ego
  - Emphasizes what the reader wants to know
- You-attitude is a matter of style. Revisions for you-attitude do not change the basic meaning of the sentence. However, revising for you-attitude may make sentences longer, since sentences become more specific.

- To create you-attitude in sentences,
  1. Talk about the reader, not about yourself.
  2. Don't talk about feelings, except to congratulate or offer sympathy.
  3. In positive situations, use *you* more often than *I*. Use *we* when it includes the reader.
  4. Avoid *you* in negative situations.
- Apply you-attitude beyond the sentence level by using organization, content, and layout as well as style to build goodwill.

Learning Applications

Questions for Comprehension

6.1   What is you-attitude?

6.2   How can you create you-attitude within sentences?

6.3   How can you create you-attitude beyond the sentence level?

Questions for Critical Thinking

6.4   Why doesn't the word *you* always create you-attitude?

6.5   Why do sentences starting "We give you" lack you-attitude?

6.6   Think of a time when you felt a business cared about you. What words or actions made you feel that way?

6.7   Can you think of situations in which the four strategies would *not* create you-attitude? If so, how would you create you-attitude in those situations?

Questions for Building Skills

6.8   What skills have you read about in this module?

6.9   What skills are you practising in the assignments you're doing for this module?

6.10   How could you further develop the skills you're working on?

Exercises and Problems

6.11 Using Passives and Impersonal Constructions to Improve You-Attitude

Revise each of these sentences to improve you-attitude, first using a passive verb, then using an impersonal construction (one in which things, not people, do the action). Are both revisions equally good? Why or why not?

1.   You did not send us your cheque

2.   You did not include all the necessary information in your letter

3.   By failing to build a fence around your pool, you have created a health hazard

6.12 Improving You-Attitude

Revise these sentences to improve you-attitude. Eliminate any awkward phrasing. In some cases, you may need to add information to revise the sentence effectively.

1.   We are pleased to offer you the ability to sign up for dental coverage online on our intranet

2.   You will be happy to know that you can use your new cell phone number anywhere in Canada

3.   After hours of hard work, I have negotiated a new employee benefit for you

4.   I urge you to attend a meeting about the new benefits package so that we can inform you about your rights and responsibilities

5.   You will be happy to learn additional cards for your spouse or child are free

6.   We have added another employee benefit for you

7. Today, we shipped the book you ordered

8. In your report, you forgot to tell how many people you surveyed

9. I hope that it is obvious to you that we want to give you the very best prices on furniture

10. You didn't order enough donuts for the meeting

6.13 Improving You-Attitude

Revise these sentences to improve you-attitude. Eliminate any awkward phrasing. In some cases, you may need to add information to revise the sentence effectively.

1. Starting next month, the company will offer you a choice of three different health plans

2. We provide dental coverage to all full-time employees

3. At the meeting, we'll explain to you how the new prescription drug plan will work

4. I have ordered a new computer for you. I expect it to arrive by the 15th, and I'll get it ready for you to use as soon as my schedule permits

5. We are happy to enrol you in our stock-purchase plan

6. You will be happy to learn that you can transfer credits from our business diploma programs to a university commerce degree

7. We give you the following benefits when you join our "Frequent Flier" program

8. We are pleased to send you a copy of "Investing in Stocks," which you requested

9. Your audit papers did not convert U.S. revenue into Canadian dollars

10. Of course we want to give you every possible service that you might need or want

6.14 Revising a Form Letter for You-Attitude

You've taken a part-time job at a store that sells fine jewellery. In orientation, the manager tells you that the store photographs jewellery it sells or appraises and mails the photo as a goodwill gesture after the transaction. However, when you see the form letter, you know that it doesn't build much goodwill—and you say so. The manager says,

"Well, you're in college. Suppose you rewrite it."

Rewrite the letter. Use square brackets for material (like the customer's name) that would have to be inserted in the form letter to vary it for a specific customer. Add information that would help build goodwill.

Dear Customer:

We are most happy to enclose a photo of the jewellery that we recently sold you or appraised for you. We feel that this added service, which we are happy to extend to our fine customers, will be useful should you wish to insure your jewellery.

We trust you will enjoy this additional service. We thank you for the confidence you have shown by coming to our store.

Sincerely,

Your Sales Associate

6.15 Evaluating You-Attitude in Documents That Cross Your Desk

Identify three sentences that use (or should use) you-attitude in documents you see as a student, consumer, or worker. If the sentences are good, write them down or attach a copy of the document(s) marking the sentence(s) in the margin. If the sentences need work, provide both the original sentence and a possible revision.

As Your Instructor Directs,

a. Share your examples with a small group of students.

b. Write a memo to your instructor discussing your examples.

c. Post an email message to the class discussing your examples.

d. Present two or three of your examples to the class in a short presentation.

e. With your small group, write a collaborative short report to your instructor about the patterns you see.

Polishing Your Prose

It's/Its

With an apostrophe, *it's* is a contraction meaning *it is*. Without an apostrophe, *its* is a possessive pronoun meaning *belonging to it*.

Contractions always use apostrophes:

It is → it's
I have → I've
You will → you'll
They are → they're

Possessive pronouns (unlike possessive nouns) do not use apostrophes:

His/hers/its
My/mine/our/ours
Your/yours
Their/theirs

Since both *it's* and *its* sound the same, you have to look at the logic of your sentence to choose the right word. If you could substitute *it is*, use *it's*.

Exercises

Choose the right word in the set of parentheses.

1. (It's/its) too bad that the team hasn't finished (it's/its) presentation.

2. The company projected that (it's/its) profits would rise during the next quarter.

3. (It's/its) going to require overtime because the data centre needs (it's/its) reports quickly.

4. I don't want responsibility for the project unless (it's/its) important.

5. The company will announce (it's/its) new name at a press conference.

6. I'm not sure whether (it's/its) a good idea to offer a conference.

7. (It's/its) a good idea to keep your travel receipts in a separate file.

8. (It's/its) good that our computer automatically backs up (it's/its) files.

9. The Saskatoon office will share (it's/its) findings with the other branch offices.

10. (It's/its) cash reserves protected the company from a hostile takeover.

Check your answers to the odd-numbered exercises on page 632.

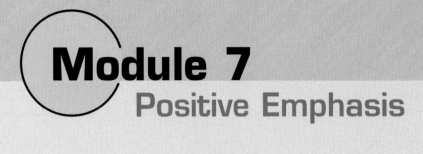

Module 7
Positive Emphasis

Topics

- How do I create positive emphasis?

- What's the best way to apologize?

- Why do I need to think about tone, politeness, and power?

Review of Key Points

Learning Applications

Polishing Your Prose: Singular and Plural Possessives

Learning Focus

After reading and applying the information in Module 7, you'll be able to demonstrate

Knowledge of

- The impact of negative information on your reader
- Techniques to convey appropriate tone in your messages

Skills to

- Continue building goodwill
- Emphasize the positive
- Use positive emphasis ethically
- Choose an appropriate tone

"Honesty remains the critical factor in all communication..."

"My job has become one of putting out timely and accurate information to help staff cope with the changes in the institution," says Scott May, communications consultant for what is now The St. Joseph's Mental Health Centre of London and St. Thomas, but what used to be the London Psychiatric Hospital.

Since 1990 the institution has been undergoing change. In the past, when people got a job in an institution like this, with a history going back 130 years, they were employed there for life. But not anymore. On the one hand, changing concepts of mental care focus on trying to get people out of institutions and into the community. On the other hand, government policies have amalgamated and/ or closed various institutions. The hospitals in St. Thomas and in London are now amalgamated along with St. Joseph's hospital. Over the next five years the current buildings will be closed and new, smaller buildings will be built in different locations.

In the meantime, the staff don't always know what lies ahead. This is where the communications office becomes important. Scott's mandate is to try to explain the nature of these changes to the staff. Eventually these changes will also affect his position. Under the new management, Scott has been made part of the Senior Leadership Team, so that he is involved in the decision-making process and can communicate what is going on more accurately.

Scott sees his role as providing both sides of the story to maintain accuracy. When asked if this means putting bad news in a good light, he said that is not what he does. "The idea of trying to make something positive out of something negative gives communicators a sense of unease, because our job demands that we communicate honestly."

Scott views his job as more of a facilitator trying to explain what is really going on. But this has to be done in a positive manner since the purpose of the information he provides is to help people function in an environment of change and uncertainty. This is no small job, which is why he must be credible.

Scott has a B.A. in administrative and commercial studies from the University of Western Ontario and a post-grad certificate in communications from the University of Guelph. He has worked with Community Living London and came to the hospital as volunteer coordinator in 1985. He has been in his current position since 1990.

When asked for parting words to other communicators in similar situations, Scott says, "Your audience always knows what to expect from you when the news is good, so they look for a commitment to accuracy when the news is bad. This is why one has to be honest in one's communication. Honesty remains the critical factor in all communication."

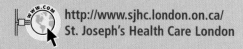

http://www.sjhc.london.on.ca/
St. Joseph's Health Care London

Sometimes negatives are necessary.

- Straightforward negatives build credibility when you have bad news to give the reader: announcements of layoffs, product defects and recalls, price increases. Being honest about the drawbacks of a job reduces turnover.
- Negatives may help people take a problem seriously. Wall Data improved the reliability of its computer programs when it eliminated the term *bugs* and used instead the term *failures*.
- In some messages, such as negative performance appraisals, your purpose is to deliver a rebuke with no alternative. In these situations, you are legally responsible for ensuring that your language conforms to organizational and governmental regulations (in a union environment, to the rules in the collective agreement; in every workplace situation, to the province's Employment Standards Act/Code and to the Human Rights Commission mandates concerning issues of harassment and discrimination). Thus there are legal as well as ethical and practical reasons to deliver negative information sensitively.
- Sometimes negatives create a "reverse psychology" that makes people look favourably at your product. Rent-a-Wreck is thriving. (The cars really don't look so bad.)[1]

In most situations, however, it's better to be positive. People respond more favourably to positive than to negative language and are more likely to act on a positively worded request.[2]

Martin Seligman's research for Met Life found that optimistic salespeople sold 37 percent more insurance than pessimistic colleagues. As a result, Met Life began hiring optimists even when they failed to meet the company's other criteria. These "unqualified" optimists outsold pessimists 21 percent in their first year and 57 percent the next.[3]

Positive emphasis is a way of looking at things. Is the bottle half empty or half full? You can create positive emphasis with the words, information, organization, and layout you choose.

How do I create positive emphasis?

De-emphasize or omit negative words and information.

The following five techniques de-emphasize negative information:

1. Avoid negative words and words with negative connotations
2. Focus on what the reader can do rather than on limitations
3. Justify negative information by giving a reason or linking it to a reader benefit
4. If the negative is unimportant, omit it
5. Put the negative information in the middle and present it compactly

In some messages, especially negative ones (◁▶ Module 11), you won't use all five techniques. Practice each of these techniques so that you can use them when they're appropriate to your purpose and the needs of your audience.

The limits of positive emphasis

Source: ONE BIG HAPPY CARTOON. By permission of Rich Detorie and Creators Syndicate.

Negative Words and Words with Negative Connotations

Figure 7.1 lists some common negative words. If you find one of these words in a draft, substitute a more positive word. When you must use a negative, use the *least negative* term that will convey your meaning.

The following examples show how to replace negative words with positive words.

Negative: We have failed to finish taking inventory.

Better: We haven't finished taking inventory.

Still better: We will be finished taking inventory Friday.

Negative: If you can't understand this explanation, feel free to call me.

Better: If you have further questions, just call me.

Still better: Omit the sentence.

Figure 7.1
Negative Words to Avoid

Negative words			Some *dis*-words:	Some *mis*-words:
afraid	except	not	disapprove	misfortune
anxious	fail	objection	dishonest	missing
avoid	fault	problem	dissatisfied	mistake
bad	fear	reject		
careless	hesitate	reluctant	**Many *in*-words:**	**Many *un*-words:**
damage	ignorant	sorry	inadequate	unclear
delay	ignore	terrible	incomplete	unfair
delinquent	impossible	trivial	inconvenient	unfortunate
deny	lacking	trouble	injury	unfortunately
difficulty	loss	wait	insincere	unpleasant
eliminate	neglect	weakness		unreasonable
error	never	worry		unreliable
	no	wrong		unsure

Southwest Airlines flight attendant Danni Abshire says, "Your occupation is approximately seventy-five percent of your life. If you go to work armed every day with a good attitude, it won't seem so much like a job. Instead, it will be a more pleasant experience." Danni's positive approach and humor made her one of Southwest's Stars of the Month in 1999.

If a sentence has two negatives, substitute one positive term.

Negative: Do not forget to back up your disks.

Better: Always back up your disks.

When you must use a negative term, use the least negative word that is accurate.

Negative: Your balance of $835 is delinquent.

Better: Your balance of $835 is past due.

Instant
Replay

Five Ways to Create Positive Emphasis

To de-emphasize negative information,

• Avoid negative words and words with negative connotations
• Focus on what the reader can do rather than on limitations
• Justify negative information by giving a reason or linking it to a reader benefit
• If the negative is truly unimportant, omit it
• Put the negative information in the middle and present it compactly

Getting rid of negatives has the added benefit of making what you write easier to understand. Sentences with three or more negatives are very hard to understand.[4]

Beware of **hidden negatives**: words that are not negative in themselves but become negative in context. *But* and *however* indicate a shift, so, after a positive statement, they are negative. *I hope* and *I trust that* suggest that you aren't sure. *Patience* may sound like a virtue, but it is a necessary virtue only when things are slow. Even positives about a service or product may backfire if they suggest that in the past the service or product was bad.

Negative: I hope this is the information you wanted.
[Implication: I'm not sure.]

Better: Enclosed is a brochure about road repairs scheduled for 2002–03.

Still better: The brochure contains a list of all roads and bridges scheduled for repair during 2002–03. Call Gwen Wong at 604-555-3245 for specific dates when work will start and stop and for alternate routes.

Negative: Please be patient as we switch to the automated system.
[Implication: you can expect problems.]

Better: If you have questions during our transition to the automated system, call Melissa Morgan.

Still better: You'll be able to get information instantly about any house on the market when the automated system is in place. If you have questions during the transition, call Melissa Morgan.

Negative: Now Crispy Crunch tastes better.
                [Implication: it used to taste terrible.]

Better: Now Crispy Crunch tastes even better.

Removing negatives does not mean being arrogant or pushy.

Negative: I hope that you are satisfied enough to place future orders.

Arrogant: I look forward to receiving all of your future business.

Better: Call Mercury whenever you need transistors.

When you eliminate negative words, be sure to maintain accuracy. Words that are exact opposites will usually not be accurate. Instead, use specifics to be both positive and accurate.

Negative: The exercycle is not guaranteed for life.

Not true: The exercycle is guaranteed for life.

True: The exercycle is guaranteed for 10 years.

Negative: Customers under 60 are not eligible for the Prime Time discount.

Not true: You must be over 60 to be eligible for the Prime Time discount.

True: If you're 60 or older, you can save 10 percent on all your purchases with RightWay's Prime Time discount.

Legal phrases also have negative connotations for most readers and should be avoided whenever possible. The idea will sound more positive if you use everyday English.

Negative: If your account is still delinquent, a second, legal notice will be sent to you informing you that cancellation of your policy will occur 30 days after the date of the legal notice if we do not receive your cheque.

Better: Even if your cheque is lost in the mail and never reaches us, you still have a 30-day grace period. If you do get a second notice, you will know that your payment hasn't reached us. To keep your account in good standing, stop payment on the first cheque and send a second one.

Focus on What the Reader Can Do Rather Than on Limitations

Sometimes, positive emphasis is a matter of the way you present something: is the glass half empty or half full? Sometimes it's a matter of eliminating double negatives. When there are limits, or some options are closed, focus on the alternatives that remain.

Negative: We will not allow you to charge more than $1,500 on your VISA account.

Better: You can charge $1,500 on your new VISA card.

or: Your new VISA card gives you $1,500 in credit that you can use at thousands of stores nationwide.

Instant Replay

Definition of Hidden Negatives

Hidden negatives are words that are not negative in themselves but become negative in context.

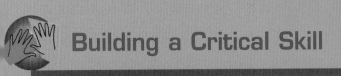

Building a Critical Skill

Using Positive Emphasis Ethically

Several of the methods to achieve positive emphasis can be misused.

Consider omission.

A bank notified customers that chequing account fees were being "revised" but omitted the amounts. Customers had to go into the bank and copy down the new (higher) fees themselves.

In another case, a condominium resort offered an "all-terrain vehicle" as a prize for visiting. (Winners had to pay $29.95 for "handling, processing, and insurance.") The actual "prize" was a lawn chair with four wheels that converted into a wheeled cart. The company claims it told the truth: "It is a vehicle. It's a four-wheel cart you can take anywhere—to the beach, to the pool. It may not be motorized, but [we] didn't say it was motorized."

In both cases, full disclosure might have affected decisions: some customers might have chosen to change banks; some customers would have declined the condominium visit. It isn't ethical to omit information that people need to make decisions.

Presenting information compactly can also go too far. A credit card company mailed out a letter with the good news that the minimum monthly payment was going down. But a separate small flyer explained that interest rates (on the charges not repaid) were going up. The print was far too small to read: 67 lines of type were crowded into five vertical inches of text.

Sources: Carmella M. Padilla, "It's a . . . a . . . a . . . All-Terrain Vehicle, Yeah, That's It, That's the Ticket," *The Wall Street Journal,* July 17, 1987, 17; and Donna S. Kienzler, "Visual Ethics," *The Journal of Business Communication* 34 (1997): 175–76.

As you focus on what will happen, **check for you-attitude** (◀▶ Module 6). In the last example, "We will allow you to charge $1,500" is positive, but it lacks you-attitude.

When you have a benefit, and a requirement the reader must meet to get the benefit, the sentence is usually more positive if you put the benefit first.

Negative: You will not qualify for the student membership rate of $25 a year unless you are enrolled for at least 10 hours.

Better: You get all the benefits of membership for only $25 a year if you're enrolled for 10 hours or more.

Justify Negative Information by Giving a Reason or Linking It to a Reader Benefit

A reason can help your reader see that the information is necessary; a benefit can suggest that the negative aspect is outweighed by positive factors. Be careful, however, to make the logic behind your reason clear and to leave no loopholes.

Negative: We cannot sell computer disks in lots of less than 10.

Loophole: To keep down packaging costs and to help you save on shipping and handling costs, we sell computer disks in lots of 10 or more.

Suppose the customer says, "I'll pay the extra shipping and handling. Send me seven." If you can't or won't sell in lots of less than 10, you need to write:

Better: To keep down packaging costs and to help customers save on shipping and handling costs, **we sell computer disks** only **in lots of 10 or more.**

If you link the negative element to a benefit, be sure that it is a benefit the reader will acknowledge. Avoid telling people that you're doing things "for their own good." They may have a different notion of what their own good is. You may think you're doing customers a favour by limiting their credit so they don't get in over their heads and go bankrupt. They may feel they'd be better off with more credit so they could expand in hopes of making more sales and more profits.

If the Negative Is Truly Unimportant, Omit It

Omit negatives entirely only when

- The reader does not need the information to make a decision
- You have already given the reader the information and he or she has access to the previous communication
- The information is trivial

The following examples suggest the kind of negatives you can omit:

Negative: A one-year subscription to *Canada Business* is $49.97. That rate is not as low as the rates charged for some magazines.

Better: A one-year subscription to *Canada Business* is $49.97.

Still better: A one-year subscription to *Canada Business* is $49.97. You save 43 percent off the newsstand price of $87.78.

Negative: If you are not satisfied with Sunlife Insurance, you do not have to renew your policy.

Better: Omit the sentence.

Bury the Negative Information and Present It Compactly

The beginning and end are always positions of emphasis. Put negatives here only if you want to emphasize the negative, as you may in a negative message (◀▶ Module 11). To de-emphasize a negative, put it in the middle of a paragraph rather than in the first or last sentence and/or in the middle of the message rather than in the first or last paragraphs.

When a letter or memo runs several pages, remember that the bottom of the first page is also a position of emphasis, even if it is in the middle of a paragraph, because of the extra white space of the bottom margin. (The first page gets more attention since it is on top and the reader's eye may catch lines of the message even when he or she isn't consciously reading it; the tops and bottoms of subsequent pages don't get this extra attention.) If possible, avoid placing negative information at the bottom of the first page.

Giving a topic plenty of space emphasizes it. Therefore, you can de-emphasize negative information by giving it as little space as possible. Give negative information only once in your message. Don't list negatives vertically on the page since lists take space and emphasize material.

What's the best way to apologize?

Early, briefly, and sincerely.

When you are at fault, you may build goodwill by admitting that fact promptly. However, apologies may have legal implications, so some organizations prefer that their employees not offer apologies to customers.

- **No explicit apology is necessary if the error is small and if you are correcting the mistake.**

Negative: I'm sorry the clerk did not credit your account properly.

Better: Your statement has been corrected to include your payment of $263.75.

- Do not apologize when you are not at fault.

When you have done everything you can and when a delay or problem is due to circumstances beyond your control, you aren't at fault and don't need to apologize. It may be appropriate to include an explanation so the reader knows you weren't negligent. If the news is bad, put the explanation first. If you have good news for the reader, put it before your explanation.

Negative: I'm sorry that I could not answer your question sooner. I had to wait until the sales figures for the second quarter were in.

Better (neutral or bad news): We needed the sales figures for the second quarter to answer your question. Now that they're in, I can tell you that . . .

Better (good news): The new advertising campaign is a success. The sales figures for the second quarter are finally in, and they show that . . .

If the delay or problem is long or large, it is good you-attitude to ask the reader whether he or she wants to confirm the original plan or make different arrangements.

Negative: I'm sorry that the chairs will not be ready by August 25 as promised.

Better: Due to a strike against the manufacturer, the desk chairs you ordered will not be ready until November. Do you want to keep that order, or would you like to look at the models available from other suppliers?

- **When you apologize, do it early, briefly, and sincerely.**

Apologize only once, early in the message. Let the reader move on to other, more positive information.

Even if major trouble or inconvenience has resulted from your error, you don't need to go on about all the horrible things that happened. The reader already knows this negative information, and you can omit it. Instead, focus on what you have done to correct the situation.

If you don't know whether or not any inconvenience has resulted, don't raise the issue at all.

FYI

People who "put on a happy face," or behave cheerfully even when they don't particularly feel that way can actually cause their mood to become more positive.

Source: Don Oldenburg, "Act Optimistic to Turn Frown Upside Down, Researcher Says," *Columbus Dispatch,* August 12, 1999, E1.

Negative: I'm sorry I didn't answer your letter sooner. I hope that my delay has not inconvenienced you.

Better: I'm sorry I didn't answer your letter sooner.

Why do I need to think about tone, politeness, and power?

So you don't offend people by mistake.

No one likes to deal with people who seem condescending or rude. Poorly chosen words can create that sense, whether the sender "meant" to be rude or not. Message **tone** is the attitude of the writer toward the reader, conveyed implicitly through document format and organization, word choice, and sentence and paragraph length. Status and power also affect message tone: the words that might seem friendly from a superior to a subordinate may seem uppity if used by the subordinate to the superior. Norms for politeness are cultural and generational. Language that is acceptable within one group may be unacceptable if used by someone outside the group (◀▶ Module 3).

The desirable tone for business writing is businesslike but not stiff, friendly but not phoney, confident but not arrogant, polite but not grovelling. The following guidelines will help you achieve the tone you want:

- **Use courtesy titles** Canadian organizations use first names for everyone, whatever their age or rank. But many people don't like being called by their first names by people they don't know or by someone much younger. When you talk or write to people outside your organization, use first names only if you've established a personal relationship. If you don't know someone well, use a courtesy title (◀▶ Module 9):

  Dear Mr. Reynolds:

  Dear Ms. Lee:

- **Be aware of the power implications of the words you use.** "Thank you for your cooperation" is generous coming from a superior to a subordinate; it's not appropriate in a message to your superior.

Different ways of asking for action carry different levels of politeness, as Figure 7.2 shows.[5]

Figure 7.2

Forms of Request and Their Levels of Politeness

Form of request	Level of politeness	Example
Order	Lowest politeness	Turn in your time card by Monday.
Polite order	Mid-level politeness	Please turn in your time card by Monday.
Indirect request	Higher politeness	Time cards should be turned in by Monday.
Question	Highest politeness	Would you be able to turn in your time card by Monday?

FYI

In an experiment, older people walked faster after they viewed positive words about old age presented subliminally. Says one of the authors of the study, "Self-image is important to quality of life and, perhaps, to physical functioning."

Source: Avery Comarow, "Light of Heart, Swift of Foot," *U.S. News and World Report,* November 15, 1999, 135

You need to be more polite if you're asking for something that will inconvenience the reader and help you more than the person who does the action. Generally, you need to be less polite when you're asking for something small, routine, or to the reader's benefit. Most readers and some discourse communities, however, prefer that even small requests be made politely.

Lower politeness: To start the scheduling process, please describe your availability for meetings during the second week of the month.

Higher politeness: Could you let me know what times you'd be free for a meeting the second week of the month?

Higher levels of politeness may be unclear. In some cases, a question may seem like a request for information to which it's acceptable to answer, "No, I can't." In other cases, it will be an order, simply phrased in polite terms.

Generally, requests sound friendliest when they use conversational language.

Poor tone: Return the draft with any changes by next Tuesday.

Better tone: Let me know by Tuesday whether you'd like any changes in the draft.

- **When the stakes are low, be straightforward.** Messages that "beat around the bush" sound pompous and defensive.

Poor tone: Distribution of the low-fat plain granola may be limited in your area. May we suggest that you discuss this matter with your store manager.

Better tone: Our low-fat granola is so popular that there isn't enough to go around. We're expanding production to meet the demand. Ask your store manager to keep putting in orders, so that your grocery is on the list of stores that will get supplies when they become available.

Or: Store managers decide what to stock. If your store has stopped carrying our low-fat granola, the store manager has stopped ordering it. Talk to the manager. Managers try to meet customer needs, so if you say something you're more likely to get what you want.

- **When you must give bad news, consider hedging your statement.** Linguistic experts John Hagge and Charles Kostelnick have shown that auditors' suggestion letters rarely say directly that firms are using unacceptable accounting practices. Instead, they use three strategies to be more diplomatic: specifying the time ("currently, the records are quite informal"), limiting statements ("it appears," "it seems"), and using impersonal statements that do not specify who caused a problem or who will perform an action.[6]

Employability Skills 2000+ Checklist for Positive Emphasis

In this module, the key skills from The Conference Board of Canada's Employability Skills 2000+ are:

Communicate

✔ write and speak so others pay attention and understand

Manage Information

✔ assess, analyze, and apply knowledge and skills from various disciplines

Think & Solve Problems

✔ assess situations and identify problems
✔ seek different points of view and evaluate them based on facts
✔ be creative and innovative in exploring possible solutions
✔ recognize the human, interpersonal, technical, scientific and mathematical dimensions of a problem
✔ check to see if a solution works, and act on opportunities for improvement

Be Adaptable

✔ be innovative and resourceful: identify and suggest alternative ways to achieve goals and get the job done
✔ be open and respond constructively to change

Review of Key Points

- **Positive emphasis** means focussing on the positive rather than the negative aspects of a situation.

  1. Avoid negative words and words with negative connotations.

  2. State information positively. Focus on what the reader can do rather than on what you won't or can't let the reader do.

  3. Justify negative information by giving a reason or linking it to a reader benefit.

  4. If the negative is truly unimportant, omit it.

  5. Put the negative information in the middle and present it compactly.

- **Hidden negatives** are words that are not negative in themselves but become negative in context.

- Don't apologize if the error is small and if you are correcting the mistake. Don't apologize if you are not at fault. If the delay or problem is long or large, it is good you-attitude to ask the reader whether he or she wants to make different arrangements.

- When you apologize, do it early, briefly, and sincerely. However, apologies may have legal implications, so some organizations prefer that apologies not be issued to customers or the public.

- The desirable tone for business writing is businesslike but not stiff, friendly but not phoney, confident but not arrogant, polite but not grovelling. The following guidelines will help you achieve the tone you want.
  - Use courtesy titles for people outside your organization whom you don't know well

- Be aware of the power implications of the words you use
- When the stakes are low, be straightforward
- When you must give bad news, consider hedging your statement

Learning Applications

Questions for Comprehension

7.1   How can you create positive emphasis?

7.2   Which of the following are negative words that you should avoid?

anxious	hesitate
change	hope
eager	necessary
instead	unfortunately

7.3   What are your options when you need to apologize?

Questions for Critical Thinking

7.4   Some negative phrases (such as "please do not hesitate") are business clichés. Why is it better to avoid them?

7.5   Think of a situation when an apology was appropriate. What strategy was actually used? Would another strategy have been better?

7.6   If you work for a company that claims to be egalitarian, do you still need to attend to tone, power, and politeness?

7.7   Can you think of situations in which positive emphasis might backfire or be inappropriate? What strategies would be most likely to meet the audience's needs in those situations?

Questions for Building Skills

7.8   What skills have you read about in this module?

7.9   What skills are you practicing in the assignments you're doing for this module?

7.10   How could you further develop the skills you're working on?

Exercises and Problems

7.11 Evaluating the Ethics of Positive Emphasis

The first word in each line below is negative; the second is a positive term that is sometimes substituted for it. Which of the positive terms seem ethical? Which seem unethical? Briefly explain your choices.

junk bonds	high-yield bonds
second mortgage	home-equity loan
tax	user fee
tax increase	revenue enhancement
nervousness	adrenaline
problem	challenge
price increase	price change

7.12 Focussing on the Positive

Revise each of the following sentences to focus on the options that remain not those that are closed off.

1. As a first-year employee, you are not eligible for dental insurance

2. I will be out of the country October 25 until November 10 and will not be able to meet with you then

3. You will not get your first magazine for at least four weeks

4. I'm sorry I'm away from my desk and cannot answer your call

7.13 Identifying Hidden Negatives

Identify the hidden negatives in the following sentences and revise to eliminate them. In some cases, you may need to add information to revise the sentence effectively.

1. This publication is designed to explain how your company can start a recycling program

2. I hope you find the information in this brochure beneficial to you and a valuable reference as you plan your move

3. In thinking about your role in our group, I remember two occasions where you contributed something

7.14 Revising Sentences to Improve Positive Emphasis

Revise the following sentences to improve positive emphasis. In some cases, you may need to add or omit information to revise effectively.

1. It will be necessary for you to submit Form PR-47 before you can be reimbursed for your travel expenses

2. If you have further questions, please do not hesitate to contact me

3. I'm sorry you were worried about your health insurance. It is not too late to sign up for a flexible spending account

4. You cannot return this item for a full refund if you keep it past 30 days

5. When you write a report, do not make claims that you cannot support with evidence

6. Although I was only an intern and didn't actually make presentations to major clients, I was required to prepare PowerPoint slides for the meetings and to answer some of the clients' questions

7. You will pay $30 more if you wait till after October 1 to register for the conference

8. To reduce unnecessary delays in processing your order, please check the form at the end of this letter to see that nothing is omitted or incorrect before you sign the form and return it

9. The figures for budget changes made at the meeting may be wrong, as I got lost during John's presentation. Please check the figures and let me know if they need correction

10. We cannot process your application to graduate because you did not supply all of the necessary information

7.15 Revising Sentences to Improve Positive Emphasis

Revise the following sentences to improve positive emphasis. In some cases, you may need to add or omit information to revise effectively.

1. No subcontractor shall be employed without the previous consent of the director

2. To avoid unnecessary delays, call for an appointment before coming in to the office

3. I realize that Wednesday at 10 A.M. is not a convenient time for everyone, but I was unable to arrange a time that is good for everyone

4. I'm sorry you were worried about the résumé you emailed us. We did not have any problems scanning it into our system.

5. I am anxious to talk with you about the job

6. People who come to work late may be perceived as unreliable

7. I hope that you receive the April spreadsheet (3 pages) that follows and that the fax quality isn't too poor

8. I was treasurer of the accounting club. Of course, we didn't have much money so I didn't have much responsibility, but I was able to put into practice principles I learned in the classroom

9. If you have any problems using your e-mail account, I will try to explain it so that you can understand

10. If you submitted a travel request, as you claim, we have failed to receive it

7.16 Revising a Memo to Improve Positive Emphasis

Revise the following memo to improve you-attitude and positive emphasis.

Subject: Status of Building Renovations

The renovation of the lobby is not behind schedule. By Monday, October 9, we hope to be ready to open the west end of the lobby to limited traffic.

The final phase of the renovation will be placing a new marble floor in front of the elevators. This work will not be finished until the end of the month.

Insofar as is possible, the crew will attempt to schedule most of the work during the evenings so that normal business is not disrupted.

Please exercise caution when moving through the construction area. The floor will be uneven and steps will be at unusual heights. Watch your step to avoid accidental tripping or falling.

7.17 Identifying Positive Emphasis in Ads and Documents

Look at print advertisements and at documents you receive from your college or university, from your workplace, and from organizations to which you belong. Identify five sentences that either (a) use positive emphasis or (b) should be revised to be more positive.

As Your Instructor Directs,

a. Share your examples with a small group of students

b. Write a memo to your instructor discussing your examples

c. Post an email message to the class discussing your examples

d. Present two or three of your examples to the class in a short presentation

e. With your small group, write a collaborative short report to your instructor about the patterns you see

Polishing Your Prose

Singular and Plural Possessives

With an apostrophe, *it's* is a contraction meaning *it is*. Without an apostrophe, *its* is a possessive pronoun meaning *belonging to it*.

To show possession when a noun is singular, put the apostrophe right after the word; then add s:

> Allen's
> The manager's
> The company's

If the possessing noun is plural, put the apostrophe right after the word:

> Customers'
> Employees'
> Companies'

In names that end with *s*, style books permit either form:

> Thomas'
> Thomas's
> Linux'
> Linux's

Often, the location of the apostrophe tells the reader whether the noun is singular or plural.

Singular Possessive	Plural Possessive
The employee's	The employees'
Product's	Products'

Because the singular and plural possessives sound the same, look at the logic of your sentence to choose the right word. Also note that when you have plural possessive nouns, other words in the sentence will also become plural.

Plural *employees* have plural *opinions*. Plural *products* have plural *prices*.

We listen to our employees' opinions.

You can find all of our products' prices on our Web site.

Exercises

Choose the correct word in each set of parentheses.

1. We design products based on our (customer's/customers') needs.

2. The winter holiday season can account for one-quarter to one-half of a (store's/stores') annual profits.

3. (Canadian's/Canadians') views of the economy reflect their confidence in the stock market.

4. In order to sell in another country, you need to understand its (people's/peoples') culture.

5. We meet the local, provincial, and federal (government's/governments') standards for quality control.

6. Two of our (computer's/computers') monitors need to be repaired.

7. The (committee's/committees') duties will be completed after it announces its decision.

8. Employees who have worked as Big Sisters have enjoyed seeing the (girl's/girls') progress.

9. We'll decide whether to have more computer training sessions based on (employee's/employees') feedback.

10. The (company's/companies') benefit plan is excellent.

Check your answers to the odd-numbered exercises on page 632.

Module 8

Reader Benefits

Topics

- Why do reader benefits work?
- How do I identify reader benefits?
- How detailed should each benefit be?
- How many different benefits do I need?
- What else do reader benefits need?

Review

Learning Applications

Polishing Your Prose: Plurals and Possessives

Learning Focus

After reading and applying the information in Module 8, you'll be able to demonstrate

Knowledge of

- Maslow's Hierarchy of Needs
- Elements of reader-centred messages
- The importance of identifying audience benefits

Skills to

- Use audience analysis to identify and choose reader benefits
- Develop reader benefits with logic and detail
- Match the benefit to the audience

"First, never forget your audience..."

"When I entered this field I found that there was very little written material about the industry that was suitable for the average person," says Elaine Kergoat, manager of internal communications for Cameco Corporation, a uranium mining and processing firm based in Saskatoon, Saskatchewan.

Elaine always wanted to work as writer and has a B.A. in French and history from the University of Saskatchewan in Saskatoon, and a B.A. in journalism from the University of Regina. She worked in journalism for three years before joining Cameco's communications department in 1989. The company has operations in Ontario, United States, and Australia as well as in Saskatchewan, and also mines gold in the Republic of Kyrgyzstan in central Asia. Since it was formed in 1988, Cameco has gone through many changes, including the merging of two crown corporations (one federal, one provincial), further restructuring, downsizing, privatization, and growth.

To make uranium industry information more accessible to the general public, Elaine developed a full-colour, tabloid-style, eight-page newsletter that included articles on industry issues as well as profiles of people in the company, thereby putting a human face on the subject. This newsletter was entitled *The Source* and won a Silver Leaf award from the International Association of Business Communicators as the best newsletter in Canada in 1992. Now as manager of internal communications, Elaine focuses on helping different departments achieve efficient, professional communications.

Her core work during the past decade has been writing, including print publications, news releases, and speeches. Elaine makes an interesting point about the differences between writing for the eye, as for print media, and writing for the ear, as for speech writing or for broadcasting. Each form of writing requires different techniques or styles. But in every case, the writer must keep the needs of the readers or listeners in mind.

"When writing anything, whether a speech, a news release or an annual report, especially if you are pooling information from a variety of sources and people, you must blend it in a consistent style, make it acceptable to variety of people who have had input, yet never forget your readers' needs." In the corporate world, the different sources of information can be from the different divisions of the company such as marketing, engineering, safety, and environment. The writer must focus not only on the reader, but also on the sources of information.

Elaine says that working at Cameco has allowed her to grow within the field of communications and believes that writing is the most important component of good communications. In addition, by focussing on writing, "I have been lucky to be able to get a lot of personal satisfaction from my work. It is something that no one can take away from you and something you can use for the rest of your life."

When asked for words of advice to someone entering the communications field, Elaine responds, "First, never forget your audience. Then remember that the quality of your research will determine the quality of your writing. The ability to weave solid research data into an informative, readable piece is what separates the good writers from the mediocre ones."

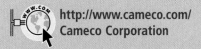

http://www.cameco.com/
Cameco Corporation

FYI

Leading the Way

"Calgary and Edmonton are home to 1.5 million people and counting. Both centres offer a high degree of 'livability'—a cultured cosmopolitan environment that is also friendly, safe, and affordable. The residents of Calgary and Edmonton are the driving force behind Canada's strongest economy (the Alberta economy is forecast to grow by 3.6 in the next year). This, combined with low housing costs and consistently low tax rates (Alberta is well-known for being the only province without a provincial sales tax), allows Calgarians and Edmontonians to enjoy one of the highest standards of living and per capita disposable incomes in the nation."

Source: Computing, High-Tech & Telecommunications Careers Handbook, 1999 Edition (Toronto: The Marskell Group, 1999), 18.

Reader benefits describe to the reader the advantages of

- Using your services
- Buying your products
- Following your policies
- Adopting your ideas

Reader benefits "sell" both informative and persuasive messages. In informative messages, reader benefits give reasons to comply with the policies you announce and suggest how and why the policies are good ones. In persuasive messages, reader benefits provide reasons to act, in order to reduce reader resistance. Negative messages (◀▶ Module 11) may not give reader benefits; however, negative messages are organized to provide maximum reader appeal.

The best reader benefits are

- Adapted specifically to the audience
- Based on intrinsic advantages
- Supported clearly and comprehensively
- Phrased in you-attitude

Why do reader benefits work?

Reader benefits improve the audience's attitudes and actions.

Reader benefits appeal to both the attitudes and the behaviour of your audience. When you provide benefits that focus on readers' needs and wants, people feel more positive about you and your request. Providing reader benefits makes it easier for you to accomplish your goals.

Expectancy theory says most people try to do their best only when they believe that they can succeed and when they want the rewards that success brings. Reader benefits tell readers that they can do the job successfully and that they will be rewarded.[1] Reader benefits help overcome two problems that reduce motivation: people may not think of all the possible benefits, and they may not understand the relationships among efforts, performance, and rewards.[2]

How do I identify reader benefits?

Know your reader and brainstorm!

Sometimes reader benefits are obvious and easy to describe. When they are harder to identify, brainstorm:

1. Think of the feelings, values, fears, and needs that may motivate your reader. Then identify features of your product or policy that meet those values or needs.
2. Identify the objective features of your product or policy. Then think how these features could benefit the audience.

Try to brainstorm at least three to five possible benefits for every informative message and five to seven benefits for every persuasive message. The more benefits you think of, the easier it will be to choose ones that will appeal directly to your reader.

1. Think of Feelings, Fears, and Needs That May Motivate Your Reader

One of the best-known analysis of needs is Abraham H. Maslow's hierarchy of needs.[3] Physical needs are the most basic, followed by needs for safety and security, for love and a sense of belonging, for esteem and recognition, and finally for self-actualization or self-fulfillment. All of us go back and forth between higher- and lower-level needs. Whenever lower-level needs make themselves felt, they take priority.

Maslow's model is a good starting place to identify the feelings, fears, and needs that may motivate your audience. Figure 8.1 shows organizational motivators for each of the levels in Maslow's hierarchy. Often a product or idea can meet needs on several levels. Focus on the ones that your audience analysis suggests are most relevant for your audience. But remember: even the best analysis may not reveal all of a reader's needs. For example, a well-paid manager may be worried about security needs if her spouse has lost his job or if the couple is supporting kids in college or an elderly parent.

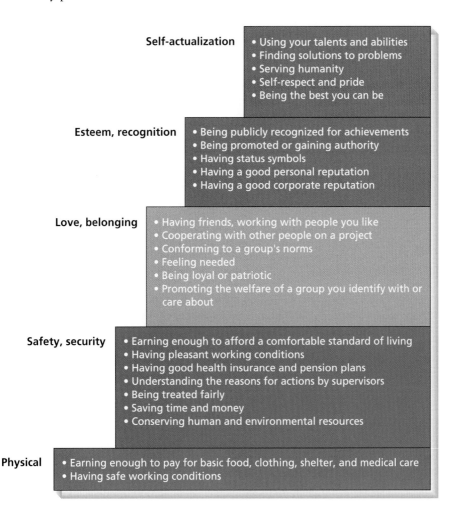

Self-actualization
- Using your talents and abilities
- Finding solutions to problems
- Serving humanity
- Self-respect and pride
- Being the best you can be

Esteem, recognition
- Being publicly recognized for achievements
- Being promoted or gaining authority
- Having status symbols
- Having a good personal reputation
- Having a good corporate reputation

Love, belonging
- Having friends, working with people you like
- Cooperating with other people on a project
- Conforming to a group's norms
- Feeling needed
- Being loyal or patriotic
- Promoting the welfare of a group you identify with or care about

Safety, security
- Earning enough to afford a comfortable standard of living
- Having pleasant working conditions
- Having good health insurance and pension plans
- Understanding the reasons for actions by supervisors
- Being treated fairly
- Saving time and money
- Conserving human and environmental resources

Physical
- Earning enough to pay for basic food, clothing, shelter, and medical care
- Having safe working conditions

Figure 8.1
Organizational Motivations for Maslow's Hierarchy of Needs

The Rousing Creativity Group sells the solid brass Benefit Finder™ to help salespeople develop benefits for the features of their products or services; www.rousingcreativity.com/ool_frameBF.html

2. Identify the Features of Your Product or Policy. Then Think How These Features Could Benefit the Audience

A feature by itself is not a benefit. Often, a feature has several possible benefits.

Feature: Bottled water

Benefits: Is free from chemicals, pollutants

Tastes good

Has no calories

Is easy to carry to class; can be used while biking, driving, hiking

Feature: Closed captions on TV

Benefits: Enables hard-of-hearing viewers to follow dialogue

Helps speakers of English as a second language learn phrases and idioms

Helps small children learn to read

Feature: Flextime

Benefits: Enables workers to accommodate personal needs

Helps organization recruit, retain workers

Makes more workers available in early morning and in evening

Enables office to stay open longer—more service to clients, customers

Enables workers to communicate with colleagues in different time zones more easily

Different features may benefit different subgroups in your audience. Depending on the features a restaurant offers, you could appeal to one or more of the following subgroups:

Subgroup	Features to meet the subgroup's needs
People who work outside the home	A quick lunch; a relaxing place to take clients or colleagues
Parents with small children	High chairs, child-size portions, and things to keep the kids entertained while they wait for their order
People who eat out a lot	Variety both in food and in decor
People on tight budgets	Economical food; a place where they don't need to tip (cafeteria or fast food)
People on special diets	Low-sodium and low-calorie dishes; vegetarian food; kosher food
People to whom eating out is part of an evening's entertainment	Music or a floor show; elegant surroundings; reservations so they can get to a show or event after dinner; late hours so they can come to dinner after a show or game

To develop your benefits, think about the details of each one. If your selling point is your relaxing atmosphere, think about the specific details that make the restaurant relaxing. If your strong point is elegant dining, consider all the details that contribute to that elegance. Sometimes you may offer features that do not meet any particular need but are still good benefits. In a sales letter for a restaurant, you might also want to mention the non-smoking section, your free coatroom, your convenient location, free parking or a drive-up window, and speedy service.

Whenever you're writing to customers or clients about features that are not unique to your organization, it's wise to present both benefits of the features themselves and benefits of dealing with your company. If you talk about the benefits of dining in a relaxed atmosphere but don't mention your own restaurant, people may go somewhere else!

> **Instant Replay**
>
> **Reader benefits** are benefits or advantages that the reader gets by using your services, buying your products, following your policies, or adopting your ideas.

An example of poor reader benefits. Good reader benefits show how the product or service features meet the audience's needs.

"This CD player costs less than players selling for twice as much."

Source: © The New Yorker Collection 1989 Robert Webber from Cartoonbank.com

How detailed should each benefit be?

Use strong, vivid details. Paint a mental picture.

You'll usually need at least three to five sentences to give enough details about a reader benefit. If you develop two or three reader benefits fully, you can use just a sentence or two for less important benefits. Develop reader benefits by linking each feature to the readers' needs—and provide details to make the benefit vivid!

Weak: We have placemats with riddles.

Better: Answering all the riddles on Caesar's special placemats will keep the kids happy till your pizza comes. If they don't have time to finish (and they may not, since your pizza is ready so quickly), just take the riddles home—or answer them on your next visit.

Make your reader benefits specific.

Weak: You get quick service.

Better: If you only have an hour for lunch, try our Business Buffet. Within minutes, you can choose from a variety of main dishes, vegetables, and a make-your-own-sandwich-and-salad bar. You can put together a lunch that's as light or filling as you want, with time to enjoy it—and still be back to the office on time.

Psychological description is a technique you can use to develop vivid, specific reader benefits. **Psychological description** means creating a scenario rich with sense impressions—what the reader sees, hears, smells, tastes, feels—so readers can picture themselves using your product or service and enjoying its benefits. You can also use psychological description to describe the problem your product will solve. Psychological description works best early in the message to catch readers' attention.

Feature:	Snooze alarm
Benefit:	When you press the snooze button, the alarm goes off and comes on again nine minutes later.
Psychological description:	Some mornings, you really want to stay in bed just a few more minutes. With the Sleepytime Snooze Alarm, you can snuggle under the covers for a few extra winks, secure in the knowledge that the alarm will come on again to get you up for that breakfast meeting with an important client. If you want to sleep in, you can keep hitting the snooze alarm for up to an additional 63 minutes of sleep. With Sleepytime, you're in control of your mornings.
Feature:	Tilt windows
Benefit:	Easier to clean
Psychological description	It's no wonder so many cleaners "don't do windows." Balancing precariously on a rickety ladder to clean upper-story windows . . . shivering outside in the winter winds and broiling in the summer

FYI

According to a Gallup survey, four employee attitudes correlate with higher profits:

1. My work gives me the opportunity to do what I do best
2. My opinion counts
3. My fellow workers are committed to quality
4. I see a direct connection between my work and the company's mission

Source: Linda Grant, "Happy Workers, High Returns," *Fortune,* January 12, 1998, 81.

sun as you scrub away . . . running inside, then outside, then inside again to try to get the spot that always seems to be on the other side. Cleaning traditional windows really is a chore.

You'll find cleaning a breeze with Tilt-in Windows. Just pull the inner window down and pull the bottom toward you. The whole window lifts out! Repeat for the outer window. Clean inside in comfort (sitting down or even watching TV if you choose). Then replace the top of the outer window in its track, slide up, and repeat with the inner window. Presto! Clean windows!

In psychological description, you're putting your reader in a picture. If the reader doesn't feel that the picture fits, the technique backfires. To prevent this, psychological description often uses subjunctive verbs ("if you like . . . " "if you were . . . ") or the words *maybe* and *perhaps*.

Psychological description means creating a scenario rich with sense impressions—what the reader sees, hears, smells, tastes, feels—so readers can picture themselves using your product or service and enjoying its benefits.

You're hungry but you don't want to bother with cooking. Perhaps you have guests to take to dinner. Or it's 12 noon and you only have an hour for lunch. Whatever the situation, the Illini Union has a food service to fit your needs. If you want convenience, we have it. If it's atmosphere you're seeking, it's here too. And if you're concerned about the price, don't be. When you're looking for a great meal, the Illini Union is the place to find it.

—*Illini Union brochure*

How do I decide which benefits to use?

Use the following three principles to decide.

Three principles guide your choice of reader benefits:

1. Use at least one benefit for each part of your audience
2. Use intrinsic benefits
3. Use the benefits you can develop most fully

1. Use at Least One Benefit for Each Part of Your Audience.

Most messages go to multiple audiences. In a memo announcing a company-subsidized day care program, you want to describe benefits not only for parents who might use the service but also for people who don't have children or whose children are older. Reader benefits for these last two audiences help convince them that spending money on day care is a good use of scarce funds.

In a letter to "consumers" or "voters," different people will have different concerns. The more of these concerns you speak to, the more persuasive you'll be.

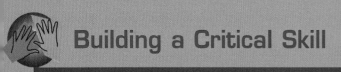

Matching the Benefit to the Audience

Suppose that you manufacture a product and want to persuade dealers to carry it. The features you may cite in ads directed toward customers—stylish colours, sleek lines, convenience, durability, good price—won't convince dealers. Shelf space is at a premium, and no dealer carries all the models of all the brands available for any given product. Why should the dealer stock your product? To be persuasive, talk about the features that are benefits from the dealer's point of view: turnover, profit margin, a national advertising campaign to build customer awareness and interest, special store displays that will draw attention to the product.

Depending on their demographic and cultural circumstances (◄|► Modules 2 and 3), consumers value different benefits. The Hudson's Bay Company, for example, targets its Bay and Zellers department stores' features to different shoppers. Zellers promises "budget-minded" Canadians low prices and rewards customer loyalty with its Club Z program. Savings realized through self-service and central checkouts are passed on to consumers. The more upscale Bay stores across Canada offer in-store events customized to their specific communities: the Calgary and Edmonton stores promote monthly events different from those in Ottawa and Toronto, which are different again from those held in stores in Montreal and Vancouver.

The Wall Street Journal asked subscribers to renew their subscriptions for two more years rather than just for one. The cost of the second year was 66 percent of the cost of the first year. The mailing admitted that renewing for two years would tie up the money but presented the cost of the second year as "a 34 percent tax-free return on your money." The benefit was highly appropriate for an audience concerned about returns on investments and aware of the risk that normally accompanies high returns.

Garbage magazine urged subscribers to respond to the first renewal notice to save the paper that an additional mailing would take. This logic was appropriate for an audience concerned about the disposal of solid waste.

Michael Turczyniak of Microsystems, a small business offering hardware and software solutions to a variety of Canadian businesses, focusses on the long-term benefits his customers will receive.

Even in your own organization, different audiences may care about different things. For example, to create an intranet for Xerox, Cindy Casselman needed support from a variety of divisions. She had to persuade her own supervisor to let her work on the project. He said "yes" but told her she had to raise the $250,000 herself. She got the money and the programming talent she needed by showing other managers how they would benefit from the proposed intranet. The CIO cared about the enormous financial investment the company had already made in its computer infrastructure. Cindy told him that the intranet would put content there. The director of education and training cared about learning at Xerox. Cindy pointed out that the intranet would provide a place for learning to happen. She raised the $250,000 by showing people how her idea would benefit the aspects of the company they cared most about.

Sources: Mike Duff, "A Seasoned Helmsman From A to Club Z," *Discount Store News*, May 24, 1999, visited Web site July 28 2001, http://www.findarticles.com/m3092/10_38/54737802/p1/article.jhtml; "Shopping is Good With a Brand New Bay Destination", Hudson's Bay Press Release, visited Web site July 28, 2001, www.newswire.ca/releases/November2000/22/c7073.html; Gregory A. Patterson, "Different Strokes: Target 'Micromarkets' It's Way to Success: No 2 Stores Are Alike," *The Wall Street Journal*, May 31, 1995, A1, A9; and Michael Warshaw, "The Good Guy's and Gal's Guide to Office Politics," *Fast Company*, April-May 1998, 156-78.

2. Use Intrinsic Benefits

Intrinsic benefits come automatically from using a product or doing something. **Extrinsic benefits** are "added on." Someone in power decides to give them; they do not necessarily come from using the product or doing the action. Figure 8.2 gives examples of extrinsic and intrinsic rewards for four activities.

Activity	Extrinsic Reward	Intrinsic Reward
Making a sale	Getting a commission	Pleasure in convincing someone; pride in using your talents to create a strategy and execute it
Turning in a suggestion to a company suggestion system	Getting a monetary reward when the suggestion is implemented	Solving a problem at work; making the work environment a little pleasanter
Writing a report that solves an organizational problem	Getting praise; a good performance appraisal, and maybe a raise	Pleasure in having an effect on an organization; pride in using your skills to solve problems; pleasure in solving the problem itself

Figure 8.2

Extrinsic and Intrinsic Rewards

Intrinsic rewards or benefits are better than extrinsic benefits for two reasons:

1. There just aren't enough extrinsic rewards for everything you want people to do. You can't give a prize to every customer every time he or she places an order or to every subordinate who does what he or she is supposed to do.
2. Research suggests that you'll motivate subordinates more effectively by stressing the intrinsic benefits of following policies and adopting proposals.

In a groundbreaking study of professional employees, Frederick Herzberg found that the things people said they liked about their jobs were all *intrinsic* rewards— pride in achievement, an enjoyment of the work itself, responsibility. Extrinsic features—pay, company policy—were sometimes mentioned as things people disliked, but they were never cited as things that motivated or satisfied them. People who made a lot of money still did not mention salary as a good point about the job or the organization.[4] A 2000 study of worker loyalty found that Canadian workers were among the least committed to their employers in the world, ranking 16 of out 32 countries surveyed. Yet while fewer than 50 percent of the Canadians surveyed revealed feelings of attachment to their employer, 58 percent said their payment was fair. The survey authors concluded, "Companies have to spend time and energy managing their work forces… Our results show that money is a satisfier, not a solution."[5] Many family-friendly companies have discovered that a culture of care keeps turnover low. The higher salary that a competitor might pay just doesn't overcome the advantage of working at a supportive, flexible company that values its employees.[6] In the current competitive job market, different candidates want different things. But many accept lower salaries to get flextime, stock options, interesting work, or people they want to work with.[7]

Since money is not the only motivator, choose reader benefits that identify intrinsic as well as extrinsic motivators for following policies and adopting ideas. Such benefits almost always acknowledge your reader's value to you and your organization.

FYI

As a professional headhunter, Gary Quick interviewed thousands of people, always asking why they were leaving the current job. "Most people said the same thing: 'My company doesn't care about me.' "

Source: "Clean My House, and I'll Be Yours Forever," *1999 Inc. 500,* 214.

Site *to* **See**

Go to
http://www.bpa.
arizona.edu/midsize
business/quarterly
3-3/livitup.html

Human nature hasn't changed since Hertzberg's 1963 study: achievement, recognition, and the nature of the work itself—all intrinsic rewards—continue to motivate employees.

Good reader benefits are
- Adapted to the audience
- Based on intrinsic advantages
- Phrased in you-attitude

3. Use the Benefits You Can Develop Most Fully.

One-sentence benefits don't do much. Use the benefits that you can develop in three to five sentences or more.

A reader benefit is a claim or assertion that the reader will benefit if he or she does something. Convincing the reader, therefore, requires two steps: ensuring that the benefit appeals to your reader, and really will result, and explaining it to the reader.

If the logic behind a claimed reader benefit is faulty or inaccurate, there's no way to make that particular reader benefit convincing. Revise the benefit to make it logical.

Faulty logic: Using a computer will enable you to write letters, memos, and reports much more quickly.

Analysis: If you've never used a computer, in the short run it will take you *longer* to create a document using a computer than it would to type it. Even after you know how to use a computer and its software, the real time savings comes when a document incorporates parts of previous documents or goes through several revisions. Creating a first draft from scratch will still take planning and careful composing; the time savings may or may not be significant.

Revised reader benefit: Using a computer allows you to revise and edit a document more easily. It eliminates retyping as a separate step and reduces the time needed to proofread revisions. It allows you to move the text around on the page to create the best layout.

If the logic is sound, making that logic evident to the reader is a matter of providing enough evidence and showing how the evidence proves the claim that there will be a benefit. Always provide enough detail to be vivid and concrete. You'll need more detail in the following situations:

- The reader may not have thought of the benefit before
- The benefit depends on the difference between the long run and the short run
- The reader will be hard to persuade, and you need detail to make the benefit vivid and emotionally convincing

Does the following statement have enough detail?

> You'll save money by using our shop-at-home service.

Readers always believe their own experience. Readers who have never used a shop-at-home service may think, "If somebody else does my shopping for me, I'll have to pay that person. I'll save money by doing it myself." They may not think of the savings in gas and parking, in travel time, and in less car wear and tear. Readers who already use shop-at-home services may believe you if they compare your items and services with another company's to see that your cost is lower. Even then, you could make saving money seem more forceful and more vivid by telling readers how much they could save and mentioning some of the ways they could use your service.

What else do reader benefits need?

Check for you-attitude.

If reader benefits aren't in you-attitude (◀▷ Module 6), they'll sound selfish and won't be as effective as they could be. A Xerox letter selling copiers with strong you-attitude as well as reader benefits got a far bigger response than did an alternate version with reader benefits but no you-attitude.[8] It doesn't matter how you phrase reader benefits while you're brainstorming and developing them, but in your final draft, edit for you-attitude.

Lacks you-attitude: We have the lowest prices in town.

You-attitude: At Brantford Toyota, you get the best deal in town.

Employability Skills 2000+ Checklist for Reader Benefits

In this module, the key skills from The Conference Board of Canada's Employability Skills 2000+ are:

Communicate
✔ listen and ask questions to understand and appreciate the points of view of others
✔ write and speak so others pay attention and understand

Manage Information
✔ access, analyze and apply knowledge and skills from various disciplines (e.g., the arts, languages, science, technology, mathematics, social sciences, and the humanities)

Think & Solve Problems
✔ assess situations and identify problems
✔ seek different points of view and evaluate them based on facts
✔ recognize the human, interpersonal, technical, scientific, and mathematical dimensions of a problem
✔ be creative and innovative in exploring possible solutions

Demonstrate Positive Attitudes & Behaviours
✔ deal with people, problems, and situations with honesty, integrity, and personal ethics
✔ show interest, initiative, and effort

Learn Continuously
✔ be willing to continuously learn and grow
✔ identify and access learning sources and opportunities

Review of Key Points

- **Reader benefits** are benefits or advantages that the reader will get by using your services, buying your products, following your policies, or adopting your ideas. Reader benefits can exist for policies and ideas as well as for goods and services. Reader benefits tell readers that they can do the job and that success will be rewarded.

- Good reader benefits are adapted to the audience, based on **intrinsic** rather than **extrinsic** advantages, supported by clear logic and explained in adequate detail, and phrased in you-attitude. Extrinsic benefits simply aren't available to reward every desired behaviour; further, they reduce the satisfaction in doing something for its own sake.

- To create reader benefits,
  1. Identify the values, feelings, fears, and needs that may motivate your reader

  2. Show how the reader can meet his or her needs with the features of the policy or product

- **Psychological description** means creating a scenario rich with sense impressions—what the reader sees, hears, smells, tastes, feels— so readers can picture themselves using your product or service and enjoying its benefits.

- Brainstorm twice as many reader benefits as you'll need for a message.
  1. Use at least one benefit for each part of your audience
  2. Use intrinsic benefits
  3. Use the benefits you can develop most fully

- Make sure reader benefits are phrased in you-attitude.

Learning Applications

Questions for Comprehension

8.1 What are reader benefits?

8.2 In a message with reader benefits, how many different benefits should you use?

8.3 What is the difference between internal and external reader benefits? Which are better? Why?

8.4 What is psychological description?

Questions for Critical Thinking

8.5 If you are writing to multiple audiences with different needs, should you include all the reader benefits you can think of in the message?

8.6 Why do reader benefits need to be in you-attitude?

8.7 How do reader benefits help you achieve your goals?

Questions for Building Skills

8.8 What skills have you read about in this module?

8.9 What skills are you practicing in the assignments you're doing for this module?

8.10 How could you further develop the skills you're working on?

Exercises and Problems

8.11 Identifying and Developing Reader Benefits

Listed here are five things an organization might like its employees to do:

1. Use less paper
2. Attend a brown bag lunch to discuss ways to improve products or services
3. Become more physically fit
4. Volunteer for community organizations
5. Ease a new hire's transition into the unit

As Your Instructor Directs,

a. Identify the motives or needs that might be met by each of the activities.

b. Develop each need or motive as a reader benefit in a full paragraph. Use additional paragraphs for the other needs met by the activity. Remember to use you-attitude!

8.12 Identifying Objections and Reader Benefits

Think of an organization you know something about, and answer the following questions for it.

1. Your organization is thinking of creating a training video. What objections might people have? What benefits could videos offer your organization? Which people would be easiest to convince?

2. The advisory council of Nunavut Arctic College recommends that business faculty have three-month internships with local organizations to learn material. What objections might people in your organization have to bringing in faculty interns? What benefits might your organization receive? Which people would be easiest to convince?

3. Your organization is thinking of buying laptop computers for all employees who travel. What fears or objections might people have? What benefits might your organization receive? Which people would be easiest to convince?

As Your Instructor Directs,

a. Share your answers orally with a small group of students.

b. Present your answers in an oral presentation to the class.

c. Email your answers to class members.

d. Write a paragraph developing the best reader benefit you identified. Remember to use you-attitude.

8.13 Identifying and Developing Reader Benefits for Different Audiences

Assume that you want to encourage people to do one of the activities listed below.

1. Hire a personal trainer

   Audiences: Professional athletes

   Busy managers

   Someone trying to lose weight

   Someone making a major lifestyle change after a heart attack

2. Buy a cellular phone

   Audiences: People who do a lot of big-city driving

   People who do a lot of driving in rural areas

   People who do a lot of flying

3. Get advice about interior decorating

   Audiences: Young people with little money to spend

   Parents with small children

   People upgrading or adding to their furnishings

   Older people moving from single-family homes into smaller apartments or condominiums

Builders furnishing model homes

4. Get advice on investment strategies

Audiences: New college or university graduates

People earning over $100,000 annually

People responsible for investing funds for a church, synagogue, or temple

Parents with small children

People within 10 years of retirement

5. Garden

Audiences: People with small children

People in apartments

People concerned about reducing pesticides

People on tight budgets

Retirees

Teenagers

6. Buy a laptop computer

Audiences: College and university students

Financial planners who visit clients at home

Sales representatives who travel constantly

People who make PowerPoint presentations

7. Teach adults to read

Audiences: Retired workers

Business people

Students who want to become teachers

High school and college students

People concerned about poverty

8. Vacation at a luxury hotel

Audiences: Stressed-out people who want to relax

Tourists who like to sightsee and absorb the local culture

Business people who want to stay in touch with the office even on vacation

Parents with small children

Weekend athletes who want to have fun

9. Attend a fantasy sports camp (you pick the sport), playing with and against retired players who provide coaching and advice

10. Attend a health spa where clients get low-fat and low-calorie meals, massages, beauty treatments, and guidance in nutrition and exercise

As Your Instructor Directs.

a. Identify needs that you could meet for the audiences listed here. In addition to needs that several audiences share, identify at least one need that would be particularly important to each group.

b. Identify a product or service that could meet each need.

c. Write a paragraph or two of reader benefits for each product or service. Remember to use you-attitude.

d. Develop one or more of the benefits using psychological description.

Hints:

• For this assignment, you can combine benefits or programs as if a single source offered them all

• Add specific details about particular sports, cities, tourist attractions, activities, etc., as material for your description

• Be sure to move beyond reader benefits to vivid details and sense impressions

• Put your benefits in you-attitude

Polishing Your Prose

Plurals and Possessives

Singular possessives and plurals sound the same but are spelled differently. A possessive noun will always have an apostrophe. Most possessives of singular nouns are formed by adding 's to the word.

Singular Possessive	Plural
company's	companies
computer's	computers
family's	families
job's	jobs
manager's	managers
team's	team

Since singular possessive nouns and plurals sound the same, you will have to look at the logic of your sentence to choose the right word.

Exercises

Choose the right word in each set of parentheses.

1. Canadian (companies, company's) are competing effectively in the global market.

2. We can move your (families, family's) furniture safely and efficiently.

3. The (managers, manager's) ability to listen is just as important as his or her technical knowledge.

4. A (memos, memo's) style can build goodwill.

5. (Social workers, social worker's) should tell clients about services available in the community.

6. The (companies, company's) benefits plan should be checked periodically to make sure it continues to serve the needs of employees.

7. Information about the new community makes the (families, family's) move easier.

8. The (managers, manager's) all have open-door policies.

9. (Memos, memo's) are sent to other workers in the same organization.

10. Burnout affects a (social workers, social worker's) productivity as well as his or her morale.

Check your answers to the odd-numbered exercises on page 632.

CBC Video Case

 CBC

Go to www.mcgrawhill.ca/college/locker for "Schmoozing", an online CBC Video Case that discusses the increasing importance of proper professional etiquette. Don't miss the following quiz at http://cbc.ca/business/programs/venture/onventure/022399.html.

Unit Three

Letters, Memos, and Email Messages

Module 9

Formats for Letters, Memos, and Email Messages

Topics

- **What are the standard business formats?**
- **What courtesy titles should I use?**
- **How should I set up memos?**
- **How should I set up email messages?**

Review

Learning Applications

Polishing Your Prose: Making Subjects and Verbs Agree

Learning Focus

After reading and applying the information in Module 9 you'll be able to demonstrate

Knowledge of

- The interdependence of purpose, audience, and form
- Basic business formats

Skills to

- Choose and use standard formats
- Use nonsexist courtesy titles
- Create a professional image

"...Be concise. Don't write a novel. And be sure to use your spell checker."

"In email it is important to get your point across quickly and effectively," says Ed Herr, a digital designer for SKYmedia Internet Broadcasting Services. "Because I get so many emails, if I don't find anything useful in the first couple of sentences, it is gone."

Ed studied communications at university but left to work in retail as a computer consultant. After three years he decided to go into business for himself and he enrolled in a college accounting program. When money got tight he returned to his old job. But by this time he had an established network and was contacted for his current position as digital designer.

SKYmedia is a new company that fills two primary needs. Their main service, for corporate express clients, is a data express service. Ed likens this to an electronic courier service. Since SKYmedia uses a satellite link instead of cable or phone lines, they can transmit greater amounts of data in less time over greater spaces. As Ed says, "This proves that communications is making the world smaller." The company is capable of serving international clients. They can also set up Internet and communications services for companies who either can't afford or don't want to spend money on infrastructure. SKYmedia's second service is a consumer line. The company can provide broad band Internet services, including movies on demand. A customer can phone SKYmedia and have a movie downloaded in minutes.

Ed points out that given the nature of the business, SKYmedia's Web page is the portal to company. As a result, email is the dominant form of communication. "Working on the Web makes you detail conscious. It also makes you aware of how other people are—or are not—attentive to detail. Because of the speed of response, you tend to send more email messages, so they have to be concise and accurate."

Part of effective email communication involves working within and around its technical limitations. Ed is often conscious of how the browser forces the user into a set format. Ed also is aware of the need to be safety conscious. For example, when he sends an email to its addressee, he will copy it to others if necessary and to himself as well, to ensure that it has been sent properly and to remember all the details. In this way Ed uses technology as a failsafe device. If everything works, then he has two copies of his message. If he does not receive his copy, he knows there has been a transmission problem and must send it again. Ed's parting words of advice to email users? "If you are sending a lot of email, be concise. Don't write a novel. And be sure to use your spell checker."

http://www.skymedia.com
SKYmedia IBS Inc.

When deciding **how** to deliver your message, remember the principle of all good design: **form follows function**. This design principle is essential to communication success: you achieve intended results when you shape your message to meet the needs of your audience and your purpose (see Figure 9.1, PAIBOC Questions for analysis).

When you write, the format of your document is as important as the wording. Format—the parts of the document and the way these parts are arranged on the page—provides a **context** for the reader, signalling *what kind* of message the audience is reading. Because text layout and organization establish reader expectation, the way you format your document is an integral part of establishing your credibility as a writer.

Business communication—letters, memos, and reports—conforms to very specific formats.

Letters and memos are both brief business messages, similar in formality, length, style, and organization. Letters, however, go to people outside the organization, whereas memos are internal letters, and are sent to people within the organization. Because they have a different *audience*, therefore, letters and memos differ in format.

What are the standard formats for letters?

Block and modified block.

The two most common letter formats are **block**, sometimes called full block (see Figure 9.3 on page 169), and **modified block** (see Figure 9.4 on page 170). Your organization may make minor changes in margins or spacing.

Use the same level of formality in the **salutation**, or greeting, as you would in talking to someone on the phone: *Dear Glenn* if you're on a first-name basis, *Dear Mr. Helms* if you don't know the reader well enough to use the first name.

Sincerely and *Cordially* are standard **complimentary closes**. When you are writing to people in special groups or to someone who is a friend as well as a business acquaintance, you may want to use a less formal close. Depending on the circumstances, the following informal closes might be acceptable: *Yours for a better environment*, or even *Ciao*.

In **two-point** or **mixed punctuation**, a colon follows the salutation and a comma follows the close. In a sales or fund-raising letter, it is acceptable to use a comma after the salutation to make the letter look like a personal letter rather than like a business letter. In **open punctuation**, omit all punctuation after the salutation and the close. Mixed punctuation is traditional. Open punctuation is faster to type.

Figure 9.2

Differences between Letter Formats

	Block	**Modified Block**
Date and signature block	Lined up at left margin	Lined up 1/2 or 2/3 over to the right
Paragraph indentation	None	Optional
Subject Line	Optional	Rare

Figure 9.3

Block Format on Letterhead (mixed punctuation; collection letter)

727 Empress Street
Winnipeg, MB R39 2P5

Northwest Hardware Warehouse

(204) 779 -0703

Line up everything at left margin

↕ 2–6 spaces depending on length of letter

June 20, 2002

1"–1 1/2"

Mr. James E. Murphy, Accounts Payable   *Title could be on a separate line*
Red River Equipment Rentals
560 Wasatch Boulevard
Red River, MB R9H 6A9

Use first name in salutation if you'd use it on the phone

Dear Jim: *Colon in mixed punctuation*

The following items totaling $393.09 are still open on your account. *¶ 1 never has a heading*

Invoice #01R-784391 *Bold heading*

After the bill for this invoice arrived on May 14, you wrote saying that the material had not been delivered to you. On May 29, our Claims Department sent you a copy of the delivery receipt signed by an employee of Red River Equipment. You have had proof of delivery for over three weeks, but your payment has not yet arrived. *5/8" – 1"*

Single-space paragraphs
Double-space between paragraphs

Please send a cheque for $78.42.

Triple-space before new heading

Voucher #59351

Do not indent paragraphs

The reference line on your voucher #59351, dated June 11, indicates that it is the gross payment for invoice #01G-002345. However, the voucher was only for $1171.25, while the invoice amount was $1246.37. Please send a cheque for $75.12 to clear this item.

Voucher #55032

Voucher #55032, dated June 15, subtracts a credit for $239.55 from the amount due. Our records do not show that any credit is due on this voucher. Please send either an explanation or a cheque to cover the $239.55 immediately.

Total Amount Due   *Headings are optional in letters*

Please send a cheque for $393.09 to cover these three items and to bring your account up to date.

↕ 2–3 spaces

Sincerely, *Comma in mixed punctuation*

3–4 spaces

Neil Hutchinson
Credit Representative

cc: Joan Stottlemyer, Credit Manager

*↑ Leave bottom margin of 3–6 spaces—
more if letter is short*

Figure 9.4

Modified Block Format on Letterhead (mixed punctuation; letter of recommendation)

Capital
Information Systems

151 Bayview Road
Ottawa, ON K1S 2C5

2–6 spaces

2–4 spaces

September 14, 2002

*Line up date with signature block
1/2 or 2/3 of the way over to the right*

Ms. Mary E. Arcas
Personnel Director
Cyclops Communication Technologies
1050 Bonita Avenue
Moncton, NB E1C 4M6 *Postal code on same line*

1"–1½"

Dear Ms. Arcas: *Colon in mixed punctuation*

5/8" – 1"

Indenting ¶ is optional in modified block

      Let me respond to your request for an evaluation of Colleen Kangas. Colleen was hired as a clerk-typist by Capital Information Systems on April 4,1999, and was promoted to Administrative Assistant on August 1, 2000. At her review in June, I recommended that she be promoted again. She is an intelligent young woman with good work habits and a good knowledge of computer software.

Single-space paragraphs

      As an Adminstrative Assistant, Colleen not only handles routine duties such as processing time cards, ordering supplies, and entering data, but also screens calls for two marketing specialists, answers basic questions about Capital Information Systems, compiles the statistics I need for my monthly reports, and investigates special assignments for me. In the past eight months, she has investigated freight charges, inventory department hardware, and microfiche files. I need only to give her general directions: she has a knack for tracking down information quickly and summarizing it accurately.

Double-space between paragraphs

      Although the department's workload has increased during the year, Colleen manages her time so that everything gets done on schedule. She is consistently poised and friendly under pressure. Her willingness to work overtime on occasion is particularly remarkable considering that she has been going to college part-time ever since she joined our firm.

      At Capital Information Systems, Colleen uses Microsoft Word and Access software. She tells me that she has also used WordPerfect and PowerPoint in her community college classes.

      If Colleen were staying in Ottawa, we would want to keep her. She has the potential either to become an Executive Secretary or to move into line or staff work, especially once she completes her degree. I recommend her highly.

2–3 spaces

Sincerely, *Comma in mixed punctuation*

Headings are optional in letters

3–4 spaces

Jeanne Cederlind
Jeanne Cederlind
Vice President, Marketing

2–4 spaces

Encl.: Evaluation Form for Colleen Kangas

Line up signature block with date

Leave at least 3–6 spaces at bottom of page—more if letter is short

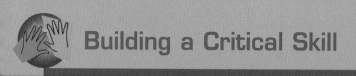
Creating a Professional Image, 1

The way you and your documents look affects the way people respond to you and to them. Every organization has a dress code. One young man was upset when an older man told him he should wear wing-tip shoes. He was wearing leather shoes but not the kind that said "I'm promotable" in that workplace. Dress codes are rarely spelled out; the older worker was doing the young man a favour by being direct. If you have a mentor in the organization, ask him or her if there are other ways you can make your appearance even more professional. If you don't have a mentor, look at the people who rank above you. Notice clothing, jewellery, and hairstyles. If you're on a budget, go to stores that sell expensive clothing to check the kind of buttons, the texture and colours of fabric, the width of lapels and belts. Then go to stores in your price range and choose garments that imitate the details of expensive clothing.

Documents need to look professional, too. Now that most documents are keyed on computers and printed with laser printers, we don't need to worry about whited-out errors or uneven key strokes. We do need to make sure that the ink or toner is printing evenly and that the document uses a standard format.

Some organizations prescribe a standard format for documents. If your organization does, follow it. If you have your choice, use one of the formats in this book. They're widely used in businesses, so they communicate a message of competence.

A **subject line** tells what the letter is about. Subject lines are required in memos; they are optional in letters. If you do use a subject line in your letter, place it after the salutation. Good subject lines are specific, concise, and appropriate for your purposes and the response you expect from your reader.

- When you have good news, put it in the subject line
- When your information is neutral, summarize it concisely in the subject line
- When your information is negative, use a negative subject line if the reader may not read the message or needs the information to act, or if the negative is your error
- When you have a request that will be easy for the reader to grant, put either the subject of the request or a direct question in the subject line
- When you must persuade a reluctant reader, use a common ground, a reader benefit, or a directed subject line (◁▶ Module 12) that makes your stance on the issue clear

For examples of subject lines in each of these situations, ◁▶ see Modules 10, 11, and 12.

A **reference line** refers the reader to the number used on previous correspondence, or the order or invoice number that this letter is about. Government organizations, such as the Canada Customs and Revenue Agency, use numbers on every piece of correspondence they send out so that it is possible quickly to find the earlier document to which an incoming letter refers.

Although not every example uses the same devices to provide visual impact, both block and modified block formats use headings, lists, and indented sections (known as "telegraphing", "highlighting" or "bulleting") for emphasis.

Site *to* **See**

Go to
http://www.canada post.ca
If you have the address, the Canada Post site gives you the postal code.

Use the format your reader expects

Source: PEANUTS reprinted by permission of United Feature Syndicate, Inc.

Each format has advantages. Block format is the format most frequently used for business letters; readers expect it; it can be typed quickly since everything is lined up at the left margin. Speed-readers maintain that it is easier to read. Modified block format creates a visually attractive page by moving the date and signature block over into what would otherwise be empty white space. Modified block is a traditional format; readers are comfortable with it.

The examples of the formats in Figures 9.3 and 9.4 on pages 169 and 170 show one-page letters on company letterhead. **Letterhead** is preprinted stationery with the organization's name, logo, address, and phone number. Figure 9.5 on page 173 shows how to set up modified block format when you do not have letterhead. (It is also acceptable to use block format without letterhead.)

When your letter runs two or more pages, use a heading on the second page to identify it. Putting the reader's name helps the writer, who may be printing out many letters at a time, to make sure the right second page gets in the envelope. Note even when the signature block is on the second page, it is still lined up with the date.

| Reader's Name |
| Date |
| Page Number |

or

| Reader's Name | Page Number | Date |

When a letter runs two or more pages, use letterhead only for page 1. (See Figures 9.6 and 9.7 on pages 174 and 175.) For the remaining pages, use plain paper that matches the letterhead in weight, texture, and colour.

Figure 9.5

Modified Block Format without Letterhead (open punctuation; claim letter)

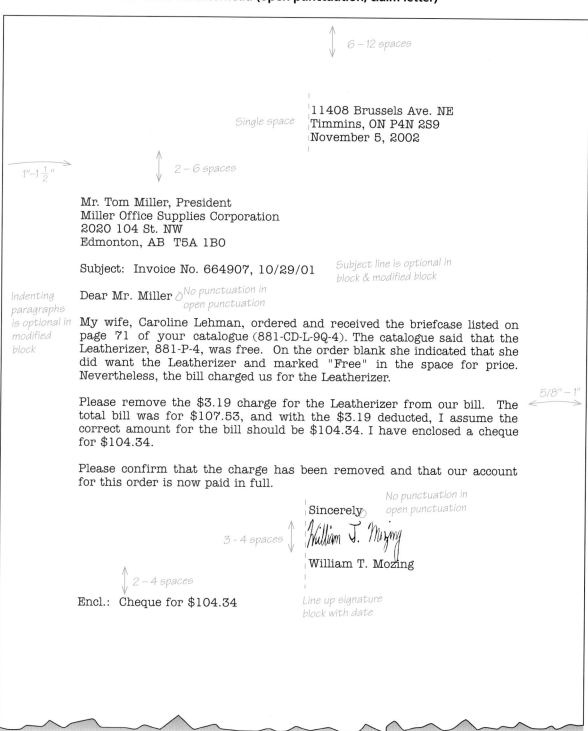

6 – 12 spaces

Single space

11408 Brussels Ave. NE
Timmins, ON P4N 2S9
November 5, 2002

1"–1 1/2 "

2 – 6 spaces

Mr. Tom Miller, President
Miller Office Supplies Corporation
2020 104 St. NW
Edmonton, AB T5A 1B0

Subject: Invoice No. 664907, 10/29/01

Subject line is optional in block & modified block

Indenting paragraphs is optional in modified block

Dear Mr. Miller

No punctuation in open punctuation

My wife, Caroline Lehman, ordered and received the briefcase listed on page 71 of your catalogue (881-CD-L-9Q-4). The catalogue said that the Leatherizer, 881-P-4, was free. On the order blank she indicated that she did want the Leatherizer and marked "Free" in the space for price. Nevertheless, the bill charged us for the Leatherizer.

5/8" – 1"

Please remove the $3.19 charge for the Leatherizer from our bill. The total bill was for $107.53, and with the $3.19 deducted, I assume the correct amount for the bill should be $104.34. I have enclosed a cheque for $104.34.

Please confirm that the charge has been removed and that our account for this order is now paid in full.

Sincerely

No punctuation in open punctuation

3 - 4 spaces

William T. Mozing

2 – 4 spaces

Encl.: Cheque for $104.34

Line up signature block with date

Figure 9.6

Second Page of a Two-Page Letter, Block Format (two-point punctuation; informative letter)

45226 Bernard Avenue
Chilliwack, BC V2P 1H1
Adrienne@hotmail.ca

May 4, 2002

1" - 1 1/2"

Stephanie Voight
Director
Corporate Communications
Spincity Incorporated
715 2nd Avenue East
Moose Jaw, SK S9X 1G9

2– 3 spaces

Indenting paragraphs is optional in modified block.

Dear Stephanie Voight: *Colon in mixed punctuation*

Thank you for your prompt response to my inquiry about co-operative opportunities at Spincity. My academic qualifications and previous work experience meet the criteria you designated in your letter.

5/8" - 1"

Academic Qualifications

I have only one semester remaining in the Honours Media and Communications program at Simon Fraser University. Our rigorous curriculum includes Writing for Publication,

Plain paper for page 2

1/2" – 1"

Stephanie Voigt   *Reader's name*   *Center* 2   May 4, 2002

Also OK to line up page number date at left under reader's name

My B.A., Journalism from the University of Western Ontario allowed me direct entry into the fourth year of the program.

Triple space before each new heading

Work Experience   *Bold headings*

Use same margins as p 1.

For the past three summers I have worked in the public relations department of Chang Design Solutions, writing ad copy and creating media relations kits for this design firm. As special events coordinator I was responsible for the company's grand opening, attended by 300 retail managers from Canada, the Northwestern United States and Hong Kong. I have additional, related experience that I would be happy to discuss with you in person.

Enclosed you will find my most recent grades transcript and press clippings from the Chang Design Solutions opening gala.

Please call me at (604) 626-5445, to arrange a meeting time at your convenience.

Sincerely,   *Comma in mixed punctuation*

3 – 4 spaces

Headings are optional in letters

Adrienne Lee

2 – 4 spaces

Enclosure: Transcript, press releases

Figure 9.7

Second Page of a Two-Page Letter, Modified Block Format (two-point; goodwill letter)

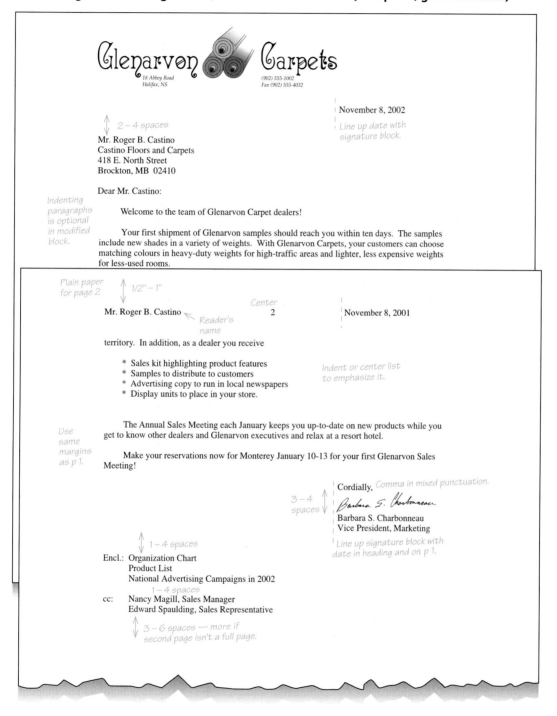

Glenarvon Carpets

18 Abbey Road
Halifax, NS

(902) 555-1002
Fax (902) 555-4032

November 8, 2002

Line up date with signature block.

2 – 4 spaces

Mr. Roger B. Castino
Castino Floors and Carpets
418 E. North Street
Brockton, MB 02410

Dear Mr. Castino:

Indenting paragraphs is optional in modified block.

Welcome to the team of Glenarvon Carpet dealers!

Your first shipment of Glenarvon samples should reach you within ten days. The samples include new shades in a variety of weights. With Glenarvon Carpets, your customers can choose matching colours in heavy-duty weights for high-traffic areas and lighter, less expensive weights for less-used rooms.

Plain paper for page 2

1/2" – 1"

Center

Mr. Roger B. Castino ← *Reader's name*   2   November 8, 2001

territory. In addition, as a dealer you receive

* Sales kit highlighting product features
* Samples to distribute to customers
* Advertising copy to run in local newspapers
* Display units to place in your store.

Indent or center list to emphasize it.

Use same margins as p 1.

The Annual Sales Meeting each January keeps you up-to-date on new products while you get to know other dealers and Glenarvon executives and relax at a resort hotel.

Make your reservations now for Monterey January 10-13 for your first Glenarvon Sales Meeting!

Cordially, *Comma in mixed punctuation.*

3 – 4 spaces

Barbara S. Charbonneau

Barbara S. Charbonneau
Vice President, Marketing

Line up signature block with date in heading and on p 1.

1 – 4 spaces

Encl.: Organization Chart
       Product List
       National Advertising Campaigns in 2002

1 – 4 spaces

cc: Nancy Magill, Sales Manager
      Edward Spaulding, Sales Representative

3 – 6 spaces — more if second page isn't a full page.

FYI

A University of British Columbia long-term study validates the direct correlation between communications skills and salary. For each additional year of education, Canadians earn an additional 8.3 percent, or $2,490 in salary, of which $772 is attributed to literacy.

Sources: Statistics Canada, The Daily, visited Web site 27 June 2001, http://www.statcan.ca/Daily/English/010319/d010319a.htm; The *Toronto Star*, Monday, March 19, 2001, A11.

Set side margins of 1" to 1½" on the left and ¾" to 1" on the right. If your letterhead extends all the way across the top of the page, set your margins even with the ends of the letterhead for the most visually pleasing page. The top margin should be three to six lines under the letterhead, or 2" down from the top of the page if you aren't using letterhead. If your letter is very short, you may want to use bigger side and top margins so that the letter is centred on the page.

Many letters are accompanied by other documents. Whatever these documents may be—a multi-page report or a two-line note—they are called **enclosures**, since they are enclosed in the envelope. The writer should refer to the enclosures in the body of the letter: "As you can see from my résumé, ..." The enclosure line is usually abbreviated: *Encl.* (see Figure 9.4). The abbreviation reminds the person who seals the letter to include the enclosure(s).

Sometimes you write to one person but send copies of your letter to other people. If you want the reader to know that other people are getting copies, list their names on the last page. The abbreviation *cc* originally meant *carbon copy* but now means *computer copy*. Other acceptable abbreviations include *pc* for *photocopy* or simply *c* for *copy*. You can also send copies to other people without telling the reader. Such copies are called **blind copies**. Blind copies are not mentioned on the original; they are listed on the copy saved for the file with the abbreviation *bc* preceding the names of people getting these copies.

You do not need to indicate that you have shown a letter to your superior or that you are saving a copy of the letter for your own files. These are standard practices.

Use two capital letters with no punctuation to abbreviate province and state names in letters and memos. See Figure 9.8 on page 177.

What courtesy titles should I use?

Research your reader's preference.

Today, most salutations use "Dear *first name last name*". However, some people prefer their professional titles: Director Chadraba, President Mauricio. Use *Ms., Mr.,* or *Mrs.* when your audience has signed their correspondence that way.

1. Use professional titles when they're relevant.

> Dr. Kristen Sorenson is our new company physician.
>
> The Rev. Robert Townsley gave the invocation.

2. If a woman prefers to be addressed as *Mrs.* or *Miss*, rather than *Ms.*, use the title she prefers. (You-attitude ◀▶ Module 6 takes precedence over nonsexist language: address the reader as she—or he—prefers to be addressed.)
   To find out if a woman prefers a traditional title,

   a. Check the signature block in previous correspondence. If a woman types her name as *(Miss) Elaine Anderson* or *(Mrs.) Kay Royster*, use the title she designates.

Province/Territory Name	Postal Service Abbreviation	State/Territory Name	Postal Service Abbreviation
Alberta	AB	Maine	ME
British Columbia	BC	Maryland	MD
Manitoba	MB	Massachusetts	MA
New Brunswick	NB	Michigan	MI
Newfoundland	NF	Minnesota	MN
Northwest Territories	NT	Mississippi	MS
Nunavut	NU	Missouri	MO
Nova Scotia	NS	Montana	MT
Ontario	ON	Nebraska	NE
Prince Edward Island	PE	Nevada	NV
Quebec	QC	New Hampshire	NH
Saskatchewan	SK	New Jersey	NJ
Yukon Territory	YT	New Mexico	NM
		New York	NY
State/Territory Name	**Postal Service Abbreviation**	North Carolina	NC
		North Dakota	ND
Alabama	AL	Ohio	OH
Alaska	AK	Oklahoma	OK
Arizona	AZ	Oregon	OR
Arkansas	AR	Pennsylvania	PA
California	CA	Rhode Island	RI
Colorado	CO	South Carolina	SC
Connecticut	CT	South Dakota	SD
Delaware	DE	Tennessee	TN
District of Columbia	DC	Texas	TX
Florida	FL	Utah	UT
Georgia	GA	Vermont	VT
Hawaii	HI	Virginia	VA
Idaho	ID	Washington	WA
Illinois	IL	West Virginia	WV
Indiana	IN	Wisconsin	WI
Iowa	IA	Wyoming	WY
Kansas	KS	Guam	GU
Kentucky	KY	Puerto Rico	PR
Louisiana	LA	Virgin Islands	VI

Figure 9.8
Postal Abbreviations for Canadian Provinces and U.S. States

b. Notice the title a woman uses in introducing herself on the phone. If she says, "This is Robin Stine," use Dear Robin Stine when you write to her. If she says, "I'm Mrs. Stine," use the title she specifies.

c. Check your company directory. In some organizations, women who prefer traditional titles list them with their names.

d. When you're writing job letters or other crucial correspondence call the company and ask the receptionist which title your reader prefers.

Ms. is particularly useful when you do not know a woman's marital status. However, when you know that a woman is married or single, **use courtesy titles only when your audience requests them.**

In addition to using parallel courtesy titles, use parallel forms for names. See Figure 9.9 on the next page.

Figure 9.9
Use Parallel Forms for Names

Not Parallel	Parallel
Members of the committee will be Mr. Jones, Mr. Yacone, and Lisa	Members of the committee will be Mr. Jones, Mr. Yacone, and Ms. Melton
	or
	Members of the committee will be Irving, Ted, and Lisa

When You Know the Reader's Name but Not the Gender

When you know your reader's name but not the gender, either

1. Call the company and ask the receptionist, or
2. Use the reader's full name in the salutation:

Dear Chris Crowell:
Dear J. C. Meath:

When You Know neither the Reader's Name nor Gender

When you know neither the reader's name nor gender, you have three options:

1. Use an attention line:

Attention: Customer Service
Attention: Human Resources
Attention: Office of the Registrar

2. Use the reader's position or job title:

Dear Loan Officer:
Attention: Registrar:

3. Use a general group to which your reader belongs:

Dear Investor:
Attention: Admissions Committee:

FYI

The word "dear" in the salutation of a letter or email reflects the sender's knowledge of standard business convention rather than the writer's relationship to the reader. "The word deore or diore in Old English meant glorious, honourable, noble, worthy. Initially an adjective, it was used throughout the thirteenth, fourteenth, and fifteenth centuries when addressing somebody....Since the seventeenth century "dear" has been used as a polite term of addressing an equal when writing to them."

Source: Laurence Urdang, editor, *Verbatim*, quoted in *The Daily Mail*, cited by Michael Kesterton, "Social Studies", *The Globe and Mail*, August 28, 2001, p. A22.

4. Omit the salutation and use a subject line in its place:

Subject:	Recommendation for Ben Wandell

Using **bolded** attention and subject lines is acceptable.

How should I set up memos?

> The standard memo uses block format but has no salutation, close, or signature.

Memos omit both the salutation and the close. Memos never indent paragraphs. Subject lines are required; headings are optional. Each heading must cover all the information until the next heading. Never use a separate heading for the first paragraph.

Figure 9.10 illustrates the standard memo format typed on a plain sheet of paper. Note that the first letters of the reader's name, the writer's name, and the subject phrase are lined up vertically. Note also that memos are usually initialled beside the To/From block. Initialling tells the reader that you have proofread the memo and prevents someone else sending out a memo you did not write with your name on it.

Some organizations have special letterhead for memos. When *Date/To/From/Subject* are already printed on the form, the date, writer's and reader's names, and subject may be set at the main margin to save typing time. (See Figure 9.11 on page 181.)

Some organizations alter the order of items in the *Date/To/From/Subject* block. Some organizations ask employees to sign memos rather than simply initialling them. The signature goes below the last line of the memo, starting halfway over on the page, and prevents anyone adding unauthorized information.

If the memo runs two pages or more, use a heading at the top of the second and subsequent pages (see Figure 9.12 on page 182). Since many of your memos go to the same people, putting a brief version of the subject line will be more helpful than just using "All Employees."

Brief Subject Line Date Page Number

or

Brief Subject Line	Page Number	Date

Figure 9.10
Memo Format (on plain paper; direct request)

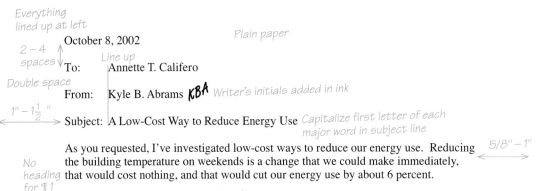

Everything lined up at left

Plain paper

October 8, 2002

2 – 4 spaces

Line up

To: Annette T. Califero

Double space

From: Kyle B. Abrams **KBA** *Writer's initials added in ink*

1" – 1½ "

Subject: A Low-Cost Way to Reduce Energy Use *Capitalize first letter of each major word in subject line*

No heading for ¶ 1

As you requested, I've investigated low-cost ways to reduce our energy use. Reducing the building temperature on weekends is a change that we could make immediately, that would cost nothing, and that would cut our energy use by about 6 percent. *5/8" – 1"*

Triple space before each new heading

The Energy Savings from a Lower Weekend Temperature *Bold headings*

Single-space paragraphs; double-space between paragraphs

Lowering the temperature from 20° to 15.5° from 8 P.M. Friday evening to 4 A.M. Monday morning could cut our total consumption by 6 percent. It is not feasible to lower the temperature on weeknights because a great many staff members work late; the cleaning crew also is on duty from 6 P.M. to midnight. Turning the temperature down for only four hours would not result in a significant heat saving.

Turning the heat back up at 4 A.M. will allow the building temperature to be back to 20° by 9 A.M. Our furnace already has computerized controls which can be set to automatically lower and raise the temperature.

Triple space

How a Lower Temperature Would Affect Employees *Capitalize first letter of each major word of heading*

A survey of employees shows that only 7 people use the building every weekend or almost every weekend. Eighteen percent of our staff have worked at least one weekend day in the last two months; 52 percent say they "occasionally" come in on weekends.

Do not indent paragraphs

People who come in for an hour or less on weekends could cope with the lower temperature just by wearing warm clothes. However, most people would find 15.5° too cool for extended work. Employees who work regularly on weekends might want to instal space heaters.

Action Needed to Implement the Change

Would you also like me to check into the cost of buying a dozen portable space heaters? Providing them would allow us to choose units that our wiring can handle and would be a nice gesture towards employees who give up their weekends to work. I could have a report to you in two weeks.

We can begin saving energy immediately. Just authorize the lower temperature, and I'll see that the controls are reset for this weekend.

Memos are initialled by To/From/Subject block — no signature

Headings are optional in memos

Figure 9.11
Memo Format (on memo letterhead; good news)

Kimball,
Walls, and
Morganstern

Date: March 15, 2002   *Line up horizontally with printed Date/To/From/Subject*

To: Annette T. Califero

From: Kyle B. Abrams *KBA*   *Writer's initials added in ink*

Capitalize first letter of each major word in subject line

Subject: The Effectiveness of Reducing Building Temperatures on Weekends

Triple space

Margin lined up with items in To/From/Subject block to save typing time

Reducing the building temperature to 20° on weekends has cut energy use by 4 percent compared to last year's use from December to February and has saved our firm $22,000.

This savings is particularly remarkable when you consider that this winter has been colder than last year's, so that more heat would be needed to maintain the same temperature.

5/8" – 1"

Fewer people have worked weekends during the past three months than during the preceding three months, but snow and bad driving conditions may have had more to do with keeping people home than the fear of being cold. Five of the 12 space heaters we bought have been checked out on an average weekend. On one weekend, all 12 were in use and some people shared their offices so that everyone could be in a room with a space heater.

Fully 92 percent of our employees support the lower temperature. I recommend that we continue turning down the heat on weekends through the remainder of the heating season and that we resume the practice when the heat is turned on next fall.

Headings are optional in memos

Figure 9.12

Option 2 for Page 2 of a Memo (direct request)

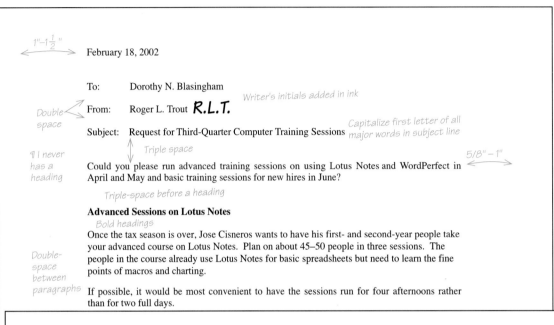

1"–1½"

February 18, 2002

To: Dorothy N. Blasingham

Double space From: Roger L. Trout **R.L.T.**   *Writer's initials added in ink*

Subject: Request for Third-Quarter Computer Training Sessions   *Capitalize first letter of all major words in subject line*

¶ I never has a heading   *Triple space*

Could you please run advanced training sessions on using Lotus Notes and WordPerfect in April and May and basic training sessions for new hires in June?

5/8" – 1"

Triple-space before a heading

Advanced Sessions on Lotus Notes
Bold headings

Once the tax season is over, Jose Cisneros wants to have his first- and second-year people take your advanced course on Lotus Notes. Plan on about 45–50 people in three sessions. The people in the course already use Lotus Notes for basic spreadsheets but need to learn the fine points of macros and charting.

Double-space between paragraphs

If possible, it would be most convenient to have the sessions run for four afternoons rather than for two full days.

Plain paper for page 2

1/2" – 1"

Dorothy N. Blasingham ← *Brief subject line or reader's name*   2 *Page number*   February 18, 2002

Also OK to line up page number, date at left under reader's name

Same margins as p 1. before the summer vacation season begins.

Orientation for New Hires *Capitalize first letter of all major words in heading*

With a total of 16 fulltime and 34 part-time people being hired either for summer or permanent work, we'll need at least two and perhaps three orientation sessions. We'd like to hold these the first, second, and third weeks in June. By May 1, we should know how many people will be in each training session.

Would you be free to conduct training sessions on how to use our computers on June 8, June 15, and June 22? If we need only two dates, we'll use June 8 and June 15, but please block off the 22nd too in case we need a third session.

Triple-space before a heading

Request for Confirmation

Let me know whether you're free on these dates in June, and which dates you'd prefer for the sessions on Lotus Notes and WordPerfect. If you'll let me know by February 25, we can get information out to participants in plenty of time for the sessions.

Thanks!

Memos are initialed by To/From/Subject block   *Headings are optional in memos*

How should I set up email messages?

Formats are still evolving.

Most email programs prompt you to supply the various parts of the format. For example, a blank Eudora screen prompts you to supply the name of the person the message goes to and the subject line (◀ ▶ Module 13). Cc denotes computer copies; the recipient will see that these people are getting the message. Bcc denotes blind computer copies; the recipient does not see the names of these people. Most email programs also allow you to attach documents from other programs. You can send someone a document with formatting, drafts of PowerPoint slides, or the design for a brochure cover. The computer program supplies the date and time automatically. Some programs allow you to write a message now and program the future time at which you want it to be sent.

Some aspects of email format are still evolving. Some writers treat email messages as if they were informal letters; some treat them as memos. Even though the email screen has a "To" line (as do memos), some writers still use an informal salutation, as in Figure 9.13 on page 184. The writer in Figure 9.13 ends the message with a signature block. You can store a signature block in the email program and set the program to insert the signature block automatically. In contrast, the writer in Figure 9.14 also on page 184 omits both the salutation and his name. When you send a message to an individual or a group you have set up, the "From:" line will have your name and email address. If you post a message to a group someone else has set up, such as a listserv, be sure to give at least your name and email address at the end of your message, as some listservs strip out identifying information when they process messages.

When you hit "reply," the email program automatically uses "Re:" (Latin for *about*) and the previous subject. The original message is set off with carats. You may want to change the subject line to make it more appropriate for your message.

If you prepare your document in a word processor, use two-inch side margins to create short line lengths. If the line lengths are too long, they'll produce awkward line breaks. Use two- or three-space tab settings to minimize the wasted space on the screen.

Site *to* **See**

Go to
http://www.mapquest.com/
Want to *see* exactly where in the world your letter or email is going?

FYI

The volume of printing in an office goes up 40 percent when email is introduced.

Source: "Fast Facts", *Fast Company,* July-August 1999, 80.

Site *to* **See**

Go to
http://www.emailreplies.com/index.html
Tips on implementing email policies and a guide to email etiquette are included at this site.

Figure 9.13
A Basic Email Message in Eudora (direct request)

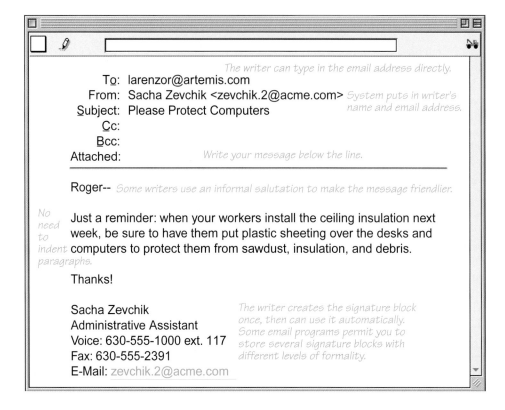

Figure 9.14
An Email Message with an Attachment (direct request)

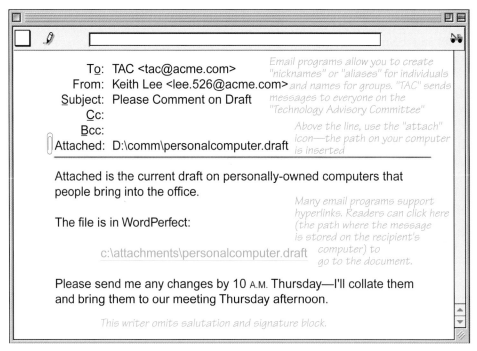

Employability Skills 2000+ Checklist for Format for Letters, Memos, and Email Messages

In this module, the key skills from The Conference Board of Canada's Employability Skills 2000+ are:

Communicate

✔ write and speak so others pay attention and understand

Manage Information

✔ locate, gather, and organize information using appropriate technology and information systems

Think & Solve Problems

✔ assess situations and identify problems
✔ seek different points of view and evaluate them based on facts
✔ recognize the human, interpersonal, technical, scientific, and mathematical dimensions of a problem

Participate in Projects & Tasks

✔ work to agreed quality standards and specifications
✔ adapt to changing requirements and information

Review of Key Points

- Block and modified block are the two standard letter formats.
- Use courtesy titles according to audience expectation.
- In a list of several people, use parallel forms for names. Use first names, first and last names or courtesy titles and last names for everyone. It's sexist to use "Mr." for each man in a document that calls all the women by their first names.

- Memos omit both the salutation and the close. Memos never indent paragraphs. Subject lines are required; headings are optional. Each heading must cover all the information until the next heading. Never use a separate heading for the first paragraph.

Learning Applications

Questions for Comprehension

9.1   When do you send a letter? When do you send a memo?

9.2   What are the differences between block and modified block letter formats?

9.3   What are the differences between block format for letters and the formats for memos?

9.4   What is the Postal Service abbreviation for your province?

Questions for Critical Thinking

9.5   Which letter format do you prefer? Why?

9.6   What are the advantages in telling your reader who is getting copies of your message?

9.7   Does following a standard format show a lack of originality and creativity?

Questions for Building Skills

9.8   What skills have you read about in this module?

9.9   What skills are you practising in the assignments you're doing for this module?

9.10   How could you further develop the skills you're working on?

Polishing Your Prose

Making Subjects and Verbs Agree

Make sure the subjects and verbs in your sentences agree. Subjects and verbs agree when they are both singular or both plural:

Correct: The laser printer no longer works.

Correct: The nonworking laser printers are in the storeroom.

Often, subject-verb errors occur when other words come between the subject and verb. Learn to correct errors by looking for the subject—who or what is doing the principal action—and the verb—the action itself:

Correct: A team of marketing researchers is reviewing our promotional campaign.

Correct: The four-colour brochures, which cost about $1,000 to print and ship, were sent to our Vancouver affiliate.

Canadian and American usage treats company names and the words *company* and *government* as singular nouns. In England and countries adopting the British system, these nouns are plural:

Correct: (Canada) Clarica is headquartered in Waterloo, Ontario.

Correct: (U.S.) Nationwide Insurance is headquartered in Columbus, Ohio.

Correct: (U.K.) Lloyds of London are headquartered in London.

Use a plural verb when two or more singular subjects are joined by and.

Correct: Mr. Simmens, Ms. Lopez, and Mr. Yee were in Seoul for a meeting last week.

Use a singular verb when two or more singular subjects are joined by *or*, *nor*, or *but*.

Correct: Neither Dr. Hroscoe nor Mr. Jamieson is in today.

When the sentence begins with *There* or *Here*, make the verb agree with the subject that follows the verb:

Correct: There were blank pages in the fax we received.

Correct: Here is the information on the job candidate you requested.

Some words that end in s are considered singular and require singular verbs:

Correct: The World Series features advertisements of our product in the stadium.

When you encounter situations that don't seem to fit the rule, or when following the rules produce an awkward sentence, rewrite the sentence to avoid the problem:

Problematic: The grant co-ordinator in addition to the awarding agency (is, are?) happy with the latest proposal we submitted.

Better: The grant co-ordinator and the awarding agency are happy with the latest proposal we submitted.

Exercises

Choose the correct verb or rewrite the sentence.

1. Each of us (is, are) entitled to company health care benefits.

2. KPMG, a leading management consulting firm, (operate, operates) locations in nine Canadian provinces.

3. The price of our stocks (is, are) increasing.

4. Every project team (train, trains) for at least 90 days before projects (is, are) started.

5. We (order, orders) a dozen new toner cartridges each month.

6. A series of meetings (is, are) planned for February.

7. Ms. Schiff as well as her assistant (is, are) attending the conference in Halifax.

8. Make it a point to (has, have) your report ready by Monday.

9. Professor Beauparlant, Mr. Kincaid, and Ms. Carolla (is, are) on the guest list and (plan, plans) to sit at the same table.

10. The offices in Buenos Aries (report, reports) a 19 percent increase in employee turnover for the past year.

Check your answers to the odd-numbered exercises on page 632.

Module 10

Informative and Positive Messages

Topics

- What's the best subject line for an informative or positive message?

- How should I organize informative and positive messages?

- When should I use reader benefits in informative and positive messages?

- What kinds of informative and positive messages am I likely to write?

- How can the PAIBOC formula help me write informative and positive messages?

Review of Key Points

Learning Applications

Polishing Your Prose: Dangling Modifiers

Learning Focus

After reading and applying the information in Module 10, you'll be able to demonstrate

Knowledge of

- The criteria that define positive messages
- The "good news" message structure
- The persuasive component present in all effective messages

Skills to

- Continue to analyze business communication situations
- Organize and write positive messages
- Write standard informative and positive messages

"Every communication program must combine thoughtful, flawless, and innovative planning, and targeted tactics..."

"My goal is to is to provide comprehensive communications strategies that help meet corporate strategies," says Kim Spirou, a partner in Media Street Communications of Windsor, a full service communications consulting firm with clients in both the private and public sector. According to Kim, Media Street's value "is in our ability to provide strategic counsel and to deliver creative communication strategies and programs to our clients."

Kim has worked in the communications and public relations field for over a decade. Prior to joining Media Street she managed the communications department for the Windsor Board of Education where she developed and implemented an award-winning public relations program. At Media Street, Kim spearheads the company's PR and research wing. One of her main roles is to conduct both quantitative and qualitative research for clients to meet their needs.

Media Street develops complete communications packages including print and video materials. With four partners, each specialising in a different area, the company provides services in video production, crisis management, strategic communications planning, research, and community relations. "We believe every communication program must combine thoughtful, flawless, and innovative planning, and targeted tactics to assist clients in developing communication programs that cut through the clutter of today's world."

An excellent example of Kim's work is a job she took on for the Windsor-Essex County Hospital Foundation. In response to government cuts and the need to eliminate duplication, five hospitals were merging into three. The challenge was to raise the local share of $40 million, in order to carry out the renovations and expansion—a campaign that would represent the largest fundraising initiative ever undertaken in the community. As chair of the Communications Division of the campaign, Kim's role was "to recruit a strong volunteer team of professionals, devise an appropriate communications plan, and guide the plan forward."

The first step was to establish campaign goals and objectives, and devise a communications program to test public opinion and find out if community rate payers would agree to have a special levy, averaging $25, added to their taxes to support the local hospitals. Results of a poll showed that health care was the number one issue in the community. So a two-pronged campaign involving mass media and interpersonal strategies was launched. The focus of the campaign was to generate community support for the levy. The goals of the campaign included raising the awareness of the need for hospital renovations and construction, building positive public opinion about the levy, and motivating and educating community leaders.

As a result of the campaign, the message got out. People supported the levy, City Council passed the necessary by-laws, and, to date, most of the money has been raised.

When asked for advice to someone entering public relations Kim said, "Public relations boils down to reputation management. Practitioners need to focus on building relationships through interpersonal communications. So you must become a language guru. Learn to write in a clear, simple language free of jargon, and keep your comments focussed on your themes and messages."

http://www.mediastreet.ca
Media Street Communications

Competent communicators classify messages as neutral, positive, or negative, depending on the audience's anticipated reaction. When we convey information that the reader will receive neutrally, the message is **informative**. If we anticipate that the reader will respond positively to our information, the message is a **positive** or **good news message**.

Positive and informative messages make no demands on the reader's time or wallet, although the writer may want the reader to save the information and act on it later. Regardless of your purpose, in every writing situation you want to build positive attitudes about yourself and the information you are presenting. Informative and positive messages, therefore, contain persuasive elements.

Informative and positive messages include

- News that is advantageous to the reader
- Acceptances
- Positive answers to reader requests
- Information about procedures, products, services, or options
- Announcements of changes that are neutral or positive

Even a simple informative or good news message usually has several purposes.

Primary Purposes:

To give information or good news to the reader or to reassure the reader

To have the reader read the message, understand it, and view the information positively

To de-emphasize any negative elements

Underlying Purposes:

To build a good image of the writer

To build a good image of the writer's organization

To cement a good relationship between the writer and reader

To reduce or eliminate future correspondence on the same subject so the message doesn't create more work for the writer

What's the best subject line for an informative or positive message?

One that contains the basic information or good news.

A **subject line** is the title of a document. It aids in filing and retrieving the document, tells readers why they need to read the document, and provides a framework or **context** in which to set what you're about to say.

Subject lines are standard in memos. Letters are not required to have subject lines (see ◄▶ Module 9). However, since a subject line saves the reader's time (and builds the writer's credibility), most business people consider a subject line in a letter to be very important. A good subject line meets three criteria: it is specific, concise, and appropriate to the kind of message (positive, negative, persuasive).

Instant Replay

Primary and Secondary Purposes

You want to build positive attitudes toward the information you are presenting, so in that sense, even an informative message has a persuasive element.

Site to See

Go to http://www.info-canada.com/gov.html Peruse federal government Web sites.

Good news comes in many forms.

Source: MOTHER GOOSE & GRIM. © Tribune Media Services, Inc. All rights reserved. Reprinted with permission.

Making Subject Lines Specific

The subject line needs to be specific enough to differentiate that message from others on the same subject, but broad enough to cover everything in the message.

Too general: Training Sessions

Better: Technical Training Sessions Dates

or   Evaluation of Training Sessions on Conducting Interviews

or   Should We Schedule a Short Course on Proposal Writing?

Making Subject Lines Concise

Most subject lines are relatively short—usually no more than 10 words, often only three to seven words.[1]

Wordy: Survey of Student Preferences in Regards to Various Pizza Factors

Better: Students' Pizza Preferences

or: The Feasibility of a Pizza Hut Branch on Campus

or: What Students Like and Dislike about Pizza Pizza

If you can't make the subject both specific and short, be specific.

Making Subject Lines Appropriate for the Pattern of Organization

In general, do the same thing in your subject line that you would do in the first paragraph.

When you have good news for the reader, build goodwill by **highlighting** it in the subject line. When your information is neutral, summarize it concisely for the subject line.

Subject: Discount on Rental Cars Effective January 2

Starting January 2, as an employee of Amalgamated Industries you can get a 15 percent discount on cars you rent for business or personal use from Roadway Rent-a-Car.

Subject: Update on Arrangements for Videoconference with France

In the last month, we have chosen the participants and developed a tentative agenda for the videoconference with France scheduled for March 21.

How should I organize informative and positive messages?

Consider your audience's needs: put the good news and a summary of the information first.

Using the appropriate pattern can help you compose more quickly and create a more effective final product. The patterns of organization described in this module and the modules that follow will work for 70 to 90 percent of business writing situations.

- Be sure you understand the rationale behind each pattern so that you can modify the pattern if necessary. (For example, when you write instructions, any warnings should go up front, not in the middle of the message.)
- Sometimes you can present several elements in one paragraph. Sometimes you'll need several paragraphs for just one element.

Present informative and positive messages in the following order:

1. **Give any good news and summarize the main points.** Share good news immediately. Include details such as the date policies begin and the percent of a discount. If the reader has already raised the issue, make it clear that you're responding.
2. **Give details, clarification, and background.** Don't repeat information from the first paragraph. Do answer all the questions your reader is likely to have; provide all the information necessary to achieve your purposes. Present details in **the order of importance to the reader.**

3. **Present any negative elements as positively as possible.** A policy may have limits; information may be incomplete; the reader may have to satisfy requirements to get a discount or benefit. Make these negatives clear, but present them as positively as possible.

4. **Explain any reader benefits.** Most informative memos need reader benefits. Show that the policy or procedure helps readers, not just the company. Give enough detail to make the benefits clear and convincing. In letters, you may want to give benefits of dealing with your company as well as benefits of the product or policy (◀▶ Module 8). In a good news message, it's often possible to combine a short, reader benefit with a goodwill ending in the last paragraph.

5. **Use a goodwill ending: positive, personal, and forward-looking.** Shifting your emphasis away from the message to the specific reader suggests that serving the reader is your real concern.

Figure 10.1 summarizes the pattern. Figures 10.2 and 10.3 on the following pages, illustrate two ways to apply the pattern.

The letter in Figure 10.2 authorizes a one-year foreign appointment that the reader and writer have already discussed, and describes the organization's priorities. Since the writer knows that the reader wants to accept the job, the letter doesn't need to persuade. The opportunity for the professor to study records that aren't available to the public is an implicit reader benefit; the concern for the reader's needs builds goodwill.

The memo in Figure 10.3 announces a new employee benefit. The first paragraph summarizes the policy. Paragraphs 2 to 5 give details. Negative elements are in paragraphs 3 to 5, stated as positively as possible. The last section of the memo gives reader benefits and shows that everyone—even part-timers who are not eligible for reimbursement—will benefit from the new program.

When should I use reader benefits in informative and positive messages?

> When you want readers to view your policies and your organization positively.

Not all informative and positive messages need reader benefits (◀▶, refer to last page of Module 8).

You don't need reader benefits when

- You're presenting factual information only
- The reader's attitude toward the information doesn't matter
- Stressing benefits may make the reader sound selfish
- The benefits are so obvious that to restate them insults the reader's intelligence

You do need reader benefits when

- You are presenting policies
- You want to shape readers' attitudes toward the information or toward your organization
- Stressing benefits presents readers' motives positively
- Some of the benefits may not be obvious to readers

Figure 10.1
How to Organize an Informative or Positive Message

FYI

The top five problems supervisors had in writing on the job were

- Meeting deadlines
- Deciding what information to include
- Organizing information
- Writing clear instructions
- Summarizing information from other sources

Source: Mark Mabrito, "Writing on the Front Line: A Study of Workplace Writing," *Business Communication Quarterly* 60, no. 3 (September 1997): 66; also visited Web site June 29, 2001. http://www. bethel.edu/wcb/schools/BC /ges/thomara/5/files/Mabri to's_study.htm

Figure 10.2
A Positive Letter

International
Fidelity
Insurance Company

100 Interstate Plaza
Atlanta, GA 30301
404-555-5000
Fax: 404-555-5270

March 8, 2002

Professor Adrienne Prinz
Department of History
The University of Toronto
Toronto, ON M5A 4K8

Dear Professor Prinz:

Good news — Your appointment as archivist for International Fidelity Insurance has been approved. When you were in Atlanta in December, you said that you could begin work June 1. Please let me know if that date is still good for you.   *Tactful*

The Board has outlined the following priorities for your work: *Assumes reader's primary interest is the job*

Negative about lighting and security presented impersonally

1. **Organize and catalogue the archives.** You'll have the basement of the Palmer Building for the archives and can requisition the supplies you need. You'll be able to control heat and humidity; the budget doesn't allow special lighting or security measures.

Details

2. **Prepare materials for a four-hour training session in October** for senior-level managers. We'd like you to cover how to decide what to send to the archives. If your first four months of research uncover any pragmatic uses for our archives (like Wells Fargo's use of archives to teach managers about past pitfalls), include those in the session.

3. **Write an article each month for the employee newsletter** describing the uses of the archives. When we're cutting costs in other departments, it's important to justify committing funds to start an archive program.

These provisions will appeal to the reader

4. **Study the IFI archives to compile** information that (a) can help solve current management problems, (b) could be included in a history of the company, and (c) might be useful to scholars of business history.

5. **Begin work on a corporate history of IFI.** IFI will help you find a publisher and support the book financially. You'll have full control over the content.

Salary is de-emphasized to avoid implying that reader is "just taking the job for the money"

Negative that reader will have to reapply presented as normal procedure

Your salary will be $23,000 for six months; your contract can be renewed twice for a total of 18 months. You're authorized to hire a full-time research assistant for $8,000 for six months; you'll need to go through the normal personnel request process to request that that money be continued next year. A file clerk will be assigned full-time to your project. You'll report to me. At least for the rest of this calendar year, the budget for the Archives Project will come from my department.

Figure 10.2

A Positive Letter (Continued)

Professor Adrienne Prinz
March 8, 2002
Page 2

IFI offices are equipped with Pentium computers with FoxPro, WordPerfect, and Excel. Is there any software that we should buy for cataloguing or research? What office supplies should we have on hand June 1 to make your work easier?

In the meantime,

1. Please send your written acceptance right away

2. Let me know if you need any software or supplies

3. Send me the name, address, and Social Insurance number of your research assistant by May 1 so that I can process his or her employment papers

Goodwill ending

4. If you'd like help finding a house or apartment in Atlanta, let me know. I can give you the name of a real estate agent

On June 1, you'll spend the morning in Personnel. Stop by my office at noon. We'll go out for lunch and then I'll take you to the office you'll have while you're at IFI.

Welcome to IFI!

Cordially,

Cynthia Yen

Cynthia Yen
Director of Education and Training

Messages to customers or potential customers sometimes include a sales paragraph promoting products or services you offer in addition to the product or service that the reader has asked about. Sales promotion in an informative or positive message should be low-key, not "hard sell."

Reader benefits are hardest to develop when you are announcing policies. The organization has probably decided to adopt the policy because it appears to help the organization; the people who made the decision may not have thought about whether it would help or hurt employees. Yet reader benefits are most essential in this kind of message so readers see the reason for the change and support it.

When you present reader benefits, be sure to present advantages ***to the reader***. Most new policies help the organization in some way, but few workers will see their

Figure 10.3

A Positive Memo

Memo

Date: January 26, 2002

To: All Crossroads Counselling Centre Employees

From: Darlene Bonifas, Director of Human Resources *DB*

Subject: New Tuition Reimbursement Program   *Good news in subject line and first paragraph*

Starting February 1st, fulltime employees who have worked at Crossroads three months or more can be reimbursed for up to $2,500 a year for tuition and fees when you take courses related to your current position (including courses needed to keep your licences), courses that would prepare you for another position you might someday hold at Crossroads, or courses required for a job-related degree program.

You can take the courses at any level: high school, college, university, or graduate school. You can find a selection of catalogues from nearby schools, colleges, and universities in the Office of Human Resources.

How to Apply for the Program   *Headings chunk material and provide good visual impact*

To apply, pick up an application form in the Office of Human Resources, fill it out, and have it signed by your immediate supervisor. Return it to the Office of Human Resources at least two weeks before classes start: your application must be approved before classes start.

How to Get Reimbursed   *Negatives presented as positively as possible*

You'll be reimbursed when you earn a "C" grade or better in the course. Just bring the following documents to the Office of Human Resources:

    1. A copy of the approved application
    2. An official grade report
    3. A statement of the tuition and fees paid

If you are eligible for other financial aid (scholarships, grants, or veterans' benefits), you will be reimbursed for the tuition and fees not covered by that aid, up to $2,500 during one calendar year. Reimbursements for undergraduate and basic education programs are currently tax-free.

Figure 10.3
A Positive Memo (Continued)

All Employees—New Tuition Reimbursement Program
January 26, 2002
Page 2

*page 2 of memo
doesn't use
letterhead*

Goals of the Program

This program will help us stay on top of developments in our field. For example, we're working with more and more people who have tested HIV-positive. Some counsellors might want to take courses on medical treatments for AIDS. The more we understand about the physical pressures our clients are under, the better we can help them cope with their emotional challenges. Knowing that AIDS leaves patients exhausted may help us understand why someone needs a little extra time or tolerance during an appointment.

Courses about anxiety and stress could help us deal with the increasing number of clients who fear that their jobs will disappear. Perhaps someone would like to take a course in money management or career counselling so that we could offer practical as well as psychological advice. Counsellors may want to become registered to administer the MBTI or learn how to use computers to score the MMPI.

*Jargon appropriate
for the audience*

*Reader
Benefits*

Counsellors can use this program to earn their doctorates so that they can be the primary psychologist seeing a patient. Having more certified counsellors would enable us to enlarge our practice.

*Including
Benefits
for
people
who are
not
eligible
to
partici-
pate*

But courses don't have to relate to psychology and counselling. Maybe someone would like to learn how to use advanced features in Word, Access, or Excel. (Could someone learn how to improve our database or chart our client profiles?) Management courses might help us run a tighter ship. And interpersonal courses might sharpen our skills so that we do an even better job of working together to solve problems.

In spite of cutbacks by some insurance providers last fall, Crossroads continues to be financially as well as professionally strong. This program gives us the opportunity to build on our strength as we prepare to help people face the challenges of the new millennium.

Goodwill ending

Some companies put on their own talk shows to inform employees and answer their questions about company strategies.

own interests as identical with those of the organization. Even if the organization saves money or increases its profits, workers will benefit directly only if they own stock in the company, if they are to receive bonuses, if the savings enables a failing company to avoid layoffs, or if all of the savings goes directly to employee benefits. In many companies, any money saved will go to executive bonuses, shareholder profits, or research and development.

To develop reader benefits for informative and positive messages, use the steps suggested in Module 8. Be sure to think about the **intrinsic benefits** (◀▶ p. 157) of your policy: what benefits come from the activity or policy itself, apart from any financial benefits? How does a policy improve the hours people spend at work?

Instant Replay

Organizing Informative and Positive Messages

1. Give any good news and summarize the main points
2. Give details, clarification, background
3. Present any negative elements—as positively as possible
4. Explain any reader benefits
5. Use a goodwill ending: positive, personal, and forward-looking

What kinds of informative and positive messages am I likely to write?

Transmittals, confirmations, summaries, adjustments, and thank-you notes.

Messages are informative, negative, or persuasive depending on how the reader will perceive what you have to say. A transmittal, for example, can be positive when you're sending glowing sales figures or persuasive when you want the reader to act on the information. A performance appraisal is positive when you evaluate someone who's doing superbly, negative when you want to compile a record to justify firing someone, and persuasive when you want to motivate a satisfactory worker to continue to improve. A collection letter is persuasive; it becomes negative in the last stage when you threaten legal action. Each of these messages is discussed in the module for the pattern it uses most frequently. However, in some cases you will need to use a pattern from a different module.

Transmittals

When you send someone something in an organization, attach a memo or letter of transmittal explaining what you're sending. A transmittal can be as simple as a small yellow Post-it™ note with "FYI" written on it ("For Your Information") or it can be a separate typed document, especially when it transmits a formal document such as a report (◀▶ Module 24).

Organize a memo or letter of transmittal in this order:

1. Tell the reader what you're sending.
2. Summarize the main point(s) of the document.
3. Indicate any special circumstances or information that would help the reader understand the document. Is it a draft? Is it a partial document that will be completed later?

4. Tell the reader what will happen next. Will you do something? Do you want a response? If you do want the reader to act, specify exactly what you want the reader to do and give a deadline.

Frequently, transmittals have important secondary purposes, such as building goodwill and showing readers that you're working on projects they value.

Confirmations

Many informative messages record oral conversations. These messages are generally short and give only the information shared orally; they go to the other party in the conversation. Start the message by indicating that it is a confirmation, not a new message:

As we discussed on the phone today, . . .

As I told you yesterday, . . .

Attached is the meeting schedule we discussed earlier today.

Summaries

You may be asked to summarize a conversation, document, or an outside meeting for colleagues or superiors. (Minutes of an internal meeting are usually more detailed. See Module 18 for advice on writing minutes of meetings.)
In a summary of a conversation for internal use, identify

- Who was present
- What was discussed
- What was decided
- Who does what next

To summarize a document

1. Start with the main point.
2. Give supporting evidence and details.
3. Evaluate the document, if your audience asks for evaluation.
4. Identify the actions that your organization should take based on the document. Should others in the company read this book? Should someone in the company write a letter to the editor responding to this newspaper article? Should your company try to meet with someone in the organization that the story is about?

Adjustments and Responses to Complaints

A study sponsored by Travelers Insurance showed that when people had gripes but didn't complain, only 9 percent would buy from the company again. But when people did complain—and their problems were resolved quickly—82 percent would buy again.[2]

When you grant a customer's request for an adjusted price, discount, replacement, or other benefit to resolve a complaint, do so in the very first sentence.

Thank-you notes can be written on standard business stationery, using standard formats. But one student noticed that his advisor really liked cats and had pictures of them in her office. So he found a cat card for his thank-you note.

> Your Visa bill for a night's lodging has been adjusted to $63. Next month a credit of $37 will appear on your bill to reimburse you for the extra amount you were originally asked to pay.

Don't talk about your own process in making the decision. Don't say anything that sounds grudging. Give the reason for the original mistake only if it reflects credit on the company. (In most cases, it doesn't, so the reason should be omitted.)

Thank-You and Congratulatory Notes

Sending a **thank-you note** recognizes and acknowledges a person's contribution and is invaluable in fostering goodwill. Furthermore, your recognition of others will make people more willing to help you again in the future. Thank-you letters are short and prompt. They need to be specific to sound sincere.

Congratulating someone can cement good feelings between you and the reader and enhance your own visibility. Again, specifics help.

Avoid language that may seem condescending or patronizing. A journalism professor was offended when a former student wrote to congratulate her for a feature article that appeared in a major newspaper. As the professor pointed out, the letter's language implied that the writer had more status than the person being praised. The former student was "quite impressed," congratulated the professor on reaching a conclusion that the writer had already reached, and assumed that the professor would have wanted to discuss matters with the writer. To the reader, "Keep up the good work!" implied that the one cheering her on had been waiting for ages at the finish line.[3]

How can the PAIBOC formula help me write informative and positive messages?

> The PAIBOC questions help you examine the points your message should include.

Before you tackle the assignments for this module, examine the following problem. See how the PAIBOC questions in Figure 10.4 probe the basic points required for a solution. Study the two sample solutions to see what makes one unacceptable and the other one good. Note the recommendations for revision that could make the good solution excellent.[4] The checklist at the end of the module in Figure 10.7 can help you evaluate a draft.

Problem

Sunwest Insurance uses computers to handle its payments and billings. There is often a time lag between receiving a payment from a customer and recording it on the computer. Sometimes, while the payment is in line to be processed, the computer sends out additional notices: past due notices, collection letters, even threats to sue. Customers are frightened or angry and write asking for an explanation. In most cases, if customers just waited a little longer, the situation would be straightened out. But policyholders are afraid that they'll be without insurance because the company thinks the bill has not been paid.

Sunwest doesn't have the time to check each individual situation to see if the cheque did arrive and has been processed. It wants you to write a letter that will persuade customers to wait. If something is wrong and the payment never reached Sunwest, the company would send a legal notice to that effect saying that the policy would be cancelled by a certain date (which the notice would specify) at least 30 days after the date on the original premium bill. Continuing customers always get this legal notice as a third chance (after the original bill and the past-due notice).

Prepare a form letter that can go out to every policyholder who claims to have paid a premium for automobile insurance and resents getting a past-due notice. The letter should reassure readers and build goodwill for Sunwest.

Analysis of the Problem

P   What are your **purposes** in writing or speaking?

To reassure readers: they're covered for 30 days. To inform them they can assume everything is OK unless they receive a second notice. To avoid further correspondence on this subject. To build goodwill for Sunwest : (a) we don't want to suggest Sunwest is error-prone or too cheap to hire enough people to do the necessary work; (b) we don't want readers to switch companies; (c) we do want readers to buy from Sunwest when they're ready for more insurance.

A   Who is (are) your **audience(s)**? How do the members of your audience differ from each other? What characteristics are relevant to this particular message?

Automobile insurance customers who say they've paid but have still received a past-due notice. They're afraid they're no longer insured. Since it's a form letter, different readers will have different situations: in some cases payment did arrive late, in some cases the company made a mistake, in some the reader never paid (cheque lost in mail, unsigned, bounced, etc.)

I   What **information** must your message include?

Readers are still insured. We cannot say whether their cheques have now been processed (company doesn't want to check individual accounts). Their insurance will be cancelled if they do not pay after receiving the second past-due notice (the legal notice).

B   What reasons or reader **benefits** can you use to support your position?

Computers help us provide personal service to policyholders. We offer policies to meet all their needs. Both of these points would need specifics to be interesting and convincing.

O   What **objections** can you expect your reader(s) to have? What negative elements of your message must you de-emphasize or overcome?

Computers appear to cause errors. We don't know if the cheques have been processed. We will cancel policies if their cheques don't arrive.

C   How will the **context** affect the reader's response? Think about your relationship to the reader, morale in the organization, the economy, the time of year, and any special circumstances

The insurance business is highly competitive—other companies offer similar rates and policies. The customer could get a similar policy for about the same money from someone else. Most people find that money is tight, so they'll want to keep insurance costs low. On the other hand, the fact that prices are steady or rising means that the value of what they own is higher—they need insurance more than ever.

Many insurance companies are refusing to renew policies (car, liability, malpractice insurance). These refusals to renew have received lots of publicity, and many people have heard horror stories about companies and individuals whose insurance has been cancelled or not renewed after a small number of claims. Readers don't feel very kindly toward insurance companies.

In Canada, drivers are legally required to have car insurance. If their insurance policies are cancelled because of a computer error, drivers have a legitimate worry.

Writing a Goodwill Ending

Goodwill endings focus on the business relationship you share with your reader. When you write to one person, tailor the last paragraph to that person specifically. When you write to someone who represents an organization, the last paragraph can refer to your company's relationship with the reader's organization. When you write to a group (for example, to "All Employees") your ending should apply to the whole group.

Possibilities include complimenting the reader for a job well done, describing a reader benefit, or looking forward to something positive that relates to the subject of the message.

For example, consider possible endings for a responding to an information query about tours of Wikwemikong Indian reserve on Manitoulin Island. The People of the Three Fires community offer group tours for special interest groups.

Weak closing paragraph: Should you have any questions regarding this matter, please feel free to call me.

Goodwill ending: Upon request, People of the Three Fires Tours can develop custom tours for educational institutions and corporate retreats. Please contact us for further information.

Some writers end every message with a standard invitation:

If you have questions, please do not hesitate to ask.

That sentence lacks positive emphasis (◀▶ Module 7). But saying "feel free to call"—though more positive—is rarely a good idea. Most of the time, the writer should omit the sentence. Don't make more work for yourself by inviting calls to clarify simple messages.

One of the reasons you write is to save the time needed to tell everyone individually. People in business aren't shrinking violets; they will call if they need help. Do make sure your phone number is in the letterhead or is typed below your name. You can also add your email address below your name.

Discussion of the Sample Solutions

The solution in Figure 10.5 on the next page, is unacceptable. The red marginal comments show problem spots. Since this is a form letter, we cannot tell customers we have their cheques; in some cases, we may not. The letter is far too negative. The explanation in paragraph 2 makes Sunwest look irresponsible and uncaring. Paragraph 3 is far too negative. Paragraph 4 is too vague; there are no reader benefits; the ending sounds selfish.

A major weakness with the solution is that it lifts phrases straight out of the problem; the writer does not seem to have thought about the problem or about the words he or she is using. Measuring the draft against the answers to the questions for analysis suggests that this writer should start over.

The solution in Figure 10.6 is much better. The blue marginal comments show the letter's strong points. The message opens with the good news that is true for all readers. (Whenever possible, one should use the good news pattern of organization.) Paragraph 2 explains Sunwest 's policy. It avoids assigning blame and ends on a positive note. The negative information is buried in paragraph 3 and is presented positively: The notice is information, not a threat; the 30-day extension is a "grace period." Telling the reader now what to do if a second notice arrives eliminates the

Figure 10.5

An Unacceptable Solution to the Sample Problem

Need date

Not personalized: not you-focussed

Dear Customer:

Not necessarily true.
Reread problem.

This explanation makes company look bad.

Relax. We got your cheque.

There is always a time lag between the time payments come in and the time they are processed. While payments are waiting to be processed, the computer with super-human quickness is sending out past-due notices and threats of cancellation.

Too negative

Need to present this positively

Cancellation is not something you should worry about. No policy would be cancelled without a legal notice to that effect giving a specific date for cancellation which would be at least 30 days after the date on the original premium notice.

If you want to buy more insurance, just contact your local Sunwest Life Assurance agent. We will be happy to help you.

This paragraph isn't specific enough to work as a reader benefit. It lacks you-attitude and positive emphasis.

Sincerely,

need for a second exchange of letters. Paragraph 4 offers benefits for using computers, since some readers may blame the notice on computers, and offers benefits for being insured by Sunwest. Paragraph 5 promotes other policies the company sells and prepares for the last paragraph.

As the red comments indicate, this good solution could be improved by personalizing the salutation and by including the name and number of the local agent. Computers could make both of those insertions easily. This good letter could be made excellent by revising paragraph 4 so that it doesn't end on a negative note, and by using more reader benefits. For instance, do computers help agents advise clients of the best policies for them? Does Sunwest offer good service—quick, friendly, nonpresssured—that could be stressed? Are agents well trained? All of these might yield ideas for additional reader benefits.

Figure 10.6
A Good Solution to the Sample Problem

Need date

Dear Amjit Sunder: *Use computer to personalize. Put in name and address of a specific reader*

Your auto insurance is still in effect.   *Good paragraph #1. True for all readers*

Good to treat notice as information, tell reader what to do if it arrives   Past-due notices are mailed out if the payment has not been processed within three days after the due date. This may happen if a cheque is delayed in the mail or arrives without a signature or account number. When your cheque arrives with all the necessary information, it is promptly credited to your account.   *Good you-attitude*

Even if a cheque is lost in the mail and never reaches us, you still have a 30-day grace period. If you do get a second notice, you'll know that we still have not received your cheque. To keep your insurance in force, just stop payment on the first cheque and send a second one.

Benefits of using computers   Computer processing of your account guarantees that you get any discounts you're eligible for: multicar, accident-free record, good student. If you have a claim, your agent uses computer tracking to find matching parts quickly, whatever car you drive. You get a check quickly—usually within 3 working days—without having to visit dealer after dealer for time-consuming estimates.   *Better to put in agent's name, phone number*
Too negative

Need to add benefits of insuring with IFI   Today, your home and possessions are worth more than ever. You can protect them with Sunwest Insurance's homeowners' and renters' policies. Let your local agent show you how easy it is to give yourself full protection. If you need a special rider to insure a personal computer, a coin, or stamp collection, or a fine antique, you can get that from Sunwest, too.   *Good specifics*

Whatever your insurance needs—auto, home, life, or health—one call to Sunwest can do it all.   *Acceptable ending*

Sincerely,

Figure 10.7

Checklist for Informative and Positive Messages

☐ In positive messages, does the subject line give the good news? In either message, is the subject line specific enough to differentiate this message from others on the same subject?

☐ Does the first paragraph summarize the information or good news? If the information is too complex to fit into a single paragraph, does the paragraph list the basic parts of the policy or information in the order in which the memo discusses them?

☐ Is all the information given in the message? (What information is needed will vary depending on the message, but information about dates, places, times, and anything related to money usually needs to be included. When in doubt, ask!)

☐ In messages announcing policies, is there at least one reader benefit for each segment of the audience? Are all reader benefits ones that seem likely to occur in this organization?

☐ Is each reader benefit developed, showing that the benefit will come from the policy and why the benefit matters to this organization? Do the benefits build on the job duties of people as this organization and the specific circumstances of the organization?

☐ Does the message end with a positive paragraph—preferably one that is specific to the readers, not a general one that could fit any organization or policy?

And, for all messages, not just informative and positive ones,

☐ Does the message use you-attitude and positive emphasis?

☐ Is the style easy to read and friendly?

☐ Is the visual design of the message inviting?

☐ Is the format correct?

☐ Does the message use standard grammar? Is it free from typos?

Originality in a positive or informative message may come from

☐ Creating good headings, lists, and visual impact.

☐ Developing reader benefits.

☐ Thinking about readers and giving details that answer their questions and make it easier for them to understand and follow the policy.

Employability Skills 2000+ Checklist for Informative and Positive Messages

In this module, the key skills from The Conference Board of Canada's Employability Skills 2000+ are:

Communicate

✔ write and speak so others pay attention and understand
✔ share information using a range of information and communications technologies (e.g., voice, email, computers)
✔ use relevant scientific, technological, and mathematical knowledge and skills to explain or clarify ideas

Manage Information

✔ locate, gather, and organize information using appropriate technology and information systems

Work with Others

✔ contribute to a team by sharing information and expertise

Review of Key Points

- A subject line is the title of a document. A good subject line meets three criteria: it's specific; it's reasonably short; and it's adapted to the kind of message (positive, negative, persuasive). If you can't make the subject both specific and short, be specific.

- The subject line for an informative or positive message should highlight any good news and summarize the information concisely.

- Informative and positive messages normally use the following pattern of organization:

  1. Give any good news and summarize the main points

  2. Give details, clarification, and background

  3. Present any negative elements—as positively as possible

  4. Explain any reader benefits

  5. Use a goodwill ending: positive, personal, and forward-looking

- Use reader benefits in informative and positive messages when

  - You are presenting policies

  - You want to shape readers' attitudes toward the information or toward your organization

  - Stressing benefits presents readers' motives positively

  - Some of the benefits may not be obvious to readers

- Use the PAIBOC questions listed in Figure 10.4 on page 203 to examine the basic points needed for successful informative and positive messages.

Learning Applications

Questions for Comprehension

10.1 What are the three criteria for good subject lines?

10.2 How should you organize a positive or informative message?

10.3 How do specific varieties of informative and positive messages adapt the basic pattern?

Questions for Critical Thinking

10.4 What's wrong with the subject line "New Policy"?

10.5 Is it unethical to "bury" any negative elements in an otherwise positive or informative message?

10.6 Why is it important to recognize the secondary as well as the primary purposes of your message?

10.7 Are you more likely to need reader benefits in informative letters or memos? Why?

Questions for Building Skills

10.8 What skills have you read about in this module?

10.9 What skills are you practising in the assignments you're doing for this module?

10.10 How could you further develop the skills you're working on?

Exercises and Problems

10.11 Revising a Letter

Your assistant gives you the following letter to sign:

Dear Ms. Hebbar:

I received your request to send a speaker to participate in "Career Day" at King Elementary School next month. I am pleased to be able to send Audrey Lindstrom to speak at your school about her job at the child care centre.

Audrey has been working in the child care centre for over five years. She trains contracted centre personnel on policies and procedures of the department.

Another commitment later that day will make it impossible for her to spend the whole day at your school. She will be happy to spend two hours with your class participating in the event.

Call Audrey to coordinate the time of the program, the expected content, and the age group of the audience.

Your students will see the importance of trained day care providers in our neighbourhoods.

Thank you for asking our agency to be part of your school's special event. Our future lies in the hands of today's students.

Sincerely,

This draft definitely needs some work. It lacks you-attitude and positive emphasis, it isn't well organized, and it doesn't have enough details. "Ms. Lindstrom" would be more professional than "Audrey." And more information is needed. Exactly when should she show up? Will she be giving a speech (how long?), speaking as a member of a panel, or sitting at a table to answer questions? Will all grade levels be together, or will she be speaking to specific grades? Will all students hear each speaker, or will there be several concurrent speakers from which to choose?

As Your Instructor Directs,

a. Write a memo to your subordinate, explaining what revisions are necessary

b. Revise the letter

10.12   Responding to a Supervisor's Request

You've received this email message from your supervisor:

Answer the message, describing something that you or others in your unit do well.

> Subject: Need "Best Practices"
>
> Please describe something our unit does well—ideally something that could be copied by or at least applied to other units. Our organization is putting together something on "Best Practices" so that good ideas can be shared as widely as possible.
>
> Be specific. For example, don't just say "serve customers"—explain exactly what you do and how you do it to be effective. Anecdotes and examples would be helpful.
>
> Also indicate whether a document, a videotape, or some other format would be the best way to share your practice. We may use more than one format, depending on the response.
>
> I need your answer asap so that I can send it on to my boss.

10.13   Accepting Suggestions

Your municipal government encourages money-saving suggestions to help balance the city budget. The suggestion committee, which you chair, has voted to adopt five suggestions:

1. Direct deposit paycheques to save distribution and printing costs. Suggested by Poh-Kim Lee, in Recreation and Parks.

2. Buy supplies in bulk. Suggested by Jolene Zigmund, in Maintenance.

3. Charge nearby towns and suburbs a fee for sending their firefighters through the city fire academy. Suggested by Charles Boxell, in Fire Safety.

4. Set up an honour system for employees to reimburse the city for personal photocopies or phone calls. Suggested by Maria Echeverria, in Police.

5. Install lock boxes so meter readers don't have to turn off water valves when people move. This causes wear and tear, and broken valves must be dug up and replaced. Suggested by Travis Gratton, in Water Line Maintenance.

Each suggester gets $100. The Accounting Department will cut cheques the first of next month; cheques should reach people in interoffice mail a few days later.

As Your Instructor Directs,

a. Write to one of the suggesters, giving the good news

b. Write to all employees, announcing the award winners

10.14   Giving Good News

Write to a customer or client, to a vendor or supplier, or to your boss announcing good news. Possibilities include a product improvement, a price cut or special, an addition to your management team, a new contract.

10.15   Easing New Hires' Transition into Your Unit

Prepare a document to help new hires adjust quickly to your unit. You may want to focus solely on work procedures; you may also want to discuss aspects of the corporate culture.

10.16   Announcing a Change in Group Life Insurance Rates

Your organization provides group life insurance to your salaried employees, worth 2.5 times the employee's annual salary. Hourly employees who worked 30 hours or more a week in the last year receive life insurance equal to what the person was paid in the last year. The premium that the organization pays has been considered taxable income. The exact value is listed on the pay stub in the box labelled "Employer-Paid Benefits." Now, the Ministry of Finance has announced a reduction in the rates used to calculate the taxable value of this employer-provided life insurance. As a result, the value of the insurance will be slightly lower, and therefore all of the taxes based on pay will be slightly lower: federal, provincial, city, provincial hospitalization insurance, and school district taxes. These changes will be effective in the paycheque issued at the end of this month for employees paid monthly and in the paycheque issued 10 days from now for employees paid biweekly.

Write a memo to all employees, explaining the change.

10.17   Introducing a Wellness Program

Your company has decided to launch a comprehensive wellness program in an effort to get employees to adopt healthier lifestyles. Studies show that people who smoke, who are moderate or heavy drinkers, who are overweight, and who do not exercise regularly have higher rates of absence due to illness. They visit doctors more often, need more prescription drugs, and are hospitalized more often and for longer periods of time.

You'll give a $100 rebate (annually) to each employee who doesn't smoke or use chewing tobacco. Employees who don't drink to excess (more than an average of at least 170 ml of beer or 85 ml of wine or 42 ml of hard liquor a day) and who don't use illegal drugs can also get $100, as can those whose cholesterol isn't over 150. Employees who exercise at least 30 minutes a day, three times a week will get rebates of $50. Exercise doesn't have to be difficult: walking and gardening count. Another rebate of $50 is available for a waist-to-hip ratio not over 0.8 for women or 0.95 for men.

As part of the wellness program, the company cafeteria will focus on serving healthier foods and the company will offer twice-yearly health fairs with free routine immunizations and flu shots for employees and dependants. These parts of the program will begin next month.

Write a memo to all employees informing them about the wellness program.

Hints:

- Pick an organization you know something about to use for this message.
- If the organization saves money through reduced absenteeism, will employees benefit?
- Why don't people already follow healthy practices? What can you do to overcome these objections?

- Saving money may not motivate everyone. Offer intrinsic benefits as well.

- Use the analysis that you developed for 2.13 in Module 2 on page 46.

10.18   Explaining Packing Material

Your organization ships thousands of boxes to fill orders from catalogues and from your Web site. To cushion items, you fill the empty spaces around the items with plastic "popcorn." Some customers have written to complain about the plastic, which is not biodegradable. Some have asked you to use real popcorn, paper, or starch (which will degrade when wet). However, these materials do not cushion as well as plastic does (so that more items are damaged during shipment) and weigh more (so that shipping costs are higher). In addition, popcorn is subject to Canadian Food Inspection Agency regulations, which you do not want to monitor; paper fill creates dust and thus is a health hazard for packers; and starch doesn't work in very humid or very dry climates. You want to use one packing material for all boxes, wherever they are going.

Customers could save and reuse the plastic packaging material. If they can't reuse it, they may be able to recycle it. They can call their local solid waste department to find out. Or they could check The Internet Consumer Recycling Guide, an online guide for Canadian and U.S. consumers, at http://www.obviously.com/recycle/guides/hard.html

As Your Instructor Directs,

a. Write a letter to one customer who has complained, showing why you are continuing to use plastic fill

b. Prepare a one-page document to be included in every package, explaining your decision about packaging

10.19   Reminding Guests about the Time Change

Twice a year the switch to and from daylight-saving time affects people in Canada. The time change can be disruptive for hotel guests, who may lose track of the date, forget to change the clocks in their rooms, and miss appointments as a result.

Prepare a form letter to leave in each hotel room reminding guests of the impending time change. What should guests do?

Write the letter.

Hints:

- Use an attention-getting page layout so readers don't ignore the message.

- Pick a specific hotel or motel chain you know something about.

- Use the letter to build goodwill for your hotel or motel chain. Use specific references to services or features the hotel offers, focussing not on what the hotel does for the reader, but on what the reader can do at the hotel.

10.20   Confirming a Reservation

You work in reservations at Basin Hot Springs Lodge in Banff National Park. Most travellers phone 13 months in advance to reserve a room and once you process the credit card payment for the first night, you then write to them to confirm the reservation.

The confirmation contains the amount charged to the credit card, the date on which

the reservation was made, the confirmation number, the kind of room (Lakefront Retreat or Mountainview Retreat), and the dates the guest will be arriving and leaving.

In addition, the letter needs to give several pieces of general information. The amount of the deposit and the amount quoted per night are the rates for the current calendar year.

However, the guest will be charged the rate for the calendar year of the stay, and that amount is likely to increase by about 4 to 5 percent. In addition to paying the new rate for each additional night, the guest will need to pay the difference between the amount of the deposit and the new rate for the first night.

Anyone who wants a refund must cancel the reservation in writing four days prior to the scheduled arrival date. Cancellations may be faxed: the fax number is on the letterhead the letter will be printed on.

Parking is limited. People who bring big motorhomes, boats, or camp trailers may have to park in the main parking area rather than right by their cabins.

All of the rooms are cabin style with three to four rooms in each building. There are no rooms in a main lodge. People will need to walk from their cabins to the restaurants, unless they do their own cooking.

Both Lakefront and Mountainview Retreats have kitchenettes with microwaves, but guests must bring their own cooking utensils, dishes, supplies, and food. The bedroom area (with a king-size bed in the Lakefront Retreats and a queen-size bed in the Mountainview Retreats) has a sliding divider that can separate it from the sitting area, which has a sofa bed.

Since the deposit pays for the first night (less any increase in room rate), the room will be held regardless of the time of arrival. Check-in time is 3 P.M.; earlier room availability cannot be guaranteed. Checkout time is 11 A.M.

All cabins are nonsmoking. Smoking is permitted on the decks of the Lakefront Retreats or the porches of the Mountainview Retreats.

The guest should present the confirmation letter when checking in.

As Your Instructor Directs,

a. Write a form letter that can be used for one type of room (either Lakefront or Mountainview Retreat). Indicate with square brackets material that would need to be filled in for each guest: for instance, arriving [date of arrival] and departing [date of departure].

b. Write a letter to Stephanie Lafleur, who has reserved a Lakefront Retreat room arriving September 18 and departing September 20. Her credit card is being billed for $187.25 ($175 plus GST—the current rate). Her address is 3122 Rue Laurier, Québec City, QC, G1R 3M7.

10.21   Lining up a Consultant to Teach Short Courses in Presentations

As director of education and training, you oversee all in-house training programs. Five weeks ago, Runata Hartley, vice president for human resources, asked you to set up a training course on oral presentations. After making some phone calls, you tracked down Brian Barreau, a professor of communications at a nearby college.

"Yes, I do short courses on oral presentations," he told you on the phone. "I would want at least a day and a half with participants—two full days would be better. They need time to practice the skills they'll be learning. I'm free Thursdays and Fridays.

I'm willing to work with up to 20 people at a time. Tell me what kind of presentations they make, whether they know how to use PowerPoint, and what kinds of things you want me to emphasize. I'll need a videocamera to record each participant's presentations and a tape for each person. My fee is $2,000 a day."

You told him you thought a two-day session would be feasible, but you'd have to get back to him after you got budget approval. You wrote a quick memo to Runata explaining the situation and asking about what the session should cover.

Two weeks ago, you received this memo.

> I've asked the veep for budget approval of $4,000 for a two-day session plus no more than $500 for all expenses. I don't think there will be a problem.
>
> We need some of the basics: how to plan a presentation, how to deal with nervousness. Adapting to the audience is a big issue: our people give presentations to varied audiences with very different levels of technical knowledge and interest. Most of our people have PowerPoint on their computers, but the slide shows I've seen have been pretty amateurish.
>
> I don't want someone to lecture. I don't want some ivory tower theorist. We need practical exercises that can help us practice skills that we can put into effect immediately.
>
> Attached is a list of 18 people who can attend a session Thursday and Friday of the second week of next month. Note that we've got a good mix of people. If the session goes well, I may want you to schedule additional sessions.

Today, you got approval from the vice president to schedule the session and pay Professor Barreau's fee and reimburse him for expenses to a maximum of $500. He will have to keep all receipts and turn in an itemized list of expenses to be reimbursed; you cannot reimburse him if he does not have receipts.

You also need to explain the mechanics of the session. You'll meet in the Conference Room, which has a screen and flip charts. You have an overhead projector, a slide projector, a video camera, and a VCR, but you need to reserve these if he wants to use them. Will he bring his own laptop computer, or does he want you to provide the computer?

Write to Professor Barreau. You don't have to persuade him to come since he's already informally agreed, but you do want him to look forward to the job and to do his best work.

Hints:

- Choose an organization you know something about.
- What audiences do people speak to? How formal are these talks? What are their purpose(s)?
- Is this session designed to hone the skills of people who are competent, or is it designed to help people who are very weak, perhaps even paralysed by fright?
- What role do presentations play in the success of the organization and of individuals in it?
- Check the calendar to get the dates. If there's any ambiguity about what "the second week of next month" is, "call" Runata to check.

10.22 Answering an International Inquiry

Your business, government, or non-profit organization has received the following inquiries from international correspondents. (You choose the country the inquiry originated from.)

1. Please tell us about a new product, service, or trend so that we can decide whether we want to buy, licence, or imitate it in our country.

2. We have heard about a problem [technical, social, political, or ethical] that occurred in your organization. Could you please tell us what really happened and estimate how it is likely to affect the long-term success of the organization?

3. Please tell us about college or university programs in this field. We are interested in sending some of our managers to your country to complete a degree.

4. We are considering setting up a plant in your city. We have already received adequate business information. However, we would also like to know how comfortable our nationals would feel. Do people in your city speak our language? How many? What opportunities exist for our nationals to improve their English? Does your town already have people from a wide mix of nations? Which are the largest groups?

5. Our organization would like to subscribe to an English-language trade journal. Which one would you recommend? Why? How much does it cost? How can we order it?

As Your Instructor Directs,

a. Answer one or more of the inquiries. Assume that your reader either reads English or can have your message translated.

b. Write a memo to your instructor explaining how you've adapted the message for your audience.

Hints:

- Even though you can write in English, English may not be your reader's native language. Write a letter that can be translated easily.

- In some cases, you may need to spell out background information that might not be clear to someone from another country.

10.23   Writing a Thank-You Letter

Write a thank-you letter to someone who has helped you achieve your goals.

As Your Instructor Directs,

a. Turn in a copy of the letter

b. Mail the letter to the person who helped you

c. Write a memo to your instructor explaining the choices you made in writing the thank-you letter

10.24   Evaluating Web Pages

Today you received this email from your boss:

Subject: Evaluating Our Web Page

Our CEO wants to know how our Web page compares to those of our competitors. I'd like you to do this in two steps. First, send me a list of your criteria. Then give me an evaluation of two of our competitors and of our own pages. I'll combine your memo with others on other Web pages to put together a comprehensive evaluation for the next Executive Meeting.

As Your Instructor Directs,

a. List the generic criteria for evaluating a Web page. Think about the various audiences for the page and the content that will keep them coming back, the way the page is organized, how easy it is to find something, the visual design, and the details, such as a creation/update date.

b. List criteria for pages of specific kinds of organizations. For example, a non-profit organization might want information for potential and current donors, volunteers, and clients. A financial institution might want to project an image both of trustworthiness and as a good place to work.

c. Evaluate three Web pages of similar organizations. Which is best? Why?

Hint:

Review the information on Web page design in Module 5 on page 109.

10.25   Creating a Human Resources Web Page

As firms attempt to help employees balance work and family life (and as employers become aware that personal and family stresses affect performance at work), human resource departments sponsor an array of programs and provide information on myriad subjects. However, some people might be uncomfortable asking for help, either because the problem is embarrassing (who wants to admit needing help to deal with drug or spousal abuse or addiction to gambling?) or because they feel that focussing on nonwork issues (e.g., child care) might lead others to think they aren't serious about their jobs. The World Wide Web allows organizations to post information that employees can access privately—even from home.

Create a Web page that could be posted by human resources to help employees with one of the challenges they face. Possible topics include

- Appreciating an ethnic heritage
- Buying a house
- Caring for dependants: child care, helping a child learn to read, living with teenagers, elder care, and so forth
- Dealing with a health issue: exercising, having a healthy diet, and so forth
- Dealing with a health problem: alcoholism, cancer, diabetes, heart disease, obesity, and so forth
- Dressing for success or dressing for casual days
- Managing finances: basic budgeting, deciding how much to save, choosing investments, and so forth
- Nourishing the spirit: meditation, religion
- Planning for retirement
- Planning vacations

- Reducing stress
- Resolving conflicts on the job or in families

Assume that this page can be accessed from another of the organization's pages. Offer at least seven links. (More is better.) You may offer information as well as links to other pages with information. At the top of the page, offer an overview of what the page covers. At the bottom of the page, put the creation/update date and your name and email address.

As Your Instructor Directs

a. Turn in two laser copies of your page(s). On another page, give the URLs for each link.

b. Turn in one laser copy of your page(s) and a disk with the HTML code and .gif files.

c. Write a memo to your instructor (1) identifying the audience for which the page is designed and explaining (2) the search strategies you used to find material on this topic, (3) why you chose the pages and information you've included, and (4) why you chose the layout and graphics you've used.

d. Present your page orally to the class.

Hints:

- Pick a topic you know something about.
- Realize that audience members will have different needs. You could explain the basics of choosing day care or stocks, but don't recommend a specific day care centre or a specific stock.
- If you have more than nine links, chunk them in small groups under headings.
- Create a good image of the organization.
- Review the information on Web page design in Module 5.

Polishing Your Prose

Dangling Modifiers

Modifiers are words or phrases that give more information about parts of a sentence. For instance, an adjective is a modifier that usually describes a noun. **Dangling modifiers** make no sense to readers because the word they modify is not in the sentence. If you diagrammed the sentence, the modifier would not be attached to anything; it would dangle.

Dangling: Confirming our conversation, your Hot Springs Hot Tub Spa is scheduled for delivery April 12.
(This sentence says that the spa is doing the confirming.)

Correct a dangling modifier in either of these ways:

1. Rewrite the modifier as a subordinate clause.

Correct: As I told you yesterday, your Hot Springs Hot Tub Spa is scheduled for delivery April 12.

2. Rewrite the main clause so its subject or object can be modified correctly.

Correct: Talking on the phone, we confirmed that your Hot Springs Hot Tub Spa is scheduled for delivery April 12.

Exercises

Correct the dangling modifiers in these sentences.

1. After working a year, dental insurance covers you.

2. Using the fax machine, new orders are processed quickly.

3. At the age of 10, I bought my daughter her first share of stock.

4. Working in teams, projects can be completed quickly.

5. Calling ahead of time, the reservations can be made efficiently.

6. Before joining our company, your résumé shows a good deal of experience with computer software.

7. Confirming our telephone call, your order was shipped on April 1.

8. A simple notebook filled with thoughts and ideas, you can keep a journal of your business experiences.

9. Sharing files with our legal department, our attorneys can work better with you.

10. As a new employee, your supervisor can answer your questions.

Check your answers to the odd-numbered exercises on page 633.

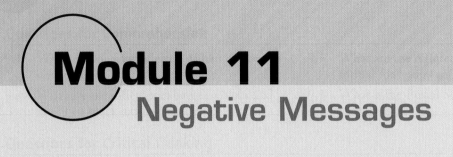

Module 11
Negative Messages

Topics

- What's the best subject line for a negative message?
- How should I organize negative messages?
- Why should I give an alternative, if one is available?
- What are the most common kinds of negative messages?
- How can PAIBOC help me write negative messages?

Review of Key Points

Learning Applications

Polishing Your Prose: Parallel Structure

Learning Focus

After reading and applying the information in Module 11, you'll be able to demonstrate

Knowledge of
- The criteria that define negative messages
- The "bad news" message structure

Skills to
- Organize negative messages
- Give bad news while retaining goodwill
- Continue to write effective subject lines
- Write common kinds of negative messages
- Continue to analyze business communication situations

"Be honest and know your audience."

"What do you do when you have eight crises happening simultaneously and you are new to the job?" asks Jan Graves, director of development and communications for London Regional Cancer Centre. The answer is to take chances and try new solutions.

Before obtaining employment with the cancer centre, Jan was communications director at Canada's largest privately operated medical-research institute. Her job there, as for the cancer centre, was to translate high-tech information to low-tech readers. "The important thing in both jobs is to know your audience," states Jan. In order to make sure she was communicating effectively she would run material past neighbours and relatives to see if they understood.

Jan has a joint bachelor's degree in petroleum geology and life sciences. Her first job was community relations coordinator at a conservation authority. This led to her interest in communications and her job at the research institute. While working at the conservation authority, she insisted on being allowed to attend board meetings so that she would hear the information first-hand. But nothing quite prepared her for the challenges at the cancer institute.

Cancer is on the rise worldwide. There is an international shortage of trained staff in the area, especially in radiation therapy. Years ago the education system decided that there were too many specialists and started focussing instead on preparing general practitioners. Now, with changing demographics, more specialists are needed, but cancer treatment is not a first choice for medical or technology students. And with recent increases in cancer rates, more treatment centres are being built, requiring even more staff. In addition to these global issues, the centre also had an image problem—the lack of an image!

Jan attacked these challenges by sitting down with the new CEO in order to come up with an action plan. They recognized that the London Regional Cancer Centre's challenges were not unique, but experienced by other treatment centres on the international scene. They took into account new developments, such as university medical students doing rotations at the centre. And they listed possible solutions, such as the development of new technologies and education programs for the public.

Then came the risk-taking part. Jan called in the media to explain the situation. Jan says that the centre had to be honest in dealing with the public, so she let the media know the big picture, the problems, and the possible solutions. The media's reaction was, "How can we help?" Jan's response was to encourage the media to contact her to confirm the facts when people called the media to complain. As Jan says, "Even though the situation for the next six months was gloomy, now our coverage isn't negative.... and we still have excellent media cooperation."

What are the keys to the success of this communications campaign? Jan's answer is succinct: "Be honest and know your audience!"

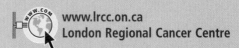

www.lrcc.on.ca
London Regional Cancer Centre

FYI

Recent studies indicate that work/life balance has become the dominant concern for Canadian employees. Employees' hierarchy of needs follows Maslow's model: if people do not feel physically and emotionally secure, the organization's investment in compensation and professional development programs is wasted. In fact, people's commitment to their work is directly related to their perception of how committed their company is to them.

Sources: "Companies slow to make employees' work/life harmony a priority," The Training Report, Jan/Feb 2001, pp. 12; Patricia Chisholm, "Redesigning Work," *Maclean's*, March 5, 2001, 34–38.

Messages are positive or negative based on audience impact. Negative messages contain information that will cost the reader: comfort, time, money, esteem, resources. When we expect the reader to be disappointed or angry at the information, we are composing a negative message.

Negative messages include

- Rejections and refusals
- Announcements of policy changes that do not benefit customers or consumers
- Requests the reader will see as bothersome, insulting, or intrusive
- Negative performance appraisals and disciplinary notices
- Product recalls or notices of defects

A negative message always has several purposes:

Primary Purposes:

- To give the reader the bad news
- To have the reader read, understand, and accept the message
- To maintain as much goodwill as possible

Secondary Purposes:

- To build a good image of the writer
- To build a good image of the writer's organization
- To reduce or eliminate future correspondence on the same subject so the message doesn't create more work for the writer

Although readers may not be happy with the news we must convey, we still want readers to feel that

- They have been taken seriously
- Our decision is fair and reasonable
- If they were in our shoes, they would make the same decision

What's the best subject line for a negative message?

Only use negative subject lines if you think the reader may otherwise ignore the message.

Letters don't require subject lines (◀▶ pp. 170 and 190). Omit a subject line in negative letters unless you think readers may ignore what they think is a routine message. (See, for example, Figure 11.2 on p. 224 of this module.)

When you give bad news, use a subject line that focusses on solutions, not problems.

> Subject: Improving Our Subscription Letter

Or, you can put the topic (but not your action on it) in the subject line:

> Subject: Status of Conversion Table Program
>
> Due to heavy demands on our time, we have not yet been able to write programs for the conversion tables you asked for.

How should I organize negative messages?

It depends on your purposes and audiences. But for optimum meaning exchange, follow the indirect, inductive, or bad news pattern.

"Meaning" resides in people, not words. Whatever your purpose—compliance, agreement, action—your audience's emotional or affective response is vital to getting the results you want. Whether notifying a client about a price increase or emailing colleagues about extra work they must complete, you want to convey information and maintain goodwill. Otherwise, you'll lose time and money in terms of lost customers and disruptive work relationships

Giving Bad News to Customers and Other People Outside Your Organization

The following pattern helps writers maintain goodwill:

1. **Start with a neutral statement, or buffer.** These openings are meant to orient the readers and psychologically prepare them for news that they are not going to like. Whether writing or speaking, the best buffers begin with areas that both you and your audience can agree upon. Buffer statements such as "Thank you for your letter," in response to a complaint and/or query, acknowledge that you have read, understood, and are responding to your reader's concern.

2. **Explain.** A good reason prepares the reader to expect the refusal.

3. **Give the negative just once, clearly.** Inconspicuous refusals can be missed, making it necessary to say *no* a second time.

4. **Always present an alternative or compromise, if one is available.** An alternative not only gives readers another way to get what they want but also suggests that you care about readers and helping them solve their problems.

5. **End with a positive, forward-looking statement.**

Figure 11.1 summarizes the pattern. Figure 11.2 uses the basic pattern.

The Buffer

A **buffer** is a neutral or positive statement that allows you to delay the negative. You'll want to begin messages with a neutral statement or buffer when the reader (individually or culturally) values harmony or when the buffer serves another purpose. For example, when you must thank the reader somewhere in the letter, putting the "thank you" in the first paragraph allows you to start on a positive note.

To be effective, a buffer must put the reader in a good frame of mind, not give the bad news but not imply a positive answer either, and provide a natural transition to the body of the letter. The kinds of statements most often used as buffers are good news, facts and chronologies of events, references to enclosures, thanks, and statements of principle.

Figure 11.1

How to Organize a Negative Letter

Figure 11.2
A Negative Letter

Nature's Lifesource Incorporated
111 Pleasant Street
Stephen NB E3L 1B4
506-825-1376 http://naturlif@origin.ca

2002 August 15

Fairmont Neutraceuticals Inc
3373 Forbes Avenue
Rosemount, PA 19010

Buffer

Dear Alyssa Scarangella:
Re: **Shipments # 3101-3105 inclusive**

Neutral Statement

Thank you for your time yesterday afternoon and for the information you provided.

Explanation

As I mentioned to you during our telephone conversation, the last three shipments have arrived with product damage. Moreover, both our transportation service suppliers and warehouse personnel have expressed concerns about the security of the loading. The quality of pallets supporting the products and the shipment fastening could lead to load shifts, creating dangerous highway travelling conditions.

And Proof

Please find enclosed the photographs of the damages to shipments #3103, 3104, and 3105, as you requested. These photographs demonstrate the condition of the pallets and the manner in which the load was secured: our research indicates these two factors lead to the damage.

Negative: reader expected to ensure adherence to safety standards and to pay for damaged shipments

Thank you for your assistance in ensuring that the quality of pallets and the fastening of all future shipments will provide a safe, secure load. I would also appreciate your help in recouping our costs for the damaged products.

Please let me know if you require further information.   *Positive ending*

Sincerely,

Leovee Yang

Leovee Yang

Encl.

1. Start with any good news or positive elements the letter contains

> Starting Thursday, June 26, you'll have access to your money 24 hours a day at Canada Trust.

Letter announcing that the drive-up windows will be closed for two days while automatic teller machines are installed

2. State a fact or provide a chronology of events

> As a result of the new graduated dues schedule—determined by vote of the Delegate Assembly last December and subsequently endorsed by the Executive Council—members are now asked to establish their own dues rate and to calculate the total amount of their remittance.

Announcement of a new dues structure that will raise most members' dues

3. Refer to enclosures in the letter

> Enclosed is a new sticker for your car. You may pick up additional ones in the office if needed. Please destroy old stickers bearing the signature of "L.S. LaVoie."

Letter announcing increase in parking rental rates

4. Thank the reader for something he or she has done

> Thank you for scheduling appointments for me with so many senior people at the Bank of Montreal. My visit there March 14 was very informative.

Letter refusing a job offer

5. State a general principle

> Good drivers should pay substantially less for their auto insurance. The Good Driver Plan was created to reward good drivers (those with 5-year accident-free records) with our lowest available rates. A change in the plan, effective January 1, will help keep those rates low.

Letter announcing that the company will now count traffic tickets, not just accidents, in calculating insurance rates—a change that will raise many people's premiums

Buffers are hard to write. Even if you think the reader would prefer to be let down easily, use a buffer only when you can write a good one.

It's better *not* to use a buffer (1) if the reader might ignore a letter with a bland first paragraph, (2) if the reader or the organization prefers "bottom-line-first messages," (3) if the reader is suspicious of the writer, or (4) if the reader "won't take *no* for an answer."

Reasons

Make the reason for the refusal clear and convincing in terms of the audience's needs and wants. Your readers would find the following reason emotionally unconvincing:

Weak reason: The goal of the ValuDrug CHARGE-ALL Centre is to provide our customers faster, more personalized service. Since you now live outside the Halifax ValuDrug CHARGE-ALL service area, we can no longer offer you the advantages of a local CHARGE-ALL Centre.

If the reader says, "I don't care if my bills are slow and impersonal," will the company let the reader keep the card? No. The real reason for the negative is that the drugstore's franchise allows it to have cardholders only in a given geographical region.

Better reason: Each local CHARGE-ALL Centre offers accounts to customers in a specific regional area. The Nova Scotia ValuDrug CHARGE-ALL Centre serves customers east of Québec. You can continue to use your current card until it expires. When that happens, you'll need to open an account with a CHARGE-ALL Centre that serves Québec.

Don't hide behind "company policy": readers will assume the policy is designed to benefit you at their expense. If possible, show how the readers benefit from the policy. If they do not benefit, don't mention policy.

Weak reason: I cannot write an insurance policy for you because company policy does not allow me to do so.

Better reason: General Insurance insures cars only when they are normally garaged at night. Standard insurance policies cover a wider variety of risks and charge higher fees. Limiting the policies we write gives General's customers the lowest possible rates for auto insurance.

Avoid saying that you *cannot* do something. Most negative messages exist because the writer or company has chosen certain policies or cutoff points. In the example above, the company could choose to insure a wider variety of customers if it wanted to do so.

Often you will enforce policies that you did not design. Don't pass the buck by saying, "This is a terrible policy." Carelessly criticizing your superiors is never a good idea. If you really think a policy is bad, try to persuade your superiors to change it. If you can't think of convincing reasons to change the policy, maybe it isn't so bad after all.

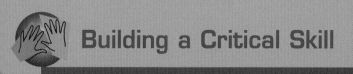

Building a Critical Skill

Thinking about the Legal Implications of What You Say

Any message that is recorded—on paper (even a napkin), on a disk or hard drive, on voice-mail—can be subpoenaed in a legal case. During the American government's months-long case against Microsoft in the late 1990s, email messages figured prominently as evidence. Even an electronic message that has been erased can be reconstituted by experts. In any message you write, however informal or hurried, you need to be sure to say exactly what you mean. The Supreme Court of Canada and provincial defamation legislation protect individuals' dignity, right to privacy, and reputation. Libel and slander liability can include everyone who participates in disseminating injurious material.

Thinking about the legal implications of what you say is particularly important in nega-

tive messages. In an effort to cushion bad news, writers sometimes give reasons that create legal liabilities. For example, as Elizabeth McCord has shown, the statement that a plant is "too noisy and dangerous" for a group tour could be used as evidence against the company in a worker's compensation claim. In another case, a writer telling a job candidate that the firm had hired someone else said that he thought she was the best candidate. She sued and won.

You need to assume your audience's point of view to figure out what to say—or not to say. Think about how a reasonable person might interpret your words. If that interpretation isn't what you mean, revise the passage so that it says what you mean, in a way that you would find acceptable.

Sources: "ARCHIVE - Internet Content-Related Liability Study," Web site visited June 29, 2001, http://strategis.ic.gc.ca/SSG/sf03241e.html#E13E6 ; Elizabeth A. McCord, "The Business Writer, the Law, and Routine Business Communication: A Legal and Rhetorical Analysis," *Journal of Business and Technical Communication* 5, no. 2 (1991): 173–99.

If you have several reasons for saying no, use only those that are strong and watertight. If you give five reasons and readers dismiss two of them, readers may feel that they've won and should get the request.

Weak reason: You cannot store large bulky items in the dormitory over the summer because moving them into and out of storage would tie up the stairs and the elevators just at the busiest times when people are moving in and out.

Way to dismiss the reason: We'll move large items before or after the two days when most people are moving in or out.

If you do not have a good reason, omit the reason rather than use a weak one. Even if you have a strong reason, omit it if it reflects poorly on your organization.

Reason that reflects poorly on company: Our company is not hiring at the present time because profits are down. In fact, the downturn has prompted top management to reduce the salaried staff by 5 percent just this month, with perhaps more reductions to come.

Better: Our company does not have any openings now.

Instant Replay

Organizing Letters to Customers

1. Start with a neutral statement or buffer
2. Explain
3. Give the news clearly
4. Present an alternative or compromise, if one is available
5. End with a positive, forward-looking statement

Psychological reactance in action

Refusals

De-emphasize the refusal by putting it in the same paragraph as the reason, rather than in a paragraph by itself.

Sometimes you may be able to imply the refusal rather than stating it directly.

Direct refusal: You cannot get insurance for just one month.

Implied refusal: The shortest term for an insurance policy is six months.

Be sure that the implication is crystal clear. Any message can be misunderstood, but an optimistic or desperate reader is particularly unlikely to understand a negative message. One of your purposes in a negative message is to close the door on the subject. You do not want to have to write a second letter saying that the real answer is *no*.

Alternatives

Giving the reader an alternative or a compromise, if one is available:

- Offers the reader another way to get what he or she wants
- Suggests that you really care about the reader and about helping to meet his or her needs
- Enables the reader to reestablish the psychological freedom you limited when you said no
- Allows you to end on a positive note and to present yourself and your organization as positive, friendly, and helpful

When you give an alternative, give readers all the information they need to act on it, but don't take the necessary steps. Let readers decide whether to try the alternative.

Negative messages limit the reader's freedom. People may respond to a limitation of freedom by asserting their freedom in some other arena. University of Kansas psychology professor Jack W. Brehm calls this phenomenon **psychological reactance.**[1] Psychological reactance is at work when a customer who has been denied credit no longer buys even on a cash basis or a subordinate who has been passed over for a promotion gets back at the company by deliberately doing a poor job.

Figure 11.3

A Refusal with an Alternative

"Serving the needs of Canada since 1890"
1800 Sandringham Way · Calgary, AB T3K 3V7· 403·555·7800 · Fax:

April 27, 2002

Mr. Marco Novelli
Canton Corporation
319 Sweetwater Bay
Winnipeg, MB R2J 3G4

Subject: Bid Number 5853, Part Number D-40040

Dear Mr. Moody:

Buffer   Thank you for requesting our quotation on your Part No. D-40040.

Reason   Your blueprints call for flame-cut rings 1/2" thick A516 grade 70. To use that grade, we'd have to grind down from 1" thick material. However, if you can use A515 grade 70, which we stock in 1/2" thick, you can cut the price by more than half.

Quantity	Description	Gross Weight	Price/Each
75	Rings Drawing D-40040, A516 Grade 70 1" thick x 6" O.D. x 2.8" I.D. ground to .5" thick.	12 lbs.	$15.08
75	Rings Drawing D-40040, A515 Grade 70 1/2" thick x 6" O.D. x 2.8" I.D.	6 lbs.	$6.91

Alternative (Depending on circumstances, different alternatives may exist.)

If you can use A515 grade 70, let me know.   *Leaves decision up to reader to re-establish psychological freedom*

Sincerely,

Valerie Prynne

Valerie Prynne
VP:wc

An alternative allows the reader to react in a way that doesn't hurt you. By letting readers decide for themselves whether they want the alternative, you allow them to reestablish their sense of psychological freedom.

The specific alternative will vary depending on the circumstances. In Figure 11.3, the company is unwilling to quote a price on an item on which it cannot be competitive. In different circumstances, the writer might offer different alternatives.

Endings

If you have a good alternative, refer to it in your ending: "Let me know if you can use A515 grade 70."

The best endings look to the future, as in this letter refusing to continue a charge account for a customer who has moved.

> Wherever you have your account, you'll continue to get all the service you've learned to expect from CHARGE-ALL, and the convenience of charging items at over a thousand ValuDrugs stores, in Canada —and in Halifax, too, whenever you come back to visit!

To maintain goodwill and retain a positive business relationship, end sincerely:

> Please call me at (403) 727-7700 if you need further clarification.

Avoid endings that seem insincere.

> We are happy to have been of service, and should we be able to assist you in the future, please contact us.

This ending lacks you-attitude and would not be good even in a positive message. In a situation where the company has just refused to help, it's likely to sound sarcastic or mean.

Giving Bad News to Superiors

Your superior expects you to solve minor problems by yourself. But sometimes, solving a problem requires more authority or resources than you have. When you give bad news to a superior, recommend a way to deal with the problem. Turn the negative message into a persuasive one.

1. **Describe the problem.** Tell what's wrong, clearly and unemotionally.
2. **Tell how it happened.** Provide the background. What underlying factors led to this specific problem?

3. **Describe the options for fixing it.** If one option is clearly best, you may need to discuss only one. But if the reader will think of other options, or if different people will judge the options differently, describe all the options, giving their advantages and disadvantages.
4. **Recommend a solution and ask for action.** Ask for approval so that you can go ahead to make the necessary changes to fix the problem.

Figure 11.4 summarizes the pattern.

Giving Bad News to Peers and Subordinates

When sending serious bad news to peers and subordinates, use a variation of the pattern to superiors:

1. **Describe the problem.** Tell what's wrong, clearly, and unemotionally.
2. **Present an alternative or compromise, if one is available.** An alternative gives readers another way to get what they want and also suggests that you care about readers and helping them meet their needs.
3. **If possible, ask for input or action.** People in the audience may be able to suggest solutions. And workers who help make a decision are far more likely to accept the consequences.

Figure 11.5 summarizes this pattern.

No serious negative (such as being downsized or laid off) should come as a complete surprise. Managers can prepare for possible negatives by giving full information as it becomes available. It is also possible to let the people who will be affected by a decision participate in setting the criteria. Someone who has bought into the criteria for awarding cash for suggestions or retaining workers is more likely to accept decisions using such criteria. And in some cases, the synergism of groups may make possible ideas that management didn't think of or rejected as "unacceptable." Some workplaces, for example, might decide to reduce everyone's pay slightly rather than laying off some individuals. To avoid firing workers during a recession, Scherer Brothers Lumber in Minneapolis, Minnesota, saved money by temporarily cutting top officers' pay 25 percent, eliminating fresh flowers on receptionists' desks, and no longer buying professional sports tickets.[2]

When the bad news is less serious, as in Figure 11.6, use the bad news organizational pattern (buffer, explanation, bad news, positive ending) unless your knowledge of the reader(s) suggests that another pattern will be more effective.

For memos, the context of communication is crucial. The reader's reaction is influenced by the following factors:

- Do you and the reader have a good relationship?
- Does the organization treat people well?
- Have readers been warned of possible negatives?
- Have readers "bought into" the criteria for the decision?
- Do communications after the negative build goodwill?

Figure 11.4

How to Organize a Negative Memo to Your Superior

Figure 11.5

How to Organize a Negative Memo to Peers or Subordinates

Instant Replay

Organizing Bad News to Peers and Subordinates

1. Describe the problem
2. Present an alternative or compromise, if one is available
3. If possible, ask for input or action

Figure 11.6

A Negative Memo to Subordinates

Memo

Brampton Board of Trade
Peel County, Brampton, ON

Date: January 10, 2001

To: All Employees

From: Floyd E. Loer, Dorothy A. Walters, and Stewart Mattson

Subject: Accounting for Work Missed Due to Bad Weather

Reason

As you know, our office is always open for our customers, whatever the weather. Employees who missed work during the snowstorm last week may count the absence as vacation, sick day(s), or personal day(s).

Refusal, stated as positively as possible

Hourly workers who missed less than a day have the option of taking the missed time as vacation, sick, or personal hours or of being paid only for the hours they worked.

One small positive

Approval of vacation or personal days will be automatic; the normal requirement of giving at least 24 hours' notice is waived.

Goodwill ending

Thanks for all the efforts you have made to continue giving our customers the best possible service during one of the snowiest winters on record.

What are the most common kinds of negative messages?

Rejections and refusals, disciplinary notices, negative performance appraisals, and layoffs and firings.

Three of the most difficult kinds of negative messages to write are rejections and refusals, disciplinary notices and negative performance appraisals, and layoffs and firings.

Rejections and Refusals

When you refuse requests, try to use a buffer. Give an alternative if one is available. For example, if you are denying credit, it may still be possible for the reader to put an expensive item on layaway.

Politeness and length help. An experiment using a denial of additional insurance found that subjects preferred a rejection letter that was longer, more tactful, and more personal. The preferred letter started with a buffer, used a good reason for the refusal, and offered sales promotion in the last paragraph.[3]

Since English-speaking Canadians and Canadian immigrants from high-context cultures (Chinese, Japanese, Indian, Pakistan) value courtesy, they would prefer this organizational structure.[4]

When you refuse requests within your organization, use your knowledge of the organization's culture and of the specific individual to craft your message. In some organizations, it may be appropriate to use company slogans, offer whatever help already established departments can give, and refer to the individual's good work. In less personal organizations, a simple negative without embellishment may be more appropriate.

Disciplinary Notices and Negative Performance Appraisals

Present disciplinary notices and negative performance appraisals directly, with no buffer. A buffer might encourage the recipient to minimize the message's importance—and might even become evidence in a court case that the employee had not been told to shape up "or else." Cite quantifiable observations of the employee's behaviour, rather than generalizations or inferences based on it. If an employee is disciplined by being laid off without pay, specify when the employee is to return.

Performance appraisals are discussed in detail in ◀▶ Module 12 on persuasive messages. Performance appraisals will be positive when they are designed to help a good employee improve. But when an employee violates a company rule or fails to improve after repeated appraisals, the company may discipline the employee or build a dossier to support firing him or her.

Layoffs and Firings

Information about layoffs and firings is normally delivered orally but accompanied by a written statement explaining severance pay or unemployment benefits that may be available. The written statement should start either with the reason or with the decision itself. A buffer would not be appropriate.

If a company is in financial trouble, management needs to communicate the problem clearly long before it is necessary to lay anyone off. Sharing information and enlisting everyone's help in finding solutions may make it possible to save jobs. Sharing information also means that layoff notices, if they become necessary, will be a formality; they should not be new information to employees.

Before you fire someone, double-check the facts. Make sure that the employee has been told about the problem and that he or she will be fired if the problem is not corrected. Give the employee the real reason for the firing. Offering a face-saving reason unrelated to poor performance can create legal liabilities. But avoid broadcasting the reason to other people: to do so can leave the company liable to a defamation suit.[5]

Site *to* **See**

Go to
http://www.mapnp.
org/library/commskls
/cmm_writ.htm
The Business Writer's Free Library, a rich resource, gives specific guidelines for writing bad news letters.

http://www.work91
1.com/articles/posla
n.htm
This Web site offers tips on persuading with positive language.

Figure 11.7
PAIBOC Questions for Analysis

PAIBOC

Use the PAIBOC questions to analyze business communication problems:

P   What are your **purposes** in writing?

A   Who is (are) your **audience(s)**? How do members of your audience differ? What characteristics are relevant to this particular message?

I   What **information** must your message include?

B   What reasons or reader **benefits** can you use to support your position?

O   What **objection(s)** can you expect your reader(s) to have? What negative elements of your message must you de-emphasize or overcome?

C   How will the **context** affect reader response? Think about your relationship to the reader, morale in the organization, the economy, the time of year, and any special circumstances.

How can PAIBOC help me write negative messages?

The PAIBOC questions help you examine the points your message should include.

Before you tackle the assignments for this module, examine the following problem. As in Module 10, the PAIBOC questions probe the basic points required for a solution. Study the two sample solutions to see what makes one unacceptable and the other one good.[6] The checklist at the end of the module in Figure 11.9 can help you evaluate a draft.

Problem

You're director of employee benefits for a Fortune 500 company. Today, you received the following memo:

From: Michelle Jagtiani

Subject: Getting My Retirement Benefits

Next Friday will be my last day here. I am leaving [name of company] to take a position at another firm.

Please process a cheque for my retirement benefits, including both the deductions from my salary and the company's contributions for the last three and a half years. I would like to receive the cheque by next Friday if possible.

You have bad news for Michelle. Although the company does contribute an amount to the retirement fund equal to the amount deducted for retirement from the employee's paycheque, employees who leave with less than five years of employment get only their own contributions. Michelle will get back only the money that has been deducted from her own pay, plus 4 percent interest compounded quarterly. Her payments and interest come to just over $17,200; the amount could be higher depending on the amount of her last paycheque, which will include compensation for any unused vacation days and sick leave. Furthermore, since the amounts deducted were not considered taxable income, she will have to pay income tax on the money she will receive.

You cannot process the cheque until after her resignation is effective, so you will mail it to her. You have her home address on file; if she's moving, she needs to let you know where to send the cheque. Processing the cheque may take two to three weeks.

Write a memo to Michelle.

Analysis of the Problem

P   What are your **purposes** in writing or speaking?

To tell her that she will get only her own contributions, plus 4 percent interest compounded quarterly; that the cheque will be mailed to her home address two to three weeks after her last day on the job; and that the money will be taxable as income.
   To build goodwill so that she feels that she has been treated fairly and consistently. To minimize negative feelings she may have.
   To close the door on this subject.

A   Who is (are) your **audience(s)**? How do the members of your audience differ from each other? What characteristics are relevant to this particular message?

   Michelle Jagtiani. Unless she's a personal friend, I probably wouldn't know why she's leaving and where she's going.
   There's a lot I don't know. She may or may not know much about taxes; she may or may not be able to take advantage of tax-reduction strategies. I can't assume the answers because I wouldn't have them in real life.

I   What **information** must your message include?

   When the cheque will come. The facts that the cheque will be based on her contributions, not her employer's, and that the money will be taxable income. How lump-sum retirement benefits are calculated. The fact that we have her current address on file but need a new address if she's moving.

B   What reasons or reader **benefits** can you use to support your position?

   Giving the amount currently in her account may make her feel that she is getting a significant sum of money. Suggesting someone who can give free tax advice (if the company offers this as a fringe benefit) reminds her of the benefits of working with the company. Wishing her luck with her new job is a nice touch.

O   What **objections** can you expect your reader(s) to have? What negative elements of your message must you de-emphasize or overcome?

   She is getting about half the amount she expected, since she gets no matching funds.
   She might have been able to earn more than 4 percent interest if she had invested the money herself. Depending on her personal tax situation she may pay more tax on the money as a lump sum than would have been due had she paid it each year as she earned the money.

C   How will the **context** affect the reader's response? Think about your relationship to the reader, morale in the organization, the economy, the time of year, and any special circumstances.

   The stock market has been doing well; 4 percent interest is not going to seem high. However, since the economy is flagging, she may be worried about her financial position.

Figure 11.8

An Unacceptable Solution to the Sample Problem

April 20, 2002

To: Michelle Jagtiani

From   Lisa Niaz   *LN*

Subject   Denial of Matching Funds

Give reason before refusal   You cannot receive a cheque the last day of work and you will get only your own contributions, not a matching sum from the company, because you have not worked for the company for at least five full years.

Better to be specific

This is lifted straight from the problem. The language in problems is often negative and stuffy; information is disorganized.

Your payments and interest come to just over $17,200; the amount could be higher depending on the amount of your last paycheck, which will include compensation for any unused vacation days and sick leave. Furthermore, since the amounts deducted were not considered taxable income, you will have to pay income tax on the money you receive.

The cheque will be sent to your home address. If the address we have on file is incorrect, please correct it so that your check is not delayed.   *Negative*

Think about the situation and use your own words to create a satisfactory message.

How will reader know what you have on file? Better to give current address as you have it.

Discussion of the Sample Solutions

The solution in Figure 11.8 is not acceptable. The subject line gives a bald negative with no reason or alternative. The first sentence has a condescending tone that is particularly offensive in negative messages. The last sentence focusses on what is being taken away rather than what remains. Paragraph 2 lacks you-attitude and is vague. The memo ends with a negative. There is nothing anywhere in the memo to build goodwill.

The solution in Figure 11.9, in contrast, is very good. The policy serves as a buffer and explanation. The negative is stated clearly but is buried in the paragraph to avoid overemphasizing it. The paragraph ends on a positive note by specifying the amount in the account and the fact that the sum might be even higher.

Figure 11.9

A Good Solution to the Sample Problem

April 20, 2002

To: Michelle Jagtiani

From: Lisa Niaz *LN*

Subject: Receiving Employee Contributions from Retirement Accounts

Good to state reason in third-person to deemphasize negative.

Employees who leave the company with at least five full years of employment are entitled both to the company contributions and the retirement benefit paycheque deductions contributed to retirement accounts. Those employees who leave the company with less than five years of employment will receive the employee paycheque contributions made to their retirement accounts.

Good to be specific

You now have $17,240.62 in your account which includes 4% interest compounded quarterly. The amount you receive could be even higher since you will also receive payment for any unused sick leave and vacation days.

Good to show how company can help

Because you now have access to the account, the amount you receive will be considered taxable income. Beth Jordan in Employee Financial Services can give you information about possible tax deductions and financial investments which can reduce your income taxes.

Good to be specific

The cheque will be sent to your home address on May 16. The address we have on file is 2724 Merriman Road, Kingston, ON K7L 3N7. If your address changes, please let us know so you can receive your cheque promptly.

Positive

Good luck with your new job!

Forward-looking

Paragraph 3 contains the additional negative information that the amount will be taxable but offers the alternative that it may be possible to reduce taxes. The writer builds goodwill by suggesting a specific person the reader could contact.

Paragraph 4 tells the reader what address is in the company files (Michelle may not know whether the files are up to date), asks that she update it if necessary, and ends with the reader's concern: getting her check promptly.

The final paragraph ends on a positive note. This generalized goodwill is appropriate when the writer does not know the reader well.

Figure 11.10

Checklist for Negative Messages

☐ Is the subject line appropriate?
☐ If a buffer is used, does it avoid suggesting either a positive or a negative response?
☐ Is the reason presented before the refusal? Is the reason relevant to the reader?
☐ Is the negative information clear?
☐ Is an alternative given if a good one is available? Does the message provide all the information needed to act on the alternative but leave the choice up to the reader?
☐ Does the last paragraph avoid repeating the negative information?
☐ Is tone acceptable—not defensive, but not cold, preachy, or arrogant either?

And, for all messages, not just negative ones,
☐ Does the message use you-attitude and positive emphasis?
☐ Is the style easy to read and friendly?
☐ Is the visual design of the message inviting?
☐ Is the format correct?
☐ Does the message use standard grammar? Is it free from typos?

Originality in a negative message may come from
☐ An effective buffer, if one is appropriate.
☐ A clear, complete statement of the reason for the refusal.
☐ A good alternative, clearly presented, which shows that you're thinking about what the reader really needs.
☐ Adding details that show you're thinking about a specific organization and the specific people in that organization.

Employability Skills 2000+ Checklist for Negative Messages

In this module, the key skills from The Conference Board of Canada's Employability Skills 2000+ are:

Communicate

✔ write and speak so others pay attention and understand
✔ share information using a range of information and communications technologies (e.g., voice, email, computers)
✔ use relevant scientific, technological, and mathematical knowledge and skills to explain or clarify ideas

Manage Information

✔ locate, gather, and organize information using appropriate technology and information systems

Think & Solve Problems

✔ assess situations and identify problems
✔ seek different points of view and evaluate them based on facts
✔ recognize the human, interpersonal, technical, scientific, and mathematical dimensions of a problem
✔ identify the root cause of a problem
✔ be creative and innovative in exploring possible solutions
✔ readily use science, technology, and mathematics as ways to think, gain and share knowledge, solve problems and make decisions
✔ evaluate solutions to make recommendations or decisions

Review of Key Points

- Organize negative letters in this way:
  1. Begin with a buffer or neutral statement
  2. Give the reason for the refusal before the refusal itself
  3. Give the negative just once, clearly
  4. Present an alternative or compromise, if one is available
  5. End with a positive, forward-looking statement

- Organize negative memos to superiors in this way:
  1. Describe the problem
  2. Tell how it happened
  3. Describe the options for fixing it
  4. Recommend a solution and ask for action

- When you must pass along serious bad news to peers and subordinates, use a variation of the pattern to superiors:

1. Describe the problem
2. Present an alternative or compromise, if one is available
3. If possible, ask for input or action

- When the bad news is less serious, use the indirect pattern for negative letters unless your knowledge of the reader(s) suggests that another pattern will be more effective.

- A good explanation offers the reader reasons that make sense from his or her point of view. Give several reasons only if all are audience-relevant and are of comparable importance. Omit the reason for the refusal if it is weak or if it makes your organization look bad.

  - Giving the reader an alternative or a compromise

  - Offers the reader another way to get what he or she wants

  - Suggests that you really care about the reader and about helping to meet his or her needs

  - Enables the reader to reestablish the psychological freedom you limited when you said no

  - Allows you to end on a positive note and to present yourself and your organization as positive, friendly, and helpful

- People may respond to limits by striking out in some perhaps unacceptable way. This effort to reestablish freedom is called **psychological reactance**.

- When you give an alternative, give the reader all the information he or she needs to act on it, but don't take the necessary steps for the reader. Letting the reader decide whether to try the alternative allows the reader to reestablish a sense of psychological freedom.

- **A buffer** is a neutral or positive statement that allows you to delay the negative message. Buffers must put the reader in a good frame of mind, not give the bad news but not imply a positive answer either, and provide a natural transition to the body of the letter. Use a buffer when the reader values harmony or when the buffer serves a purpose in addition to simply delaying the negative.

- The kinds of statements most often used as buffers are (1) good news, (2) facts and chronologies of events, (3) references to enclosures, (4) thanks, and (5) statements of principle.

- Use the PAIBOC questions listed in Figure 11.7 (page 232) to examine the basic points needed for successful informative and positive messages.

Learning Applications

Questions for Comprehension

11.1 How should a negative letter to customers or clients be organized?

11.2 Why is giving an alternative or a compromise, if one exists, a good idea?

11.3 What are the most common types of buffers?

11.4 How should a negative memo to a superior be organized?

Questions for Critical Thinking

11.5 How do specific varieties of negative messages adapt the basic pattern?

11.6 How do you use positive emphasis in a negative message?

11.7 How do you decide whether to give the negative directly or to buffer it?

Questions for Building Skills

11.8 What skills have you read about in this module?

11.9 What skills are you practising in the assignments you're doing for this module?

11.10 How could you further develop the skills you're working on?

Exercises and Problems

11.11 Rejecting Employees' Suggestions

For years, businesses have had suggestion programs, rewarding employees for money-saving ideas. Now your city government has adopted such a program. But not all of the suggestions are adopted. Today, you need to send messages to the following people. Because their suggestions are being rejected, they will not get any cash award.

1. Diane Hilgers, secretary, Mayor's office. Suggestion: Charge for 911 calls. Reason for rejection: "This would be a public relations disaster. People call because they've got emergencies. We already charge for ambulance or paramedic trips; to charge just for the call will offend people. And it might not save money. It's a lot cheaper to prevent a burglary or murder than to track down the person afterwards—to say nothing of the trauma of the loss or death. Bad idea."

2. Steve Rieneke, building and grounds supervisor. Suggestion: Fire the city's public relations specialists. Reason for rejection: "Positive attitudes toward city workers and policies make the public more willing to support public programs and taxes. In the long run, we think this is money well spent."

3. Jose Rivera, Accountant I. Suggestion: Schedule city council meetings during the day to save on light bills and staff overtime. Reason for rejection: "Having the meetings in the evening enables more citizens to attend. People have to be able to comment. Open meetings are essential so that citizens don't feel that policies and taxes are being railroaded through."

Write the messages.

11.12 Telling the Boss about a Problem

In any organization, things sometimes go wrong. Tell your supervisor about a problem in your unit and recommend what should be done.

As Your Instructor Directs,

a. Prepare notes for a meeting with your supervisor

b. Write an email message to your supervisor

c. Write a memo to your supervisor

d. Give an oral presentation on the problem.

e. Write a memo to your instructor explaining the problem, the corporate culture, and the reasons for your solution

11.13 Telling Customers That Prices Are Going Up

From time to time, organizations raise prices or impose separate fees for services that were previously free. Think of an increase in the prices your customers pay.

As Your Instructor Directs,

a. Write a letter to customers, telling them about the new fees or higher prices.

b. Examine your organization's files for messages sent out the last time prices were raised. Are the messages effective? Why or why not? Include copies of the messages with your analysis of them.

11.14 Refusing a Gift

As the head of a charitable organization, you spend a lot of your time asking for money. But today, you're turning down a gift: a time-share condominium in Florida. Time-shares are so difficult to sell that regular real-estate agents do not list them. Places that list time-shares frequently charge an up-front fee (not just a commission, which is paid if and when the unit sells). If you accepted the gift, your organization would have to pay maintenance fees charged by the homeowners' association and taxes until the unit sold (if it sold). And you'd probably have to hire someone to check on the property occasionally, since the maintenance fee covers general building maintenance, not repairs for a specific unit. You don't want the expense and hassle of something that may or may not ever yield funds for your organization, so you're going to refuse the gift.

Write a letter to the would-be donors, Benjamin and Sarah Mellon, refusing the gift.

As Your Instructor Directs,

Write letters for one or more of the following situations.

a. Yours is a well-known national charity. You have never met the Mellons, but your records show that they have given small gifts (under $100) in three of the last five years.

b. Yours is a local religious organization; the Mellons are prominent members. They don't give much money, but they're active and faithful.

c. Yours is a local charitable organization that struggles to stay open. The Mellons are major contributors. Sarah Mellon served on your board of directors, in a term ending three years ago.

d. Yours is a national charity. No one in the office has ever heard of the Mellons. They haven't contributed in the last three years—your records don't go back further.

Hints:

- Choose a charitable organization you know something about.

- Give the real reason for the refusal. You would accept real estate that seemed easy to sell.

- In situations a to c above, thank the Mellons for their past support. Be specific about what they've done.

- Use a salutation and complimentary close that are appropriate to the situation.

- In all of the situations, you want to encourage the donor to give other (more liquid) gifts to you in the future. Tell about upcoming opportunities for giving.

11.15 Refusing to Participate on a Panel

As a prominent executive, you get many requests to appear before various groups. Today, you've received a request to participate in a panel of three to five professionals who will talk about "Succeeding in the Real World." The session will run from 2:00 to 5:00 P.M. of the second Sunday of next month.

You're trying to cut back on outside commitments. Work continues to take much of your time; you have major obligations in a volunteer organization; and you want some time for yourself and your family. This request does not fit your priorities.

Decline the invitation.

As Your Instructor Directs,

Assume that the request is from

a. A college business honour society that expects 250 students at the session

b. The youth group at the church, synagogue, temple, or mosque you attend

c. The Chinese Student Association at the local college or university

11.16   Announcing Cost-Savings Measures

Your company has to cut costs but would prefer to avoid laying off workers. Therefore, you have adopted the following money-saving ideas. Some can be implemented immediately; some will be implemented at renewal dates. The company will no longer pay for

- Flowers at the receptionist's desk and in executive offices
- Skyboxes for professional sporting events
- Employees' dues for professional and trade organizations
- Liquor at business meals

Only essential business travel will be approved. The company will pay only for the lowest cost of air travel (coach, reservation 7 to 14 days in advance, stay over Saturday night).

The company will no longer buy tables or blocks of tickets for charitable events and will not make any cash donations to charity until money is less tight.

Counters will be put on the photocopiers. People must have access numbers to make photocopies; personal photocopies will cost $.10 a page.

As the chief financial officer, write a memo to all employees, explaining the changes.

11.17   Closing Bill-Payment Offices

For many years, Caraquet Public Utilities Commission had five office locations where people could take their payments. On the first of the month following next month, you're closing these offices. On that date, 100 local merchants, such as grocers, will begin to accept utility payments. Closing the

freestanding offices will save your municipality almost $1 million a year. Customers will still be able to mail in payments or have them deducted automatically from their paycheques.

Write a notice that can be inserted in utility bills this month and next month.

11.18   Giving a Customer Less Credit Than She Wants

Yang-Ming Lee applied for your Visa card, asking for a credit limit of $15,000 and a separate card for her husband, Chad Hoang. You've checked the credit references, and they're good enough to merit granting a credit card. But you generally give new customers only a $7,500 limit, even when the family income is very high, as it is in this case. You might make an exception if your bank

had a previous relationship with the client, but no such relationship exists here. While you have no set policy for reviewing and raising credit limits, normally you would expect at least six months of paying the minimum amount promptly.

Write a letter to Ms. Lee, granting her a credit card with a $7,500 limit.

11.19   Rejecting a Member's Request

All non-supervisory workers in your province are union members. As a paid staff person for the union, you spend about a third of your

time writing and editing the monthly magazine, *Public [Your Province] Employee*. You receive this letter:

Dear Editor:

Every month, we get two copies of the union magazine—one addressed to me, one to my husband. We have different last names, so your computer may not realize that we're connected, but we are, and we don't need two copies. Sending just one copy will save printing and postage costs and reduce environmental waste. My name is Dorothy Livingston; my husband is Eric Beamer. Please combine our listings to send just one copy.

Sincerely,

Dorothy Livingston

As it happens, a couple of years ago you investigated possible savings of sending just one mailing to couples who both work for the province. Sophisticated computerized merge/purge programs to eliminate duplicates are far too expensive for the union's tight budget. And going through the mailing list manually to locate and change duplications would cost more than would be saved in postage. Printing costs wouldn't necessarily drop either, since it actually costs less for each copy to print big runs.

But you want to build goodwill—both to this writer and for the union in general. Extra copies of the magazine (whether a double mailing or simply a copy someone is finished with) could be given to a non-member or taken to a doctor's or dentist's waiting room or a barber or beauty shop. Such sharing would help spread public support for the union and state workers.

Write a letter to Ms. Livingston, explaining why you can't combine mailings.

Polishing Your Prose

Parallel Structure

Use **parallel structure** in lists, headings, and subheadings in documents by using the same grammatical form for ideas that have the same relationship in your sentence.

Not parallel: Good reports are factual, logical, and demonstrate clarity.

It may be easier to see faulty parallelism by listing parts that need to be parallel. Check to make sure each component fits with the words that introduce the list.

Not parallel: Good reports are
Factual
Logical
Demonstrate clarity

Parallel: Good reports are
Factual
Logical
Clear

Make sure all of the list is horizontal or vertical. Don't start a list horizontally and finish it vertically.

Incorrect: As department manager, I supervised eight employees.
• Wrote the department budget.
• Presented our sales strategy to the Board of Directors.

Correct: As department manager, I supervised eight employees, wrote the department budget, and presented our sales strategy to the Board of Directors.

Also correct: As department manager, I
• Supervised eight employees.
• Wrote the department budget.
• Presented our sales strategy to the Board of Directors.

Headings must be parallel throughout the document, but subheads need only be parallel to other subheads in the same section.

Not parallel: Should Ogden Industries Purchase Blue Chip International in 2002?
Short-Term Costs
What Are Long-Term Gains?

Parallel: Should Ogden Industries Purchase Blue Chip International in 2002?
Short-Term Costs
Long-Term Gains

In addition to grammatical parallelism, also check your sentences for logical parallelism.

Incorrect: The group ranges from males and females to people in their 20s, 30s, and 40s.

Better: We interviewed men and women ranging in age from 20 to 50.

Gender is one category; age is another.

Exercises
Rewrite the following sentences or headings to make them parallel.

1. Last week, Alain and Rochelle flew to Toronto, Montréal, Québec City, and the capital of the State of Michigan.

2. Ask Ms. Liken, Mr. Fitzgerald, Bill Anderson, and Professor Timmons to join us for the meeting.

3. To ship a package
   1. Fill out an address form.
   2. Specify on the form how the package should be sent.
   3. If you want to send a package by overnight mail, your supervisor must initial the appropriate box on the address form.

4. Make sure benefits announcements get routed to managers, supervisors, and the folks in the Human Resources Department.

5. Appointments can be scheduled in 5-minute, 10-minute, quarter-hour, or 20-minute intervals.

6. The project's fixed costs include material, salaries, advertising, bonus packages for anyone who goes above and beyond the call of duty, and the cost of travel to different cities.

7. This report discusses
   Why We Should Upgrade Capital Equipment
   Why We Should Increase Staff by 25 percent
   The Benefits of Decreasing Employee Turnover
   The Importance of Identifying New Product Markets

8. The selection committee reviews each job applicant based on education, experience, extracurricular activities, the awards the employee has received, and the strength of the applicant's personal statement.

9. Use the telephone to answer customer questions, email to send order confirmations, and take orders using our Web page.

10. Each agency should estimate
    Annual Costs
    Costs Per Month
       Salaries
       New Equipment Costs
       How Much You Need in a Reserve Fund for Unexpected Expenses

Check your answers to the odd-numbered exercises on page 633.

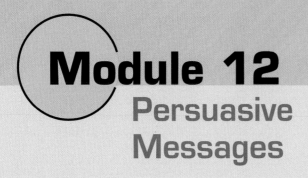

Module 12
Persuasive Messages

Topics

- What is the best persuasive strategy?

- What's the best subject line for a persuasive message?

- How should I organize persuasive messages?

- How do I identify and overcome objections?

- What other techniques can make my messages more persuasive?

- What kinds of persuasive messages am I likely to write?

- How can PAIBOC help me write persuasive messages?

Review of Key Points

Learning Applications

Polishing Your Prose: Narrative Voice

Learning Focus

After reading and applying the information in Module 12, you'll be able to demonstrate

Knowledge of
- Direct and indirect persuasion organization
- Persuasive appeals
- Narrative voice

Skills to
- Choose and implement a persuasive strategy
- Write effective subject lines for persuasive messages
- Organize persuasive messages
- Identify and overcome objections
- Write common kinds of persuasive messages
- Continue to analyze business communication situations

"Great communication requires taking the time to consider the needs of the donors..."

What are key aspects of a persuasive strategy? Helen Connell, executive director of the United Way of London and Middlesex, discusses her experience in the non-profit sector. Helen was the former editor of The London Free Press and remains a columnist with the paper. Besides her journalism training, Helen also has an M.B.A from the Richard Ivey School of Business.

Competition. Continuous improvement. Change. Customer driven.

Today these catch phrases are as true for non-profits as they are for corporate Canada, and nowhere do these words apply more than in marketing and communications strategies with donors.

Donors are the life-blood for non-profit organizations, but there are so many voices asking for money, it's easy to get lost in the din. This has prodded many non-profits to become far more donor focussed in their communications.

Instead of beginning with the writer-focussed "What do I want to tell the donors?" good communication starts with the reader-focussed question, "What kinds of information do donors require to make decisions and what format would be best suited to their needs?"

That challenge is magnified for United Way since donors come from all walks of life, including corporations and unions, entrepreneurs, homemakers, students, and retirees. Donations range from $10 a year to more than $100,000 a year. Communications methods differ with each donation but not the need to treat all donors with respect, honesty, and sincerity.

Cost control takes on new meaning for United Way. People who give money to assist those in poverty are particularly sensitive as to how donations are used. The cost of every piece of correspondence not paid through sponsors comes out of administrative costs.

The process begins by listening to people knowledgeable about community needs and about their perception of United Way's role in meeting those needs. We also assess annually where we were last year and where we want to be next year.

Then a "case for support" is created. This is an internal document that includes a mission and vision statement and details all the services and programs funded or supported in other ways. While time-consuming, it keeps the organization focussed, ensuring consistent messages. It also provides a handy reference source to staff and volunteers who require information for other communications or public speaking.

Communication vehicles need to be respectful of donors' time. The shift is away from long, narrative letters to brief statements highlighted by bullets. This crisper format requires a skilled writer to carry it off well but it stands a much better chance of being read.

Another major shift among non-profits is the move away from harping primarily on needs in the community to focussing on outcomes and results. Today's donors are looking to invest their hard-earned money in making a real difference in the lives of people in the community. While we still outline need in the community, we must now also speak clearly about our accomplishments in the past and about results from their continued support.

Great communication requires taking the time to consider the needs of the donors, as much as those of your organization. While a solid strategy is critical, it must also remain flexible enough to change quickly with the needs of donors. When communication is done well, you'll see the results in better donor relationships.

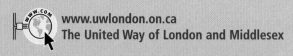

www.uwlondon.on.ca
The United Way of London and Middlesex

Site *to* **See**

Go to
http://www.as.wvu.
edu/~sbb/comm221/
primer.htm

This site is "Steve's
Primer of Practical
Persuasion and
Influence."

Site *to* **See**

Go to
http://www.class.
ewu.edu/class/comp
/201ethos.htm

This Web page
describes the four
significant appeals.

FYI

In 2000, Canadians'
contributions to
the annual Terry
Fox Run accounted
for 15 million of
the 21 million
raised worldwide.

Source: The Terry Fox
Foundation Web site,
visited July 9, 2001;
http://www.terryfoxrun.or
g/main/site_map.htm

In our knowledge-based economy, where brains are capital, businesses depend on persuasion and "buy-in" to get quality work done. You can command people to make widgets. You can't command knowledge workers to be creative. And even if you're making widgets, just going through the motions isn't enough. You want people to make high-quality widgets, while reducing scrap and other costs. Internal commitment is needed to make that happen.

External motivation doesn't last. Some people will buy a certain brand of pizza if they have a "2 for 1" coupon. But if the coupon expires, or if another company offers the same deal, customers may leave. In contrast, if customers like your pizza better—in other words, if they are motivated internally to choose it—then you may keep your customers even if another company comes in with a lower price.

In general, people begin to change attitudes and behaviours when they believe both the message and the messenger. Your audience will attend to your message if they perceive you to be a trustworthy or *credible* person; they will act on your message if the *facts*, and *the way* you present those facts appeal to their deepest values and beliefs. Aristotle identified these rhetorical (persuasive) fundamentals as *ethos*, or the audience's perception of the speaker/writer's trustworthiness, *pathos* or the message's appeal to the audience emotions, and *logos*, the message's rational or logical appeal.

Because all successful communication contains a persuasive element, the ability to persuade others is a fundamental interpersonal leadership skill. Knowing the elements of persuasion and your audience's needs enables you to convince others effectively.

Persuasive messages include

- Orders and requests
- Proposals and recommendations
- Sales and fund-raising letters
- Job application letters
- Reports, if they recommend action
- Efforts to change people's behaviour, such as collection letters, criticisms or performance appraisals where you want the subordinate to improve behaviour, and public-service ads designed to reduce drunken driving, drug use, and so on

All persuasive messages have several purposes.

Primary Purposes:

- To have the reader act
- To provide enough information so that the reader knows exactly what to do
- To overcome any objections that might prevent or delay action

Secondary Purposes:

- To build a good image of the writer
- To build a good image of the writer's organization
- To cement a good relationship between the writer and reader
- To reduce or eliminate future correspondence on the same subject so the message doesn't create more work for the writer

What is the best persuasive strategy?

It depends on how much and what kinds of resistance you expect.

Four basic short-term strategies exist: direct request, problem-solving persuasion, sales,[1] and reward and punishment. This book will focus on the first two strategies. Rewards and punishment have limited use, in part because they don't produce permanent change and because they produce psychological reactance (◀▶ p. 221). To effect a major change, no single message will work, as anti-smoking lobbyists are well aware. To change attitudes and behaviours, you will need a campaign with a series of messages, preferably from a variety of sources.

Your organizational pattern is part of your message's persuasive element, because specific patterns meet the audience's expectations, and are, therefore, logically and emotionally appealing.

Use the **direct (deductive or good news) request pattern** when

- The audience will do as you ask without any resistance
- You need a response only from the people who are willing to act
- The audience is busy and may not read all the messages received
- Your organization's culture prefers direct requests

Use the **indirect (problem-solving, inductive, bad news) pattern** when

- The audience is likely to object to doing as you ask
- You need action from everyone
- You trust the audience to read the entire message
- You expect logic to be more important than emotion in the decision

Of course, to make the best persuasive choices, you need to apply PAIBOC analysis (see Figure 12.1), to clarify your purpose and the needs of your audience.

Your message strategy must also conform to the values and norms of your corporate culture. A persuasive strategy that works in one organization may be unacceptable elsewhere.

Corporate culture (◀▶ p. 39), conveyed through multiple spoken and unspoken messages, is learned by imitation and observation. Observe the style of powerful people in your organization: when you show a draft to your boss, are you told to tone down your statements or to make them stronger? Role models and advice are two of the ways organizations communicate their cultures to newcomers.

Different ethnic and national cultures also have different preferences for gaining compliance. Canada's international reputation as a welcoming nation of courteous peacekeepers is reflected in English Canadians cultural preference for indirect requests. Canadian newcomers emigrating from Southeast Asia, India, Pakistan, and the Philippines also communicate using indirect requests; high context cultures see direct requests as rude and aggressive.

Figure 12.1
PAIBOC Questions for Analysis

PAIBOC

Use the PAIBOC questions to analyze business communication problems:

P   What are your purposes in writing?

A   Who is (are) your audience(s)? How do members of your audience differ? What characteristics are relevant to this particular message?

I   What information must your message include?

B   What reasons or reader benefits can you use to support your position?

O   What objection(s) can you expect your reader(s) to have? What negative elements of your message must you de-emphasize or overcome?

C   How will the context affect reader response? Think about your relationship to the reader, morale in the organization, the economy, the time of year, and any special circumstances.

FYI

Drawing and keeping good people tops the priority list of Canada's CEOs. Perhaps this focus on human resource management explains why information technology workers feel they are better treated than do employees in other sectors. IT employees were more likely than others to agree that they worked in exciting environments, offered fair salaries, bonuses and reward incentives, had opportunities for promotion, kept in the know by management, and offered benefits to help them do the job. As a result, IT employees agreed, they felt pride in their work, more personally committed to the company, and more convinced that their employer was committed to their personal success.

Sources: "Canadian Business Corporate Priorities in the New Economy," *Angus Reid Report*, March/April 2000, Volume 15, Number 2 p. 31–34; "Vive la tech difference," Managing + Careers, *The Globe and Mail*, May 16, 2001, M1.

Surrey Metro Savings Credit Union in B.C. proudly placed fifth in the "35 best companies to work for in Canada" survey featured in the *Report on Business* magazine. The company recognizes employees' involvement in their communities and contributes generously to local organizations—resulting in a committed, proud, and enthusiastic team. See http: www.metrosavings.com/ for more information.

What's the best subject line for a persuasive message?

For direct requests, use the request, the topic, or a question.

For problem-solving messages, use a directed subject line or a reader benefit.

In a direct request, put the request, the topic of the request, or a question in the subject line.

> Subject: Request for Updated Software
>
> My copy of HomeNet does not accept the aliases for Magnus accounts.

Subject: Status of Account #3548-003

Please get me the following information about account #3548-003.

Subject: Do We Need an Additional Training Session in October?

The two training sessions scheduled for October will accommodate 40 people. Last month, you said that 57 new staff accountants had been hired. Should we schedule an additional training session in October? Or can the new hires wait until the next regularly scheduled session in February?

When you have a reluctant reader, putting the request in the subject line just gets a quick *no* before you've had a chance to give all your arguments. One option is to use a **directed subject line** that makes your stance on the issue clear.[2] In the following examples, the first is the most neutral. The remaining two increasingly reveal the writer's preference.

Subject: A Proposal to Change the Formula for Calculating Retirees' Benefits

Subject: Arguments for Expanding the Bramalea Plant

Subject: Why Cassano's Should Close Its West Side Store

Another option is to use common ground or a reader benefit—something that shows readers that this message will help them.

Subject: Reducing Energy Costs in the Office

Energy costs in our office have risen 12 percent in the last three years, even though the cost of gas has fallen and the cost of electricity has risen only 5 percent.

Although your first paragraph may be negative in a problem-solving message, your subject line should be neutral or positive, to show that you are solving a problem, not just reporting one.

Both directed subject lines and benefit subject lines can also be used as report titles.

Figure 12.2

How to Organize a Direct Request

> Request for Action
>
> Details
>
> Request for Action

How should I organize persuasive messages?

In direct requests, start with the request.

In a problem-solving message, start with the problem you share.

Start with the request only when you anticipate ready agreement, when you fear that a busy reader may not read a message whose relevance isn't clear, or when your organization's culture prefers direct requests.

Writing Direct Requests

When you expect quick agreement, save the reader's time by presenting the request directly.

1. **Consider asking immediately for the information or service you want.** Delay the request if it seems too abrupt or if you have several purposes in the message.

2. **Give readers all the information and details they will need to act on your request.** Number your questions or set them off with bullets so the reader can check to see that all of them have been answered.

   In a claim (where a product is under warranty or a shipment was defective), explain the circumstances so that the reader knows what happened. Be sure to include all the relevant details: date of purchase, model or invoice number, and so on.

   In more complicated direct requests, anticipate possible responses. Suppose you're asking for information about equipment meeting certain specifications. Explain which criteria are most important so that the reader can recommend an alternative if no single product meets all your needs. You may also want to tell the reader what your price constraints are and ask whether the item is in stock or must be special ordered.

3. **Ask for the action you want.** Do you want a cheque? A replacement? A catalogue? Answers to your questions? If you need an answer by a certain time, say so. If possible, show the reader why the time limit is necessary.

Figure 12.2 summarizes this pattern. Figure 12.3 on the next page, illustrates the pattern. Note that direct requests do not contain reader benefits and do not need to overcome objections: they simply ask for what is needed.

Direct requests should be direct. Don't make the reader guess what you want.

Indirect request: Is there a newer version of the 2001 *Accounting Reference Manual?*

Direct request: If there is a newer version of the 2001 *Accounting Reference Manual*, please send it to me.

In some direct requests, your combination of purposes may suggest a different organization. For example, in a letter asking an employer to reimburse you for expenses after a job interview, you'd want to thank your hosts for their hospitality and cement the good impression you made at the interview. To do that, you'd spend the first two paragraphs talking about the trip and the interview. Only in the last third of the letter (or even in the postscript) would you put your request for reimbursement.

Figure 12.3
A Direct Request

---

the Bay   la Baie

Eva Pavlinic
532 Heath Street East
TORONTO, ON M5W 3M1

Card Number: 503 913 248 1
Balance: $36.28   *Request topic in subject line*
Payment Required: $33.00

Dear Ms. Eva Pavlinic,
                                          Courteous opening saves
                                             reader's face

Perhaps you missed making your recent payment because the balance on your account
is so small? It is not difficult to do and many of us overlook small balance accounts.

However, we would appreciate it if you would take a few minutes and mail us your   *Ask for actions.*
cheque for $33.00.   *Make action*
                                                                                      easy.

If your payment has already been made, thank you. *Positive, friendly*
                                                        close

Credit Department
Tel: 416-335-3888

Similarly, in a letter asking about a graduate program, a major purpose might be
to build a good image of yourself so that your application for financial aid would be
viewed positively. To achieve that goal, you would provide information about your
qualifications and interest in the field before you ask questions.

Organizing Problem-Solving Messages

Use an indirect approach and the problem-solving (inductive or bad news) pattern
of organization when you expect resistance from your reader—because your solution will cost the reader time or money—but you can show that doing what you
want will solve a problem that you and your reader share. This pattern allows you
to disarm opposition by showing all the reasons in favour of your position before
you give your readers a chance to say *no*.

1. **Mention the problem you share (which your request will solve).** Because
   you're interested in solving the problem, mention the problem objectively: it's a
   waste of time and ink to assign blame or mention personalities.

Figure 12.4

How to Organize a Problem-Solving Persuasive Message

Shared Problem

Details

Solution

Negatives

Reader Benefits

Request for Action

2. **Detail the results of the problem *as they impact your reader*.** Be specific about the cost in money, time, lost goodwill, inconvenience, and so on. Persuade your readers that *something* has to be done before you convince them that your solution is the best one.
3. **Explain the solution to the problem.** If you know that the reader will favour another solution, start with that solution and show why it won't work before you present your solution.

    Present your solution focussing on practicality, workability, and/or desirability without using the words *I* or *my*. Appeal to the reader's wallet or sense of enlightened self-interest.
4. **Prove that any negative elements (cost, time, etc.) are outweighed by the advantages.**
5. **Summarize any additional benefits of the solution.** The main benefit—solving the problem—can be presented briefly since you described the problem in detail. However, if there are any additional benefits, mention them.
6. **Ask for the action you want.** Often your reader will authorize or approve something; other people will implement the action. Give your reader a reason to act promptly, perhaps offering a new reader benefit. ("By buying now, we can avoid the next quarter's price hikes.")

Figure 12.4 summarizes the pattern. Figure 12.5 on the next page, implements the pattern. Reader benefits can be brief in this kind of message since the biggest benefit comes from solving the problem.

How do I identify and overcome objections?

Know your audience. Talk to your audience. Then try these strategies.

The easiest way to learn about objections your audience may have is to ask knowledgeable people in your organization or your network.

Toyota responded to North American brand loyalty by customizing its automotive products, promotions and services to the Canadian market. Besides the products developed specifically for Canadian winters, the company's Canadian investments include financial support in local community organizations and Canada's Special Olympics, and partnerships with the Evergreen Learning Grounds Program and community colleges' technical training programs.

Figure 12.5
A Problem-Solving Persuasive Message

Memorandum

Date: February 15, 2002

To: All Staff Members

From: Melissa J. Gutridge *MJG*

Subject: Why We Are Implementing a New Sign-Out System   *Directed subject line indicates writer's position*

Shared problem

Successfully mainstreaming our clients into the community is very important and daily interaction with the public is necessary. Our clients enjoy the times they get to go to the mall or out to lunch instead of remaining here all day.   Recently, however, clients have been taken out on activities without a staff member's knowing where the client is and whom the client is with.

Specific example of problem

We need to know where all clients are at all times because social workers, psychologists, and relatives constantly stop by unannounced. Last week Janet's father stopped by to pick her up for a doctor's appointment and she was not here. No one knew where she was or whom she was with. Naturally her father was very upset and wanted to know what kind of program we were running. Staff members' not knowing where our clients are and whom they are with is damaging to the good reputation of our staff and program.

Solution presented impersonally

Additional reader benefit

Starting Monday, February 25, a sign-out board will be located by Betty's desk. Please write down where you and the client are going and when you expect to be back. When signing out, help clients sign themselves out. We can turn this into a learning experience for our clients. Then when a social worker stops by to see someone who isn't here, we can simply look at the sign-out board to tell where the client is and when he or she will return.

Ask for action

Please help keep up the superb reputation you have helped Weststar earn as a quality center for adults with handicaps. Sign out yourself and clients at all times.

- **Use open questions and phrase your questions neutrally,** so that people feel encouraged to express their opinions openly: "What concerns would you have about a proposal to do x?" "Who makes a decision about y?" "What do you like best about [the supplier or practice you want to change]?"
- **Ask follow-up questions** to be sure you understand: "Would you be likely to stay with your current supplier if you could get a lower price from someone else? Why?"

FYI

Expert writers show how evidence proves the claims they make, limits their claims, and rebuts counter-arguments.

Source: Joanna G. Crammond, "The Uses and Complexity of Argument Structures in Expert and Student Persuasive Writing," *Written Communication* 15, no. 2 (April 1998): 230–68.

People are most aware of and willing to share objective constraints such as time and money. We are all less willing to disclose emotional anxieties. We all have a vested interest in something when we benefit directly from keeping things as they are. For example, those in power have a **vested interest** in retaining the system that gives them their power. Someone who designed a system has a vested interest in protecting that system from criticism. To admit that the system has faults is to admit that the designer made mistakes. In such cases, you'll need to probe to find out what the real reasons are.

The best way to deal with an objection is to eliminate it. To sell Jeep Cherokees in Japan, Mitsuru Sato convinced Chrysler to put the driver's seat on the right side, to make an extra preshipment quality check, and to rewrite the instruction booklet in Japanese style, with big diagrams and cartoons.[3]

If an objection is false, based on misinformation, give the response to the objection without naming the objection. In a brochure, you can present responses with a "question/answer" format. When objections have already been voiced, you may want to name the objection so that your audience realizes that you are responding to that specific objection. However, to avoid solidifying the opposition, don't attribute the objection to your audience. Instead, use a less personal attribution and neutral language: "some people wonder . . ."; "Some citizens are concerned that . . ."

If real objections remain, try one or more of the following strategies to counter objections:

1. Specify how much time and/or money is required—it may not be as much as the reader fears

> Distributing flyers to each house or apartment in your neighbourhood will probably take two afternoons.

2. Put the time and/or money in the context of the benefits they bring

> The additional $152,500 will (1) allow The Open Shelter to remain open 24 rather than 16 hours a day, (2) pay for three social workers to help men find work and homes, and (3) keep the Neighbourhood Bank open, so that men don't have to cash welfare cheques in bars, and so that they can save up the $800 they need to have up front to rent an apartment.

3. Show that money spent now will save money in the long run

> By replacing the boiler now, we'll no longer have to release steam that the overflow tank can't hold. Depending on how severe the winter is, we could save $100 to $750 a year in energy costs. If energy costs rise, we'll save even more.

4. Show that doing as you ask will benefit a group or cause the reader supports, even though the action may not help the reader directly

> By being a Big Brother or a Big Sister, you'll give a child the adult attention he or she needs to become a well-adjusted, productive adult.

5. Show the reader that the sacrifice is necessary to achieve a larger, more important goal to which he or she is committed

> These changes will mean more work for all of us. But we've got to cut our costs 25 percent to keep the plant open and to keep our jobs.

6. Show that the advantages as a group outnumber or outweigh the disadvantages as a group

> None of the locations is perfect. But the Québec City location gives us the most advantages and the fewest disadvantages.

7. Turn a disadvantage into an opportunity

> With the hiring freeze, every department will need more lead time to complete its own work. By hiring another person, the Planning Department could provide that lead time.

Instant Replay

Organizing a Problem-Solving Message

1. Describe a problem you both share (which your request will solve)
2. Give the details of the problem
3. Explain the solution to the problem
4. Show that any negative elements (cost, time, etc.) are outweighed by the advantages
5. Summarize any additional benefits of the solution
6. Ask for the action you want

What other techniques can make my messages more persuasive?

> Build credibility and emotional appeal. Use the right tone, and offer a reason to act promptly.

Persuasive messages—whether short-term or long-term—will be more effective if you build credibility and emotional appeal, use the right tone, and offer a reason to act promptly.

Build Credibility

Credibility is the audience's response to the source of the message. People are more easily persuaded by someone they see as expert, powerful, attractive, or trustworthy. We are also more easily persuaded by people whom we perceive to be like us (similar in class, values, and age) and by those who are articulate, confident, and likeable.

Build Rational Appeal

When you don't yet have the credibility that comes from being an expert or being powerful, build credibility by the language and strategy you use:

To persuade, be prepared to appeal to emotions as well as to logic.

Source DILBERT reprinted by permission of United Features Syndicate Inc.

- **Be factual:** Use concrete language, supportive stats, and exact dollar or time requirements. Don't exaggerate.
- **Be specific.** If you say "X is better," show in detail *how* it is better. Show the reader exactly where the savings or other benefits come from so that it's clear that the proposal really is as good as you say it is.
- **Be reliable.** If you suspect that a project will take longer to complete, cost more money, or be less effective than you originally thought, tell your audience *immediately*. Negotiate a new schedule that you can meet.

Build Emotional Appeal

Emotional appeal means making the reader *want* to do what you ask. People make decisions—even business decisions—logically *and* emotionally.[4]

During his summer job, for example, an engineering student asked to evaluate his company's waste treatment system saw a way that the system could be redesigned to save the company over $200,000 a year. He wrote a report recommending the change and gave it to his boss. Nothing happened. Why not? His supervisor wasn't about to send up a report that would require him to explain why *he'd* been wasting over $200,000 a year of the company's money.[5]

Stories and psychological description (◀ ▶ p. 155) are effective ways of building emotional appeal. Emotional appeal works best when people want to be persuaded. Even when you need to provide statistics or numbers to convince the careful reader that your anecdote is a representative example, telling a story first makes your message more persuasive. Recent research suggests that stories are more persuasive because people remember them.[6]

Use the Right Tone

When you ask for action from people who report directly to you, you have several choices. Although orders ("Get me the Ervin file") and questions ("Do we have the third-quarter numbers yet?") might work, you'll get greater compliance with courtesy. When you need action from co-workers, superiors, or people outside the organization, you may need to be firm but you must always be polite.

Avoiding messages that sound parental or preachy is often a matter of tone. Saying "please" is important, especially to people on your level or outside the organization. Tone works better when you give reasons for your request.

Parental: Everyone is expected to comply with these regulations. I'm sure you can see that they are commonsense rules needed for our business.

Better: Even on casual days, visitors expect us to be professional. So please let's leave the gym clothes at home!

When you write to people you know well, humour can work. Just make sure that the message isn't insulting to anyone who doesn't find the humour funny.

Writing to superiors is trickier. You may want to tone down your request by using subjunctive verbs and explicit disclaimers that show you aren't taking a yes for granted.

Arrogant: Based on this evidence, I expect you to give me a new computer.

Better: If department funds permit, I would like a new computer.

Passive verbs and jargon sound stuffy. Use active imperatives—perhaps with "Please" to create a friendlier tone.

Stuffy: It is requested that you approve the above-mentioned action.

Better: Please authorize us to create a new subscription letter.

Offer a Reason for the Reader to Act Promptly

The longer people delay, the less likely they are to carry through with the action they had decided to take. In addition, you want a fast response so you can go ahead with your own plans.

Request action by a specific date. Always give people at least a week or two: they have other things to do besides respond to your requests. Set deadlines in the middle of the month, if possible. If you say, "Please return this by March 1," people will think, "I don't need to do this until March." Ask for the response by February 28 instead. If you can use a response even after the deadline, say so. Otherwise, people who can't make the deadline may not respond at all.

Show why you need a quick response:

- **Show that the time limit is real.** Perhaps you need information quickly to use it in a report that has a due date. Perhaps a decision must be made by a certain date to catch the start of the school year, the holiday selling season, or an election campaign. Perhaps you need to be ready for a visit from out-of-town or international colleagues.
- **Show that acting now will save time or money.** If business is slow and your industry isn't doing well, then your company needs to act now (to economize, to better serve customers) in order to be competitive. If business is booming and everyone is making a profit, then your company needs to act now to get its fair share of the available profits.
- **Show the cost of delaying action.** Will labour or material costs be higher in the future? Will delay mean more money spent on repairing something that will still need to be replaced?

FYI

A $250,000 (U.S.) study, commissioned by the Las Vegas Convention and Visitors Authority, convinced casino operators to launch an ad campaign focussing on the freedom available only in Vegas. The $18.5 million TV and print campaign, aimed at the 59 percent adult U.S. population who have never visited Vegas, suggests the city's naughty attractions

Source: "Nice is out as Las Vegas flaunts the naughty," *The Globe and Mail,* January 6, 2001, T7

Site to See

Go to http://erg.environics. net/sexsnow/

In his book *Sex in the Snow,* author Michael Adams argues that the majority of Canadians qualify as rebels and reformers; we value autonomy and are more suspicious of authority than our American neighbours.

Preparing for a Performance Appraisal

Your performance appraisal constitutes a persuasive message for both you and the savvy supervisor: formative evaluation is a key retention technique. People crave performance feedback; indeed, top performers are primarily motivated by the recognition inherent in the performance appraisal. If your organization does not appraise or evaluate your performance at least once a year, ask for this feedback.

And use the occasion to

- Identify your boss's specific opinions about your performance
- Communicate your ambitions
- Ask for the training and experience you want

Some supervisors don't know how to talk about subordinates' performance strengths and the skills they need to improve. If your supervisor doesn't specify them, ask, "What am I doing well?" and "Specifically, what are the two or three things I could do that would most improve my performance?"

In the twentieth-first century, most of us will change employers a minimum of seven times. Even supposedly staid accountants will job-hop an average of five times during their careers. "Employers are impressed by people who make strategic career moves at various stages of their careers to improve or broaden their skills," according to Kathryn Bolt, district president of the Canadian division responsible for recruiting and placing accountants at Robert Half International Inc. To remain employable, therefore, you need to add to your current skill set and get new experiences (not just keep doing the same old thing). Be ready to name one or two training programs you'd like to take in the next six months. Indicate the kinds of projects you'd like a chance to try.

Let your boss know that you want to contribute even more to the organization; make it clear that you're interested in lateral or vertical moves. Ask, "What kinds of things should I do now so that I'm promotable a year (or two) from now?

Having frequent discussions about work is a sign that your supervisor sees you as promotable. If your supervisor just asks you "yes/no" questions, he or she may not think of you as someone who has the ability or desire to advance. Use the performance appraisal to change the way your supervisor sees you and to prepare the job you really want.

Source: Virginia Galt, "Job-hopping now an accepted principle," *The Globe and Mail*, May 29, 2001, B15.

Molson's "Anthem" follows up the stunning success of the Joe Canadian "Rant" by tapping into Canadians' often understated pride in their country. Inspired by the catchy melody and quick succession of iconic Canadian moments, beer drinkers can go to the www.iam.ca Web site and create their own version of the "Anthem."

What are the most common kinds of persuasive messages?

> Orders, collection letters, performance appraisals, and letters of recommendation

Orders, collection letters, performance appraisals, and letters of recommendation are among the most common varieties of persuasive messages.

Orders

Orders may be written on forms, phoned in, or made by clicking on boxes on the Web. When you write an order,

- Be specific. Give model or page numbers, colours, finishes, and so forth.
- Tell the company what you want if that model number is no longer available.
- Double-check your arithmetic, and add sales tax and shipping charges.

Collection Letters

Most businesses find that phoning rather than writing results in faster payment. But as more and more companies install voicemail systems, you may sometimes need to write letters when leaving messages doesn't work.

Collection letters ask customers to pay (as they have already agreed to do) for the goods and services they have already received. Good credit departments send a series of letters. Letters in the series should be only a week or two apart. Waiting a month between letters implies that you're prepared to wait a long time—and the reader will be happy to oblige you!

Early letters are gentle, assuming that the reader intends to pay but has met with temporary reverses or has forgotten. However, the request should assume that the cheque has been mailed but did not arrive. A student who had not yet been reimbursed by a company for a visit to the company's office put the second request in the P.S. of a letter refusing a job offer:

P.S. The cheque to cover my expenses when I visited your office in March hasn't come yet. Could you check to see whether you can find a record of it? The amount was $490 (airfare $290, hotel room $185, taxi $15).

If one or two early letters don't result in payment, call the customer to ask if your company has created a problem. It's possible that you shipped something the customer didn't want or sent the wrong quantity. It's possible that the invoice arrived before the product and was filed and forgotten. It's possible that the invoice document is poorly designed, so customers set it aside until they can figure it out. If any of these situations apply, you'll build goodwill by solving the problem rather than arrogantly asking for payment.[7]

Middle letters are more assertive in asking for payment. Figure 9.2 (◀▶ p. 168) gives an example of a middle letter. This form letter is merged with a database containing information about the customer's name, the amount due, and the magazine the customer is receiving. Other middle letters offer to negotiate a schedule for repayment if the reader is not able to pay the whole bill immediately, may remind the reader of the importance of a good credit rating (which will be endangered if the bill remains unpaid), educate the reader about credit, and explain why the creditor must have prompt payment.

Unless you have firm evidence to the contrary, assume that readers have some legitimate reason for not yet paying. Even people who are "juggling" payments because they do not have enough money to pay all their bills or people who will put payment off as long as possible will respond more quickly if you do not accuse them. If a reader is offended by your assumption that he or she is dishonest, that anger can become an excuse to continue delaying payment.

Late letters threaten legal action if the bill is not paid. **Under federal law**, the writer cannot threaten legal action unless he or she actually intends to sue. Other regulations also spell out what a writer may and may not do in a late letter.

Many small businesses find that establishing personal relationships with customers is the best way to speed payment.

Performance Appraisals

At regular intervals, supervisors evaluate, or appraise the performance of their subordinates. In most organizations, employees have access to their files; sometimes they must sign the appraisal to show that they've read it. The supervisor normally meets with the subordinate to discuss the appraisal.

As a subordinate, you should prepare for the appraisal interview by listing your achievements and goals. Where do you want to be in one year or five years? What training and experience do you need to reach your goals? Also think about any skills you'd like to improve. If you need training, advice, or support from the organization to build on your strengths, the appraisal interview is a good time to ask for this help.

Appraisals both motivate the employee and protect the organization. But these two purposes may conflict. People, particularly top performers, need praise and reassurance to believe that they're valued and can do better. But the praise that motivates someone to improve can come back to haunt the company if the person does not eventually do acceptable work. An organization is in trouble if it tries to fire someone whose evaluations never mention mistakes.

Avoid labels (*wrong, bad*) and inferences. Instead, cite specific observations that describe behaviour.

Inference:	Sam is an alcoholic.
Vague observation:	Sam calls in sick a lot. Subordinates complain about his behaviour.
Specific observation:	Sam called in sick a total of 12 days in the last two months. After a business lunch with a customer last week, Sam was walking unsteadily. Two of his subordinates have said that they would prefer not to make sales trips with him because they find his behaviour embarrassing.

Sam might be an alcoholic. He might also be having a reaction to a physician-prescribed drug; he might have a mental illness; he might be showing symptoms of a physical illness other than alcoholism. A supervisor who jumps to conclusions creates ill will, closes the door to solving the problem, and may provide grounds for legal action against the organization.

Be specific in an appraisal.

Too vague: Sue does not manage her time as well as she could.

Specific: Sue's first three weekly sales reports have been three, two, and four days late, respectively; the last weekly sales report for the month is not yet in.

Without specifics, Sue won't know that her boss objects to late reports. She may think that she is being criticized for spending too much time on sales calls or for not working 80 hours a week. Without specifics, she might change the wrong behaviours in a futile effort to please her boss.

Good managers try not only to identify the specific problems in subordinates' behaviour but also to discover the causes of the problem and to provide resources for change. Does the employee need more training? Perhaps a training course or a mentor will help. Does he or she need to work more effectively? Perhaps this is a time-management, organization or motivational problem.

Performance appraisals are motivational and therefore useful when they occur frequently and regularly, when managers' behaviours are consistent with organizational values and when employees feel engaged in the process. Persuasive performance appraisals focus on specific attitudes and behaviours relevant to department and company goals. When evaluating others' performances, it's vital to clarify the most important areas and to elicit specific recommendations for improvement from the employee. No one can improve 17 weaknesses at once. Which two should the employee work on this month? Is getting in reports on time more important than increasing sales? Supervisors should explicitly identify these priorities during the appraisal interview.

Identify goals and benchmarks in specific, measurable, achievable, relevant, and time-lined terms. Achieving "considerable progress toward completing" a report could mean anything when the manager thinks that "considerable progress" means 50 percent or 85 percent of the total work. When the manager and employee articulating and agree on concrete goals, both the employee and the organization benefit.

Letters of Recommendation

In an effort to protect themselves against lawsuits, some companies state only how long they employed someone and the position that person held. Such bare-bones letters have themselves been the target of lawsuits when employers did not reveal relevant negatives. Whatever the legal climate, there may be times when you want to recommend someone for an award or for a job.

Letters of recommendation must be specific. General positives that are not backed up with specific examples and evidence are seen as weak recommendations. Letters of recommendation that focus on minor points also suggest that the person is weak.

Figure 9.4 (p. 170) is a letter of recommendation. Either in the first or the last paragraph, summarize your overall evaluation of the person. To establish your credibility, show how well and how long you've known the person early in the letter, perhaps in the first paragraph. In the middle of the letter, offer specific details about the person's performance. At the end of the letter, indicate whether you would be willing to rehire the person and repeat your overall evaluation.

FYI

Canada's aging population demographics will result in a skilled labour shortage and a profound shift in the balance of power between workers and employers. Organizations will soon have to sell themselves to prospective employees, says Roger Martin, dean of the Joseph L. Rotman School of Management, University of Toronto.

Source: Andrea Gordon, "The Thirty-five Best Companies to Work for," *Report on Business Magazine,* Web site visited July 9, 2001; http://www.robmagazine.com/archive/2000ROBfebruary/html/cover35_best.html

A Performance Appraisal

February 13, 2002

To: Barbara Buchanan

From: Brittany Papper BAP

Subject: Your Performance Thus Far in Our Collaborative Group

Subject line indicates that memo is a performance appraisal

Overall evaluation You have been a big asset to our group. Overall, our business communication group has been one of the best groups I have ever worked with, and I think that only minor improvements are needed to make our group even better.

What You're Doing Well

Specific observations provide dates, details of performance You demonstrated flexibility and compatibility at our last meeting, before we turned in our proposal on February 12, by offering to type the proposal since I had to study for an exam in one of my other classes. I really appreciated this because I really did not have the time to do it. I will remember this if you are ever too busy with your other classes and cannot type the final report.

Another positive critical incident occurred February 5. We had discussed researching the topic of sexual discrimination in hiring and promotion at Northern Insurance. As we read more about what we had to do, we became uneasy about reporting the information from our source who works at Northern. I called you later that evening to talk about changing our topic to a less personal one. You were very understanding and said that you agreed that the original topic was a touchy one. You offered suggestions for other topics and had a positive attitude about the adjustment. Your suggestions ended my worries and made me realize that you are a positive and supportive person.

Other strengths Your ideas definitely contribute to our group. You're good at brainstorming ideas, yet you're willing to go with whatever the group decides. That's a nice combination of creativity and flexibility.

Areas for Improvement

Two minor improvements could make you an even better member.

Specific recommendations for improvement The first improvement is to be more punctual to meetings. On February 5 and February 8 you were about 10 minutes late. This makes the meetings last longer. Your ideas are valuable to the group, and the sooner you arrive the sooner we can share in your suggestions.

Specific behaviour to be changed The second suggestion is one we all need to work on. We need to keep our meetings positive and productive. I think that our negative attitudes were worst at our first group meeting February 5. We spent about half an hour complaining about all the work we had to do and about our busy schedules in other classes. In the future if this happens, maybe you could offer some positives about the assignment to get the group motivated again.

Overall Compatibility

Positive, forward-looking ending I feel that this group has gotten along very well together. You have been very flexible in finding times to meet and have always been willing to do your share of the work. I have never had this kind of luck with a group in the past and you have been a welcome breath of fresh air. I don't hate doing group projects any more!

Experts are divided on whether you should include negatives. Some people feel that any negative weakens the letter. Other people feel that presenting but not emphasizing honest negatives makes the letter more convincing.

How can PAIBOC help me write persuasive messages?

> The PAIBOC questions help you examine the points your message should include.

Before you tackle the assignments for this module, examine the following problem. As in Modules 10 and 11, the PAIBOC questions in Figure 12.1 probe the basic points required for a solution. Study the two sample solutions to see what makes one unacceptable and the other one good.[8] The checklist, at the end of the module, in Figures 12.11 and 12.12 can help you evaluate a draft.

Problem

In one room in the production department of Golden Electronics Company, employees work on computer monitors in conditions that are scarcely bearable due to the heat. Even when the temperature outside is only 23° C, it is over 37°C in the monitor room. In June, July, and August, 24 out of 36 workers quit because they couldn't stand the heat. This turnover happens every summer.

In a far corner of the room sits a quality control inspector in front of a small fan (the only one in the room). The production workers, in contrast, are carrying 10 kg monitors. As production supervisor, you tried to get air-conditioning two years ago, before Golden acquired the company, but management was horrified at the idea of spending $500,000 to insulate and air-condition the warehouse (it is impractical to air-condition the monitor room alone).

You're losing money every summer. Write a memo to Jennifer M. Kirkland, operations vice president, renewing your request.

Analysis of the Problem

P   What are your **purposes** in writing or speaking?

To persuade Kirkland to authorize insulation and air-conditioning. To build a good image of myself.

A   Who is (are) your **audience(s)**? How do the members of your audience differ from each other? What characteristics are relevant to this particular message?

The operations vice president will be concerned about keeping costs low and keeping production running smoothly. Kirkland may know that the request was denied two years ago, but another person was vice president then; Kirkland wasn't the one who said no.

I   What **information** must your message include?

The cost of the proposal. The effects of the present situation.

B   What reasons or reader **benefits** can you use to support your position?

Cutting turnover may save money and keep the assembly line running smoothly. Experienced employees may produce higher-quality parts. Putting in air-conditioning would relieve one of the workers' main complaints; it might make the union happier.

O   What **objections** can you expect your reader(s) to have? What negative elements of your message must you de-emphasize or overcome?

The cost. The time operations will be shut down while installation is taking place.

C   How will the **context** affect the reader's response? Think about your relationship to the reader, morale in the organization, the economy, the time of year, and any special circumstances.

Prices on computer components are falling; interest rates are rising. The company will be reluctant to make a major expenditure. Unemployment is low, and filling vacancies in the monitor room is hard—we are getting a reputation as a bad place to work. Summer is over, but the problem will reoccur next year.

Discussion of the Sample Solutions

Solution 1, shown in Figure 12.7 on page 265, is unacceptable. By making the request in the subject line and the first paragraph, the writer invites a *no* before giving all the arguments. The writer does nothing to counter the objections that any manager will have to spending a great deal of money. By presenting the issue in terms of fairness, the writer creates defensiveness rather than finding a common ground. The writer doesn't use details or emotional appeal to show that the problem is indeed serious. The writer asks for fast action but doesn't show why the reader should act now to solve a problem that won't occur again for eight months.

Solution 2, shown in Figure 12.8 on pages 266 and 267, is an effective persuasive message. The writer chooses a positive subject line. The opening sentence is negative, catching the reader's attention by focussing on a problem the reader and writer share. However, the paragraph makes it clear that the memo offers a solution to the problem. The problem is spelled out in detail. Emotional impact is created by taking the reader through the day as the temperature rises. The solution is presented impersonally. There are no *I*'s in the memo.

The memo stresses reader benefits: the savings that will result once the investment is recovered. The last paragraph tells the reader exactly what to do and links prompt action to a reader benefit. The memo ends with a positive picture of the problem solved.

Figures 12.9 and 12.10 on pages 267 and 268, provide checklists for direct requests and problem-solving persuasive messages.

Figure 12.7

An Unacceptable Solution to the Sample Problem

Date: October 12, 2002

To: Jennifer M. Kirkland, Operations Vice President

From: Arnold M. Morgan, Production Supervisor *AMM*

Subject: Request for Air-Conditioning the Monitor Room *Request in subject line stiffens resistance when reader is reluctant*

Please put air-conditioning in the monitor room. This past summer, 2/3 of our employees quit because it was so hot. It's not fair that they should work in unbearable temperatures when management sits in air-conditioned comfort. *attacks reader*

Inappropriate emphasis on writer I propose that we solve this problem by air-conditioning the monitor room to bring down the temperature to 26°.

Insulating and air-conditioning the monitor room would cost $500,000.

Please approve this request promptly.

Cost sounds enormous without a context

Memo sounds arrogant.
Logic isn't developed.
This attacks reader instead of enlisting reader's support.

Figure 12.8

A Good Solution to the Sample Problem

Date: October 12, 2002

To: Jennifer M. Kirkland, Operations Vice President

From: Arnold M. Morgan, Production Supervisor *AMM*

Subject: Improving Summer Productivity

Reader benefit in subject line

Shared problem

Golden forfeited a possible $186,000 in profits last summer due to a 17 percent drop in productivity. That's not unusual: Golden has a history of low summer productivity. But we can reverse the trend and bring summer productivity in line with the rest of the year's.

Good to show problem can be resolved

Cause of problem

The problem starts in the monitor room. Due to high turnover and reduced efficiency from workers who are on the job, we just don't make as many monitors as we do during the rest of the year.

Additional reason to solve problem

Both the high turnover and reduced efficiency are due to the unbearable heat in the monitor room. Temperatures in the monitor room average 20° over the outside temperature. During the summer, when work starts at 8:00 A.M., it's already 29° in the tube room. By 11:30 A.M., it's at least 40°. On six days last summer, it hit 48°. When the temperatures are that high, we may be violating Occupational Health and Safety regulations.

Production workers are always standing, moving, or carrying 10 kg. monitors. When temperatures hit 32°, they slow down. When no relief is in sight, many of them take sick days or quit.

We replaced 24 of the 36 employees in the monitor room this summer. When someone quits, it takes an average of five days to find and train a replacement; during that time, the trainee produces nothing. For another five days, the new person can work at only half speed. And even "full speed" in the summer is only 90 percent of what we expect the rest of the year.

More details about problem

Here's where our losses come from:

Normal production = 50 units a person each day (upd)

Loss due to turnover:
loss of 24 workers for 5 days =	6,000 units
24 at $^1/_2$ pace for 5 days =	3,000 units
Total loss due to turnover =	9,000 units

Shows detail— Set up like an arithmetic problem

Loss due to reduced efficiency:
loss of 5 upd x 12 workers x 10 days =	600 units
loss of 5 upd x 36 x 50 days =	9,000 units
Total loss due to reduced efficiency =	9,600 units

Total Loss =   18,600 units

Figure 12.8

A Good Solution to the Sample Problem (continued)

Jennifer M. Kirkland   2   October 12, 2001

According to the accounting department, Golden makes a net profit of $10 on every *Shows where numbers in paragraph 1 come from* monitor we sell. And, as you know, with the boom in computer sales, we sell every monitor we make. Those 18,600 units we don't produce are costing us $186,000 a year.

Additional benefit Bringing down the temperature to 25° (the minimum allowed under provincial guidelines) from the present summer average of 44° will require an investment of $500,000 to insulate and air-condition the warehouse. Extra energy costs for the air-conditioning will run about $30,000 a year. We'll get our investment back in less than three years. Once the investment is recouped, we'll be making an additional $150,000 a year—all without buying additional equipment or hiring additional workers.

Tells reader what to do By installing the insulation and air-conditioning this fall, we can take advantage of *Reason to act promptly* lower off-season rates. Please authorize the Purchasing Department to request bids for the system. Then, next summer, our productivity can be at an all-time high.

Ends on positive note of problem solved, reader enjoying benefit

---

Figure 12.9

Checklist for Direct Requests

- ☐ If the message is a memo, does the subject line indicate the request? Is the subject line specific enough to differentiate this message from others on the same subject?
- ☐ Does the first paragraph summarize the request or the specific topic of the message?
- ☐ Does the message give all of the relevant information? Is there enough detail?
- ☐ Does the message answer questions or overcome objections that readers may have without introducing unnecessary negatives?
- ☐ Does the last paragraph ask for action? Does it give a deadline if one exists and a reason for acting promptly?

continued

Figure 12.9 (continued)

And, for all messages, not just direct requests,

☐ Does the message use you-attitude and positive emphasis?
☐ Is the style easy to read and friendly?
☐ Is the visual design of the message inviting?
☐ Is the format correct?
☐ Does the message use standard grammar? Is it free from typos?

Originality in a direct request may come from

☐ Good lists and visual impact.
☐ Thinking about readers and giving details that answer their questions, overcome any objections, and make it easier for them to do as you ask.
☐ Adding details that show you're thinking about a specific organization and the specific people in that organization.

Figure 12.10

Checklist for Problem-Solving Persuasive Messages

☐ If the message is a memo, does the subject line indicate the writer's purpose or offer a reader benefit? Does the subject line avoid making the request?
☐ Is the problem presented as a joint problem both writer and reader have an interest in solving, rather than as something the reader is being asked to do for the writer?
☐ Does the message give all of the relevant information? Is there enough detail?
☐ Does the message overcome objections that readers may have?
☐ Does the message avoid phrases that sound dictatorial, condescending, or arrogant?
☐ Does the last paragraph ask for action? Does it give a deadline if one exists and a reason for acting promptly?

And, for all messages, not just persuasive ones,

☐ Does the message use you-attitude and positive emphasis?
☐ Is the style easy to read and friendly?
☐ Is the visual design of the message inviting?
☐ Is the format correct?
☐ Does the message use standard grammar? Is it free from typos?

Originality in a problem-solving persuasive message may come from

☐ A good subject line and common ground.
☐ A clear and convincing description of the problem.
☐ Thinking about readers and giving details that answer their questions, overcome objections, and make it easier for them to do as you ask.
☐ Adding details that show you're thinking about a specific organization and the specific people in that organization

Employability Skills 2000+ Checklist for Persuasive Messages

In this module, the key skills from The Conference Board of Canada's Employability Skills 2000+ are:

Communicate
✔ read and understand information presented in a variety of forms (e.g., words, graphs, charts, diagrams)
✔ write and speak so others pay attention and understand
✔ share information using a range of information and communications technologies (e g., voice, email, computers)
✔ use relevant scientific, technological, and mathematical knowledge and skills to explain or clarify ideas

Manage Information
✔ locate, gather, and organize information using appropriate technology and information systems

Use Numbers
✔ decide what needs to be measured or calculated
✔ observe and record data using appropriate methods, tools, and technology
✔ make estimates and verify calculations

Think & Solve Problems
✔ assess situations and identify problems
✔ seek different points of view and evaluate them based on facts
✔ recognize the human, interpersonal, technical, scientific, and mathematical dimensions of a problem
✔ identify the root cause of a problem
✔ be creative and innovative in exploring possible solutions
✔ readily use science, technology, and mathematics as ways to think, gain and share knowledge, solve problems, and make decisions
✔ evaluate solutions to make recommendations or decisions

Work with Others
✔ understand and work within the dynamics of a group

Review of Key Points

- Use the **direct request pattern** when
  - The audience will do as you ask without any resistance
  - You need a response only from the people who are willing to act
  - The audience is busy and may not read all the messages received
  - Your organization's culture prefers direct requests
- Use the **problem-solving pattern** when
  - The audience is likely to object to doing as you ask
  - You need action from everyone
  - You trust the audience to read the entire message
  - You expect logic to be more important than emotion in the decision
- In a direct request, put the request, the topic of the request, or a question in the subject line. Do not put the request in the subject line of a problem-solving persuasive message. Instead, use a **directed subject line** that reveals your position on the issue or a reader benefit. Use a positive or neutral subject line even when the first paragraph will be negative.
- In a direct request, consider asking in the first paragraph for the information or service you want. Give readers all the information or details they will need to act on your request. In the last paragraph, ask for the action you want.
- Organize a problem-solving persuasive message in this way:
  1. Describe a problem you both share (which your request will solve)
  2. Give the details of the problem
  3. Explain the solution to the problem
  4. Show that any negative elements (cost, time, etc.) are outweighed by the advantages
  5. Summarize any additional benefits of the solution
  6. Ask for the action you want
- Readers have a vested interest in something if they benefit directly from keeping things as they are.
- Use one or more of the following strategies to counter objections:
  - Specify how much time and/or money is required
  - Put the time and/or money in the context of the benefits they bring
  - Show that money spent now will save money in the long run
  - Show that doing as you ask will benefit some group the reader identifies with or some cause the reader supports
  - Show the reader that the sacrifice is necessary to achieve a larger, more important goal to which he or she is committed
  - Show that the advantages as a group outnumber or outweigh the disadvantages as a group
  - Turn the disadvantage into an opportunity
- To encourage readers to act promptly, set a deadline. Show that the time limit is real, that acting now will save time or money, or that delaying action will cost more.
- Use the PAIBOC questions from Figure 12.1 on page 247 to analyze persuasive situations.

Learning Applications

Questions for Comprehension

12.1 How do you decide whether to use a direct request or a problem-solving persuasive message?

12.2 How do you organize a problem-solving persuasive message?

12.3 How can you build credibility?

12.4 How do specific varieties of persuasive messages adapt the basic patterns?

Questions for Critical Thinking

12.5 What do you see as the advantages of positive and negative appeals? Illustrate your answer with specific messages, advertisements, or posters.

12.6 Is it dishonest to "sneak up on the reader" by delaying the request in a problem-solving persuasive message?

12.7 Think of a persuasive message (or a commercial) that did not convince you to act. Could a different message have convinced you? Why or why not?

Questions for Building Skills

12.8 What skills have you read about in this module?

12.9 What skills are you practising in the assignments you're doing for this module?

12.10 How could you further develop the skills you're working on?

Exercises and Problems

12.11   Revising a Form Memo

You've been hired as a staff accountant; one of your major duties will be processing expense reimbursements. Going through the files, you find this form memo:

Subject: Reimbursements

Enclosed are either receipts that we could not match with the items in your request for reimbursement or a list of items for which we found no receipts or both. Please be advised that the Accounting Department issues reimbursement cheques only with full documentation. You cannot be reimbursed until you give us a receipt for each item for which you desire reimbursement. We must ask that you provide this information. This process may be easier if you use the Expense Report Form, available in your department.

Thank you for your attention to this matter. Please do not hesitate to contact us with questions.

You know this memo is horrible. In addition to wordiness, a total lack of positive emphasis and you-attitude, and a vague subject line, the document design and organization of information bury the request.

Create a new memo that could be sent to people who do not provide all the documentation necessary in order to be reimbursed.

12.12 Recommending a Co-worker for a Bonus or an Award

Recommend someone at your workplace for a bonus or an award. The award can be something bestowed by the organization itself (Employee of the Month, Dealership of the Year, and so forth), or it can be a community or campus award (Business Person of the Year, Volunteer of the Year, an honorary degree, and so forth).

As Your Instructor Directs,

a. Create a document or presentation to achieve the goal

b. Write a memo to your instructor describing the situation at your workplace and explaining your rhetorical choices (medium, strategy, tone, wording, graphics or document design, and so forth)

12.13 Asking for a Raise or Reclassification

Do you deserve a raise? Should your job be reclassified to reflect your increased responsibilities (with more pay, of course!)? If so, write a memo to the person with the authority to determine pay and job titles, arguing for what you want.

As Your Instructor Directs,

a. Create a document or presentation to achieve the goal

b. Write a memo to your instructor describing the situation at your workplace and explaining your rhetorical choices (medium, strategy, tone, wording, graphics or document design, and so forth)

12.14 Persuading Guests to Allow Extra Time for Checkout

Your hotel has been the headquarters for a convention, and on Sunday morning you're expecting 1,000 people to check out before noon. You're staffing the checkout desk to capacity, but if everyone waits till 11:30 A.M. to check out, things will be a disaster.

So you want to encourage people to allow extra time. And they don't have to stand in line at all: by 4:00 A.M., you'll put a statement of current charges under each guest's door. If

that statement is correct and the guest is leaving the bill on the credit card used at check-in, the guest can just leave the key in the room and leave. You'll mail a copy of the final bill together with any morning charges by the end of the week.

Write a one-page message that can be put on pillows when the rooms are made up Friday and Saturday night.

12.15 Persuading an Organization to Expand Flextime

Municipal government offices are open from 9:00 A.M. to 5:00 P.M. Employees have limited flextime: they can come in and leave half an hour early or half an hour late. But employees want much more flexible hours. Some people want to start at 6:00 A.M. so they can leave at 2:00 P.M.; others want to work from 11:00 A.M. to 7:00 P.M.

When the idea has been proposed, supervisors have been very negative. "How will we hold staff meetings? How can we supervise people if everyone works different

hours? We have to be here for the public, and we won't be if people work whatever hours they please."

But conversations with co-workers and a bit of research show that there are solutions. Many firms that use flextime require everyone to be at work (or at lunch) between 10:00 A.M. and 2:00 P.M. or 11:00 A.M. and 2:00 P.M., so that staff meetings can be scheduled. Right now, when clients call, a representative is frequently on the phone and has to call back. Voice mail and better message forms could solve the problem. And flextime might actually let offices stay open longer hours—say 8:00 A.M. to 6:00 P.M., which would be helpful for taxpayers who themselves work 9:00 A.M. to 5:00 P.M. and now can come in only on their own lunch hours.

Write a memo to the Mayor and Municipal Council, persuading them to approve a change in work hours.

Hints:

* Assume that this situation is happening in your own municipal government. What services does the municipality offer?

* Use any facts about your municipality that are helpful (for example, being especially busy right now, having high turnover, dealing with tax issues.

* Use what you know about managing to allay managers' fears.

* Use the analysis that you developed for 2.15 in Module 2 on page 47.

12.16   Persuading Disability Services to Increase the Handivan's Hours

The local community college has a "Handivan" that takes students in wheelchairs from their residences or apartments to campus locations and back again. But the van stops at 6:00 P.M. (even though there are evening classes, lectures, and events). And it doesn't take people to off-campus restaurants, movies, grocery stores, or shopping centres. Write to the director of disability services, urging that the Handivan's services be increased.

12.17   Handling a Sticky Recommendation

As a supervisor in a not-for-profit provincial agency, you have a dilemma. You received this email message today:

From: John Inoye, Director of Personnel, Department of Taxation

Subject: Need Recommendation for Peggy Chafez

Peggy Chafez has applied for a position in the Department of Taxation. On the basis of her application and interview, she is the leading candidate. However, before I offer the job to her, I need a letter of recommendation from her current supervisor.

Could you please let me have your evaluation within a week? We want to fill the position as quickly as possible

Peggy has worked in your office for 10 years. She designed, writes, and edits a monthly newsletter that your office puts out; she designed and maintains the department Web site. Her designs are creative; she's a very hard worker; she seems to know a lot about computers.

However, Peggy is in many ways an unsatisfactory staff member. Her standards are so high that most people find her intimidating. Some find her abrasive. People have complained to you that she's only interested in her own work; she seems to resent requests to help other people with projects. And yet both the newsletter and the Web page are projects that need frequent interaction. She's out of the office a lot. Some of that is required by her job (she takes the newsletters to the post office, for example), but some people don't like the fact that she's out of the office so much. They also complain that she doesn't return voice mail and email messages.

You think managing your office would be a lot smoother if Peggy weren't there. You can't fire her: employees' jobs are secure once they get past the initial six-month probationary period. Because of budget constraints, you can hire new employees only if vacancies are created by resignations. You feel that it would be pretty easy to find someone better.

If you recommend that John Inoye hire Peggy, you will be able to hire someone you want. If you recommend that John hire someone else, you may be stuck with Peggy for a long time.

As Your Instructor Directs,

a. Write an email message to John Inoye

b. Write a memo to your instructor listing the choices you've made and justifying your approach

Hints:

- What are your options? Consciously look for more than two.
- Is it possible to select facts or to use connotations so that you are truthful but still encourage John to hire Peggy? Is it ethical? Is it certain that John would find Peggy's work as unsatisfactory as you do? If you write a strong recommendation and Peggy doesn't do well at the new job, will your credibility suffer? Why is your credibility important?

12.18 Writing Collection Letters

You have a small desktop publishing firm. Today, you've set aside some time to work on overdue bills.

As Your Instructor Directs,

Write letters for one or more of the following situations.

a. A $750 bill for producing three monthly newsletters for a veterinarian to mail to her clients. The agreement was that you'd bill her $250 each month. But somehow you haven't sent out bills for the last two months, so they'll go on this month's bill. You'd like payment for the whole bill, and you want to continue this predictable income of $250 a month.

b. A $200 bill for creating flyers for a rock band to post. You've called twice and left messages on an answering machine, but nothing has happened. The bill is only three weeks overdue, but the band doesn't seem very stable, and you want to be paid now.

c. A $3,750 bill, three weeks past due, for designing and printing a series of brochures for Creative Interiors, a local interior decorating shop. When you billed Creative Interiors, you got a note saying that the design was not acceptable and that you would not be paid until you redesigned it (at no extra charge) to the owner's satisfaction. The owner had approved the preliminary design on which the brochures were based; he did not explain in the note what was wrong with the final product. He's never free when you are; indeed, when you call to try to schedule an appointment, you're told the owner will call you back—but he never does. At this point, the delay is not your fault; you want to be paid.

12.19   Getting Permission from Parents for a School Project

As part of a community cleanup program, all public school students will spend the afternoon of the second Friday of April picking up trash. Younger students will pick up trash on school grounds, in parks, and in parking lots; older students will pick up trash downtown. Schoolteachers will supervise the students; where necessary, school buses will transport them. After students are finished, they'll return to their school's playground, where they'll be supervised until the end of the school day. Each school will maintain a study hall for any students whose parents do not give them permission to participate. Trash bags and snacks have been donated by local merchants.

Write a one-page cover letter that students can take home to their parents telling them about the project and persuading them to sign the necessary permission form. You do not need to create the permission form, but do refer to it in your letter.

Hints:

- What objections may parents have? How can you overcome these?
- Where should parents who drive their kids to school pick them up?
- Should students wear their normal school clothing?
- When must the form be returned? Who gets it? Whom can parents call if they have questions before they sign the form?

12.20   Asking an Instructor for a Letter of Recommendation

You're ready for the job market or for transfer to a college or university, and you need letters of recommendation.

As Your Instructor Directs,

a. Assume that you've orally asked an instructor for a recommendation, and he or she has agreed to write one. "Why don't you write up something to remind me of what you've done in the class? Tell me what else you've done, too. And tell me what they're looking for. Be sure to tell me when the letter needs to be in and whom it goes to."

b. Assume that you've been unable to talk with the instructor whose recommendation you want. When you call, no one answers the phone; you stopped by once and no one was in. Write asking for a letter of recommendation.

c. Assume that the instructor is no longer on campus. Write him or her a letter asking for a recommendation.

Hints:

- Detail the points you'd like the instructor to mention.
- How well will this instructor remember you? How much detail about your performance in his or her class do you need to provide?
- Specify the name and address of the person to whom the letter should be written; specify when the letter is due. If there's an intermediate due date (for example, if you must sign the outside of the envelope to submit the recommendation to law school), say so.

12.21   Recommending Investments*

Recommend whether your instructor should invest in a specific stock, piece of real estate, or other investment. As your instructor directs, assume that your instructor has $1,000, $10,000, or $100,000 to invest.

Hints:

- Pick a stock, property, or other investment you can research easily.
- What are your instructor's goals? Is he or she saving for a house? For retirement?

For the kids' post-secondary education expenses? To pay off his or her own student loans? When will the money from the investment be needed?

- How much risk is your instructor comfortable with?

- Is your instructor willing to put time into the investment (as managing a rental house would require)?

*Based on an assignment created by Cathy Ryan, The Ohio State University

12.22   Retrieving Your Image

As director of business communication, you get this letter from Sharon Davis, a member of your college advisory board and a major donor:

> My bank received this letter from one of your soon-to-be graduates. It seems as though a closer look at writing skills is warranted.
>
> To Whom It May Concern:
>
> This is in reference to the loan soliciation that I received in the mail. This is the second offer that I am now inquiring about. The first offer sent to my previous address I did not respond. But aftersome careful thought and consideration I think it wise to consolidate my bills. Therefore I hope the information provided is sufficient to complete a successful application. I think the main purpose of this loan is to enable me to repair my credit history. I have had problems in the past because of job status as part-time and being a student. I will be graduating in June and now I do have a full-time job. I think I just need a chance to mend the past credit problems that I have had.
>
> (The next two inches of the letter are blocked out, and both the signature and typed name are crossed out so that they cannot be read.)

As Your Instructor Directs,

Write to

a. The faculty who teach business communication, reminding them that the quality of student writing may affect fund-raising efforts

b. Ms. Davis, convincing her that indeed your school does make every effort to graduate students who can write

12.23   Persuading Employees to Join the Company Volleyball Team

Your company has decided to start a company volleyball team to play in the city recreation league. Now, you need to get people to sign up for the team. Ideally, you'd like to have several teams to involve as many people as possible and build company loyalty. If you have enough teams, they can play each other once a week in a round-robin company tournament.

Write a memo to all employees persuading them to sign up.

Hints:

- How young and how athletic are your employees? How busy are they? Will this be an easy or a difficult thing to persuade them to do?

- Some people may be reluctant to join because their skills are rusty. How can you persuade people that you want everyone to participate even if they're not athletic?

- Will the people who sign up have to pay anything or buy uniforms?

- How do people sign up? Is there a deadline?

12.24   Persuading Tenants to Pay the Rent

As the new manager of an apartment complex, you find this message in the files:

ATTENTION!

DERELICTS

If you are a rent derelict (and you know if you are) this communique is directed to you!

RENT IS DUE THE 5TH OF EACH MONTH AT THE LATEST!

LEASE HAS A 5-DAY GRACE PERIOD UNTIL THE 5TH OF THE MONTH NOT THE 15TH.

If rent is not paid in total by the 5th, you will pay the $25 late charge. You will pay the $25

late charge when you pay your late rent or your rent will not be accepted.

Half of you people don't even know how much you pay a month. Please read your lease instead of calling up to waste our time finding out what you owe per month! Let's get with the program so I can spend my time streamlining and organizing maintenance requests. My job is maintenance only.

RENT PAYMENT IS YOUR JOB!

If you can show up for a test on time, why can't you make it to the rental office on time or just mail it.

P.S. We don't take cash any longer due to a major theft.

This message is terrible. It lacks you-attitude and may even encourage people who are now paying on the first to wait until the 5th.

Write a message to go to people who have been slow to pay in the past.

12.25   Writing a Performance Appraisal for a Member of a Collaborative Group

During your collaborative writing group meetings, keep a log of events. Record specific observations of both effective and ineffective things that group members do. Then evaluate the performance of the other members in your group. (If there are two or more other people, write a separate appraisal for each of them.)

In your first paragraph, summarize your evaluation. Then, in the body of your memo, give the specific details that lead to your evaluation by answering the following questions:

- What specifically did the person do in terms of the task? Brainstorm ideas? Analyze the information? Draft the text? Suggest revisions in parts drafted by others? Format the document or create visuals? Revise? Edit? Proofread? (In most cases, several people will have done each of these activities together. Don't overstate

what any one person did.) What was the quality of the person's work?

- What did the person contribute to the group process? Did he or she help schedule the work? Raise or resolve conflicts? Make other group members feel valued and included? Promote group cohesion? What roles did the person play in the group?

Support your generalizations with specific observations. The more observations you have and the more detailed they are, the better your appraisal will be.

As Your Instructor Directs,

a. Write a midterm performance appraisal for one or more members of your collaborative group. In each appraisal, identify the two or three things the person should try to improve during the second half of the term.

b. Write a performance appraisal for one or more members of your collaborative group at the end of the term. Identify and justify the grade you think each person should receive for the portion of the grade-based group process.

c. Give a copy of your appraisal to the person about whom it is written.

Polishing Your Prose

Narrative Voice

Narrative voice refers to the "personality" of a narrator. Words, phrases, expressions, and tone convey narrative voice. Like fiction and composition, business communication uses narrative voice. The voice in memos, letters, and reports can be friendly, assertive, bureaucratic, threatening, or confident, to name just a few possibilities.

Consider the following eighteenth-century collection letter.

Sir,

I find myself constrained by a present exigence, to beg you to balance the account between us. Though matters have run into some length, yet I would not have applied to you, had I known so well to answer my pressing occasions any other way. If it suits you not to pay the whole, I beg, sir, you will remit me as much towards it as you can, without prejudice to your own affairs; and it will extremely oblige

Your most humble Servant

What phrases sound 250 years old? Is the narrator educated? How do you know? Does the narrator sound like anyone you know? Would this letter work today?

Narrative voice is as individual as personality. However, we have some control over narrative voice as we can choose the language with which we communicate. Knowing your own voice can help you to understand the "personality" it demonstrates.

Exercises

Read the following passages. How would you characterize the narrative voice in each? Which voices seem appropriate for good business communication? Try using your own words to communicate the same basic message.

1. Employees will clock in at their designated hour. Employees will follow their assigned schedules to the letter. There will be NO EXCEPTION to these rules.

2. Hi, Mr. Mills! Just stop in to pick up your order when you get a chance. Give us a ring if you want delivery. Thanks!!

3. Please find enclosed my résumé, which speaks to my superlative and most relevant qualities as candidate for the advertised position of account executive with your illustrious organization.

4. Get your act together or you're fired. Got it?

5. It's, like, one of the biggest, like, ideas our department has ever had, you know? For sure.

6. Pertaining to the party of the first part, hereafter called "party first," and excepting any and all objections from the party of the second part, hereafter called "party second," this amendment shall be considered null and void with proper written notice three (3) days prior to the execution of the original agreement.

7. Congratulations on your recent promotion to district manager, Rita. All of us in Accounting look forward to working with you in the near future.

8. I QUIT.

9. In the event of catastrophic LAN failure, users will

   1. Perform SYS/MD-3 shutdown for affected systems.

   2. Engage standard recovery matrix (SRM), per #4105.1 in SYS/MD Manual (2000: H3-H12).

   3. Record time and date, RE: LAN Failure, in compliance log, cc. MEISNER.

   4. Notify Data Services at ext. 5547, ATTN: J.J. MEISNER.

10. Nope. This idea won't work. It's not very good. I'm not sure the project is even worth our time anymore. I'm definitely not interested in having a meeting to discuss it. Don't call me unless you eggheads hatch something better.

Check your answers to the odd-numbered exercises on page 633.

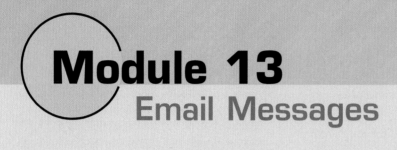

Module 13
Email Messages

Topics

- Should I write email messages the same way I write paper messages?

- What email "netiquette" rules should I follow?

- What kinds of subject lines should I use for email messages?

- Should I worry about viruses?

Review of Key Points

Learning Applications

Polishing Your Prose: Making Nouns and Pronouns Agree

Learning Focus

After reading and applying the information in Module 13, you'll be able to demonstrate

Knowledge of
- How the principles of good writing apply to email messages
- How to make the most of your time

Skills to
- Use email effectively
- Write effective subject lines for email messages
- Begin to plan how best to use your time

"Even my grandmother has email ..."

"The nature of the job is that you get so busy you don't always have time to get back to last week's project," says Jeff Tandy, computer support person at Fanshawe College.

Jeff started out hoping to be a probation officer and earned a B.A. in criminology. But by the time he graduated he realized that this was not the job for him. While in school he had taught himself how to repair computers and he decided that this was something he would enjoy. He took some computer courses at a local business college and then got his industry certification by doing the Microsoft certification program.

The job keeps Jeff hopping. He describes his position as being a "go to" person. He is responsible for setting up and maintaining computers used by faculty, support staff, and students for two of the divisions, or about 20 percent of the college. In addition to the help tasks, Jeff is also responsible for setting policies and procedures for the use of the computers, especially with regards to Internet and email use. He likes to point out that fixing computers also has a human component since he must deal with the people who use the computers. "This is where my criminology training comes in handy," he says partly in jest. "I have to be able to read people."

Jeff thinks that email is a great invention and a great first step for people getting involved with other forms of technology. "Even my grandmother has email," he says proudly. However, because of the simplicity of email usage, once people use email they have to get involved with trouble shooting. "They have to learn to open attachments and download items," he adds. From this it is a short step to troubleshooting and to other forms of technology. Jeff thinks that email is the first step toward truly digital communications where we can videoconference and have a record of the conference.

"Email is more accountable than phone calls," he adds. "In a phone call, people talk past each other, but with email there is a written record. If the receiver denies something, the sender still has a record of what was sent so the recipient cannot deny having received it. Someone could erase the phone message and say it was never received, but since the sender has a copy of the email, this cannot happen. In this way email makes us more accountable." Jeff goes on to say that since "email provides you with a written document, email is perceived as sending a letter so detailed information is contained in the message the way it would not be in a phone message.

When asked for words of advice, Jeff concludes: "Be aware of what you are opening. Remember the 'I love you' virus. If it has an interesting title and you don't know where it came from, don't open it."

Figure 13.1
PAIBOC Questions for Analysis

PAIBOC

Use the PAIBOC questions to analyze business communication problems:

P What are your **purposes** in writing?

A Who is (are) your **audience(s)**? How do members of your audience differ? What characteristics are relevant to this particular message?

I What **information** must your message include?

B What reasons or reader benefits can you use to support your position?

O What **objection(s)** can you expect your reader(s) to have? What negative elements of your message must you de-emphasize or overcome?

C How will the **context** affect reader response? Think about your relationship to the reader, morale in the organization, the economy, the time of year, and any special circumstances.

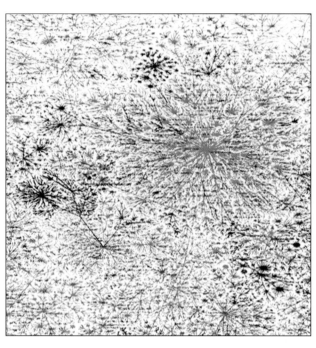

This image shows the paths an email message can take. Special software graphed the shortest path taken by the test messages sent on May 3, 1999, from a computer in Murray ill, NJ, to each of the world's 95,800 networks. The path can branch at each network. Orange lines show educational networks; purple ones show North American networks; green lines show European networks.

When you start a new job, your employer will probably expect you to be electronically literate. It's likely that you'll respond to—and perhaps initiate—email messages during your very first week at work. Although email has revived the social letter while providing us with immediate, inexpensive, and global contact, experienced writers exercise caution when composing electronic mail.

As you write email messages, keep these guidelines in mind:

- **Remember that all writing is for the record.** Although people perceive email to be as informal as conversation, it is not. Nor is it private, as a conversation might be. All writing is for the record and has intellectual, psychological, and legal implications. Your written words can be printed out or forwarded to anyone or everyone without your knowledge or consent. Organizational email messages can be tracked and your employer may legally check your messages. Email is permanent; be discreet.

- **Apply PAIBOC analysis.** All the principles of good business writing apply to email messages. Remember you-attitude (◀▷ Module 6) and positive emphasis (◀▷ Module 7). Use the language and pattern of organization that fits your audience and purpose (◀▷ Module 2). Use reader benefits (◀▷ Module 8) when they're appropriate.

- **Consider the limitations of the medium.** Email or cyberspace correspondence, unlike paper, text documents, has no tactile component; email messages carry a "just-in-time" quality suitable for brief confirmations, but inappropriate for complex meaning-making—like negotiating and resolving conflicts. The format of email messages evolves constantly; email travels via an uncensored and deregulated channel: it's vital, therefore, to know and observe email etiquette when composing your messages. Humour, for example, does not travel well via email.

- **Reread and proofread your message before sending it out.** As is true of all your writing, your emails represent you. For credible and convincing messages, therefore, check that your documents are correct and comprehensive (you've included all the necessary information).Because email feels like talking, some writers give less attention to spelling, grammar, and proofreading. Many email programs have spell checkers; use them.

- **Be clear and concise.** Email messages have to interest the reader in the subject line and first paragraph. If your message is longer than one screen, write a memo or letter instead, and send the document as an attachment.

What kinds of subject lines should I use for email messages?

Be specific, concise, and catchy.

Subject lines in email are even more important than those in letters and memos because it's so easy for the recipient to hit the delete key. Subject lines must be specific, concise, and catchy. Many email users get so many messages that they don't bother reading messages if they don't recognize the sender or if the subject doesn't catch their interest.

Try to keep the subject line short. If that's difficult, put the most important part into the first few words because some email programs only show the first 28 characters of the subject line.

If your message is very short, you may be able to put it in the subject line. "EOM" (end of message) tells your reader that there is no additional information in the body of the message.

> Subject: Will Attend 3:00 P.M. Meeting EOM

Subject Lines for Informative and Positive Email Messages

If you have good news to convey, be sure it's in the subject line. Be as brief as you can.

The following subject lines would be acceptable for informative and good news email messages:

> Subject: Travel Plans for Sales Meeting
>
> Subject: Your Proposal Accepted
>
> Subject: Reduced Prices During February

When you reply to a message, the email system automatically creates a subject line "Re: [subject line of message to which you are responding]." If the subject line is appropriate, that's fine. If it isn't appropriate, you may want to create a new subject line. And if a series of messages arises, create a new subject line. "Re: Re: Re: Re: Question" is not an effective subject line.

Go to
mesa.rrzn.uni-
hannover.de

This site will help
you find email
addresses—fast!

Subject Lines for Negative Email Messages

When you say "no" to an email request, just hit "reply" and use "Re:" plus whatever the original subject line was for your response. When you write a new message, you will have to decide whether to use the negative in the subject line. The subject line should contain the negative when

- The negative is serious. Many people do not read all their email messages. A neutral subject line may lead the reader to ignore the message.
- The reader needs the information to make a decision or act.
- You report your own errors (as opposed to the reader's).

Thus the following would be acceptable subject lines in email messages:

FYI

Email Acronyms
ASAP   As soon as
       possible
BTW   By the way
EOM   End of
       message
FAQ   Frequently
       asked
       questions
FYI   For your
       information
IMHO   In my
       humble
       opinion
TMOT   Trust me on
       this

Subject: We Lost McDonald's Account

Subject: Power to Be Out Sunday, March 12

Subject: Error in Survey Data Summary

When you write to people whom you know well, exaggerated subject lines are acceptable:

Subject: Gloom, Despair, and Agony

In other situations, a neutral subject line is appropriate.

Subject: Results of 360° Performance Appraisals

Subject Lines for Persuasive Email Messages

The subject line of a persuasive email message should make it clear that you're asking for something. If you're sure that the reader will read the message, something as vague as "Request" may work. Most of the time, it's better to be more specific.

Subject: Move Meeting to Tuesday?

Subject: Need Your Advice

Subject: Want You for United Way Campaign

Instant Replay

Keep Subject Lines Short

Try to keep the subject line short. If that's difficult, put the most important part into the first few words because some email programs only show the first 28 characters of the subject line

Should I write email messages the same way I write paper messages?

> Negative and persuasive messages will be more direct.

Negative and persuasive messages are more efficiently delivered face-to-face, because the important nuances added through non-verbal communication speak volumes and can save time and energy. If, however, you must deliver negative information electronically, write so that it's easy for readers to understand and act on the information quickly.

Writing Positive and Informative Email Messages

Email is especially appropriate for positive and informative messages. Figures 9.13 and 9.14 (pp. 184) are examples of an informative message and a positive response to a customer complaint, respectively.

Email allows you to be a bit playful in language, as Figure 13.2 on the next page shows.

Writing Negative Email Messages

Major negatives, such as firing someone, should be delivered in person, not by email. But email is appropriate for many less serious negatives.

Never write email messages when you're angry. If a message infuriates you, wait till you're calmer before you reply—and even then, reply only if you must. Writers using email are much less inhibited than they would be on paper or in person, sending insults, swearing, name-calling, and making hostile statements.[1] **Flaming** is the name given to this behaviour. Flaming reflects on the sender: it does not make you look like a mature, level-headed candidate for bigger things. And since employers have the right to read all email, flaming—particularly if directed at co-workers, regulators, suppliers, or customers—may cause an employee to be fired.

In the body of the email message, give a reason only if it is watertight and reflects well on the organization. Give an alternative, if one exists.

Edit and proofread your message carefully. An easy way for an angry reader to strike back is to attack typos or other errors.

Remember that email messages, like any written text, can become relevant documents in lawsuits. When a negative email is hard to write, you may want to compose it offline so that you can revise and even get feedback before you send the message.

Writing Persuasive Email Messages

When you ask for something small or for something that it is part of the reader's job duties to provide, your request can be straightforward. (See Figure 9.12, p. 182.)

- In the body of the message, give people all the information they need to act.
- At the end of the message, ask for the action you want. Make the action as easy as possible, and specify when you need a response. You may want an immediate response now ("Let me know asap whether you can write a story for the newsletter so that I can save the space") and a fuller one later ("we'll need the text by March 4").

Subject Lines for Persuasive Emails

The subject line of a persuasive email message should make it clear that you're asking for something

FYI

Professor William Haskell of Stanford University calculates that workers who spend 2 1/2 minutes an hour each day sending email to co-workers instead of walking over to talk with them will gain 1.1 pounds (.5 kg) of body fat a year.

Source: "Raw Data," *Wired*, May 1999, 21; visited Web site July 9, 2001. http://www.wired.com/wired/archive/7.05/mustread.html?pg=21

FYI

According to Microsoft, the average user of Outlook Express has 1,900 stored email messages.

Source: Don Clark, "Managing the Mountain," *The Wall Street Journal*, June 21, 1999, R4

Figure 13.2
A Positive Email Message

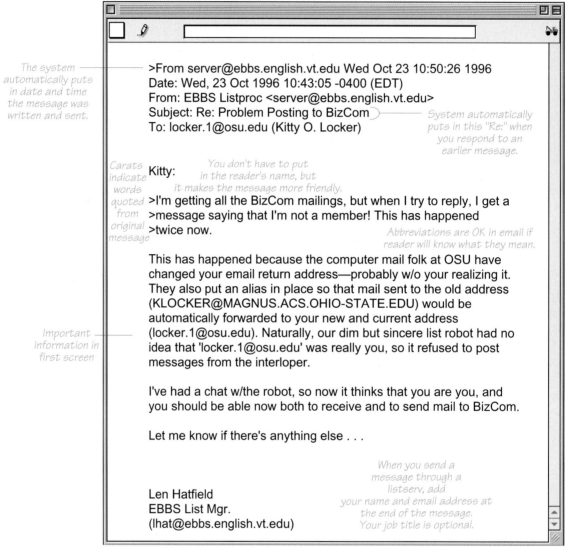

The system automatically puts in date and time the message was written and sent.

>From server@ebbs.english.vt.edu Wed Oct 23 10:50:26 1996
Date: Wed, 23 Oct 1996 10:43:05 -0400 (EDT)
From: EBBS Listproc <server@ebbs.english.vt.edu>
Subject: Re: Problem Posting to BizCom
To: locker.1@osu.edu (Kitty O. Locker)

System automatically puts in this "Re:" when you respond to an earlier message.

Carats indicate words quoted from original message

You don't have to put in the reader's name, but it makes the message more friendly.

Kitty:

>I'm getting all the BizCom mailings, but when I try to reply, I get a
>message saying that I'm not a member! This has happened
>twice now.

Abbreviations are OK in email if reader will know what they mean.

This has happened because the computer mail folk at OSU have changed your email return address—probably w/o your realizing it. They also put an alias in place so that mail sent to the old address (KLOCKER@MAGNUS.ACS.OHIO-STATE.EDU) would be automatically forwarded to your new and current address (locker.1@osu.edu). Naturally, our dim but sincere list robot had no idea that 'locker.1@osu.edu' was really you, so it refused to post messages from the interloper.

Important information in first screen

I've had a chat w/the robot, so now it thinks that you are you, and you should be able now both to receive and to send mail to BizCom.

Let me know if there's anything else . . .

When you send a message through a listserv, add your name and email address at the end of the message. Your job title is optional.

Len Hatfield
EBBS List Mgr.
(lhat@ebbs.english.vt.edu)

Instant Replay

What are SMART Goals?

SMART goals take a definite timeframe and describe your
Specific
Measurable
Achievable
Realistic
To-do's

When you ask for something big or something that is not a regular part of that person's duties, the first paragraph must not only specify the request but also make the reader view it positively. Use the second paragraph to provide an overview of the evidence that the rest of the message will provide: "Here's why we should do this. Let me describe the project. Then, if you're willing to be part of it, I'll send you a copy of the proposal." Use audience analysis (◀▶ p. 32) to find a reason to do as you ask that the reader will find convincing. Everyone is busy, so you need to make the reader want to do as you ask. Be sure to provide complete information that the reader will need to act on your request. Ask for the action you want.

Major requests that require changes in values, culture, or lifestyles should not be made in email messages.

Managing Your Time

Do you need more time? Welcome to the club! Although researchers claim that we have more leisure hours than we did 20 years ago, most of us feel more overworked than ever. And the number of things you'll need to do will only increase as you assume more job responsibilities.

The secret is to manage yourself, so that you feel more in control.

The first step in managing your time is to establish short- and long-term **SMART** goals, goals that **describe** your **S**pecific, **M**easurable, **A**chievable, **R**ealistic "to do's" in a definite **T**imeframe. "Starting today, I'm going to reserve a half-hour a day to read the paper, every day," is an example of a **SMART** goal. Identify your immediate and long-term **SMART** goals, write them down, and cross your daily **SMART** goals off as you achieve them. Following this process keeps you focussed and positive.

As an immediate **SMART** time management goal, divide projects or incoming mail into three piles (real or imaginary). Put urgent items in the *A* pile, important items in the *B* pile, and other items in the *C* pile. Do the *A* items first. Most people find that they never get to their *C* piles.

At the end of the day, make a list of the two most important things you need to do the next day—this list is your **SMART** goal record—and leave the paper where you'll see it when you start work the next morning.

Initiate a systematic problem-solving approach to understanding how you currently manage yourself:

1. For at least a week, log how you spend your time. Record what you're doing in 15-minute intervals.

2. Analyze your log to identify patterns, time obligations, time wasters, and frustrations. You may be surprised to find how much time you spend playing computer games. Or you may discover that answering email takes an hour every morning—not the five minutes or so that you'd estimated.

3. Clarify your **SMART** goals. What do you want to accomplish on the job and in your personal life? What strategies or steps (for example, taking a course, learning a new skill, or sending out job applications) will you need to do to reach your goals?

4. Set short-term **SMART** priorities. For the next month, what do you need to accomplish? In addition to goals for school and work, think also about building relationships, meeting personal obligations, and finding time to plan, to relax, and to think.

5. Ask for help or negotiate compromises. Maybe you and another parent can share baby-sitting so that you each have some time to yourselves. If your responsibilities at work are impossible, talk to your supervisor to see whether some of your duties can be transferred to someone else or whether you should stop trying to be excellent and settle for "good enough." You won't be willing or able to eliminate all your obligations, but sometimes dropping just one or two responsibilities can really help.

6. Schedule your day to reflect your priorities. You don't necessarily have to work on every goal every day, but each goal should appear on your schedule at least three times a week. Schedule some time for yourself, too.

7. Evaluate your new use of time. Are you meeting more of your goals? Are you feeling less stressed? If not, go back to step 1 and analyze more patterns, obligations, time wasters, and frustrations to see how you can make the best use of the time you have.

Visit http://www.mcgrawhill.ca/college/locker

Every technology brings both advantages and disadvantages

Source: Reprinted with special permission of King Features Syndicate.

What email "netiquette" rules should I follow?

Lurk before you leap.

Email communities develop their own norms. If possible, lurk a few days—read the messages without writing anything yourself—before you enter the conversation.
Follow these guidelines to be a good "netizen":

- Never send angry messages by email. If you have a conflict with someone, work it out face-to-face, not electronically.
- Use full caps only to emphasize a single word or two. Putting the whole message in caps is considered as rude as shouting.
- Send people only messages they need. Send copies to your boss or CEO only if he or she has asked you to.
- Find out how your recipient's system works and adapt your messages to it. Most people would rather get a separate short message on each of several topics, so that the messages can be stored in different mailboxes. But people who pay a fee to download each message may prefer longer messages that deal with several topics.
- When you respond to a message, include only the part of the original message that is essential so that the reader understands your posting. Delete the rest. If the quoted material is lengthy, put your response first, then the original material.
- When you compose a message in your word processor and call it up in email, use short line lengths (set the right margin at 2.5 inches or 3 inches). That's the way to avoid the awkward line breaks of Figure 9.13 (p. 184).

Should I worry about viruses?

Yes, in attachments.

A computer virus is a script that harms your computer or erases your data. You can't get a virus through email, but viruses can infect files that are "attached" to email messages or that you download. To stay virus-free,[2]

- Install an anti-virus program on your computer, and keep it up to date
- Ask people who send you attachments to include their names in the document titles; virus titles aren't that specific
- If you're in doubt about an attachment, don't open it
- Forward email messages only when you're sure of the source and contents

Site *to* **See**

Go to
www.kumite.com/myths

Learn whether a rumoured virus is real or a hoax.

Employability Skills 2000+ Checklist for Email Messages

In this module, the key skills from The Conference Board of Canada's Employability Skills 2000+ are:

Communicate
✔ share information using a range of information and communications technologies (e.g., voice, email, computers)
✔ write and speak so others pay attention and understand
✔ use relevant scientific, technological, and mathematical knowledge and skills to explain or clarify ideas

Manage Information
✔ locate, gather, and organize information using appropriate technology and information systems

Think & Solve Problems
✔ recognize the human, interpersonal, technical, scientific, and mathematical dimensions of a problem
✔ readily use science, technology, and mathematics as ways to think, gain and share knowledge, solve problems and make decisions

Be Responsible
✔ set goals and priorities balancing work and personal life
✔ plan and manage time, money, and other resources to achieve goals

Be Adaptable
✔ be innovative and resourceful: identify and suggest alternative ways to achieve goals and get the job done
✔ cope with uncertainty

Participate in Projects & Tasks
✔ work to agreed quality standards and specifications
✔ adapt to changing requirements and information

Review of Key Points

- All of the principles of good writing apply to email. Use you-attitude, positive emphasis, and reader benefits when you'd use them in paper messages
- Subject lines for email messages must be specific, concise, and catchy

- Create email messages that people can read and act on quickly
- Compose important messages offline to allow time for thought and revision

Learning Applications

Questions for Comprehension

13.1 How do subject lines for email messages differ from those for paper messages?

13.2 Should email messages use you-attitude, positive emphasis, and reader benefits?

13.3 What is flaming?

Questions for Critical Thinking

13.4 Why are spelling and punctuation still important in email?

13.5 Why should you compose important email messages offline?

13.6 Why should negative and persuasive email messages be more direct than their paper counterparts?

13.7 Why is it OK for your boss to send you a message with the subject line "To Do," even though that wouldn't work when you need to ask a colleague to do something?

Questions for Building Skills

13.8 What skills have you read about in this module?

13.9 What skills are you practising in the assignments you're doing for this module?

13.10 How could you further develop the skills you're working on?

Exercises and Problems

13.11 Saying Yes to a Subordinate

Today, you get this request from a subordinate.

> Subject: Request for Leave
>
> You know that I've been feeling burned out. I've decided that I want to take a three-month leave of absence this summer to travel abroad. I've got five weeks of vacation time saved up; I would take the rest as unpaid leave. Just guarantee that my job will be waiting when I come back!

Write an email message granting the request.

13.12 Calming an Angry Co-worker

You're a member of a self-managed team on a factory assembly line. When you check the team's email, you find this message from the factory's quality assurance manager:

> Subject: Holes in Your Heads?
>
> Yesterday in the scrap bin I found a casting with three times too many holes in it. How could a machinist make such a mistake? What's going on?

The answer is simple. The extra holes come not from crazy machinists but from crafty ones. Your team uses old machines that aren't computerized. When you make a part on those machines, you have to drill a test piece first to be sure that the alignment and size of the holes are correct. This testing has to be done every time you set up for a new run.

Your team has figured out that you can use less material by reusing the test piece until it resembles Swiss cheese, rather than throwing it away after a single testing. Your team is one of the most efficient in the plant, thanks to creative moves like this one.

Write an email response.

13.13 Refusing to Provide Graduates' Addresses on Your Web Page

You maintain the Web page for your university or community college department. Today, you get the following email message:

> Subject: Add Graduates' Names?
>
> I really like your Web site. Could you please add the names and addresses (snail and email) of recent graduates? That would help us keep in touch and would be really useful for networking.

You don't want to do this. Probably someone has this information, but you don't know who. You've got enough to do without tracking down the information, posting it on the Web, and updating it as people move. But you don't want to offend the person who asked, since recent graduates are asked to help in many ways (sponsor internships, give money, etc.). So you need to say *no* while maintaining goodwill.

Write the message.

13.13 Telling an Employee that a Workshop Is Full

As director of human resources, you sponsor a variety of workshops for employees. You received this email message today:

> Subject: Re: Oral Presentation Workshops
>
> Please register me for the workshop on giving oral presentations next week. My supervisor has told me I should attend this.

The workshop is full, however, and you already have three people on a waiting list to fill vacancies if anyone should cancel. You would repeat the workshop only if you have guarantees for at least 15 participants.

Write the message.

13.15 Telling Employees to Remove Personal Web Sites

You're director of management and information systems (MIS) in your organization. At your monthly briefing for management, a vice president complained that some employees have posted personal Web pages on the company's Web server. "It looks really unprofessional to have stuff about cats and children and musical instruments. How can people do this?"

You took the question literally. "Well, some people have authorization to post material—price changes, job listings, marketing information. Someone who has authorization could put up anything."

Another manager said, "I don't think it's so terrible—after all, there aren't any links from our official pages to these personal pages."

A third person said, "But we're paying for what's posted—so we pay for server space and connect time. Maybe it's not much right now, but as more and more people become Web-literate, the number of people putting up unauthorized pages could spread. We should put a stop to this now."

The vice president agreed. "The Web site is carefully designed to present an image of our organization. Personal pages are dangerous. Can you imagine the flak we'd get if someone posted links to pornography?"

You said, "I don't think that's very likely. If it did happen, as system administrator, I could remove the page."

The third speaker said, "I think we should remove all the pages. Having any at all suggests that our people have so much extra time that they're playing on the Web. That suggests that our prices are too high and may make some people worry about quality. In fact, I think that we need a new policy prohibiting personal pages on the company's Web server. And any pages that are already up should be removed."

A majority of the managers agreed and told you to write a write a message to all employees. Create an email message to tell employees that you will remove the personal pages already posted and that no more will be allowed.

Hint:

- Suggest other ways that people can post personal Web pages. Commercial services such as CompuServe and America Online are possibilities. Students at Plugged in <www.pluggedin.org> can also provide Web access for a fee. (Check to be sure that the groups you recommend are still offering Web sites. If possible, get current prices.)

13.16   Saying No to the Boss

Today, you received this email from your boss.

Subject: Oversee United Way

I'm appointing you to be the company representative to oversee United Way. You've done a good job the last three years, so this year should be a piece of cake.

It's true that you know exactly what to do. The job wouldn't be hard for you. But that's just the problem. You wouldn't learn anything, either. You'd rather have an assignment that would stretch you, teach you new skills, or enable you to interact with new people. Continuing to grow is your insurance of continued employability and mobility. Three upcoming projects in your division might offer growth: creating videos for a "town meeting" for all employees to be held at the beginning of next quarter, creating an intranet for the company, or serving on the diversity committee. Any of these would be time-consuming, but no more time-consuming than running the United Way campaign.

Write to your boss, asking for something more challenging to do.

13.17   Persuading the CEO to Attend Orientation

As the director of education and training of your organization, you run orientation sessions for new hires. You're planning next quarter's session (new quarters start in January, April, July, and October) for a big group of new college graduates. You'd really like the organization's president and CEO to come in and talk to the group for at least 15 minutes. Probably most of the employees have seen the CEO, but they haven't had any direct contact. The CEO could come any time during the three-day session. Speaking just before or after lunch would be ideal, because then the CEO could also come to lunch and talk informally with at least a few people. Next best would be speaking just before or after the midmorning or midafternoon breaks. But the CEO is busy, and you'll take what you can get.

As Your Instructor Directs,

a. Assume that your instructor is your CEO, and send an email message persuading him or her to come to orientation

b. Send an email message to your instructor, asking him or her to address new members of a campus organization

c. Address the CEO of your university, college or workplace, asking him or her to speak to new employees

13.18   Asking for More Time and/or Resources

Today, this message shows up in your email inbox from your boss:

Subject: Re: Want Climate Report

This request has come down from the CEO. I'm delegating it to you. See me a couple of days before the Board meeting—the first Monday of next month—so we can go over your presentation.

I want a report on the climate for underrepresented groups in our organization. A presentation at the last Board of Directors' meeting showed that while we do a good job of hiring women and minorities, few of them rise to the top. The Directors suspect that our climate may not be supportive and want information on it. Please prepare a presentation for the next meeting. You'll have 15 minutes.

Making a presentation to the company's Board of Directors can really help your career. But preparing a good presentation and report will take time. You can look at exit reports filed by Human Resources when people leave the company, but you'll also need to interview people—lots of people. And you're already working 60 hours a week on three major projects, one of which is behind schedule. Can one of the projects wait? Can someone else take one of the projects? Can you get some help? Should you do just enough to get by? Ask your boss for advice—in a way that makes you look like a committed employee, not a slacker.

13.19 Asking for Volunteers

You have an executive position with one of the major employers in town. (Pick a business, non-profit organization, or government office you know something about.) Two years ago, your company "adopted" a local school. You've provided computers and paid for Internet access; a small number of workers have signed up to be mentors. Today you get a call from the school's principal, a friend of yours. "I'd like to talk to you about the mentoring program. You're providing some mentors, and we're grateful for them, but we need 10 times that number."

(You wince. This program has not been one of your successes.) "I know that part of the program hasn't worked out as well as we hoped it would. But people are really busy here. Not all that many people have two or three hours a week to spend with a kid."

"So you think the time it takes is really the problem."

(Maybe your friend will appreciate that you can't force people to do this.) "Pretty much."

"Do you think people would be willing to be mentors if we could find a way for it to take less time?"

"Maybe." (You sense that a hook is coming, and you're wary.)

"Your people spend a lot of time on email, don't they?"

"Yes. Two to three hours a day, for most of them."

"What if we created a new mentoring structure, where people just emailed their mentees instead of meeting with them? That way they could still provide advice and support, but they could do it at any time of the day. And it wouldn't have to take long."

(This sounds interesting.) "So people would just have email conversations. That would be a lot easier, and we'd get more people. But can they really have a relationship if they don't meet the kids?"

"Maybe we could have a picnic or go to a game a couple of times a year so people could meet face-to-face."

"And all the kids have computers?"

"Not necessarily at home. But they all have access to email at school. Writing email to professionals will also give them more practice and more confidence. People like to get email."

"Not when they get 200 messages a day, they don't."

"Well, our kids aren't in that category. What do you say?"

"I think it will work. Let's try it."

"Great. Just send me a list of the people who are willing to do this, and we'll match them up with the kids. We'd like to get this started as soon as possible."

Write an email message to all employees asking them to volunteer.

13.20 Asking for Something Different for Administrative Professionals' Week

Your clerical job gives you flexibility you need while you're in school. Administrative Assistants' (formerly Secretaries') Week is approaching, and you really don't want flowers or a free lunch. You'd much rather have a bonus or at least time off to attend an educational seminar (resourced by the company). You're interested in learning advanced features of a computer program or in assertive behaviour techniques.

Write an email to the person who supervises clerical workers in your unit, asking that Administrative Professionals Week give you something useful.

Hints:

- Assume that you work in an organization you know something about
- Specify one or more seminars you'd like to attend
- Some seminars may cost a lot more than flowers or lunch; some may cost less. How much financial flexibility does the organization have?
- Are there other clerical workers? Would they also like bonuses or seminars, or do some prefer flowers or lunch?
- How well does the person who will make the decision know you? How positively does he or she view you and any other clerical workers?

▶ Polishing Your Prose

Making Nouns and Pronouns Agree

Pronouns must agree with the nouns to which they refer in two ways: (1) person and (2) number—singular or plural.

	Singular	**Plural**
First-person	I, my, mine, me, myself	we, our, us, ourselves
Second-person	you, your, yourself	you, your, our, ours, yourselves
Third-person	he, she, it, him, her, his, hers	they, their, them, themselves

Incorrect: In my internship, I learned that you have to manage your time wisely.

Correct: In my internship, I learned to manage my time wisely.

Incorrect: The sales team reached their goal.

Correct: The sales team reached its goal.

Canadian and U.S. usage treats company names and the words company and government as sin-gular nouns. In Great Britain, these nouns are plural and require plural pronouns:

Correct (Canadian): Clarica trains its agents well.

Correct (U.S.): Nationwide Insurance trains its agents well.

Correct (U.K.): Lloyd's of London train their agents well.

Exercises

Identify and correct any errors. Note that some sentences do not contain errors.

1. A secretary should help his or her boss work efficiently.

2. The mayor should give themselves credit for doing a good job.

3. The company announces their quarterly profits today.

4. Most new employees find that they need to learn a new culture.

5. A CEO's pay is often based on the performance of their company.

6. The union votes today on whether they will go on strike.

7. In my first month of work, I learned that you need to check email at least three times a day.

8. One of the features of my corporate culture is a willingness to share ideas.

9. The team will present its recommendations to the Executive Committee.

10. Every employee is interested in improving their technical skills.

Check your answers to the odd-numbered exercises on page 633.

 CBC Video Case

 CBC

Go to www.mcgrawhill.ca/college/locker for "Cyberslacking," an online CBC Video Case that explores the use of email in Canadian workplaces—and why companies monitor employees' messages.

Unit Four

Polishing Your Writing

Module 14
Editing for Grammar and Punctuation

Topics

- What grammar errors do I need to be able to fix?

- Should I put a comma every place I'd take a breath?

- How can I find sentence boundaries?

- What punctuation should I use inside sentences?

- What do I use when I quote sources?

- How should I write numbers and dates?

- How do I mark errors I find in proofreading?

Review of Key Points

Learning Applications

Polishing Your Prose: Using Spell and Grammar Checkers

Learning Focus

After reading and applying the information in Module 14, you'll be able to demonstrate

Knowledge of

- The connection between correctness and credibility
- Contemporary language usage

Skills to

- Use standard edited English
- Fix common grammatical errors
- Use punctuation correctly
- Mark errors as you proofread

"Writing is like driving. ...We need to remind ourselves of the rules to avoid syntactical crashes."

"Punctuation is important because how a sentence is punctuated can determine its meaning," says Otte Rosenkrantz, freelance journalist, author and, more recently, communications teacher. To demonstrate this assertion to his students, Otte writes "**woman without her man is a savage**" on the board and asks students to punctuate the phrase, with fascinating results. The men in the class usually punctuate it as, "Woman, without her man, is a savage," while the women usually punctuate it as "Woman: without her, man is a savage." Here is a clear example of how with different punctuation the same words can give opposite meanings.

Otte was born in Denmark and came to Canada as a teenager. Since English is Otte's second language he finds it fascinating because the structure is so different from Danish. There are different rules about punctuation—Otte mentions that the semicolon is a particular challenge.

Working in a second language has not been a barrier to Otte's success in communication. He began a career as a freelance journalist over twenty years ago. Otte has an M.A. in history and is currently working on his M.Ed in adult education. Otte's work has appeared in virtually every newspa-per in the country. He has written on such diverse topics as the effects of TV violence on children and outdoor experiences for *Outdoor Canada* magazine and his humorous columns have won an award from the Ontario Community Newspaper Association. Otte also has four books in print, including collections of columns, short stories, and essays, and a corporate history.

Otte says that as a freelance journalist he must first come up with an idea and then try to sell it. He's found that once editors know a writer is accurate and can meet deadlines, they start calling. Otte's approach to writing is to do the research first and then to sit down and write the whole piece. Then he edits—first for content, then for syntax. "I pay special attention to syntax," he says, "because, for example, a misplaced modifier or incorrect punctuation can mislead the reader."

"Get a good reference book and use it," Otte advises student writers. "Writing is like driving. It is too easy to develop bad habits. We need to remind ourselves of the rules to avoid syntactical crashes."

http://www.homestead.com/otte/
Otte Rosenkrantz's Homepage

Building a Professional Image, 2

Grammar and mechanics present a paradox. On the one hand, grammar and punctuation are the least important part of any message: the clarity and organization of your ideas matter much more.

On the other hand, grammatical "errors" cause the audience to doubt or ignore your ideas. Grammar, like clothing and table manners, is used to estimate social class. Business people expect documents to use standard edited English. Writers and speakers who use other varieties of English may be seen as unpromotable, poorly trained, or even unintelligent. Readers see errors as a sign of carelessness: "If you don't care enough to get your documents right, how do I know you'll care about the quality of the work you do for me?" Because they convey the quality of your ideas, grammar and punctuation can be the most important part of your message.

Occasionally, errors in grammar and punctuation hide the writer's meaning. More often, it's possible to figure out what the writer probably meant, but the mistake still sends the wrong message (and can be an excuse for a hostile reader or an opposing attorney).

Remember editing for correctness is part of the polishing or editing process, best done on your penultimate draft. The brain can't attend both to big ideas and to sentence-level concerns at the same time, so don't try to fix errors in your first and second drafts. But do save time to check your almost-final draft to eliminate any errors in grammar, punctuation, and word choice.

Most writers make a small number of grammatical errors repeatedly. Most readers care deeply about only a few grammatical points. Keep track of the feedback you get (from your instructors now, from your supervisor later) and put your energy into correcting the errors that bother the people who read what you write. A command of standard grammar will help you build the credible, professional image you want to create with everything you write

With the possible exception of spelling, grammar is the aspect of writing that writers seem to find most troublesome. Faulty grammar is often what executives are objecting to when they complain that college graduates or M.B.A.s "can't write." Indeed, your credibility is on the line whenever you write for an audience. When readers receive your written message, you're not there to explain, "What I really mean is…" Your document represents you and your organization; it's a permanent record of your capability. Letters, memos, emails, and reports with mechanical errors interfere with readability, reflect poorly on the quality of your work, and, ultimately, cost time and money.

What grammatical errors do I need to be able to fix?

Learn how to fix these six errors.

Good writers can edit to achieve subject-verb and noun-pronoun agreement, to use the right case for pronouns, to avoid dangling and misplaced modifiers, and to correct predication errors.

Subject-verb Agreement

Site *to* **See**

Go to
http://www.gramm
ar.english-at-
home.com/

This site will help
you learn grammar
in real language.

Singular subjects use singular verbs; plural subjects use plural verbs

Incorrect: The accountants who conducted the audit was recommended highly.

Correct: The accountants who conducted the audit were recommended highly.

Subject-verb agreement errors often occur when other words come between the subject and the verb. Edit your draft by finding the subject and the verb of each sentence.

Canadian and American usage treats company names and the words company and government as singular nouns. British usage treats them as plural:

Correct (Canada): Clarica Insurance trains its agents well.

Correct (U.S.):   Allstate Insurance trains its agents well.

Correct (U.K.)   Lloyd's of London train their agents well.

Site *to* **See**

Go to
http://writing.englis
hclub.com/spelling_
ukus.htm

This site identifies
the differences
between Canadian,
and American
spelling.

Use a plural verb when two or more singular subjects are joined by *and*.

Correct: Larry McGreevy and I are planning to visit the client.

Use a singular verb when two or more singular subjects are joined by *or*, *nor*, or *but*.

Correct: Either the shipping clerk or the superintendent has to sign the order.

When the sentence begins with *Here* or *There*, make the verb agree with the subject that follows the verb.

Correct: Here is the booklet you asked for.

Correct: There are the blueprints I wanted.

Note that some words that end in s are considered to be singular and require singular verbs.

Correct: A series of meetings is planned.

When a situation doesn't seem to fit the rules, or when following a rule produces an awkward sentence, revise the sentence to avoid the problem.

Problematic: The plant manager in addition to the sales representative (was, were?) pleased with the new system.

Better: The plant manager and the sales representative were pleased with the new system.

Problematic: None of us (is, are?) perfect.

Better: All of us have faults.

Errors in **noun-pronoun agreement** occur if a pronoun is of a different number (singular or plural) or person than the word it refers to.

Incorrect: All drivers of leased automobiles are billed $100 if damages to his automobile are caused by a collision.

Correct: All drivers of leased automobiles are billed $100 if damages to their automobiles are caused by collisions.

Incorrect: A manager has only yourself to blame if things go wrong.

Correct: As a manager, you have only yourself to blame if things go wrong.

The following words require a singular pronoun:

everybody	neither
each	nobody
either	a person
everyone	

Correct: Everyone should bring his or her copy of the manual to the next session on changes in the law.

Because pronoun pairs necessary to avoid sexism (his/hers) seem cumbersome, use words that take plural pronouns (people, employees, persons) or use second-person *you*.

Each pronoun must refer to a specific word. If a pronoun does not refer to a specific term, add a word to correct the error.

Incorrect: We will open three new stores in the suburbs. This will bring us closer to our customers.

Correct: We will open three new stores in the suburbs. This strategy will bring us closer to our customers.

Hint: Make sure *this* and *it* refer to a specific noun in the previous sentence. If either refers to an idea, add a noun ("this strategy") to make the sentence grammatically correct.

Use *who* and *whom* to refer to people and *which* to refer to objects. *That* can refer to anything: people, animals, organizations, and objects.

Correct: The new Executive Director, who moved here from Laval, is already making friends.

Correct: The information that she wants will be available tomorrow.

Correct: This confirms the price that I quoted you this morning.

Case

Case refers to the grammatical role a noun or pronoun plays in a sentence. Figure 14.1 on the next page, identifies the case of each personal pronoun.

Use subjective or **nominative** pronouns for the **subject** of a clause.

Correct: Shannon Weaver and I talked to the customer, who was interested in learning more about integrated software.

Use **possessive** pronouns to show who or what something belongs to.

Correct: Microsoft Office 2000 will exactly meet her needs.

Use **objective** pronouns as **objects** of verbs or prepositions.

Correct: When you send in the quote, thank her for the courtesy she showed Shannon and me.

Site *to* See

Go to
http://www.grammarbook.com/grammar/whoVwhVt.html

http://hometown.aol.com/drcarlperrin/whoquiz.html

The first Web site offers a quick review of when to use who, which, and that; the second presents the Grammar Doctor's quiz on who vs. whom.

	Nominative (subject of clause	Possessive	Objective	Reflexive/intensive
Singular				
1st person	I	my, mine	me	myself
2nd person	you	your, yours	you	yourself
3rd person	he/she/it	his/her(s)/its	him/her/it	himself/herself/itself
	one/who	one's/whose	one/whom	oneself/(no form)
Plural				
1st person	we	our, ours	us	ourselves
2nd person	you	your, yours	you	yourselves
3rd person	they	their, theirs	them	themselves

Figure 14.1

The Case of the Personal Pronoun

Hint: Use *whom* when *him* would fit grammatically in the same place in your sentence.

> I am writing this letter to (who/whom?) it may concern.
> I am writing this letter to him.

Correct: Whom is correct.

> Have we decided (who, whom?) will take notes?
> Have we decided he will take notes?

Correct: Who is correct.

Reflexive pronouns emphasize a noun or pronoun that has already appeared in the sentence.

Correct: I myself think the call was a very productive one.

Reflexive pronouns are used **very infrequently** in Canadian business practice, since they emphasize the writer/speaker unnecessarily.
Do not use reflexive pronouns as subjects of clauses or as objects of verbs or propositions.

Incorrect: Elaine and myself will follow up on this order.

Correct: Elaine and I will follow up on this order.

Incorrect: He gave the order to Dan and myself.

Correct: He gave the order to Dan and me.

Note that the first-person pronoun comes *after* names or pronouns that refer to other people.

Dangling Modifier (DM)

Modifiers are words or phrases that give more information about the subject, verb, or object in a clause. A modifier **dangles** when the word it modifies is not actually in the sentence. The solution is to reword the modifier so that it is grammatically correct.

Incorrect: Confirming our conversation, the truck will leave Monday.

> [The speaker is doing the confirming. But the speaker isn't in the sentence.]

FYI

People's perceptions of you begin with your appearance. You make the most favourable impression when you match your attire to the company culture and to your clients' expectations. And experts agree that dressing for success means dressing for the job you want.

Source: Catalina Marguilis, "You Are What You Wear," *Your Office,* June/July, 2001 Volume 8, edition 2 Toronto, ON, 25

Incorrect: At the age of eight, I began teaching my children about business.

[This sentence says that the author was eight when he or she had children who could understand business.]

Correct a dangling modifier in one of these ways:

• Recast the modifier as a subordinate clause.

Correct: As I told you, the truck will leave Monday.

Correct: When they were eight, I began teaching my children about business.

• Revise the main clause so its subject or object can be modified by the now-dangling phrase.

Correct: Confirming our conversation, I have scheduled the truck to leave Monday.

Correct: At the age of eight, my children began learning about business.

Hint: Whenever you use a verb or adjective that ends in *-ing*, make sure it modifies the grammatical subject of your sentence. If it doesn't, reword the sentence.

Misplaced Modifier (MM)

A **misplaced modifier** is a word, phrase, or clause that appears beside different element of the sentence than the writer intended, causing confusion or misinterpretation.

Incorrect: Customers who complain often alert us to changes we need to make. [Does the sentence mean that customers must complain frequently to teach us something? Or is the meaning that frequently we learn from complaints?]

Correct a misplaced modifier by moving it closer to the word it modifies or by adding punctuation to clarify your meaning. If a modifier modifies the whole sentence, use it as an introductory phrase or clause; follow it with a comma.

Correct: Often, customers who complain alert us to changes we need to make.

Parallelism

Items in a series or list must have the same grammatical structure.

Not parallel: In the second month of your internship, you will
1. Learn how to resolve customers' complaints.
2. Supervision of desk staff.
3. Interns will help plan store displays.

Parallel: In the second month of your internship, you will
1. Learn how to resolve customers' complaints.
2. Supervise desk staff.
3. Plan store displays.

Instant Replay

Dangling Modifiers

A modifier dangles when the word it modifies is not actually in the sentence.

Site *to* See

Go to
www.1dressup.com
www.harryrosen.com

Compare your sartorial choices with the experts' advice.

Also parallel: Duties in the second month of your internship include resolving customers' complaints, supervising desk staff, and planning store displays.

Hint: When you have two or three items in a list (whether the list is horizontal or vertical) make sure the items are in the same grammatical form. Put lists vertically to make them easier to see.

Predication Errors

The predicate of a sentence must fit grammatically and logically with the subject. In sentences using is and other linking verbs, the complement must be a noun, an adjective, or a noun clause.

Incorrect: The reason for this change is because the OSC now requires fuller disclosure.

Correct: The reason for this change is that the OSC now requires fuller disclosure.

Make sure that the verb describes the action done by or done to the subject.

Incorrect: Our goals should begin immediately.

Correct: Implementing our goals should begin immediately.

Should I put a comma every place I'd take a breath?

No! Commas are not breaths.

Commas, like other punctuation marks, are road signs to help readers predict what comes next, thereby contributing to ease and speed of reading, or **readability**. The easier you make it for the reader to scan and understand the text, the more credible you appear and the more likely the reader will be persuaded to your point of view.

When you move from the subject to the verb, you're going in a straight line; no comma is needed. When you end an introductory phrase or clause, the comma tells readers the introduction is over and you're turning to the main clause. When words interrupt the main clause, like this, commas tell the reader when to turn off the main clause for a short side route and when to return.

Mark	Tells the Reader
Period	We're stopping.
Semicolon	What comes next is another complete thought, closely related to what I just said.
Colon	What comes next is an illustration, example or a qualification of what I just said.
Dash	What comes next is a dramatic example of or a shift from what I just said.
Comma	What comes next is a slight turn, but we're going in the same direction

Figure 14.2
What Punctuation Tells the Reader

FYI

Forty-seven percent of business people take their laptops on vacation.

Source: Tony Schwartz, "Making Waves," *Fast Company*, October 1999, 347.

How can I find sentence boundaries?

Learn to recognize main clauses.

A **sentence** contains at least one main clause. A **main** or **independent clause** is a complete statement, with a subject and a verb. A **subordinate** or **dependent clause** contains both a subject and verb but is not a complete statement and cannot stand by itself; it depends on an independent clause (a sentence or complete thought for meaning. A phrase is a group of words that does not contain a verb.

Main/Independent Clauses

Your order will arrive Thursday.

He dreaded talking to his supplier.

I plan to enrol for summer school classes.

Subordinate/Dependent Clauses

If you place your order by Monday

Because he was afraid the product would be out of stock

Since I want to graduate next spring

Although I was prepared for the test

Phrases

With our current schedule

As a result

A clause with one of the following words will be subordinate:

after

although, though

because, since

before, until

if

until

when, whenever

while, as

Using the correct punctuation will enable you to avoid three major sentence errors: comma splices, run-on sentences, and sentence fragments.

Comma Splices (CS)

A **comma splice** or **comma fault** occurs when two main clauses are joined only by a comma (instead of by a comma and a coordinating conjunction).

Incorrect: The contest will start in June, the date has not been set.

Correct a comma splice in one of the following four ways:

- If the ideas are closely related, use a semicolon rather than a comma.

Correct: The contest will start in June; the exact date has not been set.

- If they aren't closely related, start a new sentence.

Correct: The contest will start in June. We need to determine the exact date.

- Add a coordinating conjunction (and, but or, for, nor).

Correct: The contest will start in June, but the exact date has not been set.

- Subordinate one of the clauses.

Correct: Although the contest will start in June, the date has not been set.

Remember that you cannot use just a comma with the following transitional words:

however

therefore

nevertheless

moreover

Instead, use a semicolon to separate the clauses or start a new sentence.

Incorrect: Computerized grammar checkers do not catch every error, however, they may be useful as a first check before an editor reads the material.

Correct: Computerized grammar checkers do not catch every error; however, they may be useful as a first check before an editor reads the material.

Run-on Sentences (RO)

A **run-on sentence** strings together several main clauses using *and*, *but*, *or*, *so*, and *for*. Run-on sentences and comma splices are "mirror faults." A comma splice uses *only* the comma and omits the coordinating conjunction, while a run-on sentence uses *only* the conjunction and omits the comma. Correct a short run-on sentence by adding a comma. Separate a long run-on sentence into two or more sentences. Consider subordinating one or more of the clauses.

Incorrect: We will end up with a much smaller markup but they use a lot of this material so the volume would be high so try to sell them on fast delivery and tell them our quality is very high.

Correct: Although we will end up with a much smaller markup, volume would be high since they use a lot of this material. Try to sell them on fast delivery and high quality.

Site to See

Go to
http://webster.com
mnet.edu/grammar/
runons.htm#splice

A review of comma splices and online quizzes to test your skills.

Instant Replay

Comma Splices

A **comma splice** or **comma fault** occurs when two main clauses are joined only by a comma (instead of by a comma and a coordinating conjunction).

Instant Replay

Sentence Fragments

In a sentence fragment, a group of words that is not a complete sentence is punctuated as if it were a complete sentence.

Sentence Fragments (Frag)

In a **sentence fragment**, a group of words that is not a complete sentence is punctuated as if it were a complete sentence. Sentence fragments often occur when a writer thinks of additional detail that the reader needs. Fragments are acceptable in résumés and sales letters, but they're rarely acceptable in other business documents.

Incorrect: Observing these people, I have learned two things about the program. The time it takes. The rewards it brings.

To fix a sentence fragment, either add whatever parts of the sentence are missing or incorporate the fragment into the sentence before it or after it.

Correct: Observing these people, I have learned that the program is time-consuming but rewarding.

Remember that clauses with the following words are not complete sentences. Join them to a main clause.

> after
>
> although, though
>
> because, since
>
> before, until
>
> if
>
> when, whenever
>
> while, as

Incorrect: We need to buy a new computer system. Because our current system is obsolete.

Correct: We need to buy a new computer system because our current system is obsolete.

Instant Replay

Sentence Fragments

In a **sentence fragment**, a group of words that is not a complete sentence is punctuated as if it were a complete sentence.

Site to See

Go to
http://www.nuff.ox.ac.uk/Users/Martin/APOST/Apostrop.htm

The Home for Abused Apostrophes offers visual proof of apostrophe abuse.

What punctuation should I use inside sentences?

Use punctuation to clarify meaning for your reader.

The good business and administrative writer knows how to use the following punctuation marks: apostrophes, colons, commas, dashes, hyphens, parentheses, periods, and semicolons.

Apostrophe

1. Use an apostrophe in a contraction to indicate that a letter has been omitted.

   We're trying to renegotiate the contract.

   The '90s were years of restructuring for our company.

2. To indicate possession, add an apostrophe and an s to the word.

   The corporation's home office is in Vancouver, British Columbia.

Treasure the poor apostrophe

Source: Reprinted with special permission of King Features Syndicate.

Apostrophes to indicate possession are especially essential when one noun in a comparison is omitted.

This year's sales will be higher than last year's.

When a word already ends in an *s*, add only an apostrophe to make it possessive.

The meeting will be held at St. Johns' convention centre.

With many terms, the placement of the apostrophe indicates whether the noun is singular or plural.

Incorrect: The program should increase the participant's knowledge.
[Implies that only one participant is in the program.]

Correct: The program should increase the participants' knowledge.
[Many participants are in the program.]

Hint: Use *of* in the sentence to see where the apostrophe goes.

The figures of last year = last year's figures

The needs of our customers = our customers' needs

Possessive pronouns (e.g., *his*, *ours*) usually do not have apostrophes. The only exception is *one's*.

The company needs the goodwill of its stockholders.

His promotion was announced yesterday.

One's greatest asset is the willingness to work hard.

3. Use an apostrophe to make plurals that could be confused for other words.
I earned A's in all my business courses.
However, other plurals do not use apostrophes.

Site *to* **See**

Go to
**http://inst.santafe.
cc.fl.us/~bhirschf/
aposrule.htm**
Apostrophes rules
made easy.

Colon

1. Use a colon to separate the main clause (sentence) and a list, explanation or qualification that explains the last element in the clause. The items in the list are specific examples of the word that appears immediately before the colon.

> Please order the following supplies:
>
>   printer ribbons
>
>   computer paper (20-lb. white bond)
>
>   bond paper (25-lb., white, 25% cotton)
>
>   company letterhead
>
>   company envelopes

Because English is a living language, grammar, punctuation, and usage rules evolve over time; however, current contemporary Canadian usage indicates a preference for lowercase after the colon.

> Please order the following supplies: printer ribbons, computer paper (20-lb. white bond), bond paper (25-lb., white, 25% cotton), company letterhead, and company envelopes.

Avoid using a colon when the list is grammatically part of the main clause.

Incorrect: The rooms will have coordinated decors in natural colours such as: eggplant, moss, and mushroom.

Correct: The rooms will have coordinated decors in natural colours such as eggplant, moss, and mushroom.

Correct: The rooms will have coordinated decors in a variety of natural colours: eggplant, moss, and mushroom.

If the list is presented vertically, some authorities suggest introducing the list with a colon even though the words preceding the colon are not a complete sentence.

2. Use a colon to join two independent clauses when the second clause explains or restates the first clause.

Selling is simple: Give people the service they need, and they'll come back with more orders.

Comma

1. Use commas to separate the main clause from an introductory clause, the reader's name, or words that interrupt the main clause. Note that commas both precede and follow the interrupting information.

J. Camaya, the new Sales Manager, comes to us from the Saskatoon office.

A **nonessential clause** gives extra information that is not needed to identify the noun it modifies. Because nonessential clauses give extra information, they need extra commas.

Sue Decker, who wants to advance in the organization, has signed up for the company training program in sales techniques.

Do not use commas to set off information that restricts the meaning of a noun or pronoun. **Essential clauses** give essential, not extra, information.

Anyone ☐ who wants to advance in the organization ☐ should take advantage of on-the-job training.

Do not use commas to separate the subject from the verb, even if you would take a breath after a long subject.

Incorrect: Laws requiring anyone collecting $5,000 or more on behalf of another person, apply to schools and private individuals as well to charitable groups and professional fund-raisers.

Correct: Laws requiring anyone collecting $5,000 or more on behalf of another person ☐ apply to schools and private individuals as well to charitable groups and professional fund-raisers.

2. Use a comma after the first clause in a compound sentence if the clauses are long or if they have different subjects.

This policy eliminates all sick leave credit of the employee at the time of retirement, and payment will be made only once to any individual.

Do not use commas to join independent clauses without a conjunction. Doing so produces comma splices.

3. Use commas to separate items in a series. Using a comma before the *and* or *or* is not required by some authorities, but using a comma always adds clarity. The comma is essential if any of the items in the series themselves contain the word *and*.

The company contributes equally to full hospital coverage for eligible employees, spouses, and unmarried dependent children under age 21.

Dash

Use dashes to emphasize an aside, or break in thought.

Ryertex comes in 30 grades—each with a special use.

To type a dash, use two hyphens with no space before or after.

Hyphen

1. Use a hyphen to indicate that a word has been divided between two lines.

Attach the original receipts for lodging, transportation, and registration fees.

Divide words at syllable breaks. If you aren't sure where the syllables divide, look up the word in a dictionary. When a word has several syllables, divide it after a vowel

Site *to* **See**

Go to
http://elza.lpi.ru/Wri
tersGuide/mastertoc
.html
Here's a handy
online reference for
the editing process.

or between two consonants. Don't divide words of one syllable (e.g., *used*); don't divide a two-syllable word if one of the syllables is only one letter long (e.g., *acre*).

2. Use hyphens to join two or more words used as a single adjective.

Order five 10- or 12-metre lengths.

It's a ten-year-old plan.

The computer-prepared Income and Expense statements will be ready next Friday.

The hyphen clarifies meaning. In the first example, five lengths are needed, not lengths of 5, 10, or 12 feet. In the second example, without the hyphen, the reader might think that *computer* was the subject and *prepared* was the verb.

Parentheses

1. Use parentheses to set off words, phrases, or sentences used to explain or comment on the main idea.

For the thinnest Ryertex (.015") only a single layer of the base material may be used, while the thickest (10") may contain over 600 greatly compressed layers of fabric or paper. By varying the fabric used (cotton, asbestos, glass, or nylon) or the type of paper, and by changing the kind of resin (phenolic, melamine, silicone, or epoxy), we can produce 30 different grades.

Any additional punctuation goes outside the second parenthesis when the punctuation applies to the whole sentence. It goes inside when it applies only to the words in the parentheses.

Please check the invoice to see if credit should be issued. (A copy of the invoice is attached.)

2. Use parentheses for the second of two numbers presented both in words and in figures.

Construction must be completed within two (2) years of the date of the contract.

Period

1. Use a period at the end of a sentence. Leave one space before the next sentence.

2. Use a period after some abbreviations. When a period replaces a person's name, leave one space after the period before the next word. In other abbreviations, no space is necessary.

P. Chow has been named vice president for marketing.

The B.C. division plans to hire 10 new M.B.A.s in the next year.

The tendency today is to reduce the use of punctuation. It would also be correct to write

The BC division plans to hire 10 new M.B.A.s in the next year.

Semicolon

1. Use semicolons to join two independent clauses when they are closely related.

   We'll do our best to fill your order promptly; however, we cannot guarantee a delivery date.

Using a semicolon suggests that the two ideas are very closely connected. Using a period and a new sentence is also correct but implies nothing about how closely related the two sentences are.

2. Use semicolons to separate items in a series when the items themselves contain commas.

   The final choices for the new plant are Edmonton, Alberta; Sydney, Nova Scotia; Mississauga, Ontario; Québec City, Québec; Winnipeg, Manitoba; Yellowknife, Northwest Territories; and Victoria, British Columbia.

   Hospital benefits are also provided for certain specialized care services such as diagnostic admissions directed toward a definite disease or injury; normal maternity delivery, Caesarean-section delivery, or complications of pregnancy; and in-patient admissions for dental procedures necessary to safeguard the patient's life or health.

Hint: A semicolon could be replaced by a period and a capital letter. It has a sentence on both sides.

What do I use when I quote sources?

Quotation marks, square brackets, and ellipses.

Quotation marks, square brackets, ellipses, and underlining are necessary when you use quoted material.

Quotation Marks

1. Use quotation marks around the names of brochures, pamphlets, and magazine articles.

   Enclosed are thirty copies of our pamphlet "Saving Energy."

   You'll find articles like "How to Improve Your Golf Game" and "Can You Keep Your Eye on the Ball?" in every issue.

In Canada and the U.S., punctuation, periods, and commas go inside quotation marks. Colons and semicolons go outside. Question marks go inside if they are part of the material being quoted.

2. Use quotation marks around words to indicate that you think the term is misleading.

   These "pro-business" policies actually increase corporate taxes.

3. Use quotation marks around words that you are discussing as words.

   Forty percent of the respondents answered "yes" to the first question.

Use "Ms." as a courtesy title for a woman unless you know she prefers another title.

It is also acceptable to use underlining or italicize words instead of using quotation marks.

4. Use quotation marks around words or sentences that you quote from someone else.

"The Fog Index," says its inventor, Robert Gunning, is "an effective warning system against drifting into needless complexity."

Square Brackets

Go to
http://www.juvalam
u.com/qmarks/

The "Gallery of 'Misused' Quotation Marks" offers sardonic commentary and plenty of examples of poor use of quotation marks.

Use square brackets to add your own additions to or changes in quoted material.

MPP Smith's statement: "These measures will increase the deficit."

Your use of Smith's statement: According to MPP Smith, "These measures [in the new tax bill] will increase the deficit."

The square brackets show that Smith did not say these words; you add them to make the quotation make sense in your document.

Ellipses

Ellipses are spaced dots. In typing, use three spaced periods for an ellipsis. When an ellipsis comes at the end of a sentence, use a dot immediately after the last letter of the sentence for a period. Then add three spaced dots. A space follows the last of the four dots.

1. Use ellipses to indicate that one or more words have been omitted in the middle of quoted material. You do not need ellipses at the beginning or end of a quote.

The Wall Street Journal notes that Japanese magazines and newspapers include advertisements for a "$2.1 million home in New York's posh Riverdale section . . . 185 acres of farmland [and] . . . luxury condos on Manhattan's Upper East Side."

2. In advertising and direct mail, use ellipses to imply the pace of spoken comments.

If you've ever wanted to live on a tropical island . . . cruise to the Bahamas . . . or live in a castle in Spain . . .

. . . you can make your dreams come true with Vacations Extraordinaire.

Italics vs. Underlining

1. Underlining causes the reader's eye to *fixate*, or stop unnecessarily, thereby interfering with both reading speed and retention. Unless you're typing or handwriting documents, it is preferable to use italics to indicate titles or emphasis:

Calgary Sun
Maclean's
Boom, Bust and Echo 2000

Titles of brochures and pamphlets are put in quotation marks.

2. Italicize words to emphasize them.

Here's a bulletin that gives you, in handy chart form, *workable data* on over 50 different types of tubing and pipe.

Note: If you have a printer that has a bold typeface, you may also use **bold** to emphasize words.

How should I write numbers and dates?

Spell out numbers under 10 and at the beginning of sentences.

Spell out **numbers** from one to nine. Use figures for numbers 10 and over in most cases. Always use figures for amounts of money.

Numbers (for example **19%**) do not begin sentences. Spell out any number that appears at the beginning of a sentence. If spelling it out is impractical, revise the sentence so that it does not begin with a number.

Fifty students filled out the survey.

The year 1992 marked the official beginning of the European Economic Community.

When two numbers follow each other, use words for the smaller number and figures for the larger number.

In **dates**, use figures for the day and year. The month is normally spelled out. Be sure to spell out the month in international business communication. Canadian usage puts the year first: 01/01/10 means *January 10, 2001*. U.S. usage puts the month first, so *1/10/01* means *January 10, 2001*. European usage puts the day first, so *10/01/01* means *January 10, 2001*.

Modern punctuation uses a comma before the year only when you give both the month and the day of the month:

May 1, 1998

but

Summers 1998-00

August 2002

Fall 1997

No punctuation is needed in military or European usage, which puts the day of the month first: 13 July 2002. Do not space before or after the slash used to separate parts of the date: 5/99-10/01.

Use a hyphen to join inclusive dates.

March-August 1999 (**or write out:** March to August 1999)

'98-'02

1996-2000

Note that you do not need to repeat the century in the date that follows the hyphen: 1998-99. But do give the century when it changes: 1999-2001.

How do I mark errors I find in proofreading?

Use these standard proofreading symbols.

Use the proofreading symbols in Figure 14.3 to make corrections when you no longer have access to a typewriter. Figure 14.4 shows how the symbols can be used to correct a typed text.

Figure 14.3
Proofreading Symbols

✄	delete	⌐	move to left
⦣	insert a letter	⌐	move to right
¶	start a new paragraph here	⌐	move up
(stet)	stet (leave as it was before the marked change)	⌐	move down
(tr) ⌐	transpose (reverse)	#	leave a space
(lc)	lower case (don't capitalize)	⌒	close up
≡	capitalize	//	align vertically

Figure 14.4
Marked Text

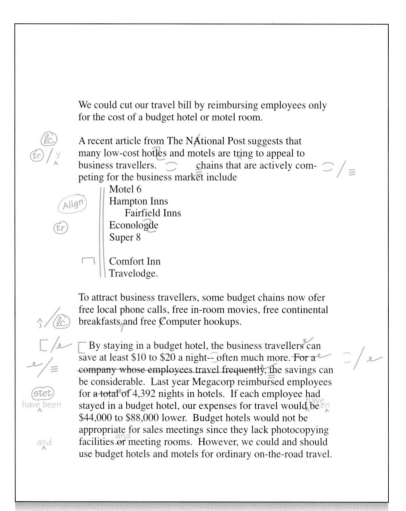

Visit http://www.mcgrawhill.ca/college/locker

Employability Skills 2000+ Checklist for Editing for Grammar and Punctuation

In this module, the key skills from The Conference Board of Canada's Employability Skills 2000+ are:

Communicate
✔ write and speak so others pay attention and understand
✔ share information using a range of information and communications technologies (e.g., voice, email, computers)
✔ use relevant scientific, technological, and mathematical knowledge and skills to explain or clarify ideas

Manage Information
✔ locate, gather, and organize information using appropriate technology and information systems

Participate in Projects & Tasks
✔ work to agreed quality standards and specifications
✔ select and use appropriate tools and technology for a task or project
✔ adapt to changing requirements and information

Review of Key Points

- Check for six kinds of grammatical errors:
    1. agreement
    2. case
    3. dangling modifier
    4. misplaced modifier
    5. parallel structure
    6. predication errors
- Use correct punctuation to avoid three major sentence errors:
    1. comma splices
    2. run-on sentences
    3. sentence fragments
- Use the following eight punctuation marks correctly:
    1. apostrophes
    2. colons
    3. commas
    4. dashes
    5. hyphens
    6. parentheses
    7. periods
    8. semicolons
- When quoting sources, use the following punctuation:
    - quotation marks
    - square brackets
    - ellipses
    - italics

- Spell out numbers under 10 and at the beginning of sentences

- Use standard proofreading symbols to mark errors.

Learning Applications

Questions for Comprehension

14.1 What words make clauses subordinate and thus require more than a comma to join clauses?

14.2 What is parallel structure? When should you use it?

14.3 What is a sentence fragment? How do you fix it?

14.4 Why is it better to fix errors in grammar and punctuation only after you've revised for content, organization, and style?

Questions for Critical Thinking

14.5 Consuela sees a lot of errors in the writing of managers at her workplace. If they don't know or don't care about correctness, why should she?

14.6 After surveying readers in her workplace (problem 14.19 below), Camilla finds that most of them are not bothered by errors in grammar and punctuation. Does that mean that she doesn't need to fix surface errors?

14.7 Joe knows that his variety of English isn't the privileged variety, but he is afraid that using standard edited English will make him "uppity" to people in his home community. Should he try to use standard grammar and pronunciation? Why or why not?

Questions for Building Skills

14.8 What skills have you read about in this module?

14.9 What skills are you practising in the assignments you're doing for this module?

14.10 How could you further develop the skills you're working on?

Exercises and Problems

14.11 Making Subjects and Verbs Agree

Identify and correct the errors in the following sentences.

1. My education and training has prepared me to contribute to your company.

2. I know from my business experience that good communication among people and departments are essential in running a successful corporation.

3. A team of people from marketing, finance, and production are preparing the proposal.

4. The present solutions that has been suggested are not adequate.

5. There has also been suggestions for improving the airflow in the building.

14.12   Using the Right Pronoun

Identify and correct the errors in the following sentences.

1. A new employee should try to read verbal and non-verbal signals to see which aspects of your job are most important.

2. With people like yourself giving gifts, the Habitat for Humanity program will be able to grow.

3. If a group member doesn't complete their assigned work, it slows the whole project down.

4. Todd drew the graphs after him and I discussed the ideas for them.

5. Thank you for the help you gave Joanne Jackson and myself.

14.13   Fixing Dangling and Misplaced Modifiers

Identify and correct the errors in the following sentences.

1. As one of the students in a good program, our company is interested in interviewing you.

2. By making an early reservation, it will give us more time to coordinate our trucks to better serve your needs.

3. Children are referred to the Big Brother/Big Sister program by their school social workers, often from underprivileged homes.

4. At times while typing and editing, the text on your screen may not look correct.

5. All employees are asked to cut back on energy waste by the manager.

14.14   Creating Parallel Structure

Identify and correct the errors in the following sentences.

1. We help clients
   • Manage change
   • Marketing/promotion
   • Developing better billing systems

2. Volunteers need a better orientation to Planned Parenthood as a whole, to the overall clinic function, and to the staff there is also a need to clarify volunteer responsibilities.

3. The benefits of an online catalogue are
   1. We will be able to keep records up-to-date;
   2. Broad access to the catalogue system from any networked terminal on campus;
   3. The consolidation of the main catalogue and the catalogues in the departmental and branch libraries;
   4. Cost savings.

4. You can get a reduced rate on your life insurance if you have an annual medical exam. Another rebate is available to employees who do not use tobacco. Exercising for 30 minutes a day three times a week also entitles employees to an insurance rebate.

5. The ideal job candidate will be able to
   • Create and maintain Web pages
   • The ability to create PowerPoint slides is expected
   • It would be best if the candidate could speak a second language

14.15   Marking Sentence Boundaries

Identify and correct the errors in the following sentences.

1. Videoconferencing can be frustrating. Simply because little time is available for casual conversation.

2. Not everyone is promoted after six months some people might remain in the training program a year before being moved to a permanent assignment.

3. Pay yourself with the Automatic Savings Account, with this account any amount your choose will be transferred automatically from your chequing account to your savings account each month.

4. You can take advantage of several banking services. Such as automatic withdrawal of a house or car payment and direct deposit of your paycheque.

5. Our group met seven times outside of class, we would have met even more if we could have found times when we could all get together.

14.16   Providing Punctuation within Sentences

Provide the necessary punctuation in the following sentences. Note that not every box requires punctuation.

1. The system□s□ user□friendly design□ provides screen displays of work codes□ rates□ and client information.

2. Many other factors also shape the organization□s□ image□ advertising□ brochures□ proposals□ stationery□ calling cards□ etc.

3. Miss Manners □ author of □Miss Manners□s□ Book of Modern Manners□□ says□ □Try to mention specifics of the conversation to fix the interview permanently in the interviewer□s□ mind and be sure to mail the letter the same day□ before the hiring decision is made□□

4. What are your room rates and charges for food service□

5. We will need accommodations for 150 people□ five meeting rooms□one large room and four small ones□□coffee served during morning and afternoon breaks□ and lunches and dinners.

6. The Operational Readiness Inspection□ which occurs once every three years□ is a realistic exercise□ which evaluates the □ Royal Canadian Air Cadet □s□ ability to mobilize□ deploy□ and fight.

7. Most computer packages will calculate three different sets of percentages□ row percentages□ column percentages□ and table percentages□

8. In today□s□ economy□ it□s almost impossible for a firm to extend credit beyond iths regular terms.

9. The Ministry of Transportation does not have statutory authority to grant easements□ however□ we do have authority to lease unused areas of highway right□of□way.

10. The program has two goals□ to identify employees with promise□ and to see that they get the training they need to advance.

14.17   Providing Punctuation

Provide the necessary punctuation in the following sentences. Note that not every box requires punctuation.

1. To reduce executive assistants □ overtime hours□ the office should hire part□time secretaries to work from 5:00 to 9:00 P.M.

2. Since memberships can begin at any time during the year□ all member□s□ dues are recognized on a cash basis when they are received.

3. I would be interested in working on the committee□ however□ I have decided to

do less community work so that I have more time to spend with my family.

4. One of the insurance companies□ Allstate Insurance □□ Fredericton □ □NB□ said it hopes to persuade the provincial government to reconsider the rule.

5. The city already has five□ two□ hundred□bed hospitals.

6. Students run the whole organization□ and are advised by a Board of Directors from the community.

7. I suggest putting a bulletin board in the rear hallway with all the interviewer□s□ pictures on it.

8. □Most small businesses just get enough money to open the doors□□ says Mr. Quinn□ adding □that the $10,000 or so of savings he used to start up simply wasn□t enough□□

9. Otis Conward Jr□□ who grew up in this area□ now heads the Council for Economic Development.

10. Volunteers also participate in a one□on□ one pal program.

14.18   Fixing Errors in Grammar and Punctuation

Identify and correct the errors in the following passages.

a. Company's are finding it to their advantage to cultivate their suppliers. Partnerships between a company and its suppliers can yield hefty payoffs for both company and supplier. One example is Bombardier, a Montreal headquartered company. Bombardier makes airplanes, subway cars and control systems. They treat suppliers almost like departments of their own company. When a Bombardier employee passes a laser scanner over a bins bar code the supplier is instantly alerted to send more parts.

b. Entrepreneur Trip Hawkins appears in Japanese ads for the video game system his company designed. "It plugs into the future! he says in one ad, in a cameo spliced into shots of U.S kids playing the games. Hawkins is one of several U.S. celebrities and business people whom plug products on Japanese TV.

c. Between 1989 and 1999 the number of self-employed grew by more than 40 per cent to 2.4 million; but this growth includes a huge increase of one person operations. "The self-employed sector now accounts for more than 16 percent of all workers; an increase from 13 percent in 1989. According to bizSmarts report Self-Employment in Canada, Trend's and Prospect's, over the next ten years, self-employment will become even more dominant in the Canadian labour market

14.19   Identifying Audience Concerns about Grammar

Most readers care passionately about only a few points of grammar. Survey one or more readers (including your boss, if you have a job) to find out which kinds of errors concern them. Use a separate copy of this survey for each reader.

Directions: Each of the following sentences contains some error. Please circle Y if the error bothers you a good bit; S if the error bothers you slightly; and N if you would not be bothered by the error (or perhaps even notice it).

Y S N   1. She brung her secretary with her.

Y S N   2. Him and Richard were the last ones hired.

Y S N   3. Wanted to tell you that the meeting will be November 10.

Y S N 4. Each representative should bring a list of their clients to the meeting.

Y S N 5. A team of people from administration, human services, and animal control are preparing the proposal.

Y S N 6. We cannot predict, how high the number of clients may rise.

Y S N 7. He treats his clients bad.

Y S N 8. She asked Eva and I to give a presentation.

Y S N 9. Update the directory by reviewing each record in the database and note any discrepancies.

Y S N 10. He has went to a lot of trouble to meet our needs.

Y S N 11. She gave the report to Davlic and myself.

Y S N 12. I was unable to complete the report. Because I had a very busy week.

Y S N 13. The benefits of an online directory are
   a. We will be able to keep records up-to-date;
   b. Access to the directory from any terminal with a modem in the county.
   c. Cost savings.

Y S N 14. By making an early reservation, it will give us more time to plan the session to meet your needs.

Y S N 15. She don't have no idea how to use the computer.

Y S N 16. The change will not effect our service to customers.

Y S N 17. Confirming our conversation, the truck will leave Monday.

Y S N 18. The sessions will begin January 4 we will pass around a sign-up sheet early in December.

Y S N 19. I will be unable to attend the meeting, however I will send someone else from my office.

Y S N 20. Its too soon to tell how many proposals we will receive.

Compare your responses with those of a small group of students.

- Which errors were most annoying to the largest number of readers?
- How much variation do you find in a single workplace? In a single type of business?

As Your Instructor Directs,

a. Present your findings to the class in a short group report

b. Present your findings to the class in an oral presentation

Polishing Your Prose

Using Spell and Grammar Checkers

Most word processing programs come with spelling and grammar checkers. While these computer tools can be useful, remember that they have limitations.

Spelling checkers identify words that don't match their dictionary. If the word is a real word, the spelling checker can't tell if it's the right word for the context (e.g., "their" versus "there," as in "We will review there report when we get their.")

Grammar checkers only suggest possible errors and solutions; you must make the final decision. That is, a grammar checker may tell you that you've used passive voice, but the checker can't tell you whether the passive is appropriate in that particular sentence.

Therefore, use spelling and grammar checkers as one of several tools to make your writing better. In addition, keep a dictionary, thesaurus, and stylebook handy. Work to improve your command of spelling and grammar; take a class or work with a college writing centre for help.

Exercises

Type the following into your word processor. Are all the words or constructions that show up as errors really wrong? Are there any errors that don't show up?

1. There product is sitting over their.

2. The project will have been completed by next Thursday?

3. Its not really a good idea to have had lunch before the flight.

4. The solution was created in the '90s using a new chemical process.

5. Martika is happy with her purchase; shell order online again.

6. I call your office because were needed in in the mailroom.

7. Les says, "Less is more.

8. Kadji is looking in to buying more property but it won't happen really soon.

9. The Internet is a powerfull research tool—so what?

10. This computers spellchecker did a pretty good job.

Check your answers to the odd-numbered exercises on page 633.

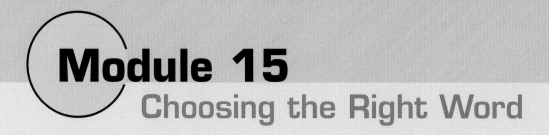

Module 15
Choosing the Right Word

Topics

- Does using the right word really matter?
- How do words get their meanings?
- Is it OK to use jargon?
- What words confuse some writers?

Review of Key Points

Learning Applications

Polishing Your Prose: Run-on Sentences

Learning Focus

After reading and applying the information in Module 15, you'll be able to demonstrate

Knowledge of
- The power of words

Skills to
- Choose words precisely
- Choose words ethically
- Choose words with appropriate connotations
- Identify critical-thinking skills

"A good editor must be able to communicate with the writer and develop a rapport with the intended reader."

"I sell words and I service sentences and paragraphs," says May Lee-Jarvis, London, Ontario-based freelance copy editor and writer. " In order to communicate properly, you must not only use the correct words, but you must use them correctly."

May has always had a love for language. Her father worked as a technical writer and marketing expert and was recognized in his field in his native Ireland as well as in England, United States, and Canada. He shared his love and respect for language with his daughter. May's love for language is limitless. It includes searching for new words, researching old words, and for relaxation, grammar texts. For outright fun May loves to do word puzzles and thinks puns are a sublime form of literary art.

May has a B.A. in linguistics and anthropology, and has taught English as a second language in addition to her editing work. She has worked on projects such as a newsletter for local businesswomen and a local monthly newspaper, and recently took on the challenge of a textbook, written by three different people, on the use of 3D ophthalmological ultra sound equipment. May's challenge as editor was to make the three writing styles flow smoothly—a task she accomplished by focussing on meaning. What did an author mean when he used a particular term? Did all three writers mean the same thing by the same technical term? Would the reader of the text understand what was being said?

Work on the textbook confirmed for May that the editor must not only focus on what the writer has written but on what the reader understands. The editor must become a critical reader in order to edit. Once the editor knows how the piece should be read, she can sell the writer her words and fix the sentences and paragraphs that need fixing.

When asked to define what skills an editor needs, May replies, "An editor needs to know language. This includes a good vocabulary and a knowledge of grammar, spelling, punctuation, and usage rules. It also means knowing when, where, and how to break these rules. In addition to these technical skills you also need good interpersonal skills. A good editor must be able to communicate with the writer and develop a rapport with the intended reader."

May goes on to emphasize that " the purpose of business writing is the message contained in it." This message can be anything from technical information to a sales pitch. "Language can make or break the message. This is where the editor can enhance the writer's expertise."

What is the highest compliment an editor can receive? May explains that good editing is transparent. You do not see the editor's work, only the finished product. Upon meeting for the first time a writer whose work she had edited for over a year, May introduced herself as "the person who edits your work." The writer replied," Do you?"

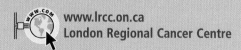

www.lrcc.on.ca
London Regional Cancer Centre

Site *to*
See

Go to
http://www.clearcf.
uvic.ca/writersguide
/Pages/DictionUsage
Toc.html

More confusable
words with
explanations are
listed at the English
department Web
site of the University
of Victoria.

Using the "best" words depends on context: the situation, your purposes, your audience, and the words you have already used.

To communicate most effectively

1. Use words that are accurate, appropriate, and familiar. Accurate words mean exactly what you want to say. Appropriate words convey the attitudes you want and fit well with the other words in your document. Familiar words are easy to read and understand.
2. Use technical jargon only when it is essential and known to the reader. Eliminate business jargon.

Does using the right word really matter?

> The right word helps you look good and get the response you want.

Using the right word helps to demonstrate that you're part of a discourse community ( p. 37). Using simple words helps to create a friendly image of yourself and your organization. Using words that are part of standard edited English helps to build credibility and demonstrate professionalism.

Site *to*
See

Go to
http://www.executi
veplanet.com/comm
unity/default.asp?se
ction=Canada

Look at how a U.S.
resource for business
travellers views
Canada and its
culture.

Getting Your Meaning Across

When the words on the page don't say what you mean, the reader has to work harder to figure out your meaning. Sometimes your audience can figure out what you mean. Sometimes, your meaning will be lost. Sometimes the wrong word can cause a lawsuit.

Denotation is a word's literal or dictionary meaning. Most common words in English have more than one denotation. The word *pound*, for example, means, or denotes, a unit of weight, a place where stray animals are kept, a unit of money in the British system, and the verb to *hit*. Coca-Cola spends an estimated $20 million a year to protect its brand names so that *Coke* will denote only that brand and not just any cola drink.

When two people use the same word to mean, or denote, different things, **bypassing** occurs. For example, negotiators for the oil company Amoco and the U.S. Environmental Protection Agency (EPA) used *risk* differently when they tried to develop rules for controlling pollution in the early 1990s. At Amoco, *risk* was an economic term dealing with efficiency; for the EPA, the term "was a four-letter word that meant political peril or health risk."[1] Progress was possible only when they agreed on a meaning.

Accurate denotations can make it easier to solve problems. In one production line with a high failure rate, the largest category of defects was *missed operations*. At first, the supervisor wondered if the people on the line were lazy or irresponsible. But some checking showed that several different problems were labelled *missed operations:* parts installed backwards, parts that had missing screws or fasteners, parts whose wires weren't connected. Each of these problems had different solutions. Using accurate words redefined the problem and enabled the production line both to improve quality and cut repair costs.[2]

FYI

In Canadian
meetings, to *table*
an item means to
postpone
discussing it. In the
United Kingdom,
to *table* an item
means to bring it
out for immediate
discussion.

Getting the Response You Want

Using the right word helps you shape the audience's response to what you say. **Connotation** means the emotional colourings or associations that accompany a word. A great many words carry connotations of approval or disapproval, disgust or delight. In Figure 15.1, words in the first column below suggest approval; words in the second column suggest criticism.

Figure 15.1

Words with Positive and Negative Connotations

Positive Word	Negative Word
assume	guess
curious	nosy
negotiate	haggle
cautious	fearful
careful	nit-picking
firm	obstinate
flexible	wishy-washy

A supervisor can "tell the truth" about a subordinate's performance and yet write either a positive or a negative performance appraisal, based on the connotations of the words in the appraisal. Consider an employee who pays close attention to details. A positive appraisal might read, "Terry is a meticulous team member who takes care of details that others sometimes ignore." But the same behaviour might be described negatively: "Terry is hung up on trivial details."

Advertisers carefully choose words with positive connotations. Expensive cars are never *used*; instead, they're *pre-owned*, *experienced*, or even *preloved*. An executive for Rolls-Royce once said, "A Rolls never, never breaks down. Of course," he added, with a twinkle in his eye, "there have been occasions when a car has failed to proceed."[3]

Words may also connote status or class distinctions. Both *salesperson* and *sales representative* are nonsexist job titles. But the first sounds like a clerk in a store; the second suggests someone selling important items to corporate customers.

Use familiar words that are in almost everyone's vocabulary. Try to use specific, concrete words. They're easier to understand and remember.[4] Short, common words sound friendlier. Figure 15.2 gives a few examples of short, simple alternatives.

Stuffy: Please give immediate attention to insure that the pages of all reports prepared for distribution are numbered sequentially and in a place of optimum visibility.[5]

Simple: Please put page numbers on all reports in the top outer corner.

Instant Replay

Denotation, Bypassing, and Connotation

Denotation is a word's literal or dictionary meaning. **Bypassing** occurs when two people use the same word to mean, or denote, different things. **Connotation** means the emotional colourings or associations that accompany a word.

FYI

According to *Advertising Age* magazine, the top ten American advertising slogans of the twentieth century include *Diamonds are forever* (DeBeers), *Just do it* (Nike), *The pause that refreshes* (Coca-Cola), *We try harder* (Avis), *Good to the last drop* (Maxwell House), and *Does she...or doesn't she?* (Clairol). Honourable mentions went to *Look, Ma, no cavities* (Crest toothpaste) and *Let your fingers do the walking* (Yellow Pages).

Source: "Social Studies", *The Globe and Mail,* January 29, 2001, A14.

Thinking Critically

Like many terms, critical thinking has more than one meaning.

In its most basic sense, critical thinking means using precise words and asking questions about what you read and hear.

Vague: This *Vancouver Sun* story discusses international business.

Precise: This *Vancouver Sun* story
tells how Bombardier plans to expand into Europe.
challenges the claim that a Canadian company needs a native partner to succeed in international business.
gives examples of translation problems in international business.
compares and contrasts accounting rules in Europe and in Asia.
tells how three women have succeeded in international business.

Questions about a *Vancouver Sun* story might include

- What information is the story based on? Did the reporter interview people on both sides of the issue?

- When was the information collected? Is it still valid?
- Does evidence from other newspapers and magazines and from your own experience tend to confirm or contradict this story?
- How important is this story? Does it call for action on your part?

In a more advanced sense, critical thinking means the ability to analyze and identify problems, gather and evaluate evidence, identify and evaluate alternate solutions, and recommend or act on the best choice—while understanding that information is always incomplete and that new information might change one's judgment of the "best" choice.

In its most advanced sense, critical thinking means asking about and challenging fundamental assumptions. For example, stories in business magazines and newspapers like *The Wall Street Journal* and *The Globe and Mail* generally assume that capitalism is good, that a major goal of any business is to make money, and that it's OK for top executives to make much more money than other workers.

Source: Carol Roever and Gerry Hines, "Teaching the Two C's Needed for Business Success: Critical Thinking and Creativity," Conference on Teaching Communication, Ohio State University, July 30–31, 1999.

Figure 15.2
Formal Words and Their Simple Alternatives

Formal and Stuffy	Short and Simple
ameliorate	improve
commence	begin
enumerate	list
finalize	finish, complete
prioritize	rank
utilize	use
viable option	choice

There are four exceptions to the general rule that "shorter is better."

1. Use a long word if it is the only word that expresses your meaning exactly.
2. Use a long word if it is more familiar than a short word. *Send out* is better than *emit* and a *word in another language for a geographic place or area* is better than *exonym* because more people know the first item in each pair.
3. Use a long word if its connotations are more appropriate. *Exfoliate* is better than *scrape off dead skin cells*.
4. Use a long word if the discourse community (Module 2) prefers it.

Although connotations rarely appear in a dictionary, they are not individual or idiosyncratic. The associations a word evokes will be consistent in any one culture but may differ among cultures. One scholar reports that while "the term 'discussion' is connotatively neutral for North Americans, it possesses a negative connotation for Latin Americans, who view it as an attempt to change someone else's mind."[6] Even within a culture, connotations may change over time. The word *charity* had acquired such negative connotations by the nineteenth century that people began to use the term *welfare* instead. Now, *welfare* has acquired negative associations.

How positively can we present something and still be ethical? *Pressure-treated lumber* sounds acceptable. But naming the product by the material injected under pressure—*arsenic-treated lumber*—may lead the customer to make a different decision. We have the right to package our ideas attractively, but we have the responsibility to give the public or our superiors all the information they need to make decisions.

How do words get their meanings?

Most meanings depend on usage.

You can find the meaning of standard words in dictionaries. Some dictionaries are *descriptive*, that is, their definitions describe the way people actually use words. In such a dictionary, the word *verbal* might be defined as *spoken, not written*, because many people use the word that way. In a *prescriptive* dictionary, words are defined as they are supposed to be used, according to a panel of experts. In such a dictionary, *verbal* would be defined as *using words*—which of course includes both writing and speaking. *The Oxford Encyclopedic English Dictionary* is an example of a prescriptive dictionary, whereas *Merriam-Webster's Collegiate Encyclopedia* is a descriptive one. Check the introduction to your dictionary to find out which kind it is.

When a word has more than one meaning or isn't in the dictionary at all, we learn meanings by context, by being alert and observant. Some terms will have a specialized meaning in a social or work group. We learn some meanings by formal and informal study: "generally accepted accounting principles" or what the trash can on an email screen symbolizes. Some meanings are negotiated as we interact one-on-one with another person, attempting to communicate. Some words persist, even though the reality behind them has changed. In Canada's two largest cities, so-called "minorities" are already in the majority.[7] Some people are substituting the term *traditionally underrepresented groups* for *minorities*, but the old term is likely to remain in use for some time.

FYI

Communications and leadership consultants Ellinor and Gerard maintain that *"dialogue"*—the language of listening—more effectively encourages genuine communication than does *"discussion"*—a word with the same root as percussion and concussion—that connotes a fragmenting or shattering.

Source: Linda Ellinor and Glenna Gerard, *Dialogue* (Toronto: John Wiley & Sons, Inc., 1998), p. 18–20.

Go to http://www.takeourword.com

This interactive site traces the etymological, or historical origins of words.

Many words are easily confused

Source: ONE BIG HAPPY CARTOON. By permission of Rich Detorie and Creators Syndicate.

Is it OK to use jargon?

If it's essential.

Two Kinds of Jargon

Technical jargon includes words that have specific technical meanings. Use this kind of jargon only in job application letters. Avoid other technical jargon unless it's essential. **Business jargon** or **businessese** are words that do not have specialized meanings. Avoid these terms.

There are two kinds of **jargon**. The first kind of jargon is the specialized terminology of a technical field. *LIFO* and *FIFO* are technical terms in accounting; *byte* and *baud* are computer jargon; *scale-free* and *pickled* and *oiled* designate specific characteristics of steel. A job application letter is the one occasion when it's desirable to use technical jargon: Using the technical terminology of the reader's field helps suggest that you're a peer who also is competent in that field. In other messages, use technical jargon only when the term is essential. Define the term when you're not sure whether the reader knows it.

If a technical term has a "plain English" equivalent, use the simpler term:

Jargon: Foot the average monthly budget column down to Total Variable Cost, Total Management Fixed Cost, Total Sunk Costs, and Grand Total.

Better: Add the figures in the average monthly budget column for each category to determine the Total Variable Costs, the Total Management Fixed Costs, and the Total Sunk Costs. Then add the totals for each category to arrive at the Grand Total.

The revision here is longer but better because it uses simple words. The original will be meaningless to a reader who does not know what *foot* means.

Business slang includes terms that are borrowed from technical fields but are used in a more general sense: *bottom line*, *GIGO*, *blindsiding*, and *downsize*. These terms are appropriate in job application letters and in messages for people in your own organization, who are likely to share the vocabulary.

General slang includes words like *awesome*, *diss*, and *going postal*. Slang is sometimes used in business conversations and presentations, but it is too casual for business and administrative writing.

The second kind of jargon is the **businessese** that some writers still use: *as per your request*, *enclosed please find*, *please do not hesitate*. None of the words in this second category of jargon is necessary. Indeed, some writers call these terms *deadwood*, since they are no longer living words. Some of these terms, however, seem to float through the air like germs. If any of the terms in the first column of Figure 15.1 show up in your writing, replace them with contemporary language.

Site *to* **See**

Go to
http://www.rightwords.co.nz/backnews.html

For the New Zealand-based *Right Words* newsletter.

Figure 15.3

Getting Rid of Business Jargon

Instead of	Use	Because
At your earliest convenience	The date you need a response	If you need it by a deadline, say so. It may never be convenient to respond.
As per your request; 60 km per hour	As you requested; 60 km an hour	*Per* is a Latin word for *by* or *each*. Use *per* only when the meaning is correct; avoiding mixing English and Latin.
Enclosed please find	Enclosed is; Here is	An enclosure isn't a treasure hunt. If you put something in the envelope, the reader will find it.
Forward same to this office	Return it to this office	Omit legal jargon.
Hereto, herewith	Omit	Omit legal jargon.
Please be advised; Please be informed	Omit—simply state your response	You don't need a preface. Go ahead and start
Please do not hesitate	Omit	Omit negative words.
Pursuant to	According to; or omit	*Pursuant* does not mean *after*. Omit legal jargon.
Said order	Your order	Omit legal jargon.
This will acknowledge receipt of	Omit—start your response.	If you answer a letter, the your letter reader knows you got it.
Trusting this is satisfactory, we remain	Omit	Eliminate *-ing* endings. When you are through, stop.

Employability Skills 2000+ Checklist for Choosing the Right Word

In this module, the key skills from The Conference Board of Canada's Employability Skills 2000+ are:

Communicate
✔ write and speak so others pay attention and understand
✔ share information using a range of information and communications technologies (e.g., voice, email, computers)
✔ use relevant scientific, technological, and mathematical knowledge and skills to explain or clarify ideas

Manage Information
✔ locate, gather, and organize information using appropriate technology and information systems

Be Adaptable
✔ be open and respond constructively to change
✔ cope with uncertainty

Participate in Projects & Tasks
✔ work to agreed quality standards and specifications
✔ select and use appropriate tools and technology for a task or project
✔ adapt to changing requirements and information

Review of Key Points

- Use words that are accurate, appropriate, and familiar.
- **Denotation** is a word's literal or dictionary meaning.
- **Bypassing** occurs when two people use the same word to mean, or denote, different things.
- **Connotation** means the emotional colourings or associations that accompany a word.

- Generally, short words are better. But use a long word when
  1. It is the only word that expresses your meaning exactly
  2. It is more familiar than a short word
  3. Its connotations are more appropriate
  4. The discourse community prefers it
- Use technical jargon only when it is essential. Eliminate business jargon.

Learning Applications

Questions for Comprehension

15.1 What is the difference between *denotation* and *connotation*?

15.2 What is *bypassing*?

15.3 What are the two kinds of jargon? Which is OK to use at times?

15.4 Why are short, simple words generally best?

Questions for Critical Thinking

15.5 If you were going to buy a new dictionary, would you want a descriptive or a prescriptive one? Why?

15.6 Why is it desirable to use technical jargon in a job letter and a job interview?

15.7 Is it possible to avoid connotations entirely?

Questions for Building Skills

15.8 What skills have you read about in this module?

15.9 What skills are you practising in the assignments you're doing for this module?

15.10 How could you further develop the skills you're working on?

Exercises and Problems

15.11 Identifying Words with Multiple Denotations

a. Each of the following words has several denotations. How many can you list without going to a dictionary? How many additional meanings does a good dictionary list?

browser   log

court   table

b. List five words that have multiple denotations.

15.12   Explaining Bypassing

Show how different denotations make bypassing possible in the following examples:

a. France and Associates: Protection from Professionals

b. We were not able to account for the outstanding amount of plastic waste generated each year.

c. I scanned the résumés when I received them.

15.13   Evaluating Connotations

a. Identify the connotations of each of the following metaphors for a multicultural nation.

melting pot	garden salad
mosaic	stew
tapestry	tributaries
crazy quilt	

b. Which connotations seem most positive? Why?

15.14   Evaluating the Ethical Implications of Connotations

In each of the following pairs, identify the more favourable term. Is its use justified? Why or why not?

1. wastepaper   recovered fibre
2. feedback   criticism
3. deadline   due date
4. scalper   ticket reseller
5. budget   spending plan

15.15   Correcting Errors in Denotation and Connotation

Identify and correct the errors in denotation or connotation in the following sentences.

1. I will take credit for the mistake.
2. The technology for virtual reality looms over the horizon.
3. The three proposals are diametrically opposed to each other.
4. In her search for information, she literally devours *The Globe and Mail* and several business magazines each week.
5. Approximately 489 customers answered our survey.

15.16   Using Connotations to Shape Response

Write two sentences to describe each of the following situations. In one sentence, use words with positive connotations; in the other, use negative words.

1. Lee talks to co-workers about subjects other than work, such as last weekend's ball game.
2. Lee spends a lot of time sending email messages and monitoring email newsgroups.
3. As a supervisor, Lee rarely gives specific instructions to subordinates.

15.17 Choosing Levels of Formality

Identify the more formal word in each pair. Which term is better for most business documents? Why?

1. adapted to   geared to
2. befuddled   confused
3. assistant   helper
4. pilot project   testing the waters
5. cogitate   think

15.18 Identifying Jargon

How many of these business jargon terms do you know?

1. Sticky Web site
2. Alpha geek
3. Road warrior
4. Think outside the box
5. Be on the same page
6. A new paradigm

15.19 Eliminating Jargon and Simplifying Language

Revise these sentences to eliminate jargon and to use short, familiar words. In some sentences, you'll need to reword, reorganize, or add information to produce the best revision.

1. Computers can enumerate pages when the appropriate keystroke is implemented.
2. Any alterations must be approved during the 30-day period commencing 60 days prior to the expiration date of the agreement.
3. As per your request, the undersigned has compiled a report on claims paid in 1996. A copy is attached hereto.
4. Please be advised that this writer is unable to attend the meeting on the fifteenth due to an unavoidable conflict.
5. Enclosed please find the schedule for the training session. In the event that you have alterations, which you would like to suggest, forward same to my office at your earliest convenience.

15.20 Choosing the Right Word

Choose the right word for each sentence.

1. Exercise is (good, well) for patients who have had open-heart surgery.
2. This response is atypical, but it is not (unique, unusual).
3. The personnel department continues its (roll, role) of compiling reports for the federal government.
4. The Accounting Club expects (its, it's) members to come to meetings and participate in activities.
5. Part of the fun of any vacation is (cite, sight, site)-seeing.
6. The (lectern, podium) was too high for the short speaker.
7. The (residence, residents) of the complex have asked for more parking spaces.
8. Please order more letterhead (stationary, stationery).
9. The closing of the plant will (affect, effect) housing prices in the area.
10. Better communication (among, between) design and production could enable us to produce products more efficiently.

15.21   Choosing the Right Word

Choose the right word for each sentence.

1. The audit revealed a small (amount, number) of errors.

2. Diet beverages have (fewer, less) calories than regular drinks.

3. In her speech, she (implied, inferred) that the vote would be close.

4. We need to redesign the stand so that the catalogue is eye-level instead of (laying, lying) on the desk.

5. (Their, There, They're) is some evidence that (their, there, they're) thinking of changing (their, there, they're) policy.

6. The settlement isn't yet in writing; if one side wanted to back out of the (oral, verbal) agreement, it could.

7. In (affect, effect), we're creating a new department.

8. The firm will be hiring new (personal, personnel) in three departments this year.

9. Several customers have asked that we carry more campus merchandise, (i.e., e.g.,) pillows and mugs with the college seal.

10. We have investigated all of the possible solutions (accept, except) adding a turning lane.

15.22   Choosing the Right Word

Choose the right word for each sentence.

1. The author (cites, sights, sites) four reasons for computer phobia.

2. The error was (do, due) to inexperience.

3. (Your, you're) doing a good job motivating (your, you're) subordinates.

4. One of the basic (principals, principles) of business communication is "Consider the reader."

5. I (implied, inferred) from the article that interest rates would go up.

6. Working papers generally are (composed, comprised) of working trial balance, assembly sheets, adjusting entries, audit schedules, and audit memos.

7. Eliminating time clocks will improve employee (moral, morale).

8. The (principal, principle) variable is the trigger price mechanism.

9. (Its, It's) (to, too, two) soon (to, too, two) tell whether the conversion (to, too, two) computerized billing will save as much time as we hope.

10. Formal training programs (complement, compliment) on-the-job opportunities for professional growth.

Polishing Your Prose

Run-on Sentences

A sentence with too many ideas, strung together by coordinating conjunctions that lack the required comma, is a *run-on*. (Remember that coordinating conjunctions such as *and*, *or*, and *but* need a comma to connect independent clauses.)

While most run-on sentences are long, length is not the real problem. In fact, don't confuse run-ons with grammatically correct long sentences, whose ideas are still clear to readers.

Run-ons confound readers because there are too many ideas competing for attention and because the missing commas make the ideas harder to follow. The effect is similar to listening to a speaker who does not pause between sentences—where does one point begin and another end?

Test for run-ons by looking for more than two main ideas in a sentence and a lack of commas with coordinating conjunctions:

We installed the new computers this morning and they are running fine but there weren't enough computers for everyone so we are going to purchase more on Wednesday and we will install them and then the department will be fully operational.

Count the number of things going on in this sentence. Where are the commas?

Fix a run-on in one of three ways:

1. For short run-ons, add the missing commas:

   Incorrect: The Purchasing Department sent order forms but we received too few so we are requesting more.

   Correct: The Purchasing Department sent order forms, but we received too few, so we are requesting more.

2. Rewrite the sentence using subordination:

   Correct: Because we received too few order forms, we are requesting more from the Purchasing Department.

3. For longer run-ons, break the run-on into two or more sentences, add missing commas, and subordinate where appropriate.

   Correct: We installed the new computers this morning. They are running fine, but because there weren't enough computers for everyone, we are going to purchase more on Wednesday. We will install them, and then the department will be fully operational.

Exercises

Fix the following run-on errors.

1. The marketing department ordered new brochures that are really nice and the brochures are in four-colour.

2. All expense accounts should be itemized based on type and cost so remember to include the appropriate shipping confirmation number.

3. Work into your schedule some time to meet next week and we can talk about your promotion so you can transition easily into the new job.

4. We will take a final product inventory on December 1 and managers will report any lost stock so employees should make sure any broken items are reported and managers should record this information in their computer databases.

5. Employees may request benefits changes during the annual enrollment period and supervisors should pass out the required forms and employees should have them completed by the deadline on the form.

6. Ian leaves his computer on overnight but Aaron turns his off and Marilyn leaves hers on, too, and so does Tashi.

7. Mohammed should make sure he specifies 20- rather than 15- paper stock and Jenna should call the print shop and ask them if

they need anything and Bruce needs to tell Ms. Winans we appreciate her letting us know we originally ordered the wrong stock.

8. The office is planning a new marketing campaign so the St. John's office will help with the promotion but office is coordinating the product show.

9. A few customers are concerned about the shipping date but the mailroom is sure we can ship overnight and I think there's no reason to be concerned.

10. Last week I went to Montréal and Haj went to Miami and this week Tony took a trip too so our travel budget is almost gone.

Check your answers to the odd-numbered exercises on page 633.

Module 16

Editing Sentences and Paragraphs

Topics

- What is "good" style?
- Are there rules I should follow?
- What should I look for when I revise sentences?
- What should I look for when I revise paragraphs?
- How does corporate culture affect style?

Review of Key Points

Learning Applications

Polishing Your Prose: End Punctuation

Learning Focus

After reading and applying the information in Module 16, you'll be able to demonstrate

Knowledge of
- The components of style
- Specific revision strategies

Skills to
- Build a forceful style
- Choose between active and passive voice
- Make your writing concise
- Vary sentence patterns
- Choose the right tone

"All too often people think they are being precise when in fact they are waffling."

"How do I present the facts in such a way so I can sell the benefits of the proposal?" is the first question Melissa Hardy-Trevenna asks herself when she sits down to write a report or a speech for someone else.

Melissa is the communications officer for the regional London-St. Thomas Real Estate Board and manages, facilitates, and writes, all internal and external communications for the board. This involves writing reports and speeches for members of the board as well as lobbying on behalf of the real estate industry on both provincial and federal levels.

Along with people from other jurisdictions, Melissa was involved in lobbying the federal government to allow first-time home buyers to borrow from their RRSPs without penalty. This became the RRSP Home Buyer's Plan, enacted in 1992.

Returning from Ottawa, Melissa wrote a report on what had transpired. This report was presented by the chair of the committee that oversaw the lobbying, and Melissa's challenge was to write the report in the style of the person who would be reading it. This meant writing a report that reflected the presenter's interests and mannerisms.

At annual meetings where there are a number of speakers, Melissa finds it humorous that she has written all of the speeches, especially when people say that the speech really sounded like the person who delivered it. Melissa accomplishes this by paying attention to the ways in which the respective speakers use language, and by including references to their respective interests. A generic speech gets a personalized treatment and the person reading feels comfortable presenting it.

The same process is used in writing reports. Melissa begins with the information and organizes it according to who will be the presenter. Then she personalizes the report from the standpoint of the presenter. Melissa is very concerned about the precise use of language. She says that she "works very hard to ensure that my language is very precise. All too often people think they are being precise when in fact they are waffling."

Melissa brings a varied background to this position. She has a B.A. in English and creative writing, an M.A. in medieval history and did further grad work in ecclesiastical history. She is also a fiction writer and has two collections of short stories and a novel in print. In 1995 she won the Journey Prize for the best short fiction of the year. Before coming to the real estate board she also worked as a journalist. It is easy to see, that with her varied background, language is very important to Melissa.

"Because of the nature of specialization today, business students don't learn basic communication skills," Melissa concludes. "The role of the communicator has become like the medieval scribe in that the professional communicator does the job of communicating for other people." Her final advice? "Don't be afraid of choosing the right words."

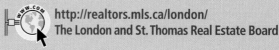

http://realtors.mls.ca/london/
The London and St. Thomas Real Estate Board

Writing *style* refers to the combined choices—of page layout, format, words, sentence construction and length, punctuation, and paragraph organization—that writers make to convey meaning. Competent writers choose consciously, based on their analysis of audience and purpose. They also recognize that all writing is rewriting: the most effective writing is the product of many, many revisions.

What is "good" style?

It's both businesslike and friendly.

Good business and administrative writing sounds like one person talking to another. Much of the writing produced in organizations today seems to have been written by faceless bureaucrats rather than by real people.

The writing style that has traditionally earned high marks in university essays and term papers is arguably more formal than good business and administrative writing. (See Figure 16.1.) However, professors also like term papers that are easy to read and that make a good visual impact.

Most people have several styles of talking, which they vary instinctively depending on the audience. Good writers have several styles, too. A memo to your boss complaining about the delays from a supplier will be informal, perhaps even chatty; a letter to the supplier demanding better service will be more formal.

Keep the following points in mind as you choose a level of formality for a specific document:

- Use a friendly, informal style for someone you've talked with.
- Avoid contractions, slang, and even minor grammatical lapses in paper documents to people you don't know. Abbreviations are acceptable in email messages if they're part of the group's culture.
- Pay particular attention to your style when you have to write uncomfortable messages: when you write to people you fear or when you must give bad news.

Figure 16.1

Different Levels of Style

Feature	Conversational Style	Good Business Style	Traditional Term Paper Style
Formality	Highly informal	Conversational; sounds like a real person talking	More formal than conversation would be, but retains a human voice
Use of contractions	Many contractions	OK to use occasional contractions	Few contractions, if any
Pronouns	Uses *I*, first- and second-person pronouns	Uses *I*, first- and second-person pronouns	First- and second-person pronouns kept to a minimum
Level of friendliness	Friendly	Friendly	No effort to make style friendly
How personal	Personal; refers to specific circumstances of conversation	Personal; may refer to reader by name; refers to specific circumstances of readers	Impersonal; may generally refer to *readers* but does not name them or refer to their circumstances
Word choice	Short, simple words; slang	Short, simple words but avoids slang	Many abstract words; scholarly, technical terms
Sentence and paragraph length	Incomplete sentences; no paragraphs	Short sentences and paragraphs	Sentences and paragraphs usually long
Grammar	Can be ungrammatical	Uses standard edited English	Uses standard edited English
Visual impact	Not applicable	Attention to visual impact of document	No particular attention to visual impact

Using the Right Tone

Your tone indicates your attitudes about your audience. Business writing tone should be businesslike and friendly. But what exactly does "friendly" mean? Well, it depends. It depends on norms and expectations of your audience, the culture of your workplace, even the part of the country where you work.

Over the past 50 years, Canadian and American social distance has decreased. In many workplaces, people call each other by their first names, whatever their age or rank. But even in cultures that pride themselves on their egalitarianism, differences in status do exist. When you're a newcomer in an organization, when you're a younger person speaking to someone older, or when you're a subordinate speaking to a superior, you're wise to show your awareness of status in the tone you use.

If you're the boss, it may be appropriate to email your subordinates, "Let me know when you're free next week for a meeting." But if you're a subordinate trying to line up people on your own level or higher up, respect and courtesy pay: "Would you be able to meet next week? Could you let me know what times you have free?"

The difficulty, of course, is that norms for politeness, like those for friendliness, can differ from organization to organization, from group to group, and even in different parts of the country and of the world (◀▶ p. 140). Furthermore, the same words that seem polite and friendly coming from a superior to a subordinate can seem pushy or arrogant coming from a subordinate to a superior. "Keep up the good work!" is fine coming from your boss. It isn't, however, something you would say to your boss.

As in other communication situations, you have to analyze the situation. Who are your audiences (◀▶ Module 2)? What are your purposes? How do other people in the organization talk and write? What kind of response do you get? If a customer winces when you return her credit card and say, "Have a nice day, Mary," maybe she doesn't appreciate hearing a cliché or being called by her first name. Talk to your peers in the organization about communication. What seems to work? What doesn't? And talk to a superior you trust. How do you come across? If you're creating the image you want to create, good. But if people think that you're rude, stuck-up, or arrogant, they may be reacting to your tone. A tone that worked for you in some situations in the past may need to be changed if you're to be effective in a new workplace, a new organization.

Relying on nouns rather than on verbs and a general deadening of style increase when people are under stress or feel insecure.[1] Confident people are more direct. Edit your writing so that you sound confident, whether you feel that way or not.

Good business style allows for individual variation. Figures 16.2 and 16.3 on page 342 show letters from two different CEOs. Jack Welch's direct, hard-hitting style in Figure 16.2 conveys an image of energy and drive. Warren Buffett's wry, self-deprecating style in Figure 16.3 suggests homespun intelligence and integrity.

Figure 16.2
Jack Welch's Letter Uses the Standard Business Style

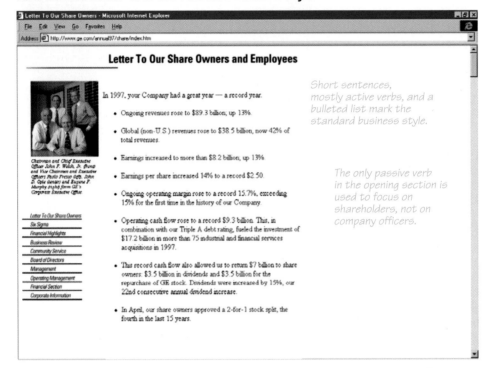

Figure 16.3
Warren Buffett's Letter Uses a More Individual Style

Are there rules I should follow?

Most "rules" are really guidelines.

Some "rules" are grammatical conventions. For example, standard edited English requires that each sentence has a subject and verb and that they agree. Business writing normally demands standard grammar, but exceptions exist. Promotional materials such as brochures, advertisements, and sales and fund-raising letters may use sentence fragments to gain the effect of speech.

Other "rules" may be conventions adopted by an organization so that its documents will be consistent. For example, a company might decide to capitalize job titles (e.g., *Production Manager*), although grammar doesn't require the capitals, or always to use a comma before *and* in a series, though a sentence can be grammatical without the comma. A different company might make different choices.

Still other "rules" are attempts to codify "what sounds good." "Never use *I*" and "use big words" are examples of this kind of "rule." These "rules" must be applied selectively, if at all. Think about your audience (p. 28), the discourse community (p. 37), your purposes, and the situation. If you want the effect produced by an impersonal style and polysyllabic words, use them. But use them only when you want the distancing they produce.

To improve your style,

- Read widely and write a *lot*.
- Get a clean page or screen, so that you aren't locked into old sentence structures.
- Try WIRMI: *What I Really Mean Is.*[2] Then write the words.
- Try reading your draft aloud to someone sitting nearby. If the words sound stiff, they'll seem stiff to a reader, too.
- Ask someone else to read your draft out loud. Readers stumble because the words on the page aren't what they expect to see. The places where that person stumbles are places where you'll want to revise for clarity.

FYI

Many first-year college and university students address their women professors as "Miss," a respectful honourific drilled into them in high school. The teachers, however, perceive the ubiquitous "Miss" as disrespectful and prefer to be addressed by name (Ms. Braun, Mrs. Braun, Marta) or title (Doctor Braun). We're usually experts on tone of voice, especially the tones of other people's voices who don't seem to respect us. But sometimes it's harder for us to hear the lack of respect in our own voices as we talk or write to others.

What should I look for when I revise sentences?

Try these six techniques.

At the sentence level, you can do many things to make your writing easy to read.

1. Use Active Verbs Most of the Time.

"Who does what" sentences that accentuate the action make your writing clearer and more interesting.

A verb is **active** if the grammatical subject of the sentence does the action the verb describes. Contemporary business communications favour the use of active verbs. A verb is **passive** if the subject is acted upon. Passives are usually made up of a form of the verb *to be* plus a past participle. *Passive* has nothing to do with *past*. Passives can be past, present, or future:

were received	(in the past)
is recommended	(in the present)
will be implemented	(in the future)

Site *to* **See**

Go to http://www.io.com/ ~eighner/writing_co urse/oldquestions/q a050152.html

This writer's site explains how to think of strong verbs

People who wish to avoid responsibility while delivering bad news tend to use s passive verbs.

To spot a passive, find the verb. If the verb describes something that the grammatical subject is doing, the verb is active. If the verb describes something that is being done to the grammatical subject, the verb is passive.

Active	**Passive**
The customer received 500 widgets.	Five hundred widgets were received by the customer.
I recommend this method.	This method is recommended by me.
The provincial agencies will implement the program.	The program will be implemented by the provincial agencies.

Verbs can be changed from active to passive by making the direct object (in the oval) the new subject (in the box). To change a passive verb to an active one, you must make the agent ("by ___ " in<>.) the new subject. If no agent is specified in the sentence, you must supply one to make the sentence active.

Active	**Passive**
The plant manager approved the request.	The request was approved by the <plant manager>.
The committee will decide next month.	A decision will be made next month. No agent in sentence.
[You] send the customer a letter informing her about the change.	A letter will be sent informing the customer of the change. No agent in sentence.

If the sentence does not have a direct object in its active form, no passive equivalent exists.

Active	**No Passive Exists**
I would like to go to the conference.	
The freight charge will be about $1,400.	
The phone rang.	

Passive verbs have at least three disadvantages:

1. If all the information in the original sentence is retained, passive verbs make the sentence longer. Passives take more time to understand.[3]
2. If the agent is omitted, it's not clear who is responsible for doing the action.
3. When many passive verbs are used, or when passives are used in material that has a lot of big words, the writing can be boring and pompous.

Passive verbs are desirable in these situations:

- Use passives to emphasize the object receiving the action, not the agent.

  Your order was shipped November 15.

The customer's order, not the shipping clerk, is important.

Ways to Improve Style

- Read widely and write a lot.
- Get a clean page or screen.
- Try WIRMI: What I Really Mean Is.
- Read your draft out loud to someone sitting about three feet away.
- Ask someone else to read your draft out loud. Revise passages where readers stumble.

- Use passives to provide coherence within a paragraph. A sentence is easier to read if "old" information comes at the beginning of a sentence. When you have been discussing a topic, use the word again as your subject even if that requires a passive verb.

> The bank made several risky loans in the late 1990s. These loans were written off as "uncollectible" in 2001.

Using *loans* as the subject of the second sentence provides a link between the two sentences, making the paragraph as a whole easier to read.

- Use passives to avoid assigning blame.

> The order was damaged during shipment.

An active verb would require the writer to specify who damaged the order. The passive here is more tactful.

FYI

Strong verbs make sentences more forceful and up to 25 percent easier to read.

Sources: E. B. Coleman, "The Comprehensibility of Several Grammatical Transformations," *Journal of Applied Psychology* 48, no. 3 (1964): 186–90; Keith Raynor, "Visual Attention in Reading: Eye Movements Reflect Cognitive Processes," *Memory and Cognition* 5 (1977): 443–48

2. Use Strong, Action Verbs to Carry the Weight of Your Sentence.

Since the verb is the most important word in any sentence, put the weight of your sentence in the verb. When the verb is a form of the verb *to be*, revise the sentence to use a more forceful verb.

Weak: The financial advantage of owning this equipment instead of leasing it is 10 percent after taxes.

Better: Owning this equipment rather than leasing it will save us 10 percent after taxes.

Nouns ending in *-ment*, *-ion*, and *-al* often hide verbs.

make an adjustment	adjust
make a payment	pay
make a decision	decide
reach a conclusion	conclude
take into consideration	consider
make a referral	refer
provide assistance	assist

Use verbs to present the information more forcefully.

Weak: We will perform an investigation of the problem.

Better: We will investigate the problem.

Weak: Selection of a program should be based on the client's needs.

Better: Select the program that best fits the client's needs.

3. Tighten Your Writing.

Writing is **wordy** if the same idea can be expressed in fewer words. Unnecessary words increase typing time, bore your reader, and make your meaning more difficult to follow, since the reader must hold all the extra words in mind while trying to understand your meaning.

Good writing is tight. Tight writing may be long because it is packed with ideas. In ◀▶ Modules 6–8, we saw that revisions to create you-attitude and positive emphasis and to develop reader benefits were frequently *longer* than the originals because the revision added information not given in the original.

Sometimes you may be able to look at a draft and see immediately how to tighten it. When wordiness isn't obvious, try the following strategies for tightening your writing.

   a. Eliminate words that say nothing
   b. Use gerunds (the *-ing* form of verbs) and infinitives to make sentences shorter and smoother
   c. Combine sentences to eliminate unnecessary words
   d. Put the meaning of your sentence into the subject and verb to cut the number of words

The purpose of eliminating unnecessary words is to save the reader's time, not simply to see how few words you can use. You aren't writing a telegram, so keep the little words that make sentences complete. (Incomplete sentences are fine in lists where all the items are incomplete.)

The following examples show how to use these methods.

a. Eliminate Words That Say Nothing.

Cut words that are already clear from other words in the sentence. Substitute single words for wordy phrases.

Wordy: Keep this information on file for future reference.

Tighter: Keep this information for reference.

or: File this information.

Wordy: Ideally, it would be best to put the billing ticket just below the screen and above the keyboard.

Tighter: If possible, put the billing ticket between the screen and the keyboard.

Phrases beginning with *of*, *which*, and *that* can often be shortened.

Wordy: the question of most importance

Tighter: the most important question

Wordy: the estimate which is enclosed

Tighter: the enclosed estimate

Sentences beginning with *There is/are* or *It is* delay the information and bore the reader. Tighten these sentences for readability.

Instant Replay

Active and Passive Verbs

If the verb describes something that the grammatical subject is doing, the verb is active. If the verb describes something that is being done to the grammatical subject, the verb is passive.

Instant Replay

Wordiness

Writing is **wordy** if the same idea can be expressed in fewer words.

Wordy: There are three reasons for the success of the project.

Tighter: Three reasons explain the project's success.

Wordy: It is the case that college and university graduates advance more quickly in the company.

Tighter: College and university graduates advance more quickly in the company.

Check your draft. If you find these phrases, or any of the unnecessary words shown in ◀▶ Figure 15.1, eliminate them.

b. Use Gerunds and Infinitives to Make Sentences Shorter and Smoother.

A **gerund** is the -ing form of a verb; grammatically, it is a verb used as a noun. In the sentence, "Running is my favourite activity," *running* is the subject of the sentence. An **infinitive** is the form of the verb that is preceded by *to: to run* is the infinitive.

In the revision below, a gerund (*purchasing*) and an infinitive (*to transmit*) tighten the revision.

Wordy: A plant suggestion has been made where they would purchase a fax machine for the purpose of transmitting test reports between plants.

Tighter: The plant suggests purchasing a fax machine to transmit test reports between plants.

Even when gerunds and infinitives do not greatly affect length, they often make sentences smoother and more conversational.

c. Combine Sentences to Eliminate Unnecessary Words.

In addition to saving words, combining sentences focusses the reader's attention on key points, makes your writing sound more sophisticated, and sharpens the relationship between ideas, thus making your writing more coherent.

Wordy: I conducted this survey by telephone on Sunday, April 21. I questioned two groups of juniors and seniors—male and female—who, according to the Student Directory, were still living in the dorms. The purpose of this survey was to find out why some juniors and seniors continue to live in the dorms even though they are no longer required by the university to do so. I also wanted to find out if there were any differences between male and female juniors and seniors in their reasons for choosing to remain in the dorms.

Tighter: On Sunday, April 21, I phoned male and female juniors and seniors living in the dorms to find out (1) why they continue to live in the dorms even though they are no longer required to do so, and (2) whether men and women had the same reasons for staying in the dorms.

d. Put the Meaning of Your Sentence into the Subject and Verb to Cut the Number of Words.

Put the core of your meaning into the subject and verb of your main clause. Think about what you mean and try saying the same thing in several different ways. Some alternatives will be tighter than others. Choose the tightest one.

Energy and enthusiasm are good. Add standard grammar and accuracy to create good sentences

Source: ONE BIG HAPPY CARTOON. By permission of Rich Detorie and Creators Syndicate.

Wordy: The reason we are recommending the computerization of this process is because it will reduce the time required to obtain data and will give us more accurate data.

Better: We are recommending the computerization of this process because it will save time and give us more accurate data.

Tight: Computerizing the process will give us more accurate data more quickly.

Wordy: The purpose of this letter is to indicate that if we are unable to mutually benefit from our seller/buyer relationship, with satisfactory material and satisfactory payment, then we have no alternative other than to sever the relationship. In other words, unless the account is handled in 45 days, we will have to change our terms to a permanent COD basis.

Better: A good buyer/seller relationship depends upon satisfactory material and satisfactory payment. You can continue to charge your purchases from us only if you clear your present balance in 45 days.

4. Vary Sentence Length and Sentence Structure.

Readable prose mixes sentence lengths and varies sentence structure. Most sentences should be 20 words or fewer. A really short sentence (under 10 words) can add punch to your prose. Really long sentences (over 30 or 40 words) are danger signs.

You can vary sentence patterns in several ways. First, you can mix simple, compound, and complex sentences. **Simple sentences** have one main clause:

We will open a new store this month.

Compound sentences have two main clauses joined with *and, but, or,* or another conjunction. Compound sentences work best when the ideas in the two clauses are closely related.

We have hired staff, and they will complete their training next week.

We wanted to have a local radio station broadcast from the store during its grand opening, but the DJs were already booked.

Site *to* **See**

Go to
www.bartleby.com/ 141/ index.html

For the online version of Strunk and White's classic guide to writing well, *The Elements of Style.*

Complex sentences have one main and one subordinate clause; they are good for showing logical relationships.

> When the stores open, we will have balloons and specials in every department.

> Because we already have a strong customer base in the north, we expect the new store to be just as successful as the store in the City Centre Mall.

Compound-complex sentences have two main clauses with one or more subordinate clause; these sentences combine interdependent, complex ideas:

> Although we have a strong customer base in the north, we expect the new store to attract younger, urban professionals, and, therefore, we'll be focussing our promotional efforts on this particular demographic.

You can also vary sentences by changing the order of elements. Normally the subject comes first.

> We will survey customers later in the year to see whether demand warrants a third store on campus.

To create variety, occasionally begin the sentence with some other part of the sentence.

> Later in the year, we will survey customers to see whether demand warrants a third store on campus.

> To see whether demand warrants a third store on campus, we will survey customers later in the year.

Use these guidelines for sentence length and structure:

- Always edit sentences for tightness. Even a 17-word sentence can be wordy.
- When your subject matter is complicated or full of numbers, make a special effort to keep sentences short.
- Use long sentences

  > To show how ideas are linked to each other

  > To avoid a series of short, choppy sentences

  > To reduce repetition

- Group the words in long and medium-length sentences into chunks that the reader can process quickly.[4]
- When you use a long sentence, keep the subject and verb close together.

Let's see how to apply the last three principles.

Use Long Sentences to Show How Ideas Are Linked to Each Other, to Avoid a Series of Short, Choppy Sentences, and to Reduce Repetition.

The sentence on the next page is hard to read not simply because it is long but also because it is shapeless. Just cutting it into a series of short, choppy sentences doesn't help. The best revision uses medium-length sentences to show the relationship between ideas.

Instant Replay

Sentence Length and Sentence Structure

Readable prose mixes sentence lengths and varies sentence structure. Most sentences should be 20 words or fewer.

Too long: It should also be noted in the historical patterns presented in the summary, that though there were delays in January and February which we realized were occurring, we are now back where we were about a year ago, and that we are not off line in our collect receivables as compared to last year at this time, but we do show a considerable over-budget figure because of an ultraconservative goal on the receivable investment.

Choppy: There were delays in January and February. We knew about them at the time. We are now back where we were about a year ago. The summary shows this. Our present collect receivables are in line with last year's. However, they exceed the budget. The reason they exceed the budget is that our goal for receivable investment was very conservative.

Better: As the summary shows, although there were delays in January and February (of which we were aware), we have now regained our position of a year ago. Our present collect receivables are in line with last year's, but they exceed the budget because our goal for receivable investment was very conservative.

Group the Words in Long and Medium-Length Sentences into Chunks.

The "better" revision above has seven chunks. In the list below, the chunks starting immediately after the numbers are main clauses. The chunks that are indented are subordinate clauses and parenthetical phrases.

1. As the summary shows,
2. although there were delays in January and February
3. (of which we were aware),
4. we have now regained our position of a year ago.
5. Our present collect receivables are in line with last year's,
6. but they exceed the budget
7. because our goal for receivable investment was very conservative.

The first sentence has four chunks: an introductory phrase (1), a subordinate clause (2) with a parenthetical phrase (3), followed by the main clause of the first sentence (4). The second sentence begins with a main clause (5). The sentence's second main clause (6) is introduced with *but*, showing that it will reverse the first clause. A subordinate clause explaining the reason for the reversal completes the sentence (7). At 27 and 24 words, respectively, these sentences aren't short, but they're readable because no chunk is longer than 10 words.

Any sentence pattern will get boring if it is repeated sentence after sentence. Use different sentence patterns—different kinds and lengths of chunks—to keep your prose interesting.

Keep the Subject and Verb Close Together.

Often you can move the subject and verb closer together if you put the modifying material in a list at the end of the sentence. For maximum readability, present the list vertically.

Hard to read: Movements resulting from termination, layoffs and leaves, recalls and reinstates, transfers in, transfers out, promotions in, promotions out, and promotions within are presently documented through the Payroll Authorization Form.

Smoother: The following movements are documented on the Payroll Authorization Form: termination, layoffs and leaves, recalls and reinstates, transfers in and out, and promotions in, out, and within.

Still better: The following movements are documented on the Payroll Authorization Form:

- Termination
- Layoffs and leaves
- Recalls and reinstates
- Transfers in and out
- Promotions in, out, and within

Sometimes you will need to change the verb and revise the word order to put the modifying material at the end of the sentence.

Hard to read: The size sequence code, which is currently used for sorting the items in the NOSROP lists and the composite stock list is not part of the online file.

Smoother: The online file does not contain the size sequence code, which is currently used for sorting the items in the composite stock lists and the NOSROP lists.

5. Use Parallel Structure.

Words or ideas that share the same logical role in your sentence must also be in the same grammatical form. Parallelism is also a powerful device for making your writing smoother and more forceful. Note the parallel portions in the following examples:

Faulty: I interviewed juniors and seniors and athletes.

Parallel: I interviewed juniors and seniors. In each rank, I interviewed athletes and non-athletes.

Faulty: Errors can be checked by reviewing the daily exception report or note the number of errors you uncover when you match the lading copy with the file copy of the invoice.

Parallel: Errors can be checked by reviewing the daily exception report or by noting the number of errors you uncover when you match the lading copy with the file copy of the invoice.

Also Parallel To check errors, note
1. The number of items on the daily exception report.
2. The number of errors discovered when the lading copy and the file copy are matched.

Note that a list in parallel structure must fit grammatically into the umbrella sentence that introduces the list.

6. Put Your Readers in Your Sentences.

Use second-person pronouns (*you*) rather than third-person (*he, she, one*) to give your writing more impact. *You* is both singular and plural; it can refer to a single person or to every member of your organization.

Third-person: Funds in a participating employee's account at the end of each six months will automatically be used to buy more stock unless a "Notice of Election Not to Exercise Purchase Rights" form is received from the employee.

Second-person: Once you begin to participate, funds in your account at the end of each six months will automatically be used to buy more stock unless you turn in a "Notice of Election Not to Exercise Purchase Rights" form.

Be careful to use *you* only when it refers to your reader.

Incorrect: My visit with the outside sales rep showed me that your schedule can change quickly.

Correct: My visit with the outside sales rep showed me that schedules can change quickly.

What should I look for when I revise paragraphs?

Check for topic sentences and transitions.

Paragraphs are visual and logical units. Use them to chunk your sentences.

1. Begin Most Paragraphs with Topic Sentences.

A good paragraph has **unity**: it is about only one idea, or topic. The **topic sentence** states the main idea and provides a scaffold to structure your document. Your writing will be easier to read if you make the topic sentence explicit and put it at the beginning of the paragraph.[5]

Hard to read (no topic sentence):   In fiscal 2000, the company filed claims for refund of federal income taxes of $3,199,000 and interest of $969,000 paid as result of an examination of the company's federal income tax returns by the Canada Customs and Revenue Agency for the years 1997 through 1999. It is uncertain what amount, if any, may ultimately be recovered.

Better (paragraph starts with topic sentence):   The company and the Canada Customs and Revenue Agency disagree about whether the company is liable for back taxes. In fiscal 2000, the company filed claims for a refund of federal income taxes of $3,199,000 and interest of $969,000 paid as a result of an examination of the company's federal income tax returns by the Canada Customs and Revenue Agency for the years 1997 through 1999. It is uncertain what amount, if any, may ultimately be recovered.

A good topic sentence forecasts the structure and content of the paragraph.

Plan B also has economic advantages.
(Prepares the reader for a discussion of B's economic advantages.)

We had several personnel changes in June.
(Prepares the reader for a list of the month's terminations and hires.)

Employees have complained about one part of our new policy on parental leaves.
(Prepares the reader for a discussion of the problem.)

When the first sentence of a paragraph is not the topic sentence, readers who skim may miss the main point. Move the topic sentence to the beginning of the paragraph. If the paragraph does not have a topic sentence, you will need to write one. If you can't think of a single sentence that serves as an "umbrella" to cover every sentence, the paragraph lacks unity. To solve the problem, either split the paragraph into two, or eliminate the sentence that digresses from the main point.

2. Use Transitions to Link Ideas.

Transition words and sentences signal the connections between ideas to the reader. Transitions tell whether the next sentence continues the previous thought or starts a new idea; they can tell whether the idea that comes next is more or less important than the previous thought. Figure 16.4 lists some of the most common transition words and phrases.

How does corporate culture affect style?

Different cultures may prefer different styles.

Different organizations and bosses may legitimately have different ideas about what constitutes good writing. If the style the company prefers seems reasonable, use it. If the style doesn't seem reasonable—if you work for someone who likes flowery language or wordy paragraphs, for example—you have several choices.

Figure 16.4
Transition Words and Phrases

To Show Addition or Continuation of the Same Idea	To Introduce an Example	To Show That the Contrast Is More Important Than the Previous Idea	To Show Time
and	for example (e.g.)	but	after
also	for instance	however	as
first, second, third	indeed	nevertheless	before
in addition	to illustrate	on the contrary	in the future
likewise	namely		next
similarly	specifically	**To Show Cause and Effect**	then
		as a result	until
To Introduce the Last or Most Important Item	**To Contrast**	because	when
finally	in contrast	consequently	while
furthermore	on the other hand	for this reason	
moreover	or	therefore	**To Summarize or End**
			in conclusion
			in summary
			finally

Site *to* **See**

Go to

www.vuse.vanderbi lt.edu/˜jgray/funny.h tml

A collection of ambiguous and often funny sentences from ads, church bulletins, and insurance forms. (Scroll down past the long first page.)

- Go ahead and use the techniques in this chapter. Sometimes seeing good writing changes people's minds about the style they prefer.
- Help your organization learn about writing. Add up-to-date writing reference texts to the company library. (If your company doesn't already offer employees a reference library, start one).
- Recognize that a style serves many communication purposes. An abstract, hard-to-read style may forge group identity or emphasize exclusivity. Government, medical, and legal writing, for example, reflects highly specialized knowledge accessible only to the initiated. James Suchan and Ronald Dulek have shown that U.S. navy officers preferred a passive, impersonal style because they saw themselves as followers. An aircraft company's engineers saw wordiness as the verbal equivalent of backup systems. A backup is redundant but essential to safety, because parts and systems do fail.[6] When big words, jargon, and wordiness are central to a group's self-image, change will be difficult, since changing style will mean changing the corporate culture.
- Ask. Often the documents that end up in files aren't especially good. Later, other workers may find these documents and imitate them, thinking they represent a corporate standard. Bosses may in fact prefer better writing.

Building your own writing style takes energy and effort, but it's well worth the work. Good style makes every document more effective; moreover, developing a good style builds confidence and competence and makes you the writer so valuable to every organization.

Employability Skills 2000+ Checklist for Revising Sentences and Paragraphs

In this module, the key skills from The Conference Board of Canada's Employability Skills 2000+ are:

Communicate
- ✔ write and speak so others pay attention and understand
- ✔ use relevant scientific, technological, and mathematical knowledge and skills to explain or clarify ideas

Manage Information
- ✔ locate, gather, and organize information using appropriate technology and information systems
- ✔ access, analyze, and apply knowledge and skills from various disciplines (e.g., the arts, languages, science, technology, mathematics, social sciences, and the humanities)

Think & Solve Problems
- ✔ assess situations and identify problems
- ✔ seek different points of view and evaluate them based on facts

Review of Key Points

- Good style in business and administrative writing is friendlier and more informal and personal than the style usually used for term papers.
- To improve your style,
  - Read and write a lot.
  - Get a clean page or screen, so that you aren't locked into old sentence structures.
  - Try WIRMI: *What I Really Mean Is*. Then write the words.
  - Try reading your draft out loud to someone sitting about three feet away. If the words sound stiff, they'll seem stiff to a reader, too.
  - Ask someone else to read your draft out loud. Readers stumble because the words on the page aren't what they expect to see. The places where that person stumbles are places where your writing can be better.
- As you write and revise sentences,
  1. Use active verbs most of the time. Active verbs are better because they are shorter, clearer, and more interesting.
  2. Use strong verbs to carry the weight of your sentence.

3. Tighten your writing. Writing is **wordy** if the same idea can be expressed in fewer words.
   a. Eliminate words that say nothing
   b. Use gerunds and infinitives to make sentences shorter and smoother
   c. Combine sentences to eliminate unnecessary words
   d. Put the meaning of your sentence into the subject and verb to cut the number of words
4. Vary sentence length and sentence structure.
5. Use parallel structure. Use the same grammatical form for ideas that have the same logical function.
6. Put your readers in your sentences.
- As you write and revise paragraphs,
  1. Begin most paragraphs with topic sentences so that readers know what to expect in the paragraph
  2. Use transitions to link ideas
- Different organizations and bosses may legitimately have different ideas about what constitutes good writing.

Learning Applications

Questions for Comprehension

16.1 What problems do passive verbs create? When are passive verbs desirable?

16.2 List two ways to tighten your writing.

16.3 What is parallel structure?

16.4 How do topic sentences help readers?

Questions for Critical Thinking

16.5 Do you prefer Jack Welch's style in Figure 16.2 or Warren Buffet's style in Figure 16.3? Why? Could you use the style you prefer as a model for your own business writing? Why or why not?

16.6 Would your other instructors like the style you're learning to use in this class?

16.7 Can a long document be tight rather than wordy?

Questions for Building Skills

16.8 What skills have you read about in this module?

16.9 What skills are you practising in the assignments you're doing for this module?

16.10 How could you further develop the skills you're working on?

Exercises and Problems

16.11 Changing Verbs from Passive to Active

Identify the passive verbs in the following sentences and convert them to active verbs. In some cases, you may need to add information to do so. You may use different words as long as you retain the basic meaning of the sentence. Remember that imperative verbs are active, too.

1. The marketing plan was prepared by Needra Smith.

2. With the assistance of computers, inventory records are updated and invoices are automatically issued when an order is entered by one of our customers.

3. When the Web page is finalized it is recommended that it be routed to all managers for final approval.

4. As stated in my résumé, I speak Polish fluently.

5. All employees being budgeted should be listed by name and position. Any employee whose name does not appear on the "September Listing of Salaried Employees" must be explained. If this employee is a planned replacement, indicate who will be replaced and when. If it is an addition, the reason must be explained.

16.12 Using Strong Verbs

Revise each of the following sentences to use stronger verbs.

1. The advantage of using colour is that the document is more memorable.

2. Customers who make payments in cash will receive a 1 percent rebate on all purchases.

3. When you make an evaluation of media buys, take into consideration the demographics of the group seeing the ad.

4. We provide assistance to clients in the process of reaching a decision about the purchase of hardware and software.

5. We maintain the belief that Web ads are a good investment.

16.13   Reducing Wordiness

1. Eliminate words that say nothing. You may use different words.

   a. It is necessary that we reach a decision about whether or not it is desirable to make a request that the office be allowed the opportunity and option of hiring additional workers.

   b. The purchase of a new computer will allow us to produce form letters quickly. In addition, return-on-investment could be calculated for proposed repairs. Another use is that the computer could check databases to make sure that claims are paid only once.

   c. There are many subjects which interest me.

2. Use gerunds and infinitives to make these sentences shorter and smoother.

   a. The completion of the project requires the collection and analysis of additional data.

   b. The purchase of laser printers will make possible the in-house production of the newsletter.

   c. The treasurer has the authority for the investment of assets for the gain of higher returns.

3. Combine sentences to show how ideas are related and to eliminate unnecessary words.

   a. Some buyers want low prices. Other buyers are willing to pay higher prices for convenience or service.

   b. We projected sales of $34 million in the third quarter. Our actual sales have fallen short of that figure by $2.5 million.

   c. We conducted this survey by handing out questionnaires January 10, 11, and 12. Our office surveyed 100 customers. We wanted to see whether they would like to be able to leave voicemail messages for their representatives. We also wanted to find out if our hours are convenient for them. Finally, we asked whether adequate parking was available.

16.14   Improving Parallel Structure

Revise each of the following sentences to create parallelism.

1. Training programs

   - Allow employees to build skills needed for current and future positions

   - Employees enjoy the break from routine work

   - Training programs are a "fringe benefit" that helps to attract and retain good employees

2. Newsletters enhance credibility, four times as many people read them as read standard ad formats, and allow soft-sell introduction to prospective customers.

3. When you leave a voicemail message,

   - Summarize your main point in a sentence or two

   - The name and phone number should be given slowly and distinctly

   - The speaker should give enough information so that the recipient can act on the message

   - Tell when you'll be available to receive the recipient's return call

16.15   Editing Sentences to Improve Style

Revise these sentences to make them smoother, less wordy, and easier to read. Eliminate jargon and repetition. Keep the information; you may reword or reorganize it. If the original is not clear, you may need to add information to write a clear revision.

1. The table provided was unclear due to hard-to-understand headings.

2. By working a co-op or intern position, you may have to be in school an additional year to complete the requirements for graduation, but this extra year is paid for by the income you make in the co-op or intern position.

3. There is a seasonality factor in the workload, with the heaviest being immediately prior to quarterly due dates for estimated tax payments.

4. Informational meetings will be held during next month at different dates and times. These meetings will explain the health insurance options. Meeting times are as follows:

   October 17, 12:00 P.M.–1:00 P.M.

   October 20, 4:00 P.M.–5:00 P.M.

   October 23, 2:00 P.M.–3:00 P.M.

5. Listed below are some benefits you get with OHIP:

   1. Routine doctors' visits will charge only a $10 co-payment.

   2. No hassle of prescription reimbursements later. You only pay the co-payment when you fill your prescription.

   3. Hospitalization is covered 100 percent.

16.16   Putting Readers in Your Sentences

Revise each of the following sentences to put readers in them. As you revise, use active verbs and simple words.

1. Mutual funds can be purchased from banks, brokers, financial planners, or from the fund itself.

2. Every employee will receive a copy of the new policy within 60 days after the labour agreement is signed.

3. Another aspect of the university is campus life, with an assortment of activities and student groups to participate in and lectures and sports events to attend.

16.17   Using Topic Sentences

Make each of the following paragraphs more readable by opening each paragraph with a topic sentence. You may be able to find a topic sentence in the paragraph and move it to the beginning. In other cases, you'll need to write a new sentence.

1. At Disney World, a lunch put on an expense account is "on the mouse." McDonald's employees "have ketchup in their veins." Business slang flourishes at companies with rich corporate cultures. Memos at Procter & Gamble are called "reco's" because the model P&G memo begins with a recommendation.

2. The first item on the agenda is the hiring for the coming year. George has also asked that we review the agency goals for the next fiscal year. We should cover this early in the meeting since it may affect our hiring preferences. Finally, we need to announce the deadlines for grant proposals, decide which grants to apply for, and set up a committee to draft each proposal.

3. Separate materials that can be recycled from your regular trash. Pass along old clothing, toys, or appliances to someone else who can use them. When you purchase products, choose those with minimal packaging. If you have a yard, put your yard waste and kitchen scraps (excluding meat and fat) in a compost pile. You can reduce the amount of solid waste your household produces in four ways.

16.18 Writing Paragraphs

Write a paragraph on each of the following topics.

a. Discuss your ideal job.

b. Summarize a recent article from a business magazine or newspaper.

c. Explain how technology is affecting the field you plan to enter.

d. Explain why you have or have not decided to work while you attend college.

e. Write a profile of someone who is successful in the field you hope to enter.

As Your Instructor Directs

a. Label topic sentences, active verbs, and parallel structure

b. Edit a classmate's paragraphs to make the writing even tighter and smoother

Polishing Your Prose

End Punctuation

Sentences normally end with one of three forms of punctuation: a period, a question mark, or an exclamation point.

Periods end most statements:

The report is on your desk.

Question marks end questions:

Have you read it?

Exclamation marks end statements with strong emphasis or emotion:

The report is on fire!

Overusing exclamation points creates a "gushy" tone instead of the business-like tone we want.

Exercises

Use appropriate punctuation at the end of each of the following sentences.

1. Where is the file on the Richman proposal

2. Would you send me a copy of that memo

3. Ms. Amarotti will arrive by plane tomorrow

4. Watch out

5. Take a moment to read the instructions before completing the form

6. Are you sure that the times on this meeting roster are correct

7. Congratulations on your recent promotion to line manager

8. Please fax the invoices to us at (519) 555-2222

9. Remember, when we turn on the breakroom lights, everyone is to yell, "Happy Birthday, Susharita"

10. I can never remember what is the purpose of making three copies of each purchase order

Check your answers to the odd-numbered exercises on page 633.

CBC Video Case

Go to www.mcgrawhill.ca/college/locker to view "A Science Project," this Unit's online CBC Video Case. You'll get a critical view of how companies search for impressive "scientific" terms to promote their products—and find out how the consumer audience reacts to this specialized vocabulary.

Unit Five

Interpersonal Communication

Module 17
Listening

Topics

- **What do good listeners do?**
- **What is active listening?**
- **How do I show people that I'm listening to them?**
- **Can I use these techniques if I really disagree with someone?**

Review of Key Points

Learning Applications

Polishing Your Prose: Combining Sentences

Learning Focus

After reading and applying the information in Module 17, you'll be able to demonstrate

Knowledge of

- The fundamentals of good listening practice
- Active listening as a core communication competency

Skills to

- Listen actively
- Continue to learn how to build goodwill

"There is no point in asking a question unless you are prepared to hear the answer."

"Listening involves not just words but the context in which the words are spoken, and the speaker's body language," says Marion Boyd, whose various jobs over the last fifteen years have depended on good listening skills.

Marion, who has a B.A. in English and history from York University, held various jobs, including staff representative for the Faculty Association at York, administrator for a child care centre, and college instructor before she became the executive director of the Battered Women's Advocacy Clinic in London. Here listening skills are extremely important in order to establish empathy and trust with students, colleagues, and clients.

Marion was a member of the Ontario provincial legislature from 1990 to 1999 and served as a Cabinet member for five years. In this position listening skills were needed both in the legislature and in the home constituency office. During Question Period, when the opposition questions the government, Marion says "it is essential to listen carefully to the question that is being asked." All too often, politicians get into trouble because they don't respond to what is being asked. One must be especially careful since "you have to listen differently when the speaker is not on your side."

In the constituency office, Marion had to listen and show that she was listening. This was accomplished by body language. Marion's behaviour let the speaker know she cared, even if there wasn't anything she could do to help. Sometimes a truly sympathetic ear, with an explanation of why nothing could be done is all that was required. This way the person at least had a fair hearing. Marion uses a medical analogy to make her point. All too often a doctor will ask a patient how she is, but the body language of the doctor will show that she really isn't interested. As Marion says, "There is no point in asking a question unless you are prepared to hear the answer. Your body language must be consistent with your verbal language."

Since leaving politics Marion has been involved with three projects. She has her own consulting business; she is working on a special project with the board of health to develop proper practices in the screening of abused women and the long-term effects of abuse on women's health; and she is an adjudicator with the Criminal Injury Compensation Board.

It is essential in all of these situations to listen to what is being said. Sometimes you have to go beyond words and listen for context. In many cases, a good verbal memory is needed. In other cases, such as with the CIC Board, notes can be taken and documents are used in determining the outcome. But a major factor in determining what is important depends on how the adjudicator listens to the person before the board.

When asked for words of advice, Marion says, "You must learn to listen to your own words when speaking so that you can understand what the other person is hearing."

http://www.marionboyd.net/about
marion.htm
Marion Boyd's homepage

FYI

A recent survey by Select Appointments North America found that 80 percent of responding executives rated listening as the most important skill in the workforce. Soft skills such as listening and problem solving ranked far higher than technical skills. However, listening skills were also rated by 28 percent of executives as the most lacking in the workforce.

Source: Jennifer Salopek, "Is Anyone Listening?" visited Web site July 21, 2001; http://www.astd.org/CMS/templates/index.html?template_id=1&articleid=23760

Despite the universal "You weren't listening!" lament of friends, lovers, parents, teachers, co-workers, and employers, we rarely receive formal training in this key skill. In fact, active listening is an acquired skill that takes a lifetime of practice and requires enormous energy. Listening may be even more difficult on the job than it is in the classroom:

- In class you're encouraged to take notes. But you can't whip out a notepad every time your boss speaks.
- Many classroom lectures are well-organized, with signposts (◀▶ Module 24) and repetition of key points to help hearers follow. But conversations usually wander. A key point about when a report is due may be sandwiched in among statements about other due dates for other projects.
- In a classroom lecture you're listening primarily for information. In interchanges with friends and co-workers, you need to listen for feelings, too. Feelings of being rejected or overworked need to be dealt with as they arise. But you can't deal with a feeling unless you are aware of it.

As Module 2 explains (◀▶ p. 30), to receive a message, the receiver must first perceive the message, then decode it (that is, translate the symbols into meaning), and then interpret it. In interpersonal communication, **hearing** denotes perceiving sounds. **Listening** means decoding and interpreting them correctly.

What do good listeners do?

They consciously follow four practices.

Good listeners pay attention, focus on the other speaker(s) in a generous way rather than on themselves, avoid making assumptions, and listen for feelings as well as for facts.

Pay Attention.

Good listening requires energy. You have to resist distractions and tune out noise (◀▶ Module 2), whether the rumble of a truck going by or your own worry about whether your parking meter is expiring.

Some listening errors happen because the hearer doesn't attend closely enough to a key point. After a meeting with a client, a consultant waited for the client to

Polish your listening skills. You'll need them on the job as well as in your personal life

Source: FRANK & ERNEST reprinted by permission of United Feature Syndicate, Inc.

send her more information that she would use to draft a formal proposal to do a job for the client. It turned out that the client thought the next move was up to the consultant. The consultant and the client had met together, but they hadn't remembered the same facts.

To avoid listening errors caused by inattention,

- Before the conversation anticipate the answers you need to get. Make a mental or paper list of your questions. When is the project due? What resources do you have? What is the most important aspect of this project, from the other person's point of view? During a conversation, listen for answers to your questions.
- At the end of the conversation, check your understanding with the other person. Especially check who does what next.
- After the conversation, write down key points that affect deadlines or work assessment.

Focus on the Other Speaker(s) in a Generous Way.

Most of us half hear while we listen to our own internal monologues. We focus on factors incidental to the topic, or look for flaws: "What an ugly tie." "She sounds like a little girl." "There's a typo in that slide." Often we listen only for the pause that signifies it's our turn to speak, or as if the discussion were a war, collecting weapons to attack the other speaker. "Ah hah! You're wrong about *that*!"

Good listeners, in contrast, are more generous. They realize that people who are not polished speakers may nevertheless have something to say. Rather than pouncing on the first error they hear and tuning out the speaker while they wait impatiently for their own turn to speak, good listeners weigh all the evidence before they come to judgment. They realize that they can learn something even from people they do not like.

To avoid listening errors caused by self-absorption,

- Focus on the substance of what the speaker says, not his or her appearance or delivery
- Spend your time evaluating what the speaker says, not just planning your rebuttal
- Consciously work to learn something from every speaker

Avoid Making Assumptions.

Many listening errors come from making faulty assumptions. In 1977 when two Boeing 747 jumbo jets ran into each other on the ground in Tenerife, the pilots seem to have heard the control tower's instructions. The KLM pilot was told to taxi to the end of the runway, turn around, and wait for clearance. But the KLM pilot didn't interpret the order to wait as an order he needed to follow. The Pan Am pilot interpreted *his* order to turn off at the "third intersection" to mean the third *unblocked* intersection. He didn't count the first blocked ramp, so he was still on the main runway when the KLM pilot ran into his plane at 186 miles an hour. The planes exploded in flames; 576 people died.[1]

In contrast, asking questions can provide useful information. Superb salespeople listen closely to client questions and objections, to better identify and respond to

Instant Replay

Hearing and Listening

Hearing denotes perceiving sounds **Listening** means decoding and interpreting them correctly

the sticking points of a sale. Magazine advertising account representative Beverly Jameson received a phone call from an ad agency saying that a client wanted to cancel the space it had bought. Jameson saw the problem as an opportunity: "Instead of hearing 'cancel,' I heard, 'There's a problem here—let's get to the root of it and figure out how to make the client happy.' " Jameson met with the client, asked the right questions, and discovered that the client wanted more flexibility. She changed some of the markets, kept the business, and turned the client into a repeat customer.[2]

To avoid listening errors caused by faulty assumptions,

- Consider the other person's background and experiences. Why is this point important to the speaker? What might he or she mean by it? How can its importance to the speaker benefit you?
- Don't ignore instructions you think are unnecessary. Before you do something else, check with the order giver to see if in fact there is a reason for the instruction.
- Paraphrase what the speaker has said, giving him or her a chance to correct your understanding.

Listen for Feelings as Well as Facts.

Sometimes, someone just needs to blow off steam, to vent (◀|▶ p. 406). Sometimes, people just want to have a chance to fully express themselves; "winning" or "losing" may not matter. Sometimes, people may have objections that they can't quite put into words.

To avoid listening errors caused by focussing solely on facts,

- Consciously listen for feelings
- Pay attention to tone of voice, facial expression, and body language (◀|▷ p. 59)
- Don't assume that silence means consent. Invite the other person to speak

What is active listening?

Feeding back the literal meaning, or the emotional content, or both.

In **active listening**, receivers actively demonstrate that they've heard and understood a speaker by feeding back either the literal meaning or the emotional content, or both. Other techniques in active listening are asking for more information and stating one's own feelings.

Five strategies create active responses:

1. Paraphrase the content. Feed back the meaning, as you understand it, in your own words.
2. Mirror the speaker's feelings. Identify the feelings you think you hear.
3. State your own feelings. This strategy works especially well when you are angry.
4. Ask for information or clarification.
5. Ask how you can help.

Blocking Response	Possible Active Response
Ordering, threatening "I don't care how you do it. Just get that report on my desk by Friday."	**Paraphrasing content** "You're saying that you don't have time to finish the report by Friday."
Preaching, criticizing "You should know better than to air the department's problems in a general meeting."	**Mirroring feelings** "It sounds like the department's problems really bother you."
Interrogating "Why didn't you tell me that you didn't understand the instructions?"	**Stating one's own feelings** "I'm frustrated that the job isn't completed yet, and I'm worried about getting it done on time."
Minimizing the problem "You think that's bad. You should see what I have to do this week."	**Asking for information or clarification** "What parts of the problem seem most difficult to solve?"
Advising "Well, why don't you try listing everything you have to do and seeing which items are most important?"	**Offering to help solve the problem together** "Is there anything I could do that would help?"

Figure 17.1

Blocking Responses versus Active Listening

Source: The 5 responses that block communication are based on a list of 12 in Thomas Gordon and Judith Gordon Sands, *P.E.T. in Action* (New York: Wyden, 1976), 117–18

Instead of mirroring what the other person says, many of us respond to our own needs by attempting to analyze, solve, or dismiss the problem. People with problems need to know above all that we hear that they're having a rough time. Figure 17.1 lists some of the responses that block communication. Ordering and interrogating tell the other person that the listener doesn't want to hear what he or she has to say.

Preaching attacks the other person. Minimizing the problem suggests that the other person's concern is misplaced. Even advising shuts off discussion. Giving a quick answer minimizes the pain the person feels and puts him or her down for not seeing (what is to us, because it's not our problem) the obvious answer. Even if it is a good answer from an objective point of view, the other person may not be ready to hear it. And sometimes, the off-the-top-of-the-head solution doesn't address the real problem.

Active listening takes time and energy. Even people who are skilled active listeners can't do it all the time because the listener's feelings interfere with open reception. Furthermore, as experts have pointed out, active listening works only if you genuinely accept the other person's ideas and feelings. Active listening can reduce the conflict that results from miscommunication, but it alone cannot reduce the conflict that comes when two people want apparently inconsistent things or when one person wants to change someone else.[3]

Four Habits of Good Listeners

Good listeners

- Pay attention
- Focus on the other speaker(s) in a generous way
- Avoid making assumptions
- Listen for feelings as well as for facts

How do I show people that I'm listening to them?

Acknowledge their comments in words, in nonverbal symbols, and in actions.

Active listening is a good way to show people that you are listening. Referring to another person's comment is another way: "I agree with Diana that . . ."

Leading by Listening

Enormous energy, stamina, and curiosity characterize the best managers. And they draw on these resources ceaselessly, since over 90 percent of their day is spent communicating. Canadian, American, British, and Swedish managers demonstrate a marked preference for gathering information by word-of-mouth, through conversations, telephone calls and meetings, rather than by reading documents. These managers lead by putting themselves in the centre of the organization's information flow. Listening to "soft" data, including opinions and gossip, allows them to recognize problems and opportunities, make decisions, motivate and negotiate. To accumulate and disseminate the information necessary to do their job, these leaders spend most of their day listening.

In fact, experts and practitioners agree that the most effective leaders apply sophisticated interpersonal skills, not management theory, to manage people. Major-General Lewis MacKenzie, chief of staff of the United Nations Protection force in Yugoslavia, espouses leadership tenets he learned first-hand. Significantly, MacKenzie believes that learning to listen became one of his most powerful leadership techniques.

According to an article in *the training report*, "MacKenzie said that early in his career he always thought that he knew more than the person talking to him, and often didn't hear what they were saying to him because he was constructing his response midway through their sentence. It was a slap in the face when he finally realized that half the people who worked for him knew more than he did. But then he learned that if he listened to a subordinate's idea, implemented it, and gave that person credit..." he'd look just as good, the subordinate would gain in recognition and morale and the organization would be improved. To get people talking, MacKenzie also had to listen: "...he found out what their passions were and used those interests as a threshold to open com-

munication." Peacekeeper MacKenzie "commanded a multinational force that spoke 16 different languages and hailed from 31 different countries." Despite the obvious communication difficulties, "MacKenzie and his troops opened the airport in Sarajevo in 1992, sidestepping normal channels and allowing for the daily delivery of 250 to 300 tons of desperately needed food and medicine."

The key to active listening is preparedness. How prepared are most of us to listen, most of the time?

In 1996, out-of-work stagehand Sam Holman, disabled from a chronic knee injury and ineligible for disability insurance, was casually talking baseball with friend Bill MacKenzie in The Mayflower, an Ottawa pub. MacKenzie, a baseball scout for over 20 years, commented on the number of bats that major leaguers broke each season. Then he suggested that Holman use his carpentry skills to do something about the problem: 'Why don't you start making bats?' Hundreds of hours of research later, Holman carved the prototype Sam Bat, the first maple bat in the history of baseball. Although its original price didn't cover production costs, by August 1977 the Sam Bat had attracted important converts: Blue Jays' Joe Carter loved the bat and began to lobby the league to approve it. In 1998, the Sam Bat received approval—the first maple bat in major-league history to do so. Meanwhile heavy hitters on all the major league teams began ordering Holman's bats, which many credited for their improved batting averages. By 1999, not only the majors, but college, little league, Taiwanese, and Mexican teams were also ordering Sam Bats. Today Holman custom-makes 200 different bat models while overseeing the four employees of the Original Maple Bat Corporation.

Sources: Henry Mintzberg, "The Manager's Job: Folklore and Fact," http://www.uu.edu/personal/bnance/318/mintz.html, visited Web site July 21, 2001; "Lessons in Leadership," *the training report*, May/June 2001; Alex Gillis, "Batman," *National Post Business*, October 1999, 60-69.

Acknowledgment responses or *conversation regulators*—nods, uh huh's, smiles, frowns—also help carry the message that you're listening. Remember, however, that listening responses vary from culture to culture.

European Canadians indicate attention and involvement by making eye contact, leaning forward, and making acknowledgment responses. However, as Module 3 shows (◀▶ p. 60), some cultures show respect by looking down. In a multicultural workforce, you won't always know whether a colleague who listens silently as you talk agrees with what you say or disagrees violently but is too polite to say so. The best thing to do is to observe the behaviour, without assigning a meaning to it: "You aren't saying much." Then let the other person speak.

Of course, if you go through the motions of active listening but then act with disrespect, people will feel that you have not heard them. Acting on what people say is necessary for people to feel completely heard.

Can I use these techniques if I really disagree with someone?

Yes!

Most of us do our worst listening when we are in highly charged emotional situations, such as talking with someone with whom we really disagree, getting bad news, or being criticized. Certainly you don't need to listen to a radio talk show host whose views you deplore. But at work, you do need to listen, even to people with whom you have major conflicts.

At a minimum, good listening enables you to find out why your opponent objects to the programs or ideas you support. Understanding the objections to your ideas is essential if you are to create a persuasive campaign to overcome those objections.

Good listening is crucial when you are criticized, especially by your boss. You need to know which areas are most important and exactly what kind of improvement counts. Otherwise, you might spend your time and energy changing your behaviour, but changing it in a way not valued by your organization.

Listening can do even more. Listening to people is an indication that you're taking them seriously. If you really listen to the people you disagree with, you show that you respect them. And taking that step may enable them to respect you and listen to you.

Instant Replay

Strategies for Active Listening

- Paraphrase the content
- Mirror the speaker's feelings
- State your own feelings
- Ask for information or clarification
- Offer to help solve the problem

Employability Skills 2000+ Checklist for Listening

In this module, the key skills from The Conference Board of Canada's Employability Skills 2000+ are:

Communicate
✔ listen and ask questions to understand and appreciate the points of view of others
✔ share information using a range of information and communications technologies (e.g., voice, email, computers)

Think & Solve Problems
✔ seek different points of view and evaluate them based on facts
✔ recognize the human, interpersonal, technical, scientific, and mathematical dimensions of a problem

Be Adaptable
✔ cope with uncertainty
✔ be open and respond constructively to change

Learn Continuously
✔ be willing to continuously learn and grow
✔ assess personal strengths and areas for development

Work with Others
✔ be flexible: respect, be open to and supportive of the thoughts, opinions and contributions of others in a group
✔ recognize and respect people's diversity, individual differences, and perspectives
✔ accept and provide feedback in a constructive and considerate manner

Review of Key Points

- In interpersonal communication, **hearing** denotes perceiving sounds. **Listening** means decoding and interpreting them correctly.

- Good listeners pay attention, focus on the other speaker(s) in a generous way rather than on themselves, avoid making assumptions, and listen for feelings as well as for facts.

- To avoid listening errors caused by inattention,
  - Be conscious of the points you need to know and listen for them
  - At the end of the conversation, check your understanding with the other person
  - After the conversation, write down key points that affect deadlines or how work will be evaluated

- To avoid listening errors caused by self-absorption,
  - Focus on the substance of what the speaker says, not his or her appearance or delivery
  - Spend your time understanding and assessing what the speaker says, not planning your rebuttal
  - Consciously work to learn something from every speaker
- To reduce listening errors caused by misinterpretation,
  - Don't ignore instructions you think are unnecessary
  - Consider the other person's background and experiences. Why is this point important to the speaker?
  - Paraphrase what the speaker has said, giving him or her a chance to correct your understanding

- To avoid listening errors caused by focusing solely on facts,
  - Consciously listen for feelings
  - Attend to tone of voice, facial expression, and body language (p. 59)
  - Don't assume that silence means consent. Invite the other person to speak
- In **active listening**, receivers actively demonstrate that they've heard and understood a speaker by feeding back either the literal meaning or the emotional content or both. To do this, hearers can
  - Paraphrase the content
  - Mirror the speaker's feelings
  - State their own feelings
  - Ask for information or clarification
  - Ask what they can do to help

Learning Applications

Questions for Comprehension

17.1   What is the difference between hearing and listening?

17.2   What do good listeners do?

17.3   What is active listening?

Questions for Critical Thinking

17.4   Why is listening such hard work?

17.5   How do you show someone that you are listening?

17.6   What are the people and circumstances in your life where you find it most difficult to listen? Why do you find it difficult?

17.7   Think of a time when you really felt that the other person listened to you, and a time when you felt unheard. Describe the verbal and non-verbal content in each situation. How did you know the other person was listening? What behaviours and words caused you to feel unheard? Now describe your feelings in each situation. What was different in each situation?

Questions for Building Skills

17.8   What skills have you read about in this module?

17.9   What skills are you practising in the assignments you're doing for this module?

17.10   How could you further develop the skills you're working on?

Exercises and Problems

17.11 Identifying Responses That Show Active Listening

Which of the following responses show active listening? Which block communication?

1. Comment: Whenever I say something, the group ignores me.

   Responses: a. That's because your ideas aren't very good. Do more planning before group meetings.

   b. Nobody listens to me, either.

   c. You're saying that nobody builds on your ideas.

2. Comment: I've done more than my share of work on this project. But the people who have been freeloading are going to get the same grade I worked so hard to earn.

   Responses: a. Yes, we're all going to get the same grade.

   b. Are you afraid we won't do well on the assignment?

   c. It sounds like you feel resentful.

3. Comment: My parents are going to kill me if I don't have a job lined up at the end of this term.

   Responses: a. You know they're exaggerating. They won't *really* kill you.

   b. Can you blame them? I mean, you've been in school for six years. Surely you've learned something to make you employable!

   c. If you act the way in interviews that you do in our class, I'm not surprised. Companies want people with good attitudes and good work ethics.

17.12 Practising Active Listening

Go around the room for this exercise. In turn, let each student complain about something (large or small) that really bothers him or her. Then the next student(s) will

a. Offer a statement of limited agreement that would buy time

b. Paraphrase the statement

c. Check for feelings that might lie behind the statement

d. Offer inferences that might motivate the statement

17.13 Interviewing Workers about Listening

Interview someone who works in an organization about his or her on-the-job listening. Possible questions to ask include the following:

• Whom do you listen to as part of your job? Your superior? Subordinates? (How many levels down?) Customers or clients? Who else?

• How much time a day do you spend listening?

• What people do you talk to as part of your job? Do you feel they hear what you say? How do you tell whether or not they're listening?

• Do you know of any problems that came up because someone didn't listen? What happened?

• What do you think prevents people from listening effectively? What advice would you have for someone on how to listen more accurately?

As Your Instructor Directs,

a. Share your information with a small group of students in your class

b. Present your findings orally to the class

c. Present your findings in a memo to your instructor

d. Join with other students to present your findings in a group report or presentation

17.14   Reflecting on Your Own Listening

Keep a listening log for a week. Record how long you listened, what barriers you encountered, and what strategies you used to listen more actively and more effectively. What situations were easiest? Which were most difficult? Which parts of listening do you need to work hardest on?

As Your Instructor Directs,

a. Share your information with a small group of students in your class

b. Present your findings orally to the class

c. Present your findings in a memo to your instructor

d. Join with other students to present your findings in a group report or presentation

17.15   Reflecting on Acknowledgment Responses

Try to be part of at least three conversations involving people from more than one culture. What acknowledgment responses do you observe? Which seem to yield the most positive results? If possible, talk to the other participants about what verbal and nonverbal cues show attentive listening in their cultures.

As Your Instructor Directs,

a. Share your information with a small group of students in your class

b. Present your findings orally to the class

c. Present your findings in a memo to your instructor

d. Join with other students to present your findings in a group report or presentation

Polishing Your Prose

Combining Sentences

Combining sentences is a powerful tool to make your writing tighter and more forceful.

When too many sentences in a passage have fewer than 10 words and follow the same basic pattern, prose is **choppy**. Choppy prose seems less unified and either robot-like or frenzied in tone. Combining short sentences to create longer, flowing ones can eliminate this problem.

Choppy: I went to the office supply store. I purchased a computer, a fax machine, and a laser printer. I went to my office. I installed the equipment. I am more efficient.

Better: At the office supply store, I purchased a computer, a fax machine, and a laser printer. After installing the equipment in my office, I am more efficient.

There are several ways to combine sentences.

1. Use **transitions**: words and phrases that signal connections between ideas. Common transitions are *first, second, third, finally, in addition, likewise, for example, however, on the other hand, nevertheless, because, therefore, before, after, while,* and *in conclusion.*

Choppy: Neil drove the truck to the warehouse. Charlie loaded it with cement. Phil supervised the work.

Better: First, Neil drove the truck to the warehouse. Then Charlie loaded it with cement while Phil supervised the work.

2. Rewrite sentences using **subordinate clauses**. A clause with one of the following words will be subordinate: *after*, *although*, *though*, *because*, or *since*.

Better: After Neil drove the truck to the warehouse, Charlie loaded it with cement. Phil supervised the work.

3. Join simple sentences together with **coordinating conjunctions**, like *and*, *but*, or *or*. These conjunctions can also function as transitional words. Be sure to use the comma before the conjunction when combining two independent clauses.

Better: Neil drove the truck to the warehouse, Charlie loaded it with cement, and Phil supervised the work.

4. Create a **list** using commas and coordinating conjunctions.

Choppy: Sam put our old files in the storeroom. Sam placed extra copies of the company telephone directory in the storeroom. Sam put boxes of three-ring binders in the storeroom.

Better: Sam put old files, extra copies of the telephone directory, and boxes of three-ring binders in the storeroom.

Exercises

Combine the following sentences to make them easier to read.

1. You can get promoted quickly at our company. Being organized and on time will help. Not meeting deadlines will not.

2. There are many reasons to choose Canadian Human Resource Planners as your human resources consulting firm. Our organization has over 20 years in the business. We have regional offices in Calgary and Toronto. Canadian Human Resource Planners has an international membership of members from industry, government, non-profit groups, educational institutions, and consulting firms.

3. Changing the toner cartridge on the photocopier is simple. Open the front panel. Find the green tabs. Depress the green tabs with your thumbs. Pull the black toner cartridge out. Put the toner cartridge in the recycling box. Slide a new toner cartridge into the compartment. The green tabs will snap back into place. Close the panel.

4. The development team members took a plane to Victoria. That was on Friday. They attended a conference. That was on Saturday. They came home. That was on Sunday. On Friday it rained. The team members used umbrellas. The other two days it did not rain. They did not need our umbrellas on those days.

5. The tornado plan for our building has five parts. One part is to go to your designated shelter area in the basement of the building. One part is to listen for the tornado alert siren. One part is to sit down on the floor. One part is to take the stairs and not the elevator. One part is to cover your head with your arms.

Check your answers to the odd-numbered exercises on page 633.

Module 18

Planning, Managing, and Recording Meetings

Topics

- **What planning should precede a meeting?**

- **When I'm in charge, how do I keep the meeting on track?**

- **What decision-making strategies work well in meetings?**

- **How can I be an effective meeting participant?**

- **What should go in meeting minutes?**

- **How can I use informal meetings to advance my career?**

- **Do virtual meetings require special consideration?**

Review of Key Points

Learning Applications

Polishing Your Prose: Hyphens and Dashes

Learning Focus

After reading and applying the information in Module 18, you'll be able to demonstrate

Knowledge of

- Meeting management
- Networking opportunities

Skills to

- Plan a meeting
- Lead a meeting
- Participant in meetings
- Take good meeting minutes
- Network effectively

"I even attend meetings to prepare for meetings..."

"Everything is 80 percent preparation and 20 percent execution," says Sandi Ellis, a regional representative of the Canadian Labour Congress.

The Canadian Labour Congress (CLC) is an umbrella organization comprised of most unions in the country. Unions pay dues to the CLC for services provided on local levels by people like Sandi. One of the main services provided by the CLC is education. Local reps help to organize weekend schools so that union members can learn more about how to be stewards, how to be health and safety reps, or just more about what unions do, how they do it, and how to get more involved.

Sandi began her union career when she became a letter carrier twenty-five years ago. She was elected secretary of her union and became the health and safety rep for her local. She became involved in helping to develop the Employee Assistance Program for her union. This, in turn, got her involved with the United Way. She volunteered for all kinds of positions with the United Way and this service soon led to her becoming the labour staff representative for the United Way. She joined the Steelworkers union, who in turn appointed her as a CLC rep, and when her current job opened up six years ago she jumped at the chance. "I always dreamed of working locally but being on the national stage," says Sandi of her dream job.

Sandi's main responsibility is to attend labour council meetings. Labour councils are the local organizations of the CLC. In her area there are eight councils, which means eight full membership meetings a month, plus eight executive meetings a month, and various committee meetings. "I even attend meetings to prepare for meetings," says Sandi, emphasising her first point. "Meetings are the meat of my life", she jokes, "But they are also my bread and butter."

In addition to providing services, she sees her job as enabling people in the labour movement. The 80 percent of her preparation often involves encouraging, enabling, and assisting others so that they will be prepared for the tasks they choose to pursue.

Most meetings are similar in structure since the structure comes from the umbrella organization, but local councils can alter things to suit their needs. Helping the local councils to do this is one of Sandi's jobs. She provides information, support, resources, an ear, and a shoulder to council members. She says that in order to do this kind of job you have to like people because each council is different, each executive is different, and each member is different. You also have to understand the community each council represents, especially if the council plans any political action.

When asked for words of advice to people working in this kind of environment, Sandi says, "You have to be open and accessible and you have to be a good listener. Then people will relate to you, talk to you, respect you, and trust your leadership."

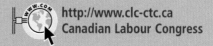

http://www.clc-ctc.ca
Canadian Labour Congress

FYI

The average time spent in a single meeting is 68 minutes.

Source: "Why Making Meetings Better Matters," *Selling Power,* June 1999, 78

Site *to* **See**

Go to
http://www.robertsrules.com/
http://www.bartleby.com/176/

The first Web site is the "official" Robert's Rules of Order site, presenting information about the most current version of this classic of meeting procedures. The 1915 edition (in public domain) is available at the second Web site.

In the evolution from Old to New Economy, information exchange proliferates. Although meetings have always comprised the largest proportion of the average manager's day, emphasis on team productivity means that meetings are even more frequent. On average, employees attend three meetings a week; as people rise in the organization, they attend many more meetings. Ipsos-Reid's May 2001 survey indicated that, because sharing information with co-workers had become so important, Canadian office workers spent an average of 5.2 hours per week in meetings. In larger organizations with 500 or more employees, people averaged almost seven hours per week in meetings.[1]

Business, non-profit, and government organizations hold several types of meetings:

- **Parliamentary meetings** are run according to strict rules, like the rules of parliamentary procedure summarized in *Robert's Rules of Order*. Formal rules help the meeting run smoothly if the group is large or the agenda long. Participants must make formal motions before a topic can be debated. Each point is settled by a vote. **Minutes** record each motion and the vote on it. Parliamentary meetings are often used by boards of directors and by legislative bodies such as the municipal, provincial and federal governments, but they are rarely part of the day-to-day meetings common in most businesses and non-profit organizations.

- **Regular staff meetings** are held to announce new policies and products, answer questions, share ideas, and motivate workers. For example, Microsoft Exchange Group's development team meets every morning to review daily software builds and to identify any issues that have come up in the last 24 hours. At Industrial Light & Magic's "Computer Graphics Weeklies," project teams present special-effects problems that they have solved or that they need help with. Other teams learn from them or help them solve it. On the first Friday of every month, all the employees of Employease, a four-year-old firm that helps companies automate Human Resource functions, gather to review financial updates, welcome new employees, build the corporate culture, and connect raw data to the company's long-term vision. The meetings mix "straight talk, town-hall discussion, and vaudeville."[2] A financial services company holds quarterly town-hall meetings for all employees, complete with staging, professional-quality videos, and question-and-answer sessions with the executive team.[3]

- **Team meetings** bring together team members to brainstorm, solve problems, and create documents. Meetings may be called on short notice when a problem arises that needs input from several people.

- **Informal**, **hall** or **one-on-one meetings** continue to comprise the most significant meetings of all. Employees talk by the water cooler or the refrigerator or ride up an elevator together. One person walks into another's office or cubicle to ask a question. A supervisor stops by a line worker to see how things are going and to "manage by walking around." These highly informal meetings create or reinforce the company culture, support networking and facilitate advancement.

Organizations hold many other kinds of meetings. Many companies hold sales meetings for their sales staff. Conventions bring together workers in the same field from many different employers. Retreats allow a small group to get away for team-building, brainstorming, or long-range planning.

These meetings may be supported with computers. Many organizations display proceedings for all the participants to see. "People literally see themselves being heard. Related comments are identified, linked, and edited on screen. The digressions and tangents quickly become apparent." The resulting document can be posted on the company intranet for further discussion and comments.[4]

Informal meetings are even more common than formal meetings in most organizations. Here, the cofounders of Excite plan their next corporate move. Even in an informal meeting, someone should record decisions made and note who is responsible for actions that have been agreed upon.

A variety of meetings are held in business, non-profit, and government organizations. Other organizations use group support software. Each person sits at a workstation. Participants key in their own brainstorming ideas and comments. People can vote by ranking items on a 1-to-10 scale; the software calculates the averages.[5]

Speakerphones and conference calls allow people in different locations to participate in the same conversation. Online meetings, such as those hosted by WebEx <www.webex.com>, allow you to bring together five other participants for a simultaneous email conversation in your own private chat room. Some computer systems support video as well as data or audio transmissions. Videoconferences provide high-quality video and audio transmissions.

The organizational culture, the length and purposes of the meeting, the people who attend, the budget, and the available technology all affect outcomes. However, a number of principles structure successful meetings.

What planning should precede a meeting?

> Identify the purpose(s) and create an agenda.

Meetings can have at least six purposes:

1. To share information
2. To brainstorm ideas
3. To evaluate ideas
4. To make decisions
5. To create a document
6. To motivate members

When meetings combine two or more purposes, it's useful to make the purposes explicit. For example, in the meeting of a university student government or a company's board of directors, some items are presented for information. Discussion is possible, but the group will not be asked to make a decision. Other items are presented for action; the group will be asked to vote. A business meeting might specify that the first half-hour will allotted for brainstorming, with the second half-hour devoted to evaluation.

FYI

Pay is not the prime motivator for knowledge workers. According to Anil Verma, professor of industrial relations, University of Toronto, knowledge workers seek a high degree of job satisfaction. Talented workers leave employers who do not accommodate their need for control over their own careers, organizational involvement, and professional development opportunities.

Source: Virginia Galt, "Pay is not enough: expert", *The Globe and Mail,* February 22, 2001, B14.

Intel's agendas also specify *how* decisions will be made. The company recognizes four different decision-making processes:

- Authoritative (the leader makes the decision alone)
- Consultative (the leader hears group comments, but then makes the decision alone)
- Voting (the majority wins)
- Consensual (discussion continues until everyone can "buy into" the decision)[6]

Articulating how input will be used clarifies expectations and focusses the conversation.

Once you've identified your purposes, think about how you can make them happen. Perhaps participants need to receive and read materials before the meeting. Perhaps people should bring drafts to the meeting so that creating a document can go more quickly.

For team meetings called on short notice, the first item of business is to create an agenda. This kind of agenda can be informal, simply listing the topics or goals.

For meetings with more lead time, distribute an agenda several days before the meeting. (*Agenda* is Latin for "to be done.") If possible, give participants a chance to comment and revise the agenda in response to those comments. A good agenda indicates

- Where and when: time and place of the meeting
- What: agenda items
- Why: each item flagged for purpose; information, discussion, or decision
- Who: participants and individuals sponsoring or introducing each item
- How: meeting duration and time allotted for each item

Many groups first deal with routine items on which agreement will be easy. If there's a long list of routine items, save them till the end or, in a parliamentary meeting, dispense with them in an omnibus motion. An **omnibus motion** allows a group to approve many items together rather than voting on each separately. A single omnibus motion might cover multiple changes to operational guidelines, or a whole slate of candidates for various offices, or various budget recommendations.

Schedule controversial items early in the meeting, when people's energy level is high, and to allow enough time for full discussion. Giving a controversial item only half an hour at the end of the meeting leads people to suspect that the leaders are trying to manipulate them.

If you're planning a long meeting, for example, a training session or a conference, recognize that networking is part of the value of the meeting. Allow short breaks at least every two hours and generous breaks twice a day so participants can talk informally to each other. If participants will be strangers, include some social functions so they can get to know each other. If participants have different interests or different levels of knowledge, plan concurrent sessions on different topics or for people with different levels of expertise. Don't forget that the best meetings—such as the "best practices" of successful organizations—encourage participation, creativity and fun.

Finally, you may want to leave five minutes at the end of the meeting to evaluate it. What went well? What could be better? What do you want to change next time?

Networking

Build your interpersonal relationships. Recent studies validate that networking continues to be the most successful job-search process. Informal professional and social links provided 48 percent of Canadian and 66 percent of U.S. executives with new jobs last year.

What are the secrets to networking? Getting to know people within and beyond your own organization builds contacts of colleagues and friends.

In your own organization,

- Most days, have lunch with other people in your organization. At least once a month (more often is better) invite someone whom you don't know well. You can go someplace inexpensive or even bring brown-bag lunches. But don't work through lunch more than twice a week. Use the time to widen your circle of acquaintances at the place where you work.
- At a meeting, sit by someone you don't know well. Introduce yourself, and find out something about the other person.

To get to know other business people in your community,

- Participate in your community: Canadians value community involvement. Canvass for charity, coach little league, join your neighbourhood ratepayers' association, your town's business association, arts council, Toastmaster's, Lion's Club, Knights of Columbus, Big Brother/Sister organization, chamber of commerce or board of trade. You can start your own book club or become a member of local bookstores' clubs. Every person you meet knows a minimum of three other people, so every volunteer activity, association, and club membership expands your network.
- At events, sit with people you don't yet know. For example, if your company buys a table of ten seats at a charity luncheon, ask the organizers to put two of you at each of five tables, so that you can use the lunch to network.

- Attend meetings of the trade association for your industry and meetings of business people specifically designed to network or to share ideas.

Join a listserv to get to know other people in your field. To find the appropriate listserv, visit www.topica.com, with links to many business listservs.

Consider everyone a customer. Prepare for every networking opportunity. Read widely and pay attention to local news of interest. When you meet new people, express interest: ask what they and their companies do. And listen! (◄|► Module 17) When you know someone's specialty, ask his or her opinion about challenges or events in that industry. After you find out about the other person, give a short, 60-second description of your work and your company. Then probe more deeply into the other person's experience and ideas. Find out what his or her position is. Exchange business cards. And ask for the names of other people in that organization whom you should talk to, depending on your own interests and your job.

Nurture your contacts. Some business people like to send a short follow-up message right after the first meeting. In some cases, you may want to set up occasional lunches with people—in your own or in other organizations—who are particularly interesting. The very best follow-up is to send something the other person can truly use—information about a book or article, a URL, the address for a listserv you find useful. Think of networking not only as a way to meet people who can be useful to you but also as a way to be more useful and visible in your own organization and in the community in which you live and work.

Sources: Virginia Galt, "Networking tops Web in CEO job search," *The Globe and Mail*, April 4, 2001, M1; Robert Sheppard. "We Are Canadian," *Maclean's*, December/January, 2001, 26–32; Marc Kramer, *Power Networking: Using the Contacts You Didn't Even Know You Have to Succeed in the Job You Want* (Lincolnwood, IL: VGM Career Horizons, 1998).

Only 16 percent of the people attending meetings are "extremely prepared."

Source: "Why Making Meetings Better Matters," *Selling Power*, June 1999, 78.

When I'm in charge, how do I keep the meeting on track?

Pay attention both to task and to process.

The chair's role is to clarify the meeting's significance and goal(s) and to encourage participation in a timely and comprehensive way. When the issues are simple and clear-cut, you may only need to introduce the speaker on each issue, recognize people who want to speak, and remind the group of its progress. "We're a bit behind schedule. Let's see if we can get through the committee reports quickly." When the issues are complex, or when members have major disagreements, you may need to acknowledge and negotiate conflict, shape the discussion or summarize issues: "We're really talking about two things: whether the change would save money and whether our customers would like it. Does it make sense to keep those two together, or could we talk about customer reaction first, and then deal with the financial issues?"

As chair, you may want to make ground rules explicit. Based on the corporate culture, ground rules vary considerably from company to company and sometimes even within organizations (◀▶ Module 2). In some meetings, participants are expected to stay for the entire session, even if not all agenda items are relevant to them. In others, people are free to attend just part of the meeting. In some cultures, participants are expected to give their full attention to the discussion. In others, it may be acceptable to check one's email or even work on other projects during the meeting. Some organizations ask senior people to wait to speak until after junior people have spoken; others may expect senior people to speak first. If the issue is contentious, the chair may ask that speakers for and against a motion alternate. If no one remains on one side, then the discussion can stop.

A good chairperson attends to both the ***task*** and ***maintenance*** functions of the meeting. ***Task*** functions include all communications (stating objectives, clarifying topics, questioning, summarizing, tracking time) devoted to meeting task or purpose. Paying attention to people and process—the ***maintenance*** of the participants' emotional engagement is equally important for success. At informal meetings, a good leader observes non-verbal feedback and invites everyone to participate. If conflict seems to be getting out of hand, a leader may want to focus attention on the group process and ways that it could deal with conflict (◀▶ Module 19), before getting back to the substantive issues.

If the group doesn't formally vote, summarize the group's consensus after each point so that it is clear to everyone what decision has been made and who is responsible for implementing or following up on each item.

Go to http://www.ecac.uni melb.edu.au/project /team/mod2b.html

This site explores team dynamics in depth.

What decision-making strategies work well in meetings?

Try the standard agenda or dot planning.

Probably the least effective decision-making strategy is to let the person who talks first, last, loudest, or most determine the decision. Voting is quick but may leave people in the minority unhappy with and uncommitted to the majority's plan.

Meetings depend on social interaction as well as a good agenda

Source: FOR BETTER OR WORSE reprinted by permission of United Feature Syndicate, Inc.

Coming to consensus takes time but results in speedier implementation of ideas. Two strategies that are often useful in organizational groups are the standard agenda and dot planning.

The **standard agenda** is a seven-step decision-making process for solving problems.

1. Understand what the group has to deliver, in what form, by what due date. Identify available resources.
2. Identify the situation. What question(s) is the group trying to answer? What exactly is wrong?
3. Gather information, share it with all group members, and examine it critically.
4. Establish criteria. What would the ideal solution include? Which elements of that solution would be part of a less-than-ideal but still acceptable solution? What legal, financial, moral, or other limitations might keep a solution from being implemented?
5. Generate alternate solutions. Brainstorm and record ideas for the next step.
6. Measure the alternatives against the criteria.
7. Choose the best solution.[7]

Dot planning offers a way for large groups to choose priorities quickly. First, the group brainstorms ideas, recording each on pages that are put on the wall. Then each individual gets two strips of three to five adhesive dots in different colours. One colour represents high priority, the other lower priority. People then walk up to the pages and affix dots by the points they care most about. Some groups allow only one dot from one person on any one item; others allow someone who is really passionate about an idea to put all of his or her dots on it. As Figure 18.1 on the next page shows, the dots make it easy to see which items the group believes are most important.

Instant Replay

Agenda

A good agenda indicates

• The date, time, place, and length of the meeting
• The meeting content: topics listed chronologically and identified as presented for information, for discussion, or for a decision
• The people: the name of each individual who is sponsoring or introducing each item
• The time allotted for each item

Figure 18.1

Dot Planning Allows Groups to Set Priorities Quickly

Here, green dots mean "high priority;" blue dots mean "low priority." One can see at a glance which items have widespread support, which are controversial, and which are low priority.

Directory of Resources ●	Marketing Materials
● Group Health Plan	●● Develop two rep tracks: independent & Franchise
● Have all reps use FAFN name	Directory of reps & specialties
One-page Social Analysis	● Reps pay nominal costs for specialized materials
● Conference: 5 minutes for each rep to talk	Having more rep-only sessions at conference
Increase Fee account compensation	● Write Product Manuals
System of compensating mentors	Handbook on how to set up Fee Business
● Free Basic Brochure to reps	● Increased Insurance Production
Create rep advisory council	New Product R & D ●

Source: "The Color-Coded Priority Setter," *Inc.*, June 1995, 70–71; online version at http://mothra.inc.com/virtualconsult/goodforms/forms/0695gf.html; visited Web site June 26, 2001.

How can I be an effective meeting participant?

Be prepared.

Take the time to prepare for meetings. Read the materials distributed before the meeting and think about the issues to be discussed. Bring those materials to the meeting, along with something to write on, and with, even if you're not the secretary.

In a small meeting, you'll probably get several chances to speak. Research indicates that the most influential people in a meeting are those who say something in the first five minutes of the meeting (even just to ask a question), who talk most often, and who talk at greatest length.[8]

In a large meeting, you may get just one chance to speak. Make notes of what you want to say so that you can be succinct, fluent, and complete.

It's frustrating to speak in a meeting and have people ignore what you say. Here are some tips for being taken seriously.[9]

- Show that you've done your homework. Laura Sloate, who is blind, establishes authority by making sure her first question is highly technical: "In footnote three of the 10K, you indicate. . . ."
- Link your comment to the comment of a powerful person. Even if logic suffers a bit, present your comment as an addition, not a challenge. For example, say, "John is saying that we should focus on excellence, AND I think we can become stronger by encouraging diversity."
- Find an ally in the organization and agree ahead of time to acknowledge each other's contributions to the meeting, whether you agree or disagree with the point being made. Explicit disagreement signals that the comment is worth taking seriously: "Duane has pointed out. . . , but I think that. . . ."

What should go in meeting minutes?

Topics discussed, decisions reached, and who does what next.

Meeting expert Michael Begeman suggests recording three kinds of information:

1. Decisions reached
2. Action items, where someone needs to implement or follow up on something
3. Open issues—issues raised but not resolved[10]

Minutes of formal meetings indicate who was present and absent and the wording of motions and amendments as well as the vote. Committee reports are often attached for later reference. For less formal meetings, brief minutes are fine. The most important notes are the decisions and assignments. Long minutes will be most helpful if assignments are set off visually from the narrative.

Site *to* See

Go to
http://www.fis.utoronto.ca/courses/LIS/2133/legisour.htm#fed-leg

Information on Canadian federal and provincial legislation is provided in this one-page chart of Internet links and print sources at the University of Toronto.

We discussed whether we should switch from road to rail shipment.
Action: Laya will get figures on cost for the next meeting.
Action: Jaffer will conduct survey of current customers online to ask their opinions

---

How can I use informal meetings with my boss to advance my career?

Plan scripts to present yourself positively.

You'll see your supervisor several times a week. Some of these meetings will be accidental: you'll meet by the coffeepot or ride up the elevator together. Some of them will be deliberately initiated: your boss will stop by your area, or you'll go to your boss's area to ask for something.

You can take advantage of these meetings by planning for them. These informal meetings are often short. An elevator ride, for example, may last about three minutes. So plan 90-second scripts that you can use to give your boss a brief report on what you're doing, ask for something you need, or lay the groundwork for an important issue.

Instant Replay

Decision-Making Strategies
The **standard agenda** is a seven-step process for solving problems. **Dot planning** offers a way for large groups to choose priorities quickly.

Planning scripts is especially important if your boss doesn't give you much feedback or mentoring. In this case, your boss probably doesn't see you as promotable. You need to take the initiative. Make statements that show the boss you're thinking about ways to work smarter. Show that you're interested in learning more so that you can be more valuable to the organization.

Do virtual meetings require special consideration?

Yes. Watch interpersonal communication.

For important projects, build in some real meetings as well.

When you meet technologically rather than in person, you lose the informal interactions of going to lunch or chatting during a break. Those interactions not only create bonds, so that people are more willing to work together, but also give people a chance to work out dozens of small issues. Listening (◀▶ Module 17), teamwork, and the ability to resolve conflicts constructively (◀▶ Module 19) become even more crucial.

Be aware of the limitations of your channel. When you are limited to email, you lose both tone of voice and body language. In addition, email messages are often more brusque than comments in person (◀▶ Module 13). Audio messages provide tone of voice but not the non-verbal signals that tell you whether someone wants to make a comment or understands what you're saying. Even videoconferencing gives you only the picture in the camera's lens. With any of these technologies, you'll need to attend specifically to interpersonal skills.

For an important project, North Americans continue to rely on telephone and in-person meetings. Tom Vassos, vice president of ebusiness with IBM Canada and M.B.A. instructor at the University of Toronto, prefers the telephone to virtual meetings using Web conferencing software. Because of our preference for a human voice, Web-based conferencing software has had a negligible business impact. The telephone and email are the preferred long-distance meeting media, according to 66 percent of a sample of 500 Canadian companies surveyed last year.[11]

Employability Skills 2000+ Checklist for Planning, Conducting, and Recording Meetings

In this module, the key skills from The Conference Board of Canada's Employability Skills 2000+ are:

Communicate

✔ write and speak so others pay attention and understand
✔ listen and ask questions to understand and appreciate the points of view of others
✔ share information using a range of information and communications technologies (e.g., voice, email, computers)
✔ use relevant scientific, technological, and mathematical knowledge and skills to explain or clarify ideas

Manage Information

✔ locate, gather, and organize information using appropriate technology and information systems

Demonstrate Positive Attitudes and Behaviours

✔ feel good about yourself and be confident
✔ deal with people, problems, and situations with honesty, integrity, and personal ethics

Be Responsible

✔ plan and manage time, money, and other resources to achieve goals
✔ be accountable for your actions and the actions of your group
✔ be socially responsible and contribute to your community

Be Adaptable

✔ work independently or as a part of a team
✔ carry out multiple tasks or projects
✔ be innovative and resourceful: identify and suggest alternative ways to achieve goals and get the job done
✔ cope with uncertainty

Work with Others

✔ understand and work within the dynamics of a group
✔ ensure that a team's purpose and objectives are clear
✔ be flexible: respect, be open to and supportive of the thoughts, opinions, and contributions of others in a group
✔ recognize and respect people's diversity, individual differences, and perspectives

Participate in Projects & Tasks

✔ work to agreed quality standards and specifications
✔ select and use appropriate tools and technology for a task or project
✔ adapt to changing requirements and information

Review of Key Points

- A good agenda indicates
  - The date, time, place, and length of the meeting
  - The meeting content: topics listed chronologically and identified as presented for information, for discussion, or for a decision
  - The people: the name of each individual who is sponsoring or introducing each item
  - The time allotted for each item
- To make meetings more effective,
  - State the purpose of the meeting at the beginning
  - Distribute an agenda that indicates whether each item is for information, for discussion, for action, and how long each is expected to take
  - Allow enough time to discuss controversial issues
- Pay attention to people and process as well as to the task at hand
- If you don't take formal votes, summarize the group's consensus after each point. At the end of the meeting, summarize all decisions and remind the group who is responsible for implementing or following up on each item.
- The **standard agenda** is a seven-step process for solving problems. In **dot planning** the group brainstorms ideas. Then each individual affixes adhesive dots by the points or proposals he or she cares most about.
- Minutes should record
  - Decisions reached
  - Action items, where someone needs to implement or follow up on something
  - Open issues—issues raised but not resolved

Learning Applications

Questions for Comprehension

18.1 What should go in an agenda?

18.2 What are the seven steps in the standard meeting agenda?

18.3 When would dot planning be most effective?

18.4 What should go in minutes of a meeting?

Questions for Critical Thinking

18.5 What opportunities do you have to network?

18.6 In the groups of which you're a member (at school, at work, and in volunteer organizations), what kinds of comments are most valued in meetings?

18.7 What is the best meeting you ever attended? What made it so effective?

Questions for Building Skills

18.8   What skills have you read about in this module?

18.9   What skills are you practising in the assignments you're doing for this module?

18.10 How could you further develop the skills you're working on?

Exercises and Problems

18.11   Writing an Agenda

Write an agenda for your next collaborative group meeting.

As Your Instructor Directs,

a. Write a memo to your instructor, explaining the choices you made.

b. Share your agenda with the ones developed by others in your group. Use the agendas as drafts to help you create the best possible agenda.

c. Present your best agenda to the rest of the class in a group oral presentation.

18.12   Taking Minutes

As Your Instructor Directs,

Have two or more people take minutes of each class or collaborative group meeting for a week. Compare the accounts of the same meeting.

- To what extent do they agree on what happened?

- Does one contain information missing in other accounts?

- Do any accounts disagree on a specific fact?

- How do you account for the differences you find?

18.13   Writing a Meeting Manual*

Create a procedures manual for students next term, describing how to have effective meetings as they work on collaborative projects.

*Adapted from Miles McCall, Beth Stewart, and Timothy Clipson, "Teaching Communication Skills for Meeting Management," *1998 Refereed Proceedings*, Association for Business Communication Southwestern United States, ed. Marsha L. Bayless (Nacogdoches, TX), p. 68.

18.14   Planning Scripts for 3-Minute Meetings

Create a script for a 90-second statement to your boss

1. Describing the progress on a project you're working on

2. Providing an update on a problem the boss already knows about

3. Telling about a success or achievement

4. Telling about a problem and asking approval for the action you recommend

5. Asking for resources you need for a project

6. Asking for training you'd like to get

7. Laying the groundwork for a major request you need to make

As Your Instructor Directs,

a. Discuss your scripts with a small group of other students

b. Present your script to the class

c. Write a memo to your instructor explaining the choices you have made in terms of content, arrangement, and word choice

Polishing Your Prose

Hyphens and Dashes

Hyphens and dashes are forms of punctuation used within sentences. Use a **hyphen** to

1. Indicate that a word has been divided between two lines.

   Correct: Our biggest competitor announced plans to introduce new models of computers into the European market.

   Divide words only at syllable breaks. If you aren't sure where the syllables break, look up the word in a dictionary. When a word has several syllables, divide it after a vowel or between two consonants.

   While many word processing programs automatically hyphenate for you, knowing where and when to divide words is important for words the program may not recognize or for special cases. For instance, don't divide words of one syllable (e.g., *used*), and don't divide a two-syllable word if one of the syllables is only one letter long (e.g., *acre*).

2. Join two or more words used as a single adjective.

   Correct: After a flurry of requests, we are marketing new lines of specialty dinners for Asian- and Jamaican-Canadian customers.

   Order five 10- or 12-metre lengths.

   Here, hyphens prevent misreading. Without the hyphen, readers might interpret *Asian-Canadian* incorrectly as Asian. (Typically, compound adjectives such as *Asian-Canadian* and *Jamaican-Canadian* are not hyphenated when used as nouns.) In the second sentence, five lengths are needed, not lengths of 5, 10, or 12 metres.

3. Use a **dash** to emphasize a break in thought.

   Correct: Despite our best efforts—which included sending a design team to Paris and increasing our promotional budget—sales are lagging.

Create a dash by typing the hyphen key twice. With some word processors, this "double hyphen" will automatically be replaced with a longer, single dash (called an "em-dash"), which is acceptable.

Exercises

Supply necessary dashes or hyphens in the following sentences. If no punctuation is needed—if a space is correct—leave the parentheses blank.

1. Our biggest competitors( )including those in the Asian and European markets( )intro ( )duced more product models during the fourth quarter.

2. Our cutting ( )edge fashions sell best in French( )Canadian cities like Montréal.

3. Please pick up three( )2( )by( )4 posts at the lumberyard.

4. Next Monday, *The Aboriginal Times* ( )magazine will do a cover story on a thriving new business created by Native( )Canadians.

5. Painters from the building( )services department plan to give Tarik's office two ( )coats of paint.

6. Our gift certificates come in 5( ), 10( ), and 15( )dollar denominations.

7. The latest weather reports suggest that travel over South( )and Latin( )America may be interrupted by storms.

8. We need to work on more cost( )effective versions of our best( )selling software programs.

9. You can email the results to my office in the early( )morning.

10. Katrina gave us four( )options during the sales( )meeting on Friday afternoon.

Check your answers to the odd-numbered exercises on page 634.

Module 19

Working and Writing in Teams

Topics

- **What kinds of communications happen in groups?**
- **What roles do people play in groups?**
- **How should we handle conflict?**
- **How can we create the best co-authored documents?**

Review of Key Points

Learning Applications

Polishing Your Prose: Delivering Criticism

Learning Focus

After reading and applying the information in Module 19, you'll be able to demonstrate

Knowledge of
- The ground rules for working well with others
- Group roles
- The characteristics of successful work teams

Skills to
- Work in a team
- Lead productively
- Resolve conflicts constructively
- Write collaborative documents

"Our employees can be our greatest ambassadors."

"Each year we spend months putting our business plan together, based on every available input. Then the communications challenge begins," says Nigel Miller, Halifax, Nova Scotia-based director of marketing for Labatt in Atlantic Canada. "In writing any plan, I always advise that one begins by analysing the audience. Be very clear about what your stakeholders need to know. Be conscious of the audience's level of knowledge about your topic and avoid unnecessary jargon along the way."

Before Nigel became director of marketing, he was director of public affairs, responsible for all internal and external communications. Prior to working at Labatt he was senior vice president at Weber Shandwick in Toronto and also worked as account director for McDonald's. Nigel brings a great deal of communications experience to his position as director of marketing. Marketing, after all, is about communications. "In my current role, communications plays a key role. Public relations is part of the marketing mix in bringing our brands to life in the communities where our consumers live and work. Additionally, communications plays a key role in ensuring our employees all know what we have planned to support our brands. Our employees can be our greatest ambassadors. Good internal communication ensures those employees are well informed and represent the brewery with pride in the communities where they live and play."

Nigel's comments give new meaning to the phrase "communications highway." He must receive input from his stakeholders and he must be aware of his audience's level of knowledge. "Our stakeholders include the entire selling organization in the region, our employees, our customers, and ultimately, our consumers." Then he must assemble his team to develop a marketing plan to present his products to the public. Marketing is clearly a form of team communication, with the communications going in many different directions at once. As team manager, Nigel must maintain control of this process.

The process of writing a marketing plan is a very lengthy one. As Nigel states, "Each year we spend months putting our business plan together. Once we have made our choices, based on every available input, the communications challenge begins." Nigel emphasizes that the plan must avoid jargon and must inspire his stakeholders.

Nigel confirms that his long and varied background as a communications professional "has set me up well for this challenge, and it is one that I find most gratifying when I see audiences smiling, nodding their heads, and even cheering at the conclusion of a plan presentation."

When asked to give advice to students entering the marketing field, Nigel notes that one should "never underestimate the value of clear, concise communication. In any marketing role you will find yourself communicating to a myriad of important stakeholders. Your ability to clearly articulate your message—your vision—will be critical to achieving alignment of your plan."

http://www.labatt.com/
Labatt

Employers hire for attitude and train for skill. In fact, Canadian employers ranked "willingness to learn" and "customer service skills" as the best employee traits, well above technical and computer skills.[1] The Conference Board of Canada also identifies the ability to work well with others as one of the three top employability skills. Obviously, teamwork is crucial to success in an organization.

Some teams produce products, provide services, or recommend solutions to problems. Other teams—perhaps in addition to providing a service or recommending a solution—also produce documents.

Interpersonal communication is communication between people. Interpersonal skills such as listening (◀▶ Module 17) and dealing with conflict are used in one-on-one conversations, in problem solving, and in writing groups. Continuing improvement in these skills builds confidence and contributes to your personal and professional success. In writing groups, careful attention to group process and writing processes (◀▶ Module 4) improves both productivity and members' satisfaction with the group.

Teams are often most effective when they adopt explicit ground rules. Figure 19.1 lists some of the most common ground rules used by workplace teams.

What kinds of communications happen in groups?

> Different messages occur at different points in a group's development.

Group messages fall into three categories:

1. **Informational** messages focus on content: the problem or challenge, data, and possible solutions.
2. **Procedural** messages focus on method and process. How will the group make decisions? Who will do what? When will assignments be due?
3. **Interpersonal** messages focus on people, promoting friendliness, cooperation, and group loyalty. Informational and procedural messages are both considered *task*-related messages. Interpersonal messages are *maintenance*-related messages.

Different messages dominate during the various stages of group development. During **orientation**, when members meet and begin to define their task, groups

Figure 19.1

Possible Group Ground Rules

- Start on time; end on time
- Come to the meeting prepared
- Focus comments on the issues
- Avoid personal attacks
- Listen to and respect members' opinions
- NOSTUESO (No One Speaks Twice Until Everybody Speaks Once)
- If you have a problem with another person, tell that person, not everyone else
- Everyone must be 70 percent comfortable with the decision and 100 percent committed to implementing it
- If you agree to do something, do it
- Communicate immediately if you think you may not be able to fulfill an agreement.

Sources: Nancy Schullery and Beth Hoger, "Business Advocacy for Students in Small Groups," Association for Business Communication Annual Convention, San Antonio, November 9–11, 1998; "An Antidote to Chronic Cantankerousness," *Fast Company*, February/March 1998, 176; John Grossmann, "We've Got to Start Meeting Like This," *Inc.*, April 1998, 70; Gary Dessler, "Winning Commitment," quoted in *Team Management Briefings*, preview issue (September 1998), 5; and 3M Meeting Network, "Groundrules and Agreements," www.3M.com/meetingnetwork/readingroom/meetingguide_grndrules.html visited Web site July 21, 2001.

need to develop some sort of social cohesiveness and to agree on procedures for meeting and acting. Interpersonal and procedural communications reduce tension and begin building the trust necessary for teamwork. Insistence on information in this first stage can hurt the group's long-term productivity.

During **formation**, conflicts almost always arise when the group chooses a leader and defines the problem. Successful leaders make the procedure clear so that each member knows what he or she is supposed to do. Interpersonal communication is needed to articulate and resolve the conflict that surfaces during this phase. Successful groups analyze the problem carefully before they begin to search for solutions.

Coordination is the longest phase, during which most of the group's work is done. Procedural and interpersonal communication maintains the trust necessary to gather and focus on the task information. Good information is essential to a good decision. Creative conflict re-occurs as the group debates alternate solutions.

In **formalization**, the group seeks consensus. The success of this phase determines how well the group's decision will be implemented. In this stage, the group seeks to forget earlier conflicts.

What roles do people play in groups?

People play both task and maintenance roles, and every role can be positive or negative.

Positive roles and actions that help the group achieve its task goals include the following:[2]

- **Seeking information and opinions.** Asking questions, identifying gaps in the group's knowledge
- **Giving information and opinions.** Answering questions, providing relevant information
- **Summarizing.** Restating major points, pulling ideas together, summarizing decisions
- **Evaluating.** Comparing group process and products to standards and goals
- **Coordinating.** Planning work, giving directions, and fitting together contributions of group members

Positive maintenance roles and actions that help the group build loyalty, resolve conflicts, and function smoothly include the following:

- **Listening actively.** Showing group members that they have been heard and that their ideas are being taken seriously (◀▶ Module 17)
- **Encouraging participation.** Demonstrating openness and acceptance, recognizing the contributions of members, calling on quieter group members

Eagle's Flight® is a leader in experiential training for the business community. Here, participants investigate a realistic crime scene, an environment designed to teach the critical elements of effective communication through sharing, evaluation, and organization of information.

FYI

Less than a third of small companies use virtual teams, while 52 percent of large companies do.

Source: Eleena de Lisser, "Firms with Virtual Environments Appeal to Workers," *The Wall Street Journal,* October 5, 1999, B2.

- **Relieving tensions.** Joking and suggesting breaks and fun activities
- **Checking feelings.** Asking members how they feel about group activities and sharing one's own feelings with others
- **Solving interpersonal problems.** Opening discussion of interpersonal problems in the group and suggesting ways to solve them

Negative roles and actions that hurt the group's product and process include the following:

- **Blocking.** Disagreeing with everything that is proposed
- **Dominating.** Trying to run the group by ordering, shutting out others, and insisting on one's own way
- **Clowning.** Making unproductive jokes and diverting the group from the task
- **Withdrawing.** Being silent in meetings, not contributing, not helping with the work, not attending meetings

Each of these roles can be positive or negative, depending on context, group culture and the organization's culture. Criticizing ideas is necessary if the group is to produce the best solution, but criticizing every single idea without suggesting possible solutions blocks a group. Jokes can defuse tension and make the group more creative. Too many jokes or inappropriate jokes can frustrate or offend team members, or impede progress.

Leadership in Groups

You may have noted that "leader" was not one of the roles listed above. Leadership is based on communication and interpersonal effectiveness. Being a leader does not mean doing all the work yourself. Indeed, someone who implies that he or she has the best ideas and can do the best work is likely playing the negative roles of blocking and dominating.

Effective groups balance three kinds of leadership, which parallel the three group development dimensions:

1. Informational leaders generate and evaluate ideas and text
2. Interpersonal leaders monitor the group's process, check people's feelings, and resolve conflicts
3. Procedural leaders set the agenda, make sure that everyone knows what's due for the next meeting, communicate with absent group members, and check to be sure that assignments are carried out

While it's possible for one person to take on all of these responsibilities, in many groups, three (or more) different people take on the three kinds of leadership. Some groups formally or informally rotate or share these responsibilities, so that everyone—and no one—is a leader.

Several studies have shown people who talk a lot, listen effectively, and respond non-verbally to other members in the group are considered to be leaders.[3]

Characteristics of Successful Student Groups

A case study of six student groups completing class projects found that students in successful groups were not necessarily more skilled or more experienced than students in less successful groups. Instead, successful and less successful groups communicated differently in three ways.[4]

Site *to* **See**

Go to
www.workteams.un
t.edu
The Center for the Study of Work Teams offers abstracts of research reports, newsletter archives, and an extensive list of links.

Instant
Replay

Positive Roles in Groups
Task Roles

- Seeking information and opinions
- Giving information and opinions
- Summarizing
- Evaluating
- Coordinating

Interpersonal Maintenance Roles

- Encouraging participation
- Relieving tensions
- Checking feelings
- Solving interpersonal problems
- Listening actively

Leading Without Being Arrogant

Sometimes when groups form, no one wants to "lead." Perhaps that's because we've seen "leaders" who seemed dictatorial, implied that no one else's work would be up to their high standards, and generally antagonized the people unfortunate enough to have to work with them.

You don't have to be arrogant to be a leader. Here are some things that you can do to get your group started on the right track.

- **Smile.** Get to know the other members of your group as individuals. Invite members to say something about themselves, perhaps what job they're hoping to get and one fact about their lives outside school.
- **Share.** Tell people about your own work style and obligation, and ask others to share their styles and obligations. Savvy group members play to each other's strengths and devise strategies for dealing with differences. The earlier you know what those differences are, the easier it will be to deal with them.

- **Suggest.** "Could we talk about what we see as our purposes in this presentation?" "One of the things we need to do is...." "One idea I had for a project is...." Presenting your ideas as suggestions gets the group started without suggesting that you expect your views to prevail.
- **Think.** Leaders look at the goal and identify the steps needed to get there. "Our proposal is due in two weeks. Let's list the tasks we need to do in order to write a rough draft."
- **Volunteer.** Volunteer to take notes, or to gather some of the data the group will need, or to prepare the charts after the data are in. Volunteer not just for the fun parts of the job (such as surfing the Web to find visuals for your PowerPoint presentation) but also for some of the dull but essential work, such as proofreading.
- **Ask.** Bring other people into the conversation. Learn about their knowledge, interests, and skills, so that you'll have as much as possible to draw on as you complete your group projects

1. In the successful groups, the leader set clear deadlines, scheduled frequent meetings, and dealt directly with conflict that emerged in the group. In less successful groups, members had to ask the leader what they were supposed to be doing. The less successful groups met less often, and they tried to pretend that conflicts didn't exist.
2. The successful groups listened to criticism and made important decisions together. Perhaps as a result, everyone in the group could articulate the group's goals. In the less successful groups, a subgroup made decisions and told other members what had been decided.
3. The successful groups had a higher proportion of members who worked actively on the project. The successful groups even found ways to use members who didn't like working in groups. For example, one student who didn't want to be a "team player" functioned as a "freelancer" for her group, completing assignments by herself and giving them to the leader. The less successful groups had a much smaller percentage of active members and each had some members who did very little on the final project.

Teamwork expert Rebecca Burnett has shown that student groups produce better documents when they disagree over substantive issues of content and document

FYI

British Columbia, New Brunswick, Ontario, and Quebec offer confidential, 24-7 telephone access to registered nurses for free health advice and general health information. Telehealth Ontario's bilingual service includes translation support in 14 other languages. British Columbia's provincial government also provides residents with a comprehensive medical guide (*Health Guide*), and an Internet site—www.bchealthguid e.org—available nationally.

Source: Telehealth Ontario, Queen's Printer for Ontario, 2001, and Caroline Alphonso, "Patient, heal thyself," *The Globe and Mail,* March 13, 2001, R5.

design. The disagreement does not need to be angry: A group member can simply say, "Yes, and here's another way we could do it." Deciding among two (or more) alternative options forces the proposer to explain the rationale for an idea. Even when the group adopts the original idea, considering alternatives rather than quickly accepting the first idea produces better writing.[5]

Writer Kimberly Freeman found that the students who spent the most time meeting with their groups had the highest grades—on their individual as well as on group assignments.[6]

Peer Pressure and Groupthink

Groups that never express conflict may be experiencing groupthink. **Groupthink** is the tendency for groups to put such a high premium on agreement that they directly or indirectly punish dissent.

Groups that "go along with the crowd" and suppress conflict ignore the full range of alternatives, seek only information that supports the positions they already favour, and fail to prepare contingency plans to cope with foreseeable setbacks. A business suffering from groupthink may launch a new product that senior executives support but for which there is no demand. Student groups suffering from groupthink turn in inferior documents.

The best correctives to groupthink are to

- Brainstorm for additional alternatives
- Test assumptions against those of a range of other people
- Encourage disagreement, perhaps even assigning someone to be "devil's advocate"
- Protect the right of people in a group to disagree

How should we handle conflict?

Get at the real issue, and repair bad feelings.

Conflicts will arise in any group of intelligent people who care about the task. Yet many of us feel so uncomfortable with conflict that we pretend it doesn't exist. However, unacknowledged conflicts rarely go away: they fester, impeding progress and making the next interchange more difficult.

To reduce the number of conflicts in a group,

- Make responsibilities and ground rules clear at the beginning
- Acknowledge verbal and non-verbal messages of discomfort, anger, and/or hostility
- Discuss problems as they arise, rather than letting them fester till people explode
- Realize that group members are not responsible for each others' feelings

Figure 19.2 on the next page, suggests several possible solutions to frequent sources of group conflict. Often the symptom arises from a feeling of not being respected or appreciated by the group. Problems can be averted if people advocate for their ideas in a positive way. The best time to advocate for an idea is when the group has not yet identified all possible options, seems dominated by one view, or

Figure 19.2

Troubleshooting Group Problems

Symptom	Possible Solutions
We can't find a time to meet that works for all of us.	a. Find out why people can't meet at certain times. Some reasons suggest their own solutions. For example, if someone has to stay home with small children, perhaps the group could meet at that person's home. b. Assign out-of-class work to "committees" to work on parts of the project. c. Use email to share, discuss, and revise drafts.
One person isn't doing his or her fair share.	a. Find out what is going on. Is the person overcommitted? Does he or she feel unappreciated? Those are different problems you'd solve in different ways. b. Early on, do things to build group loyalty. Get to know each other as writers and as people. Sometimes, do something fun together. c. Encourage the person to contribute. "Maria, what do you think?" "Savio, which part of this would you like to draft?" Then find something to praise in the work. "Thanks for getting us started." d. If someone misses a meeting, assign someone else to bring the person up to speed. People who miss meetings for legitimate reasons (job interviews, illness) but don't find out what happened may become less committed to the group. e. Consider whether strict equality is the most important criterion. On a given project, some people may have more knowledge or time than others. Sometimes the best group product results from letting people do different amounts of "work." f. Even if you divide up the work, make all decisions as a group: what to write about, which evidence to include, what graphs to use, what revisions to make. People excluded from decisions become less committed to the group.
I seem to be the only one in the group who cares about quality.	a. Find out why other members "don't care." If they received low grades on early assignments, stress that good ideas and attention to detail can raise grades. Perhaps the group should meet with the instructor to discuss what kinds of work will pay the highest dividends. b. Volunteer to do extra work. Sometimes people settle for something that's just OK because they don't have the time or resources to do excellent work. They might be happy for the work to be done—if they didn't have to do it. c. Be sure that you're respecting what each person can contribute. Group members sometimes withdraw when one person dominates and suggests that he or she is "better" than other members.
People in the group don't seem willing to disagree. We end up going with the first idea suggested.	a. Appoint someone to be a "devil's advocate." b. Brainstorm so you have several possibilities to consider. c. After an idea is suggested, have each person in the group suggest a way it could be improved. d. Have each person in the group write a draft. It's likely the drafts will be different, and you'll have several options to mix and match. e. Talk about good ways to offer criticism. Sometimes people don't disagree because they're afraid that other group members won't tolerate disagreement.
One person just criticizes everything.	a. Ask the person to follow up the criticism with a suggestion for improvement. b. Talk about ways to express criticism tactfully. "I think we need to think about x" is more tactful than "You're wrong." c. If the criticism is about ideas and writing (not about people), value it. Ideas and documents need criticism to improve them.

Three Kinds of Group Leadership

Informational leaders generate and evaluate ideas and text. Interpersonal leaders monitor the group's process, check people's feelings, and resolve conflicts. Procedural leaders set the agenda, make sure that everyone knows what's due for the next meeting, communicate with absent group members, and check to be sure that assignments are carried out.

Go to
http://www.intrepid
software.com/fallacy
/toc.htm
A complete compendium of frequently heard logical fallacies is offered here.

Go to
http://www.ozemail.
com.au/~caveman/
Creative/Techniques/
For insights into your own creative processes.

seems unable to choose among solutions. A tactful way to advocate for the position you favour is to recognize the contributions others have made, to summarize, and then to hypothesize: "What if … ? "Let's look six months down the road." "Let's think about x."[7]

Steps in Conflict Resolution

Dealing successfully with conflict requires attention to both the issues and to people's feelings. This five-step procedure will help you resolve conflicts constructively.

1. Make Sure That the People Involved Really Disagree.

Sometimes someone who's under a lot of pressure may explode. But the speaker may just be **venting** anger and frustration; he or she may not in fact be angry at the person who receives the explosion. One way to find out if a person is just venting is to ask, "Is there something you'd like me to do?"

2. Check to See That Everyone's Information Is Correct.

Sometimes different conversational styles (◀▶ p. 63) or cultural differences (◀▶ p. 56) create apparent conflicts when in fact no real disagreement exists. Similarly, misunderstanding can arise from faulty assumptions.

3. Discover the Needs Each Person Is Trying to Meet.

Sometimes identifying the real need makes it possible to see a new solution. The **presenting problem** that surfaces as the subject of dissension may or may not be the real problem. For example, a worker who complains about the hours he's putting in may in fact be complaining not about the hours themselves but about not feeling appreciated. A supervisor who complains that the other supervisors don't invite her to meetings may really feel that the other managers don't accept her as a peer. Sometimes people have trouble seeing beyond the presenting problem because they've been taught to suppress their anger, especially toward powerful people. One way to tell whether the presenting problem is the real problem is to ask, "If this were solved, would I be satisfied?" If the answer is no, then the problem that presents itself is not in fact the real problem. Solving the presenting problem won't solve the conflict. Keep probing until you get to the real conflict.

4. Search for Alternatives.

Sometimes people are locked into conflict because they see too few alternatives. Indeed, people often see only two polarized choices—known as the ***either-or logical fallacy***. Robert Moran tells the story of a large U.S. high technology company that was having trouble in the Japanese market. At a meeting called to discuss the problem, the president wrote two alternatives on the board: "GET OUT" and "MAKE THEM DO WHAT WE WANT". Moran suggested a third alternative: "LEARN TO WORK WITH THE JAPANESE".

Creative people train themselves to think in terms of possibilities—the more the better. This technique, known as brainstorming, is an essential part in every step of the problem-solving process!

5. Repair Bad Feelings.

Conflict can emerge without anger and without escalating the disagreement, as the next section shows. But if people's feelings have been hurt, the group needs to deal with those feelings to resolve the conflict constructively. Only when people feel respected and taken seriously can they take the next step of trusting others in the group.

Responding to Criticism

Conflict is particularly difficult to resolve when someone else criticizes or attacks us directly. When we are criticized, our natural reaction is to defend ourselves—perhaps by counterattacking. The counterattack prompts the critic to defend him- or herself. The conflict escalates; feelings are hurt; issues become muddied and more difficult to resolve.

Just as resolving conflict depends upon identifying the needs each person is trying to meet, so dealing with criticism depends upon understanding the real concern of the critic. Constructive ways to respond to criticism and get closer to the real concern include

- Paraphrasing
- Checking for feelings
- Checking inferences
- Buying time with limited agreement

Paraphrasing

To **paraphrase**, repeat in your own words the verbal content of the critic's message. The purposes of paraphrasing are (1) to be sure that you have heard the critic accurately, (2) to let the critic know what his or her statement means to you, and (3) to communicate the feeling that you are taking the critic and his or her feelings seriously.

Criticism: You guys are stonewalling my requests for information.

Paraphrase: You think that we don't give you the information you need quickly enough.

Checking for Feelings

When you check the critic's feelings, you identify the emotions that the critic seems to be expressing verbally or non-verbally. The purposes of checking feelings are to try to understand (1) the critic's emotions, (2) the importance of the criticism for the critic, and (3) the unspoken ideas and feelings that may actually be more important than the voiced criticism.

Criticism: You guys are stonewalling my requests for information.

Feeling check: You sound pretty angry.

Always *ask* the other person if you are right in your perception. Even the best reader of non-verbal cues is sometimes wrong.

FYI

In 1993, Statistics Canada counted 600,000 teleworkers. Four years later, in 1997, telecommuting grew by 40 percent to 1,000,000 teleworkers. By 2001, Statistics Canada, predicts, telecommuting will grow by 50 percent to 1,500,000 teleworkers.

Source: Canadian Telework Association, http://www.ivc.ca/part12.html#statsfacts, visited Web site July 21, 2001.

Site *to* **See**

Go to http://www.edwdebono.com

Edward DeBono is the authority on creative or lateral thinking

Checking for Inferences

When you check the inferences you draw from criticism, you identify the implied meaning of the verbal and non-verbal content of the criticism, taking the statement a step further than the words of the critic to try to understand *why* the critic is bothered by the action or attitude under discussion. The purposes of checking inferences are (1) to identify the real (as opposed to the presenting) problem and (2) to communicate the feeling that you care about resolving the conflict.

Criticism: You guys are stonewalling my requests for information.

Inference: Are you saying that you need more information from our group?

Inferences can be faulty. In the above interchange, the critic might respond, "I don't need more information. I just think you should give it to me without my having to file three forms in triplicate every time I want some data."

Buying Time with Limited Agreement

Buying time is a useful strategy for dealing with criticisms that really sting. When you buy time with limited agreement, you avoid escalating the conflict (as an angry statement might do) but also avoid yielding to the critic's point of view. To buy time, restate the part of the criticism that you agree to be true. (This is often a fact, rather than the interpretation or evaluation the critic has made of that fact.) *Then let the critic respond, before you say anything else.* The purposes of buying time are (1) to allow you time to think when a criticism really hits home and threatens you, so that you can respond to the criticism rather than simply reacting defensively, and (2) to suggest to the critic that you are genuinely listening to what he or she is saying.

Criticism: You guys are stonewalling my requests for information.

Limited agreement: It's true that the cost projections you asked for last week still aren't ready.

DO NOT go on to justify or explain. A "Yes, but ..." statement is not a time-buyer.

You-Attitude in Conflict Resolution

You-attitude (p. 122) means looking at things from the audience's point of view, respecting the audience, and protecting the audience's ego. The *you* statements that many people use when they're angry attack the audience; they do not illustrate you-attitude. Instead, substitute statements about your own feelings. In conflict, *I* statements show good you-attitude!

Lacks you-attitude: You never do your share of the work.

You-attitude: I feel that I'm doing more than my share of the work on this project.

Lacks you-attitude: Even you should be able to run the report through a spell checker.

You-attitude: I'm not willing to have my name on a report with so many spelling errors. I did lots of the writing, and I don't think I should have to do the proofreading and spell-checking, too.

How can we create the best co-authored documents?

Talk about your purposes and audience(s).

Discuss drafts and revisions as a group.

Whatever your career, it is likely that some of the documents you produce will be written with a group. Indeed, 87 percent of the 700 professionals in seven fields who were surveyed responded that they sometimes wrote as members of a team or a group.[8] Collaboration is often prompted by one of the following situations:

- The task is too big or the time is too short for one person to do all the work
- No one person has all the knowledge required to do the task
- A group representing different perspectives must reach a consensus
- The stakes for the task are so high that the organization wants the best efforts of as many people as possible; no one person wants the sole responsibility for the success or failure of the document

Collaborative writing can be done by two people or by a much larger group. The group can be democratic or run by a leader who makes decisions alone. The group may share or divide responsibility for each of the eight stages in the writing process (◀▶ Module 4).

Research in collaborative writing is beginning to tell us about the strategies that produce the best writing. Rebecca Burnett found that student groups that voiced disagreements as they analyzed, planned, and wrote a document produced significantly better documents than those that suppressed disagreement, going along with whatever was first proposed.[9] A case study of two collaborative writing teams in a state agency found that the successful group distributed power equally, worked to soothe hurt feelings, and was careful to involve all group members. In terms of writing process, the successful group understood the task as a response to a rhetorical situation, planned revisions as a group, saw supervisors' comments as legitimate, and had a positive attitude toward revision.[10]

Professors Ede and Lunsford's detailed case studies of collaborative teams in business, government, and science create an "emerging profile of effective collaborative writers." The profile reflects those interpersonal competency skills so sought after by employers: "They are flexible; respectful of others; attentive and analytical listeners; able to speak and write clearly and articulately; dependable and able to meet deadlines; able to designate and share responsibility, to lead and to follow; open to criticism but confident in their own abilities; ready to engage in creative conflict."[11]

Planning the Work and the Document

Collaborative writing is most successful when the group articulates its understanding of the document's purposes and audiences and explicitly discusses the best way to achieve these rhetorical goals. Businesses schedule formal planning sessions for large projects to set up a time line specifying intermediate and final due dates, meeting dates, who will attend each meeting, and who will do what. Putting the plan in writing reduces misunderstandings during the project.

FYI

On July 1, 2000, Canada's population was an estimated 30,750,000. In 25 years, it is expected to be between 34 million and 39 million. Although Canada's population will continue to grow over the next twenty-five years, it will age considerably while the proportion of young people will shrink significantly. New population projections forecast that half the population will be over the age of 43.6 by 2026, up substantially from 36.8 in 2000. By 2051, the projected median age will be 46.2.

Source: Statistics Canada, *The Daily*, March 13, 2001; visited Web site July 23, 2001. http://www.statcan.ca/Daily/English/010313/td010313.htm

Instant **Replay**

Responding to Criticism

Constructive ways to respond to criticism and get closer to the real concern include paraphrasing, checking for feelings, checking inferences, and buying time with limited agreement.

When you plan a collaborative writing project,

- Make your analysis of the problem, the audience, and your purposes explicit so you know where you agree and where you disagree.
- Plan and agree on the organization, format, and style of the document before anyone begins to write, to make it easier to blend sections written by different authors.
- Consider your work styles and other commitments. A writer working alone can stay up all night to finish a single-authored document. But members of a group need to work together to accommodate each other's styles and to enable members to meet other commitments.
- Build in project-management time lines.
- Build some leeway into your deadlines. It's harder for a group to finish a document when one person's part is missing than it is for a single writer to finish the last section of a document on which he or she has done all the work.

Composing the Drafts

Most writers find that composing alone is faster than composing in a group. However, composing together may reduce revision time later, since the group examines every choice as it is made.

When you draft a collaborative writing project,

- Use word processing to make it easier to produce the many drafts necessary in a collaborative document
- If the quality of writing is crucial, have the best writer(s) draft the document after everyone has gathered the necessary information

Revising the Document

Revising a collaborative document requires attention to content, organization, and style. The following guidelines can make the revision process more effective:

- Evaluate the content and discuss possible revisions as a group. Brainstorm ways to improve each section so the person doing the revisions has some guidance.
- Recognize that different people favour different writing styles. If the style satisfies the demands of standard English and the conventions of business writing, accept it even if you wouldn't say it that way.
- When the group is satisfied with the content of the document, one person— probably the best writer—should make any changes necessary to make the writing style consistent throughout.

Editing and Proofreading the Document

Since writers' mastery of standard English varies, a group report needs careful editing and proofreading.

- Have at least one person check the whole document for correctness in grammar, mechanics, and spelling and for consistency in the way that format elements, names, and numbers are handled

- Run the document through a spell checker
- After you use a computerized spell checker, have at least one person proofread the document again.

Making the Group Process Work

When you create a co-authored document,

- Allow plenty of time to discuss problems and find solutions. Students writing group reports spend six to seven hours a week outside class in group meetings—not counting the time they spend gathering information and writing their drafts.[12]
- Take the time to get to know group members and to build group loyalty. Group members will work harder and the final document will be better if the group is important to members.
- Be a responsible group member. Attend all the meetings; do what you've committed to do, and plan so you will meet deadlines.
- Be aware that people have different ways of experiencing reality and of expressing themselves.
- Because talking is "looser" than writing, people in a group can think they agree when they don't. Don't assume that because the discussion went smoothly, a draft written by one person will necessarily be acceptable.

Show that you're willing and able to work in teams

© 1993 Farcus Cartoons   WAISGLASS/COULTHART

"We've had a few complaints that you're not a team player."

Employability Skills 2000+
Working and Writing in Teams

In this module, the key skills from The Conference Board of Canada's Employability Skills 2000+ are:

Communicate
✔ write and speak so others pay attention and understand

Think & Solve Problems
✔ assess situations and identify problems
✔ seek different points of view and evaluate them based on facts
✔ recognize the human, interpersonal, technical, scientific, and mathematical dimensions of a problem
✔ check to see if a solution works, and act on opportunities for improvement

Demonstrate Positive Attitudes & Behaviours

✔ deal with people, problems, and situations with honesty, integrity, and personal ethics
✔ recognize your own and other people's good efforts
✔ show interest, initiative, and effort

Be Adaptable

✔ work independently or as part of a team
✔ carry out multiple tasks or projects
✔ be innovative and resourceful: identify and suggest alternative ways to achieve goals and get the job done
✔ be open and respond constructively to change
✔ cope with uncertainty

Work with Others

✔ understand and work within the dynamics of a group
✔ ensure that a team's purpose and objectives are clear
✔ be flexible: respect, be open to and supportive of the thoughts, opinions, and contributions of others in a group
✔ recognize and respect people's diversity, individual differences, and perspectives
✔ accept and provide feedback in a constructive and considerate manner
✔ contribute to a team by sharing information and expertise
✔ lead or support when appropriate, motivating a group for high performance
✔ understand the role of conflict in a group to reach solutions
✔ manage and resolve conflict when appropriate

Participate in Projects & Tasks

✔ work to agreed quality standards and specifications
✔ select and use appropriate tools and technology for a task or project
✔ adapt to changing requirements and information

Review of Key Points

- Effective groups balance information leadership, interpersonal leadership, and procedural leadership.
- Students in successful groups have leaders who set clear deadlines, schedule frequent meetings, and deal directly with conflict that emerges in the group; an inclusive decision-making style; and a higher proportion of members who work actively on the project.

- Students who spend the most time meeting with their groups get the highest grades.
- **Groupthink** is the tendency for groups to put such a high premium on agreement that they directly or indirectly punish dissent. The best correctives to groupthink are to consciously search for additional alternatives, to test one's assumptions against those of a range of other people, and to protect the right of people in a group to disagree.

- To resolve conflicts, first make sure that the people involved really disagree. Next, check to see that everyone's information is correct. Discover the needs each person is trying to meet. The **presenting problem** that surfaces as the subject of dissension may or may not be the real problem. Search for alternatives.

- Constructive ways to respond to criticism include paraphrasing, checking for feelings, checking inferences, and buying time with limited agreement.

- Use statements about the speaker's feelings to own the problem and avoid attacking the audience. In conflict, *I* statements reflect good you-attitude!

- **Collaborative writing** means working with other writers to produce a single document. Writers producing a joint document need to pay attention not only to the basic steps in the writing process but also to the processes of group formation and conflict resolution.

Learning Applications

Questions for Comprehension

19.1 What are the three kinds of group leadership?

19.2 What is groupthink?

19.3 How do you use you-attitude during conflict?

19.4 What strategies produce the best co-authored documents?

Questions for Critical Thinking

19.5 Why are so many people so afraid of conflict in groups? What can a group do to avoid groupthink?

19.6 Why is it better for groups to deal with conflicts, rather than just trying to ignore them?

19.7 What is the most successful group or team you've been part of? What made it effective?

Questions for Building Skills

19.8 What skills have you read about in this module?

19.9 What skills are you practising in the assignments you're doing for this module?

19.10 How could you further develop the skills you're working on?

Exercises and Problems

19.11 Keeping a Journal about a Group

As you work in a collaborative writing group, keep a journal after each group meeting.
- What happened?
- What roles did you play in the meeting?
- What conflicts arose? How were they handled?
- What strategies could you use to make the next meeting go smoothly?

- Record one observation about each group member.

In 19.12 through 19.15, assume that your group has been asked to recommend a solution.

As Your Instructor Directs,

a. Send email messages to group members laying out your initial point of view on the issue and discussing the various options

b. Meet as a group to come to a consensus

c. As a group, answer the message

d. Write a memo to your instructor telling how satisfied you are with
- The decision your group reached
- The process you used to reach it

e. Write a memo describing your group's dynamics (19.18)

19.12   Recommending a Fair Way to Assign Work Around the Holidays

You are on the labour-management committee. This email arrives from the general manager:

Subject: Allocating Holiday Hours

As you know, lots of people want to take extra time off around holidays to turn three-day weekends into longer trips. But we do need to stay open. Right now, there are allegations that some supervisors give the time off to their friends. But even "fair" systems, such as giving more senior workers first choice at time off, or requiring that workers with crucial skills work, also create problems. And possibly we need a different system around Christmas, when many people want to take off a week or more, than around other holidays, when most people take only an extra day or two.

Please recommend an equitable way to decide how to assign hours.

Write a group response recommending the best way to assign hours.

Hint:

Agree on an office, factory, store, hospital, or other workplace to use for this problem.

19.13   Recommending an Internet Use Policy

You're on the information technology integration committee. You get this message from your manager.

Subject: Need Internet Use Policy

We have no policy on Internet use. Is it OK for people to play games or surf the Web during work hours? Should we block access to certain Web sites?

The biggest problem may be responses to listservs and comments on electronic bulletin boards. There's no problem when people log on from home. But if they post responses from their workstations here, people might think the comment represents the official organizational stance on the issue—and it doesn't

---

Write a group response recommending a policy.

Hint:

Agree on an office, factory, store, hospital, or other workplace to use for this problem.

19.14   Recommending Ways to Retain Workers

You are on the recruitment and retention committee. This email arrives from the vice president for human resources:

> Subject: Retaining Workers
>
> As you know, it's a challenge to find employees with the skills we want. To limit the need to hire new people, we want to reduce turnover. What could we do to keep people happy? Please divide your recommendations into low-cost and high-cost solutions

Write a group response recommending ways to retain workers.

Hint:

Agree on an office, factory, store, hospital, or other workplace to use for this problem.

19.15   Judging Suggestions

You're on the suggestion committee. employees submit suggestions that will save money or improve quality, procedures, or morale. Your committee must decide whether to accept, partially accept, or reject each suggestion.

Write a message to each suggester, informing him or her of your decision.

1.
> From: Ewelena Kusznirewicz, Human Resources
>
> Subject: Suggestion to Change Sick-Leave Policy
>
> Right now, employees can "cash in" their unused sick-leave days each year and many people do that. The trouble with that is that people have too few days left if they need to have major surgery or chemotherapy. I recommend that we change the policy to allow people to "cash in" unused sick-leave days only when they retire or quit their jobs.

2.
> From: Ivan Lin, Call Centre
>
> Subject: Suggestion—Open Corporate Store
>
> We should have a store. I visited a friend whose company had a store with company-logo clothing, toys, and sundries (mugs, mouse pads, etc.) as well as greeting cards, snacks, and so forth.

3.
> From: Mohammed Chaar, Accounts Receivable
>
> Subject: Suggestion: Allow Pets at Work
>
> We should let people bring pets to work. Pets reduce stress and blood pressure. People like Justin's seeing-eye dog.

19.16   Planning a Game*

Many companies are using games and contests to solve problems in an enjoyable way. One company promised to give everyone $30 a month extra if they got the error rate below 0.5 percent. The rate improved immediately. After several successful months, the incentive went to $40 a month for getting it under .3 percent and finally to $50 a month for getting it under .2 percent. Another company offered workers two "well hours" if they got in by 7 A.M. every day for a month. An accounting and financial-services company divided its employees into two teams. The one that got the most referrals and new accounts received a meal prepared and served by the losing team (the firm paid for the food). Games are best when the people who will play them create them. Games need to make business sense and give rewards to many people, not just a few. Rewards should be small.

Think of a game or contest that could improve productivity or quality in your classroom, on campus, or in a workplace you know well.

As Your Instructor Directs,

a. Write a message to persuade your instructor, boss, or other decision maker to authorize the game or contest

b. Write a message announcing the game and persuading people to participate in it

*Based on John Case, *The Open-Book Experience: Lessons from Over 100 Companies Who Successfully Transformed Themselves* (Reading, MA: Addison-Wesley, 1998), 129–201.

19.17   Creating Brochures

In a collaborative group, create a series of brochures for an organization and present your design and copy to the class in a group oral presentation. Your brochures should work well as a series but also be capable of standing alone if a reader picks up just one. They should share a common visual design and be appropriate for your purposes and audience. You may use sketches rather than photos or finished drawings. Text, however, should be as it will appear in the final copy.

As you prepare your series, talk to a knowledgeable person in the organization.

For this assignment, as long as the person is knowledgeable, he or she does not have to have the power to approve the brochures.

In a manila folder, turn in

1. Two copies of each brochure

2. A copy of your approved proposal (◀▶ Module 21)

3. A narrative explaining (a) how you responded to the wishes of the person in the organization who was your contact and (b) five of the choices you made in terms of content, visuals, and design and why you made these choices

19.18   Analyzing the Dynamics of a Group

Analyze the dynamics of a task group of which you are a member. Answer the following questions:

1. Who was the group's leader? How did the leader emerge? Were there any changes in or challenges to the original leader?

2. Describe the contribution each member made to the group, and the roles each person played.

3. Did any members of the group officially or unofficially drop out? Did any one join after the group had begun working? How did you deal with the loss or addition of a group member, both in terms of getting the work done and in terms of helping people work together?

4. What planning did your group do at the start of the project? Did you stick to the plan or revise it? How did the group decide that revision was necessary?

5. How did your group make decisions? Did you vote? Reach decisions by consensus?

6. What problems or conflicts arose? Did the group deal with them openly? To what extent did they interfere with the group's task?

7. Evaluate your group both in terms of its task and in terms of the satisfaction members felt. How did this group compare with other task groups you've been part of? What made it better or worse?

As you answer the questions,

- Be honest. You won't lose points for reporting that your group had problems or did something "wrong."

- Show your knowledge of good group dynamics. That is, if your group did something wrong, show that you know what *should* have been done. Similarly, if your group worked well, show that you know *why* it worked well.

- Be specific. Give examples or anecdotes to support your claims.

As Your Instructor Directs,

a. Discuss these questions with the other group members

b. Present your findings orally to the class

c. Present your findings in an individual memo to your instructor

d. Join with the other group members to write a collaborative memo to your instructor

Polishing Your Prose

Delivering Criticism

None of us likes to be told that our work isn't good. But criticism is necessary if people and documents are to improve (Module 12 ◀▶ p. 247).

Depending on the situation, you may be able to use one of these strategies,

1. Notice what's good as well as what needs work.

   The charts are great. We need to make the text as good as they are.

   I really like the builds you've used in the slides. We need to edit the bullet points so they're parallel.

2. Ask questions.

   Were you able to find any books and articles, in addition to sources on the Internet?

   What do you see as the most important revisions to make for the next draft?

3. Refer to the textbook or another authority.

   The module on design says that italic type is hard to read.

   Our instructor told us that presentations should have just three main points.

4. Make statements about your own reaction.

   I'm not sure what you're getting at in this section.

   I wouldn't be convinced by the arguments here.

5. Criticize what's wrong, without making global attacks on the whole document or on the writer as a person.

   There are a lot of typos in this draft.

   You begin almost every sentence with *um*.

Exercises

Rewrite each criticism to make it less hurtful. You may add or omit information as needed.

1. This is the worst report I've ever seen.

2. My 10-year-old can spell better than you do.

3. I can't believe that you didn't go to the library to get any sources.

4. You've used four different fonts in this report. Didn't you read the book? Don't you know that we're not supposed to use more than two?

5. This design is really lame. It looks like every other brochure I've ever seen.

6. There's no way we'll get a passing grade if we turn this in.

7. Were you asleep? Didn't you hear our instructor say that we had to use at least five sources?

8. This is really creative. You've written the perfect illustration for "How to Fail This Course."

9. This proposal makes no sense.

10. This clip art is sexist. There's no way we should use it.

Check your answers to the odd-numbered exercises on page 634.

Module 20
Making Oral Presentations

Topics

- What decisions do I need to make as I plan a presentation?

- How should I organize a presentation?

- How can I create a strong opening and close?

- What are the keys to delivering an effective presentation?

- How should I handle questions from the audience?

- What are the guidelines for group presentations?

Review of Key Points

Learning Applications

Polishing Your Prose: Choosing Levels of Formality

Learning Focus

After reading and applying the information in Module 20, you'll be able to demonstrate

Knowledge of

- The differences between written and oral messages
- Types of presentations
- Effective presentations' criteria

Skills to

- Reframe written material into an oral presentation
- Plan and deliver oral presentations
- Develop a good speaking voice
- Prepare and deliver group presentations

"Writing is a more logical process than speaking. Take the time to write as much as you can..."

"Although I seem to be writing constantly, it isn't a primary role for me," says Janet Maaten, public affairs associate for Imperial Oil. "Much of my time is spent developing communications strategies, acting as company spokesperson, or ensuring the company has a well-established crisis communications plan."

Janet has a bachelor of journalism from Carleton University and has worked for Imperial for nineteen years, mostly in public affairs. In addition to her fulltime job, Janet also finds time to serve on the board of directors of the Lambton County Branch of the Canadian Mental Health Association. She is a past board member of the Victoria Order of Nurses Foundation and the local YMCA.

Imperial Oil is one of Canada's largest corporations, with a history going back over a hundred years, and is the largest producer of crude oil in the country as well as a major producer of natural gas.

Janet works at Imperial's Sarnia manufacturing site, which includes an oil refinery, chemical plant, and research department. She is part of the communications and corporate planning, public affairs division, and works as part of a team. When speaking on behalf of the company, she must ensure that her words accurately reflect what the company is doing.

Her main job is to "coordinate external relations support for clients in Imperial. This includes media, government, public relations, community outreach, issue management, and crisis communication."

Janet's work begins whenever Imperial announces a new project, like a plant, pipeline, or service station. Her first step is to prepare a media release or response statement along with some scripted questions and answers. Janet tries to write as if she were going to present orally. Then when she does have to speak on the issue, she is prepared. After the press releases are sent out, Janet follows up with interviews to answer specific questions.

Next comes the public consultation meeting. At these meetings, Janet works behind the scenes to prepare the technical people to answer questions in a way that the public can understand. Technical people include engineers, environmental specialists, and anyone else directly involved with the project; rehearsals may be held so that they are comfortable talking to the public. The purpose here is to ensure that the public's concerns are accurately addressed and that problems can be resolved. For example, if a pipeline is planned, one farmer might want it placed elsewhere because it comes too close to his well. Another person has a three-hundred-year-old oak that he doesn't want to lose. The public consultation process is a two-way street.

When asked to give advice to someone entering the field, Janet says, "The ability to write concisely and persuasively is the foundation for all communication projects. Writing is a more logical process than speaking. Take the time to write as much as you can and have your friends and your teachers edit your work."

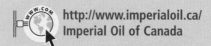

http://www.imperialoil.ca/
Imperial Oil of Canada

Some experts contend that all communication is an effort to convince someone else to our point of view (◀▷ Module 12). Effective messages, therefore, always contain some element of persuasion: if your message fails to capture people's attention and interest, how will you get your ideas across?

As do competent writers, persuasive speakers customize their presentation strategies carefully. They organize their material and adapt their delivery to suit specific purposes, audiences, and situations.

Therefore, all your effective communication strategies—analyzing the audience, using you-attitude and positive emphasis, developing reader benefits, designing slides, overcoming objections, researching and analyzing data—are relevant to your oral presentation planning.

Oral presentations inform, persuade, and build goodwill. And like written messages, most oral presentations serve more than one purpose.

Informative presentations inform or teach the audience. Health and safety training sessions in an organization are primarily informative. Secondary purposes may be to conform to legislation, to meet ISO standards, to persuade employees to follow organizational procedures, rather than doing something their own way, and to acculturalize new employees (◀▷ Module 2).

Persuasive presentations motivate the audience to act or to believe. Giving information and evidence persuade through appeals to credibility and reason (◀▷ Module 12). Moreover, the speaker must build goodwill by appearing to be credible and sympathetic to the audience's needs. The goal in many presentations is a favourable vote or decision. For example, speakers making business presentations may try to persuade the audience to approve their proposals, to adopt their ideas, or to buy their products. Sometimes the goal is to change behaviour or attitudes or to reinforce existing attitudes. For example, a speaker at a workers compensation and benefits information meeting may stress the importance of following safety procedures. A speaker at city council meeting may talk about the problem of homelessness in the community and try to build support for community shelters for the homeless.

Goodwill presentations entertain and validate the audience. In an after-dinner speech, the audience wants to be entertained. Presentations at sales meetings may be designed to stroke the audience's egos and to validate their commitment to organizational goals.

What decisions do I need to make as I plan a presentation?

> Identify your purpose as specifically as possible. Then determine how you can transform your purpose into a benefit for your audience.

An oral presentation needs to be simpler than a written message to the same audience. For one thing, people can listen almost twice as fast as speakers talk; therefore, good presenters compensate for this *listening lag* by reinforcing their ideas through clarity, repetition and emphasis.

Identify the one idea you want the audience to take home. Once you've determined this purpose, rephrase it so that it specifically offers some benefit to the audience.

FYI

Your ability to communicate with others is the key to career advancement.

Source: Peter Urs Bender, author of the bestsellers *Secrets of Power Presentations* and *Leadership from Within* The Achievement Group (Toronto, ON: Stoddard, 2001).

Site *to* See

Go to **http://www.3m.com /meetingnetwork/pr esentations/**

3M's Presentation Corner gathers useful information on turning so-so presentations into strong ones. Many of the best articles come from *Presentations,* but they're easier to find on the 3M Web site than on www.presentations. com.

Weak: The purpose of my presentation is to discuss saving for retirement.

Better: The purpose of my presentation is to persuade my audience to put their retirement funds in stocks and bonds, not in money market accounts and CDs.

or: The purpose of my presentation is to explain how to calculate how much money someone needs to save in order to maintain a specific lifestyle after retirement.

Note: Your purpose *is not* the introduction of your talk; it is the principle that guides your decisions as you plan your presentation.

Simplify your supporting detail so it's easy to follow. Simplify visuals so they can be taken in at a glance. Simplify your words and sentences so they're easy to understand.

Analyze your audience for an oral presentation just as you do for a written message. If you'll be speaking to co-workers, talk to them about your topic or proposal to find out what questions or objections they have. For audiences inside the organization, the biggest questions are often practical ones: Will it work? How much will it cost? How long will it take?[1] And what's in it for me?

You also need to reflect on **where** and **when** you'll be speaking. What size is the room? What equipment will be available? Will the audience be tired at the end of a long day of listening? Sleepy after a big meal? Will the group be large or small? The more you know about your audience and your environment, the better you can adapt your presentation for maximum persuasive impact.

Instant Replay

Three Purposes of Presentations

- **Informative presentations** inform or teach the audience
- **Persuasive presentations** motivate the audience to act or to believe
- **Goodwill presentations** entertain and validate the audience

Most oral presentations have more than one purpose.

Choosing the Kind of Presentation

When you have identified your *purpose* in presenting—that is, you've clarified the result(s) you want—and you've analyzed the needs of your audience, you can decide on one of three basic kinds of presentations: monologue, guided discussion, or sales.

In a **monologue presentation**, the speaker functions as an expert, speaks without interruption and solicits questions at the end of the presentation. The speaker plans the presentation in advance and delivers it without deviation. This kind of presentation may represent the most common educational situation, but it's often boring for the audience. Good delivery skills are crucial, since the audience is comparatively uninvolved.

Guided discussions offer a better way to present material and encourage an audience to really engage. In a guided discussion, the speaker presents the questions or issues that both speaker and audience agree on. Rather than functioning as an expert with all the answers, the speaker serves as a facilitator to help the audience tap its own knowledge. This kind of presentation works well for adult training and for presenting the results of consulting projects, when the speaker has specialized knowledge, but the audience must implement the solution if it is to succeed. Guided discussions need more time than monologue presentations, but produce more audience response, more responses involving analysis, and more commitment to the result.[2]

A **sales presentation** is a conversation, even if the salesperson stands up in front of a group and uses charts and overheads. The sales representative uses questions to determine the buyer's needs, probe objections, and gain temporary and then final commitment to the purchase. Even in a memorized sales presentation, the buyer

Michael Goldman offers helpful advice on meetings and presentations in his bimonthly column "The Meeting Doctor" in *The Training Report* <http://www.trainingreport.ca/>. He has also edited books on facilitation and team building, and owns and operates Participative Dynamics, Canada, a consulting firm that offers training and workshops <http://www.participative-dynamics.com/>.

will talk at least 30 percent of the time. In a problem-solving sales presentation, the buyer may talk 70 percent of the time.

Michael Goldman, the Meeting Doctor, suggests the Guidelines in Figure 20.1 for deciding on your presentation format.

Figure 20.1
Michael Goldman's Guidelines for Deciding on Your Presentation Role

Chair when you want to ...	Facilitate when you want to ...
Exchange information	Increase participation
Get informal feedback	Deal with group dynamics
Hear members report back	Have members problem solve
Overview the current agenda	Get members to make decisions
Set the parameters of the discussion	Get members to create action plans
Review meeting objectives with members	Shift ownership and commitment levels

Source: Michael Goldman, "To chair or to facilitate, that is the question," *The Training Report*, Jan/Feb 2001, page 13.

Adapting Your Ideas to the Audience

Remember that *people can take in only so much information before they shut down*! Measure the message you'd like to send against where your audience is now. If your audience is indifferent, skeptical, or hostile, focus on the part of your message the audience will find most interesting and easiest to accept.

Don't seek a major opinion change in a single oral presentation. If the audience has already decided to hire some advertising agency, then a good presentation can convince them that your agency is the one to hire. But if you're talking to a small business that has always done its own ads, limit your purpose. You may be able to prove that an agency can earn its fees by doing things the owner can't do and by freeing the owner's time for other activities. A second presentation may be needed to prove that an ad agency can do a *better* job than the small business could do on its own. Only after the audience is receptive should you try to persuade the audience to hire your agency rather than a competitor.

Make your ideas relevant to your audience by linking what you have to say to the audience's experiences interests and needs. Showing your audience members that the topic affects them directly is the most effective strategy. When you can't do that, at least link the topic to some everyday experience.

> When was the last time you were hungry? Maybe you remember being hungry while you were on a diet, or maybe you had to work late at a lab and didn't get back to the dorm in time for dinner.

Speech about world hunger to an audience of college students

Instant Replay

Simplify
An oral presentation needs to be simpler than a written message to the same audience

Planning Visuals and Other Devices to Involve the Audience

Visuals can give your presentation a professional image. A 1986 study found that presenters using overhead transparencies were perceived as "better prepared, more professional, more persuasive, more credible, and more interesting" than speakers who did not use visuals. They were also more likely to persuade a group to adopt their recommendations. Coloured overhead transparencies were most effective in persuading people to act.[3]

A 2000 study found that in an informative presentation, multimedia (PowerPoint slides with graphics and animation) produced 5 percent more learning than overheads made from the slides and 16 percent more learning than text alone. In a sales presentation, multimedia (PowerPoint slides with graphics, animation, and video) motivated 58 percent more students to choose that bank compared to overheads and 60 percent more compared to text alone. Although the two banks offered identical fees and services, students said that the bank represented by the multimedia presentation "was more credible, was more professional, and offered better services and fees."[4]

To maximize readability, use a sans serif font (Ariel, Helvetica, Technical) and at least 18-point type for visuals you prepare with a word processor. When you prepare slides with PowerPoint, Corel, or another presentation program, use at least 24-point type for the smallest words (◀▶ See Module 5, especially Figure 5.4, for a discussion of fonts).

Well-designed visuals can serve as an outline for your talk (see Figure 20.2 on the next page), eliminating the need for additional notes. Plan at most one visual for every minute of your talk, plus two visuals to serve as title and conclusion. Don't try to put your whole talk on visuals. Visuals should highlight your main points, not give every detail.

Use these guidelines to create and show visuals for presentations:

- Keep it simple
- Replace text with illustrations—charts, graphs, tables, clipart—whenever possible
- Make only one point with each visual. Break a complicated point down into several visuals
- Give each visual a title that makes a point connected to your presentation main point
- Limit the amount of text: aim for five lines per slide and five words per line, maximum

Figure 20.2

PowerPoint Slides for an Informative Presentation

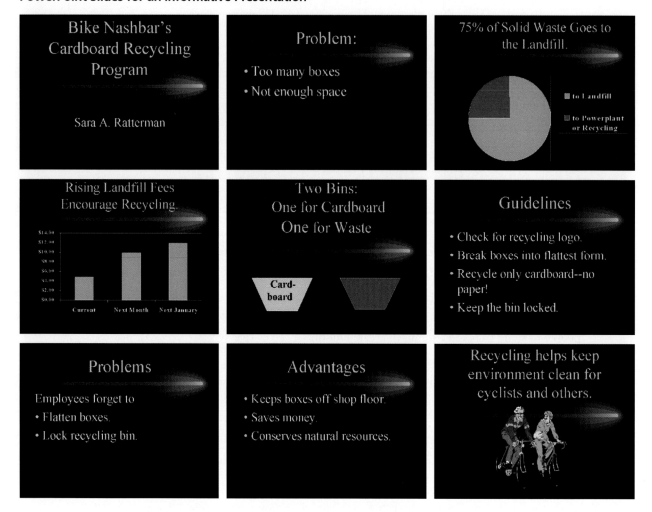

- Put your visual up when you're ready to talk about it
- Leave it up until your next point; don't turn the projector or overhead off

See ◁▷ Module 25 for information on how to present numerical data through visuals.

Visuals work only if the technology they depend on works. When you give presentations in your own office, check the equipment in advance. When you make a presentation in another location or for another organization, arrive early so that you'll have time not only to check the equipment but also to track down a service worker if the equipment isn't working. Be prepared with a backup plan to use if you're unable to show your slides or videotape.

Remember too that PowerPoint presentations have become commonplace. If you're going to attract and hold your audience's attention, you must also engage them in a variety of other ways:

- Students presenting on intercultural business communications demonstrated the way Chinese, Japanese, and Canadians exchange business cards by asking audience members to role-play the differences.

- Another student discussing the need for low-salt products brought in a container of Morton salt, a measuring cup, a measuring spoon, and two plates. As he discussed the body's need for salt, he measured out three teaspoons onto one plate: the amount the body needs in a month. As he discussed the amount of salt the average diet provides, he continued to measure out salt onto the other plate, stopping only when he had .5 kg of salt—the amount in the average North American diet. The demonstration made the discrepancy clear in a way words or even a chart could not have done.[5]

Some presenters use quizzes and games formats—like *Family Feud* or *Who Wants to be a Millionaire*—to encourage audience members to share their expertise with others.

- To make sure that his employees understood where money went, the CEO of a specialty printing shop printed up $2 million in play money and handed out big cards to employees marked *Labour*, *Depreciation*, *Interest*, and so forth. Then he asked each "category" to come up and take its share of the revenues. The action was more dramatic than a colour pie chart could ever have been.[6]

- Another speaker who was trying to raise funds used the simple act of asking people to stand to involve them, to create emotional appeal, and to make a statistic vivid:

> [A speaker] was talking to a luncheon club about contributing to the relief of an area that had been hit by a tornado. The news report said that 70 percent of the people had been killed or disabled. The room was set up ten people at each round table. He asked three persons at each table to stand. Then he said, ". . . You people sitting are dead or disabled. You three standing have to take care of the mess. You'd need help, wouldn't you?"[7]

How can I create a strong opening and close?

Brainstorm several possibilities.

The following four hooks can help.

The beginning and end of a presentation, like the beginning and end of a written document, are positions of emphasis. Use those key positions to interest the audience and emphasize your key point. You'll sound more natural and more effective if you talk from notes but write out your opener and close in advance and memorize them. (They'll be short: just a sentence or two.)

Brainstorm several possible openers for each of the four modes: startling statement, narration or anecdote, question, or quotation. The more you can do to personalize your opener for your audience, the better. Recent events are better than things that happened long ago; local events are better than events at a distance; people they know are better than people who are only names.

FYI

In 1999, an online survey of 3,400 business, education, and government professionals showed that nearly half gave three or more presentations a month. Five percent of those surveyed gave more than 16 presentations a month.

Source: Jon Hanke, "Survey Offers Glimpse of the Average Presenter," *Presentations*, June 1999, 13.

FYI

More than three-quarters of the business people surveyed scan in photos and art work to customize their presentations.

Source: Jon Hanke, "Slideshow Bouillabaisse," *Presentations*, June 1999, 14.

Startling Statement

> Twelve of our customers have cancelled orders in the past month.

This presentation to a company's executive committee went on to show that the company's distribution system was inadequate and to recommend a third warehouse located in the west.

Narration or Anecdote

> A mother was having difficulty getting her son up for school. He pulled the covers over his head.
>
> "I'm not going to school," he said. "I'm not ever going again."
>
> "Are you sick?" his mother asked.
>
> "No," he answered. "I'm sick of school. They hate me. They call me names. They make fun of me. Why should I go?"
>
> "I can give you two good reasons," the mother replied. "The first is that you're 42 years old. And the second is *you're the school principal*."[8]

This speech given at a seminar for educators went on to discuss "the three knot-tiest problems in education today." Educators had to face those problems; they couldn't hide under the covers.

Question

> Are you going to have enough money to do the things you want to when you retire?

This presentation to a group of potential clients discusses the value of using the services of a professional financial planner to achieve one's goals for retirement.

Quotation

> According to Towers Perrin, the profits of Fortune 100 companies would be 25 percent lower—they'd go down $17 billion—if their earnings statements listed the future costs companies are obligated to pay for retirees' health care.

This presentation on options for health care for retired employees urges executives to start now to investigate options to cut the future cost.

Your opener must interest the audience and establish rapport. Some speakers use humour to achieve those goals. However, an inappropriate joke can turn the audience against the speaker. Never use humour that's directed against the audience. In contrast, speakers who make fun of themselves almost always succeed:

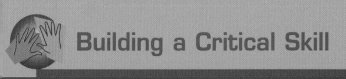

Finding Your Best Voice

Paralanguage—*how* we say what we say—accounts for over 30 percent of the meaning in our messages. Next to your face, therefore, your voice is your most important visual aid! Effective speakers use their voices to support and enhance content. Your best voice will manipulate pitch, intonation, tempo, and volume to express energy and enthusiasm.

Pitch

Pitch measures whether a voice uses sounds that are low (like the bass notes on a piano) or high. Low-pitched voices project more credibility than do high-pitched voices. Low-pitched presenters are perceived as being more authoritative, sexier, and more pleasant to listen to. Most voices go up in pitch when the speaker is angry or excited; some people raise pitch when they increase volume. Women whose normal speaking voices are high may need to practice projecting their voices to avoid becoming shrill when they speak to large groups.

To find your best pitch, try humming. The pitch where the hum sounds loudest and most resonant is your best voice.

Intonation

Intonation marks variation in pitch, stress, or tone. Speakers who use many changes in pitch, stress, and tone usually seem more enthusiastic; often they also seem more energetic and more intelligent. Someone who speaks in a mono-

tone may seem apathetic or unintelligent. Non-native speakers whose first language does not use tone, pitch, and stress to convey meaning and attitude may need to practice varying these voice qualities.

Avoid raising your voice at the end of a sentence, since in English a rising intonation signals a question. Therefore, speakers who end sentences on a questioning or high tones—known as *up-talk* or *Valley-speak*—sound immature and/or uncertain of the validity of what they're saying.

Tempo

Tempo is a measure of speed. In a conversation, match your tempo to the other speaker's to build rapport. In a formal presentation, vary your tempo. Speakers who speak quickly and who vary their volume during the talk are more likely to be perceived as competent.

Volume

Volume is a measure of loudness or softness. Very soft voices, especially if they are also breathy and high-pitched, give the impression of youth and inexperience. People who do a lot of speaking to large groups need to practice projecting their voices so they can increase their volume without shouting.

Sources: George B. Ray, "Vocally Cued Personality Prototypes: An Implicit Personality Theory Approach," *Communication Monographs* 53, no. 3 (1986): 266–76; and Jacklyn Boice, "Verbal Impressions," *Selling Power*, March 2000, 69.

It's both a privilege and a pressure to be here.[9]

Humour isn't the only way to set an audience at ease and establish a positive emotional connection. Smile at your audience before you begin; let them see that you're a real person and a nice one.

The end of your presentation should be as strong as the opener. For your close, you do one or more of the following:

- Restate your main point
- Refer to your opener to create a frame for your presentation

- End with a vivid, positive picture
- Tell the audience exactly what to do to solve the problem you've discussed

The following close from a fund-raising speech combines a restatement of the main point with a call for action, telling the audience what to do.

> Plain and simple, we need money to run the foundation, just like you need money to develop new products. We need money to make this work. We need money from you. Pick up that pledge card. Fill it out. Turn it in at the door as you leave. Make it a statement about your commitment . . . make it a big statement.[10]

When you write out your opener and close, remember that listeners can take in only so much information; then they disengage and tune out. When preparing your presentation, apply the **KISS formula: keep it simple, sweetheart**. As you can see in the example close above, speaking style uses shorter sentences and shorter, simpler words than writing does. Oral style can even sound a bit choppy when it is read by eye. Oral style uses more personal pronouns, a less varied vocabulary, and much more repetition.

How should I organize a presentation?

Start with the main point. Often, one of five standard patterns will work.

Most presentations use a direct pattern of organization, even when the goal is to persuade a reluctant audience. In a business setting, the audience members are in a hurry and know that you want to persuade them. Be honest about your goals, but prepare your opening to demonstrate that your goal meets the audience's needs too.

In a persuasive presentation, start with your strongest point, your best reason. If time permits, give other reasons as well and respond to possible objections. Put your weakest point in the middle so that you can end on a strong note.

Often one of five standard patterns of organization will work.

1. **Chronological.** Start with the past, move to the present, and end by looking ahead.
2. **Problem-Causes-Solution.** Explain the symptoms of the problem, identify its causes, and suggest a solution. This pattern works best when the audience will find your solution easy to accept.
3. **Excluding alternatives.** Explain the symptoms of the problem. Explain the obvious solutions first and show why they won't solve the problem. End by discussing a solution that will work. This pattern may be necessary when the audience will find the solution hard to accept.
4. **Pro-Con.** Give all the reasons in favour of something, then those against it. This pattern works well when you want the audience to see the weaknesses in its position.
5. **1-2-3.** Discuss three aspects of a topic. This pattern works well to organize short informative briefings. "Today I'll review our sales, production, and profits for the last quarter."

Early in your talk—perhaps immediately after your opener—provide an agenda or **overview of the main points** you will make.

> First, I'd like to talk about who the homeless in Vancouver are. Second, I'll talk about the services The Open Shelter provides. Finally, I'll talk about what you—either individually or as a group—can do to help.

An overview provides a mental peg that hearers can hang each point on. It also can prevent someone missing what you are saying because he or she wonders why you aren't covering a major point that you've saved for later.[11]

Offer a clear signpost as you come to each new point. A **signpost** is an explicit statement of the point you have reached. Choose wording that fits your style. The following statements are four different ways that a speaker could use to introduce the last of three points:

> Now we come to the third point: what you can do as a group or as individuals to help homeless people in Vancouver.

> So much for what we're doing. Now let's talk about what you can do to help.

> You may be wondering, what can I do to help?

> As you can see, the Shelter is trying to do many things. We could do more things with your help.

What are the keys to delivering an effective presentation?

Turn your fear into energy, look at the audience, and use natural gestures.

Audience members want you to succeed in your presentation out of a vested self-interest: they don't want to feel uncomfortable for you. They also want the sense that you're talking directly to them, that you've taken the time and trouble to prepare, that you're interested in your subject and that you care about their interest.

They'll forgive you if you get tangled up in a sentence and end it ungrammatically. They won't forgive you if you seem to have a "canned" talk that you're going to deliver no matter who the listeners are or how they respond. You convey a sense of caring to your audience by making direct eye contact and by using a conversational style.

Instant Replay

Humour

An inappropriate joke can turn the audience against the speaker. Never use humour that's directed against the audience. In contrast, speakers who can make fun of themselves almost always succeed.

Site *to* See

Go to www.toastmasters. org/tips.htm

Toastmasters International suggests ways to deal with nervousness. The clubs—available North America—provide forums where members can practice their speaking skills

Tricks for dealing with nervousness work less well than planning your talk and practicing, practicing, practicing

"It seems you misunderstood when I said you should visualize the audience naked."

Source: FARCUS®. Reprinted with permission from LaughingStock Licensing, Inc. Ottawa, Canada. All rights reserved.

Using Fear

The best and most experienced speakers get butterflies. Even great actors like Sir Laurence Olivier have attested to experiencing paralytic fear before every performance. Feeling nervous is normal. But you can harness that nervous energy to do your best work. As one student said, you don't need to get rid of your butterflies. All you need to do is make them fly in formation.

To calm your nerves as you prepare to give an oral presentation,

- Be prepared; analyze your audience, organize your thoughts, prepare visual aids, practice your opener and close, check out the arrangements.
- Practice, practice, practice.
- Use only the amount of caffeine you normally use. More or less may make you jumpy.
- Avoid alcoholic beverages.
- Relabel your nerves. Instead of saying, "I'm scared," try saying, "My adrenaline is up." Adrenaline sharpens our reflexes and helps us do our best.

Just before your presentation,

- Consciously contract and then relax your muscles, starting with your feet and calves and going up to your shoulders, arms, and hands
- Take several deep breaths from your diaphragm

During your presentation,

- Pause and look at the audience before you begin speaking
- Concentrate on communicating well
- Channel your body energy into emphatic gestures and movement

Using Eye Contact

Site *to* See

Go to http://www.llrx.com /columns/guide14. htm

For tips on relaxation techniques that will help you handle stage fright.

Look directly at the people you're talking to. Speakers who looked more at the audience during a seven-minute informative speech were judged to be better informed, more experienced, more honest, and friendlier than speakers who delivered the same information with less eye contact.[12] An earlier study found that speakers judged sincere looked at the audience 63 percent of the time, while those judged insincere looked at the audience only 21 percent of the time.[13]

The point in making eye contact is to establish one-on-one contact with the individual members of your audience. People want to feel that you're talking to them. Looking directly at individuals also enables you to be more conscious of feedback from the audience, so that you can modify your approach if necessary.

Standing and Gesturing

Stand with your feet far enough apart for good balance, with your knees flexed. Unless the presentation is very formal or you're on camera, you can walk if you want to. Some speakers like to come out from the lectern to remove that barrier between themselves and the audience.

Build on your natural style for gestures. Gestures usually work best when they're big and confident.

Using Notes and Visuals

Instant Replay

Overviews and Signposts
Immediately after your opener, provide an **overview of the main points** you will make. Offer a clear signpost as you come to each new point. A **signpost** is an explicit statement of the point you have reached.

Unless you're giving a very short presentation, you'll probably want to use notes. Even experts use notes. The more you know about the subject, the greater the temptation to add relevant points that occur to you as you talk. Adding an occasional point can help to clarify something for the audience, but adding too many points will overwhelm the audience, destroy your outline and put you over the time limit.

Put your notes on cards or on sturdy pieces of paper. Most speakers like to use 10-by-15-centimetre or 12.5-by-17.5-centimetre cards because they hold more information. Your notes need to be complete enough to help you if you go blank, so use long phrases or complete sentences. Under each main point, jot down the evidence or illustration you'll use. Indicate where you'll refer to visuals.

Look at your notes infrequently. Most of your gaze time should be directed to members of the audience. Hold your notes high enough so that your head doesn't bob up and down like a yo-yo as you look from the audience to your notes and back again.

If you have lots of visuals and know your topic well, you won't need notes. If possible, put the screen to the side so that you won't block it. Face the audience, not the screen. With transparencies, you can use colour marking pens to call attention to your points as you talk. Show the entire visual at once: don't cover up part of it. If you don't want the audience to read ahead, prepare several visuals that build up. In your overview, for example, the first visual could list your first point, the second the first and second, and the third all three points.

Keep the room lights on if possible; turning them off makes it easier for people to fall asleep and harder for them to concentrate on you.

How should I handle questions from the audience?

> Anticipate questions that might be asked. Be honest.
>
> Rephrase biased or hostile questions.

Prepare for questions by listing every fact or opinion you can think of that challenges your position. Treat each objection seriously and try to think of a way to deal with it. If you're talking about a controversial issue, you may want to save one point for the question period, rather than making it during the presentation. Speakers who have visuals to answer questions seem especially well prepared.

During your presentation, tell the audience how you'll handle questions. If you have a choice, save questions for the end. In your talk, answer the questions or objections that you expect your audience to have.

Of the respondents to an online survey, 55 percent said they spent at least five hours creating visuals for a new presentation. That doesn't count time spent planning and practicing.

Source: "Presentation Carpentry," *Presentations*, April 1999, 12.

During the question period, acknowledge questions by looking directly at the questioner. As you answer the question, expand your focus to take in the entire group.

If the audience may not have heard the question or if you want more time to think, repeat the question before you answer it. Link your answers to the points you made in your presentation. Keep the purpose of your presentation in mind, and select information that advances your goals.

If a question is hostile or biased, rephrase it before you answer it. "You're asking whether . . . ." Or suggest an alternative question: "I think there are problems with both the positions you describe. It seems to me that a third possibility is . . . ."

Sometimes people will ask a question really designed to state the their own position. Respond to the question if you want to. Another option is to say, "I'm not sure what you're asking" or "That's a clear statement of your position. Let's move to the next question now." If someone asks about something that you already explained in your presentation, simply answer the question without embarrassing the questioner. Even when actively participating, audiences remember only about 70 percent of what you say.

If you don't know the answer to a question, say so and promise to get the information and respond as soon as possible. Write down the question so that you can look up the answer before the next session. You may want to refer the question to your audience, which both involves and flatters them. If it's a question to which you think there is no answer, ask if anyone in the room knows. When no one does, your "ignorance" is vindicated.

At the end of the question period, take two minutes to summarize your main point once more. (This can be a restatement of your close.) Questions may or may not focus on the key point of your talk. Take advantage of having the floor to repeat your message briefly and forcefully.

What are the guidelines for group presentations?

In the best presentations, voices take turns within each point.

Plan carefully to involve as many members of the group as possible in speaking roles.

The easiest way to make a group presentation is to outline the presentation and then divide the topics, giving one to each group member. Another member can be responsible for the opener and the close. During the question period, each member answers questions that relate to his or her topic.

In this kind of divided presentation, be sure to

- Plan transitions
- Strictly enforce time limits
- Coordinate your visuals so that the presentation seems a coherent whole
- Choreograph the presentation: plan each member's movement and seating arrangements as the group transfers from speaker to speaker; take turns managing the visual support so that each speaker can focus on content and delivery, without worrying about changing slides or transparencies
- Practice the presentation as a group at least once; more is better

The best group presentations are even more fully integrated: together, the members of the group

- Write a very detailed outline
- Choose points and examples
- Create visuals

Then, *within* each point, speakers take turns. This presentation is most effective because each voice speaks only a minute or two before a new voice comes in. However, it works only when all group members know the subject well and when the group plans carefully and practices extensively.

Whatever form of group presentation you use, introduce each member of the team to the audience at the beginning of the presentation and at each *transition*: use the next person's name when you change speakers: "Now, Jason will explain how we evaluated the Web pages."

As a team member, pay close attention to your fellow speaker; don't ever indulge in sidebar conversations with others in the group. If other members of the team seem uninterested in the speaker, the audience gets the sense that that speaker isn't worth listening to.

Employability Skills 2000+ Checklist for Making Oral Presentations

In this module, the key skills from The Conference Board of Canada's Employability Skills 2000+ are:

Communicate
✔ write and speak so others pay attention and understand
✔ share information using a range of information and communications technologies (e.g., voice, email, computers)
✔ use relevant scientific, technological, and mathematical knowledge and skills to explain or clarify ideas

Manage Information
✔ locate, gather, and organize information using appropriate technology and information systems

Participate in Projects & Tasks
✔ plan, design, or carry out a project or task from start to finish with well-defined objectives and outcomes
✔ develop a plan, seek feedback, test, revise, and implement
✔ select and use appropriate tools and technology for a task or project
✔ adapt to changing requirements and information

Review of Key Points

- Most oral presentations have more than one purpose and all contain an element of persuasion. **Informative presentations** inform or teach the audience. **Sales presentations** motivate the audience to act or to believe. **Goodwill presentations** entertain and validate the audience.

- An oral presentation needs to be simpler than a written message to the same audience.

- In a **monologue presentation**, the speaker plans the presentation in advance and delivers it without deviation. In a **guided discussion**, the speaker presents the questions or issues that both speaker and audience have agreed on in advance. Rather than functioning as an expert with all the answers, the speaker serves as a facilitator to help the audience tap its own knowledge. A **sales presentation** is a conversation using questions to determine the buyer's needs, probe objections, and gain provisional and then final commitment to the purchase.

- Adapt your message to your audience's beliefs, experience, and interests.

- Plan the beginning and end of the presentation to interest the audience and emphasize your key point.

- Use visuals to make your presentation seem more prepared, more interesting, and more persuasive.

- Use a direct pattern of organization. Put your strongest reason first.

- Limit your talk to three main points. Early in your talk—perhaps immediately after your opener—provide an **overview of the main points** you will make. Offer a clear signpost as you come to each new point. A **signpost** is an explicit statement of the point you have reached.

- To calm your nerves as you prepare to give an oral presentation,

- Be prepared. Analyze your audience, organize your thoughts, prepare visual aids, practice your opener and close, check out the arrangements.

- Use only the amount of caffeine you normally use.

- Avoid alcoholic beverages.

- Relabel your nerves. Instead of saying, "I'm scared," try saying, "My adrenaline is up." Adrenaline sharpens our reflexes and helps us do our best.

Just before your presentation,

- Consciously contract and then relax your muscles, starting with your feet and calves and going up to your shoulders, arms, and hands.

- Take several deep breaths from your diaphragm.

During your presentation,

- Pause and look at the audience before you begin speaking.

- Concentrate on communicating well.

- Use body energy in strong gestures and movement.

- Convey a sense of caring to your audience by making direct eye contact with them and by using a conversational style.

- Treat questions as opportunities to give more detailed information than you had time to give in your presentation. Link your answers to the points you made in your presentation.

- Repeat the question before you answer it if the audience may not have heard it or if you want more time to think. Rephrase hostile or biased questions before you answer them.

- The best group presentations result when the group writes a very detailed outline, chooses points and examples, and creates visuals together. Then, within each point, voices trade off.

Learning Applications

Questions for Comprehension

20.1 How are monologue presentations, guided discussions, and sales presentations alike and different?

20.2 What are four possible openers?

20.3 What does maintaining eye contact and smiling do for a presentation?

Questions for Critical Thinking

20.4 If you use presentation software, will you automatically have strong visuals?

20.5 Why should you plan a strong close, rather than just saying, "Well, that's it"?

20.6 Why does an oral presentation have to be simpler than a written message to the same audience?

20.7 What are the advantages and disadvantages of using humour?

Questions for Building Skills

20.8 What skills have you read about in this module?

20.9 What skills are you practising in the assignments you're doing for this module?

20.10 How could you further develop the skills you're working on?

Exercises and Problems

20.11   Making a Short Oral Presentation

As Your Instructor Directs,

Make a short (2- to 5-minute) presentation, with three to eight slides, on one of the following topics:

a. Explain how what you've learned in classes, in campus activities, or at work will be useful to the employer who hires you after graduation.

b. Profile someone who is successful in the field you hope to enter and explain what makes him or her successful.

c. Describe a specific situation in an organization in which communication was handled well or badly.

d. Make a short presentation based on another problem in this book, such as,

1.13   Discuss three of your strengths

2.17   Analyze your boss

10.12 Explain a "best practice" in your organization

11.12 Tell your boss about a problem in your unit and recommend a solution

26.12 Explain one of the challenges (e.g., technology, ethics, international competition) that the field you hope to enter is facing

28.12 Profile a company you would like to work for and explain why you think it would be a good employer

29.11 Explain your interview strategy

20.12 Making a Longer Oral Presentation

As Your Instructor Directs,

Make a 5- to 12-minute presentation on one of the following. Use visuals to make your talk effective.

a. Show why your unit is important to the organization and either should be exempt from downsizing or should receive additional resources

b. Persuade your supervisor to make a change that will benefit the organization

c. Persuade your organization to make a change that will improve the organization's image in the community

d. Persuade classmates to donate time or money to a charitable organization (Read Module 11)

e. Persuade an employer that you are the best person for the job

f. Use another problem in this book as the basis for your presentation, such as,

2.18 Analyze a discourse community

2.20 Analyze an organization's corporate culture

10.25 Present a Web page you have designed

22.15 Summarize the results of a survey you have conducted

23.15 Summarize the results of your research

20.13 Making a Group Oral Presentation

As Your Instructor Directs,

Make a 5- to 12-minute presentation using visuals.

3.13 Show how cultural differences can lead to miscommunication

5.15 Evaluate the design of three Web pages

12.21 Recommend an investment for your instructor

19.14 Recommend ways to retain workers

19.17 Present brochures you have designed to the class

24.15 Summarize the results of your research

29.12 Share the advice of students currently on the job market

Polishing Your Prose

Choosing Levels of Formality

Some words are more formal than others. Generally, business messages call for a middle-of-the-road formality, not too formal, but not so casual as to seem sloppy.

Formal and stuffy	Short and simple
ameliorate	improve
commence	begin, start
enumerate	list
finalize	finish, complete
prioritize	rank
utilize	use
viable option	choice

Sloppy	Casual
befuddled	confused
diss	criticize
guess	assume
haggle	negotiate
nosy	curious
wishy-washy	indecisive, flexible

What makes choosing words so challenging is that the level of formality depends on your purposes, the audience, and the situation. What's just right for a written report will be too formal for an oral presentation or an advertisement. The level of formality that works in one discourse community may be inappropriate for another.

Listen to the language that people in your discourse community use. What words seem to have positive connotations? What words persuade? As you identify these terms, use them in your own messages.

Exercises

In each sentence, choose the better word or phrase. Justify your choice.

1. On Monday, I [took a look at/inspected] our [stuff/inventory].

2. [Starting/commencing] at 5 P.M., all qualifying employees may [commence/begin] their [leave times/vacations].

3. Though their [guy/representative] was [firm/stubborn], we eventually [hashed out/negotiated] a settlement.

4. Call to schedule [some time/a meeting] with me to [talk about/deliberate on the issues in] your memo.

5. The manager [postponed making /waited until she had more information before making] a decision.

6. Rick has [done his job/performed] well as [top dog/manager] of our Sales Department.

7. In my last job, I [ran lots of errands/worked as a gofer] for the marketing manager.

8. Please [contact/communicate with] [me/the undersigned] if you [have questions/desire further information or knowledge].

9. This report [has problems/stinks].

10. In this report, I have [guessed/assumed] that the economy will continue to grow.

Check your answers to the odd-numbered questions on page 634.

CBC Video Case

CBC

Go to www.mcgrawhill.ca/college/locker for "Small Talk" and "The Trouble with Teams", two online CBC Video Cases that highlight key issues from Unit 5. "Small Talk" looks in as an M.B.A. class is coached on one of the toughest skills for students to master—the art of making conversation in a business setting. And "The Trouble with Teams" explores recent studies indicating that perhaps team work—once seen as a sure-fire way to boost productivity and creativity—is not as successful as previously thought.

Unit Six

Research, Reports, and Visuals

Module 21
Proposals and Progress Reports

Topics

- What is a "report"?
- How do I identify a problem to study?
- What should go in a proposal?
- What should go in a progress report?

Review of Key Points

Learning Applications

Polishing Your Prose: Who/Whom and I/Me

Learning Focus

After reading and applying the information in Module 21, you'll be able to demonstrate

Knowledge of
- The variety of report types
- The communications purposes that reports address

Skills to
- Write purpose statements
- Identify your audiences' "hot buttons"
- Write proposals
- Write progress reports

"Provide multiple means for people to respond ..."

"The planning process involves exploring how to provide the future-needed services that have been identified from within the community," says Richard Zelinka, partner and principal planner in a consulting firm.

Richard has a B.A. in urban studies and a master's degree in environmental studies. He worked as a municipal planner for twelve years. He then spent another twelve years as a junior partner in a planning consulting firm before starting his own business.

Richard's firm works on such diverse projects as developing new official municipal plans and plan policies regarding types and location of development, planning residential subdivisions and commercial plazas, and developing recreation master plans for municipalities. Recreational planning involves a variety of stakeholder groups and requires a wide range of communication and feedback strategies.

The first step in recreational planning is to undertake a background study, which can involve a review of demographics, existing facilities, and the condition of structures. Then the firm looks at how the services will be delivered. Will some facilities be built and managed by stakeholder groups such service clubs, and other not-for-profit organizations, or will everything be built and operated by the municipality? Depending on the involvement of the different groups, Richard will form various partnerships among groups involved in recreation.

Once it has been established what facilities and services exist, Richard has to determine future needs within the community. Richard's firm conducts questionnaires, talks to stakeholder groups, and sets up steering committees that reflect the various interests in the community. It is important at this point to identify the shortcomings of the existing system to determine "the things that prevent the most effective delivery of the services."

The firm also conducts random surveys across the population, not only to achieve statistically valid data, but also because "we want to reach people who are not currently users so we can find where the system is not fulfilling needs."

When all this information is gathered the interim report is written. This report is a way of testing the assumptions underlying the process that results in the plan. This step is crucial since it leads to the final report that will make the recommendations. Richard likes to use an open-house approach since it is informal and allows for the widest range of input from both stakeholders and interested members of the public. Also this approach allows the widest methods of responding to the report. When all the information and feedback is processed, the final report is written.

What kind of advice does Richard offer to people involved in this process? "Provide multiple means for people to respond to ensure the widest cross-section of the population can participate."

Reports provide the information that people in organizations need to communicate, plan, and problem-solve.

The report-writing process includes five basic steps:

1. Define the problem
2. Gather the necessary information
3. Analyze the information
4. Organize the information
5. Write the report

For most writers, this process is recursive rather than linear: after you've gathered and analyzed your information, you may need to circle back to redefine the problem. Your initial problem definition, or working thesis, may change as a result of your information gathering and analysis.

After reviewing the varieties of reports, this module focusses on the first step. ◀▶ Module 22 discusses the second and third steps. Modules 23 and 24 illustrate the fourth and fifth steps.

Other modules that are useful for writing reports are ◀▶ Modules 12, 19, 20, and ◀▶ Module 25.

What is a "report"?

Any kind of documentation can be a report.

In some organizations, a report is a long document or a document that contains numerical data. In others, one- and two-page memos are called *reports*. A proposal to your supervisor in memo format or to a client in letter format is an example of a report. **Formal reports** contain formal elements such as a title page, a transmittal, a table of contents, and a list of illustrations. **Informal reports** may be letters and memos, or even computer printouts of production or sales figures.

Figure 21.1
Three Levels of Reports

> **Reports Can Provide**
> *Information only*
> - **Sales reports** (sales figures for the week or month)
>
> - **Quarterly reports** (figures showing a plant's productivity and profits for the quarter)
>
> *Information plus analysis*
> - **Annual reports** (financial data and an organization's accomplishments during the past year)
>
> - **Audit reports** (interpretations of the facts revealed during an audit)
>
> - **Make-good** or **pay-back reports** (calculations of the point at which a new capital investment will pay for itself)
>
> *Information plus analysis plus a recommendation*
> - **Feasibility reports** evaluate two or more alternatives and recommend which alternative the organization should choose
>
> - **Justification reports** justify the need for a purchase, an investment, a new personnel line, or a change in procedure
>
> - **Problem-solving reports** identify the causes of an organizational problem and recommend a solution

Reports can provide information, provide information and analyze it, or provide information and analysis to support a recommendation (see Figure 21.1). Reports can be called **information reports** if they collect data for the reader, **analytical reports** if they interpret data but do not recommend action, and **recommendation reports** if they recommend action or a solution.

How do I identify a problem to study?

Pick something real, important, and specific.

Good report problems grow out of real situations: incongruence between reality and the ideal vision, lack of information to make an informed decision, the need to make a choice. When you write a report as part of your job, your role or organizational demands define the topic. To identify a problem for a class or course report, pick a topic that's important and relevant to you. Consider organizational or communication problems at work. Identify challenges that face your college or university; housing on campus; social, religious, and professional groups on campus and in your city; local businesses; and municipal, city, provincial, and federal governments and their agencies. Read your campus and local papers and newsmagazines; watch the news on TV or listen to it on the CBC or your local radio station.

A good report problem meets the following criteria:

1. The problem is
   - Real
   - Important enough to be worth solving
   - Narrow but challenging
2. The audience for the report is
   - Real
   - Interested in and affected by the information
   - Able to implement recommended action
3. The data, evidence, and facts are
   - Sufficient to document the severity of the problem
   - Sufficient to support the recommendation that will solve the problem
   - Available to *you*
   - Comprehensible to *you*

Often you need to narrow your problem perspective. For example, the topic "improving the college experiences of international students studying in Canada" is far too broad. **First**, choose one college or university. **Second**, identify the specific problem. Do you want to increase the language and cultural resources available to international students? Increase the social interaction between English-speaking Canadians and international students? Help international students find housing? Increase the number of ethnic grocery stores and restaurants? **Third**, identify the specific audience with a vested interest in or power to implement your recommendations. Depending on the topic, the audience might be the academic vice president, the Office of International Studies, the residence hall counsellors, or service organizations on campus or in town.

Pick a problem you can solve in the time available. Six months of fulltime (and overtime) work and a team of colleagues might allow you to look at all the ways to make a store more profitable. If you're producing a report in six to twelve weeks for a

A research think tank writes proposals to do research for the federal government and private corporations. Proposals used to run 250 pages. Now, clients request 90-minute oral presentations supplemented with 50-page summaries of qualifications.

Source: Ruth Ann Hendrickson to Kitty Locker, March 5, 1997.

class that is only one of your responsibilities, limit the topic. Depending on your interests and knowledge, you could examine the store products' prices and styles, its inventory procedures, its overhead costs, its layout and decor, or its advertising budget.

Remember the key tenet of the decision-making process: ***How you define the problem shapes the solutions you find.*** For example, suppose that a manufacturer of frozen foods isn't making money. If the researcher defines the situation as a marketing problem, he/she may analyze the product's price, image, advertising, and position in the market. But perhaps the real problem is that overhead costs are too high due to poor inventory management, or that an inadequate distribution system doesn't get the product to its target market. ***Defining the problem accurately is essential to finding an effective solution.***

Once you've defined your problem, you're ready to write a purpose statement. The purpose statement—or thesis—goes in both your proposal and your final report. A good **purpose statement** clearly articulates

- The situation, problem or conflict
- The specific information that must be explored or questions that must be answered to solve the problem or resolve the situation
- The purpose(s) of the report, ***expressed as benefits to the audience***

The following purpose statement has all three elements. The report's audience is the Parks Canada Agency, responsible for Alberta's Elk Island National Park.

> Current management methods keep the elk population within the carrying capacity of the habitat, but require frequent human intervention. Both wildlife conservation specialists and the public would prefer methods that controlled the elk population naturally. This report will compare the current short-term management techniques (hunting, trapping and transporting, and winter-feeding) with two long-term management techniques, habitat modification and the reintroduction of predators. The purpose of this report is to recommend which techniques or combination of techniques would best satisfy the needs of conservationists, hunters, and the public.

To write a good purpose statement, you must identify and analyze the problem and, based on your experience, observation and/or research, have some idea of the questions that your report will answer. Note, however, that you can (and should) write a working purpose statement before researching the specific alternatives the report will discuss.

What should go in a proposal?

> What you're going to do, why, how and when you'll do it, and evidence that you'll do it well.

Proposals suggest a method for finding information or solving a problem.[1] (See Figure 21.2 on the next page.)

Proposals have two goals: to get the project accepted and to get you accepted to do the job. Proposals must stress reader benefits and provide specific supporting

Company's Current Situation	The Proposal Offers to	The Final Report Will Provide
We don't know whether we should change.	Assess whether change is a good idea.	Insight, recommending whether change is desirable.
We need to/want to change, but we don't know exactly what we need to do.	Develop a plan to achieve desired goal.	A plan for achieving the desired change.
We need to/want to change, and we know what to do, but we need help doing it.	Implement the plan, increase (or decrease) measurable outcomes.	A record of the implementation and evaluation process.

Figure 21.2
Relationship among Situation, Proposal, and Final Report

Source: Adapted from Richard C. Freed, Shervin Freed, and Joseph D. Romano, *Writing Winning Proposals: Your Guide to Landing the Client, Making the Sale, Persuading the Boss* (New York: McGraw-Hill, 1995), p. 21.

details. Attention to details—including good visual impact and proofreading—helps establish your professional image and suggest that you'd give the same care to the project if your proposal were accepted.

To write a good proposal, you need to have a clear view of the problem you hope to solve and the kind of research or other action needed to solve it. A proposal must answer the following questions convincingly:

- What problem are you going to solve?
- How are you going to solve it?
- What exactly will you provide for us?
- Can you deliver what you promise?
- What benefits can you offer?
- When will you complete the work?
- How much will you charge?

Government agencies and companies often issue Requests for Proposals, known as **RFP**s. Follow the RFP exactly when you respond to a proposal. Competitive proposals are often scored by giving points in each category. Evaluators look only under the heads specified in the RFP. If information isn't there, the proposal gets no points in that category.

Proposals for Class Research Projects

A proposal for a student report usually has the following sections:

1. In your first paragraph (no heading), summarize in a sentence or two the topic and purposes of your report.

2. **Problem.** What product/service problem exists? What needs to change? What needs to improve? Who needs information? Why? What background is relevant?

3. **Feasibility.** Can a solution be found, given the available resources? How do you know?

4. **Audience.** Who in the organization has the power to implement your recommendation? What secondary audiences might be asked to evaluate your report? What audiences would be affected by your recommendation? Will anyone serve as a gatekeeper, determining whether your report is sent to decision makers? What watchdog audiences might read the report?

Purpose Statements

A good **purpose statement** makes three things clear:

- The organizational problem or conflict
- The specific technical questions that must be answered to solve the problem
- The rhetorical purpose the report is designed to achieve

Make your proposal persuasive by using benefits that your audience finds important

"Your Majesty, my voyage will not only forge a new route to the spices of the East but also create over three thousand new jobs."

Source: © The New Yorker Collection 1992 Dana Fraden from cartoonbank.com.

For each of these audiences and for your initial audience (your instructor), give the person's name, job title, and business address and answer the following questions:

- What is the audience's major concern or priority?
- What will the audience see as advantages of your proposal? What objections, if any, is the reader likely to have?
- How interested is the audience in the topic of your report?
- How much does the audience know about the topic of your report?
- List any terms, concepts, equations, or assumptions that one or more of your audiences may need to have explained. Briefly identify ways in which your audiences may affect the content, organization, or style of the report.

5. **Topics to Investigate.** List the questions and subquestions you will answer in your report, the topics or concepts you will explain, the aspects of the problem you will discuss. Indicate how deeply you will examine each of the aspects you plan to treat. Explain your rationale for choosing to discuss some aspects of the problem and not others.

6. **Methods / Procedure.** How will you get answers to your questions? Whom will you interview or survey? What published sources will you use? What Web sites will you consult? Give the full bibliographic references. Your methods section should clearly indicate where and how you will get the information you need to answer the questions in the topics-to-investigate section.

7. **Qualifications / Facilities / Resources.** What attitudes, knowledge and skills qualify you to conduct this study? Do work in the organization? Do you have a contact or source for information? What's your professional or personal interest? How has your education prepared you for the investigation? Do you have access to the resources you will need to conduct your research (computer, books, etc.)? Where will you turn for help if you hit an unexpected snag? You'll be more convincing if you have already scheduled an interview, checked out books, or perused online sources.

8. **Work Schedule.** List both the total time you plan to spend on and the date when you expect to finish each of the following activities:

- Gathering information
- Analyzing information
- Preparing the progress report
- Organizing information

Identifying "Hot Buttons"

In a proposal, as in any persuasive document, it's crucial that you deal with the audience's "hot buttons." **Hot buttons** are the issues to which your audience has a strong emotional response.

Hot buttons sometimes cause people to make what seems like an "illogical" decision—unless you understand the real priorities. A phone company lost a $36 million sale to a university because it assumed that the university's priority would be cost. Instead, the university wanted a state-of-the-art system. The university accepted a higher bid.

When Ernst & Young prepared a proposal to provide professional services to a major automotive company, a team of 15 subject-matter experts spent two intense days working one-on-one with client personnel to learn what issues they cared most about. Reducing work and saving money were concerns, and Ernst & Young proposed redesigning the work to reduce costs and increase return on investment. The focus on value also enabled Ernst & Young to identify an opportunity related to but not part of the original RFP.

But even more important, spending time with the automotive company allowed Ernst & Young to see that a real "hot button" was that the competitor who held the current contract for services seemed to take the automotive company for granted. Ernst & Young exploited this hot button in two ways. First, the proposed work plan included steps to help stakeholders in the company to buy into and support the project. Second, the form of the oral presentation of the proposal shouted, "We understand you." Ernst & Young invited the decision makers to come to the Ernst & Young office for the presentation. Personnel wore shirts with the company logo, mirroring the uniforms worn at the automotive company. The presentation took place on an office floor that had been designed to mimic the floor plan at the automotive company.

Not only providing logical evidence but also meeting emotional needs won Ernst & Young a seven-figure contract, with the possibility of even more work.

Source: James Lane to Kitty Locker, March 8, 1999.

- Writing the draft
- Revising the draft
- Preparing the visuals
- Editing the draft
- Proofreading the report

Answer this question either in a chart or in a calendar. A good schedule provides realistic estimates for each activity, allows time for unexpected snags, and indicates that you can manage a project and complete the work on time.

9. **Close/Call to Action.** In your paragraph, indicate that you'd welcome any suggestions your instructor may have for improving the research plan. Ask your instructor to approve your proposal so that you can begin work on your report. Provide a contact number or email address for confirmation.

Figure 21.3 on the next page shows a student proposal for a long report using online, library, and survey research.

Sales Proposals

Sales proposals are the most common type of business reports, since writers use them to sell ideas, goods or services. Because proposals contain a persuasive compo-

Instant Replay

Proposal for a Student Report

Include the following sections:

- Problem
- Feasibility
- Audience
- Topics to Investigate
- Methods
- Qualifications
- Work Schedule
- Call to Action

Figure 21.3

Proposal for a Student Report Using Survey Research

October 15, 2002

To: Kitty O. Locker

From: Natalie M. Rogal *NMR*

In subject line ① indicate that this is a proposal
② specify the kind of report
③ specify the topic.

Subject: Proposal to Write a Report Recommending the Best Summer Internship
            Program for FFI Health Services

Summarize topic and purposes of report. Many companies use summer internship programs to recruit and "try out" students who will eventually become permanent employees. FFI Health Services does not have such a program. It is interested in creating a program that will attract quality applicants. Using survey data, materials available on campus and on the Web, and my own experience, I will design an internship program that will meet FFI's needs.

Background on FFI Health Services   *Background gives your reader information needed to understand the problem.*

FFI Health Services is a small prescription benefit management company based in Edmonton, Alberta. Started five years ago with only two employees, it has experienced explosive growth. It now has 43 employees in the Edmonton office and seven in Surrey, British Columbia. Gross profits this year will be approximately $60 million. One of the founders, Mr. Paul Wutz, sees the company as a sort of "niche player" in the private health care industry. He describes his company as no longer simply providing traditional prescription benefits but rather as being an entrepreneurial marketing company working with pharmacy retailers and manufacturers.

Background on Summer Internships   *Not all proposals need background sections.*

Student advisors strongly encourage students to pursue co-ops and internships for a variety of reasons, including developing career interests and establishing career goals. The best students aggressively seek internships and use their summer experiences to narrow the field of possible employers. Without an internship program, a company is cutting itself off from some of the most determined and well-rounded undergraduates. Companies can use internship programs to screen permanent hires. Watching a person for three months gives much more information about a person's work ethic and his or her ability to interact with customers or clients than can any interview. Student workers have proven an excellent resource for filling temporary or special needs. They are positively motivated because the work relates to their educational objectives and career interests.

Problem   *This problem is unusually simple. Many problems need several paragraphs of explanation.*

FFI Health Services does not have an internship program that would help it attract high-potential undergraduate students. Currently the company conducts national searches for managerial positions and runs classified ads in local papers for lower-level jobs. An internship program would enable the company to "grow" its own managers.

If "Problem" section is detailed and well-written, you may be able to use it unchanged in your report.

Figure 21.3

Proposal for a Student Report Using Survey Research (continued)

Proposal to Write a Recommendation Report on Internships
October 15, 2002
Page 2

Feasibility *Convince your instructor that you have a backup plan if your original proposal proves unworkable.*

I expect that my research will enable me to recommend a program for FFI. However, if FFI is unable to fund the kind of program necessary, or if none of the models I can find will work for FFI, I will recommend that the company delay implementing a program until circumstances change.

Audiences *Identify the kinds of audiences and the major concerns or priority of each.*

All of my audiences are at least somewhat interested in the topic of my report. None of them are hostile to it, so I will be able to present information straightforwardly. The topic is not particularly technical, so everyone should be able to understand my report easily.

My primary audience is Mr. Paul Wutz, partner of FFI Health Services, Edmonton, Alberta. He has the power to approve my plan. He describes himself as the Human Resources Department and is concerned about the time that would be needed for current staff to train and supervise interns. Still, he is open to the idea and currently views an internship program as a kind of philanthropic effort. He also appreciates the fact that I am acting as an outside consultant at no charge to conduct this study for his company.

You are my initial audience. You've told me that you know a moderate amount about internship programs and are interested in them.

Secondary audiences for my report include the workers at FFI who would train and supervise interns, the students who might apply for internships, and the campus placement offices that help students find internships. Most of these people would welcome additional internship programs.

Topics to Investigate *Indicate what you'll discuss briefly and what you'll discuss in more detail. This list should match your audience's concerns.*

I will investigate the following topics in detail:
1. What do students want from the internship experience?
   - How do students view internships? (a chance to get experience? build a résumé? make connections? a way to get a permanent job?)
   - What do interns want from a summer experience?
   - How willing would out-of-province students be to accept internships at FFI? (interest in managed health care as a field, willingness to spend the summer in Edmonton.)

   All items in list must be grammatically parallel. Here, all are questions.

2. What kinds of internship experiences can the company offer?
   - What resources are available to train, mentor, and supervise interns?
   - What interesting, meaningful assignments could the company have interns do?
3. What models of internships are available?
   - What do interns typically do?
   - What features should a program have?
   - What are common problems and how can FFI avoid them?

   If it is well-written, "Topics to Investigate" section will become the "Scope" section of the report —with minor revisions.

I will briefly discuss the advantages to students and the company of summer internships and how interns and internship programs can be evaluated.

Figure 21.3

Proposal for a Student Report Using Survey Research (continued)

Proposal to Write a Recommendation Report on Internships
October 15, 2002
Page 3

Indicate any topics relevant to your report that you choose not to discuss.

I do not plan to discuss how the internship program should be publicized or at what schools the company should focus its recruiting efforts.

If you'll administer a survey or conduct interviews, tell how many subjects you'll have, how you'll choose them, and what you'll ask them.

Methods

If you're writing a report based on library research, list 10-15 sources that look relevant. Give full bibliographic citations.

I expect to get data from three sources: (1) a survey of Athabasca students to learn what features are important to them in an internship; (2) interviews with Mr. Wutz and other workers at FFI to discover the company's needs and resources; and (3) material on internships from the Fisher College of Business Placement Office, the Web, and my own experience coordinating an internship program last summer.

A draft of my survey questions is attached. Ideally, I would like to get a list of business students and send the survey to a random sample of about 200 students (hoping for at least 100 responses). If that is not possible, I will need to use a convenience sample.

Qualifications

Cite knowledge and skills from other classes, jobs, and activities that will will enable you to conduct the research and interpret your data.

As a student in Rhetoric and Composition at Athabasca University with a focus in business writing, I have done much research and writing. I am also employed by a large international law firm for which I do administrative and analytical work. Last summer I coordinated and evaluated the summer internship program. I am familiar with strategies involved in organizing and maintaining an internship program.

Work Schedule

The following schedule will enable me to complete the report by the due date.

Activity	Total Time	Completion Date
Gathering information	25 hours	Nov. 12
Analyzing information	10 hours	Nov. 19
Preparing the progress report	3 hours	Oct. 26
Organizing information	5 hours	Nov. 21
Writing the draft/Drafting visuals	15 hours	Nov. 29
Revising draft and visuals	12 hours	Dec. 5
Editing	7 hours	Dec. 8
Proofreading	3 hours	Dec. 10

Time needed will depend on the length and topic of the report, your knowledge of the topic, and your writing skills.

Allow plenty of time! Good reports need good revision, editing, and proofreading as well as good research.

Call to Action

Could we set up a conference to discuss my proposal and survey draft? I would welcome any suggestions you may have for improving the research plan or making the report better. Please approve this proposal so that I can begin work on my report.

It's tactful to indicate you'll accept suggestions. End on a positive note.

Figure 21.3

Proposal for a Student Report Using Survey Research (continued)

In your introductory pargraph,
① tell how to return the survey
② tell how the information will be used

Survey on Internships

Please answer the following questions and return the completed survey to the person who gave it to you. All information will be confidential and used only for a class project examining the feasibility of establishing an internship program for a particular business.

1. Major/Program _____

2. Rank:　First Year _____

Start with easy-to-answer questions

　　　　　Second Year _____
　　　　　Third Year _____
　　　　　Fourth Year _____

3. How important it is to you to have one or more internships before you graduate?
　___ Very important
　___ Somewhat important
　___ Not important

Put directions in parentheses to separate them from the question itself.

Branch questions allow readers to skip questions.

4. Did you have an internship last summer?
　___ Yes　___ No (Skip to Question 6.)

5. What were the most beneficial aspects of your internship? (Check all that apply.)
　___ Work related to my major
　___ Likely to get a job offer/got a job offer
　___ Chance to explore my interests
　___ Made connections
　___ Worked with clients
　___ Looks good on my résumé
　___ Other (Please explain.)

6. How much money did you make last summer? (Approximate hourly rate, before taxes.)

Give readers information _____ they need to understand your question.

　❏ Check here if you did not make any money last summer.

7. For next summer, could you afford to take an unpaid internship?
　___ Yes　___ No

8. For next summer, could you afford to take an internship paying only the minimum wage?
　___ Yes　___ No

10. How important is each of the following criteria in choosing whether to accept a specific internship?

These abbreviations are OK when you survey skilled readers

	Very impt.	Some impt.	Not impt.
a. Money	❏	❏	❏
b. Prestige of company	❏	❏	❏
c. Location near where you live now	❏	❏	❏
d. Quality of mentoring	❏	❏	❏
e. Building connections	❏	❏	❏
f. Chance of getting a job with that company	❏	❏	❏
g. Gaining experience	❏	❏	❏

Make sure to break up the lines. Leaving an extra space makes it more likely that the respondent will check the right line.

11. How interested are you in a career in managed care?
　___ Very interested
　___ Somewhat interested
　___ Not interested

12. Could you take a job in Edmonton next summer?
　___ Definitely
　___ Maybe
　___ No

13. Have you heard of FFI Managed Care?
　___ Yes
　___ No

14. I invite any other comments you would like to make regarding internships.

Using columns gets the survey on one side, saving money in copying and eliminating the problem of people missing questions on the back. But it leaves almost no room to write in comments.

Thank you for taking the time to answer this survey. Please return to the person who gave it to you.

Repeat where to turn in or mail completed surveys.

nent, you must convey you-attitude (◀ ▶ Module 6) and demonstrate reader benefits (◀ ▶ Module 8) for everything you offer. Consider using psychological description (p. 157) to make the benefits vivid.

Use language appropriate for your audience. Even if the buyers want a state-of-the-art system, they may not want the level of detail that your staff could provide; they may not understand or appreciate technical jargon (◀ ▶ Module 15).

With long proposals, provide a one-page cover letter. Organize the cover letter in this way:

1. Catch the reader's attention and summarize up to three major benefits you offer
2. Discuss each of the major benefits in the order in which you mentioned them in the first paragraph
3. Deal with any objections or concerns the reader may have
4. Mention other benefits briefly
5. Ask the reader to approve your proposal and provide a reason for acting promptly

Proposals for Funding

If you need money for a new or continuing public service project, you may want to submit a proposal for funding to a foundation, a corporation, a government agency, or a religious agency. In a proposal for funding, stress the needs your project will meet and show how your project helps fulfill the goals of the organization you are asking to fund it. Every funding source has certain priorities; most post lists of the projects they have funded in the past.

Figuring the Budget

A good budget is crucial to making the winning bid. Ask for everything you need to do a quality job. Asking for too little may backfire, leading the funder to think that you don't understand the scope of the project.

Read the RFP to find out what is and isn't fundable. Talk to the program officer and read successful past proposals to find out

- What size projects will the organization fund in theory?
- Does the funder prefer making a few big grants or many smaller grants?
- Does the funder expect you to provide in-kind or matching funds from other sources?

Think about exactly what you'll do and who will do it. What will it cost to get that person? What supplies or materials will he or she need? Also think about indirect costs for using office space, about retirement and health benefits as well as salaries, about office supplies, administration, and infrastructure.

Detail the specifics of your estimates.

Weak: 75 hours of transcribing interviews $1,125

Better: 25 hours of interviews; a skilled transcriber can complete an hour of interviews in 3 hours; 75 hours @ $15/hour   **$1,125**

Without inflating your costs, give yourself a cushion. For example, if the going rate for skilled transcribers is $15 an hour, but you think you might be able to train someone and pay only $10 an hour, use the higher figure. Then, even if your grant is cut, you'll still be able to do the project well.

What should go in a progress report?

What you've done, why it's important, and what you will do next.

When you're assigned to a single project that will take a month or more, you'll probably be asked to file one or more progress reports. A progress report reassures the funding agency or employer that you're making progress and allows you and the agency or employer to resolve problems as they arise. Different readers may have different concerns. An instructor may want to know whether you'll have your report in by the due date. A client may be more interested in what you're learning about the problem. Adapt your progress report to meet the needs of the audience.

Progress reports can do more than just report progress. You can use progress reports to

- **Enhance your image.** Provide details about the number of documents you've read, people you've surveyed, or experiments you've conducted to create a picture of a hardworking person doing a thorough job.
- **Float trial balloons.** Explain, "I could continue to do X [what you approved]; I could do Y instead [what I'd like to do now]." The detail in the progress report can help back up your claim. Even if the idea is rejected, you don't lose face because you haven't made a separate issue of the alternative.
- **Minimize potential problems.** As you do the work, it may become clear that implementing your recommendations will be difficult. In your regular progress reports, you can alert your boss or the funding agency to the challenges that lie ahead, enabling them to prepare psychologically and physically to act on your recommendations.

A study of the progress reports in a large research and development organization found that poor writers tended to focus on what they had done and said very little about the value of their work. Good writers, in contrast, spent less space writing about the details of what they'd done but much more space explaining the value of their work for the organization.[2]

Subject lines for progress reports are straightforward. Specify the project on which you are reporting your progress.

> Subject: Progress on Developing a Marketing Plan for TCBY

> Subject: Progress on Group Survey on Campus Parking

If you are submitting weekly or monthly progress reports on a long project, number your progress reports or include the time period in your subject line. Include dates for the work completed since the last report and to be completed before the next report.

Make your progress report as positive as you honestly can. You'll build a better image of yourself if you show that you can take minor problems in stride and that you're confident of your own abilities.

FYI

According to management guru C.K.Prahalad, formulator of the core competencies concept (*Competing for the Future*, 1994), today's leaders manage through human resource skills. Prahalad credits the Internet for the revolution in the role of modern management. Today's successful leaders emphasize the "network of dialogues"—communications among employees, suppliers and customers—over corporate structures.

Source: C.K. Prahalad and Venkatran Ramaswamy "Co-opting Customer Competence," *Harvard Business Review*, January-February, 2000.

FYI

Only 7.2 percent of small businesses are financed by venture capitalists and "angel" investors. Bank loans and equity from owners and their families and friends are the major funding sources.

Source: "Where's the Cash?" *Business Week,* June 7, 1999, 8.

Negative: I have not deviated markedly from my schedule, and I feel that I will have very little trouble completing this report by the due date.

Positive: I am back on schedule and expect to complete my report by the due date.

Progress reports can be organized in three ways: by chronology, by task, and to support a recommendation.

Chronological Progress Reports

The following pattern of organization focuses on what you have done and what work remains.

1. **Summarize your progress in terms of your goals and your original schedule.** Use measurable statements.

   Poor: My progress has been slow.

   Better: The research for my report is about one-third complete.

2. Under the heading Work Completed, describe what you have already done. Be specific, both to support your claims in the first paragraph and to allow the reader to appreciate your hard work. Acknowledge the people who have helped you. Describe any serious obstacles you've encountered and tell how you've dealt with them.

   Poor: I have found many articles about Procter & Gamble on the Web. I have had a few problems finding how the company keeps employees safe from chemical fumes.

   Better: On the Web, I found Procter & Gamble's home page, its annual report, and mission statement. No one whom I interviewed could tell me about safety programs specifically at P&G. I have found seven articles about ways to protect workers against pollution in factories, but none mentions P&G.

3. **Under the heading Work to Be Completed, describe the work that remains.** If you're more than three days late (for school projects) or two weeks late (for business projects) submit a new schedule, showing how you will be able to meet the original deadline. You may want to discuss "Observations" or "Preliminary Conclusions" if you want feedback before writing the final report or if your reader has asked for substantive interim reports.

4. **Either express your confidence in having the report ready by the due date or request a conference to discuss extending the due date or limiting the project.** If you are behind your original schedule, show why you think you can still finish the project on time.

Figure 21.4

A Student Chronological Progress Report

October 29, 2002

To: Kitty O. Locker

From: David G. Bunnel *DGB*

Subject: Progress on CAD/CAM Software Feasibility Study for the Architecture Firm, Patrick and Associates, Inc.

¶ 1: Summarize results in terms of purpose, schedule.

I have obtained most of the information necessary to recommend whether CADAM or CATIA is better for Patrick and Associates, Inc. (P&A). I am currently analyzing and organizing this information and am on schedule.

Work Completed *Underline Headings or Bold.*

Be very specific about what you've done.

To learn how computer literate P&A employees are, I interviewed a judgment sample of five employees. My interview with Bruce Ratekin, the director of P&A's Computer-Aided Design (CAD) Department on October 15 enabled me to determine the architectural drafting needs of the firm. Mr. Ratekin also gave me a basic drawing of a building showing both two- and three-dimensional views so that I could replicate the drawing with both software packages.

Show how you've overcome minor problems.

I obtained tutorials for both packages to use as a reference while making the drawings. First I drew the building using CADAM, the package designed primarily for two-dimensional architectural drawings. I encountered problems with the isometric drawing because there was a mistake in the manual I was using; I fixed the problem by trying alternatives and finally getting help from another CADAM user. Next, I used CATIA, the package whose strength is three-dimensional drawings, to construct the drawing. I am in the process of comparing the two packages based on these criteria: quality of drawing, ease of data entry (lines, points, surfaces, etc.) for computer experts and novices, and ease of making changes in the completed drawings. Based on my experience with the packages, I have analyzed the training people with and without experience in CAD would need to learn to use each of these packages.

Indicate changes in purpose, scope, or recommendations. Progress report is a low-risk way to bring the readers on board.

Work to Be Completed

Making the drawings has shown that neither of the packages can do everything that P&A needs. Therefore, I want to investigate the feasibility of P&A's buying both packages.

Specify the work that remains.

As soon as he comes back from an unexpected illness that has kept him out of the office, I will meet with Tom Merrick, the CAD systems programmer for Georgian Gollege, to learn about software expansion flexibility for both packages as well as the costs for initial purchase, installation, maintenance, and software updates. After this meeting, I will be ready to begin the first draft of my report.

Whether I am able to meet my deadline will depend on when I am able to meet with Mr. Merrick. Right now, I am on schedule and plan to submit my report by the December 10th deadline.

End on a positive note.

Task Progress Reports

In a task progress report, organize information under the various tasks you have worked on during the period. For example, a task progress report for a group report project might use the following headings:

Finding Background Information on the Web and in Print

Analyzing Our Survey Data

Working on the Introduction of the Report and the Appendices

Under each heading, the group could discuss the tasks it has completed and those that remain.

Recommendation Progress Reports

Recommendation progress reports recommend action: increasing the funding for a project, changing its direction, cancelling a project that isn't working out. When the recommendation will be easy for the reader to accept, use the Direct Request pattern of organization from Module 12 (◀|▶ p. 250). If the recommendation is likely to meet strong resistance, the Problem-Solving pattern (◀|▶ p. 251) may be more effective.

Employability Skills 2000+ Checklist for Proposals and Progress Reports

In this module, the key skills from The Conference Board of Canada's Employability Skills 2000+ are:

Communicate
✔ write and speak so others pay attention and understand
✔ share information using a range of information and communications technologies (e.g., voice, email, computers)
✔ use relevant scientific, technological, and mathematical knowledge and skills to explain or clarify ideas

Manage Information
✔ locate, gather, and organize information using appropriate technology and information systems

Think & Solve Problems
✔ assess situations and identify problems
✔ seek different points of view and evaluate them based on facts
✔ recognize the human, interpersonal, technical, scientific, and mathematical dimensions of a problem
✔ identify the root cause of a problem

Employability Skills 2000+ Checklist
for Proposals and Progress Reports (continued)

✔ be creative and innovative in exploring possible solutions
✔ readily use science, technology, and mathematics as ways to think, gain, and share knowledge, solve problems, and make decisions
✔ evaluate solutions to make recommendations or decisions

Participate in Projects and Tasks

✔ plan, design or carry out a project or task from start to finish with well-defined objectives and outcomes
✔ develop a plan, seek feedback, test, revise, and implement
✔ work to agreed quality standards and specifications
✔ adapt to changing requirements and information
✔ continuously monitor the success of a project or task and identify ways to improve

Review of Key Points

- **Information reports** collect data for the reader; **analytical reports** present and interpret data; **recommendation reports** recommend action or a solution.

- A good purpose statement must make three things clear:
  1. The organizational problem or conflict
  2. The specific technical questions that must be answered to solve the problem
  3. The rhetorical purpose (to explain, to recommend, to request, to propose) the report is designed to achieve

- A proposal must answer the following questions:
  - What problem are you going to solve?
  - How are you going to solve it?
  - What exactly will you provide for us?
  - Can you deliver what you promise?
  - When will you complete the work?
  - How much will you charge?

- In a proposal for a class research project, use the following headings:

  - Problem
  - Feasibility
  - Audience
  - Topics to Investigate
  - Methods
  - Qualifications
  - Work Schedule
  - Call to Action

- Use the following pattern of organization for the cover letter for a sales proposal.
  1. Catch the reader's attention and summarize up to three major benefits you offer
  2. Discuss each of the major benefits in the order in which you mentioned them in the first paragraph
  3. Deal with any objections or concerns the reader may have
  4. Mention other benefits briefly
  5. Ask the reader to approve your proposal and provide a reason for acting promptly

- In a proposal for funding, stress the needs your project will meet. Show how your project helps fulfil the goals of the organization you are asking to fund it.
- To focus on what you have done and what work remains, organize a progress report in this way:
  1. Summarize your progress in terms of your goals and your original schedule
  2. Under the heading "Work Completed," describe what you have already done

3. Under the heading "Work to Be Completed," describe the work that remains
4. Either express your confidence in having the report ready by the due date or request a conference to discuss extending the due date or limiting the project

- Use positive emphasis in progress reports to create an image of yourself as a capable, confident worker.

Learning Applications

Questions for Comprehension

21.1 What three components belong in a purpose statement?

21.2 What is an RFP?

21.3 How does the RFP relate to the organization of the proposal?

Questions for Critical Thinking

21.4 How can you learn your audience's hot buttons?

21.5 What should you do if you have information you want to put in a proposal that the RFP doesn't call for?

21.6 In the budget for a proposal, why isn't it to your advantage to try to ask for the smallest amount of money possible?

21.7 How do you decide whether to write a chronological, task, or recommendation progress report?

Questions for Building Skills

21.8 What skills have you read about in this module?

21.9 What skills are you practising in the assignments you're doing for this module?

21.10 How could you further develop the skills you're working on?

Exercises and Problems

21.11 Writing a Proposal for a Student Report

Write a proposal to your instructor to do the research for a formal or informal report. (See Problems 23.12, 23.13, 23.14, 24.11, 24.12, and 24.13.)

The headings and the questions in the section titled "Proposals for Class Research Projects" are your RFP; be sure to answer every question and to use the headings exactly as stated in the RFP. Exception: Where alternate heads are listed, you may choose one, combine the two ("Qualifications and Facilities"), or treat them as separate headings in separate categories.

21.12   Writing a Chronological Progress Report

Write a memo summarizing your progress on your report.

In the introductory paragraph, summarize your progress in terms of your schedule and your goals. Under a heading titled "Work Completed," list what you have already done. (This is a chance to toot your own horn: If you have solved problems creatively, say so! You can also describe obstacles you've encountered that you have not yet solved.) Under "Work to Be Completed," list what you still have to do. If you are more than two days behind the schedule you submitted with your proposal, include a revised schedule, listing the completion dates for the activities that remain.

In your last paragraph, either indicate your confidence in completing the report by the due date or ask for a conference to resolve the problems you are encountering.

As Your Instructor Directs,

Send the email or paper progress report to

a. The other members of your group

b. Your instructor

21.13   Writing a Task Progress Report

Write a memo summarizing your progress on your report in terms of its tasks.

As Your Instructor Directs,

Send the email or paper progress report to

a. The other members of your group

b. Your instructor

21.14   Writing a Chronological Progress Report for a Group Report

Write a memo to your instructor summarizing your group's progress.

In the introductory paragraph, summarize the group's progress in terms of its goals and its schedule, your own progress on the tasks for which you are responsible, and your feelings about the group's work thus far.

Under a heading titled "Work Completed," list what has already been done. Be most specific about what you yourself have done. Describe briefly the chronology of group activities: number, time, and length of meetings; topics discussed and decisions made at meetings.

If you have solved problems creatively, say so! You can also describe obstacles you've encountered that you have not yet solved. In this section, you can also comment on problems that the group has faced and whether or not they've been solved. You can comment on things that have gone well and have contributed to the smooth functioning of the group.

Under "Work to be Completed," list what you personally and other group members still have to do. Indicate the schedule for completing the work.

In your last paragraph, either indicate your confidence in completing the report by the due date or ask for a conference to resolve the problems you are encountering.

Polishing Your Prose

Who/Whom and I/Me

Even established writers sometimes get confused about when to use *who* versus *whom* and *I* versus *me*. These pronouns serve different functions in a sentence or part of a sentence.

Use who or I as the subject of a sentence or clause.

Correct: Who put the file on my desk?
(*Who* did the action, *put*.)

Correct: Keisha and I gave the presentation at our annual meeting.
(Both *Keisha* and *I* did the action, *gave*.)

Correct: Ai-Lan, who just received a Ph.D. in management science, was promoted to vice president.
(*Who* is the subject of the clause "who just received a Ph.D. in management science.")

Use *whom* and *me* as the object of a verb or a preposition.

Correct: Whom did you write the report for?
(*Whom* is the object of the preposition *for*.)

Correct: She recommended Thuy and me for promotions.
(*Me* is an object of the verb *recommend*.)

Though some print sources may use *who* and *whom* interchangeably, stick to the rules until this practice becomes widely acceptable.

If you're not sure whether a pronoun is being used as a subject or object, try substituting *he* or *him*. If *he* would work, the pronoun is a subject. If *him* sounds right, the pronoun is an object.

Correct: He wrote the report.

Correct: I wrote the report for him.

Exercises

Choose the correct word in each set of brackets.

1. Karen and [I/me] visited St Francis Xavier University last week.

2. For [who/whom] is this letter intended?

3. Dr. Jacobsen, [who/whom] serves on the board of directors, is retiring.

4. Take it from Les and [I/me]: it pays to be prepared in business.

5. [Who/Whom] is the most experienced person on your staff?

6. There was only about an hour for Kelly, Maria, and [I/me] to get to the airport.

7. My supervisor told me the committee will decide [who/whom] gets the promotion.

8. It is the customer for [who/whom] we make our product.

9. Three people at the firm [who/whom] can speak a second language are Van, Chang, and [I/me].

10. Trust [I/me]: it's not a good idea to begin a letter with "To [who/whom] it may concern," even if people frequently do.

Check your answers to the odd-numbered exercises on page 634.

Module 22

Finding, Analyzing, and Documenting Information

Topics

Learning Focus

After reading and applying the information in Module 22, you'll be able to demonstrate

Knowledge of
- Research techniques
- Electronic resources
- Quantitative information analysis

Skills to
- Find information online and in print
- Write questions for surveys and interviews
- Analyze information
- Document sources
- Use the Internet for research

"Documentation ... generally represents a measure of the writer's credibility and competence."

"No matter which method of documentation you use, the process begins with how you take notes and how you provide details. At the outset, decide on which convention you are going to use," says Professor Bruce Lundgren of the English department at the University of Western Ontario.

Bruce has been at Western for over thirty years. He is a specialist in nineteenth century literature with a special love for the work of Charles Dickens. His career took what he calls "an interesting turn" with the arrival of computers and has as a result of his interest in computer technology his career actually had a few more interesting turns.

The first turn was Bruce's realization that computers offered new methods and new sources of research. Pursuing these new sources led Bruce to the insight that business communication and technical writing had something to offer traditional researchers. He began teaching technical writing. In addition to his regular teaching duties, Bruce is the director of the certificate writing program at Western, which offers courses such as Introduction to College Writing, Advanced Exposition, Rhetoric, and Persuasion, Writing for Publication, and, of course, Technical Writing. The second turn was Bruce's editing of the Canadian edition of the *Harbrace Handbook*, a guide to writing for college and university students. Finally, Bruce's interest in the combination of technical writing and computer technology has led him to help develop a Web site to help Western students with grammar. The Web site has a seven-module grammar program designed "to meet the needs of students who had been ill served in the teaching of grammar."

When asked about the implications of different styles of documentation, Bruce comments that "it is important to know that these conventions exist. They are applied by people who make decisions on publication." He further states that writers must research the publications they write for so they can use the appropriate method. Bruce likens this process to researching the job market. When applying for a job, the applicant must keep in mind what the employer wants. When documenting research, keep in mind what the publisher of the document wants. "Documentation becomes an issue with regard to authenticity, but generally it represents a measure of the writer's credibility and competence." One must be particularly vigilant when taking notes, Bruce points out, as careless note-taking can lead to inadvertent plagiarism.

Bruce's advice to students is succinct: "Take pride in your document, take care in its preparation, and take praise for its quality."

 http://publish.uwo.ca/~lundgren
Bruce Lundgren's home page

Research can be as simple as documenting your observations of a workplace situation, or getting a computer printout of sales for the last month. Research may also mean finding online or published material, or surveying or interviewing people. **Secondary research** retrieves information that someone else has gathered: library research and online searches are the best-known kinds of secondary research. **Primary research** gathers new information. Surveys, interviews, and observations are common methods for gathering new information for business reports.

How can I find information online and in print?

Learn how to do keyword searches.

Figures 22.1, 22.2, and 22.3 list a few of the hundreds of online and print resources.

Figure 22.1
Sources for Electronic Research

These CD-ROM databases are available in many university and college libraries:

AB/Inform (indexes and abstract 800 journals in management and business)

Biological and Agricultural Index

Canadian Government Sources:
  Canadian Federal Government
  Canadian Government Information (National Library of Canada)
  Canadian Government Information on the Internet
  Government of Canada Web site
  Parliament of Canada
  Industry Canada's Strategis: The Information Site that Means Business
  Government of Canada Depository Services Program

CINAHL (nursing and allied health)

ComIndex (indexes and abstracts journals in communication)

ERIC (research on education and teaching practices in Canada and other countries)

Foreign Trade and Economic Abstracts

International Film Archive

LEXIS/NEXIS Services

McGraw-Hill Encyclopedia of Science

Newspaper Abstracts

PAIS International—Public Affairs Information Service

Peterson's College Database

Social Sciences Index

Wilson Business Abstracts

Women's Resources International

Figure 22.2
Sources for Web Research
Web addresses may change. For links to the current URLs, see the Web site for this book at http://www.mcgraw hill.ca/college/locker

Subject Matter Directories

SmartPros Accounting
accounting.smartpros.com

Canada Business Service Centres
http://www.cbsc.org/

Canadian small business quarterly report
http://www.strategis.ic.ca/SSG/mi07237e.html

FINWeb
http://www.finweb.com

International business sources on the WWW
ciber.bus.msu.edu/busres.htm

Marketing, Research, Advertising, Selling, Promotion & More
http://www.knowthis.com

Technical Dictionaries for ebusiness and technology terms
http://www.globetechnology.com/site/tech_encyclopedia.html

The Webopedia dictionary
http://www.pcwebopaedia.com

The Internet Dictionary
http://www.oh-no.com/define.html

The Computer User High Tech Dictionary
http://www.computeruser.com/resources/dictionary/dictionary.html

The WWW Virtual Library
http://www.vlib.org

News Sites

AJR NewsLink (links Canadian, U.S., and international newspapers, magazines, and resources online)
ajr.newslink.org/menu.html

Business Week online
http://www.businessweek.com

CBC
http://cbc.ca/newsworld

CNN/CNNFN
http://www.cnn.com (news)
http://www.cnnfn.com (financial news)

The Globe and Mail online
http://www.globeandmail.com/

Maclean's online
http://www.macleans.ca/

The National Post online
http://www.nationalpost.com/

The New York Times on the Web
http://www.nyt.com

The Wall Street Journal Interactive Edition
http:// www.public.wsj.com/home.html

Canadian Government Information

Statistics Canada
http://www.statcan.ca

Most recent 5 years of data, constantly updated
http://www.statcan.ca/english/Pgdb/

The Daily News, with analytical summaries of current StatsCan info
http://www.statcan.ca/englishdai-quo.htm

Profile of Canadian Communities: tables for over 5,000 Canadian communities from most recent census, with the ability to create local base maps
http://www.statcan.ca/english/census96/list.htm

Download over 100 publications free
http://www.statcan.ca/cgi-bin/downpub/freepub.cgi

Canadian historical statistics
http://www.statcan.ca/english/freepub/11-516-XIE/sectiona/cover.htm

Canada's online homepage
http://www.canadaspace.com/newsmedia.htm

CBC Radio
http://cbc.ca/onair/

Reference Collections

Britannica Online
http://www.eb.com

CEO Express
http://www.ceoexpress.com

Hoover's Online (information on more than 13,000 public and private companies worldwide)
http://www.hoovers.com

Topica (mailing lists)
http://www.topica.com

Reference Desk
http://www.refdesk.com

Figure 22.2
Sources for Web Research (continued)
Web addresses may change. For links to the current URLs, see the Web site for this book at http://www.mcgraw hill.ca/college/locker

FYI

In 1999, the Web had 800 million pages. That number is expected to grow to 8 billion by 2002.

Source: "Must Read," *Wired*, November 1999, 112–16; and "A Hidden Goldmine Called Inktomi," *Business Week E-Biz*, September 27, 1999, EB74.

FYI

In 1999, the top 12 search engines together covered only 42 percent of the Web's 800 million indexable pages.

Source: "Must Read," *Wired*, November 1999, 112–16.

To use a computer database and Web search engines efficiently, identify the concepts you're interested in and choose keywords that will help you find relevant sources. Keywords are the terms that the computer searches for. If you're not sure what terms to use, check the ABI/Inform Thesaurus for synonyms and the hierarchies in which information is arranged in various databases.

How do I write questions for surveys and interviews?

Test your questions to make sure they're neutral and clear.

A survey questions a large group of people, called respondents or subjects. The easiest way to ask many questions is to create a questionnaire, a written list of questions that people fill out. Figure 21.3 in ◀▶ Module 21 shows an example of a questionnaire. An interview is a structured conversation with someone who will be able to give you useful information. Surveys and interviews can be useful only if the questions are well designed.

Site *to* **See**

Go to
http://www.lib.berk eley.edu/Teaching Lib/Guides/Internet/Strategies.html

A great tutorial on search techniques.

Figure 22.3
Print Sources for Research

Indexes:
  Accountants' Index
  Business Periodicals Index
  Canadian Business Index
  Hospital Literature Index
  Personnel Management Abstracts

Facts, figures, and forecasts (also check the Web):
  Canada Year Book
  Almanac of Business and Industrial Financial Ratios

Moody's Manuals
The Statistical Abstract of the U.S.

Canadian Census reports (also available on the Web):
  Census of Manufacturers
  Census of Retail Trade

International business and government:
  Dun and Bradstreet's *Principal International Businesses*
  European Marketing Data and Statistics
  Statistical Yearbook of the United Nations

Although survey and interview queries are based on your ideas and a theory—or *working thesis*—it's important to phrase questions in a way that won't lead the respondent or bias the response. Avoid questions that make assumptions about your subjects. The question "Does your spouse have a job outside the home?" assumes that your respondent is married.

Use words that mean the same thing to you and to the respondents. Words like *often* and *important* mean different things to different people. Whenever possible, use quantitative, measurable language.

Vague: Do you use the Web often?

Better: How many hours a week do you spend on the Web?

Closed questions—those questions to which people can only answer "yes" or "no,"—limit information. Open questions—the journalism or "W" questions (*what, who, why, where, when, how*)—encourage information and do not lock the subject into any sort of response. Figure 22.4 gives examples of closed and open questions. Closed questions are faster for subjects to answer and easier for researchers to score. However, since all answers must fit into chosen categories, closed questions cannot probe the complexities of a subject. You can improve the quality of closed questions by conducting a pretest with open questions to find categories that matter to respondents.

When you use multiple-choice questions, make sure that only one answer fits in any one category. In the following example of overlapping categories, a person who worked for a company with exactly 25 employees could check either *a* or *b*. The resulting data would be unreliable.

Overlapping categories: Indicate the number of full-time employees in your company on May 16:
  __a. 0–25
  __b. 25–100
  __c. 100–500
  __d. over 500

Discrete categories: Indicate the number of full-time employees in your company on May 16:
  __a. 0–25
  __b. 26–100
  __c. 101–500
  __d. over 500

Go to
http://home.sprint mail.com/~debflan agan/hunt.html
Debbie Flanagan offers a useful tutorial on Web search strategies. Try the Web scavenger hunt to test your search sophistication.

http://www.qesn. meq.gouv.qc.ca/cc/ inclass/scavenge.htm
The Québec English Schools Network tells you how to create your own Web scavenger hunt and offers links to a number of challenging examples.

Figure 22.4
Closed and Open Questions

Closed Questions

Are you satisfied with the city bus service? (yes/no)

How good is the city bus service?
Excellent   5   4   3   2   1   Terrible

Indicate whether you agree or disagree with each of the following statements about city bus service:

A   D   The schedule is convenient for me.

A   D   The routes are convenient for me.

A   D   The drivers are courteous.

A   D   The buses are clean.

Rate each of the following improvements in the order of their importance to you (1 = most important, 6 = least important)

_____ Buy new buses.

_____ Increase non-rush-hour service on weekdays.

_____ Increase service on weekdays.

_____ Provide earlier and later service on weekdays.

_____ Buy more buses with wheelchair access.

_____ Provide unlimited free transfers.

Open Questions

How do you feel about the city bus service?

Tell me about the city bus service.

Why do you ride the bus? (or, Why don't you ride the bus?)

What do you like and dislike about the city bus service?

How could the city bus service be improved?

Branching questions direct different respondents to different parts of the questionnaire based on their answers to earlier questions.

> 10. Have you talked to an academic advisor this year?
> yes _____ no _____
> (if "no," skip to question 14.)

Use closed multiple-choice questions for potentially embarrassing topics. Seeing their own situation listed as one response can help respondents feel that it is acceptable. However, very sensitive issues are perhaps better asked in an interview, where interviewers can build trust and reveal information about themselves to encourage the interviewee to answer.

Put questions that will be easy to answer early in the questionnaire. Put questions that are harder to answer or that people may be less willing to answer (e.g., age and income) near the end of the questionnaire. Even if people choose not to answer such questions, you'll still have the rest of the survey filled out.

Site *to* See

Go to
http://www.vuw.ac.nz/~agsmith/evaln/evaln.htm

A list of Web sites dealing with the topic of evaluating information on the Internet.

http://urbanlegends.about.com/library/blhoax.htm

A comprehensive account of Internet hoaxes.

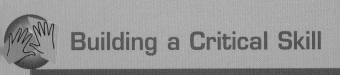

Using the Internet for Research

Most research projects today include the Internet. However, don't rely solely on the Internet for research. Powerful as it is, the Internet's just one tool. Your public or school library, experts in your company, journals and newspapers, and even information in your files are other tools that can be used.

Finding Web Pages

Use root words to find variations. A root word such as *stock* followed by the plus sign (*stock+*) will yield *stock*, *stocks*, *stockmarket*, and so forth.

Use quotation marks for exact terms. If you want only sites that use the term "business communication," put quotes around the term.

Uncapitalize words. Capitalizing words limits your search to sites where the word itself is capitalized; if the word doesn't have to be capitalized, don't.

Some search engines group related sites based on keywords. Look for these links at the top of your search engine.

If you get a broken or dead link, try shortening the URL. For example, if www.mirror.com/newinfo/index.html no longer exists, try www.mirror.com. Then check the site map to see whether it has the page you want.

Evaluating Web Pages

Anyone can post a Web site, and no one checks the information for accuracy or truthfulness. By contrast, many print sources, especially academic journals, have an editorial board that reviews manuscripts for accuracy and truthfulness. The review process helps ensure that information meets high standards.

For a list of Web sites about evaluating information, see http://www.vuw.ac.nz/~agsmith/evaln/evaln.htm.

Use reputable sources. Start with sites produced by universities and established companies or organizations. Be aware, however, that such organizations are not going to post information that makes them look bad. To get "the other side of the story," you may need to monitor listservs or to access pages critical of the organization. (Search for "consumer opinion" and the name of the organization.)

Look for an author. Do individuals take "ownership" of the information? What are their credentials? How can you contact them with questions? Remember that ".edu" sites could be from students not yet expert on a subject.

Check the date. How recent is the information?

Check the source. Is the information adapted from other sources? If so, try to get the original.

Compare the information with other sources. Internet sources should complement print sources. When facts are correct, you'll likely find them recorded elsewhere.

If subjects will fill out the questionnaire themselves, pay careful attention to the physical design of the document. Use indentations and white space effectively; make it easy to mark and score the answers. Include a brief statement of purpose if you (or someone else) will not be available to explain the questionnaire or answer questions. Pretest the questionnaire to make sure the directions are clear. One researcher mailed out a two-page questionnaire without pretesting it. Twenty-five respondents didn't answer the questions on the back of the first page.[1]

Poor questions yield poor data

How do I decide whom to survey or interview?

Use a random sample for surveys, if funds permit.

Use a judgment sample for interviews.

The population is the group you want to make statements about. Depending on the purpose of your research, your population might be all *Report on Business Top 1000* companies, all business students at your college, or all consumers.

Defining your population correctly is crucial to getting useful information. For example, Microscan wanted its sales force to interview "customer defectors." At first, salespeople assumed that a "defector" was a former customer who no longer bought anything at all. By that definition, very few defectors existed. But then the term was redefined as customers who had stopped buying *some* products and services. By this definition, quite a few defectors existed. And the fact that each of them had turned to a competitor for some of what they used to buy from Microscan showed that improvements—and improved profits—were possible.[2]

Because it is not feasible to survey everyone, you select a sample. If you take a true random sample, you can generalize your findings to the whole population from which your sample comes. In a random sample, each person in the population theoretically has an equal chance of being chosen. When people say they did something *randomly* they often mean *without conscious bias*. However, unconscious bias always exists. Someone passing out surveys in front of the library will be more likely to approach people who seem friendly and less likely to ask people who seem intimidating, in a hurry, much older or younger, or of a different race, class, or sex. True random samples rely on random digit tables, generated by computers and published in statistics texts and books such as *A Million Random Digits*.

A convenience sample is a group of respondents who are easy to get: students who walk through the student centre, people at a shopping mall, workers in your own unit. Convenience samples are useful for a rough pretest of a questionnaire. However, you cannot generalize from a convenience sample to a larger group.

A judgment sample is a group of people whose views seem useful. Someone interested in surveying the kinds of writing done on campus might ask each department for the name of a faculty member who cared about writing, and then send

Site *to* **See**

Go to
http://www.statcan.
ca/Daily/English/010
326/d010326a.htm
Canadian Internet
use is reported on
yearly by Statistics
Canada. This URL
reflects 2000 data
reported in 2001;
search
http://www.statcan.
ca/Daily for data
from other years.

FYI

IBM interviews 40,000 customers a year, in 71 countries and 26 languages.

Sources: Robert Hiebeler, Thomas B. Kelly, and Charles Ketterman, *Best Practices: Building Your Business with Customer-Focused Solutions* (New York: Simon & Schuster, 2000), 168.

surveys to those people. Judgment samples are often good for interviews, where your purpose is to talk to someone whose views are worth hearing.

How should I analyze the information I've collected?

> Look for answers to your research questions, patterns, and interesting nuggets.

As you analyze your data, look for answers to your research questions and for interesting nuggets that may not have been part of your original questions but emerge from the data. Such stories can be more convincing in reports and oral presentations than pages of computer printouts.

Understanding the Source of the Data

FYI

A Canadian Automobile Association's survey results reflect Canadians preference for practicality over luxury. Most of the 22,000 CAA members surveyed said they'd rather drive sport utility vehicles, minivans, or light trucks than luxury model cars.

Source: "Minivan please," *The Globe and Mail,* Friday, March 23, B13.

If your report is based upon secondary data from library and online research, look at the sample, the sample size, and the exact wording of questions to see what the data actually measure. Some studies bias results by limiting the alternatives. In one survey 90 percent of students surveyed by Levi Strauss & Co. said Levi's 501 jeans would be the most popular clothes that year. But the Levi's were the only brand of jeans on the list of choices.[3]

Identify the assumptions used in analyzing the data. When studies contradict each other, the explanation sometimes lies in the assumptions. For example, a study that found disposable diapers were better for the environment than cloth diapers assumed that a cloth diaper lasted for 92.5 uses. A study that found that cloth diapers were better assumed that each cloth diaper lasted for 167 uses.[4]

Evaluating online sources, especially Web pages, can be difficult, since anyone can post pages on the Web or contribute comments to chat groups. Check the identity of the writer: is he or she considered an expert? Can you find at least one source printed in a respectable newspaper or journal that agrees with the Web page? If a comment appeared in chat groups, did others in the group support the claim? Does the chat group include people who could be expected to be unbiased and knowledgeable? Especially when the issue is controversial, seek out opposing views.

Analyzing Numbers

Many reports analyze numbers—either numbers from databases and sources or numbers from a survey you have conducted.

If you've conducted a survey, your first step is to transfer the responses on the survey form into numbers. For some categories, you'll assign numbers arbitrarily. For example, you might record men as "1" and women as "2"—or vice versa. Such assignments don't matter, as long as you're consistent throughout your project. In these cases, you can report the number and percentage of men and women who responded to your survey, but you can't do anything else with the numbers.

When you have numbers for salaries or other figures, start by figuring the average, or mean, the median, and the range. The average or mean is calculated by adding up all the figures and dividing by the number of samples. The median is the number that is exactly in the middle. When you have an odd number of observations, the median will be the middle number. When you have an even number, the

Site *to* See

Go to http://www.vicc.com/

Explore insurance premiums criteria and theft costs for cars and motorcycles on Canada's Vehicle Information Centre's Web site.

median will be the average of the two numbers in the centre. The range is the high and low figures for that variable.

Finding the average takes a few more steps when you have different kinds of data. For example, it's common to ask respondents whether they find a feature "very important," "somewhat important," or "not important." You might code "very important" as "3," "somewhat important" as "2," and "not important" as "1." To find the average in this kind of data,

1. For each response, multiply the code by the number of people who gave that response.
2. Add up the figures.
3. Divide by the total number of people responding to the question.

For example, suppose you have surveyed 50 people about the features they want in a proposed apartment complex.

The average gives an easy way to compare various features. If a party room averages 2.3 while extra parking for guests is 2.5, you know that your respondents would find extra parking more important than a party room. You can now arrange the factors in order of importance:

Table 4. "How Important Is Each Factor to You in Choosing an Apartment?"	
n = 50; 3 = "Very Important"	
Extra parking for guests	2.5
Party room	2.3
Pool	2.2
Convenient to bus line	2.0

Often it's useful to simplify numerical data: round it off and combine similar elements. Then you can see that one number is about 2½ times another. Charting it can also help you see patterns in your data. Look at the raw data as well as at percentages. For example, a 50 percent increase in shoplifting incidents sounds alarming—but an increase from two to three shoplifting incidents sounds well within normal variation.

Analyzing Words

If your data include words, try to find out what the words mean to the people who said them. Respondents to Whirlpool's survey of 180,000 households said that they wanted "clean refrigerators." After asking more questions, Whirlpool found that what people really wanted were refrigerators that *looked* clean, so the company developed models with textured fronts and sides to hide fingerprints.[5] Also try to measure words against numbers. When he researched possible investments, Peter Lynch found that people in mature industries were pessimistic, seeing clouds. People in immature industries saw pie in the sky, even when the numbers weren't great.[6]

Look for patterns. If you have library sources, on which points do experts agree? Which disagreements can be explained by early theories or numbers that have now changed? By different interpretations of the same data? Having different values and criteria? In your interviews and surveys, what patterns do you see?

Site to See

Go to http://lib.nmsu.edu/instruction/evalcrit.html

This university site provides excellent evaluation criteria for Web sources.

FYI

Having enough money may well be one source of happiness reports Michael Adams, president of Environics Research and author of *Better Happy than Rich?* His research indicates that 85 percent of Canadians earning $150,000 or more annually report being happy more than unhappy, compared to people making between $40,000 to $50,000. However, Adams and other researchers identify autonomy—feelings of self-worth and a sense of being in control of one's life—as the essential ingredient to happiness.

Source: Nancy J. White. "The pursuit of perfection," *The Toronto Star*, March 24, 2001, M 1-2.

Three Kinds of Samples

In a **random sample**, each person in the population has an equal chance of being chosen.
A **convenience sample** is a group of respondents who are easy to get.
A **judgment sample** is a group of people whose views seem useful.

Go to
http://www.intrepid software.com/fallacy /welcome.htm

Examine the most common examples of faulty logic

Analyzing Numbers

The average or mean is calculated by adding up all the figures and dividing by the number of samples. The median is the number that is exactly in the middle. The range is the high and low figures for that variable.

- Have things changed over time?
- Does geography account for differences?
- What similarities do you see?
- What differences do you see?
- What confirms your hunches?
- What surprises you?

Checking Your Logic

Don't confuse causation with correlation. Causation means that one thing causes or produces another. Correlation means that two things happen at the same time. One might cause the other, but both might be caused by a third.

For example, suppose that you're considering whether to buy cell phones for everyone in your company, and suppose that your surveys show that the people who currently have cell phones are, in general, more productive than people who don't use cell phones. Does having a cell phone lead to higher productivity? Perhaps. But perhaps productive people are more likely to push to get cell phones from company funds, while less productive people are more passive. Perhaps productive people earn more and are more likely to be able to buy their own cell phones if the organization doesn't provide them.

Consciously search for at least three possible causes for each phenomenon you've observed and at least three possible solutions for each problem. The more possibilities you brainstorm, the more likely you are to find good options. In your report, mention all of the possibilities; discuss in detail only those that will occur to readers and that you think are the real reasons and the best solutions.

When you have identified patterns that seem to represent the causes of the problem or the best solutions, check these ideas against reality. Can you find support in the quotes or in the numbers? Can you answer counterclaims? If you can, you will be able to present evidence for your argument in a convincing way.

If you can't prove the claim you originally hoped to make, you will need to revisit your working thesis or modify your conclusions to fit your data. Even when your market test is a failure, you can still write a useful report.

- Identify changes that might yield a different result (for example, selling the product at a lower price might enable the company to sell enough units).
- Discuss circumstances that may have affected the results.
- Summarize your negative findings in progress reports to let readers down gradually and to give them a chance to modify the research design.
- Remember that negative results aren't always disappointing to the audience. For example, the people who commissioned a feasibility report may be relieved to have an impartial outsider confirm their suspicions that a project isn't feasible.[7]

How should I document sources?

Business documents use APA style.

The two most widely used formats for endnotes and bibliographies in reports are those of the American Psychological Association (APA) and the Modern Language

Analyzing numbers and words is important when a company tests a new product or tries to reposition an existing one. For example, sales of tennis balls have dropped 29 percent in the last 10 years. Penn Racquet Sports, test marketed "natural felt fetch toys" for dogs and created a new product category. "Ten times more people own pets than play tennis," says Penn president Gregg R. Weida.

Association (MLA). Figure 22.5 shows the APA and MLA formats for books, government documents, journal and newspaper articles, online sources, and interviews.

In a good report, sources are cited and documented smoothly and unobtrusively. Citation means attributing an idea or fact to its source in the body of the report. "According to the 1996 Census . . ." "Jane Bryant Quinn argues that . . ." Citing sources demonstrates your honesty, enhances your credibility, and protects you from charges of plagiarism. Documentation means providing the bibliographic information readers would need to go back to the original source. Note that citation and documentation are used in addition to quotation marks. If you use the source's exact words, you'll use the name of the person you're citing and quotation marks in the body of the report; you'll indicate the source in parentheses and a list of *References or Works Cited*. If you put the source's idea into your own words, or if you condense or synthesize information, you don't need quotation marks, but you still need to tell whose idea it is and where you found it.

Indent long quotations on the left and right to set them off from your text. Indented quotations do not need quotation marks; the indentation shows the reader that the passage is a quote. Since many readers skip quotes, always summarize the main point of the quotation in a single sentence before the quotation. End the sentence with a colon, not a period, since it introduces the quote.

Interrupt a quotation to analyze, clarify, or question it.

Use square brackets around words you add or change to clarify the quote or make it fit the grammar of your sentence. Omit any words in the original source that are not essential for your purposes. Use ellipses (spaced dots) to indicate omissions.

Site *to* **See**

Go to
http://www.compro
-inc.com/P3thinking
Sk.htm

This site provides a primer on analytical thinking skills.

Site *to* **See**

Go to
http://www.lrc.gmcc.
ab.ca/writing/

http://www.wisc.edu
/writing/Handbook/

Links to documents describing both the MLA and APA styles of documentation are provided at these Web pages from Grant MacEwan College in Edmonton and the University of Wisconsin.

Figure 22.5
APA and MLA Formats for Documenting Sources

APA Format

APA internal documentation gives the author's last name and the date of the work in parentheses in the text. A comma separates the author's name from the date (Pagel & Westerfelhaus, 1999). The page number is given only for direct quotations (Katz, 1998, p. 74). If the author's name is used in the sentence, only the date is given in parentheses. A list of References gives the full bibliographic citation, arranging the entries alphabetically by the author's last name and using hanging indents.

The References contain only items which are generally available. Therefore email messages, interviews, and postings on listserves to which one must subscribe are not listed. Instead, these are cited as personal communications in the body: (Kitty Locker to Mike Garafano, personal communication, June 9, 2000).

In a double-spaced document, double space References as well. In a single-spaced document, double space between entries.

Web page   *Creation/update date*   *Period after year in parentheses*

American Express. (1998). Creating an effective business plan. Retrieved June 15, 2000 from the
      World Wide Web: http://home3.americanexpress.com/smallbusiness/resources/
      starting/biz_plan   *← No punctuation*   *Break Web page address at a slash, period, or hyphen.*

Article from an electronic database   *Last name first for all authors*   *Ampersand*

Atre, T., Auns, K., Badenhausen, K., McAuliffe, K., Nikolov, C., & Ozanian, M. K. (1996, May 20).
      Sports stocks and bonds. *Financial World*, p. 53 (11). General Reference Center Gold (GPIP).
      Starting page   *Number of pages in article.*   *Name of database*

Article in an edited book

Burnett, R. E. (1993). Conflict in collaborative decision-making. In N. R. Blyler & C. Thralls (Eds.),
      Professional communication: The social perspective (pp. 144-162). Newbury Park, CA: Sage.
      In book titles, capitalize only the first words of the title and subtitle.

Book or pamphlet with a corporate author

Citibank. (1994). *Indonesia: An investment guide.* [Jakarta]: Author.
      Square brackets for information you add.

Interview

Fear, Janet, librarian, Sheridan College (2001, February 26). Interview by author. Oakville, ON.

Government document

Business Development Bank of Canada. "Financing a Small Business, A Guide For Women
      Entrepreneurs." Ottawa: Industry Canada, 1999.

Book

Katz, S. M. (1998). *The dynamics of writing review: Opportunities for growth and change in the workplace.*
      Greenwich, CT: Ablex   *Give state when city is not well known.*

Article in a scholarly journal   *Comma even when only two authors*   *Capitalize first and main words of journal, newspaper titles*

Pagel S., & Westerfelhaus, R. (1999). Read the book or attend the seminar? Charting ironies in how
      managers prefer to learn. *The Journal of Business Communication, 36*(2), 163-193.   *Repeat "1" in "193."*
      Year first   *comma*   *Volume number. Issue number.*

Article in a newspaper or magazine

Petzinger, T., Jr. (1999, April 2). New business leaders find greater profit mixing work, caring. *The
      Wall Street Journal*, p. B1.   *No quotes for title of article.*
      "p." or "pp." for newspapers and magazines when you do not give a volume number.

Figure 22.5

APA and MLA Formats for Documenting Sources (continued)

MLA Format

MLA internal documentation gives the author's last name and page number in parentheses in the text. Unlike APA, the year is not given, and no comma separates the name and page number (Katz 74). If the author's name is used in the sentence, only the page number is given in parentheses. A list of Works Cited gives the full bibliographic citation, arranging the entries alphabetically by the author's last name.

In a double-spaced document, double space Works Cited as well. In a single-spaced document, double space between entries.

Web page   *Put title in quote. Capitalize all main words.*   *Creation/ update date*   *Date you visited site*

American Express. "Creating an Effective Business Plan." 1998. 15 June 2000.   *URL in angle brackets*
        <http://home3.americanexpress.com/smallbusiness/resources/starting/biz_plan>.

Article from   *Last name first only for first author*   *"and"*

an   Atre, Tushar, Kristine Auns, Kirt Badenhausen, Kevin McAuliffe, Christopher Nikolov, <u>and</u> Michael
electronic   K. Ozanian. "Sports Stocks and Bonds." *Financial World* 20 May 1996, 53 (11). General
database   Reference Center (GPIP). 30 Mar. 1997. *Date you visited site.*   *Number of pages*
                                                                                                   in article
Posting to a listserv   *Abbreviate month*   *Page article starts*

Bowman, Joel P. "Re: 'They' as Singular." 23 Mar. 1999. Online posting. Biz<u>Com.</u>
                                        Date posted.   *Name of listserv.*

Article in an edited book

Burnett, Rebecca E. "Conflict in Collaborative Decision-Making." *Professional Communication: The*
Date after *Social Perspective.* Ed. Nancy Roundy Blyler and Charlotte Thralls. Newbury Park, CA: Sage,
publisher   1993. 144-62.   *Omit "1" in "162"*

Book or pamphlet with a corporate author

Citibank. *Indonesia: An Investment Guide.* [Jakarta:] Citibank, 1994.

Interview   *Use square brackets for information you add.*

Drysdale, Andrew. Telephone interview. 12 Apr. 1999.

Interview

Fear, Janet. Personal interview. 26 February 2001.

Book   *Capitalize all main words in book title*

Katz, Susan M. *The Dynamics of Writing Review: Opportunities for Growth and Change in the Workplace.*
        Greenwich, CT: Ablex, 1998.   *Give state when city is not well known.*

E-Mail

Locker, Kitty O. "How Do I Get Printer Fixed?" Email to Mike Garafano and Cheryl Frasch, 9 June,
        2000.

Article   *Comma*   *Period*

in a   Pagel, Sonya, and Robert Westerfelhaus. "Read the Book or Attend the Seminar? Charting Ironies in
journal   How Managers Prefer to Learn." *The Journal of Business Communication* 36.2 (1999): 163-93.

Article in a newspaper or magazine   *No punctuation*   *Period*   *Colon*

Petzinger, Thomas, Jr. "New Business Leaders Find Greater Profit Mixing Work, Caring." *The Wall*
        Street Journal, 2 April 1999: B1.   *No "p."*   *Put quotes around title of article*

Government document

Canada. Business Development Bank of Canada. "Financing a Small Business, A Guide for Women
        Entrepreneurs." Ottawa: Industry Canada, 1999.

Employability Skills 2000+ Checklist for Finding, Analyzing and Documenting Information

In this module, the key skills from The Conference Board of Canada's Employability Skills 2000+ are:

Communicate
✔ share information using a range of information and communications technologies (e.g., voice, email, computers)
✔ write and speak so others pay attention and understand
✔ use relevant scientific, technological and mathematical knowledge and skills to explain or clarify ideas

Manage Information
✔ locate, gather, and organize information using appropriate technology and information systems

Participate in Projects & Tasks
✔ work to agreed standards and specifications
✔ adapt to changing requirements and information

Review of Key Points

- To decide whether to use a Web site as a source in a research project, evaluate the site's authors, objectivity, information, and revision date.

- A survey questions a large group of people, called respondents or subjects. A questionnaire is a written list of questions that people fill out. An interview is a structured conversation with someone who will be able to give you useful information.

- Closed questions have a limited number of possible responses. Open questions do not lock the subject into any sort of response. Branching questions direct different respondents to different parts of the questionnaire based on their answers to earlier questions.

- In a random sample, each person in the population theoretically has an equal chance of being chosen. Only in a random sample is the researcher justified in inferring that the results from the sample are also true of the population from which the sample comes. A convenience sample is a group of subjects who are easy to get. A judgment sample is a group of people whose views seem useful.

- Causation means that one thing causes or produces another. Correlation means that two things happen at the same time. One might cause the other, but both might be caused by a third.

- Citation means attributing an idea or fact to its source in the body of the report. Documentation means providing the bibliographic information readers would need to go back to the original source.

Learning Applications

Questions for Comprehension

22.1 What is the difference between open and closed questions?

22.2 What is the difference between the mean and the median?

22.3 What is the difference between correlation and causation?

Questions for Critical Thinking

22.4 Why do you need to know the exact way a question was phrased before using results from the study as evidence?

22.5 How do you decide whether a Web site is an acceptable source for a report?

22.6 Why should you test a questionnaire with a small group of people before you distribute it?

22.7 Why should you look for alternate explanations for your findings?

Questions for Building Skills

22.8 What skills have you read about in this module?

22.9 What skills are you practising in the assignments you're doing for this module?

22.10 How could you further develop the skills you're working on?

Exercises and Problems

22.11   Evaluating Survey Questions

Evaluate each of the following questions. Are they acceptable as they stand? If not, how can they be improved?

a. Questionnaire on grocery purchases.

   1. Do you *usually* shop at the same grocery store?

     a. Yes

     b. No

   2. How much is your average grocery bill?

     a. Under $25

     b. $25–50

     c. $50–100

     d. $100–150

     e. Over $150

b. Survey on technology

   1. Would you generally welcome any technological advancement that allowed information to be sent and received more quickly and in greater quantities than ever before?

   2. Do you think that all people should have free access to all information, or do you think that information should somehow be regulated and monitored?

c. Survey on job skills

How important are the following skills for getting and keeping a professional-level job in Canadian business and industry today?

	Low				High
Ability to communicate	1	2	3	4	5
Leadership ability	1	2	3	4	5
Public presentation skills	1	2	3	4	5
Selling ability	1	2	3	4	5
Teamwork capability	1	2	3	4	5
Writing ability	1	2	3	4	5

22.12   Evaluating Web Sites

Evaluate seven Web sites related to the topic of your report. For each, consider

- Author(s)
- Objectivity
- Information
- Revision date

Based on these criteria, which sites are best for your report? Which are unacceptable? Why?

As Your Instructor Directs,

a. Share your results with a small group of students

b. Present your results in a memo to your instructor

c. Present your results to the class in an oral presentation

22.13   Designing Questions for an Interview or Survey

Submit either a one- to three-page questionnaire or questions for a 20- to 30-minute interview AND the information listed below for the method you choose.

Questionnaire

1. Purpose(s), goal(s)
2. Subjects (who, why, how many)
3. How and where to be distributed
4. Rationale for order of questions, kinds of questions, wording of questions

Interview

1. Purpose(s), goal(s)
2. Subject (who and why)
3. Proposed site, length of interview
4. Rationale for order of questions, kinds of questions, wording of questions, choice of branching or follow up questions

As Your Instructor Directs,

a. Create questions for a survey on one of the following topics:

- Survey students on your campus about their knowledge of and interest in the programs and activities sponsored by a student organization

- Survey students about their knowledge and use of campus services, like the counselling, health, career, or tutoring centres

- Survey workers at a company about what they like and dislike about their jobs

- Survey people in your community about their willingness to pay more to buy products using recycled materials and to buy products that are packaged with a minimum of waste

- Survey students and faculty on your campus about whether adequate parking exists

- Survey two groups on a topic that interests you

b. Create questions for an interview on one of the following topics:

- Interview an international student about the form of greetings and farewells, topics of small talk, forms of politeness, festivals and holidays, meals at home, size of families and roles of family members in his or her county

- Interview the owner of a small business about the problems the business has, what strategies the owner has already used to increase sales and profits and how successful these strategies were, and the owner's attitudes toward possible changes in product line, decor, marketing, hiring, advertising, and money management

- Interview someone who has information you need for a report you're writing

Polishing Your Prose

Mixing Verb Tenses

Normally, verb tenses within a sentence, paragraph, and document should be consistent.

Incorrect: I went to the store yesterday. There, I will buy a new computer, desk, and bookcase. Afterward, I assemble everything and arrange my new home office.

Correct: I went to the store yesterday. There, I bought a new computer, desk, and bookcase. Afterward, I assembled everything and arranged my new home office.

When you have to mix tenses in a document, do so appropriately. The reader must understand the relationship between time and action throughout your document:

Incorrect: By the time you get to the meeting, I drop off the package at FedEx.

Correct: By the time you get to the meeting, I will have dropped off the package at FedEx.

The correct example uses *future perfect tense* to indicate action that has not occurred yet, but will prior to your getting to the meeting (expressed in *simple present tense*).

In general, stick to simple verb tenses in business communication. Standard edited English prefers them. Unless you must indicate specifically when one action takes place with respect to another, the simple tenses work fine.

- Use present tense in résumés and job application letters to describe current job duties; use it in persuasive documents when you want the reader to feel close to the action.

- Use past tense in résumés and job application letters to describe previous job duties; use it in correspondence and reports where action has already occurred.
- Use future tense in messages to describe action that still needs to be completed—in a progress report, any remaining activities; in a résumé or job application letter, when you will graduate from college or complete a job certification program.

Exercises

Fix the verb tense errors in the following sentences.

1. I went to the garage yesterday and get my tires changed.

2. Many of our retirees work for the company for many years.

3. Our vice president of consumer affairs resigned last week but come into the office yesterday to clean out her desk.

4. The phone rang until I answer it.

5. I will go to college when I graduated from high school.

6. About two hundred résumés come in for the position yesterday.

7. Before we drove to the sales meeting, we get gasoline for the car.

8. After you graduate, you work for our company.

9. The warranty provided service or replacement of defective parts for the next five years.

10. I enjoy my vacation to the Bahamas last January and February.

Check your answers to the odd-numbered exercises on page 634.

Module 23
Short Reports

Topics

- What are the basic strategies for organizing information?
- How do I decide what organizational pattern to use?
- Should I use the same style for reports as for other business documents?

Review of Key Points

Learning Applications

Polishing Your Prose: Being Concise

Learning Focus

After reading and applying the information in Module 23, you'll be able to demonstrate

Knowledge of

- Strategies for organizing information
- The criteria for a specific report pattern

Skills to

- Organize information in reports
- Create a good writing style for reports
- Ask good questions on the job

"The report does not rehash the issues. 'Mediation is forward looking...'"

"When an outside mediator is hired, it usually means the problem is significant and has been going on for at least six months," says Tom Haight, a mediator who has his own practice and who also works with the Canadian Centre for Mediation. Tom notes that ongoing conflict in an organization is significant both in economic and in interpersonal terms.

Tom has a B.A. in history and is currently doing an M.A. in theology. He became interested in mediation when he himself went through the process. He then took a course on mediation training and followed up with studies through the International Mediation Institute in Kansas, whose trainers travel to Canada to provide instruction.

Tom's mediation practice involves such diverse issues as family problems, estate issues, and workplace conflict. This last category can involve anything from two people fighting over office space to harassment. Tom is also involved in mediation training and has a contract with Canada Customs and Revenue Agency to help train managers so that they can attempt to deal with issues inhouse.

In a large company, usually management will call in Tom, but in a small business anyone involved in a conflict may call. Tom must first lay out the ground rules. The mediator is in charge of the process, but tries to get the people in conflict to communicate. The people are in control of the content. "It is necessary that the people in mediation have the power to reach an agreement," says Tom. "If they finally do resolve their problems, no one then wants upper management to overrule the agreement." Tom points out that in a downsizing situation companies often don't realize the costs involved. In many cases mediation reveals it may be cheaper to keep people.

The mediation process begins by defining the problem. In a sense Tom follows the old journalistic process of identifying the who, what, where, why, and when. Sessions are held in private and neutral territory, such as a boardroom—as was important in one recent mediation that involved two people fighting over who got the window office. The mediation process led to both people realizing their status was equal, with the result that they agreed to take different office space and open the window area up as a public lounge.

When the mediation process is done, Tom must write what he calls the Draft Memorandum of Agreement. It is a draft since company lawyers usually write a final version in legal language. The draft follows a basic short report format, defining the original problem and stating the solutions. Tom points out that the report does not rehash the issues. "Mediation is forward looking. Counselling looks back." Tom adds that his report must be precise and to the point.

When asked for parting words of advice, Tom says, "Remember, you cannot mediate if the problem, or the situation leading to the problem, involves anything that is illegal, immoral, or unethical. For those issues, get the proper help. Then see a mediator."

http://www.ccmediation.com/
Canadian Centre for Mediation

Whenever you have a choice, write a short report rather than a long one. Choose to use only the information that your reader needs to make a decision. In today's information-saturated world, every extra word costs you—in credibility and goodwill.

Email has had the most significant impact on why, how, and when we write. Before email, most people's jobs didn't require writing. Now more of us have to write to communicate, and computers have reshaped writing style. Our declining attention spans demand brevity and conciseness. Twenty years ago, the average sentence length in a novel was twenty words; today, sentences consist of seven to 14 words. One-sentence paragraphs, once sparingly used for dramatic effect, are common. And bullet-point writing, a function of Internet communication, telegraphs compact information reliant on parallelism, qualities that used to characterize poetry. Cyberlanguage isn't just a new vocabulary; it's an intellectual and cultural shift.[1]

One report writer was asked to examine a building that had problems with heating, cooling, and air circulation. The client who owned the building wanted quick answers to three questions: Can we do it? What will it cost? When will it pay for itself? The client wanted a three-page report with a seven-page appendix showing the payback figures.[2] When Susan Kleimann studied reply forms for a hotel, its managers said they didn't want to read a report. So Kleimann limited the "report" to an executive summary with conclusions and recommendations. Everything else went into appendixes.[3]

Short reports normally use letter or memo format, depending on whether they are written to an external audience, or to a reader in your organization.

What are the basic strategies for organizing information?

Try one of these seven patterns.

1. General to particular or particular to general
2. Comparison/contrast
3. Problem-solution
4. Elimination of alternatives
5. Geographic or spatial
6. Functional
7. Chronological

Any of these patterns can be used to organize all or part of a report.

1. General to Particular or Particular to General

General to particular starts with the problem as it affects the organization, or as it manifests itself in general, and then moves to a discussion of the parts of the problem and solutions to each of these parts. Particular to general starts with the problem as the audience defines it and moves to larger issues of which the problem is a part. Both are useful patterns when you need to redefine the reader's perception of the problem in order to solve it effectively.

Problem-solving starts with recognizing a problem or need in your organization

"Call it a hunch, but I'd say it's about time to re-evaluate the company's hiring criteria."

Source: By permission of Leigh Rubin and Creators Syndicate.

2. Comparison/Contrast

Comparison/contrast examines each alternative in turn, discussing strengths and weaknesses. Feasibility studies usually use this pattern.

A variation of the divided pattern is the **pro and con pattern**. In this pattern, under each specific heading, give the arguments for and against that alternative.

Whatever information comes second will carry more psychological weight. This pattern is least effective when you want to de-emphasize the disadvantages of a proposed solution, for it does not permit you to bury the disadvantages between neutral or positive material.

3. Problem-Solution

Identify the problem; explain its background or history; discuss its extent and seriousness; identify its causes. Discuss the factors (criteria) that affect the decision. Analyze the advantages and disadvantages of possible solutions. Conclusions and recommendations can go either first or last, depending on the preferences of your reader. This pattern works well when the reader is neutral.

4. Elimination of Alternatives

After discussing the problem and its causes, discuss the *impractical* solutions first, showing why they will not work. End with the most practical solution. This pattern works well when the solutions the reader is likely to favour will not work, while the solution you recommend is likely to be perceived as expensive, intrusive, or radical.

5. Geographic or Spatial

In a geographic or spatial pattern, you discuss problems and solutions by units by their physical arrangement. Move from office to office, building to building, factory to factory, province to province, region to region, etc.

A sales report uses a geographic pattern of organization:

Sales Have Risen in the European Economic Community
Sales Have Fallen Slightly in Asia
Sales Are Steady in North America

6. Functional

Functional patterns discuss the problems and solutions of each functional unit. For example, a report on a new plant might divide data into sections on the costs of land and building, on the availability of personnel, on the convenience of raw materials, etc. A government report might divide data into the different functions an office performed, taking each in turn.

7. Chronological

A chronological report records events in the order in which they happened or are planned to happen.

Instant Replay

Seven Ways to Organize Information

1. General to particular or particular to general
2. Comparison/ contrast
3. Problem- solution
4. Elimination of alternatives
5. Geographic or spatial
6. Functional
7. Chronological

How do I decide what organizational pattern to use?

Establish and then meet readers' expectations.

Successful reports are organized according to readers' expectations for that kind of report.

Informative and Closure Reports

An **informative** or **closure report** summarizes completed work or research that does not result in action or recommendation.

Informative reports often include the following elements:

- **Introductory paragraph** summarizing the problems or successes of the project
- **Chronological account** of problem identification, action, and results
- **Concluding paragraph** with suggestions for later action. In a recommendation report, the recommendations would be based on proof. In contrast, the suggestions in a closure or recommendation report are not proved in detail.

Figure 23.1 on the next page presents this kind of informative report.

Feasibility Reports

Feasibility reports evaluate several alternatives and recommend one of them. (Doing nothing or delaying action can be one of the alternatives.)

Feasibility reports normally open by explaining the decision to be made, listing the alternatives, and explaining the criteria. In the body of the report, evaluate each alternative according to the criteria. Discussing each alternative separately is better when one alternative is clearly superior, when the criteria interact, and when each alternative is indivisible. If the choice depends on the weight given to each criterion, you may want to discuss each alternative under each criterion.

Whether your recommendation should come at the beginning or the end of the report depends on your reader. Most readers want the "bottom line" up front. However, if your solution will cost time or money, provide all your evidence before giving the recommendation.

FYI

English, with about 490,000 words, has the largest vocabulary of any language. Even educated people use only about 5,000 words in speech and 10,000 words in writing in their lifetime.

Source: Guinness Book of World Records: visited Web site July 27, 2001; http://www.triviastic.com/ items/807.html

Figure 23.1

An Informative Memo Report

March 27, 2002

To: Kathryn Hughes

From: Tessa Laughton

Subject: Self-Evaluation, Group Presentation Performance

First paragraph summarizes completed work

Last Thursday, my team members and I delivered out first multi-media presentation, "Bikes: More Than Just a Ride in the Park." Mark McLean, Buchanan Elliot, Scott Turbat, and I worked well together, as was evident by the class reaction to our presentation.

Identifies purpose and scope of the report

When I had the opportunity to view my performance on video, I was impressed with how much I've improved over last year. Watching the video, however, allowed me to see specific speaking habits I would like to change.

Overview of the Team's Success

Chronological background what was done, by whom, why

Our team chose this topic because it was of interest to all of us, especially Buchanan. He rides mountain bikes competitively in the summer and is now president of a board organizing a summer bike-riding camp in memory of his friend Rory Dick. We all agreed that the topic was relevant to the class because everyone has owned or ridden a bike at least once and could, therefore, find some useful information in our presentation.

Overall our presentation worked well. Of course there were some flaws, but we look forward to refining it and having the chance to present it again at the end of the semester. In general, our group worked well together, our attitudes meshed and no one tried to dominate or slack off. I felt that each of us brought an important ability to the group presentation:

❑   Buchanan is very knowledgeable about his mountain bike riding and very enthusiastic about sharing that knowledge. You could see it in his delivery: his eye contact, smile, positive manner, and so on

❑   Mark is very good at organizing information and kept us to predetermined objectives and timelines

❑   Scott's good ideas and sense of humour inspired us

❑   I contributed the technical and design aspects of the PowerPoint presentation.

My Presentation Contribution

Specific details of writer's role in the project

My team strengths included taking responsibility for the PowerPoint slide show. I took this on because I have confidence in my technical knowledge and design abilities; I knew that I could create a slide show that included all the other team members' ideas.

As I watched the video of our presentation, I noticed a number of other positives about my performance:

Figure 23.1

An Informative Memo Report (continued)

❑ I knew the information inside and out. I made sure that before I got up in front of the class and you, I knew every detail in my part. In fact, that's the only way I can feel comfortable presenting: I have to know what I am explaining and why the information is relevant

❑ While watching the video, I also noticed that my eye contact had improved. I made eye contact with members of the audience throughout the room. This was actually the first presentation I have done without holding papers or cue cards in front of my face, or on a podium. I wanted to discover if I could relax enough to present to an audience without a sheet of paper to depend on

❑ I also thought my voice modulation had improved. Obviously it's something I can work on, but I felt that my enthusiasm came across in my voice.

Plans for Continuous Improvement

Although my performance was much better than in the past, I need to improve in specific areas, as was evident when I viewed the video:

❑ I kept using "umm..." In fact, saying "umm" once or twice is too much, but I think I say it because I get nervous. Or maybe I just say it out of habit. When I watched the video, I noticed that I repeated "umm" two or three times; I was not aware that I had this habit until I watched myself on camera

Information on problems discovered

❑ Another area I intend to work on is my ability to use my voice for emphasis. I need to make my content more interesting for the listener by varying my volume and rate of speaking.

Plan for subsequent action

I've developed two strategies for change: first, I've asked family members and friends to give me immediate feedback if and when I use vocal interferences—"umm" or "like," for example—in my conversation; secondly, I've begun to record myself reading aloud, trying different tonal inflections. As you can see, both these strategies will make me conscious of these habits and enable me to develop a more powerful speaking style.

Summary repeats project's success

In summary, I was pleased with our team effort and with the presentation organization and delivery. By next month, when we have an opportunity to present formally again, my group members and I will be practised enough to take advantage of our speaking strengths and to eliminate the weaknesses. Although it felt a bit weird to watch myself on video, I sure learned a great deal about my skills and the areas that I need to build on.

Justification/Analytical Reports

Justification or analytical reports recommend or justify a purchase, investment, hiring, or change in policy. If your organization has a standard format for justification reports, follow that format. If you can choose your headings and organization, use the ***direct, deductive or good news pattern*** (◀▶ Module 12) when your recommendation will be easy for your reader to accept:

1. **Indicate what you're asking for and why it's needed** Since the reader has not asked for the report, you must link your request to organizational goals
2. **Briefly give the background of the problem or need**

3. **Explain each of the possible solutions** For each, give the cost and the advantages and disadvantages
4. **Summarize the action needed to implement your recommendation** If several people will be involved, indicate who will do what, and how long each step will take
5. **Ask for the action you want**

When the reader will be reluctant to grant your request because action will cost time or money, use the ***indirect, inductive or bad news*** variation of the problem-solving pattern described in Modules 11 and 12:

1. **Describe the organizational problem (which your request will solve)** Provide specific examples (results) to demonstrate the seriousness of the problem
2. **Prove that easier or less expensive solutions will not solve the problem**
3. **Present your solution impersonally**
4. **Show that the disadvantages of your solution are outweighed by the advantages**
5. **Summarize the action needed to implement your recommendation** If several people will be involved, indicate who will do what, and how long each step will take.
6. **Ask for the action you want**

The detail you need to give in a justification report depends on your reader's knowledge of and attitude toward your recommendation and on the corporate culture. Many organizations expect justification reports to be short—only one or two pages. Other organizations may expect longer reports with much more detailed budgets and a full discussion of the problem and each possible solution.

Should I use the same style for reports as for other business documents?

Yes, with modifications.

The advice about style in  Modules 15 and 16 also applies to reports, with these modifications:

1. **Use the third person; avoid the word *you*.** In a document to multiple audiences, it will not be clear who *you* is. Instead, use the third person ("first-year accounting students," "nursing graduates," "employees," "managers," "waste management services").
2. **Include in the report all the definitions and documents needed to understand the recommendations.** The multiple audiences for reports include readers who may consult the document months or years from now. Explain acronyms and abbreviations the first time they appear. Explain the history or background of the problem. Add as appendices previous documents on which you build.

The following points apply to any kind of writing, but they are particularly important in reports:

1. Say what you mean
2. Keep your writing tight
3. Use transitions, topic sentences, and headings to make your organization clear to your reader

Instant **Replay**

Report Style
Reports use the same style as other business documents, with three exceptions:

1. Reports use a more formal style than do many letters and memos
2. Reports rarely use the word *you*
3. Reports should be self-explanatory

FYI

North Americans' dread of conversational pauses marks our speech patterns. Vocal interferences— "like," "you know," and the all-Canadian "eh?"— and air words like "basically" create a deadly impression on listeners.

Let's look at each of these principles as they apply to reports.

1. Say What You Mean

Right word choices result in successful reports, often skimmed by readers who are looking for the bottom line, or who know very little about the subject. Putting the meaning of your sentence in the verbs will help you say what you mean.

Vague: My report revolves around the checkout lines and the methods used to get price checks when they arise.

Better: My report shows how price checks slow checkout lines, and recommends ways to reduce the number of price checks needed.

The right word can recast the sentence for maximum impact.

Incorrect: The first problem with the incentive program is that middle managers do not use good interpersonal skills in implementing it. For example, the hotel chef openly ridicules the program. As a result, the kitchen staff fear being mocked if they participate in the program.

Better: The first problem with the incentive program is that some middle managers undercut it. For example, the hotel chef openly ridicules the program. As a result, the kitchen staff fear being mocked if they participate in the program.

2. Tighten Your Writing

Eliminate unnecessary words, use gerunds and infinitives, combine sentences, and reword sentences to cut the number of words.

Wordy: Campus Jewellers' main objective is to increase sales. Specifically, the objective is to double sales in the next five years by becoming a more successful business.

Better: Campus Jewellers' objective is to double sales in the next five years.

3. Use Blueprints, Transitions, Topic Sentences, and Headings

Blueprints are overviews or forecasts that tell the reader what you will discuss in a section or in the entire report. Make your blueprint easy to read by telling readers how many points they'll be reading, and by numbering them. In the following example, the first sentence in the revised paragraph tells the reader to look for four points; the numbers separate the four points clearly. This overview paragraph also establishes readers' expectations; they now expect to read about tax benefits first and employee benefits last.

Paragraph without numbers Employee Stock Ownership Programs (ESOPs) have several advantages. They provide tax benefits for the company. ESOPs also create tax benefits for employees and for lenders. They provide a defence against takeovers. In some organizations, productivity increases because workers now have a financial stake in the company's profits. ESOPs are an attractive employee benefit and help the company hire and retain good employees.

Asking Specific and Polite Questions

Learning to *ask the right question the right way* is a critical skill in both business and interpersonal communications. ***Because people tend to answer the questions we ask***, it's crucial to ask the right questions. Good business communicators use specificity and politeness.

Specificity

Vague questions generate vague or rambling answers. Therefore, make sure you ask the right question for the kind of answer you want. To get a short answer,

- Ask closed questions (◀▮▶ Module 22):
  Do you prefer flex hours?
- Give simple choices:
  When you work extra hours, would you prefer overtime pay or comp time (the same number of hours off)?
- Ask the real question:
  Not: When do you want to meet?
  But: Which day is best for you to meet?
- Ask for a quantifiable or measurable response, such as facts, dates, statistics, and so forth.
  What percentage of our customers are repeat business?

When you want longer, more qualitative answers, make your question specific enough for your audience to understand what you're asking:

- Use one of the six Ws or journalism questions: Who, what, where, when, why, or way (how):
  How would your telecommuting contribute to our bottom line?
- Add concrete language that invites a qualified response:

What reservations do you have about my proposal?
Why do you want to work for this firm?

Politeness

Courtesy is a matter of timing, tone, language, and culture (◀▮▶ Module 3). Remember that *when* and *how* you ask the question is as important as the question itself. To increase your chances of creating goodwill and getting the information you need,

- **Time your queries.** Pay attention to others' emotional space: people respond to psychological as well as physical space. Don't assault people with questions the moment they arrive or get up to leave. If someone is upset, give him or her time to calm down. Avoid questions when it's obvious someone doesn't want them.
- **Keep questions to a minimum.** Review all the resources at your disposal first to see if the answers are there.
- **Avoid embarrassing or provocative questions.** Even if you are comfortable discussing such issues, don't assume other people are.
- **Avoid language that implies doubt, criticism, or suspicion.**
  Rude: You don't really think you can handle this project, do you?
  Polite: How do you feel about managing this project?
- **Use you-attitude and empathy.** Try to look at situations from the other person's point of view, particularly if a conflict is involved.

Because culture affects the rules of politeness—and culture changes—keep abreast of what is and isn't acceptable in society. Remember that different cultures have different concepts of politeness.

Revised paragraph with numbers Employee Stock Ownership Programs (ESOPs) provide four benefits. First, ESOPs provide tax benefits for the company, its employees, and lenders to the plan. Second, ESOPs help create a defence against takeovers. Third, ESOPs may increase productivity by giving workers a financial stake in the company's profits. Fourth, as an attractive employee benefit, ESOPs help the company hire and retain good employees.

Transitions words, phrases, or sentences signal that the discussion is continuing on the same point or shifting points.

There are economic advantages, too.
(Tells the reader that we are still discussing advantages but that we have now moved to economic advantages.)

An alternative to this plan is . . .
(Tells reader that a second option follows.)

These advantages, however, are found only in A, not in B or C.
(Prepares reader for a shift from A to B and C.)

A **topic sentence** introduces or summarizes the main idea of a paragraph. Readers follow your ideas more easily when each paragraph begins with a topic sentence.

Hard to read (no topic sentence):	Another main use of ice is to keep the fish fresh. Each of the seven kinds of fish served at the restaurant requires 3.78 litres twice a day, for a total of 52.9. An additional 22.7 litres a day are required for the salad bar.
Better (begins with topic sentence):	Seventy-six litres of ice a day are needed to keep food fresh. Of this, the biggest portion (52.9) is used to keep the fish fresh. Each of the seven kinds of fish served at the restaurant requires 3.78 litres twice a day (7X7.56 = 52.9). An additional 22.7 litres a day are required for the salad bar.

Headings are single words, short phrases, or complete sentences that indicate the topic in each section. The best writers use headings as signposts to the reader, signalling the topics or sections that are coming up next. A heading must cover all of the material under it until the next heading. For example, *Cost of Tuition* cannot include the cost of books or of room and board. You can have just one paragraph or several pages under a heading. When you have several pages between headings, consider using subheadings, particularly when you have two or more divisions within a main heading.

Topic headings focus on the structure of the report. As you can see from the following example, topic headings give very little information.

Recommendation
Problem
   Situation 1
   Situation 2
Causes of the Problem
   Background
   Cause 1
   Cause 2
Recommended Solution

Informative or **talking heads**, in contrast, tell the reader what to expect. Informative heads, like those in the examples in this chapter, provide an overview of each section and of the entire report:

Recommended Reformulation for Vibe Bleach
Problems in Maintaining Vibe's Granular Structure
   Solidifying during Storage and Transportation
   Customer Complaints about "Blocks" of Vibe in Boxes
Why Vibe Bleach "Cakes"
   Vibe's Formula
   The Manufacturing Process
   The Chemical Process of Solidification
Modifications Needed to Keep Vibe Flowing Freely

Headings must be **parallel** (◀▶ Module 16, p. 351); that is, they must use the same grammatical structure. Subheads must be parallel to each other but do not necessarily have to be parallel to subheads under other headings.

Employability Skills 2000+ Checklist for Short Reports

In this module, the key skills from The Conference Board of Canada's Employability Skills 2000+ are:

Communicate
✔ write and speak so others pay attention and understand
✔ listen and ask questions to understand and appreciate the points of view of others

Manage Information
✔ locate, gather, and organize information using appropriate technology and information systems

Think & Solve Problems
✔ assess situations and identify problems
✔ identify the root cause of a problem
✔ be creative and innovative in exploring possible solutions
✔ evaluate solutions to make recommendations or decisions

Participate in Projects & Tasks
✔ plan, design, or carry out a project or task from start to finish with well-defined objectives and outcomes
✔ work to agreed quality standards and specifications
✔ adapt to changing requirements and information
✔ continuously monitor the success of a project or task and identify ways to improve

Review of Key Points

- **General to particular** begins with the problem as it affects the organization or as it manifests itself in general, then moves to a discussion of the parts of the problem and solutions to each of these parts. **Comparison/contrast** takes up each alternative in turn. The **pro and con pattern** divides the alternatives and discusses the arguments for and against that alternative. A **problem-solving report** identifies the problem, explains its causes, and analyzes the advantages and disadvantages of possible solutions. **Elimination** identifies the problem, explains its causes, and discusses the least practical solutions first, ending with the one the writer favours. **Particular to general** starts with specific aspects of the problem, then moves to a discussion of the larger implications of the problem for the organization. **Geographical or spatial** patterns discuss the problems and solutions by units. **Functional** patterns discuss the problems and solutions of each functional unit.

- Reports use the same style as other business documents, with three exceptions:
  1. Reports use a more formal style than do many letters and memos
  2. Reports rarely use the word you
  3. Reports should be self-explanatory

- To create good report style,
  1. Say what you mean
  2. Tighten your writing
  3. Use blueprints, transitions, topic sentences, and headings

- **Headings** are single words, short phrases, or complete sentences that cover all of the material under it until the next heading. **Informative** or **talking heads** tell the reader what to expect in each section.

Learning Applications

Questions for Comprehension

23.1 What are the seven basic patterns for organizing information?

23.2 What is a blueprint?

23.3 What is a talking head?

Questions for Critical Thinking

23.4 Why shouldn't you put all the information you have into a report?

23.5 Why do reports often use a more formal style than other business documents?

23.6 Why should you avoid *you* in reports?

23.7 Why are topic sentences especially useful in reports?

Questions for Building Skills

23.8 What skills have you read about in this module?

23.9 What skills are you practising in the assignments you're doing for this module?

23.10 How could you further develop the skills you're working on?

Exercises and Problems

23.11   Explaining "Best Practices"

Write a report describing the "best practices" of a unit or team where you work. Convince your reader that these practices could be adopted by other units in your organization.

23.12   Recommending Action

Write a report recommending an action that your unit or organization should take. Address your report to the person who would have the power to approve your recommendation. Possibilities include

- Hiring an additional worker for your department

- Making your organization more employee-friendly
- Making a change that will make the organization more efficient
- Making changes to improve accessibility for customers or employees with disabilities

23.13   Writing up a Survey

Survey two groups of people on a topic that interests you. Possible groups are men and women, people in business and in English programs, younger and older students, students and townspeople. Non-random samples are acceptable.

As Your Instructor Directs,

a. Survey 40 to 50 people.

b. Team up with your classmates. Survey 50 to 80 people if your group has two members, 75 to 120 people if it has three members, 100 to 150 people if it has four members, and 125 to 200 people if it has five members.

c. Keep a journal during your group meetings and submit it to your instructor.

d. Write a memo to your instructor. (◀▶ Module 19 on working and writing in groups.)

As you conduct your survey, make careful notes about what you do so that you can use this information when you write up your survey. If you work with a group, record who does what. Use a memo format. Your subject line should be clear and reasonably complete. Omit unnecessary words such as "Survey of." Your first paragraph serves as an introduction, but it needs no heading. The rest of the body of your memo could be divided into four sections with the following headings: Purpose, Procedure, Results, and Discussion. Alternatively, make your survey report more interesting by using talking headings.

In your first paragraph, briefly summarize (not necessarily in this order) who conducted the experiment or survey, when it was conducted, where it was conducted, who the subjects were, what your purpose was, and what you found out.

In your **Purpose** section, explain why you conducted the survey. What were you trying to learn? Why did this subject seem interesting or important?

In your **Procedure** section, describe in detail *exactly* what you did.

In your **Results** section, first tell whether your results supported your hypothesis. Use both visuals and words to explain what your numbers show. (◀▶ See Module 25 on how to design visuals.) Process your raw data in a way that will be useful to your reader.

In your **Discussion** section, evaluate your survey and discuss the implications of your results. Consider these questions:

1. Do you think a scientifically valid survey would have produced the same results? Why or why not?

2. Were there any sources of bias either in the way the questions were phrased or in the way the subjects were chosen? If you were running the survey again, what changes would you make to eliminate or reduce these sources of bias?

3. Do you think your subjects answered honestly and completely? What factors may have intruded? Is the fact that you did or didn't know them, or that they were or weren't of the same gender relevant?

4. What causes the phenomenon your results reveal? If several causes together account for the phenomenon, or if it is impossible to be sure of the cause, admit this. Identify possible causes and assess the likelihood of each.

5. What action should the reader take?

The discussion section gives you the opportunity to analyze the significance of your survey. Its insight and originality lift the otherwise well-written memo from the ranks of the merely satisfactory to the ranks of the above average and the excellent.

23.14   Writing a Report Based on Your Knowledge and Experience

Write a report on one of the following topics.

1. What should Canadian managers know about dealing with workers from _____ [you fill in the country or culture]? What factors do and do not motivate people in this group? How do they show respect and deference? Are they used to a strong hierarchy or to an egalitarian setting? Do they normally do one thing at once or many things? How important is clock time and being on time? What factors lead them to respect someone? Age? Experience? Education? Technical knowledge? Wealth? Or what? What conflicts or miscommunications may arise between workers from this culture and other workers due to cultural differences? What cultural norms specific to these workers are similar to English-speaking Canadians? What cultural variation could the organization learn and benefit from?

2. Describe an ethical dilemma encountered by workers in a specific organization. What is the background of the situation? What competing loyalties exist? In the past, how have workers responded? How has the organization responded? Have "whistle-blowers" been rewarded or punished? What could the organization do to foster ethical behaviour?

3. Describe a problem or challenge encountered by an organization where you've worked. Explain why it needed to be solved, who did what to try to solve it, and how successful the efforts were. Possibilities include

- How the organization is implementing work teams, downsizing, or a change in organizational culture

- How the organization uses email or voice mail, statistical process control, or telecommuting

- How managers deal with stress, make ethical choices, or evaluate subordinates

- How the organization is responding to changing Canadian demographics, the Charter of Rights and Freedoms' equality guarantee and employees with disabilities, international competition and opportunities, or challenges from dot.com companies

Polishing Your Prose

Being Concise

Being **concise** in business writing means using only necessary words to make your point, without sacrificing politeness or clarity. Wordy sentences may confuse or slow readers:

Wordy: All of our employees at Haddenfield and Dunne should make themselves available for a seminar meeting on the 5th of August, 2002, at 10 o'clock in the morning. Please make sure you come to the conference room on the 2nd Floor of the Main Complex.

Concise: Please plan to attend a seminar at 10 A.M., August 5, 2002, in the Main Complex 2nd Floor conference room.

Being concise does not mean eliminating necessary information. Sometimes you'll have to write longer sentences to be clear.

Nor does tightening your writing mean using short, choppy sentences.

Choppy: We have a new copier. It is in the supply room. Use it during regular hours. After 5 P.M., it will be shut down.

Concise: A new copier is available in the supply room for use before 5 P.M.

Use Concrete Words.

Instead of vague nouns and verbs with strings of modifiers, use specifics.

Vague: The person who drops off packages talked about the subject of how much to charge.

Concrete: The delivery person discussed fees.

Avoid Vague or Empty Modifiers.

Words like *very*, *some*, *many*, *few*, *much*, *kind of/sort of*, and so forth usually can be cut.

Cut Redundant Words or Phrases.

Don't say the same thing twice. *Cease* and *desist*, *first* and *foremost*, the *newest* and *latest*, *official*

company policy, 24 *stories tall*, *said out loud*, and *return* the form *back* to me are all redundant.

Avoid Unnecessarily Complex Constructions.

Instead of *the bid that won the contract*, use *the winning bid*.

Stick to Simple Verb Tenses.

Standard edited English prefers them. Instead of "I *have been attending* Royal Roads University" use "I *attend* Royal Roads University." Instead of "By 2003, I *will have completed* my degree" use "I *will graduate* by 2003."

Exercises

Rewrite the following sentences to make them concise.

1. It would be in your best interest to return the order form to us as quickly as possible.

2. Our official records show that you are a very responsible person.

3. The automobile that is blue belongs to the woman in charge of legal affairs.

4. The mainframe computer is located in our subterranean basement.

5. Call us on the telephone if you want to confirm your order.

6. We faxed a reproduced copy of the application on the fax machine.

7. Enclosed along with the rest of this job application letter is a list of references that can talk about my job qualifications because I used to work for them.

8. I enjoyed the presentation very much.

9. To begin with, let me start by telling you some stories about our guest of honour.

10. The guy that runs our advertising department yelled loudly across the parking lot that a delivery truck had left its two headlights on.

Check your answers to the odd-numbered exercises on page 634.

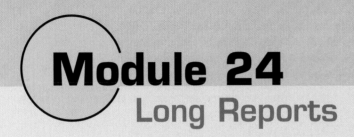

Module 24
Long Reports

Topics

- I've never written a long document. How should I organize my time?

- How do I create each of the parts of a formal report?

Review of Key Points

Learning Applications

Polishing Your Prose: Improving Paragraphs

Learning Focus

After reading and applying the information in Module 24, you'll be able to demonstrate

Knowledge of
- The components of the formal report

Skills to
- Use your time efficiently when you write reports
- Set up the parts of a full formal report
- Continue to create a professional image

"Long reports must be kept simple and crisp..."

"Visual presentation helps readers to navigate a long report," says Paige Cantle of Cantle Communications. "Long reports must be kept simple and crisp. The writer is constantly trying to bring the reader's eye through a great deal of information."

Paige, who has a honours B.A. in English and an M.B.A., owns her own communications company. Before going out on her own she was assistant vice president, communications, for Credit Union Central of Canada, the trade association of Ontario credit unions. She has also worked for Dylex Limited in the corporate communications department.

Paige's small communications firm specializes in "making complex subjects simple." Much of her work comes from her contacts in the credit union field and she specializes in financial reports. She has recently written reports for the federal task force on the Future of the Canadian Financial Services Sector and was a consultant for the London Acute Care Teaching Hospitals' Restructuring Committee. The interim version of this report won an award of excellence from the International Association of Business Communicators.

Paige says that the writer of long reports must "first focus on the main message of the report. Then you have to look at the structure of the report, which answers the question of how you are going to get your message across. And finally, you must focus on who your audience will be."

Many reports are written on behalf of committees who direct a project, lead consultations with stakeholders, and provide the "public face" of a project. A list of their names should be provided in the report, along with a brief biography of each member. A committee will often produce an interim report for the purpose of getting input from the stakeholders on the particular project. Following this consultation, a final report will be issued, with recommendations, which reflect the input received.

Since long reports are often hard to read, Paige says that how the information is presented is important. "Introduce white space," she adds. Paige is influenced by Web designs. In a long report she will often leave large margins on the left side of the page. In these margins she will have subject headings and often logos that depict sections of the report. For example, in a technical section of a report she may use a computer logo. This use of space makes it easier to read and lets the reader find the sections of the report he or she is interested in. Visual cues combat information overload and helps the reader locate and assimilate information quickly.

When asked for advice to report writers, Paige says, "Accept the fact that most people won't read your report in its entirety. Much of your audience will pick and choose from the document, so make sure the executive summary gets your main points across in an engaging and succinct manner. Also make sure your writing style is consistent and that each section can stand on its own."

Site *to* **See**

Go to
http://www.study
web.com/links/1120.
html

This site offers a
compendium of
report-writing
techniques.

Formal reports are distinguished from informal letter and memo reports by their length and by their components. Most organizations produce an annual formal report to summarize its economic performance and forecast the future for its shareholders.

A full formal report *may* contain all of the following components

- Cover
- Letter of Transmittal
- Title Page
- Table of Contents
- List of Illustrations
- Executive Summary
- Report Body
  - Introduction (May include subheadings for Purpose and Scope; may also have Limitations, Assumptions, and Methods.)
  - Background/History of the Problem (Serves as a record for later readers of the report.)
  - Body (Presents and interprets data in words and visuals. Analyzes causes of the problem and evaluates possible solutions. Specific headings will depend on the topic of the report.)
  - Conclusion (Summarizes main points of report.)
- Recommendations (Recommends actions to solve the problem. May be combined with Conclusion; may be put before body rather than at the end.)
- Appendixes (Provide additional materials, which the careful reader may want: transcript of an interview, copies of questionnaires, tallies of all the questions, computer printouts, previous reports.)
- References or Works Cited (Documents sources cited in the report.)

I've never written a long document. How should I organize my time?

Write parts as soon as you can.

Spend most of your time on sections that are important to your proof.

To use your time efficiently, think about the parts of the report before you begin writing. Much of the Introduction comes from your proposal with only minor revisions: Purpose, Scope, Assumptions, and Methods.

The bibliography from your proposal can form the first draft of your References. Save a copy of your questionnaire or interview questions to use as an appendix. As you tally and analyze the data, prepare an appendix summarizing all the responses to your questionnaire, your figures and tables, and a complete list of References.

You can write the title page and the transmittal as soon as you know what your recommendation will be.

After you've analyzed your data, write the Executive Summary, the body, and the Conclusions and Recommendations. Prepare a draft of the table of contents and the list of illustrations.

When you write a long report, list all the sections (headings) that your report will have. Mark those that are most important to your reader and your proof, and spend most of your time on them. Write the important sections early. That way,

One key to writing a good report is to start early and budget your time

Source: PEANUTS reprinted by permission of United Feature Syndicate, Inc.

you won't spend all your time on Background or History of the Problem. Instead, you'll get to the meat of your report.

How do I create each of the parts of a formal report?

Follow the sections laid out below.

As you read each section below, you may want to turn to the corresponding pages of the long report in Figure 24.1, page 493, to see how the component is set up and how it relates to the total report.

Title Page

The Title Page of a report contains four items: the title of the report, whom the report is prepared for, whom it is prepared by, and the release date.

The title of the report should be as informative as possible.

Poor title: New Office Site

Better title: Why St. John's is the Best Site for the New Info.com Office

In many cases, the title will state the recommendation in the report: "Improving Productivity at Cambridge International: Updating Communications Policies". However, the title should omit recommendations when

- The reader will find the recommendations hard to accept
- Putting all the recommendations in the title would make it too long
- The report does not offer recommendations

If the title does not contain the recommendation, it normally indicates what problem the report tries to solve.

Letter or Memo of Transmittal

Use a *memo* of transmittal if you are a regular employee of the organization for which you prepare the report; use a *letter* if you are not. The transmittal has several purposes: to transmit the report, to orient the reader to the report, and to build a good image of the report and of the writer.

Organize the transmittal in this way:

1. Tell when and by whom the report was authorized and the purpose it was to fulfill.
2. Summarize your conclusions and recommendations.
3. Indicate minor problems you encountered in your investigation and show how you surmounted them. Thank people who helped you.
4. Point out additional research that is necessary, if any.
5. Thank the reader for the opportunity to do the work and offer to answer questions. Even if the report has not been fun to do, expressing satisfaction in doing the project is expected.

Table of Contents

In the Table of Contents, list the headings exactly as they appear in the body of the report. If the report is shorter than 25 pages, list all the headings. In a very long report, list the two or three highest levels of headings.

List of Illustrations

Report visuals comprise both tables and figures. **Tables** are words or numbers arranged in rows and columns. **Figures** are everything else: bar graphs, pie charts, maps, drawings, photographs, computer printouts, and so forth. Tables and figures are numbered independently, so you may have both a "Table 1" and a "Figure 1." In a report with maps and graphs but no other visuals, the visuals are sometimes called "Map 1" and "Graph 1." Whatever you call the illustrations, list them in the order in which they appear in the report; give the name of each visual as well as its number.

See ◁▶ Module 25 for information about how to design and label visuals.

Executive Summary

An **Executive Summary** provides an overview of the whole report, including a summary of the recommendations. If your report ends with conclusions, provide the Conclusion section in the Executive Summary. If your report ends with recommendations, put these in the Summary.

> To market life insurance to mid-40s urban professionals, Great North Insurance should advertise in upscale publications and use direct mail.
>
> Network TV and radio are not cost-efficient for reaching this market. This group comprises a small percentage of the prime-time network TV audience and a minority of most radio station listeners. They tend to discard newspapers and general-interest magazines quickly, but many of them keep upscale periodicals for months. Magazines with high percentages of readers in this group include *Architectural Digest*, *Bon Appétit*, *Canadian Home*, *Canadian Garden*, *Golf Digest*, and *Smithsonian*. Most urban professionals in their mid-40s already shop by mail and respond positively to well-conceived and well-executed direct mail appeals.
>
> Any advertising campaign needs to overcome this group's feeling that they already have the insurance they need. One way to do this would be to encourage them to check the coverage their employers provide and to calculate the

Site to See

Go to
http://www.parl.gc.c a/InfoComDoc/36/1/ SINS/Studies/Reports /sinsrp05-e.htm

This site has links to Canadian government organizations and hundreds of their reports.

Instant Replay

Report Titles

Normally, the title of the report should give the recommendation. Omit the recommendations when

- The reader will find the recommendations hard to accept
- Putting all the recommendations in the title would make it too long
- The report does not offer recommendations

If the title does not contain the recommendation, it normally indicates what problem the report tries to solve.

Creating a Professional Image, 3

Even on dress-down or casual Fridays, most organizations still expect employees to take care of business. Attention to detail, organization, accuracy, economy, and courtesy are the norm. According to Max Messruer, chairman of Accountemps and author of the best-selling *Job Hunting For Dummies®* (IDG Books Worldwide), what you wear determines others' perceptions of you, and therefore directly affects your career advancement.

On casual days, wear clothes in good condition that are one or two "notches" below what you'd wear on other days. If suits are the norm, choose blazers and slacks or skirts. If blazers and slacks or skirts are the norm, choose sweaters or knit sport shirts; khakis, simple skirts, or dressier jeans; or simple dresses. Wear good shoes and always be well groomed. Avoid anything that's ill-fitting or revealing.

Other symbols also convey professionalism. Your work area, for instance, says a lot about you. If your organization allows employees to personalize their desks or offices with photographs, knickknacks, and posters, don't display so much that you seem frivolous. And never display offensive photos or slogans, even in an attempt to be funny. One supervisor, known for being strict, put a poster of Adolph Hitler on his door to make light of his reputation. He so offended others that he lost his job. The same caution goes for screen savers and radio stations. It isn't professional to play a morning "shock jock" who uses coarse language and offensive stereotypes.

If your organization allows employees to listen to music, keep the volume at a reasonable level. If your organization allows, consider wearing headphones.

Avoid playing computer games, surfing the Web inappropriately, or ordering personal items on company time.

Keep your voicemail message succinct and professional—find out what co-workers say in theirs.

Keep your desk organized. File papers; keep stacks to a minimum. Throw away anything you don't need. Don't store food in your office. Clean periodically. Water your plants.

The volume of your voice can also disturb others. While most people wouldn't shout across an office, many of us don't realize how loud our voices can be when we're excited or happy. Keep personal conversations to a minimum, in person and on the phone.

Learn the culture of your organization and fit into it as much as you can. When in doubt, follow the lead of someone the organization respects.

---

cost of their children's expenses through college graduation. Insurance plans that provide savings and tax benefits as well as death benefits would also appeal to this target market.

Introduction

The **Introduction** of the report contains a statement of purpose and scope and may include all the parts in the following list:

- **Purpose.** Identify the organizational problem the report addresses, the technical investigations it summarizes, and the rhetorical purpose (to explain, to recommend).

- **Scope.** Identify the topics the report covers. For example, Company XYZ is losing money on its line of radios. Does the report investigate the quality of the radios? The advertising campaign? The cost of manufacturing? The demand for radios? If the report was authorized to examine only advertising, then one cannot fault the report for not considering other factors.
- **Limitations.** Limitations make the recommendations less valid or valid only under certain conditions. Limitations usually arise because time or money constraints haven't permitted full research. For example, a campus pizza restaurant considering expanding its menu may not have enough money to take a random sample of students and townspeople. Without a random sample, the writer cannot generalize from the sample to the larger population. Many recommendations are valid only for a limited time. For example, a store wants to know what kinds of clothing will appeal to college men. The recommendations will remain in force only for a short time: Three years from now, styles and tastes may have changed.
- **Assumptions.** Assumptions are statements whose truth you assume and which you use to support your conclusions and recommendations. If they are wrong, the conclusion will be wrong too. For example, recommendations about what cars appeal to drivers aged 18 to 34 would be based on assumptions both about gas prices and about the economy. If gas prices radically rose or fell, the kinds of cars young adults wanted would change. If there were a major recession, people wouldn't be able to buy new cars.
- **Methods.** Tell how you chose the people for a survey, focus groups, or interviews and how, when, and where they were interviewed. Omit Methods if your report is based solely on library and online research. Instead, simply cite your sources in the text and document them in References or Works Cited. See ◀ ▶ Module 22 on how to cite and document sources.

Background or History

Even though the current audience for the report probably knows the situation, reports are filed and consulted years later. These later audiences will probably not know the background, although it may be crucial for understanding the options that are possible.

In some cases, the History may cover many years. For example, a report recommending that a Québec consortium purchase an Ontario superhighway will probably provide the history of the highway ownership from its construction date, several years before. In other cases, the Background or History is much briefer, covering just the immediate situation.

Conclusion and Recommendations

The **Conclusion** summarizes points proven in the body of the report; **recommendations** identify action items that would solve or partially solve the problem. The way you organize and present the relevant facts in the Body of the report should lead the reader to your conclusions and recommendations.

Be sure to number the recommendations to make them easy to discuss. If your readers will find your recommendations expensive, difficult, or controversial, give a brief rationale paragraph after each recommendation. If your recommendations are easy for the audience to accept, simply list them without comments or reasons. The recommendations will also be in the Executive Summary and perhaps in the title and the transmittal.

Figure 24.1

A Long Report

*You may also design
a letterhead for yourself,
especially if you're assuming
that you are doing the report
as a consultant.*

*This letter uses
block format (see Figure 9.2).
Modified block format is
also acceptable.*

1470 Highland Street
Calgary, AB T2G 5N2
December 10, 2002

Mr. Paul Wutz
Vice President
FFI Health Services
127 Street NorthWest
Edmonton, AB T5M 1H7

Dear Mr. Wutz:

*In paragraph 1, release the report.
Note when and by whom the report
was authorized. Note report's purpose.*

Here is the report you authorized in October exploring the kind of internship
program that might be best for FFI.

FFI Health Services can benefit from establishing an internship program while providing a
valuable service to students. To establish an internship program, you should

*Give
recommendations
or thesis.*

- Use the guidelines suggested by Athabasca University's Professional Experience
  Program.
- Pilot the program, focussing on finance and computer science majors the first
  summer.
- Set intern salaries at $9–$10 an hour for all majors except computer science.
  Start computer science majors at at least $15 an hour.
- Survey your staff to find out which employees would like to supervise and
  mentor interns.
- Publicize the program on the Web as well as in Athabasca's Career Services
  Centre. Conduct further research on the best way to reach computer science majors.
- Conduct further research to identify other colleges and universities that would also
  be good sources of interns.

*Thank
people
who
helped
you.*

The information for this report came from online and print sources, a survey of 150
Athabasca University's students, and an interview with Mindy Kannard of Career Services at
The Athabasca Faculty of Business. I especially appreciate the guidance of Ms. Kannard and
others involved in the Professional Experience Program.

Thank the reader for the opportunity to do the research.

Thank you for the opportunity to conduct this research. I appreciate the chance to apply my
experience helping to run an internship program last summer. If you have any questions
about the material in this report, please call me at 403-677-2443.

Sincerely,

*Offer to answer questions about the report.
Answers would be included in your fee—no extra charge!*

Natalie Rogal

Natalie Rogal

Figure 24.1
A Long Report (continued)

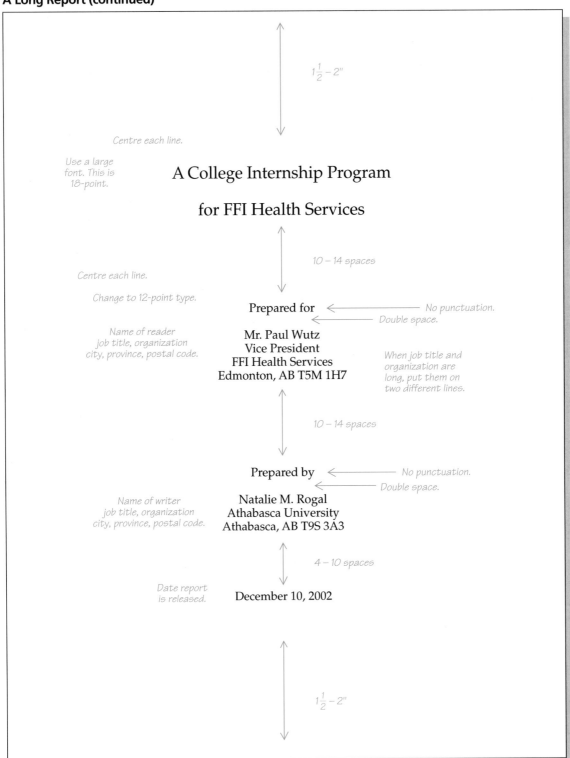

Centre each line.

Use a large font. This is 18-point.

A College Internship Program

for FFI Health Services

10 – 14 spaces

$1\frac{1}{2} - 2''$

Centre each line.

Change to 12-point type.

Prepared for   ⟵   *No punctuation.*
                      Double space.

Name of reader job title, organization city, province, postal code.

Mr. Paul Wutz
Vice President
FFI Health Services
Edmonton, AB T5M 1H7

When job title and organization are long, put them on two different lines.

10 – 14 spaces

Prepared by   ⟵   *No punctuation.*
                      Double space.

Name of writer job title, organization city, province, postal code.

Natalie M. Rogal
Athabasca University
Athabasca, AB T9S 3A3

4 – 10 spaces

Date report is released.   December 10, 2002

$1\frac{1}{2} - 2''$

Figure 24.1
A Long Report (continued)

Table of Contents does not list itself.

Use lower-case Roman numerals for front matter.

Intro begins on page "1".

Indent subheads.

Capitalize first letter of each major word in headings.

Some reports have separate sections for "Conclusions" and "Recommendations".

Headings or subheadings must be parallel within a section. Here, headings are nouns and noun (gerund) phrases. Questions and complete sentences can also be used.

Add a "List of Illustrations" at the bottom of the Table of Contents or on a separate page if the report has graphs and other visuals. Omit "List of Illustrations" if you have only tables.

Line up right margin (justify).

Figure 24.1

A Long Report (continued)

**A College Internship Program
for FFI Health Services**

*Report
title.*

Executive Summary

Start with recommendations or thesis.

FFI Health Services should create a college internship program following the model outlined in Athabasca University's Professional Experience Program. Following this program will cover the basics of a sound internship program and will enable FFI to hire interns at Athabasca University.

*Provide
brief
support
for each
recom-
mendation*

FFI can eventually offer internships in eight areas: accounting, computer science, finance, human resources, marketing, social services, transportation logistics, and Web maintenance. FFI does work in each of these areas and could benefit both from the projects that interns might complete and from the opportunity to make permanent hires in these areas. In its first year, however, the internship program should focus on two or three main areas of employment to pilot the program. Finance and computer science are FFI's areas of greatest need.

Since the best students have several options, FFI should offer interns a competitive wage. The average intern earned between $8 and $9 last summer, so FFI Health Services should set intern pay at $9–$10 an hour for all majors except computer science. To hire the best computer science majors will require starting salaries of at least $15 an hour. Providing housing would make the internships more attractive and would enlarge the pool of applicants.

At least two fulltime FFI employees should supervise the interns, even during the first summer when there may be only two or three interns. FFI will need to conduct internal research to determine how potential supervisors and mentors feel about working closely with interns. Acting as a mentor should be a voluntary position to ensure active and enthusiastic guidance for the intern.

Participating in the Professional Experience Program will mean that FFI's job descriptions will be available to students who come to the Fisher College of Business Career Services Centre looking for internships. However, other kinds of publicity are also desirable so that FFI can have the widest pool of applicants from which to choose. Announcing the internships on FFI's Web site is an obvious step and would bring up FFI's internships when students do Web searches for "internships." Many other companies already give information about internships on Web sites. If computer majors remain in such high demand, FFI will need to do something special to attract them. Further research will be needed to determine what kind of niche FFI can develop.

FFI may want to recruit at other post secondary institutions. More research needs to be done to determine the optimal places for FFI Health Services to recruit student interns. Since students may not be able to relocate for the summer or may only move if given a substantial pay incentive, recruiting at other Alberta universities may make sense. In addition, it would be useful to identify any colleges that offer majors in managed care. Such colleges would be a good source of students who would be interested in the kind of work FFI does.

*Language in Executive Summary
can come from report. Make sure
any repeated language is well-
written!*

*The Executive Summary
contains the logical skeleton of
the report: the recommendation(s)
and evidence supporting them.*

Figure 24.1
A Long Report (continued)

Here, the running head and page numbers are one point size smaller than the text used for the body of the report.

Start with introduction.

Introduction

Centre first-level heads. This author uses bold (one point larger than body).

Many companies use internship programs to recruit and "try out" students who will eventually become permanent employees. Internships are so popular that they have increased 37% in the last five years (Ferguson, 1998). FFI Health Services is interested in creating an internship program that will attract quality applicants.

Purpose

Rhetorical purpose

The purpose of this report is to recommend a post-secondary internship program that will meet FFI's needs.

Scope

Tell what you discuss and how thoroughly you discuss each topic. Scope section should match report. This section has changed a bit from the proposal because of the available information.

In this report, I will focus on three topics: models of internships, Athabasca students' internship needs, and the kinds of internship experiences FFI Health Services can offer. My information about models for internships comes largely from The Fisher College of Business' Professional Experience Program (PEP). PEP suggests activities for interns and outlines the features for an internship program. I also use anecdotal evidence about common internship problems and how FFI can avoid them.

The report discusses what Athabasca students want from the internship experience based on a survey of 150 students. I discuss how students view internships, what students want from a summer experience, and their willingness to accept internships at FFI. Finally, based on interviews with staff members, especially Paul Wutz, I discuss the kinds of internship experiences FFI can offer.

Give topics in the order in which you'll discuss them.

The report also briefly presents the general advantages of internships and describes how the internship program could be publicized.

List relevant topics that you will not discuss.

The report does not discuss the financial feasibility of the program or the schools the company should focus its recruiting efforts.

Assumptions

Assumptions cannot be proven. But if they are wrong, the report's recommendation may no longer be valid.

My recommendations are based on three assumptions:

These ideas could be presented in a paragraph. But the list provides visual variety and makes it easier for the reader to skim the page.

- The job market will remain tight, making it difficult to find qualified applicants. The tight job market makes an internship program especially desirable. If the job market changed so that there were many more applicants than jobs, FFI might be able to hire managers more easily without needed to "grow" its own managers.

- FFI's central office will remain in Edmonton, making it desirable to recruit students from the universities of Edmonton, Calgary, and Lethbridge, as well as Athabasca. If the central office moved, students from other universities might be more desirable than Alberta students as interns.

- Athabasca students' preferences regarding internships are typical of students at other universities.

Figure 24.1
A Long Report (continued)

*If you use only library and online sources, you do not need a
"Methodology" section. Instead, briefly describe your sources in
a paragraph under "Purpose."*

A College Internship Program for FFI Health Services   Page 2

Even if it focusses on Athabasca's students, FFI will hire interns from other universities as well and should
investigate preferences at other universities.

Methodology   *If you collected original data (surveys, interviews, or observations),
tell how you chose whom to study, what kind of a sample you used,
and on what date(s) you collected the information.*

Information for this report comes from print and online sources, interviews, and a survey of 150 Athabasca
University students. I was unable to take a random sample of business students because the Faculty of Business
does not make available a directory of its students. Thus it was necessary for me to use a convenience sample. I
chose to survey students on November 20, 2002, at the Student Union during a Career Fair. To get the desired
number in the sample I asked every student who walked by if he or she had a few minutes to fill out a survey.

Summarize the demographic information about your respondents.

The students who responded represent a wide variety of majors and interests. Two-thirds of the students in my
sample were juniors and seniors; 32% had an internship last summer. (See Appendix A for all of the raw data
from the survey.)   *Refer to your Appendixes in
the text of your report.*

Limitations   *If your report has limitations, state them.
Giving the number makes it easier for the reader to read the paragraph.*

My research has four limitations. First, I surveyed students only at Athabasca University, and FFI will probably
want to recruit from other universities as well. Second, at Athabasca, FFI is probably most interested in interns
from the Colleges of Business and of Engineering, where Computer Science is housed. Yet my sample covers a
wide variety of colleges and has no Engineering students at all. Third, the fact that my survey is based on a convenience sample means that we cannot generalize from my survey to all post-secondary students. Indeed,
respondents' demographics show that the students I surveyed are not representative. The College of Social and
Behavioural Sciences has the most undergraduate majors at Athabasca, yet it is not the College with the most
students in my sample. Fourth, my survey may have interviewer error, which results from the interviewer
answering questions differently for different people. Some respondents asked for clarification on some questions while others did not. I tried to answer consistently but my wording was open to interpretation and may
have affected the responses. This source of error probably did not significantly affect the accuracy.

Criteria   *Triple-space (2 empty spaces) before
new head. Double-space after
head before paragraph.*

According to Paul Wutz, the two most important criteria for an internship program are that (1) supervising
interns take as little time as possible and (2) the program yield permanent promotable workers. A less important criterion is that interns be able to complete some of the projects that full-time FFI personnel have not had
time to do.

Background on FFI Health Services

FFI Health Services contracts with companies to manage prescription benefits. FFI enables employers to give
employees prescription coverage at a very reasonable price. Employees can order deeply discounted prescription drugs on FFI's Web site.

Figure 24.1

A Long Report (continued)

A College Internship Program for FFI Health Services   Page 3

The company is five years old and started with two employees. FFI Health Services has experienced explosive growth. It now employs 50 people in two offices, one in Edmonton, Alberta, and the other in Surrey, British Columbia. Hiring qualified personnel is a challenge. Current hiring procedures include running classified advertisements or conducting nationwide searches depending on the type of position to be filled. Some specialized positions such as computer programmers are in such high demand that FFI Health Services does not always feel it is getting the best candidates.

Use talking heads. Note how much more informative this is than "Advantages".

General Benefits of College Internship Programs

Begin most paragraphs with topic sentences.

Businesses benefit enormously from hiring interns. Students are good, productive employees who are positively inclined toward work that is related to their career interests. They can serve as temporary staff or provide assistance for ongoing or special projects. Hiring interns also increases access for hiring women and minorities. Students cost less to hire than regular permanent employees and improve morale in the workplace. Furthermore, student employees bring new ideas and technology to the work site (Athabasca, 1998).

Other benefits include recruiting opportunities. When interns become fulltime employees, they need less training and orientation into the company. "Research shows that the turnover rate of employees who have had co-op/internship experience with the organization is significantly less than that for those who did not have this type of job-related opportunity" (Athabasca, 1998, "Criteria and Guidelines").

APA format calls for page numbers when you quote a source. This Web source doesn't have page numbers, but the student gives the subpage from which the quote was taken.

A Model Internship Program

When starting a new internship program, a company can benefit by following a model. The Director of the Professional Experience Program (PEP) at Athabasca works with employers to design internships that benefit both the company and the student. The PEP Employer Handbook offers extensive, specific guidelines for employers. In addition, several articles suggest general guidelines for successful internships.

Spell out term the first time you use it, with the abbreviation in parentheses. Then you can use the abbreviation by itself.

Intern Duties

When author's name is in the sentence, use only year and page number in parentheses.

Appropriate job duties are at the heart of a successful internship program. Admitting that gofer and grunt work are "ubiquitous" in internships, Martha Stone argues that the best internships provide "planned, hands-on" tasks in the field of the student's major (1998, p. 8). Some companies ask interns to do small projects that no one in the organization has time for, but that the organization wants to have done.

Another option is to give interns the same kinds of jobs that entry-level employees would have. Allegiance Healthcare (Watson, 1998), Micron Technology (King, 1997), and Aetna are three of the many companies that take this approach. Aetna's actuarial interns analyze data, improve processes, and "mak[e] things happen" (1999, "Qualifications and Rewards"). One intern reports,

Use square brackets for your changes in quoted text.

Quote when the source is especially credible for the point you want to make.

As an Aetna actuarial intern, I worked closely with the other actuaries in my area. I helped to develop a reserving system and price a new contract. I began contributing to the area on my first day, which really surprised me. I worked side-by-side with the other actuaries in the area, as well as the other non-financial areas. What I did really made a difference. My technical, communication, and analytical skills were appreciated and demanded. (1999, "On the Job with Aetna Actuarial Interns")

This quote comes from the Web and has no page number. Title of subpage makes it easy for reader to find page on which quote appears.

Figure 24.1
A Long Report (continued)

A College Internship Program for FFI Health Services

Page 4

The Professional Experience Program requires that the employer submit a one-page job description. Examples of job duties in past internships include the following:

Accounting
- Perform inventory costing and cost accounting
- Prepare monthly and year-end close-outs
- Prepare and produce financial statements for reports
- Implement and audit programs to verify accuracy
- Coordinate procurement and transmittal records for audit
- Use Excel, Lotus 1-2-3 and other business software

Periods could be used to end each line. But because this is part of a quote, give text exactly as it appears in the source.

Finance
- Prepare program management cost estimates for projects
- Perform Capital Investment Analysis—analyze the Net Present Value and Internal Rate of Return
- Gather financial and accounting data for financial planning and analysis purposes
- Prepare Cost of Capital Estimates
- Prepare Monthly Cash Budgets

This line could be tightened—"Analyze Capital Investments." But because this is part of a quote, give it exactly as in the source. If you make changes, put them in square brackets [ ].

Human Resources
- Train employees on writing and supervisory skills
- Redesign clerical salary structures
- Evaluate and track recruiting efforts
- Develop a guide for cooperative education
- Assist with targeted selection recruiting plan
- Conduct grievance and disciplinary interviews (Ohio State, 1998, "Job Descriptions")

Other duties are also possible. For example, the Professional Experience Program guidelines suggest that employers may want to ask interns to present their projects to other managers or to employees within the department, both to inform other employees and to enhance students' communication skills.

As these job descriptions suggest, interns can be assigned the same work that might be given to entry-level employees. One question that a company might have is whether interns who have not yet graduated can really do the work normally assigned to graduates. Anecdotal evidence suggests that they can. According to Mindy Kannard, Director of Athabasca's Professional Experience Program, "We have very few problems" (personal communication, November 1, 2001). Testimonials from companies that have hired interns are even more positive. According to Heidi A. Willis, Internship Coordinator

When the source is in the paragraph, the parentheses come before the period at the end of the sentence.

Long quotations are indented; no quotation marks necessary.

Implementing a successful internship program was effortless with the help of the Career Services staff. Students from the Faculty of Business selected to join our internship team have an elevated level of maturity, a hearty appetite for success, and an active desire to convert learned theories into working ideas. ("Testimonials")

Note that the source parenthesis goes after the period at the end of the sentence in indented quotes.

Program Features

Employers who work with Athabasca's Professional Experience Program must supervise and evaluate interns. Setting appropriate salaries is also important.

Figure 24.1
A Long Report (continued)

Indent third-level headings to make them distinct

Third-level headings have periods even when they are not complete sentences.

Quote when you can't think of any better words than those in the source.

Supervising Interns. Interns must receive supervision that is "on-going, consistent and positive" (Athabasca, 1998, "Criteria & Guidelines." At the beginning of the assignment, orientation should include identifying the "key players," the chain of command, office policy (for example, time sheets, overtime, and sick leave), and the corporate culture (including appropriate dress). Ideally, the supervisor or someone else should mentor the intern, not merely give an assignment and disappear. Students benefit from learning not only what is needed, but also why it's needed—how it fits into the larger picture of the company's goals. Identifying specific learning goals can help interns budget their time and also makes evaluation easier.

Mr. Wutz has assumed that since FFI does not have a Human Resources department, he would have to do all the work of supervising and evaluating interns. However, this work could be done by people in the areas in which the interns are working. Because the mentor provides guidance and acts as a "go-to" person for addressing concerns and questions, a mentor working in the same area as the student is ideal. It is important that each student be matched with an enthusiastic mentor who will take an active role in guiding the student's development and providing career advice.

Evaluating Interns. Interns should be evaluated midway through the work period and again at the end. The evaluation should be based on specific goals established earlier. Areas for evaluation might include quality of work, enthusiasm toward assignments, comprehension and knowledge, organizational skills, and judgment. Objectives set forth at the onset of the internship should be reiterated at the interim evaluation and discussed again before the student returns to school. The supervisor should discuss the evaluation with the student and provide constructive criticism and encouragement.

The Professional Experience Program provides a sample form which the employer can use (www.cob.athabascau.edu/careers/pep/EmpEvual.htm). Employers can also use another evaluation instrument but must turn in some form of written evaluation to the Faculty of Business Career Services Centre.

Setting Salary. The Professional Experience Program at Athabasca gives useful suggestions for setting interns' salaries. While the initial salary should be high enough to attract quality applicants, it should be low enough so that wages can be raised commensurate with increased responsibilities developed should the student be hired again for another internship or hired as a permanent employee.

Second-level heads are flush with the left margin and bolded. Triple-space before new head; double-space after.

Common Problems

Some of the possible problems, such as not giving interns substantive work assignments, can be prevented by following the guidelines for the Professional Experience Program. Professor Dawn Kalmuth, who teaches a class for interns, reports that most interns experience situations in which they feel uncertain. Discussions among interns are helpful in understanding situations, brainstorming alternatives, and developing strategies for implementing the preferred alternative. Some interns find that their supervisors are not in fact very knowledgeable and that they need to seek information from more active (but busier) people. Some interns have been given huge assignments which require massive overtime. Other interns are asked to pick up a project started by a former intern without adequate documentation about what has been done and why. Still other interns experience problems that might be encountered by fulltime employees, including sexual harassment (Dawn Kalmuth, personal communication, November 12, 2002). Telling the intern about company channels for dealing with problems and good communication between the intern and his or her mentor or supervisor is essential.

APA format for phone calls, conversations and other sources which the reader cannot check.

Figure 24.1

A Long Report (continued)

*Heading must cover everything under that
heading until the next head or
subhead at that level.*

Making Internships Attractive to Athabasca Students

Few of the people I surveyed—only 15%—had heard of FFI Managed Care. Companies with strong internship programs are "overwhelmed with applications" ("Internships," 1997, p. 102), but it will be a while before FFI commands that kind of interest. To get off to a good start, FFI's internship program should be attractive to Athabasca's students.

*When an article has no author,
use the first word of the title to
identify it.*

Providing Good Experience

In terms of accepting a specific internship, the students I surveyed ranked experience as most important, as Table 1 shows.

Refer to Tables in your text.

Table 1. How Important Are Various Criteria in Accepting a Specific Internship?

Rank	Criterion	Average; N = 150 (3 = Very impt., 2 = Somewhat impt., 1 = Not impt.)
1	Gaining experience	2.99
2	Quality of mentoring	2.92
3	Building connections	2.73
4	Chance of getting a job with that company	2.57
5	Prestige of company	2.43
6	Location where you live now	2.36
7	Money	2.22

*Compare Table 1 with
the raw data for Question 10
in Appendix A (p. 11 of report).
Here, the items have been
re-arranged to go from the
highest to the lowest score.*

This emphasis on gaining experience is consistent with the reports of people who had internships last summer. The top four benefits of their internships, according to the people who had them last summer, were "looks good on my résumé, work related to my major, chance to explore my interests," and "made connections." (See Table 2.) If FFI provides internships that give students experience related to their majors, it can attract interns even though it is not yet well known.

Table 2. What Were the Most Beneficial Aspects of Your Internship?

Rank	Aspect	N = 48 n	%
1	Looks good on my résumé	42	86%
2	Work related to my major	41	85%
3	Chance to explore my interests	35	73%
4	Made connections	34	71%
5	Worked with clients	22	46%
6	Likely to get a job offer/got a job offer	15	31%

*"N" is the total number of
people responding to the
question; "n" is the number
of people giving a particular
response. Giving percentages
makes it easier for readers
to understand data.*

Surprisingly, as Table 1 shows, "chance of getting a job with that company" ranked only fourth out of seven criteria. Fewer than a third of the students who had internships got or expected to get a job offer from that company (Table 2). This emphasis on experience rather than employment will work to FFI's benefit. Only 13% of the students I surveyed were "very interested" in a career in managed care, with a full 47% "not interested." But since students do not necessarily expect to work permanently at the site of their internships, they probably will be

*Quote to give the exact wording of survey questions, so reader can
interpret data accurately.*

Figure 24.1
A Long Report (continued)

A College Internship Program for FFI Health Services   Page 7

willing to accept any internship that gives them good experience. Then, a good internship experience can convince students that FFI is a good employer.

Part of providing good experience is assigning students to a good mentor. Some companies assign interns to otherwise unproductive people (Dawn Kalmuth, personal communication, November 12, 2002). However, this is a mistake. FFI should assign its most effective people as mentors, so that students have the best internship experience possible.

FFI's greatest needs are computer personnel, including a Web weaver, and finance personnel (Paul Wutz, personal communication, November 18, 2002). The company also could offer internships in accounting, fulfillment, human resources, marketing, and transportation logistics. Each of these areas could offer solid experience to college students while meeting FFI's needs.

Providing Competitive Pay

Begin most paragraphs with topic sentences. Numbering your points helps the reader.

My survey indicates three points in regards to pay. First, students who did not have internships last summer made an average of $7.67 per hour. The average wage for students with internships was $8.20. The highest-paid interns seem to be those majoring in Management Information Sciences (MIS): One respondent reported that computer science interns received $2,500 a month plus a bonus. Second, the survey demonstrates that only 20% of the respondents could afford to take an unpaid internship next summer. However, 49% could afford to take an internship paying only the minimum wage next summer. Third, while money is the least important of the seven criteria in choosing whether to accept a specific internship, it is at least "somewhat important" to most students. Therefore, FFI should offer competitive wages to attract the best students.

Here published, online, and survey data are combined.

Some internship programs provide more than just an hourly wage. Micron Technology provides corporate housing (King, 1997). Aetna provides not only housing but also round-trip travel to and from its corporate headquarters (Aetna, 1999). Only 15% of the students I surveyed said they could definitely take a job in Edmonton next summer. These may well be students who live in Calgary. Providing housing and round-trip transportation could win over many of the students who say they "could not" take a job in Edmonton.

Vary paragraph lengths to provide good visual impact.

Finding a Niche for FFI Internships

Don't need author's name in parentheses if name is used in the sentence.

Simply announcing the internships may not be enough to get high-demand students such as MIS majors. If FFI develops an image or "niche" it will stand a better chance of attracting the strongest students. Natalie Engler (1998) shows the lengths to which some companies go. Sapient Corporation conducts "Super Saturdays" eight times a year. These team-based exercises are designed not only to test students' skills but, more important, to develop a good impression of Sapient. In one exercise, teams of six were asked to design and build a gift made out of Legos for a book-writing marine biologist. Sapient has used these Super Saturdays to attract employees. The company has added 300 people in the last year and has a very low rate of turnover.

Not every idea needs a source. Use your knowledge of people and of business.

Vary sentence length and sentence structure.

What sets Allegiance Healthcare's internships apart is its on-campus "virtual internship" program. Allegiance installed workstations on campus which students used to complete Allegiance projects throughout the school year (Watson, 1998). Thus Allegiance's location was immaterial; students did not need to relocate. An added benefit to Allegiance was that the interns' work could continue year-round.

Since most students don't know about FFI and don't come to the hiring process interested in managed care, it would be useful for FFI to develop some "gimmick" that could set it apart in students' minds.

Figure 24.1

A Long Report (continued)

Conclusions repeat points made in the report.
Recommendations are actions the readers should take.

12 pt. **Conclusions and Recommendations**

11 pt. I recommend that FFI Health Services establish an internship program following the model outlined in the Professional Experience Program. Following this program will cover the basics of a sound internship program and will enable FFI to hire interns at Athabasca University. Decisions to be made include choosing which posi- *List in* tions to offer interns, deciding how much to pay them, identifying supervisors and mentors within each *the order* department, and determining how to publicize the program and at which colleges to recruit. *in which you'll discuss them.*

Some companies ask for Conclusions and
1. Choosing Positions for Interns   *Recommendations at the beginning of reports.*

FFI should eventually offer internships in eight areas: accounting, computer science, finance, human resources, marketing, social services, transportation logistics, and Web maintenance. FFI does work in each of these areas and could benefit both from the projects that interns might complete and from the opportunity to make permanent hires in these areas.

In its first year I recommend that the internship program focus on two or three main areas of employment. For instance, hiring only finance and computer science majors will give FFI Health Services the opportunity to pilot the program. This strategy will help to ensure that each intern gets the necessary attention and career-related experience. Also, FFI Health Services can detect and correct any flaws in the initial program.

2. Setting Intern Salaries

My survey indicates that only 20% of students could afford to take an unpaid internship, and 51% would not be able to work for minimum wage. Since the best students have several options, FFI should offer interns a competitive wage. Because the average intern earned between $8 and $9 last summer, I recommend that FFI Health Services set intern pay at $9–$10 an hour for all majors except computer science. To hire the best computer science majors will require starting salaries of at least $15 an hour. Providing housing would make the internships more attractive and would enlarge the pool of applicants.

Numbering the issues makes it easy
3. Choosing Supervisors and Mentors   *for readers to discuss them.*

One person should not attempt to supervise all of the interns, even during the first summer when there may be only two or three interns. I suggest conducting internal research to determine how potential supervisors and mentors feel about working closely with interns. Acting as a mentor should be a voluntary position to ensure active and enthusiastic guidance for the intern. Supervisors should be made familiar with assignment and evaluation procedures and should feel comfortable with their role in the internship program. Willing and dedicated supervisors and mentors will make for a more effective program.

4. Publicizing the Program

Participating in the Professional Experience Program will mean that FFI's job descriptions will be available to students who come to the Faculty of Business Career Services Centre looking for internships. However, other kinds of publicity are also desirable so that FFI can have the widest pool of applicants from which to choose.

Figure 24.1
A Long Report (continued)

Announcing the internships on FFI's Web site is an obvious step and would bring up FFI's internships when students do Web searches for "internships." Many other companies already give information about internships on Web sites. If computer majors remain in such high demand, FFI will need to do something special to attract them. Further research will be needed to determine what kind of niche FFI can develop.

5. Recruiting Interns

While my research focuses on Athabasca students, FFI may want to recruit at other schools. More research needs to be done to determine the optimal places for FFI Health Services to recruit student interns. Since students may not be able to relocate for the summer or may only move if given a substantial pay incentive, recruiting at colleges in Alberta and in British Columbia may make sense. In addition, it would be useful to identify any post-secondary institutions that offer majors in managed care. Such universities and colleges would be a good source of students who would be interested in the kind of work FFI does.

Because many readers turn to the "Recommendations" first, provide a brief rationale for each. The ideas in this section must be logical extensions of the points made and supported in the body of the report.

Figure 24.1
A Long Report (continued)

Tell how many people responded.

Appendix A: Raw Survey Data

N = 150. Percentages sometimes total more than 100% due to rounding.

1. Major (Grouped by College)
   Agriculture *Also give* 7 (5%)
   Arts *percentages.* 11 (7%)
   Business 35 (23%)
   Human Ecology 15 (10%)
   Humanities 41 (27%)
   Math & Physical Sciences 23 (15%)
   Social & Behav. Sciences 18 (12%)

2. Rank: First-Year   15 (10%)
           Second-Year   34 (23%)
           Third-Year   47 (31%)
           Fourth-Year   54 (36%)

3. How important is it to you to have one
   or more internships before you
   graduate?
   80 (53%) Very important
   57 (38%) Somewhat important
   14 (9%) Not important

4. Did you have an internship last summer?
   48 (32%) Yes
   103 (68%) No (skip to Question 6)

5. What were the most beneficial aspects of
   your internship? (Check all that apply.)
   41 (85%) Work related to my major
   15 (31%) Likely to get a job offer/
            got a job offer
   35 (73%) Chance to explore my interests
   34 (71%) Made connections
   22 (46%) Worked with clients
   42 (86%) Looks good on my résumé

6. How much money did you make last
   summer? (Approximate hourly rate,
   before taxes)
   Intern: average $8.20/hr
   Non-intern: average $7.67/hr

   ☐ Check here if you did not make any
   money last summer.
   3 interns; 9 non-interns

7. For next summer, could you afford to
   take an unpaid internship?
   30 (20%) Yes   120 (80%) No

8. For next summer, could you afford to
   take an internship paying only the
   minimum wage?
   73 (49%) Yes   76 (51%) No

10. How important is each of the following
    criteria in choosing whether to accept a
    specific internship?

	Very impt. (3)	Some impt. (2)	Not impt. (1)
		Average	
a. Money		2.22	
b. Prestige of company		2.43	
c. Location near where you live now		2.36	
d. Quality of mentoring		2.92	
e. Building connections		2.73	
f. Chance of getting a job with that company		2.57	
g. Gaining experience		2.99	

11. How interested are you in a career in
    managed care?
    19 (13%) Very interested
    63 (42%) Somewhat interested
    71 (47%) Not interested

12. Could you take a job in Alberta next
    summer?
    22 (15%) Definitely
    70 (47%) Maybe
    58 (39%) No

13. Have you heard of FFI Managed
    Care?
    23 (15%) Yes
    122 (81%) No

Include a copy of your survey with the raw data. Here, the format is changed a bit to make room for the data.

Figure 24.1

A Long Report (continued)

Appendix B: Responses to Open-Ended Question

"Whether or not I could take an unpaid internship or one paying minimum wage would depend on the type of internship and how relevant the experience would be."

"I wish internships would pay."

"I might sacrifice money for one summer if the internship was worth it in terms of gaining experience."

"Just as long as it dealt with my career field, I would be interested in taking an internship."

"It was told to me that internships are as important as some classes. Yet students who work themselves through college cannot afford some of these do to pay. Companies need to start making it worth the while for the working student."

Give responses verbatim, errors and all!

"Another important factor in deciding whether or not to accept a specific internship would be how enjoyable and comfortable the atmosphere is."

"I'll only work where it is warm!"

"Everyone should intern at least one quarter."

"I feel internships are *extremely* important!"

"MIS majors can make $33,000 or $2,500 + bonus a month for internships."

"Philosophy students don't do internships, too much like work."

"I think internships are very important."

"Internships give you a taste for what your career will be like and what it's like to work in the 'real world.'"

Provide the text of survey comments so readers get a sense of the flavour of responses.

Figure 24.1

A Long Report (concluded)

A College Internship Program for FFI Health Services   Page 12

Treat short Web pages like journal articles.   **References**   *APA Format*

Aetna. (1999). Actuarial internships. Retrieved November 4, 2000 from the World Wide Web: http://www.aetna.com/working/interns.htm

When you use two sets of pages that are part of one Web site, combine them in a single entry.

Engler, N. (1998, March 23). We want you! (Please?!?) *Computerworld*, pp. 72–73.

Ferguson, L. H. (1998, April). Guidelines for a safety internship program in industry. *Professional Safety*, *43*(no. 4), 22–25.

Give the page number(s) without "p." when you give the volume and issue number.

Internships identify promising future employees among college students. (1997, April). *HRMagazine*, *42*(4), 102. *Start with the title of the article when no author is given.*

King, J. (1997, February 17). Companies use interns as hiring pool. *Computerworld*, pp. 63, 65.

Use "pp." when you don't have volume and issue number.

Fisher College of Business. (1998). *The professional experience program: Employer handbook*. Retrieved November 4, 2000 from the World Wide Web: http://www.cob.ohio-state.edu/careers/pep/

Stone, M. L. (1998, June). How to offer successful internships. *Advertising Age's Business Marketing*, p. 8.

Watson, S. (1998, September 21). Changing perceptions. *Computerworld*, pp. C2–C4.

Month or date of issue goes after year.   *Underline titles of magazines, journals, and books if you don't have italics.*

List all the printed and online sources cited in your report. Do not list sources you used for background but did not cite. Do not list interviews, phone calls, or other information to which the reader has no access.

Employability Skills 2000+ Checklist for Long Reports Communicate

In this module, the key skills from The Conference Board of Canada's Employability Skills 2000+ are:

Communicate

✔ write and speak so others pay attention and understand
✔ use relevant scientific, technological, and mathematical knowledge and skills to explain or clarify ideas

Manage Information

✔ locate, gather, and organize information using appropriate technology and information systems

Think & Solve Problems

✔ assess situations and identify problems
✔ recognize the human, interpersonal, technical, scientific, and mathematical dimensions of a problem
✔ identify the root cause of a problem
✔ be creative and innovative in exploring possible solutions
✔ readily use science, technology, and mathematics as ways to think, gain and share knowledge, solve problems and make decisions
✔ evaluate solutions to make recommendations or decisions

Participate in Projects & Tasks

✔ plan, design, or carry out a project or task from start to finish with well-defined objectives and outcomes
✔ work to agreed quality standards and specifications
✔ adapt to changing requirements and information

Review of Key Points

- The Title Page of a report contains the title of the report, for whom the report is prepared, by whom the report is prepared, and the release date.
- The title of a report should contain the recommendation unless
  - The reader will find the recommendations hard to accept

- Putting all the recommendations in the title would make it too long
- The report does not offer recommendations
- If the report is shorter than 25 pages, list all the headings in the Table of Contents. In a long report, pick a level and put all the headings at that level and above in the Contents.

- Organize the transmittal in this way:
  1. Release the report.
  2. Summarize your conclusions and recommendations.
  3. Mention any points of special interest. Indicate minor problems you encountered in your investigation and show how you surmounted them. Thank people who helped you.
  4. Point out additional research that is necessary, if any.
  5. Thank the reader for the opportunity to do the work and offer to answer questions.
- The **Introduction** of the report contains a statement of Purpose and Scope. The **Purpose** statement identifies the organizational problem the report addresses,

the technical investigations it summarizes, and the rhetorical purpose (to explain, to recommend). The **Scope** statement identifies the topics the report covers. The Introduction may also include **Limitations**, problems or factors that limit the validity of the recommendations; **Assumptions**, statements whose truth you assume, and which you use to prove your final point; and **Methods**, an explanation of how you gathered your data.

- A **Background** or **History** section is included because reports are filed and may be consulted years later.
- The **Conclusion** summarizes points made in the body of the report; **Recommendations** are action items that would solve or partially solve the problem.

Learning Applications

Questions for Comprehension

24.1 What parts of the report come from the proposal, with some revision?

24.2 How do you decide whether to write a letter or memo of transmittal?

24.3 How should you organize a transmittal?

24.4 What goes in the Executive Summary?

Questions for Critical Thinking

24.5 How do you decide what headings to use in the body of the report?

24.6 How do you decide how much background information to provide in a report?

24.7 How much evidence do you need to provide for each recommendation you make?

Questions for Building Skills

24.8 What skills have you read about in this module?

24.9 What skills are you practising in the assignments you're doing for this module?

24.10 How could you further develop the skills you're working on?

Exercises and Problems

As Your Instructor Directs,

Turn in the following documents for Problems 24.11 through 24.13:

a. The approved proposal

b. Two copies of the report, including

   Cover

   Letter or Memo of Transmittal

   Title Page

   Table of Contents

List of Illustrations

Executive Summary

Body (Introduction, all information, recommendations). Your instructor may specify a minimum length, a minimum number or kind of sources, and a minimum number of visuals.

Appendixes, if useful or relevant

References or Works Cited

c. Your notes and rough drafts

24.11 Writing a Feasibility Study

Write an individual or group report evaluating the feasibility of two or more alternatives. Explain your criteria clearly, evaluate each alternative, and recommend the best course of action. Possible topics include the following:

1. Is it feasible for a local restaurant to open another branch? Where should it be?

2. Is it feasible to create a program to mentor women and traditionally underrepresented groups in your organization?

3. Is it feasible to create or enlarge a day care centre for the children of students?

4. Is it feasible to start a monthly newsletter for students in your program?

5. With your instructor's permission, choose your own topic.

24.12 Writing a Library Research Report

Write an individual or group library research report. Possible topics include your province's healthcare policies, your city's strategies for providing homeless shelters, Canadian copyright or defamation legislation related to Internet material, your province's small business support resources or your province's welfare strategies. Or, with your professor's permission, choose your own topic.

Start the project by finding the most current information available online or in print.

24.13 Writing a Recommendation Report

Write an individual or group recommendation report. Possible topics include the following:

1. **Recommending Courses.** What skills are in demand in your community? What courses at what levels should the local college offer? What accreditation courses should graduates in your programs pursue to increase their marketability and salaries?

2. **Improving Sales and Profits.** Recommend ways a small business in your community can increase sales and profits. Focus on one or more of the following: the products or services it offers, its advertising, its decor, its location, its accounting methods, its cash management, or any other aspect that may be keeping the company from achieving its potential. Address your report to the owner of the business.

3. **Increasing Student Involvement.** How could an organization on campus persuade more of the students who are eligible to join or to become active in its programs?

Do students know that it exists? Is it offering programs that interest students? Is it retaining current members? What changes should the organization make? Address your report to the officers of the organization.

4. **Evaluating a Potential Employer.** What training is available to new employees? How soon is the average entry-level person promoted? How much travel and weekend work are expected? Is there a "busy season," or is the workload consistent year-round? What fringe benefits are offered? What is the corporate culture? Is the climate nonracist and nonsexist? How strong is the company economically? How is it likely to be affected by current economic, demographic, and political trends? Address your report to a college placement office; recommend whether it should encourage students to work at this company.

5. With your instructor's permission, choose your own topic.

Polishing Your Prose

Improving Paragraphs

Good paragraphs demonstrate unity, detail, and variety.

The following paragraph from a sales letter illustrates these three qualities:

> The best reason to consider a Schroen Heat Pump is its low cost. Schroen Heat Pumps cost 25 percent less than the cheapest competitor's. Moreover, unlike the competition, the Schroen Heat Pump will pay for itself in less than a year in energy savings. That's just 12 months. All of this value comes with a 10-year unlimited warranty—if anything goes wrong, we'll repair or replace the pump at no cost to you. That means no expensive repair bills and no dollars out of your pocket.

A paragraph is **unified** when all its sentences focus on a single central idea. As long as a paragraph is about just one idea, a topic sentence expressing that idea is not required. However, using a topic sentence makes it easier for the reader to skim the document. (Essays use a *thesis statement* for the central idea of the entire document.) Sentences throughout the paragraph should support the topic sentence or offer relevant examples.

Transitions connect ideas from one point to another. Common transitions are *and, also, first, second, third, in addition, likewise, similarly, for example (e.g.), for instance, indeed, to illustrate, namely, specifically, in contrast,* and *on the other hand.*

Detail makes your points clearer and more vivid. Good details express clearly and completely what you mean. Use concrete words, especially strong nouns, verbs, adjectives, and adverbs that paint a picture in the reader's mind and say what you mean. Avoid unnecessary repetition.

Variety is expressed first in sentence length and patterns and second in the number of sentences in each paragraph. Most sentences in business writing should be 16 to 20 words, but an occasional longer or very short sentence gives punch to your writing.

The basic pattern for sentences is subject/verb/object (SVO): *Our building supervisor sent the forms.* Vary the SVO pattern by changing the order, using transitions and clauses, and combining sentences.

Also vary paragraph length. First and last paragraphs can be quite short. Body paragraphs will be longer. Whenever a paragraph runs eight typed lines or more, think about dividing it into two paragraphs.

Exercises

Rewrite the following paragraphs to improve unity, detail, and variety.

1. I used to work for McCandless Realty as a receptionist. My many experiences in the accounting field make me an ideal candidate for a position as senior administrative assistant with Graham, Chang, and Associates. I answered phones at McCandless. I typed there. I worked at Dufresne Plastics as a secretary. At McCandless, I also handled payroll. There are a lot of reasons why I liked Dufresne. These included the opportunity for training in data entry and Microsoft Word. I learned to type 70 WPM with no mistakes.

2. Mr. Walter Pruitt visited our business communication class yesterday. He spoke about the importance of co-op placements. Mr. Pruitt works for Nortel Networks. Nortel Networks provides network and service management to companies around the world. Mr. Pruitt, who works for Nortel, told us he got his first job because of a co-op. A co-op is an opportunity for students to work with a company for a period of time to get business experience. Mr. Pruitt went to college and worked at a co-op placement for Nortel. At first, Nortel only wanted him to work for 10 weeks. Mr. Pruitt did such a good job, they kept him on another 10 weeks and another. Mr. Pruitt was offered a job by Nortel when he graduated.

Check your answer to the odd-numbered exercise on page 634.

Module 25
Using Visuals

Topics

- **When and how should I use visuals?**

- **Does it matter what kind of visual I use?**

- **What design conventions should I follow?**

- **Can I use colour and clip art?**

- **What else do I need to check for?**

- **Can I use the same visuals in my document and my presentation?**

Review of Key Points

Learning Applications

Polishing Your Prose: Writing Subject Lines and Headings

Learning Focus

After reading and applying the information in Module 25, you'll be able to demonstrate

Knowledge of

- The impact of visual depiction
- Contemporary design conventions

Skills to

- Use visuals to tell stories
- Match the visual to the story
- Design visuals
- Make visuals ethical
- Use visuals in your document or presentation

"You have to guide people through the information but you cannot set your own agenda..."

"When explaining complex scientific concepts to non-scientists, it is important to use imagery," says Dr. Cecilia Hageman, a forensic scientist who works at the crime laboratory in Toronto. "Language has to be clear so that the limitations of the conclusions can be understood by non-scientists."

Cecilia earned her Ph.D in biology and then went to law school with the intent of working in the field of patent law so that she could "use law in the service of science." But, she ended up working in the crime lab where she uses science in the service of law.

The forensic laboratory is divided into divisions according to a specific science. There are departments in biology, chemistry, toxicology, and firearms. There is also a documents section where tests for forgery are performed.

The main role of the lab is to answer two questions: (1) what substance is on a piece of evidence? and (2) what is the identity of the originator of the substance (especially if it comes from a person)? General lab tests determine what the substance is, and DNA tests determine identity.

Once the tests are complete, reports are written. Here, scientists must be careful so that non-scientists reading the report will not read the wrong things into it. As Cecilia notes, "We have to be careful so that our conclusions are not over-interpreted."

This is where diagrams and analogies are used. Pictures help to explain just what a technical report means. Analogies, which use everyday imagery to explain complex scientific concepts, are very useful; they work not only in written reports but also in court when the scientist must testify. The findings and what they mean must be explained to a jury in a way that the truth is maintained but so that a non-scientist will be able to make sense of the findings.

To explain DNA findings, Cecilia uses the analogy of a price bar, which most people today are familiar with. When the lines match, the two samples in question are identical. So when presenting DNA evidence, Cecilia will show how these samples line up. If there is a match, then the test is conclusive. If there is no match, then the sample has not been obtained from the person on trial.

Cecilia concludes that the most important considerations when addressing non-scientists from the witness stand "is to answer the question that is asked. Do not go off to explain all kinds of things. You have to guide people through the information but you cannot set your own agenda. You must stick to the specific task at hand." And in doing, so, justice will be served.

http://www.solicitorgeneral.msg.gov.on.
ca/english/public/forensic.html
Centre of Forensic Sciences (Ontario)

Because the Internet enables everyone to publish, we are inundated with information. Information overload has escalated our expectations of immediacy while reducing our patience with written text. Thus, the truism that a picture is worth 1,000 words has never been more relevant.

Visuals—illustrations, charts, and graphs—readily convey and clarify information; therefore, visuals are a reader-friendly way to communicate your points. This module shows you how to turn data into charts and graphs. See ◀▶ Module 5 for a discussion of designing slides for oral presentations and ◀▶ Module 20 for a discussion of other aspects of good oral presentations.

In your rough draft, use visuals

- **To see that ideas are presented completely.** A table, for example, can show you whether you've included all the items in a comparison.
- **To find relationships.** For example, charting sales on a map may show that the sales representatives who made quota all have territories on the west coast or in the Atlantic provinces. Is the product one that appeals to coastal lifestyles? Is advertising reaching the coasts but not the Prairie provinces, Ontario, or Québec? Even if you don't use the visual in your final document, creating the map may lead you to questions you wouldn't otherwise ask.

In the final presentation or document, use visuals

- **To make points vivid.** Readers skim memos and reports; a visual catches the eye. The brain processes visuals immediately. Understanding words—written or oral—takes more time.
- **To emphasize material** that might be skipped if it were buried in a paragraph.
- **To present material more compactly and with less repetition** than words alone would require.

The number and type of visuals you need depend on your purposes, your information, and the audience. You'll use more visuals when you want to show relationships and to persuade, when the information is complex or contains extensive numerical data, and when the audience values visuals.

Your chart is only as good as the underlying data. Check to be sure that your data come from a reliable source (◀▶ Module 22).

What are stories, and how do I find them?

A story is something that is happening, according to the data.

To find stories, look for relationships and changes.

Every visual should tell a story. Stories can be expressed in complete sentences that describe something that happens or changes. The sentence can also serve as the title of the visual.

Not a story: Canadian Exports, 1995–2000

Possible stories: The U.S. Continues to be Canada's Leading Trade Partner
Exports from China Increase
Ontario Leads in Manufacturing Boom
New Customers Account for Forty Percent of Sales

Stories that tell us what we already know are rarely interesting. Instead, good stories may

- Support a hunch you have
- Surprise you or challenge so-called "common knowledge"
- Show trends or changes you didn't know existed
- Have commercial or social significance
- Provide information needed for action
- Be personally relevant to you and the audience

To find stories,

1. **Focus on a topic** (starting salaries, rock music demographics, and so forth).
2. **Simplify the data** on that topic and convert the numbers to simple, easy-to-understand units.
3. **Look for relationships and changes.** For example, compare two or more groups: do men and women have the same attitudes? Look for changes over time. Look for items that can be seen as part of the same group. For example, to find stories about TV ads, you might group ads in the same product category—ads for cars, for food, for beverages.

Use visuals only for points you want to emphasize

"It looks much worse when you see the big picture."

When you think you have a story, test it against all the data to be sure it's accurate.

Some stories are simple straight lines: "Sales Increased." But other stories are more complex, with exceptions or outlying cases. Such stories will need more nuanced titles to do justice to the story. And sometimes the best story arises from the juxtaposition of two or more stories. In Figure 25.1 on the next page, *Maclean's* magazine uses a **matrix table** to make a graphic comparison. The matrix provides a snapshot of the increasingly competitive business travellers' market among Canadian airlines.

Your audience should be able to see what the visual says:

> Does the chart support the title; and does the title reinforce the chart? So if I *say* in my title that "sales have increased significantly" I want to *see* a trend moving up at a sharp angle. If not, if the tend parallels the baseline, it's an instant clue that the chart needs more thinking.[1]

For optimum audience impact, use the "Tell, Show, Tell" rule: first, *tell* your readers or listeners what they are about to see; next, *show* your audience what you promised to show them; finally, *tell* them the significance of the visual. And, of course, the visual must depict exactly what you said it would.

Almost every data set allows you to tell several stories. You must choose the story you want to tell. Dumps of uninterpreted data confuse and frustrate your audience; they undercut the credibility and goodwill you want to create.

Figure 25.1

A Matrix Table Tells A Complete Story

	Air Canada	Canada 3000	WestJet
Headquarters:	Montreal	Toronto	Calgary
2000 Operating Revenues:	$9.3 billion	$756 million	$332 million
2000 Profit (Loss):	($82 million)	$9.5 million	$30.3 million
Airlines Taken Over:	Canadian Airlines International (2000): Roots Air (2001)	Royal Airlines: CanJet Airlines (both 2001)	None
Number of Planes:	375	36	23
Loyalty Program:	Aeroplan, powerful program with 5.7 million members, linked with credit cards and partners in the Star alliance	American Airlines AAdvantage Rewards. Points redeemable on Canada 3000, American Airlines, and other One World partners	Passengers can use AirMiles to book travel on WestJet, but no points are earned on its flights
Reasons to Fly:	Broad national coverage, frequent flights, full business class, international connections, Aeroplan program	Cheap fares, national routes. Business class starts June 1	Cheap fares, famously friendly staff. Specializes in shorter hauls, primarily in the West, where flights are relatively frequent
Reasons to Avoid:	History of poor customer service; higher fares on many routes	Cramped economy seats; limited numberof routes and flights	Limited number of routes. Uses Hamilton instead of Toronto, Canada's major hub. No onboard meals, no baggage connections to other airlines, no business class
Sample Economy Fare, Calgary-Vancouver Return:	Walk-on: $1,041 Cheapest: $226 Flights/week: 154	Walk-on: $327 Cheapest: $167 Flights/week: 17	Walk-on: $486 Cheapest: $208 Flights/week: 77

Source: Katherine Macklem, "Then there were three", *Maclean's*, May 21, 2001, 73.

Does it matter what kind of visual I use?

Yes! The visual must match the kind of story.

Visuals are not interchangeable. Choose the visual that best matches the purpose of presenting the data.

- Use **tables** when the reader needs to be able to identify exact values (See Figure 25.2a)
- Use a chart or graph when you want the reader to focus on relationships[2]
- To compare a part to the whole, use a **pie chart** (See Figure 25.2b)
- To compare one item to another item, or items over time, use a **bar chart** or a **line graph** (See Figures 25.2c and 25.2d)

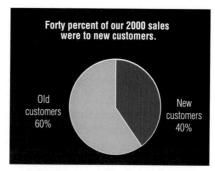

a. Tables show exact values.

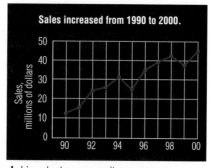

b. Pie charts compare a component to the whole.

Figure 25.2
Choose the Visual to Fit the Story

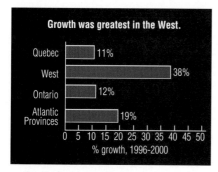

c. Bar charts compare items or show distribution or correlation.

d. Line charts compare items over time or show distribution or correlation.

What design conventions should I follow?

Check your visuals against the lists that follow.

Every visual should contain six components:

1. A title that tells the story that the visual shows.
2. A clear indication of what the data are. For example, what people *say* they did is not necessarily what they really did. An estimate of what a number will be in the future differs from numbers in the past that have already been measured.
3. Clearly labelled units.
4. Labels or legends identifying axes, colours, symbols, and so forth.
5. The source of the data, if you created the visual from data someone else gathered and compiled.
6. The source of the visual, if you reproduce a visual someone else created.

Formal visuals are divided into tables and figures. **Tables** are numbers or words arranged in rows and columns; **figures** are everything else. In a document, formal visuals have both numbers and titles, e.g., "Figure 1. The Falling Cost of Computer Memory, 1990–2000." In an oral presentation, the title is usually used without the number: "The Falling Cost of Computer Memory, 1990–2000." The title should tell the story so that the audience knows what to look for in the visual and why it is important. Informal or spot visuals are inserted directly into the text; they do not have numbers or titles.

Instant Replay

How to Find Stories

1. Focus on a topic
2. Simplify the data
3. Look for relationships and changes

The Six Components of Every Visual

1. A title that tells the story that the visual shows
2. A clear indication of what the data are
3. Clearly labelled units
4. Labels or legends identifying axes, colours, symbols, and so forth
5. The source of the data, if you created the visual from data someone else gathered and compiled
6. The source of the visual, if you reproduce a visual someone else created

Tables

Use tables only when you want the audience to focus on specific numbers. Graphs convey less specific information but are always more memorable.

- Round off to simplify the data (e.g., 35% rather than 35.27%; 34,000 rather than 33,942)
- Provide column and row totals or averages when they're relevant
- Put the items you want readers to compare in columns rather than in rows to facilitate mental subtraction and division
- When you have many rows, screen alternate entries or double space after every five entries to help readers line up items accurately.

Pie Charts

Pie charts force the audience to measure area. Research shows that people can judge position or length (which a bar chart uses) much more accurately than they judge area. The data in any pie chart can be put in a bar chart.[3] Therefore, use a pie chart only when you are comparing one segment to the whole. When you are comparing one segment to another segment, use a bar chart, a line graph, or a map—even though the data may be expressed in percentages.

- Start at 12 o'clock with the largest percentage or the percentage you want to focus on. Go clockwise to each smaller percentage or to each percentage in some other logical order.
- Make the chart a perfect circle. Perspective circles distort the data.
- Limit the number of segments to five or seven. If your data have more divisions, combine the smallest or the least important into a single "miscellaneous" or "other" category.
- Label the segments outside the circle. Internal labels are hard to read.

Bar Charts

Bar charts are easy to interpret because they ask people to compare distance along a common scale, which most people judge accurately. Bar charts are useful in a variety of situations: to compare one item to another, to compare items over time, and to show correlations. Use horizontal bars when your labels are long; when the labels are short, either horizontal or vertical bars will work.

- Order the bars in a logical or chronological order.
- Put the bars close enough together to make comparison easy.
- Label both horizontal and vertical axes.
- Put all labels inside the bars or outside them. When some labels are inside and some are outside, the labels carry the visual weight of longer bars, distorting the data.
- Make all the bars the same width.
- Use different colours for different bars only when their meanings are different: estimates as opposed to known numbers, negative as opposed to positive numbers.
- Avoid using perspective. Perspective makes the values harder to read and can make comparison difficult.

Figure 25.3

Varieties of Bar Charts

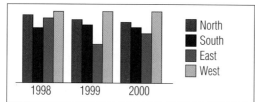
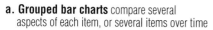

a. Grouped bar charts compare several aspects of each item, or several items over time

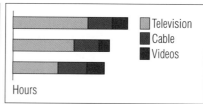

b. Segmented, subdivided, or **stacked bars** sum the components of an item

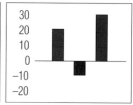

c. Deviation bar charts identify positive and negative values

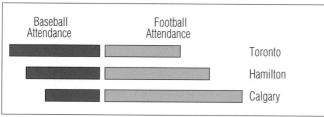

d. Paired bar charts show the correlation between two items

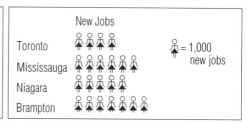

e. Histograms or **pictograms** use images to create the bars

Several varieties of bar charts exist. See Figure 25.3 for examples.

- **Grouped bar charts** allow you to compare several aspects of each item or several items over time
- **Segmented**, **subdivided**, or **stacked bars** sum the components of an item. It's hard to identify the values in specific segments; grouped bar charts are almost always easier to use
- **Deviation bar charts** identify positive and negative values, or winners and losers
- **Paired bar charts** show the correlation between two items
- **Histograms** or **pictograms** use images to create the bars

Line Graphs

Line graphs are also easy to interpret. Use line graphs to compare items over time, to show frequency or distribution, and to show correlations.

- Label both horizontal and vertical axes.
- When time is a variable, put it on the horizontal axis.
- Avoid using more than three different lines on one graph. Even three lines may be too many if they cross each other.
- Avoid using perspective. Perspective makes the values harder to read and can make comparison difficult.

Tables and Figures

Tables are numbers or words arranged in rows and columns; **figures** are everything else. In a document, formal visuals have both numbers ("Figure 1") and titles. In an oral presentation, the title is usually used without the number.

Go to
http://webdesign.ab
out.com/library/wee
kly/aa070400c.htm
Information about colour symbolism by culture and other colour studies.

http://www.paintca
fe.com/en/
A Québec Web site that includes more colour symbolism and a colour preference assessment quiz.

Can I use colour and clip art?

Use colour carefully.

Avoid decorative clip art in memos and reports.

Colour makes visuals more dramatic, but it creates at least two problems. First, readers try to interpret colour, an interpretation that may not be appropriate. Second, meanings assigned to colours differ depending on the audience's national background and profession.

Connotations for colour vary from culture to culture (◀▶ Module 3). Blue suggests masculinity in North America, criminality in France, strength or fertility in Egypt, and villainy in Japan. Red is sometimes used to suggest danger or *stop* in North American culture; it means *go* in China and is associated with festivities. Red suggests masculinity or aristocracy in France, death in Korea, blasphemy in some African countries, and luxury in many parts of the world. Yellow suggests caution or cowardice in North America, prosperity in Egypt, grace in Japan, and femininity in many parts of the world.[4]

Corporate, national, or professional associations may supersede these general cultural associations. Some people associate blue with IBM or Hewlett-Packard and red with Coca-Cola, communism, or Japan. People in specific professions learn other meanings for colours. Blue suggests *reliability* to financial managers, *water* or *coldness* to engineers, and *death* to health care professionals. Red means *losing money* to financial managers, *danger* to engineers, but *healthy* to health care professionals. Green usually means *safe* to engineers, but *infected* to health care professionals.[5]

These various associations suggest that colour is safest with a homogenous audience that you know well. In an increasingly multicultural workforce, colour may send signals you do not intend.

When you do use colour in visuals, experts suggest the following guidelines:[6]

- Use no more than five colours when colours have meanings
- Use glossy paper to make colours more vivid
- Be aware that colours on a computer screen always look brighter than the same colours on paper because the screen sends out light

In any visual, use as little shading and as few lines as are necessary for clarity. Don't clutter up the visual with extra marks. When you design black and white graphs, use shades of grey rather than stripes, wavy lines, and checks to indicate different segments or items.

In memos and reports, resist the temptation to make your visual "artistic" by turning it into a picture or adding clip art. **Clip art** is predrawn images that you can import into your newsletter, sign, or graph. A small drawing of a car in the corner of a line graph showing the number of miles driven is acceptable in an oral presentation or a newsletter, but out of place in a written report.

Chartjunk impedes readability and detracts from your credibility.[7] Turning a line graph into a highway to show miles driven makes it harder to read: it's hard to separate the data line from lines that are merely decorative. If you use clip art, you must be sensitive to your audience's pluralistic interpretations: be sure that the images of people show a good mix of both sexes, various races and ages, and various physical conditions (◀▶ Module 3).

Integrating Visuals into Your Text

Refer to every visual in your text. Normally give the table or figure number in the text but not the title. Put the visual as soon after your reference as space and page design permit. If the visual must go on another page, tell the reader where to find it:

> As Figure 3 shows (p. 10), . . .
> (See Table 2 on page 3.)

Summarize the main point of a visual *before* you present the visual itself. Then when readers get to it, they'll see it as confirmation of your point.

Weak: Listed below are the results.

Better: As Figure 4 shows, sales doubled in the last decade.

How much discussion a visual needs depends on the audience, the complexity of the visual, and the importance of the point it makes. If the material is new to the audience, you'll need a fuller explanation than if similar material is presented to this audience every week or month. Help the reader find key data points in complex visuals. If the point is important, discuss its implications in some detail. In contrast, one sentence about a visual may be enough when the audience is already familiar with the topic and the data, when the visual is simple and well designed, and when the information in the visual is a minor part of your proof.

When you discuss visuals, spell out numbers that fall at the beginning of a sentence. If spelling out the number or year is cumbersome, revise the sentence so that it does not begin with a number.

Correct: Forty-five percent of the cost goes to pay wages and salaries.

Correct: The year 1992 marked the official beginning of the European Economic Community.

What else do I need to check for?

Be sure that the visual is accurate and ethical.

Always double-check your visuals to be sure that the information is accurate. However, many visuals have accurate labels but misleading visual shapes. Visuals communicate quickly; audiences remember the shape, not the labels. If the reader has to study the labels to get the right picture, the visual is unethical even if the labels are accurate.

Figure 25.4 on the next page, is distorted by chartjunk and dimensionality. In an effort to make "Mouse Power" interesting, the artist for *Fortune* used icons rather than simple bars. Admissions to Disney theme parks were not even twice NBA admissions, but the mouse appears to be six or eight times bigger than the basketball player. The Statue of Liberty is twice the height of the White House, reflecting twice the number of admissions. But since we expect the statue to be taller than the White House, the force of the comparison is lost. Two-dimensional figures distort data by multiplying the apparent value by the width as well as by the height—four times for every doubling in value. Perspective graphs are especially hard for readers to interpret and should be avoided.[8]

Figure 25.4
**Chartjunk and
Misleading
Dimensions
Distort Data**

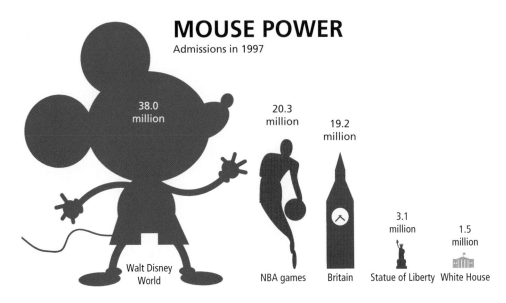

Source: Fortune, April 13, 1998, 122.

Even simple bar and line graphs may be misleading if part of the scale is missing, or **truncated**. Truncated graphs are most acceptable when the audience knows the basic data set well. For example, graphs of the stock market almost never start at zero; they are routinely truncated. This omission is acceptable for audiences who follow the market closely.

Data can also be distorted when the context is omitted. For example, a drop may be part of a regular cycle, a correction after an atypical increase, or a permanent drop to a new, lower plateau.

To make your visuals more accurate,

- Differentiate between actual and estimated or projected values
- When you must truncate a scale, do so clearly with a break in the bars or in the background
- Avoid perspective and three-dimensional graphs
- Avoid combining graphs with different scales
- Use images of people carefully in histographs to avoid sexist, racist, or other exclusionary visual statements

Can I use the same visuals in my document and my presentation?

Only if the table or graph is simple.

For presentations, simplify paper visuals. To simplify a complex table, cut out some of the information, round off the data even more, or present the material in a chart rather than a table.

Visuals for presentations should have titles but don't need figure numbers. Do know where each visual is so that you can return to one if someone asks about it during the question period. Decorative clip art is acceptable in oral presentations as long as it does not obscure the story you're telling with the visual.

Employability Skills 2000+ Checklist for Using Visuals

In this module, the key skills from The Conference Board of Canada's Employability Skills 2000+ are:

Communicate

✔ read and understand information presented in a variety of forms (e.g. words, graphs, charts, diagrams)
✔ share information using a range of information and communications technologies (e.g. voice, email, computers)
✔ use relevant scientific, technological, and mathematical knowledge and skills to explain or clarify ideas

Manage Information

✔ locate, gather, and organize information using appropriate technology and information systems
✔ access, analyze, and apply knowledge and skills from a variety of disciplines (e.g. the arts, languages, science, technology, mathematics, social sciences, and the humanities)

Think & Solve Problems

✔ assess situations and identify problems
✔ recognize the human, interpersonal, technical, scientific, and mathematical dimensions of a problem
✔ readily use science, technology, and mathematics as ways to think, gain, and share knowledge, solve problems, and make decisions

Participate in Projects & Tasks

✔ plan, design, or carry out a project or task from start to finish with well-defined objectives and outcomes
✔ work to agreed quality standards and specifications
✔ adapt to changing requirements and information

Review of Key Points

- In the rough draft, use visuals to see that ideas are presented completely and see what relationships exist. In the final report, use visuals to make points vivid, to emphasize material that the reader might skip, and to present material more compactly and with less repetition than words alone would require.

- Use more visuals when you want to show relationships and to persuade, when the information is complex or contains extensive numerical data, and when the audience values visuals.

- Pick data to tell a story, to make a point. To find stories,

1. Focus on a topic
2. Simplify the data
3. Look for relationships and changes

- **Matrices** and **paired graphs** juxtapose two or more simple stories to create a more powerful story.

- The best visual depends on the kind of data and the point you want to make with the data.

- Visuals must present data accurately, both literally and by implication. **Chartjunk** denotes decorations that at best are irrelevant to the visual and at worst mislead the reader. Truncated scales omit part of the scale and visually mislead readers. Perspective graphs and graphs with negative bases mislead readers.

- Summarize the main point of a visual before it appears in the text.

- Visuals for presentations need to be simpler than visuals on paper.

- How much discussion a visual needs depends on the audience, the complexity of the visual and the importance of the point it makes.

Learning Applications

Questions for Comprehension

25.1 How can you find stories in data?

25.2 What is the difference between a table and a figure?

25.3 What is chartjunk?

Questions for Critical Thinking

25.4 Why does each visual need to tell a story?

25.5 Why are charts more memorable than tables?

25.6 When is chartjunk most likely to be acceptable? Why?

25.7 When is a truncated scale most likely to be acceptable?

Questions for Building Skills

25.8 What skills have you read about in this module?

25.9 What skills are you practising in the assignments you're doing for this module?

25.10 How could you further develop the skills you're working on?

Exercises and Problems

25.11 Identifying Stories

Of the following, which are stories?

1. Computer Use
2. Computer Prices Fall
3. More Single Parents Buy Computers Than Do Any Other Group
4. Where Your Tax Dollars Go
5. Sixty Percent of Tax Dollars Pay Entitlements, Interest

25.12   Matching Visuals with Stories

What visual(s) would make it easiest to see each of the following stories?

1. Canada buys 35 percent of U.S. exports.
2. Undergraduate enrolment rises, but graduate enrolment declines.
3. Population growth will be greatest in southwestern Ontario, in Montréal and its suburbs, and in Mahone Bay, Nova Scotia.
4. Companies with fewer than 200 employees created a larger percentage of new jobs than did companies with more than 5,000 employees.
5. Canada's population is aging.

25.13   Evaluating Visuals

Evaluate each of the following visuals.

1.
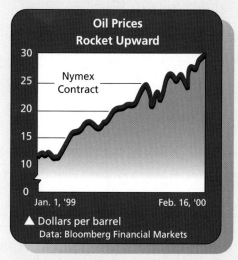

Source: *Business Week,* February 28, 2000, 37.

2.
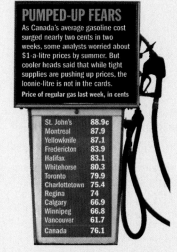

Source: *Maclean's,* May 14, 2001, 21.

3.   **How My Time Will Be Used**

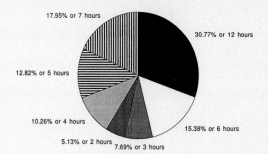

4.

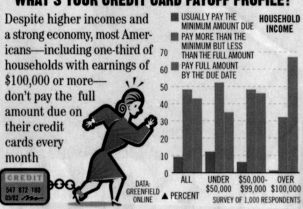

Source: *Business Week*, March 27, 2000, 10.

5.

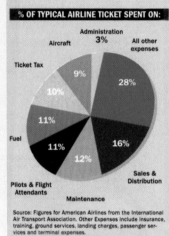

Source: *Selling Power*, October 1999, 2.

- Is the visual's message clear?
- Is it the right visual for the story?
- Is the visual designed appropriately? Is colour, if any, used appropriately?

- Is the visual free from *chartjunk*?
- Does the visual distort data or mislead the reader in any way?

25.14 Interpreting Data

As Your Instructor Directs,

a. Identify at least seven stories in one or more of the following data sets.

b. Create visuals for three of the stories.

c. Write a memo to your instructor explaining why you chose these stories and why you chose these visuals to display them.

d. Write a memo to some group that might be interested in your findings, presenting your visuals as part of a short report. Possible groups include career counsellors, radio stations, advertising agencies, and local restaurants.

e. Brainstorm additional stories you could tell with additional data. Specify the kind of data you would need.

1.

Average hours per week of television viewing
Fall 1999

	Total population	children 2-11	adolescents 12-17	men 18 and over	women 18 and over
			hours per week		
Canada	**21.6**	**15.5**	**15.5**	**20.9**	**25.5**
Newfoundland	**24.5**	19.0	16.3	23.2	29.0
Prince Edward Island	**20.7**	15.9	13.0	20.0	24.8
Nova Scotia	**22.1**	15.3	16.8	21.5	25.7
New Brunswick	**22.9**	17.0	17.5	21.8	26.7
Quebec					
Total[1]	**24.7**	19.0	16.7	23.4	29.5
English[2]	**20.7**	18.2	15.4	19.7	24.4
French[2]	**25.5**	13.4	16.9	24.1	30.6
Ontario	**20.5**	14.9	15.3	19.6	24.2
Manitoba	**20.3**	15.1	14.2	19.7	24.4
Saskatchewan	**20.8**	16.1	15.5	20.0	24.5
Alberta	**19.6**	13.7	15.0	19.3	23.1
British Columbia	**20.7**	13.1	14.5	21.3	23.6

1. Includes respondents who did not indicate a language spoken at home or who indicated a language other than English or French.

2. Language spoken at home.

Source: Statistics Canada, Catalogue no. 87F0006XIB.

2.

Households in top 15 Census Metropolitan Areas with at least one regular Internet user

	1998	1999	2000
		All locations[1] % of households	
Canada	**35.9**	**41.8**	**51.3**
Halifax	50.2	52.4	64.1
Québec	28.6	33.9	50.3
Montréal	31.6	39.1	46.6
Ottawa[2]	55.3	56.7	65.2
Toronto	42.0	48.5	57.9
Hamilton	41.2	43.1	54.9
St. Catharines-Niagara	29.3	34.4	46.0
Kitchener	42.4	43.7	52.7
London	40.4	45.9	59.2
Windsor	26.8	33.6	47.5
Winnipeg	37.9	42.1	53.9
Edmonton	43.9	48.8	59.5
Calgary	52.8	60.1	65.2
Vancouver	45.7	49.7	60.0
Victoria	48.5	56.4	59.1

1. All Internet access locations.

2. Ontario portion only of the Ottawa-Hull Census Metropolitan Area.

Source: Source: Statistics Canada, CANSIM, Matrix 7944 and Catalogue no. 63-016-XPB. Last modified: August 22, 2001.

3.

Generational Thirst
Percent of all dollars spent annually in each beverage category, by life stage

	Carbonated Beverages	Coffee	Juices, Refrigerated	Soft Drinks Non-carb.	Bottled Water	All Remain Carb. Bev/Diet	All Remain Carb. Bev/Reg	Coffee, Liquid
Young singles (age 18–34)	2%	1%	2%	2%	2%	2%	1%	3%
Childless younger couples (two adults, 18–34)	4%	3%	4%	4%	6%	4%	4%	8%
New families (2 adults, 1 or more children <6)	5%	3%	5%	8%	6%	4%	5%	4%
Maturing families (2 adults, 1 or more children, not all <6 or + 12)	26%	19%	22%	36%	22%	21%	30%	19%
Established families (1 or more children, all +12)	12%	9%	10%	10%	10%	9%	14%	12%
Middle aged singles (35–54)	7%	5%	7%	4%	9%	9%	7%	7%
Middle aged childless couples (2 adults, 35–54)	18%	17%	16%	14%	18%	19%	16%	18%
Empty nesters (2 adults, +55, no children at home)	20%	32%	24%	17%	20%	24%	17%	21%
Older singles (55+)	7%	11%	10%	6%	7%	8%	6%	8%
Total	100%	100%	100%	100%	100%	100%	100%	100%

Source: American Demographics, February 2000, 63.

25.15   Graphing Data from the Web

Find data on the Web about a topic that interests you. Sites with data include

  http://www.canoe.ca/

  http://www.statcan.ca/

  http://www.findarticles.com/cf_0/ m0FWE/11_3/57785862/print.jhtml

  American Demographics Archives: www.marketingtools.com/search.htm

  Graphic, Visualization, & Usability Center's WWW surveys: www.cc. gatech.edu/gvu/user_surveys/

  Statistical Universe (U.S. government statistics back to the 1970s): www.cispubs.com

As Your Instructor Directs,

a. Identify at least seven stories in the data

b. Create visuals for three of the stories

c. Write a memo to your instructor explaining why you chose these stories and why you chose these visuals to display them

d. Write a memo to some group that might be interested in your findings, presenting your visuals as part of a short report

e. Print out the data and include it with a copy of your memo or report

Polishing Your Prose

Writing Subject Lines and Headings

Subject lines are the title of a letter, memo, or email message. Headings within a document tell the reader what information you will discuss in that section.

Good subject lines are specific, concise, and appropriate for your purposes and the response you expect from the reader. Subject lines are required in memos, optional in letters.

- Put in good news if you have it
- If information is neutral, summarize it
- Use negative subject lines if the reader may not read the message, needs the information to act, or if the negative is your error
- In a request that is easy for the reader to grant, put the subject of that request, or a direct question in the subject line
- When you must persuade a reluctant reader, use a common ground, a reader benefit, or a directed subject line that makes your stance on the issue clear

Headings are single words, short phrases, or complete sentences that indicate the topic in a document section. Headings must be parallel—that is, they must use the same grammatical structure—and must cover all the information until the next heading.

The most useful headings are **informative**, or **talking, heads**, which sum up the content of the section.

Weak: Problem
         Cause 1
         Cause 2
         Cause 3

Better: Communication Problems Between Air
         Traffic Controllers and Pilots
         Selective Listening
         Indirect Conversational Style
         Limitations of Short-Term Memory

Exercises

For the situations in 1–5, write a good subject line. Make 6–10 into effective headings using parallel form.

1. I'm your new boss.

2. I wanted those annual enrolment forms back from you last week.

3. Blood drive.

4. Not that it will really affect you, but starting next week there will be an opportunity for non-hourly workers (you're hourly) to also get overtime compensation for extra hours worked.

5. We're going to raise your insurance rates!

6. Making the Most of Undergraduate Years; Making the Most of Graduate School; Now What?

7. Research; Logistics: What's in It for Us?

8. Pros of Investing in Short-Term Mutual Funds; Cons of Investing in Short-Term Mutual Funds; The Market

9. Clemente Research Group's Five-Year Goals; What We Want to Accomplish in Ten-Years; Our Fifteen-Year Goals

10. Overview; Budget; The Problem of Avondale Expanding into Europe

Check your answers to the odd-numbered exercises on page 634.

Unit Seven
Job Hunting

Module 26
Researching Jobs

Topics

- What do I need to know about myself to job hunt?

- What do I need to know about companies that might hire me?

- Should I do information interviews?

- What is the "hidden job market"? How do I tap into it?

- What's the best way to present non-traditional experience?

Review of Key Points

Learning Applications

Polishing Your Prose: Using Details

Learning Focus

After reading and applying the information in Module 26, you'll be able to demonstrate

Knowledge of
- Job search techniques

Skills to
- Self-assess realistically
- Find information about employers
- Use the Internet in your job search
- Find posted jobs and explore the hidden job market
- Present your non-traditional experience positively
- Decide whether to keep your current job or look for a new one

"...Don't underestimate the value of your network ..."

"Don't take things at face value, and don't underestimate the value of your network," says Kimberley Chesney, president and founder of Prime Management Group Inc., a southwest Ontario-based company that works internationally.

Kimberley founded Prime Management Group Inc. in 1990. She is a certified personnel consultant and is on the board of the National Personnel Association, an international organization, with board members from the United States, Canada, and Australia.

Since Prime Management Group Inc. works with both individual job seekers ("candidates") and with companies looking for people to fill specific jobs ("clients"). Kimberley must actively research the job market from both sides of the fence. She considers herself an "out-of-the-box-thinker"—a necessity as the changes in the labour market and in the workforce mean that the old methods are no longer effective for hiring the best staff possible.

When a new candidate contacts Prime, Kimberley's staff helps that person determine what he or she wants in a new job. Most of Prime's candidates are employed but wish to redirect their careers or work in new areas. Kimberley's job is to get candidates to focus on their inner concerns, their motives, their needs. Candidates will often remark, "I didn't know I had to answer that question." And by helping candidates focus on their needs, Kimberley helps them understand how to use their personal network to find the job they are looking for. Helping candidates network effectively is an important aspect

of Prime's work, particularly since so many opportunities are in the "hidden job market".

At the same time, however, Kimberley must consider employer needs. She is not just matching up a person to a job—it has to be the right person for the right job. Kimberley emphasizes, "We do not find people jobs. We help them understand what is out there." However, this process may lead Kimberley to recommend a candidate to one of her clients.

When dealing with corporate clients, Kimberley conducts a 360-degree process analysis. To ensure that a client gets the right person for the job, she investigates the company to understand the big picture. The president might want a financial person to head human resources, but other people in the company know that other skills are needed. By asking accountants, production managers, and other key members of the organization, as well as executive management, about the needs of the job, Kimberley can see what combination of skills and experience will work work in the company.

When asked what kind of advice she would give to someone entering the field of human resources management, Kimberley says that most people end up in the by accident. "But," she adds, "college students would make excellent candidates for human resources management, even if it is a stepping stone to another career."

http:// www.pmg.on.ca
Prime Management Group Inc.

Go to
http://www.jobhunt ersbible.com/

Visit Richard Bolles' site for more employability tips

The job market in the early twenty-first century is full of contradictions. On the one hand, workers faced with the economic slowdown and implosion of the dot-com sector now seek stable jobs in traditional industries.[1] On the other hand, work-force talent—especially communications services talent—is in such demand that many Canadian companies are holding on to their skilled employees, despite the current economy.

During the last few years of the 1990s, unemployment was at a 30-year low. Companies initiated innovative and aggressive recruitment techniques to attract talent: recruiters attended music festivals to search for likely employee prospects and some organizations offered employees cash bonuses in return for employee leads and referrals. Yet, middle managers spent 30 percent more time trying to find comparable jobs in 1999 than in 1998 and only about half of the members of the class of 2000 had jobs by graduation. Fully 60 percent of new and prospective graduates felt that finding a job would be at least somewhat difficult.[2]

Over 50 percent of current hot jobs for those with a B.A. are in the health-related and computer sectors, especially wireless services. Canadian employers are also looking for hardware engineers, human resource specialists, retail store and sales managers, networking and programming instructors, pharmacists, healthcare workers, writers, and researchers.[3]

Perhaps you already have a job waiting for you; perhaps your skills are in such demand that employers will seek *you* out. If, however, you're not sure how to secure your ideal job in a faltering economy, the modules in this unit will help you find your way.

The first step in any job search, however, is to think about your own interests and needs. Indeed, Richard Bolles, author of the classic job-hunter's guide, ***What Color Is Your Parachute?*** claims that the most successful job hunting method hasn't changed:

> Do thorough homework on yourself. Know your best skills, in order of priority. Know the fields in which you want to use those skills. Talk to people who have those kinds of jobs. Find out whether they're happy, and how they found their jobs. Then choose the places where you want to work, rather than just those places that have advertised openings. Thoroughly research these organizations before approaching them. Seek out the person who actually has the power to hire you for the job that you want. Demonstrate to that person how you can help the company with its problems. Cut no corners; take no shortcuts. That method has an 86 percent success rate.[4]

What do I need to know about myself to job hunt?

> Your need to realistically self-assess: identify your knowledge, skills, abilities, interests, and values.

Each person could do several jobs happily. Personality and aptitude tests can tell you what your strengths are, but they won't say, "You should be a _____." In preparation for the job search and for the interview you need to answer specific questions like these:

- What achievements have given you the most satisfaction? *Why* did you enjoy them?
- Would you rather have firm deadlines or a flexible schedule? Do you prefer working alone or with other people? Do you prefer specific instructions and standards for evaluation or freedom and uncertainty? How comfortable are you with pressure? How do you manage multiple deadlines? How much challenge do you want?
- Are you willing to take work home? Are you prepared to travel? How important is recognition to you? How important is money compared to having time to spend with family and friends?
- Where do you want to live? What features in terms of weather, geography, and cultural and social life do you see as ideal?
- What do you want from your work? Do you work to achieve certain purposes or values, or is work "just a way to make a living"? Are the organization's culture and ethical standards important to you?

Once you have identified in writing what is most important to you, analyze the job market to see where you can find what you want. For example, your greatest interest is athletics, but you aren't good enough for the pros. Your job market analysis might suggest several alternatives. You could teach sports and physical fitness as a high school coach or a corporate fitness director. You could cover sports for a newspaper, a magazine, a TV station, or the Web. You could go into management or sales for a professional sports team, a health club, or a company that sells sports equipment. You could create or manage a sports Web page.

What do I need to know about companies that might hire me?

Everything you can!

Organizations hire people who demonstrate motivation, energy, and critical thinking. Preparation through research demonstrates all these skills. Indeed, to adapt your letter and résumé to a specific organization and to shine at the interview, you need information both about the employer and about the job itself. You'll need to know,

- **What the job itself involves.** Notebooks at campus placement offices often have fuller job descriptions than appear in ads. Talk to friends who have graduated recently to learn what their jobs involve. Request information interviews to learn more about opportunities that interest you.
- **The name and address of the person who should receive the letter.** To get this information, check the ad or the organization's Web site, or call the company. An advantage of calling is that you can find out whether your contact prefers a courtesy title (*Mr., Ms.* or *Mrs*).
- **What the organization does and at least four or five facts about it.** Knowing the organization's larger goals enables you to describe how your specific work will help the company meet its goals. Useful facts include
  - Market share
  - Competitive position
  - New products, services, or promotions

Building a Critical Skill

Choosing Whether to Stay or Go

When your job offers financial security, it's difficult to know whether to stay or move. After all, you know all the flaws of your current situation. Any new job will have its own flaws, but you probably don't know them and certainly don't know all of them. To decide on the basis of the pluses and minuses you know, therefore, is illogical. You need a better way to compare the job you know to the one that is only a possibility.

Job-assessment guru William Morin offers a seven-question quiz. Are the following statements true or false for you?

1. Your boss likes you and advocates for you in the organization.
2. Your boss is doing well.
3. You've been promoted in the last two years.
4. Your pension plan, and other benefits are vested (or are near vesting) and growing.
5. The company is doing well and can grow further.
6. You're getting better-than-average raises. (Average for white-collar workers is about 3.5 percent a year.)
7. Your boss has mentioned within the last year that you are valued and he or she sees where you might be headed in the organization.

If most of these statements are true for you, Morin says, you should stay where you are.

Professor John Sullivan offers a different set of questions to evaluate your current job and new possibilities:

1. Do you love the work? The ideal job is one you'd want to do even if you were rich.
2. Do you have a great mentor? Your career will soar if you do.
3. Do you have opportunities to learn a lot fast? No job is forever. But if you keep learning cutting-edge skills, you'll always be employable.
4. Does the job encourage rapid change? Change encourages growth. And growth keeps you employable and promotable.
5. Is the company an employer of choice (EOC, for whom everyone wants to work) or a fun place to work (FPW)? If you're with an EOC, you get an "impeccable pedigree that will prove invaluable" the next time you're on the job market. And a FPW is its own reward.

The job with the most "yes" responses wins.

Sources: Anne Fisher, "Ask Annie," *Fortune*, February 7, 2000, 210; and John Sullivan, "What Makes a Great Job?" *Fast Company*, October 1998, 166.

- Technology or manufacturing equipment applications
- Plans for growth or downsizing
- Challenges the organization faces
- The corporate culture (◀ ▷ Module 2)

The directories listed in Figure 26.1 provide information ranging from net worth, market share, and principal products to the names of officers and directors. Ask your librarian to identify additional directories. To get specific financial data (and to see how the organization presents itself to the public), get the company's annual report on the Web. (Note: only companies whose stock is publicly traded are required to issue annual reports. In this day of mergers and buyouts, many companies are owned by other companies. The parent company may be the only one to issue an annual report.) Many company Web sites provide information about training programs and career paths for new hires. To learn about new products, plans for

General Directories

Directory of Corporate Affiliations

Dun's Million Dollar Directory

Standard & Poor's Register of Corporations,
Directors, and Executives

Thomas Register of American Manufacturers

Specialized Directories and Resource Books

Accounting Firms and Practitioners

California Manufacturers Register

Directory of Hotel and Motel Systems

Dun and Bradstreet

Franchise Annual: Handbook and Directory

Hoover's Handbook of American Business

O'Dwyer's Directory of Public Relations Firms

The Rand McNally Banker's Directory

Scott's Business Directory

Standard Directory of Advertisers ("Red Book")

Television Factbook

Traders

Figure 26.1

Where to Get Addresses and Facts About Companies

Advertising Age

Business to Business Magazine

CAmagazine

Canada Employment Weekly

Canadian Auto World

Canadian Business

The Canadian Firefighter

Canadian Musician

Computer & Entertainment Retailing

Computer Dealer News

Computing Canada

Direction Informatique

Essense (Canadian Federation of Chefs & Cooks)

Farm & Country (Ontario commercial farmer trade)

Financial Analysts Journal

Graphic Arts Monthly

HR Focus

Information highways

Medical Post's Outlook Magazine (financial advice for physicians)

Northern Miner (mining news)

The Western Producer (Saskatoon)

Figure 26.2

Examples of Trade Journals and Magazines

growth, or solutions to industry challenges, read business newspapers such as The *National Post*, *The Globe and Mail*, *The Wall Street Journal* or The *Financial Post*; business magazines such as *Report on Business*, *Canadian Business*, *Strategy Magazine*, *Fortune*, *Business Week*, and *Forbes*; and trade journals. Each of these has indexes listing which companies are discussed in a specific issue. A few of the trade journals available are listed in Figure 26.2.

The Internet has much of this information, including information about corporate culture and even anonymous statements from employees. Figure 26.3 lists some of the best sites. Check professional listservs and electronic bulletin boards. Employers sometimes post specialized jobs on them: they're always a good way to get information about the industry you hope to enter.

Should I do information interviews?

> They help any job hunter. They're crucial if you're not sure what you want to do.

In an **information interview**, you talk to someone who works in the area you hope to enter. Ostensibly the interview allows you to find out what the day-to-day work involves and how you can best prepare to enter that field. However, if you're prepared, you can use the information interview to self-recruit ("I want to work for *you*!") and to make a positive impression.

Site *to* **See**

Go to
http://www.journal
ismnet.com/business/
canada.htm#canbest

Information regarding Canadian companies and businesses.

Site *to* **See**

Go to
http://www.ryerson.
ca/library/subjects/
mktg.html

A comprehensive subject search.

An information interview can

- Let you know whether or not you'd like the job
- Give you specific information that you can use to present yourself effectively in your résumé and application letter
- Create a good image of you in the mind of the interviewer, so that he or she thinks well of you when openings arise

In an information interview, you might ask the following questions:

- Tell me about the papers on your desk. What are you working on right now?
- How do you spend your typical day?
- How does what you do make or save the organization time or money?

Figure 26.3
Career Resources on the Web

Canada One Magazine
www.canadaone.com/ezine/expert/expert39.html
This free online magazine for small business in Canada examines interpersonal networking skills.

Career Experience
www.careerexperience.com
This American site offers a wealth of career resources. Explore hundreds of careers and match your personality to occupations.

CareerMagazine
www.careermag.com

CareerMosaic
www.careermosaic.com

Career Gateway
www.edu.gov.on.ca/eng/career/descrip.html
Home page: www.edu.gov.on.ca/eng/career/
Hard-to-find occupational information organized by Canadian, American, and overseas sources.

Fast Company Working Progress
fcke.fastcompany.com
Links to *Fast Company* articles by company. The best entries also have responses from employees to questions about corporate culture, decision making, dress codes, creativity, and work-life balance.

The Foundation for Enterprise Development's site
www.fed.org

HireDiversity
www.hirediversity.com

Human Resources Development Canada
hrdc.-drhc.gc.ca

Industry Canada's Strategic site
www.strategis.lc.gc.ca

JobTrak
www.jobtrak.com

Monster Board
www.monster.ca

Non-profit Jobs
www.nonprofitexpert.com/nonprofit_jobs.htm

Rebecca Smith's eRésumés and Resources
www.eresumes.com/links_jobs.html
www.eresumes.com/tut_scanresume.html

The Riley Guide: Employment Opportunities and Job Resources on the Internet
www.dbm.com/jobguide
Good information about what to search for and where to look, with links.

SkillSearch
www.skillsearch.co.uk

Vault
vault.com
Size, profits, links to stories about a company and its Web page, "uppers," "downers," a company snapshot, the percent of women and minority employees, and even the number of rounds of interviews before someone is hired.

Wetfeet.com
www.wetfeet.com/asp/home.asp
Information about careers, job-hunting strategies, and specific companies. Includes discussion groups where you can post your résumé for feedback and talk to recruiters and employees at selected companies.

World Wide Web Employment Office
www.employmentoffice.net/index.htm

Source: "100 Top Internet Sites for learning and Employment," Youth Employment Strategy, Human Resources Development Canada, Government of Canada, 2000 Edition.

- How have your duties changed since you first started working here?
- What do you like best about your job? What do you like least?
- What do you think the future holds for this kind of work?
- How did you get this job?
- What courses, activities, or jobs would you recommend to someone who wanted to do this kind of work?

The basic principles for presenting yourself shouldn't change when you use the Internet in your job search

Source: © Ann Reinertsen Farrell. Reprinted from *Harvard Business Review.*

To set up an information interview, phone or write a letter like the one in Figure 26.4 on the next page. If you do write, phone the following week to set up a specific time.

What is the "hidden job market"? How do I tap into it?

> The "hidden market", composed of jobs that are never advertised, is accessible to those who know how to use networking techniques.
>
> Referral interviews and prospecting letters can help you find it.

Most great jobs are never advertised—and the number rises the higher up the job ladder you go. Over 60 percent of all new jobs come not from responding to an ad but from networking with personal contacts.[5] Some of these jobs are created especially for a specific person. These unadvertised jobs are called **the hidden job** market; creating your own opportunities to meet and work with others informally— through *volunteer community involvement*, for example—is the optimum method of tapping into this market. Referral interviews, an organized method of networking, offer another way to tap into these jobs. Schedule **referral** interviews to learn about current job opportunities in your field. Sometimes an interview that starts out as an information interview turns into a referral interview.

A referral interview gives you information about current opportunities available in your town in the area you're interested in, refers you to other people who can tell you about job opportunities, and enables the interviewer to see that you could make a contribution to his or her organization. Therefore, the goal of a referral interview is to put you face-to-face with someone who has the power to hire you: the president of a small company, the division vice president or branch manager of a big company, the director of the local office of a provincal or federal agency.

FYI

Networking finds executive jobs far more effectively than surfing the Internet, according to a recent North American survey. Last year, 48 percent of Canadians and 66 percent of Americans marketed themselves into new jobs through informal professional and social networks.

Source: Virginia Galt, "Networking tops Web in CEO job search," *The Globe and Mail*, April 4, 2001. M1.

Figure 26.4

Letter Requesting an Information Interview

774 Sherbrooke Street East
Montreal, PQ
H8S 1H1

April 18, 2002

Kam Yuricich
Clary Communications
1420 Sherbrooke Street East
Montréal PQ
H3G 1K9

Dear Kam Yuricich: *If starting with the request seems too abrupt, work up to it more gradually.*

You advice would be invaluable to me as I attempt to find my niche in the workforce. Could I schedule an information interview with you to learn more about how public relations consultants work with their clients?

Refer to any previous contact with reader

Your talk to McGill's PRSSA Chapter last week, about the differences between working for a PR firm and being a PR staff person within an organization, really interested me. Last summer I had a co-op placement with Management Horizons. Although some of my assignments were "go-fer" jobs, my supervisor, Jason Correila, gave me the chance to work on several brochures and to draft two speeches for managers. I enjoyed this variety and would like to learn more about the possibility of working in a PR firm.

Ask about ways to enter the field

Perhaps we could discuss the courses you think would best prepare me for PR work. I have a year and a half left before graduation and would like to choose electives that would make me most employable.

I would greatly appreciate any time that you could afford me. If it's convenient for you, perhaps we could meet some time over the next three weeks. I'll call you early next week to set up an appointment.

Sincerely,

Lee Tan

Lee Tan

Start by scheduling interviews with people you know who may know something about that field—professors, co-workers, neighbours, friends. Call your alumni office to get the names and phone numbers of alumni who now work where you would like to work. Your (purported) purpose in talking to them is to get advice about improving your résumé and about general job-hunting strategies. Your real intention: to become a known commodity and thereby get **referrals** to other people. In fact, go into the interview with the names of people you'd like to talk to. If the interviewee doesn't suggest anyone, say, "Do you think it would be a good idea for me to talk to _____ ?"

Then, armed with a referral from someone you know, call Mr. or Ms. "Big" and say, "So-and-so suggested I talk with you about job-hunting strategy." If the person says, "We aren't hiring," you say, "Oh, I'm not asking _you_ for a job. I'd just like some advice from a knowledgeable person about the opportunities in banking [or desktop publishing, or whatever] in this city." If this person does not have the power to create a position, you seek more referrals at the end of _this_ interview. (You can also polish your résumé, if you get good suggestions.)

Even when you talk to the person who could create a job for you, you _do not ask for a job_. But to give you advice about your résumé, the person has to look at it. When a powerful person focuses on your skills, he or she will naturally think about the problems and needs in that organization. When there's a match between what you can do and what the organization needs, that person has the power to create a position for you.

Remember the two truisms of job hunting: self-recruitment is still the number one way to get hired, and people hire people that they know. Prepare as carefully for these interviews as you would for a job interview. Think in advance of good questions; know something about the general field or industry; learn as much as you can about the specific company.

Always follow up information and referral interviews with personal thank-you letters. Use specifics to show that you paid attention during the interview, and enclose a copy of your revised résumé.

How do I present my non-traditional experiences?

Address the employer's potential concerns positively.

Today, people bring a variety of non-traditional experiences to the job search. However, these experiences often build the transferable skills that savvy employers search for. In a world where the ability to learn is recognized as the key to employability, your communication skills will determine whether or not you get the job.

This section gives advice on presenting your previous experience positively.

"All My Experience Is in My Family's Business."

In your résumé, simply list the company you worked for. For a reference, instead of a family member, list a supervisor, client, or vendor who can talk about your work. Since the reader may wonder whether "Jim Clarke" is any relation to "Clarke Construction Company," be ready to answer interview questions about why you're looking at other companies. Prepare an answer that stresses the broader opportunities you seek but doesn't criticize your family or the family business.

FYI

Only 4 percent of Canadians work 9 to 5; 51 percent work a routine schedule each day; only 33 percent work Monday-Friday each week.

Source: " '9 to 5' is no more, BBM study reveals"; visited Web site February 13, 2001: http://library.northernlight.com/CK1999 1118040001489.html.

Instant Replay

Information Interviews

In an **information interview** you talk to someone who works in the area you hope to enter, to find out what the day-to-day work involves and how you can best prepare to enter that field

FYI

The Alliance of Canadian Manufacturers and Exporters identified "problem solving," "communication" and interpersonal" as the top three employee skills most needing improvement.

Source: Management Issues Survey, quoted in _The Globe and Mail,_ February 12, 2001, M1.

Go to
http://www.plar.com
/english.html

Learn what you
need to know about
your job skills at this
PLAR (Prior Learning
Assessment and
Recognition) site.

FYI

The Information
Technologies (IT)
industry is one of
the fastest
growing, most
profitable, and
most competitive
industries in the
world. Companies
in Canada's major
cities are always
hiring, but so too
are expanding
communities in
every province. The
*Canadian
Biotechnology
Company Directory*
can provide leads
to potential
employers in these
fields. To apply in
the information
technologies field,
you can send your
resume via email to
*CANDIDATECH
Placing Firm Inc.*

"I've Been Out of the Job Market for a While."

You need to prove to a potential employer that you're up-to-date and motivated. To do that,

- Investigate how work in your field has changed. For example, librarians must have a much broader understanding of technology than they did even five years ago.
- Be active in professional organizations. Attend meetings; read magazines, newspapers and trade journals
- Learn the computer programs that professionals in your field use
- Find out your prospective employer's immediate priorities. If you can show you'll contribute from day one, you'll have a much easier sell. But to do that, you need to know what the employer needs: what skill sets are employers looking for?
- Show how your at-home experience relates directly to the workplace. Multi-tasking, organizing food bank drives, managing projects, chairing PTA meetings, dealing with unpredictable situations, building consensus, listening, raising money, and making presentations are all transferable skills.
- Create a portfolio of your work—even if it's for imaginary clients—to demonstrate your expertise. Most of Canada's provinces and territories offer prior learning assessment and recognition (PLAR) to adults with work experience. Based on a demonstration of the requisite knowledge and skills, you can get credit for post-secondary courses. Most high-level courses require that candidates prepare a proposal and a portfolio of work to demonstrate subject knowledge and skills.

"I Want to Change Fields."

Learn about the skills needed in the job you want. Learn the language of the industry.

Then you can identify a good reason (from the perspective employer's point of view) for choosing to explore a new field. "I want a change" or "I need to get out of a bad situation" will not convince an employer that you know what you're doing.

Think about how your experience relates to the job you want. Jack is an older-than-average student who wants to be a pharmaceutical sales representative. He has sold woodstoves, served subpoenas, and worked on an oil rig. A chronological résumé makes his work history look directionless. But a skills résumé (◁|▶ Module 27) could focus on persuasive ability (selling stoves), initiative and persistence (serving subpoenas), and technical knowledge (courses in biology and chemistry).[6]

"I Was Fired."

First, deal with the emotional baggage. You need to reduce negative feelings to a manageable level before you're ready to job hunt.

Second, try to learn from the experience. You'll be a much more attractive job candidate if you can show that you've learned from the experience—whether your lesson is improved work habits or that you need to choose a job where you can do work you can point to with pride.

Third, suggests Phil Elder, an interviewer for an insurance company, call the person who fired you and say something like this: "Look, I know you weren't pleased with the job I did at _____ . I'm applying for a job at _____ now and the personnel director may call you to ask about me. Would you be willing to give me the chance to get this job so that I can try to do things right this time?" All but the hardest of heart, says Elder, will give you one more chance. You won't get a glowing reference, but neither will the statement be so damning that no one is willing to hire you.[7]

"I Don't Have Any Experience."

Get some. You can get experience in several ways:

- Take a fast-food job—and keep it. If you do well, you may be promoted to a supervisor within a year.
  Use every opportunity to learn about the management and financial aspects of the business.
- Volunteer. Coach a community little-league, join the PTA, help out at your local food bank, canvass for charity. If you work hard, you'll quickly get an opportunity to do more: manage a budget, write fund-raising materials, and supervise other volunteers.
- Freelance. Design brochures, create Web pages, do tax returns for small businesses. Use your skills—for free, if you have to at first.
- Write. Create a portfolio of ads, instructions, or whatever documents are relevant for the field you want to enter. Ask a professional—an instructor, a local businessperson, someone from a professional organization—to critique them. Volunteer your services to local fund-raising organizations and small businesses.

Getting experience is particularly important for students with good grades. Pick something where you interact with other people, so that you can show that you can work well in an organization.

If you're in the job market now, think carefully about what you've really done. Write sentences using the action verbs in  Figure 27.3 on page 556. Think about what you've done in courses, in volunteer work, in unpaid activities. Focus especially on your communications skills: problem solving, critical thinking, managing projects, working as part of a team, persuasive speaking, and writing. Solving a problem for a hypothetical firm in an accounting class, thinking critically about a report problem in business communication, working with a group in a marketing class, and communicating with people at the senior centre where you volunteer are all valuable experiences, even if no one paid you.

If you're not actually looking for a job but just need to create a résumé for this course, ask your instructor whether you may assume that you're graduating and add the things you hope to do between now and that time.

"I'm a Lot Older Than They Want."

Even before the recent dot-com backlash, more mature workers were in demand for their sophisticated interpersonal and communications abilities. Uninformed employers are concerned that older people won't be flexible, up-to-date, or willing to be supervised by someone younger. To counter these fears,

- Keep up-to-date. Read trade journals; attend professional meetings.
- Learn the computer programs your field uses. Refer to technology in the résumé, job letter, and interview: "Yes, I saw the specifications for your new product on your Web site."

Instant Replay

The Hidden Job Market and Referral Interviews

Unadvertised jobs are called **the hidden job market**. Referral interviews, an organized method of networking, offer the most systematic way to tap into these jobs. Schedule **referral interviews** to learn about current job opportunities in your field.

Site to See

Go to
www.youth.gc.ca
www.jobboom.com
The Government of Canada's Youth Employment Strategy Web site and Québec's www.jobboom.com provide the top 100 Internet links for job searching: these sites cover every aspect of career development, from choosing the right job and building your résumé to evaluating market trends and job offers.

- Work with younger people, in classroom teams, in volunteer work, or on the job. Be able to cite specific cases where you've learned from young people and worked well with them.
- Use positive emphasis (◀▶ Module 7). Talk about your ability to relate to older customers (who have so much disposable income), the valuable perspective you bring. Focus on fairly recent events, not ones from 20 years ago.
- Show energy and enthusiasm to counter the stereotype that older people are tired and ill.

Employability Skills 2000+ Checklist for Researching Jobs

In this module, the key skills from The Conference Board of Canada's Employability Skills 2000+ are:

Communicate
✔ read and understand information presented in a variety of forms (e.g. words, graphs, charts, diagrams)
✔ write and speak so others pay attention and understand share information using a range of information and communications technologies (e.g. voice, email, computers)
✔ use relevant scientific, technological, and mathematical knowledge and skills to explain or clarify ideas

Manage Information
✔ locate, gather, and organize information using appropriate technology and information systems
✔ access, analyze, and apply knowledge and skills from a variety of disciplines (e.g. the arts, languages, science, technology, mathematics, social sciences, and the humanities)

Think & Solve Problems
✔ assess situations and identify problems
✔ recognize the human, interpersonal, technical, scientific, and mathematical dimensions of a problem
✔ readily use science, technology, and mathematics as ways to think, gain and share knowledge, solve problems, and make decisions
✔ check to see if a solution works, and act on opportunities for improvement

Participate in Projects & Tasks
✔ plan, design, or carry out a project or task from start to finish with well-defined objectives and outcomes
✔ work to agreed quality standards and specifications
✔ adapt to changing requirements and information
✔ continuously monitor the success of a project or task and identify ways to improve

Review of Key Points

- Informal preparation for job hunting should start soon after you arrive on campus. Formal preparation for job hunting should begin a full year before you begin interviewing.

- Use directories, annual reports, recruiting literature, business periodicals, trade journals, and Web pages to get information about employers and jobs to use in your letter.

- Information and referral interviews can help you tap into the **hidden job market**—jobs that are not advertised. In an **information interview** you find out what the day-to-day work involves and how you can best prepare to enter that field. **Referral interviews** are interviews you schedule to learn about current job opportunities in your field.

- If you have concerns about your employment history, brainstorm a way to address the employer's fears calmly and positively.

Learning Applications

Questions for Comprehension

26.1 What should you know about yourself before you apply for jobs?

26.2 What information should you try to learn about a company?

26.3 What is an information interview?

26.4 What is the hidden job market?

Questions for Critical Thinking

26.5 Why is it desirable to start thinking about jobs months—even years—before you'll actually be on the market?

26.6 Why is it important to research the companies you want to apply to?

26.7 What is your biggest weakness as you prepare to job hunt? How could you minimize it?

Questions for Building Skills

26.8 What skills have you read about in this module?

26.9 What skills are you practising in the assignments you're doing for this module?

26.10 How could you further develop the skills you're working on?

Exercises and Problems

26.11   Evaluating Career Web Sites*

Evaluate three or more Web sites for job hunters, considering the following questions:

- Is the site easy to navigate?
- Is it visually attractive?
- Are any ads unobtrusive?
- Does it contain good advice?

- Does it let job hunters specify who may *not* see their posted résumés (e.g., the current employer)?
- Does it have any features that you don't find in other career Web sites?

*Inspired by a problem written by Gary Kohut, University of North Carolina at Charlotte.

26.12   Networking

Write to a friend who is already in the workforce, asking about one or more of the following topics:

- Are any jobs in your field available in your friend's organization? If so, what?
- If a job is available, can your friend provide information beyond the job listing that will help you write a more detailed, persuasive letter? (Specify the kind of information you'd like to have.)
- Can your friend suggest people in other organizations who might be useful to you in your job search? (Specify any organizations in which you're especially interested.)

26.13   Gathering Information about an Industry

Use six recent issues of a trade journal to report on three to five trends, developments, or issues that are important in an industry.

As Your Instructor Directs,

a. Share your findings with a small group of other students

b. Summarize your findings in a memo to your instructor

c. Present your findings to the class

d. Email your findings to the other members of the class

e. Join with a small group of other students to write a report summarizing the results of this research

26.14   Gathering Information about a Specific Organization

Gather printed information about a specific organization, using several of the following methods:

- Use the most current edition of The Career Directory
- Check the company's Web site
- Read the company's annual report
- Talk to someone who works there
- Pick up relevant information at your local board of trade or chamber of commerce
- Read articles in trade publications and *The Globe and Mail*, The *National Post*, *The Wall Street Journal*, or The *Financial Post* that mention the organization (check the indexes)

- Get the names and addresses of its officers (from a directory or from the Web)
- Read recruiting literature provided by the company

As Your Instructor Directs,

a. Share your findings with a small group of other students

b. Summarize your findings in a memo to your instructor

c. Present your findings orally to the class

d. Email your findings to the other members of the class

e. Join with a small group of other students to write a report summarizing the results of this research

26.15 Conducting an Information Interview

Interview someone working in a field you're interested in. Use the questions listed in the module or the shorter list here:

- How did you get started in this field?
- What do you like about your job?
- What do you dislike about your job?
- Who are three other people who could give me additional information about this job?

As Your Instructor Directs,

a. Share the results of your interview with a small group of other students

b. Write up your interview in a memo to your instructor

c. Present the results of your interview orally to the class

d. Email a summary of your interview to other members of your class

e. Write to the interviewee thanking him or her for taking the time to talk to you

Polishing Your Prose

Using Details

Details are especially important in reader benefits (◀ ▶ Module 8), reports, résumés, job application, and sales letters. Customers or potential employers look for specific details to help them make decisions, such as what makes your product better than the competition's or how your experience would help the reader. Here's an example:

> I can offer your more than ten years of advertising experience, including five years of broadcast sales in Ottawa, where I generated more than $19 million in revenue, as well as three years with J. Walter Thompson, Toronto's leading advertising company. For the first four years of my career, I also wrote advertising copy, including hundreds of local and regional radio spots for such diverse products as cookies, cat food, fishing tackle, and children's toys. I also wrote print pieces, including the entire 15-month campaign for Vancouver-based "Uncle Bill's Electronics Bazaar," which increased sales by nearly 37 percent during that period.

Reader Benefits

What features or experiences make your product or service unique? Useful? Cost-effective?

Weak: With the Stereobooster, your car will sound great.

Better: The Stereobooster safely gives your car audio system a full 30 watts per channel of sheer sound excitement, double that of other systems on the market—all for under $50.

The Five Senses

Describe sight, sound, taste, touch, and smell. Some sensations are so powerful that they immediately conjure up thoughts or emotions—the smell of fresh coffee, the sound of ocean waves, the feeling of sunlight against the skin.

Concrete Nouns and Verbs

Concrete nouns and verbs are better than more general nouns and verbs combined with adjectives and adverbs. For instance, *Manager* and *15 months* are more concrete than *the person in charge* or *a while*. Concrete words make meaning clear and vivid:

Weak: At my last job, I typed stuff.

Better: As a clerk typist II until July for Hughes and Associates, I typed hundreds of memos, letters, and reports.

Increase your vocabulary by reading a variety of materials. Keep a dictionary and thesaurus handy. Do crossword puzzles or computer word games to practice what you know.

Adjectives and Adverbs That Count

Omit or replace vague or overused adjectives and adverbs: *some, very, many, a lot, kind/sort of, partly, eventually*. Increasingly, novice writers are using *so* as an adjective, as in "He was so happy about the promotion." Exactly how happy is this?

Conversational English, Not Jargon or Obscure Words.

In general, choose the more conversational option over jargon or obscure words: *exit, typical,* or *second to last* rather than *egress, quintessential,* or *penultimate*.

Exercises

Add details to the following sentences.

1. I work for a company.

2. The person in charge of our department wants some files.

3. Sometime in the future I will get a job in my field.

4. It's been a while since I went there.

5. Our product will help you.

6. There are lots of reasons why you should hire me.

7. This product is so much better than its competitors.

8. We will have a meeting in the afternoon.

9. My experience makes me a good candidate for this job.

10. We plan to travel to a couple of states sometime next month.

Check your answers to the odd-numbered exercises on page 634.

Module 27
Creating Persuasive Résumés

Topics

- How can I create an attention-getting résumé?

- What kind of résumé should I use?

- How do résumés differ?

- What parts résumés are the same?

- What should I do if the standard categories don't fit?

- Should I limit my résumé to just one page?

- How do I create a scannable résumé?

Review of Key Points

Learning Applications

Polishing Your Prose: Proofreading

Learning Focus

After reading and applying the information in Module 27, you'll be able to demonstrate

Knowledge of

- Current résumé-writing practices

Skills to

- Create the résumé that best showcases your qualifications
- Make your experience relevant to employers
- Write the strongest possible résumé
- Increase the number of "hits" your résumé receives
- Use a computer to create paper and scannable résumés

"If the résumé does not impact the reader ... neither will the person whom it represents."

"You are selling a valuable product: yourself. Your résumé must be enjoyable and you must put in it what you have to offer," says Guy Parent, president of Stellar Personnel Placement, a personnel and human resources agency serving all of southwestern Ontario with offices in London, St. Thomas, and Windsor. "Your résumé is your introduction to the business world. Make it count. This is true whether you are a general labourer or a corporate executive."

Guy Parent has worked in the industry of placing personnel since 1976. He presently owns three companies that focus respectively on the hiring of new personnel, investigating the conduct of existing personnel, and offering pre-employment screening dedicated to conducting background checks.

Stellar Personnel Placement functions both as an employment agency and as a human resources agency providing services to business clients. Stellar sales people work in the field selling its services, so they understand all aspects of the employment market. They know what works because they are out there selling themselves and the résumés they receive.

Corporations today are more conscious of who they hire. The costs and risks related to bringing an employee on board are frightening given liability issues, pension and group insurance, WSIB exposure, cost of the grievance procedure, training, and supervision, to name only a few. Placement agencies offer the employer an opportunity to extend the probation period to ensure the fit is right before a commitment is offered.

Guy remarks, "When candidates come to Stellar for an interview, our mandate is twofold. Find the candidate the employment they seek, and present the best candidate to the client."

"The résumé is your ticket to an interview. Its sole purpose is to introduce you in a favourable fashion to a prospective employer. If the résumé does not impact the reader, you can assume that neither will the person whom it represents. In short, résumés must reflect "FAB": important Facts about yourself, your Accomplishments, and how you will Benefit the employer."

"Visual presentation is also important," Guy observes. He stresses that since most résumés are copied or faxed, they should be on plain white paper and laser printed. Coloured paper should not be used unless appropriate to a particular job. Finally, language in the résumé plays an important role. "Think of the employer as a spectator at a game. You must do something to get him to rise up and cheer."

Guy concludes, "You never know what personal experience will trigger interest in a prospective employer but one thing is for sure...to manufacture, misrepresent, cheat, or lie on your résumé will cause you grief. Upfront and honest are rare qualities that I never stop looking for. If you don't get the job because you were too honest, it wasn't the job for you. Imagine working for three months and then facing your boss who brings to your attention an exaggeration on your résumé because you can't do what you said you could. Chances are you won't see your fourth month."

www.stellarplacement.com
Stellar Personnel Placement

www.gumshoes.com
Corporate Investigation Services

www.corporateinquiry.com
Corporate Inquiry Systems

Figure 27.1
PAIBOC Questions for Analysis

PAIBOC

Use the PAIBOC questions to analyze business communication problems:

P   What are your **purposes** in writing?

A   Who is (are) your **audience(s)**? How do members of your audience differ? What characteristics are relevant to this particular message?

I   What **information** must your message include?

B   What reasons or reader **benefits** can you use to support your position?

O   What **objection(s)** can you expect your reader(s) to have? What negative elements of your message must you de-emphasize or overcome?

C   How will the **context** affect reader response? Think about your relationship to the reader, morale in the organization, the economy, the time of year, and any special circumstances.

A **résumé** summarizes your qualifications so persuasively that you get an interview. When you're in the job market, having a résumé makes you prepared for every opportunity. When you're employed, having a current résumé allows you to assess your continuous improvement; this ongoing inventory makes it easier for you to take advantage of even better job opportunities that come up. Even if you're several years away from job hunting, preparing a résumé now will make you more conscious of what to do in the next two or three years to make yourself an attractive candidate. Writing a résumé is also an ego-building experience: the person who looks so good on paper is **you**!

If your skills are in great demand, you can ignore every résumé-writing guideline and still get a good job. When you must compete against many applicants, however, these guidelines can showcase your employability skills.

And, of course, the PAIBOC writing formula (see Figure 27.1) applies to all job communications. Tailor your résumé to your specific audiences and purposes, and to your unique qualifications. Adopt the wording or layout of an example if it's relevant to your own situation, but consider your résumé a lifelong work-in-progress. Your experiences, the nature of work, the labour market and the demands of the potential job change constantly; so will your résumé.

How can I encourage the employer to pay attention to my résumé?

> Write your résumé to show how your qualifications fit the job and the company.

Your résumé can be screened in two ways: electronically or by a person. If people do the reading, the employer will skim the résumés quickly, dividing the documents into two piles: "reject" and "maybe." In the first round, each résumé may get as little as 2.9 seconds of the reader's attention. Then the reader goes through the "maybe" pile again, weeding out more documents. If there are a lot of résumés (and some companies get 2,000 résumés a week), résumés may get only 10 to 30 seconds in this stage. After the initial pile has been culled to one-half or one-hundredth of the initial pile, the remaining documents will be read more carefully to choose the people who are invited for interviews.

Or your résumé may be electronically scanned into a job-applicant tracking system. Then a computer does the first set of cuts. The employer specifies the keywords from the job description, listing the knowledge, skills, and abilities that the ideal applicant would have. Sometimes personal characteristics (e.g., *hard worker*, *good writer*, *willing to travel*) may also be included. The employer receives the résumés that match the keywords, arranged with the most "hits" first. The employer then chooses the interviewees. In the current job market, you need both a paper résumé that's attractive to the human eye and a scannable résumé that serves your purposes in a job-applicant tracking system. To increase the chances that a real human being will attend to your résumé,

- Specify how you contributed to the organization. If possible, quantify your contribution: *increased sales 10 percent, saved the company $13,000, supervised five people.*

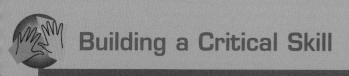

Using a Computer to Create Résumés

Even if you pay someone else to produce your résumé, *you* must specify the exact layout.

Print your résumé on a laser printer on high-quality 21-by-27 centimetre paper (never legal size). White paper is standard for business résumés; cream, pale grey, and parchment colours are also acceptable.

Play with Layout and Design

Experiment with layout, fonts, and spacing to get an attractive résumé. Consider creating a letterhead that you use for both your résumé and your application letter. (See Figure 27.4.)

Use enough white space to make your résumé easy to read but not so much that you look as if you're padding. Centre your name as the title of the document in 14-point (or bigger) type. Use 12-point for headings. To get more on a page, use 11-point type for the text. The default margins and tab settings probably are too big. Especially if you use the indented format, try a .8 inch left margin. Set tab settings at .3 inch rather than the standard .5 inch. Try rules (thin lines) or borders to see if you like their look.

Avoid Templates

Some services fit every résumé into a single template. Even if you have lots of volunteer work, you have to fit it all into an inch-high space. But if you have no volunteer work, you still have that inch—glaringly empty. Using a standard template defeats the purpose of a good résumé: to make you look as good as possible.

If a placement service requires you to use a template, do so, but also create another résumé that looks good. Take a copy to each interview. Tell the interviewer, "I thought you might like to know a little more about me."

Proofread

Employers assume that the résumé represents your best work. Proofread carefully to be sure the document is perfect. Especially check
- Spelling of your college, your employers, and your references
- Parallelism (◀▶ Module 14)
- Consistency (spell out all province names or use Postal Service abbreviations for all)
  - Dates
  - Phone numbers, email addresses, and URLs

- Emphasize achievements that
  - Are most relevant to the position for which you're applying
  - Are recent
- Identify your abilities in order of financial worth to the organization. Idea people are worth the most, because creative or innovative notions can save companies billions of dollars; cite your strategic/problem-solving accomplishments first. People skills are the next most valuable abilities; refer to your training, supervising and scheduling responsibilities. "Things" skills—software knowledge, for example—are easiest acquired and immediately obsolete; cite these last, unless these technical skills are key to the job.
- Show your superiority to other applicants.
- Use the language and terminology of the industry and the organization you want to join.
- Include transferable skills: ability to use computer programs, to write and speak well, to identify and solve problems, to work well independently and with others, to speak a second language.

FYI

The personal qualities employers want most are communication skills and self-motivation, according to a survey by the National Association of Colleges and Employers.

Source: Albert R. Karr, "Work Week," *The Wall Street Journal,* February 8, 2000, A1.

• Design one résumé to appeal to the human eye and the second to be easily processed by an electronic scanner.

The more you tailor your résumé to a specific employer, the greater your chances for securing an interview.

What kind of résumé should I use?

Use the format that makes you look best.

Depending on their experience and the audience, people use one of three kinds of résumés: chronological, functional/combination, or skills. The **chronological résumé** summarizes what you have accomplished, starting with the most recent events and going backward in reverse chronology. It emphasizes degrees, job titles, and dates. Figure 27.2 on the next page shows a chronological résumé. Use a chronological résumé when you have limited relevant work experience and your education and experience show

• A logical preparation for the position for which you're applying
• A steady progression leading to the present.

The **functional/combination résumé** emphasizes the applicant's most important (to the reader) job titles and responsibilities, or **functions**, regardless of chronology. Usually, the functional résumé reverts to the **reverse chronology** listing for information not related to paid employment, as reflected in Figure 27.3 on page 556. Use the functional/combination résumé when

• Your work experiences match the position responsibilities
• Your skills and expertise match the position requirements
• Your education and experience are not the usual route to the position for which you're applying
• you wish to de-emphasize your formal educational

The **skills résumé** emphasizes the skills you've acquired through work experience, rather than dates. Figure 27.4 on page 558, shows a skills résumé. Use a skills résumé when

• You want to combine experience from paid jobs, activities or volunteer work, and courses to show the extent of your experience in administration, finance, speaking, etc.
• Your education and experience are not the usual route to the position for which you're applying
• You're changing fields
• Your recent work history may create the wrong impression (e.g., it has gaps, shows a demotion, shows job-hopping, etc.)

The best résumés telegraph relevant details as concisely and attractively as possible. Most résumés use bullet points, omit *I*, and use sentence fragments punctuated as complete sentences. Complete sentences are acceptable, as are *me* and *my*, if they are the briefest way to present information.

Figure 27.2
A Chronological Résumé

A vertical line provides visual variety.

Jerry A. Jackson

Vary font sizes. The name is in 18-point, the main headings in 12-point, and the text in 11-point type.

Campus Address
Community College of Winnipeg
St. Mary's Road
Winnipeg, SK
R2H 1J2
(360) 555-5718
jjackson@ccw.sk.ca
hotmail.com/jackson.2495/home.htm

Permanent Address
2105 East Hill Avenue
Saskatoon, SK
S7J 3C8
(306) 731-4108

If you have a professional Web page, include its URL.

Education
A.A.S. in Finance, May 2002, Community College of Winnipeg, Winnipeg, SK
"B" Average
Courses Related to Program:

List not only major courses, but also others that will enhance your performance.

Intermediate Accounting I and II
Business Writing
Consumer Finance
Financial Management
Interpersonal Communication
Investments

Microeconomics
Presentation Skills
Public Speaking
Report and Technical Writing
Sociology of Marriage and Family
Statistics

Sports Experience
CAAD (Colonial Athletes Against Drugs)
Intramural Volleyball Team (Champions, Winter 2001)
Two-year Varsity Letterman, Community College of Winnipeg
   Men's NCAA Division II Basketball

Experience
Financial Sales Representative, Primerica Company, Winnipeg, SK, February 2001-present.
   Work with clients to plan investment strategies; recommend specific investments.
Entrepreneur, Winnipeg, SK, and Saskatoon, SK, September 2000-January 2001. Created a saleable
   product, secured financial backing, found a manufacturer, supervised production, and sold product—
   12 dozen T-shirts at a $5.25 profit each—to help pay for school expenses.   *How to handle self-employment.*
Landscape Maintenance Supervisor, Saskatoon, SK, Summers 1992-2000. Formed a company to cut
   lawns, put up fences, fertilize, garden, and paint houses. Hired, fired, trained, motivated, and paid
   friends to complete jobs.
Collector and Repairman, ACN Inc., Saskatoon, SK, Summers 1992-98. Collected and counted up to

Specify large sums of money.

   $10,000 a day. Worked with technicians to troubleshoot and repair electronic and coin mechanisms of
   video and pinball games, cigarette machines, and jukeboxes. Drove company cars and trucks
   throughout Saskatoon metro area to collect cash and move and repair machines.

Provide details to interest readers, set you apart from other applicants.

Figure 27.3
A Functional/Combination Résumé

Mohammed Shaffer

1803 Albert Road Windsor, ON N8W 3X1 705-333-8998

Fax 705-333-8991 mshaffer@sympatico.com

Attractive design element -text on left for emphasis, reader's eye does not have to travel to middle of page

CAREER HIGHLIGHTS

- ❑ Recognized top Ontario salesperson for General Foods Canada, 1994-1996
- ❑ Co-authored *Marketing for Dummies* which sold over 500,000 copies internationally
- ❑ Founded landscape design and build business, generating over $200,000 business annually
- ❑ Featured in *Canadian Gardens*, Spring 1999
- ❑ Recognized Windsor's Volunteer of the Year, 2000
- ❑ Computer literate including DOS, Windows, Linux Operating Systems
- ❑ Design using Nextel CAD
- ❑ Fluent in Spanish, Italian, French and Hindi

In order of relevance to reader, not in chronological order

Highlights identify measurable achievements related to Sales Management position

WORK EXPERIENCE

Ontario Sales Manager   Nabisco Canada
1996-1998   Windsor Ontario

- ❑ Responsible for all Ontario sales; consistently exceeded sales quotas by 10-15%
- ❑ Managed a diverse workforce of twenty-five salespeople
- ❑ Represented company at international marketing conventions
- ❑ Served as Nabisco's media liaise person, Windsor location

Salesperson   General Foods Canada
1994-1996   Windsor Ontario

- ❑ Responsible for all southern Ontario sales region
- ❑ Consistently exceeded sales quotas by 25%
- ❑ Wrote Sales Processes and Procedures Manual, used by company Canada-wide
- ❑ Recruited by Nabisco Canada

Owner/Manager   Decorative Decks LTD
1998-Present   Windsor, Ontario

- ❑ Originated landscape design and build business
- ❑ Manage four full-time, thirty seasonal employees
- ❑ Market services to over 300 clients
- ❑ Acquire 30 new clients annually
- ❑ Write weekly garden and landscape design column for The *Windsor Star*

Current employment less significant to reader

Figure 27.3

A Functional/Combination Résumé (continued)

Mohammed Shaffer

1803 Albert Road Windsor, ON N8W 3X1 705-333-8998

Fax 705-333-8991 mshaffer@sympatico.com

VOLUNTEER EXPERIENCE   *Indicates community involvement*

1997-present   sailing instructor, Windsor Sailing Academy
1994-present   coach, Windsor Soccer Club

Résumé now identifies relevant experience in reverse chronology

PUBLICATIONS

"Gardening in Paradise", The *Windsor Star's* Living section: weekly column,
"Creating a Deck for All Seasons," *Canadian Gardening*, Spring, 1998. Toronto: Southam Press.
Marketing for Dummies. (1996)Toronto: McGraw-Hill.

ASSOCIATIONS

2000-present   Editors' Association of Canada   *Indicates professional development*
1990-present   Toastmasters, Canada
1994-present   Canadian Association of Marketing Professionals
1990-1998   Association for Business Communications

EDUCATION

St. Clair College   Business Administration, Marketing
University of Windsor, Windsor, Ontario   B.A., Commerce, completed Year 2

Perhaps formal education cannot compete with other applicants. De-emphasized through placement

HONOURS AND AWARDS

Nabisco Canada's Salesperson of the Year, 1997, '98
Top Salesperson for General Foods Ontario region, 1994, '95 and '96
Valedictorian, St. Clair College Business Administration program, class of 1999

HOBBIES AND INTERESTS

Writing for publication, bridge, backgammon, poker and chess, tennis golf, sailing and skiing: downhill and slalom, gourmet cooking

REFERENCES upon request *} optional*

Figure 27.4
A Skills Résumé

Sagarika Banerjee

210 Steeles Avenue (West), Apt # 1701 Brampton, Ontario
L6Y 2K3 **905-453-3828** sagarikabanerjee@usa.net

Objective

Excellent philosophy

To find a challenging information technology position where my communication and technical skills would make a valuable and valued contribution to the organization

Profile

Highlights communication and technical skills

- Motivated team player with good organizational, communication, and people skills
- Quick learner and good problem solver
- Detail oriented and analytical
- Able to work independently and under pressure
- Meticulous and adept manager of time critical projects
- Trained and experienced in superb customer service skills

Concrete & specific details

- Unix, DOS, Win95/98, NT, VMS, VB6, Perl, Java, SQL, Novell Net Ware 5.0
- System Analysis, DataBase Design, Data Communication, and LAN
- Knowledge of Quality Control procedures and software testing
- Seismic Data processing on VAX/VMS platform

Education

- Systems Analyst Co-operative Program
  1999-present   Sheridan College, Brampton ON

- Master of Science & Technology in Applied Geophysics
  1987-1990   Indian School Of Mines, Dhanbad, India

- Bachelor of Science (Major in Physics)
  1982-1986   Scottish Church College, Calcutta University, India

Achievements

- A average in all Sheridan College courses
- First class with distinction at Masters level (OGPA 4.02/5)
- Class and Residence Prefect college and university levels

Figure 27.4
A Skills Résumé (continued)

Sagarika Banerjee
210 Steeles Avenue (West), Apt # 1701 Brampton, Ontario
L6Y 2K3 **905-453-3828** sagarikabanerjee@usa.net

Computer Skills
- MSDOS, Windows 95/98/2000, Unix, VMS, NT, Novell Netware 5.0
- Visual Basic6, Perl, Java, SQL
- MS Office 2000
- Systems Analysis, Design Methodologies & Database Design
- Data Communication and LAN
- Email & Internet Research
- Data entry, Data analysis and processing in VAX/VMS platform
- Knowledge of ODBC, OLE

Scientific and Administrative Skills
- Research, Work distribution, & scheduling
- Project documentation and analyses
- Processing of Oil Exploration Data and also data entry and analyses
- Operation of Thermal Transfer Label Printers

Client Services
- Good listening, verbal, and written communication skills
- Excellent techno-economic presentation skills
- Excellent negotiating skills

Work History

Teklynx
Software Quality Analyst   **2001-present**
Creating test plans and test scripts
- Set up/maintain test environment
- Conduct planned and ad hoc testing
- Analyze and document defects and causes of defects

Responsibilities optional

Reverse chronology

India Rainbow Community Services of Peel
Administrative Assistant   **Summer, 1999**
- General administrative duties, front desk, customer service, filling, preparing documents in MSWord and assisting in the training program on WHMIS

Sagarika includes these because they're so impressive

Computech Ispat Ltd. Calcutta, India
Senior Geophysicist   1990-1994
- Performed Seismic Data Processing on VAX/VMS platform
- PC based processing using application software from Seismic Image software, Calgary
- Interpreted sub-surface geology in oil exploration

References available on request

Résumé is a French word meaning *summary*. To create the é (e with an acute accent), pull down the "Insert" menu to "Symbol." Never use the apostrophe to replace the accent. However, you can write RESUME in full caps or use *resume* without the accent marks.

How do résumé formats differ?

They showcase you differently, depending on your experiences, your purpose (the job you're applying for) and your audience.

A chronological résumé, like the one in Figure 27.2, focusses on when, then what, and emphasizes academic qualifications. Experience is organized by dates, with the most recent job first. The functional/combination (Figure 27.3) showcases the applicant's qualifications based on relevant job functions, or responsibilities. Extensive experience, not dates or academic degrees, is the focus. Seasoned and highly qualified applicants use this format. A skills résumé, like the one in Figure 27.4, summarizes experience and acquired skills needed for the job. Under each heading, information is listed in order of importance, combining paid and unpaid work (in classes, activities, and community groups). An Employment History section lists job titles (or functions), employers, city and province.

Chronological Résumés

In a chronological résumé, start with the Education heading. Under Work Experience or Employment History, include employment dates, position or job title, organization, city, province, and other details: seasonal, full- or part-time status, job duties, special responsibilities and/or promotions with companies. Include unpaid jobs and self-employment if they provided relevant skills (e.g., supervising people, budgeting, planning, persuading). If you've held co-op or intern placements (very significant to employers), include these under a separate heading like **Co-operative Placement Experience**.

Normally, go back as far as the summer after high school. Include earlier jobs if you started working someplace before graduating from high school but continued working there after graduation. However, give minimal detail about high school jobs. If you worked fulltime after high school, make that clear.

If, as an undergraduate you've earned a substantial portion of your college expenses, say so, either under Experience or in the Interpersonal or Skills Profile section with which you can begin the résumé. (Graduate students are expected to support themselves.)

These jobs paid 40 percent of my college expenses.

Paid for 65 percent of expenses with jobs, scholarships, and loans.

Omit information about low-level jobs, unless they illustrate experience important to your reader. Use details when they display your attitudes, abilities or talents. Tell how many people you trained or supervised, how much money you budgeted or raised. Describe the aspects of the job you did.

Too vague: 2000-2002 Sales Manager, The *Daily Collegian*, Mount Royal College, AB Supervised staff; promoted ad sales.

Good details: 2000-2002 Sales Manager, The *Daily Collegian*, Mount Royal College, AB. Supervised twenty-two member sales staff; helped recruit, interview, and select staff; assigned duties and scheduled work; recommended best performer for promotion. Motivated staff to increase paid ad sales 10 percent over previous year's sales.

Verbs or gerunds (the *-ing* form of verbs) always create a more dynamic image than do nouns, so use them on résumés that will be read by people. (Rules for scannable résumés to be read by computers come later in this module.) In the revisions below, nouns, verbs, and gerunds are in bold type.

Nouns: 1999-2001 Chair, Income Tax Assistance Committee, Winnipeg, MB. Responsibilities: **recruitment** of volunteers; flyer **design**, **writing**, and **distribution** for **promotion** of program; **speeches** to various community groups and nursing homes to advertise the service.

Verbs: 1999-2001 Chair, Income Tax Assistance Committee, Winnipeg, MB. **Recruited** volunteers for the program. **Designed**, **wrote**, and **distributed** a flyer to promote the program; made presentations to various community groups and nursing homes to advertise the service.

Gerunds: 1999-2001 Chair, Income Tax Assistance Committee, Winnipeg, MB. Responsibilities included **recruiting** volunteers for the program; **designing**, **writing**, and **distributing** a flyer to promote the program; and presenting to various community groups and nursing homes to advertise the service.

Note that the items in the list must be in parallel structure (◀▶ Module 14). Figure 27.5 lists action verbs that work well in résumés.

Instant Replay

Chronological Résumés

A **chronological résumé** summarizes what you did in a timeline (starting with the most recent events, and going backward in **reverse chronology**). Use a chronological résumé when your education and experience

• Are a logical preparation for the position for which you're applying
• Show a steady progression leading to the present

accomplished	appointed	calculated	conceived	cultivated
achieved	appraised	calibrated	conducted	customized
acted	approved	canvassed	concluded	debugged
adapted	arranged	carried out	condensed	decided
addressed	ascertained	categorized	conferred	decreased
acquired	assembled	caused	constructed	dedicated
activated	assessed	changed	consulted	defined
adjusted	assigned	charted	contracted	delegated
administered	assisted	clarified	contributed	delineated
adopted	assured	classified	controlled	delivered
advised	attended	collaborated	converted	documented
advanced	audited	collected	co-operated	demonstrated
aided	authorized	combined	co-ordinated	depicted
allocated	automated	communicated	corresponded	derived
altered	began	compiled	corrected	described
analyzed	billed	completed	costed	designed
announced	budgeted	composed	counselled	detailed
answered	built	computed	created	detected

Figure 27.5
Action Verbs for Résumés

Figure 27.5
Action Verbs for Résumés (continued)

determined	forwarded	managed	produced	set
developed	founded	manipulated	programmed	set up
devised	furnished	manufactured	projected	settled
diagnosed	gathered	mapped	protected	solicited
differentiated	generated	marketed	provided	started
directed	graded	maximized	published	stimulated
discharged	graduated	measured	purchased	studied
discussed	granted	mechanized	questioned	strengthened
dispensed	guarded	mediated	qualified	submitted
displayed	guided	minimized	rated	summarized
disseminated	handled	mobilized	received	supervised
documented	helped	modeled	recommended	supplied
drafted	identified	monitored	recorded	supported
earned	implemented	motivated	rectified	surveyed
edited	illustrated	negotiated	reduced	taught
educated	imported	modified	referred	tested
elected	improved	observed	refined	theorized
eliminated	improvised	obtained	regulated	timed
employed	incorporated	officiated	related	traced
engaged	induced	operated	released	trained
engineered	inducted	orchestrated	removed	transferred
ensured	influenced	organized	reorganized	transformed
entertained	informed	oversaw	repaired	translated
equipped	initiated	packaged	reported	transmitted
estimated	inquired	paid	represented	transported
evaluated	inspected	participated	researched	transposed
examined	instituted	performed	responded	treated
exchanged	instructed	persuaded	restored	tutored
expanded	insured	planned	retained	updated
expedited	integrated	positioned	retrieved	upgraded
experimented	interfaced	practised	reviewed	used
explained	interpreted	precipitated	revised	utilized
explored	interviewed	predicted	sampled	validated
extracted	introduced	prepared	saved	valued
fabricated	invented	prescribed	scheduled	verified
facilitated	investigated	presented	screened	visited
filed	justified	preserved	searched	worked
filled	labelled	presided	secured	wrote
financed	licensed	prevented	selected	
finalized	located	priced	sold	
formed	maintained	printed	served	

Visit http://www.mcgrawhill.ca/college/locker

Good résumés provide accurate details about what you've done, rather than exaggerate

Source: FOR BETTER OR WORSE reprinted by permission of United Feature Syndicate, Inc.

Functional/Combination Résumés

The functional résumé focusses on the **what**; this format provides the flexibility to highlight relevant job responsibilities or functions, and to include disparate experiences. Mature, highly skilled people with the right job credentials use the functional résumé to describe their extensive skills sets.

Begin with Career Achievements or Career Highlights, where you summarize your primary professional accomplishments. The Employment History is most important: describe your work responsibilities and subsequent skills as they relate to the position for which you are applying. Later in the résumé, identify conferences, clubs, and professional associations in reverse chronology to demonstrate your industry currency. Unless applying for job where your education credentials are paramount (like an academic position) and you have those credentials, place Education towards the end of this format.

Skills Résumés

Skills résumés use the *skills* or *aspects* of the job you are applying for as headings, rather than the category title or the dates of the jobs you've held (as in a chronological résumé). For entries under each skill, combine experience from paid jobs, unpaid work, classes, activities, and community service.

Use headings that reflect the jargon of the job for which you're applying: *logistics* rather than *planning* for a technical job; *procurement* rather than *purchasing* for a civilian job with the military. Figure 27.6 shows a skills résumé for someone who is changing fields. Marcella suggests that she already knows a lot about the field she hopes to enter by using its jargon for the headings.

You need at least three headings related to the job in a skills résumé; six or seven is not uncommon. Give enough detail to convince the reader that you have developed the requisite skill sets through a variety of experience. Put the most important category—from the reader's perspective—first.

Instant Replay

Functional/Combination and Skills Résumés

Use a functional or skills résumé when

- Your education and experience are not the usual route to the position
- You're changing fields
- You want to combine experience from paid jobs, activities and volunteer work, and courses
- Your recent work history may create the wrong impression

Figure 27.6
A Skills Résumé for Changing Job Fields

On the first page of a skills résumé, put skills directly related to the job for which you're applying.

Centred format is eye-catching but can be hard to read. Here, bold headings draw the reader's eye.

Marcella G. Cope

370 Mahon Avenue
Vancouver, BC V7M 3E1
250-555-1997
mcope@postbox.com

Objective

To help create high quality CD-ROM products in Metatec's New Media Solutions Division

Put company's name in objective.

Editing and Proofreading Experience

Edited a textbook published by Simon and Schuster, revising with attention to format, consistency, coherence, document integrity, and document design.
Proofed training and instructor's manuals, policy statements, student essays and research papers, internal documents, and promotional materials.
Worked with authors in a variety of fields including English, communication, business, marketing, economics, education, history, sociology, biology, agriculture, computer science, law, and medicine to revise their prose and improve their writing skills by giving them oral and written feedback.

Writing Experience

Wrote training and instructor's manuals, professional papers, and letters, memos, and reports.
Co-authored the foreword to a forthcoming textbook (Fall 2002) from NCTE press.
Contributed to a textbook forthcoming (Fall 2002) from Bedford Books/St. Martin's press.

Computer Experience

Designed a Web page using Microsoft Front Page
(www.cohums.ohio-state.edu/english/People/Bracken.1/Sedgwick/)
Learned and used a variety of programs on both Macintosh and PC platforms:
Word Processing and Spreadsheets
Microsoft Project
Front Page
Pagemaker
Aspects (a form for online synchronous discussion)
Storyspace (a hypertext writing environment)
PowerPoint
Email

Centre headings only when you use a large font. Here 14 pt. is used.

Computer experience is crucial for almost every job. Specify the software and hardware you've worked with.

Other Business and Management Experience
Developed policies, procedures, and vision statements.
Supervised new staff members in a mentoring program.
Coordinated program and individual schedules, planned work and estimated costs, set goals, and evaluated progress and results.
Member of team that directed the nation's largest first-year writing program.

Figure 27.6

A Skills Résumé for Changing Job Fields (continued)

Marcella G. Cope

Page 2

Employment History

Graduate Teaching Associate, Department of English, The University of Victoria
September 1997-Present. Taught Intermediate and First-Year Composition.
Writing Consultant, University Writing Centre, Simon Fraser University, January-April 2000
Program Administrator, First-Year Writing Program, The University of Victoria
September 1998-January 2000

Honours

Phi Kappa Phi Honour Society, inducted 1998. Membership based upon performance
in top 10 percent of graduate students nationwide.
Letters of Commendation, 1997-2000. Issued by the Director of
Graduate Studies in recognition of outstanding achievement.
Dean's List

Education

Master of Arts, June 1999, The University of Victoria
Cumulative GPA: 4.0/4.0
Bachelor of Arts, June 1997, Simon Fraser University
Graduated with Honours.

A job description can give you ideas for headings. Possible headings and sub-headings for skills résumés include

Administration	Communication
Alternatives or subheadings:	Alternatives or subheadings:
Coordinating	Conducting Meetings
Evaluating	Editing
Implementing	Fund-raising
Negotiating	Interviewing
Planning	Speaking
Keeping Records	Negotiating
Scheduling	Persuading
Solving Problems	Proposal Writing
Budgeting	Report Writing
Supervising	

Many jobs require a mix of skills. Include the skills that you know will be needed in the job you want.

In a skills résumé, list your paid jobs under Employment History near the end of the résumé (see Figure 27.4). List only job title, employer, city, province, and dates. Omit details about what you did, since you will have already used them under Experience.

What parts of résumé formats are the same?

Increasingly all résumés begin with an attention-grabbing heading like Communications and Technical Skills, Interpersonal Profile, or Career Achievements.

Every résumé should have an overview of your communication skills and an Education section. Career Objective, Honours and Awards, and References are optional.

Career Objective

Career Objective statements should sound like the job descriptions an employer might use in a job listing. Keep your statement brief—two or three lines at most. Tell what you want to do and what level of responsibility you want to hold.

Ineffective career objective: To offer a company my excellent academic foundation in hospital technology and my outstanding skills in oral and written communication.

Better career objective: Selling state-of-the-art Siemens medical equipment.

Including the employer's name in the objective is a nice touch.

As an alternative to writing a Career Objective statement, put the job title or field under your name:

Joan Larson Ooyen	Terence Edward Garvey	David R. Lunde
Marketing	Technical Writer	Corporate Fitness Director

Note that many recruiters consider Career Objective statements irrelevant.

Interpersonal Profile/Communications Skills, Career Achievements

Highlight proficiency in foreign or computer languages and identify your outstanding communication skills, in order of importance to the reader

- Excellent researching, writing, and presentation skills
- Completely conversant in all software applications
- Speak, read, and write Portuguese
- Internet, Intranet, and LAN proficient

The functional/combination résumé uses career achievements to showcase measurable accomplishments

- As Western Division Sales Manager, generated revenue of 3.5 million over quota
- Implemented employee mentoring program resulting in a 40 percent retention rate increase
- Created new assembly procedure that cut production costs by 25 percent
- Developed procedures manual now used in every national and international office

Education

Education can be your first major category if you've just earned (or are about to earn) a degree, if you have a degree that is essential or desirable for the position you're seeking, or if you lack relevant work experience. Put Education later if you need all of page 1 to emphasize your skills and experience, or if you lack a degree that other applicants may have.

Include summer school if you took optional courses or extra electives to graduate early. Include study abroad, even if you didn't earn college credits. If you got a certificate for international study, give the name and explain the significance of the certificate.

Professional certifications can be listed under Education, under or after your name, or in a separate category.

Include your GPA only if it's good. Because grade point systems vary, specify what your GPA is based on: "3.4/4.0" means 3.4 on a 4.0 scale. If your GPA is under 3.0 on a 4.0 scale, use words rather than numbers: "B2 average." If your GPA isn't impressive, calculate your average in your major and your average for your last 60 hours. If these are higher than your overall GPA, consider using them.

List in reverse chronological order (most recent first) each degree earned, field of study, date, school, city, province, or state of any graduate work, short courses and professional certification courses, college, community college, or school from which you transferred.

B.S. in Personnel Management, June 2002, University of Waterloo, Waterloo, ON
A.S. in Office Management, June 1999, Georgian Community College, Barrie, ON

To fill a page, you can also list selected courses, using short descriptive titles rather than course numbers. Use a subhead such as "Courses Related to Major" or "Courses Related to Financial Management" which will allow you to list all the courses (including psychology, speech, and business communication) that will help you in the job for which you're applying.

FYI

Marks don't count as much as communication skills, focus, and drive do: a survey of 1,300 millionaires discovered that the average millionaire made Bs and Cs in college.

Source: "Book on Millionaires: High IQ No Lock to Making Big Bucks," *The Columbus Dispatch*, February 7, 2000, 1A.

Bachelor of Science in Management, May 2002, University of Guelph, Guelph, ON
GPA: 3.8/4.0
Courses Related to Management:

Personnel Administration	Business Decision-Making
Finance	International Business
Management I and II	Marketing
Accounting I and II	Legal Environment of Business
Business Report Writing	Business Speaking

Salutatorian, Eastview High School, June 1997, Toronto, ON

A third option is to list the number of hours in various subjects, especially if the combination of courses qualifies you for the position for which you're applying.

B.S. in Marketing, May 2001, St. Xavier University, Nova Scotia
30 hours in Marketing
15 hours in Spanish
9 hours in Human Resources Management

Honours and Awards

The Honours and Awards heading creates a positive impression even when the reader skims the résumé. Include this category for all awards that reflect your drive for achievement and recognition.

Include the following kinds of entries in this category:

- Listings in recognition books (e.g., *Who's Who in Web Design*).
- Academic honour societies. Specify the nature of Greek-letter honour societies so the reader understands that these are more than social clubs.
- Fellowships and scholarships.
- Awards given by professional societies and community associations.
- Major awards given by civic groups.
- Music accreditation and awards; varsity letters; selection to provincial or national sports teams; finishes in provincial, national, or Olympic meets. (These could also go under Activities but may look more impressive under Honours. Put them under one category or the other—not both.)

Site *to* See

Go to
www.eresumes.com/
tut_webrezpicks.html
Rebecca Smith posts examples of especially interesting Web résumés.

Omit honours such as "Miss Congeniality" that work against the professional image you want your résumé to create.

As a new graduate, you should try to put Honours on page 1. In a skills and functional/combination résumé, place Honours and Awards on page 2 or 3, depending on the space your Work Experience takes.

References

Including references on a separate page anticipates the employer's needs and removes a potential barrier to your getting the job. You can, however, omit this category on your résumé, since prospective employers now take it for granted that applicants will supply references when required.

When you list references, use three to five. Include at least one professor and at least one employer or advisor—someone who can comment on your work habits and leadership skills.

Always ask the person's permission to list him or her as a reference. Don't say, "May I list you as a reference?" Instead, say, "Can you speak specifically about my work?" Jog the person's mind by taking along copies of work you did for him or her and a copy of your current résumé. Tell the person what points you'd like him or her to stress in a letter. Keep your list of references up to date. If it's been a year or more since you asked someone, ask again—and tell the person about your recent achievements.

References the reader knows are by far the most impressive. In a functional and skills résumé, choose people to recommend you who can testify to your abilities in the most important skills areas.

What should I do if the standard categories don't fit?

Create new ones.

Create headings that match your qualifications: Computer Skills, Military Experience, Foreign Languages, Summer and Part-Time Jobs, Marketing Experience, Publications, Exhibitions, Professional Associations.

Education and Experience (if you use the latter term) always stand as separate categories, even if you have only one item under each head. Combine other headings so that you have at least two long or three short items under each heading. For example, if you're in one honour society, two social clubs, and on one athletic team, combine them all under Activities and Honours.

If you have more than seven items under a heading, consider using subheadings. For example, a student who had a great many activities might divide them into Student Government, Other Campus or Extracurricular Activities, and Community Service.

Put your strongest categories near the top and at the bottom of the first page. If you have impressive work experience, you might want to put that category first after your name, put Education in the middle of the page, and put your address at the bottom.

Should I limit my résumé to just one page?

Not if you've got lots of qualifications.

A one-page résumé is sufficient, but do fill the page. The average résumé is now two pages, according to career-planning consultant Marilyn Moats Kennedy. An experiment that mailed one- or two-page résumés to CPA firms showed that even readers who said they preferred short résumés were more likely to want to interview the candidate with the longer résumé.[1]

If you do use more than one page, the second page should have at least 10 to 12 lines. Use a second sheet and staple it to the first so that readers who skim see the

FYI

To see the HTML coding that someone has used to create a Web résumé, click on "View," then on "Source" or "Page Source."

FYI

By 2002, estimates Computer Economics, 16 million résumés will be online, and about 1,200 Web sites will be devoted to careers.

Source: "Must Read," *Wired,* October 1999, 102.

Site to See

Go to
www.cigna.com/wor
king/scannable.html

Cigna is one of several companies offering advice about how to create scannable résumés. Check the Web pages of companies you want to apply to. Some suggest keywords to use.

staple and know that there's more. Leave less important information for the second page. Put your name and "Page 2" or "Cont." on the second page. If the pages are separated, you want the reader to know whom the qualifications belong to and that the second page is not your whole résumé.

How do I create a scannable résumé?

Take out all your formatting.

Figure 27.7 on the next page is an example of a scannable résumé.

To increase the chances that the résumé is scanned correctly,

- Use a standard typeface: Helvetica, Futura, Optima, Times Roman, New Century Schoolbook, Courier, Univers, or Bookman[2]
- Use 12- or 14-point type
- Use a ragged right margin rather than full justification. Scanners can't always handle the extra spaces between words and letters that full justification creates
- Don't italicize or underline words—even for titles of books or newspapers that grammatically require such treatment
- Put the text in bold to make sure letters don't touch each other. Then remove the bold
- Don't use lines, boxes, script, leader dots, or borders
- Don't use two-column formats or indented or centred text
- Put each phone number on a separate line
- Use plenty of white space
- Don't fold or staple the pages
- Don't write anything by hand on your résumé
- Send a laser copy. Stray marks defeat scanners

To increase the number of matches or "hits,"

- Use a Keywords section under your name, address, and phone. In it, put degrees, job field or title, accomplishments and interpersonal strengths and attitudes: *dependable, skill in time management, leadership, sense of responsibility*.[3]
- Use industry buzzwords and jargon, even if you're redundant. For example, "Web page design and HTML coding" will "match" either "Web" or "HTML" as a keyword.
- Use nouns. Some systems don't handle verbs well.
- Use common headings such as Summary of Qualifications, Strengths, Certifications, as well as Education, Experience, and so on.
- Use as many pages as necessary.
- Mention specific software programs (e.g., Lotus Notes) you've used.
- Be specific and quantifiable. "Managed $2 million building materials account" will generate more hits than "manager" or "managerial experience." Listing Microsoft Front Page as a skill won't help as much as "Used Microsoft Front Page to design an interactive Web page for a national fashion retailer, with links to information about style trends, current store promotions, employment opportunities, and an online video fashion show."

Figure 27.7
A Scannable Résumé

Jerry A. Jackson   *Use 12- or 14-point type in a standard typeface. Here, Times Roman is used.*

Keywords: family financial management; financial planning; retirement planning; investment sales; computer modelling; competitive; self-starter; hard worker; responsible; self-managing; collegiate athletics; sales experience

In keywords, use labels and terms that employer might include in job listing.

Campus Address
St. Mary's Road
Winnipeg, SK R2H 1J2
(306) 555-5718
Email address: jjackson@ccw.sk.ca
Created a Web page on saving for life goals, such as a home, children's education, and retirement:
http://hotmail.com/jackson.2495/home.htm

Permanent Address   *Give as much information as you like. The computer doesn't care how long the document is.*
2105 East Hill Avenue
Saskatoon, SK S7J 3C8
(306) 731-4108

Education
A.A.S. in Finance, May 2002, Community College of Winnipeg, Winnipeg, SK
"B" Grade Point Average
Comprehensive courses related to program provide not only the basics of family financial management but also skills in communication, writing, speaking, small groups, and computer modelling
Intermediate Accounting I and II
Business Writing
Consumer Finance   *Don't use columns. Scanners can't handle them.*
Financial Management
Interpersonal Communication
Investments
Microeconomics
Presentation Skills
Public Speaking
Report and Technical Writing
Sociology of Marriage and Family
Statistics

Sports Experience
CAAD (Colonial Athletes Against Drugs)
Intramural Hockey Team (Champions, Winter 2001)
Two-year Varsity Letterman, Community College of Winnipeg
Men's NCAA Division II Basketball

Figure 27.7

A Scannable Résumé

Experience
Financial Sales Representative, Primerica Company, Winnipeg, SK, February 2001-present. Work
with clients to plan investment strategies; recommend specific investments, including stocks,
bonds, mutual funds, and annuities.

Entrepreneur, Winnipeg, SK, and Saskatoon, SK, September 2000-January 2001. Created a saleable
product, secured financial backing, found a manufacturer, supervised production, and sold
product—12 dozen T-shirts at a $5.25 profit each—to help pay for school expenses.

Landscape Maintenance Supervisor, Saskatoon, SK, Summers 1992-2000. Formed a company to
cut lawns, put up fences, fertilize, garden, and paint houses. Hired, fired, trained, motivated, and
paid friends to complete jobs. Managerial experience.

Collector and Repairman, ACN Inc., Saskatoon, SK, Summers 1992-98. Collected and counted up
to $10,000 a day. Worked with technicians to troubleshoot and repair electronic and coin
mechanisms of video and pinball games, cigarette machines, and jukeboxes. Drove company cars
and trucks throughout Saskatoon metro area to collect cash and move and repair machines.

Willing to relocate
Willing to travel
Canadian citizen

Don't justify margins.
Doing so creates extra spaces
which confuse scanners.

Site *to* **See**

Go to
http://canadajobsea
rch.com/resume.htm
Here you'll find
dozens of résumé
posting sites.

- Join honour societies and professional and trade organizations, since they're often used as keywords.[4] Spell out Greek letter societies (the scanner will mangle Greek characters, even if your computer has them): "Pi Sigma Alpha Honour Society." For English words, spell out the organization name; follow it with the abbreviation in parentheses: "College Newspaper Business and Advertising Managers Association (CNBAM)." That way, the résumé will be tagged whether the recruiter searches for the full name or the acronym.
- Put everything in the résumé, rather than "saving" some material for the cover letter. While some applicant tracking systems can search for keywords in cover letters and other application materials, most only extract information from the résumé, even though they store the other papers. The length of the résumé doesn't matter.

Employability Skills 2000+ Checklist for Researching Jobs

In this module, the key skills from The Conference Board of Canada's Employability Skills 2000+ are:

Communicate
✔ write and speak so others pay attention and understand
✔ share information using a range of information and communications technologies (e.g. voice, email, computers)

Manage Information
✔ locate, gather, and organize information using appropriate technology and information systems

Demonstrate Positive Attitudes & Behaviours
✔ feel good about yourself and be confident
✔ deal with people, problems, and situations with honesty, integrity, and personal ethics
✔ recognize your own and other people's good efforts

Learn Continuously
✔ be willing to continuously learn and grow
✔ assess personal strengths and areas for development
✔ identify and access learning sources and opportunities
✔ plan for and achieve your learning goals

Review of Key Points

- A résumé must fill at least one page. Use two pages if you have extensive activities and experience.

- Emphasize recent (last three years) information most relevant to the job you want and that demonstrates your superiority to other applicants.

- To emphasize key points, put them in headings, list them vertically, and provide details.

- Résumés use sentence fragments punctuated like complete sentences. Items in the résumé must be concise and parallel. Emphasize verbs and gerunds in a résumé that people will read.

- A **chronological résumé** summarizes what you did in a timeline (starting with the most recent events and going backward in **reverse chronology**). It emphasizes degrees, job titles, and dates. Use a chronological résumé when your education and experience

- Are a logical preparation for the position for which you're applying
- Show a steady progression leading to the present
- A **functional** or **combination résumé** emphasizes your relevant job roles and responsibilities. Use a functional/combination résumé when
  - You have extensive and relevant work experience
  - You have experience but lack the requisite academic qualifications
  - You're a mature worker returning to the workforce
- A **skills résumé** emphasizes the skills you've used, rather than the job in which or the date when you used them. Use a skills résumé when
  - Your education and experience are not the usual route to the position for which you're applying

- You're changing fields
- You want to combine experience from paid jobs, activities or volunteer work, and courses to show the extent of your experience in administration, finance, speaking, etc.
- Your recent work history may create the wrong impression (e.g., it has gaps, shows a demotion, shows job-hopping, etc.)
- Résumés commonly contain the applicant's name, address, phone number, education, and experience. An overview of communication, technical and interpersonal abilities, activities and honours and awards should be included if possible.
- To fill the page, list courses or list references vertically.
- To create a scannable résumé, create a "plain vanilla" text using industry jargon, buzzwords, and acronyms.

Learning Applications

Questions for Comprehension

27.1 How do you decide whether to use a chronological, a functional or a skills résumé?

27.2 In a chronological résumé, in what order do you list your experience?

27.3 Why should you think about dividing a section that has more than seven items?

Questions for Critical Thinking

27.4 Is it ethical to omit information that might hurt you, such as a low grade point average?

27.5 What are the arguments for and against listing references on your résumé?

27.6 Should someone who is having trouble creating a good résumé pay a résumé service to create a document for him or her?

27.7 Suppose that you know that people with your qualifications are in great demand. Is there any reason for you to take the time to write a strong résumé?

Questions for Building Skills

27.8 What skills have you read about in this module?

27.9 What skills are you practising in the assignments you're doing for this module?

27.10 How could you further develop the skills you're working on?

Exercises and Problems

27.11 Analyzing Your Accomplishments

List the 10 accomplishments that give you the most personal satisfaction. These could be things that other people wouldn't notice. They can be things you've done recently or things you did years ago.

Answer the following question for each accomplishment:

1. What skills or knowledge did you use?
2. What personal traits did you exhibit?
3. What about this accomplishment makes it personally satisfying to you?

As Your Instructor Directs,

a. Share your answers with a small group of other students

b. Summarize your answers in a memo to your instructor

c. Present your answers orally to the class

27.12 Remembering What You've Done

Use the following list to jog your memory about what you've done. For each, give three or four details as well as a general statement.

Describe a time when you

1. Used facts and figures to gain agreement on an important point
2. Identified a problem faced by a group or organization and developed a plan for solving the problem
3. Made a presentation or a speech to a group
4. Responded to criticism
5. Interested other people in something that was important to you and persuaded them to take the actions you wanted
6. Helped a group deal constructively with conflict
7. Demonstrated creativity

As Your Instructor Directs,

a. Identify which job(s) each detail is relevant for

b. Identify which details would work well on a résumé

c. Identify which details, further developed, would work well in a job letter

27.13 Evaluating Career Objective Statements

None of the following career objective statements is effective. What is wrong with each statement as it stands? Which statements could be revised to be satisfactory? Which should be dropped?

1. To use my acquired knowledge of accounting to eventually own my own business.

2. A progressively responsible position as a MARKETING MANAGER where education and ability would have valuable application and lead to advancement.

3. To work with people responsibly and creatively, helping them develop personal and professional skills.

4. A position in international marketing which makes use of my specialization in marketing and my knowledge of foreign markets.

5. To design and maintain Web pages.

27.14   Writing a Paper Résumé

Write a résumé on paper that you could mail to an employer or hand to an interviewer at an interview.

As Your Instructor Directs,

a. Write a résumé for the field in which you hope to find a job

b. Write two different résumés for two different job paths you are interested in pursuing

c. Adapt your résumé to a specific company you hope to work for

27.15   Writing a Scannable Résumé

Take the résumé you like best from problem 27.14 and create a scannable version of it.

Polishing Your Prose

Proofreading

Wait until the final draft is complete to edit and proofread. There is no point in proofreading words and passages that might change. (Some writers claim to proofread documents while they're composing; this practice is like trying to mow the lawn and trim the hedges at the same time.)

Editing includes checking for you-attitude and positive emphasis, fixing any sexist or biased language, and correcting grammatical errors.

Proofreading means making sure that the document is free from typos. Check each of the following aspects.

Spelling. Scan for misspelled or misused words that spell checkers don't catch: *not* instead of *now*, *you* instead of *your*, *its* instead of *it's*, *their* instead of *there* or *they're*, *one* instead of *won*, and so forth.

Consistency. Check abbreviations and special terms.

Names. Double-check the reader's name.

Punctuation. Make sure that parentheses and quotation marks come in pairs. Be on the lookout for missing or extra commas and periods.

Format. Look for errors in spacing, margins, and document design, especially if you compose your document on one computer and print it out at another. Use the correct format for citations—MLA, APA, Chicago, etc.

Numbers and dates. Double-check all numbers to make sure they add up. Make sure page numbers appear where they should and are sequential. Do the same for tables of contents or appendixes. Check dates.

How to proofread is as individual as writing style. Try these methods or invent your own:

- **Read the document from last word to first word** to catch spelling errors.
- **Read the document in stages**—first page, second page, third page—with plenty of "rest" in between so you are fresh for each page.
- **Read pages out of sequence** so you can concentrate on the characters on the page rather than the meaning.
- **Read the document aloud**, listening for awkward or incorrect phrasing.
- **Ask a friend to read the document aloud**, voicing punctuation, while you follow along with the original.

Whatever your approach, build time into the composing process for proofreading. If possible, finish the document a day or two before it's due to allow enough time. (If the document is a 100-page report, allow even more time.) If you're in a hurry, use a spell checker, proof the document yourself, *and* ask a friend or colleague to proof it as well.

Exercises

Proofread the following passages:

1. Ours are a company worth doing business with. Your can count on our promiss to provide not only the best service but, also the finest in materials, fit, and, finish. All of are products our made to exacting specifications meaning that you received the best product for the best prices. If you arent satisfied for any reason, simply call the toll-free hotline at 1-800-555-1212 to get a promp refund. Or you can right us at: The John Doe Company, 123 Main Street Anytown Canada M6V 2B4. Remember; our moto is "the customers is always's right?

2.

Resumee for Kathy Jones

332 West Long Strt.
Moncton, New Brunswick E4Z 1Z8
(614-555-8188

Objection
A management position in fullfilament services where my skills, expereince can be best be used to help your company acheeve it's goals.

Relevent Experience:
2000 to Present Day: Ass. Manager for high-end sports equipment distributor. Responsible for checking new customers out.
1895-1999: Owned and Operated Jones, Inc., a telephone order procesing company for lady's apparel.
1997: Received a plague for Must Promising Executive of the Year" from *Columbus Monthly Magazine*.
1998: Delivery address to local high school seniors on why accuracy is important in business.

Special Skills
Type 7 or more words per minute
Studied English all my life. Fluent in French.
Shot at local gun club.

Check your answers to the odd-numbered exercises on page 634.

Module 28
Job Application Letters

Topics

- **What kind of letter should I use?**
- **How are the two letters different?**
- **What parts of the two letters are the same?**
- **How long should my letter be?**
- **How do I create the right tone?**
- **How do I send an email application letter?**

Review of Key Points

Learning Applications

Polishing Your Prose: Using You and I

Learning Focus

After reading and applying the information in Module 28, you'll be able to demonstrate

Knowledge of

- Application letter formats

Skills to

- Organize job application letters
- Catch the reader's interest even when the company isn't planning to hire
- Show that you have the qualifications for the job
- Persuade the employer that you're in the very top group of applicants
- Use information about the company effectively in your letter

"Let your enthusiasm for the job come across."

"People are the bottom line in the non-profit sector," says Nancy Brown, executive director of the London Unemployed Help Centre. After thirteen years on the job, Nancy finds that every day still brings challenges. Previous to this position, she spent twenty years working in the business sector.

Nancy has a degree in English from the University of Western Ontario, but in order to upgrade her skills she has enrolled in the Non-Profit Sector management program as well as the Canadian Institute of Management program. Nancy takes her management duties and the responsibilities of her job very seriously.

The Unemployment Help Centre, with an emphasis on *Help Centre*, provides a variety of programs geared to the individual needs of people looking for jobs. Everyone has a counsellor, but after the first meeting, clients have the option of working on their own in a self-directed program or continuing to work in a structured manner with the counsellor. There are also videos and other materials available, including vocational assessments and résumé workshops. The centre also provides advocacy (paralegal) services for its clientele.

Nancy speaks passionately about the needs of the adult clients her agency works with. And she speaks passionately about the importance of covering letters. "The last time I ran an ad for a job here I received 700 applications. The process becomes looking for ways to eliminate applications. If anything is wrong with the covering letter, even it is from the most qualified person, the résumé will not get looked at." The letter must be perfect. It must also look good. Visual presentation is part of the message. If the letter is cluttered and hard to read, the writer gives the impression that is how he or she would do the job.

In a covering letter applicants have "about one minute to sell themselves." They must research the company they are applying to and make the letter specific to that job. Avoid form letters. The letter has to show the employer that the writer has done his or her homework. Nancy adds that employers can recognise insincerity very quickly, so it very important to do one's homework and to be honest.

Language is vital. While the applicants must sell themselves, they must also avoid focussing on themselves. "Never begin with 'I am writing' and never use phrases like 'as can be seen in my résumé.' Use active words; use lots of verbs," advises Nancy, "Let your enthusiasm for the job come across."

Most people don't take covering letters seriously enough. Nancy's closing advice is "It is not enough to just send a résumé. Also, make sure you are applying for the job you want. If it is not what you want, you will be looking again shortly. And remember to sell yourself. It is easier to sell yourself if you are applying for a job that is a proper fit for you."

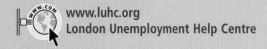

www.luhc.org
London Unemployment Help Centre

Figure 28.1
PAIBOC Questions for Analysis

PAIBOC

Use the PAIBOC questions to analyze business communication problems:

P What are your **purposes** in writing?

A Who is (are) your **audience(s)**? How do members of your audience differ? What characteristics are relevant to this particular message?

I What **information** must your message include?

B What reasons or reader **benefits** can you use to support your position?

O What **objection(s)** can you expect your reader(s) to have? What negative elements of your message must you de-emphasize or overcome?

C How will the **context** affect reader response? Think about your relationship to the reader, morale in the organization, the economy, the time of year, and any special circumstances.

The purpose of a job application letter, together with your résumé, is to get an interview. If you get a job through interviews arranged by a campus placement office or through contacts, you may not need to write a letter. However, you will need a letter if you want to work for an organization that isn't interviewing on campus, or when you change jobs. Writing a letter is also a good preparation for a job interview, because the letter is your first step in showing a specific company what you have to offer.

In your letter, focus on

- Key requirements of the job for which you're applying
- Skills and knowledge that separate you from other applicants
- Information that demonstrates your knowledge of the organization
- Qualities that every employer is likely to value: the ability to write and speak effectively, to solve problems, to get along with people

Note that the advice in this book applies to job-hunting in Canada. Conventions, expectations, and criteria differ from culture to culture: different norms apply in different countries. Even within Canada, different discourse communities (◀▶ Module 2, p. 37) may have different preferences. For example, letters applying for sales jobs might need to be more aggressive than the examples in this module. Whether you're seeking employment in your home province, nationally or internationally, however, your PAIBOC analysis (see Figure 28.1) can be vital to your success. Well-written job application letters are the most persuasive messages.

Every employer wants businesslike employees who understand professionalism. To make your application letter professional,

- Create your letter on a computer. Use a standard font (Times Roman, Palatino, Arial, or Helvetica) in 11- or 12-point type.
- Address your letter to a specific person. If the reader is a woman, call the office to find out if she prefers a courtesy title (◀▶ Module 9, p. 176).
- Use the language of the organization and the industry.
- Use contact or employee names if the reader knows them and thinks well of them, if they think well of you and will say good things about you, and if you have permission to use their names.
- Always connect an experience (coursework, co-op placement, community involvement) with a resultant skill that you know the prospective employer wants.
- Unless you're applying for a creative job in advertising or Web design, use business stationery and a conservative style: few contractions, no sentence fragments, clichés, or slang.
- Edit the letter carefully and proof it several times to make sure it's perfect.

What kind of letter should I use?

It depends on whether the company has asked for applications.

Two different hiring situations call for two different kinds of application letters. Write a **solicited letter** when you know that the company is hiring: you've seen an ad, you've been advised to apply by a professor or friend, or you've read in a trade publication that the company is expanding. Sometimes, however, the advertised positions may not be what you want, or you may want to work for an organization that has not announced that it has openings in your area. Then the situation calls for an **unsolicited** or **prospecting letter** (as in prospecting for gold.)

Prospecting letters help you tap into the hidden job market (◀▶ Module 26). In some cases, your prospecting letter may arrive at a company that has decided to hire but has not yet announced the job. In other cases, companies create positions to get a good person who is on the market. Even in a hiring freeze, jobs are sometimes created for specific individuals.

How are the two letters different?

They begin and end differently.

When you know the company is hiring, organize your letter in this way:

1. State that you're applying for the job (phrase the job title as your source phrased it). Tell where you learned about the job (ad, referral, Web). Briefly show that you have the major qualifications required by the ad: a degree, professional certification, job experience, etc. Summarize your other qualifications briefly in the same order in which you plan to discuss them in the letter. This **summary sentence** or **paragraph** then covers everything you will talk about and serves as an organizing device for your letter.

> I have a good background in standard accounting principles and procedures and a working knowledge of some of the special accounting practices of the oil industry. This working knowledge is based on practical experience in the oil fields: I've pumped, tailed rods, and worked as a roustabout.

> Let me put my creative eye, artistic ability, and experience to work for McLean Design.

2. Develop your major qualifications in detail. Be specific about what you've done; relate your achievements to the work you'd be doing in this new job. This is not the place for modesty!
3. Develop your other qualifications, even if the ad doesn't ask for them. (If the ad asks for a lot of qualifications, pick the most important three or four.) Show what separates you from the other applicants who will also answer the ad. Demonstrate your knowledge of the organization.
4. Ask for an interview; tell when you'll be available to be interviewed and to begin work. End on a positive, forward-looking note.

Figure 28.2 on the next page presents this pattern of organization visually. Figures 28.4 and 28.5 are examples of a solicited letter.

When you don't have any evidence that the company is hiring, you cannot use the pattern for solicited letters. Instead, organize your letter this way:

1. Catch the reader's interest.
2. Create a **bridge** between the attention-getter and your qualifications. Focus on what you know and can do. Since the employer is not planning to hire, he or she

Site *to* **See**

Go to
www.careerlab.com /letters/chap12.htm
Career Lab's Cover Letter Library posts letters for a variety of situations, including prospecting letters when a company has not announced openings.

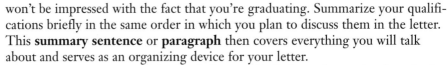

Figure 28.2

How to Organize a Solicited Job Letter

Request for Action

Details

Details

Request for Action

won't be impressed with the fact that you're graduating. Summarize your qualifications briefly in the same order in which you plan to discuss them in the letter. This **summary sentence** or **paragraph** then covers everything you will talk about and serves as an organizing device for your letter.

3. Develop your strong points in detail. Be specific. Relate what you've done in the past to what you could do for this company. Show that you know something about the company. Identify the specific niche you want to fill.

4. Ask for an interview and tell when you'll be available for interviews. (Don't tell when you can begin work.) End on a positive, forward-looking note.

Figure 28.3 presents this pattern visually. Figure 28.6 is an example of a prospecting letter.

The First Paragraph of a Solicited Letter

When you know that the firm is hiring, refer to the specific position in your first sentence. Your letter can then be routed to the appropriate person, thus speeding up consideration of your application. Identify where you learned about the job: "the position of junior accountant announced in Sunday's *Vancouver Sun*," "Kadji Kado, our placement director, told me that you are looking for. . . ."

Note how the following paragraph picks up several of the characteristics of the ad:

How to Organize a Solicited Letter

1. State that you're applying for the job and tell where you learned about it. Summarize your qualifications in the order in which you plan to discuss them in the letter.

2. Develop your major qualifications in detail.

3. Develop your other qualifications. Show what separates you from the other applicants who will also answer the ad. Demonstrate your knowledge of the organization.

4. Ask for an interview. End on a positive, forward-looking note.

Ad: Business Education Instructor at University of New Brunswick. Candidate must possess a bachelor's degree in Business Education. Will be responsible for providing in-house training to business and government leaders. . . . Candidate should have at least six months' office experience. Prior teaching experience not required.

Letter: Please consider me for the position of **Business Education Instructor**, advertised in Monday's *Telegraph-Journal*. My Business Education degree, knowledge of adult education principles and previous office experience make me ideal candidate for the position.

Good word choices can help set your letter apart from the scores or even hundreds of letters the company is likely to get in response to an ad. The following first paragraph of a letter in response to an ad by Allstate Insurance Company shows a knowledge of the firm's advertising slogan and sets itself apart from the dozens of letters that start with "I would like to apply for. . . ."

> The Allstate Insurance Company is famous for its "Good Hands Policy." I would like to lend a helping hand to many Canadians as a financial analyst for Allstate, as advertised in yesterday's *National Post*. I have an Accounting Co-op diploma from Georgian College and I have worked with figures, computers, and people.

Note that the last sentence forecasts the organization of the letter, preparing for paragraphs about the student's academic background and (in this order) experience with "figures, computers, and people."

First Paragraphs of Prospecting Letters

In a prospecting letter, asking for a job in the first paragraph is dangerous: unless the company plans to hire but has not yet announced openings, the reader is likely to throw the letter away. Instead, catch the reader's interest. Then in the second paragraph shift the focus to your skills and experience, showing how they can be useful to the employer.

Here is an effective first paragraph and the second paragraph of a letter applying to be a computer programmer for an insurance company:

> Computers alone aren't the answer to demands for higher productivity in the competitive insurance business. Merging a poorly written letter with a database of customers just sends out bad letters more quickly. But you know how hard it is to find people who can both program computers and write well.
>
> My education and training have given me this useful combination. I'd like to put my associate's degree in computer technology and my business experience writing to customers to work in Sun Canada's service approach to insurance.

Last Paragraphs

In the last paragraph, indicate when you'd be available for an interview. If you're free any time, say so. But it's likely that you have responsibilities in class and work. If you'd have to go out of town, there may be only certain days of the week or certain weeks that you could leave town for several days. Use a sentence that fits your situation.

> I could come to Thunder Bay for an interview anytime between March 17 and 21.

> Please call me at 519-842-4229, for an interview time and date at your convenience.

Should you wait for the employer to call you, or should you call the employer to request an interview? In a solicited letter, it's safe to wait to be contacted: you know the employer wants to hire someone, and if your letter and résumé show that you're one of the top applicants, you'll get an interview. However, for sales jobs, say that you'll call the employer—and do it! In a prospecting letter, also call the employer. Because the employer is not planning to hire, you'll get a higher percentage of interviews if you're aggressive. Don't, however, be rude. No one owes you a response. And when you do call, be polite to the person who answers the phone.

If you're writing a prospecting letter to a firm that's more than a few hours away by car, say that you'll be in the area the week of such-and-such and could stop by for an interview. Some companies pay for follow-up visits, but not for first interviews. A company may be reluctant to ask you to make an expensive trip when it isn't yet sure it wants to hire you.

Instant Replay

How to Organize a Prospecting Letter

1. Catch the reader's interest.
2. Create a bridge between the attention-getter and your qualifications. Summarize your qualifications in the order in which you plan to discuss them in the letter.
3. Develop your strong points in detail. Relate what you've done in the past to what you could do for this company. Show that you know something about the company. Identify the specific niche you want to fill.
4. Ask for an interview. End on a positive, forward-looking note.

Figure 28.3

How To Organize a Prospecting Letter

| Attention-Getter |
| Details |
| Details |
| Request for Action |

End the letter on a positive note that suggests you look forward to the interview and that you see yourself as a person who has something to contribute, not as someone who just needs a job.

> On Wednesday, April 25, I will call you between 9:00 and 9:30 A.M., to schedule a time when we can talk.

> I look forward to discussing with you ways in which I could contribute to The Great Western's continued growth.

What parts of the two letters are the same?

The body paragraphs discussing your qualifications.

In both solicited and prospecting letters you should

- Address the letter to a specific person
- Indicate the specific position for which you're applying
- Be specific about your qualifications
- Show what separates you from other applicants
- Demonstrate a knowledge of the company and the position
- Refer to your résumé (which you would enclose with the letter)
- Ask for an interview

Showing a Knowledge of the Position and the Company

If you could substitute another inside address and salutation and send out the letter without any further changes, it isn't specific enough. Use your knowledge of the position and the company to choose relevant evidence from what you've done to support your claims that you could help the company. (See Figures 28.5 and 28.6.)

One or two specific details usually are enough to demonstrate your knowledge. Be sure to use the knowledge, not just repeat it. Never present the information as though it will be news to the reader. After all, the reader works for the company and presumably knows much more about it than you do.

Separating Yourself from Other Applicants

Your knowledge of the company separates you from other applicants. You can also use course work, an understanding of the field, and experience in jobs and extracurricular events to show that you're unique.

- This student, example on page 585, uses summer jobs and course work to set herself apart from other applicants:

A company as diverse as Monsanto requires extensive record keeping as well as numerous internal and external communications. Both my summer jobs and my course work have prepared me for these responsibilities. As Office Manager for Safety Express Limited, I was in charge of most of the bookkeeping and letter writing for the company. I kept accurate records for each workday, and I often entered over 100 transactions in a single day. In business and technical writing I learned how to write persuasive letters and memos and how to present extensive data in reports in a simplified style that is clear and easy to understand.

How long should my letter be?

Use a full page.

A short letter throws away an opportunity to be persuasive; it may also suggest that you have little to say for yourself or that you aren't very interested in the job.

Without eliminating content, tighten each sentence (◀▶ Module 16, p. 346) to be sure that you're using space as efficiently as possible. If your letter is still slightly over a page, use smaller margins, a type size that's one point smaller, or justified proportional type to get more on the page.

However, if you need more than a page, use it. The extra space gives you room to be more specific about what you've done and to add details about your experience that separate you from other applicants. Employers don't want longer letters, but they will read them *if* the letter is well written and *if* the applicant established early in the letter that he or she has the credentials the company needs.

Instant Replay

What Job Letters Must Do

In all job letters,

- Address the letter to a specific person
- Indicate the specific position for which you're applying
- Be specific about your qualifications
- Show what separates you from other applicants
- Show a knowledge of the company and the position
- Refer to your résumé (which you would enclose with the letter)
- Ask for an interview

Figure 28.4
A Solicited Letter (1)

880 Middlegate Road
Mississauga, ON L4Y 1M3

Block format is standard in business

September 5, 2002

William Chen
Director
The Resources Corporation
2025 Sheppard Avenue East
Toronto, ON M2J 1V7

Paragraph 1 is thesis or controlling paragraph. Repeats language of the ad, and identifies the specific qualifications the rest of the letter will demonstrate.

Dear William Chen:

Please consider my application for the position of **Auditor**, advertised in The *Toronto Star*, September 3, 2002. My education and auditing experience, and my organizational, analytical, and communication skills make me an ideal candidate for the position.

Begins as few sentences as possible with "I"

Provides specific auditing experience

After graduating in Business Administration, Finance, I received my CA designation in November 1998. My Finance program focussed on the Canadian regulatory/securites industry standards and by-laws. Indeed, in my third year at Centennial College, I completed an analytical report about the Canadian regulatory and security market. During my co-operative placement with Tort, Tort and Tort, I also assisted CA's in their field examinations and in-office desk reviews of regulatory filings of association audit jurisdiction firms. Although we often worked under intense pressure, my organizational and communication skills helped me to graduate with an A+ average; furthermore, based on my performance with the firm, Tort, Tort and Tort offered me a fulltime position upon graduation.

Details demonstrate applicant has excellent communication skills

Shows self-motivation, sales and managerial skills, demonstrates active learner with transferable skills.

Instead, I chose to work as a financial sales representative for Templeton Trust. As you know financial selling is a highly competitive field, but I enjoy competing. While in high school, for example, I created a business, hired a staff, and recruited clients. Subsequently, in my landscaping business, I delegated work and motivated my employees to do the quality jobs that our clients expected. My entrepreneurial experiences taught me the value of hard work, dedication and accountability, requisite qualities for auditors.

In the last year, as financial sales representatives for Templeton Trust, I've honed my analytical and communication skills while helping clients develop financial plans and investment products tailored to their needs. I'm proud of my achievements at Templeton Trust, and would like to make a contribution to your organization.

Can we meet to discuss this possibility? Please call me at (416) 925-4415, to arrange an interview time and date at your convenience.

Ask for the interview

Sincerely,

Jerry Jackson

Jerry Jackson
Enclosure: Résumé

Figure 28.5
A Solicited Letter (2)

638 Changery Court
Lethbridge, AB
T1J 2A5
May 21, 2002

Shelley Aquina
Human Resources Manager
Home Outfitters
425 18 Avenue Northwest
Calgary AB T2N 2G6

Dear Shelly Aquina:
RE: File # 7664566-F ← *quotes file number as ad requests*

Repeats words of the ad

Please consider me for the position of Sales Manager, advertised in The *Calgary Sun*, Saturday, May 20. I possess the educational background, work experience, and exceptional organizational and communication skills for which you have advertised.

Thesis or controlling paragraph tells the reader what's going to be proven in the letter.

Specifics directly connect the experience with the resultant skill

In June I will graduate with a business administration diploma from Mount Royal College, Calgary, Alberta. Throughout my college career I worked with peers on a variety of projects, including sales proposals, formal reports, and sales presentations. In my third year I was chosen team captain for our marketing project, a year long analysis and oral and written report of possible marketing initiatives for a Calgary client, MediaWaves. My responsibilities included identifying timelines, delegating tasks, negotiating conflicts among group members, reporting to the client and our marketing professor, and revising and editing the final thirty-page report. Our team project not only secured the top grade in the class; the client accepted our recommendations, resulting in an immediate 10 percent sales increase for MediaWaves. Because I'm very aware of the importance of listening when working with others, I have made a conscious effort to improve this key communication skill. I believe that part of the success of our project can be attributed to my managing through active listening.

Since grade 11 I have worked part-time and summers at Canadian Tire, in Lethbridge Alberta. Although I started as a stock clerk, I worked my way up to sales associate. My supervisor has commented on my excellent sales skills, particularly my product knowledge and ability to up-sell. During my employment with Canadian Tire—a high energy, fast-paced environment—I learned to focus calmly on clients' concerns and to communicate confidently. As a result of my performance I was promoted to assistant manager, a job I held while finishing college. While working part-time, attending school and participating in varsity basketball, I learned to juggle multiple priorities, to manage my time and to problem-solve.

Jargon of the marketing industry

These skills would have been identified in the ad as necessary for the position

Enclosed please find my résumé with further details.

Demonstrates research and industry awareness

The market for home decorations and furnishings has become increasingly competitive, and, with the entry of American big box stores like Heritage Homes, promises to become even more so. I would like an opportunity to increase your market share while developing my own marketing career. Please call me at 525-4339 to arrange an interview time and date at your convenience.

Asks for the interview

Sincerely,

Carlos DeLeon
ENC: resume

Figure 28.6
A Prospecting Letter

Kristine Manalili
2 Inverary Court
Porters Lake, Nova Scotia B3E 1M8
902-388-6488 kmanalili@hotmail.com

Kristine creates a boxed "letterhead"

2002-06-25

Mr. John Harrobin
2653 Dublin Street
Halifax, NS B3: 3J7

In an unsolicited or prospecting letter, open with a sentence that:
① will create reader interest
② provides an natural bridge to talking about yourself

Dear Mr. Harrobin:

Refers to her enclosed résumé

Providing an athlete with physiotherapy can assist with a debilitating injury in the short term, but may not provide the long-term product and therapy information necessary for complete recovery. It can be a real challenge finding employees who are conversant with the latest injury management modalities, who are familiar with the most current injury management support equipment, and who also work well with rehabilitating clients. However, you will see from my enclosed résumé that I have this useful combination of skills.

Refers to mutual acquaintance   *Shows knowledge of the company*

Rita Haralabidis tells me that HealthRhab needs people to identify injury management therapy and equipment to meet your clients needs. My education and work experience have provided me with the injury evaluation and product knowledge that you require. While studying at Nunavut Arctic College's Sports Injury Management program, for example, I provided over 200 hours of successful client care at the college clinic.

Demon-strates skill sets she prom-ised in first paragraph

Moreover, I was able to apply the most current therapy modalities and to learn about sophisticated sports injury products and equipment while serving my four-month internship term at Wu's Sports Clinic in Victoria, British Columbia. Wu's clinic is renowned for it's progressive therapy options. My internship provided me with practical experience in injury prevention and treatment. Equally important, I learned about the latest equipment, products, and techniques available to maximize client rehabilitation and recovery.

Relates what she's done to what she could do for this company

My communication skills and product knowledge would enable me to adapt immediately to clients' specific needs, and to develop programs for your clients. I am flexible, a quick study, and committed to proactive healthcare. I will call you next week to arrange a mutually convenient time when we can discuss putting my talents to work for HealthRhab.

Promises action

Sincerely,

Enclosed: Résumé

Targeting a Specific Company in Your Letter

If your combination of skills is in high demand, a one-size-fits-all letter may get you an interview. But when you must compete against dozens—perhaps hundreds or even thousands—of applicants for an interview slot, you need to target your letter to the specific company. Targeting a specific company also helps you prepare for the job interview.

The Web makes it easy to find information about a company. The example below shows how applicants could use information posted on the Sleeman Breweries Limited Web site <http://www.sleeman.com/> on June 26, 2001.

Check for Facts about the Company.

Like most corporate Web sites <http://www.sleeman.com/> offers dozens of facts about the company. A computer network administrator might talk about helping to keep the 3,500 LANS working well. A Web weaver could talk about supporting a new Investor Relations site, or about developing even more interactive content for both national and international potential investors. Someone in corporate communication, advertising, marketing, or multimedia programs might write a prospecting letter about Sleemans' recent media campaign. An interviewee with experience in international business might pitch the company on the know-how necessary to do business in Boston, Germany, and South Africa. And someone in human resources management could talk about the electronic processing of HR data benefits for the thousands of employees joining this expanding company, or about current recruitment and retention strategies for the company CIBC World Markets Inc., reports is "...a well-managed, creative company."[1]

Check News Releases and Speeches.

Recent press releases have covered everything from the company's national expansion—across the Maritimes, into Québec, and Western Canada—to its international partnerships with U.S., German, and South African breweries. Anyone in international business could talk about helping Sleeman expand its base into China—and beyond.

An April 3, 2001 press release announced the launch of the company's second annual Writer's Craft Award, $10,000 for the best short-story collection published by an Ontario writer. Students about to complete marketing, finance, and management programs could show how their course work and experience prepare them to market this and similar community-focussed programs; or could offer technical or managerial expertise on the best way for Sleemans' to adopt e-business strategies for their continuing growth.

Check the Corporate Culture.

In his media interviews, President John Sleeman emphasizes that his family-owned business produces a quality product based on his great-great-grandfather's recipe. The company's Web site material also refers to the family beer-making tradition and the site's design reinforces this commitment to traditional values. These promotional strategies appeal to the mature consumers who buy Sleemans' beers. Yet Sleemans' partnership arrangements and media advertisements indicate the company's enthusiasm for creativity and flexibility. Successful job applicants would do well to stress their creative abilities and their support of community arts activities.

FYI

Job titles include

• **Top Dog:** Allpets.com (pet portal)
• **Cultural Czar** (nurtures corporate culture): Homestead.com (tools for building Web sites)
• **Product Evangelist:** Adventa (Silicon Valley startup)
• **Prince of Pine, Monarch of Mulch, Marquis of Machinery:** International Paper

Sources: "Job Titles of the Future," *Fast Company,* April 2000, 64, 76; "Talent from the Class of 2000," *Fortune,* May 29, 2000, 100; and "Job Titles of the Future," *Fast Company,* June 2000, 72.

How do I create the right tone?

Use you-attitude and positive emphasis.

You-attitude and positive emphasis help you sound assertive without being arrogant.

You-Attitude

Unsupported claims may sound overconfident, selfish, or arrogant. Create you-attitude (◀▶ Module 6, p. 122) by describing exactly what you have done and by showing how that relates to what you could do for this employer.

Lacks you-attitude: An inventive and improvising individual like me is a necessity in your business.

You-attitude: Building a summer house-painting business gave me the opportunity to find creative solutions to challenges. At the end of the first summer, for example, I had nearly 50 litres of exterior latex left, but no more jobs. I contacted the home economics teacher at my high school. She agreed to give course credit to students who were willing to give up two Saturdays to paint a house being renovated by Habitat for Humanity. I donated the paint and supervised the students. I got a charitable deduction for the paint and hired the three best students to work for me the following summer. I could put these skills in problem solving and supervising to work as a personnel manager for Burroughs.

Remember that the word *you* refers to your reader. Using *you* when you really mean yourself or "all people" can insult your reader by implying that he or she still has a lot to learn about business:

Since you're talking about yourself, you'll use *I* in your letter. Do so sparingly. Reduce the number of *I*'s by revising some sentences to use *me* or *my*.

Site *to* **See**

Go to http://www.world skip.com/

Check out the international marketplace, by country, and learn about specific cultures, values, and careers.

Under my presidency, the Agronomy Club . . .

Courses in media and advertising management gave me a chance to . . .

My responsibilities as a co-op student included . . .

In particular, avoid beginning every paragraph with *I*. Begin sentences with adverbs (presently, currently) prepositional phrases or introductory clauses.

Positive Emphasis

Be positive. Don't plead ("Please give me a chance") or apologize ("I cannot promise that I am substantially different from the lot").

When you job hunt, focus on positives. Show what you've learned and how your skills can meet the employer's needs.

Source: Frank & Ernest reprinted by permission of United Feature Syndicate, Inc.

Avoid word choices with negative connotations (◀▶ Module 7, p. 137). Note how the following revisions make the writer sound more confident.

Negative: I have learned an excessive amount about writing through courses in journalism and advertising.

Positive: Courses in journalism and advertising have taught me to recognize and to write good copy. My profile of a professor was published in the campus newspaper; I earned an "A" on my direct mail campaign for the Canadian Dental Association to persuade young adults to see their dentist more often.

Excessive suggests that you think the courses covered too much—hardly an opinion likely to endear you to an employer.

The company wants an email application. What should I do?

Compose a document in a word-processing program. Then attach it to a courteous email message.

When you submit an email letter (see Figure 28.7 on the next page) with an attached résumé,

- Tell in what word-processing program your scannable résumé is saved
- Put the job number or title for which you're applying in your subject line and in the first paragraph
- Prepare your letter in a word-processing program with a spell checker to make it easier to edit and proof the document
- Don't send anything in all capital letters
- Don't use smiley faces or other emoticons
- Put your name and email address at the end of the message. Most email programs send along the "sender" information at the top of the screen, but a few don't, and you want the employer to know whose letter this is!

Figure 28.7
An Email Application Letter

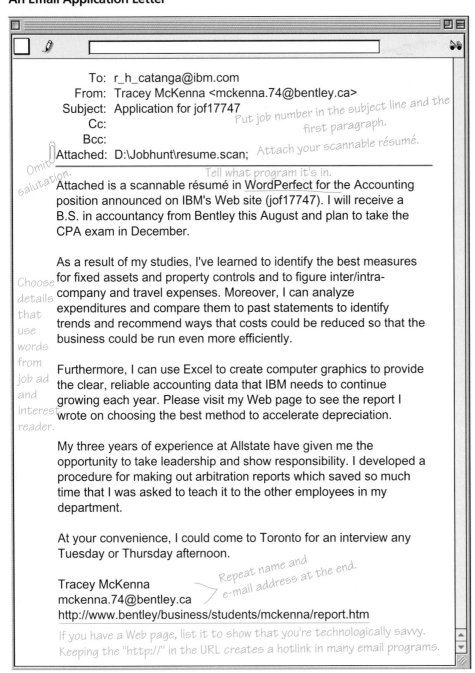

To: r_h_catanga@ibm.com
From: Tracey McKenna <mckenna.74@bentley.ca>
Subject: Application for jof17747
Cc:
Bcc:
Attached: D:\Jobhunt\resume.scan;

Put job number in the subject line and the first paragraph.

Attach your scannable résumé.

Omit salutation.

Tell what program it's in.

Attached is a scannable résumé in WordPerfect for the Accounting position announced on IBM's Web site (jof17747). I will receive a B.S. in accountancy from Bentley this August and plan to take the CPA exam in December.

Choose details that use words from job ad and interest reader.

As a result of my studies, I've learned to identify the best measures for fixed assets and property controls and to figure inter/intra-company and travel expenses. Moreover, I can analyze expenditures and compare them to past statements to identify trends and recommend ways that costs could be reduced so that the business could be run even more efficiently.

Furthermore, I can use Excel to create computer graphics to provide the clear, reliable accounting data that IBM needs to continue growing each year. Please visit my Web page to see the report I wrote on choosing the best method to accelerate depreciation.

My three years of experience at Allstate have given me the opportunity to take leadership and show responsibility. I developed a procedure for making out arbitration reports which saved so much time that I was asked to teach it to the other employees in my department.

At your convenience, I could come to Toronto for an interview any Tuesday or Thursday afternoon.

Tracey McKenna
mckenna.74@bentley.ca
http://www.bentley/business/students/mckenna/report.htm

Repeat name and e-mail address at the end.

If you have a Web page, list it to show that you're technologically savvy. Keeping the "http://" in the URL creates a hotlink in many email programs.

Employability Skills 2000+ Checklist for Job Application Letters

In this module, the key skills from The Conference Board of Canada's Employability Skills 2000+ are:

Communicate

✔ read and understand information presented in a variety of forms (e.g. words, graphs , charts, diagrams)
✔ write and speak so others pay attention and understand
✔ share information using a range of information and communications technologies (e.g. voice, email, computers)
✔ use relevant scientific, technological, and mathematical knowledge and skills to explain or clarify ideas

Manage Information

✔ locate, gather, and organize information using appropriate technology and information systems
✔ access, analyze, and apply knowledge and skills from a variety of disciplines (e.g. the arts, languages, science, technology, mathematics, social sciences, and the humanities)

Think & Solve Problems

✔ assess situations and identify problems
✔ recognize the human, interpersonal, technical, scientific, and mathematical dimensions of a problem
✔ readily use science, technology, and mathematics as ways to think, gain, and share knowledge, solve problems, and make decisions
✔ check to see if a solution works, and act on opportunities for improvement

Demonstrate Positive Attitudes & Behaviours

✔ feel good about yourself and be confident
✔ deal with people, problems, and situations with honesty, integrity, and personal ethics

Participate in Projects & Tasks

✔ plan, design, or carry out a project or task from start to finish with well-defined objectives and outcomes

Review of Key Points

- When you know that a company is hiring, send a **solicited job letter**. When you want a job with a company that has not announced openings, send a **prospecting job letter**.

- Organize a solicited letter in this way:

  1. State that you're applying for the job and tell where you learned about the job (ad, referral, etc.). Briefly show that you have the major qualifications required by the ad. Summarize your qualifications in the order in which you plan to discuss them in the letter.

  2. Develop your major qualifications in detail.

  3. Develop your other qualifications. Show what separates you from the other applicants who will also answer the ad. Demonstrate your knowledge of the organization.

  4. Ask for an interview; tell when you'll be available to be interviewed and to begin work. End on a positive, forward-looking note.

- Organize a prospecting letter in this way:

  1. Catch the reader's interest.

  2. Create a bridge between the attention-getter and your qualifications. Summarize your qualifications in the order in which you plan to discuss them in the letter.

  3. Develop your strong points in detail. Relate what you've done in the past to what you could do for this company. Show that you know something about the company. Identify the specific niche you want to fill.

  4. Ask for an interview and tell when you'll be available for interviews. End on a positive, forward-looking note.

- In both letters, you should

  - Address the letter to a specific person
  - Indicate the specific position for which you're applying
  - Be specific about your qualifications
  - Show what separates you from other applicants
  - Show a knowledge of the company and the position
  - Refer to your résumé (which you would enclose with the letter)
  - Ask for an interview

- Use your knowledge of the company, your course work, your understanding of the field, and your experience in jobs and extracurricular activities to show that you're unique.

- Use you-attitude by supporting general claims with specific examples and by relating what you've done to what the employer needs. Use positive emphasis to sound confident.

Learning Applications

Questions for Comprehension

28.1 How should you organize a letter in response to an announced job opening?

28.2 How should you organize a letter when the company has not announced openings?

Questions for Critical Thinking

28.3 Why is it important for you to separate yourself from other applicants?

28.4 Why should you *not* ask for a job in the first paragraph of a prospecting letter?

28.5 Why is a good writing style particularly important in a job application letter?

28.6 Is it ethical for someone who isn't a good writer to hire someone to "ghostwrite" the letter for him or her?

28.7 Suppose that people with your qualifications are in great demand. Is there any reason for you to take the time to write a strong letter?

Questions for Building Skills

28.8 What skills have you read about in this module?

28.9 What skills are you practising in the assignments you're doing for this module?

28.10 How could you further develop the skills you're working on?

Exercises and Problems

28.11 Analyzing First Paragraphs of Prospecting Letters

All of the following are first paragraphs in prospecting letters written by new graduates. Evaluate the paragraphs on these criteria:

- Is the paragraph likely to interest the reader and motivate him or her to read the rest of the letter?
- Does the paragraph have some content that the student can use to create a transition to talking about his or her qualifications?
- Does the paragraph avoid asking for a job?

1. Ann Gibbs suggested that I contact you.

2. Each year, the Christmas shopping rush makes more work for everyone at Zellers, especially for the Credit Department. While working for Zellers Credit Department for three Christmas and summer vacations, the Christmas sales increase is just one of the credit situations I became aware of.

3. Whether to plate a five-centimetre eyebolt with cadmium for a tough, brilliant shine or with zinc for a rust-resistant, less

expensive finish is a tough question. But similar questions must be answered daily by your salesmen. With my experience in the electro-plating industry, I can contribute greatly to your constant need of getting customers.

4. Prudential Insurance Company did much to help my college career, as the sponsor of my National Merit Scholarship. Now I think I can give something back to Prudential. I'd like to put my education, including a degree in finance from _____ College, to work in your investment department.

5. Since the beginning of Delta Electric Construction Co. in 1997, the size and profits have grown steadily. My father, being a stockholder and vice president, often discusses company dealings with me. Although the company has prospered, I understand there have been a few problems of mismanagement. I feel with my present and future qualifications, I could help ease these problems.

28.12 Improving You-Attitude and Positive Emphasis in Job Letters

Revise each of these sentences to improve you-attitude and positive emphasis. You may need to add information.

1. I understand that your company has had problems due to the mistranslation of documents during international ad campaigns.

2. Included in my résumé are the courses in Finance that earned me a fairly attractive grade average.

3. I am looking for a position that gives me a chance to advance quickly.

4. Although short on experience, I am long on effort and enthusiasm.

5. I have been with the company from its beginning to its present unfortunate state of bankruptcy.

28.13 Writing a Solicited Letter

Write a letter of application in response to an announced opening for a fulltime job that a new graduate could hold.

Turn in a copy of the listing. If you use option (a), (b), or (d) below, your listing will be a copy. If you choose option (c), you will write the listing and can design your ideal job.

a. Respond to an ad in a newspaper, a professional journal, in the placement office, or on the Web. Use an ad that specifies the company, not a blind ad. Be sure that you are fully qualified for the job.

b. Take a job description and assume that it represents a current opening. Use a directory to get the name of the person to whom the letter should be addressed.

c. If you have already worked somewhere, assume that your employer is asking you to apply for fulltime work after graduation. Be sure to write a fully persuasive letter.

d. Respond to one of the listings below. Use a directory or the Web to get the name and address of the person to whom you should write.

1. Cotts Beverages is hiring an **assistant auditor**. Minimum 12 hours of accounting experience. Work includes analysis and evaluation of operating and financial controls and requires contact with many levels of company management. Extensive travel (50 percent) required through the Canadian West, along with some international work. Effective written and oral communication skills a must, along with sound decision-making abilities. Locations: Edmonton, Toronto, Halifax, New York, Los Angeles, Dallas, Atlanta, Philadelphia, Denver, Chicago. Refer to job FA-2534.

2. Roxy Systems (Roxy.com) seeks **Internet marketing coordinators** to analyze online campaigns and put together detailed reports, covering ad impressions and click-through rates. Must have basic understanding of marketing; be organized, creative, and detail-oriented; know Microsoft Excel; have excellent communication skills; and be familiar with the Internet. Send letter and résumé to mike@roxy.com.

3. Bose Corporation seeks **public relations/communications administrative associate** (Job Code 117BD). Write, edit, and produce the in-house newsletter using desktop publishing software. Represent the company to external contacts (including the press). Provide administrative support to the manager of PR by scheduling meetings, preparing presentations, tabulating and analyzing surveys, and processing financial requests. Excellent organizational, interpersonal, and communication skills (both written and oral) required. Must be proficient in MS Office and Filemaker Pro.

4. The Gap is hiring **executive development program trainees**. After completing 10-week training programs, trainees will become assistant buyers. Prefer people with strong interest and experience in retailing. Apply directly to the store for which you want to work.

5. A local non-profit seeks a **coordinator of volunteer services**. Responsibilities for this fulltime position include coordinating volunteers' schedules, recruiting and training new volunteers, and evaluating existing programs. Excellent listening and communication skills required.

28.14   Writing a Prospecting Letter

Pick a company you'd like to work for and apply for a specific position. The position can be one that already exists or one that you would create if you could to match your unique blend of talents. Give your instructor a copy of the job description with your letter.

Address your letter to the president of a small company, the area vice president or branch manager of a large company. Use directories or the Web to get the name and address of the person with the power to create a job for you.

Polishing Your Prose

Using You *and* I

You-attitude (◀▶ Module 6) means that you'll use lots of *you's* in business messages. However, use *you* only when it refers to your reader. When you mean "people in general," use another term.

Incorrect: When I visited your office, I learned that you need to find a way to manage your email.

Correct: When I visited your office, I saw the importance of managing one's email.

Incorrect: Older customers may not like it if you call them by their first names.

Correct: Older customers may prefer being called by courtesy titles and their last names.

Omit *you* when it criticizes or attacks the reader.

Not you-attitude: You didn't turn your expense report in by the deadline.

You-attitude: Expense reports are due by the fifth of each month. We have no record of receiving your report.

When you talk about what you've done, use *I*.

Correct: In the past month, I have completed three audits.

In general, keep *I's* to a minimum. They make you sound less confident and more self-centred.

Weak: I think that we would save money if we bought a copier instead of leasing it.

Better: We would save money by buying a copier instead of leasing it.

Weak: I want to be sure that I understand how I will be affected by this project.

Better: How will this project affect our unit?

When you write a document that focusses on you (such as a progress report or a job application letter), vary sentence structure so that you don't begin every sentence with I.

Correct: This job gave me the opportunity to . . .

Correct: As an intern, I . . .

Correct: Working with a team, I . . .

When you use a first-person pronoun as part of a compound subject or object, put the first-person pronoun last.

Correct: She asked you and me to make the presentation.

Correct: You, Kelly, and I will have a chance to talk to members of the audience before the dinner.

Be sure to use the right case. Omit the other part(s) of the compound to see the case you should use:

She asked me.

I will have a chance.

Use the same form when you restore the other words.

Exercises

Revise the following sentences to eliminate errors and improve the use of *you* and *I.*

1. I worked with a team to create a class Web page. I was responsible for much of the initial design and some of the HTML coding. I also tested the page with three people to see how easily they could navigate it. I and the other team members presented the page to a committee of local business people.

2. I have taken a lot of time and trouble to get a copy of *Using Excel* for each of you.

3. If you offend someone in the team, you need to resolve the conflict you have created.

4. Please return the draft to me and Mehtap.

5. I think that it would be a good idea for us to distribute an agenda before the meeting.

6. I have asked each department head if he or she had information to announce at the meeting, collated the responses, and arranged the topics to cover in an agenda. I have indicated how much time each topic will take. I am herewith distributing the agenda for Friday's meeting.

7. You haven't made the Web page accessible to users with impaired vision.

8. My last job showed me that you have to be able to solve problems quickly.

9. I observed department meetings during my internship. I also sat in on client meetings. I designed PowerPoint slides for client presentations. I participated in strategy sessions. Finally, I drafted brochures.

10. The client asked me and my supervisor to explain our strategy more fully.

Check your answers to the odd-numbered exercises on page 635.

Module 29
Preparing for Job Interviews

Topics

- Why do I need an interview strategy?
- What details should I think about?
- Should I practice before the interview?
- How should I answer traditional interview questions?
- How can I prepare for behavioural and situational interviews?
- How can I prepare for phone or video interviews?

Review of Key Points

Learning Applications

Polishing Your Prose: Matters on Which Experts Disagree

Learning Focus

After reading and applying the information in Module 29, you'll be able to demonstrate

Knowledge of
- Job interview best practices

Skills to
- Be your best self at a job interview
- Plan and practice for the interview
- Answer traditional interview questions
- Shine in behavioural and situational interviews
- Participate in phone or video interviews
- Negotiate salary and benefits

"Everything you do needs to be viewed as a learning experience that can eventually lead to your long-term career goals."

"I train people to be able to evaluate or qualify candidates looking for employment," says Chris Bocchini, operations coordinator of training and development for Express Personnel Services. "One of the things I train employees in is to be able to teach candidates how to conduct themselves on job interviews."

Chris has an honours B.A. in French and history and started as a temporary worker for Express while in university. After University Express hired her full-time, proving that we never know where we may end up working. Chris went on to pursue her Canadian Human Resources Professional Designation.

Express Personnel Services, formerly Contact Human Resource Group, was established in London, Ontario in 1979. Currently Express Personnel Services, a franchise organization, has 425 offices in such countries as the United States, South Africa, and, of course, Canada. Express has two sides to its operation. It provides temporary workers as well as offering permanent job placement services.

When candidates come to Express they go through a multiple-step interview process that is designed to discover the strengths of the candidates. This process involves an evaluation of the candidates' experience, qualifications, soft skills, and goals so that Express refers the candidate to the appropriate job situation. Even gaps in the employment history are looked at. Gaps are not necessarily negative, for one could have acquired relevant job skills while not actually working. All this information goes into creating a can-

didate profile so that the skills on record can be matched up with the appropriate job order. The central question of the process is "What does the candidate want to do?"

During the interview process Express looks for three things in a candidate, when matching him or her to a job placement. The candidate must exhibit appropriate behaviour, show initiative, and most importantly have the necessary skills for the particular job and company.

Another very important trait that candidates must show is the right attitude. The "fit" of a candidate with a company can change from one company to another. Flexibility is the key in today's job market.

Interviews are extremely important since that is where personal impressions are made on prospective employers. As Chris states, "candidates have one to two minutes to make that first impression—which is so important. Make this time count." Express coaches candidates on how to conduct themselves in interviews. All the behaviours that Express looks for in an interview are identical to those that other employers look for. An Express staffing consultant will work with a candidate on interview technique.

Chris concludes, "It is important to know what you are looking for. Everything you do needs to be viewed as a learning experience that can eventually lead to your long-term career goals..." Chris' career has proven her own point.

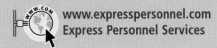

www.expresspersonnel.com
Express Personnel Services

Even when you've prepared thoroughly, job interviews are scary: you know what you want, but you don't feel in control of the situation. When you are prepared, however, you can harness the adrenaline to work for you so that you make the best possible impression to get the job you want.

Today many employers expect you to

- Be more aggressive. One employer deliberately tells the company receptionist to brush off callers who ask about advertised openings. He interviews only those who keep calling and offer the receptionist reasons why they should be interviewed. However, if you're rejected even after giving reasons, accept the rejection gracefully.
- Follow instructions to the letter. The owner of a delivery company tells candidates to phone at a precise hour. Failing to do so means that the person couldn't be trusted to deliver packages on time.[1]
- Participate in many interviews. In 1996, Xerox outsourced preliminary interviews. Applicants went through six interviews with a separate company before they actually met someone from Xerox. High-level jobs may require even more preliminary interviews. A senior vice president in a high-tech company went through 17 interviews before she was offered the job.[2]
- Have one or more interviews by phone, computer, or video.
- Take one or more tests, including aptitude tests, computer simulations, and essay exams where you're asked to explain what you'd do in a specific situation.
- Be approved by the team you'll be joining. In companies with self-managed work teams, the team has a say in who is hired.
- Provide—at the interview or right after it—a sample of the work you're applying to do. You may be asked to write a memo or a proposal, calculate a budget on a spreadsheet, or make a presentation.

Be courteous to the receptionists and secretaries you speak to. Find out the person's name on your first call and use it on subsequent calls. "Thank you for being so patient. Can you tell me when a better time might be to try to get Mr. or Ms. X? I'll try again on [date]." Sometimes, if you call after 5 P.M., executives answer their own phones since clerical staff members have gone home.

If you get voicemail, leave a concise message with your name and phone number. Even if you've called 10 times, keep your voice pleasant. If you get voicemail repeatedly, call the main company number to speak with a receptionist. Ask whether the person you're trying to reach is in the building. If he or she is on the road, ask when the person is due in.

Why do I need an interview strategy?

So that you can do everything possible to get what you want!

Develop an overall strategy based on your answers to these three questions:

1. **What do you want the interviewer to know about you?** Pick two to five points that represent your strengths for that particular job. These facts may be achievements, character traits (such as enthusiasm, attention to detail, creativity), experiences that qualify you for the job and separate you from other applicants, your passion for working for this company, and so on. For each strength, identify

To work in Nelvana's creative environment, employees are hired because they possess both the *skills* to do the job, and the *creativity* to imagine original ideas. Applicants' portfolios are expected to contain evidence of both.

and write down a specific action or accomplishment to support it. For example, be ready to give an example to prove that you're "hard working." Show how you have saved money, served customers better, or led the team in other organizations where you've worked. Then at the interview, listen to every question to see how you can make one of your key points part of your answer. If the questions don't allow you to make your points, bring them up at the end of the interview.

2. **What disadvantages or weaknesses do you need to minimize?** Expect that you may be asked to explain weaknesses or apparent weaknesses in your record: lack of experience, so-so grades, or gaps in your record.

3. **What do you need to know about the job and the organization to decide whether to accept this job if it is offered to you?**

FYI

In a 1999 survey of campus recruiters, 81 percent said that applicants should wear navy blue to interviews.

Source: Glenn Burkins, "Work Week," *The Wall Street Journal,* August 10, 1999

What details should I think about?

What you'll wear, what you'll take with you, and how to get there.

Inappropriate clothing or being late can cost you a job. Put enough time into planning details so that you can move on to substantive planning.

What to Wear

Your interview clothing should be at least as formal as the clothing of the person likely to interview you. When the interview is scheduled, ask the person who invites you whether the company has a dress policy. If the dress is "casual," wear a shirt and a good-quality skirt or pants, not jeans.

If you're interviewing for a management or office job, wear a business suit. What kind of suit? If you've got good taste and a good eye for colour, follow your instincts. If fashion isn't your strong point, read John Molloy's *New Dress for Success* (1998; men's clothes) and *New Woman's Dress for Success* (1996). Perhaps the best suggestion in the books is his advice to visit expensive stores, noting details—the exact shade of blue in a suit, the number of buttons on the sleeve, the placement of pockets, the width of lapels—and then go to stores in your price range and buy a suit that has the details found on more expensive clothing. You can also find quality clothes at bargain prices in second-hand and vintage clothing shops in your town or city.

Site *to* **See**

Go to
http://www.job-interview.net/interviewlibdress.htm
Recommended books on dressing for job interviews.

http://www.job-interview.net/interviewlibdress.htm
Hints to help college students dress for job interviews.

Interview Strategy

Plan an interview strategy based on these three questions:

1. What two to five facts about yourself do you want the interviewer to know?
2. What disadvantages or weaknesses do you need to overcome or minimize?
3. What do you need to know about the job and the organization to decide whether or not you want to accept this job if it is offered to you?

If you're interviewing for a position that involves working, visiting, or supervising muddy or dirty sites, wear sturdy clothes that suggest you're willing to get dirty.[3] In this case, looking "good" is less important than looking businesslike.

Consider the corporate culture. A woman interviewing for a job at The Gap wore a matching linen skirt and blouse that were similar to Gap clothing. Her clothing was evidence that she'd researched the job.[4]

Choose comfortable shoes. The last thing you want to be thinking about during an important interview is how much your feet hurt! You also may do a fair amount of walking during the office visit or plant trip.

Take care of all the details. Check your heels to make sure they aren't run down; make sure your shoes are shined. Have your hair cut or styled conservatively. Jewellery and makeup should be understated. Personal hygiene must be impeccable. If you wear cologne or perfume, keep it to a minimum.

What to Bring to the Interview

Bring extra copies of your résumé. If your campus placement office has already given the interviewer a data sheet, present the résumé at the beginning of the interview: "I thought you might like a little more information about me."

Bring something to write on, something to write with, and a small notepad with the questions you want to ask on it.

Bring copies of your work or a portfolio: an engineering design, a copy of a memo you wrote on a job or in a business writing class, an article you wrote for the campus paper. You don't need to present these unless the interview calls for them, but they can be very effective.

Bring the names, addresses, and phone numbers of your references if you haven't already provided them. Bring complete details about your work history and education, including dates and street addresses, in case you're asked to fill out an application form.

If you can afford it, buy a briefcase to carry these items. At the start of your career, an inexpensive briefcase is acceptable.

Note-Taking

During or immediately after the interview, write down

- The name of the interviewer (or all the people you talked to, if it's a group interview or an office visit)
- What the interviewer seemed to like best about you
- Any negative points or concerns that came up that you need to counter in your follow-up letter or phone calls
- Answers to your questions about the company
- When you'll hear from the company

The easiest way to get the interviewer's name is to ask for his or her card. You may be able to make all the notes you need on the back of the card.

How to Get There

If you're going to a place you haven't been before, do a practice run at the same time of day your interview is scheduled for. Check out bus transfers or parking fees. On the day of the interview, leave early enough so that you'll get to the interview

Go to http://jobsearchcan ada.about.com/

Click on "Interview Survival" for some helpful hints and guidelines, but don't miss the opportunity to explore other helpful information regarding jobs in Canada via other links on this Web site.

15 minutes early. Use the extra time to check your appearance in the restroom mirror and to thumb through the company publications in the waiting room. If an accident does delay you, call to say you'll be late.

Should I practice before the interview?

Absolutely!

Your interviewing skills will improve with practice. Rehearse everything you can: put on the clothes you'll wear and practice entering a room, shaking hands, sitting down, and answering questions. Ask a friend to interview you. Saying answers out loud is surprisingly harder than saying them in your head.

Some campuses have videotaping facilities so that you can watch your own sample interview. Videotaping is more valuable if you can do it at least twice, so you can modify behaviour the second time and check the tape to see whether the modification works.

How to Act

Should you "be yourself"? There's no point in assuming a radically different persona. If you do, you run the risk of getting into a job that you'll hate (though the persona you assumed might have loved it). On the other hand, all of us have several selves: we can be lazy, insensitive, bored, slow-witted, and tongue-tied, but we can also be energetic, perceptive, interested, intelligent, and articulate. Be your best self at the interview.

Interviews can make you feel vulnerable and defensive; to counter this, review your productive personality traits and accomplishments—the things you're especially proud of having done—in writing. You'll make a better impression if you have a firm sense of your own self-worth.

Every interviewer repeats the advice that mothers often give: sit up straight, don't mumble, look at people when you talk. It's good advice for interviews. Be aware that many people respond negatively to smoking.

Office visits that involve meals and semi-social occasions call for sensible choices. When you order, choose something that's easy and unmessy to eat. Watch your table manners. Eat a light lunch, with no alcohol, so that you'll be alert during the afternoon. At dinner or an evening party, decline alcohol if you don't drink or are underage. If you do drink, accept just one drink—you're still being evaluated. Be aware that some people respond negatively to applicants who drink hard liquor.

Parts of the Interview

Every interview has an opening, a body, and a close.

In the **opening** (two to five minutes), good interviewers will try to set you at ease. Some interviewers will open with easy questions about your major or interests. Others open by telling you about the job or the company. If this happens, listen so you can answer later questions to show that you can do the job or contribute to the company that's being described.

The **body** of the interview (10 to 25 minutes) is an all-too-brief time for you to highlight your qualifications and find out what you need to know to decide if you

Site *to* **See**

Go to
http://www.career
services.uwaterloo.
ca/manual-home.html
The University of
Waterloo's award-
winning Career
Development
Manual offers useful
suggestions for
managing
information
interviews.

FYI

Replacing an
employee costs the
company about 1½
times the person's
annual salary.

Source: Sue Shellenbarger,
"To Win the Loyalty of
Your Employees, Try a
Softer Touch," *The Wall
Street Journal,* January
26, 2000, B1.

want to accept a second interview. Expect questions that allow you to showcase your strong points and questions that probe any weaknesses evident from your résumé. (You were neither in school nor working last fall. What were you doing?) Normally the interviewer will also try to sell you on the company and give you an opportunity to raise questions.

Be aware of time so that you can make sure to get in your key points and questions: "We haven't covered it yet, but I want you to know that I . . . ." "I'm aware that it's almost 10:30. I do have some more questions that I'd like to ask about the company."

In the **close** of the interview (two to five minutes), the interviewer will usually tell you what happens next: "We'll be bringing our top candidates to the office in February. You should hear from us in three weeks." One interviewer reports that he gives applicants his card and tells them to call him. "It's a test to see if they are committed, how long it takes for them to call, and whether they even call at all."[5]

Close with an assertive statement. Depending on the circumstances, you could say: "I've certainly enjoyed learning more about General Electric." "I hope I get a chance to visit your Mississauga office. I'd really like to see the new computer system you talked about." "This job seems to be a good match between what you're looking for and what I'd like to do."

Stress Interviews

A **stress interview** deliberately puts the applicant under stress. If the stress is physical (for example, you're given a chair where the light is in the your eyes), be assertive: move to another chair or tell the interviewer that the behaviour bothers you.

Usually the stress is psychological. A group of interviewers fire rapid questions. A single interviewer probes every weak spot in the applicant's record and asks questions that elicit negatives. If you get questions that put you on the defensive, **rephrase** them in less inflammatory terms, if necessary, and then **treat them as requests for information**.

Q: Why did you major in physical education? That sounds like a pretty Mickey Mouse major.

A: You're asking whether I have the academic preparation for this job. I started out in physical education because I've always loved sports. I learned that I couldn't graduate on time if I officially switched to business administration because the requirements were different in the two programs. But I do have 21 hours in business administration and 9 hours in accounting. And my sports experience gives me practical training in teamwork, motivating people, and management.

Respond assertively. The candidates who survive are those who stand up for themselves and who explain why indeed they *are* worth hiring.

Silence can also create stress. One woman walked into her scheduled interview to find a male interviewer with his feet up on the desk. He said, "It's been a long day. I'm tired and I want to go home. You have five minutes to sell yourself." Since she had planned the points she wanted to be sure interviewers knew, she was able to do this. "Your recruiting brochure said that you're looking for someone with a major in accounting and a minor in finance. As you may remember from my résumé, I'm majoring in accounting and have had 12 hours in finance. I've also served as treasurer of a local campaign committee and have worked as a volunteer tax preparer through the Accounting Club." When she finished, the interviewer told her it was a test: "I wanted to see how you'd handle it."

Increasingly common is the variety of stress interview that asks you to do—on the spot—the kind of thing the job would require. An interviewer for a sales job handed applicants a ballpoint pen and said, "Sell me this pen." (It's OK to ask who the target market is and whether this is a repeat or a new customer.) Candidates who make it through the first two rounds of interviews for sales jobs at Dataflex are invited to participate in a week's worth of sales meetings, which start at 7 A.M. four times a week. The people who do participate—not merely attend—are the people who get hired.[6] AT&T asks some applicants to deliver presentations or lead meetings. Massachusetts Mutual Life asked the finalists for a vice presidency to process memos and reports in a two-hour in-basket exercise and participate in several role plays.[7]

Site *to* **See**

Go to
http://careers.msn.com/

Use this resource to explore articles on resume writing, interviewing, negotiating offers, and moving up the company ladder.

How should I answer traditional interview questions?

Choose answers that fit your qualifications and your interview strategy.

As Figure 29.1 on the next page shows, successful applicants use different communication behaviours than do unsuccessful applicants. Successful applicants are more likely to use the company name during the interview, support their claims with specific details, and ask specific questions about the company and the industry. In addition to practising the content of questions, try to incorporate these tactics.

The following questions frequently come up at interviews. Do some unpressured thinking on paper before the interview so that you'll be able to come up with answers that are responsive, honest, and paint a good picture of you. Choose answers that fit your qualifications and your interview strategy.

Site *to* **See**

Go to
http://www.ns.hrdc-drhc.gc.ca/english/career/pathways/intrview.htm

A grid prepared by Human Resources Development Canada sets out typical interview questions, analyses their purpose, and gives you suggestions on how to approach them.

1. **Tell me about yourself.**
   Don't launch into an autobiography. Instead, talk about your achievements as they relate to the organization's culture and goals. Give specific examples to prove each of your strengths.

2. **What makes you think you're qualified to work for this company? Or, I'm interviewing 120 people for 2 jobs. Why should I hire you?**
   This question may feel like an attack. Use it as an opportunity to state your strong points: your qualifications for the job, the skills, knowledge, and character traits that separate you from other alternatives.

3. **What two or three accomplishments have given you the greatest satisfaction?**
   Pick accomplishments that you're proud of, that create the image you want to project, and that enable you to share one of the things you want the interviewer to know about you. Focus not just on the end result, but on the transferable skills—teamwork, problem solving, and critical thinking—that made the achievement possible.

4. **Why do you want to work for us? What is your ideal job?**
   Even if you're interviewing just for practice, make sure you have a good answer—preferably two or three reasons you'd like to work for that company. Do your homework; know everything possible about the company and the job.

Figure 29.1

The Communication Behaviours of Successful Interviewees

Behaviour	Unsuccessful Interviewees	Successful Interviewees
Statements about the position	Had only vague ideas of what they wanted to do; changed "ideal job" up to six times during the interview	Specific and consistent about the position they wanted; were able to tell why they wanted the position
Use of company name	Rarely used the company name	Referred to the company by name four times as often as unsuccessful interviewees
Knowledge about company and position	Made it clear that they were using the interview to learn about the company and what it offered	Made it clear that they had researched the company; referred to specific brochures, journals, or people who had given them information
Level of interest, enthusiasm	Responded neutrally to interviewer's statements: "OK," I see." Indicated reservations about company or location	Expressed approval of information provided by the interviewer nonverbally and verbally; "That's great!" Explicitly indicated desire to work for this particular company
Picking up on interviewer's cues	Gave vague or negative answers even when a positive answer was clearly desired ("How are your math skills?")	Answered positively and confidently—and backed up the claim with a specific example of "problem solving" or "toughness"
Use of industry terms and technical jargon	Used almost no technical jargon	Used technical jargon: "point of purchase display," "NCR charge," "two-column approach," "direct mail"
Use of specifics in answers	Gave short answers—10 words or less, sometimes only one word; but did not elaborate. Gave general responses: "fairly well"	Supported claims with specific personal experiences, comparisons, statistics, statements of teachers and employers
Questions asked by interviewee	Asked a small number of general questions	Asked specific questions based on knowledge of the industry and the company. Personalized questions: "What would my duties be?"
Control of time and topics	Interviewee talked 37% of the interview time; initiated 36% of the comments; spent little time talking outside of question-answer sequences	Interviewee talked 55% of the total time; initiated subjects 56% of the time; gave shorter answers but spent more time talking to interviewer outside question-answers sequences

Sources: Based on research reported by Lois J. Einhorn, "An Inner View of the Job Interview: An Investigation of Successful Communicative Behaviors," *Communication Education* 30 (July 1981): 217–28; and Frederic M. Jablin, Vernon D. Miller, and Patricia M. Sias, "Communication and Interaction Processes," in *The Employment Interview Handbook*, ed. Robert W. Elder and Michael M. Harris (Thousand Oaks, CA: Sage, 1999), 297–320.

If you don't seem to be taking the interview seriously, the interviewer won't take you seriously, and you won't even get good practice.

5. **What college courses did you like best and least? Why?**
    This question may be an icebreaker; it may be designed to discover the kind of applicant the organization is looking for. If your favourite class was something outside your program, prepare an answer that shows that you have qualities that can help you in the job you're applying for: "My favourite class was Canadian

Literature. We got a chance to think on our own, rather than just regurgitate facts; we made presentations to the class every week. I found I really like sharing my ideas with other people and presenting reasons for my conclusions about something."

6. **Why are your grades so low?**
   If possible, show that the cause of low grades now has been solved or isn't relevant to the job you're applying for: "My father almost died last year, and my schoolwork really suffered." "When I started, I didn't have any firm goals. Once I discovered the program that was right for me, my grades have all been 'Bs' or better." "I'm not good at multiple-choice tests. But you need someone who can work with people, not someone who can take tests."

7. **What have you read recently? What movies have you seen recently?**
   These questions may be icebreakers; they may be designed to probe your intellectual depth. Be prepared: read at least one book or magazine (regularly) and see at least one movie that you could discuss at an interview.

8. **Show me some samples of your writing.**
   The year you're interviewing, go through your old papers and select the best ones, retyping them if necessary, so that you'll have samples if you're asked for them. Show interviewers essays, reports, or business documents, not poetry or song lyrics. If you don't have samples at the interview, mail them to the interviewer immediately after the interview.

9. **Where do you see yourself in five years?**
   Employers ask this question to find out if you are a self-starter or if you passively respond to what happens. You may want to have several scenarios for five years from now to use in different kinds of interviews. Or you may want to say, "Well, my goals may change as opportunities arise. But right now, I want to. . . ."

10. **What are your interests outside work? What campus or community activities have you been involved in?**
    While it's desirable to be well-rounded, naming 10 interests may work against you: The interviewer may wonder when you'll have time to work.
    If you mention your fiancé, spouse, or children in response to this question ("Well, my fiancé and I like to go sailing"), it is perfectly legal for the interviewer to ask follow-up questions ("What would you do if your spouse got a job offer in another town?"), even though the same question would be illegal if the interviewer brought up the subject first.

11. **What have you done to learn about this company?**
    An employer may ask this to see what you already know about the company (if you've read the recruiting literature, the interviewer doesn't need to repeat it). This question may also be used to see how active a role you're taking in the job search and how interested you are in this job.

12. **What adjectives would you use to describe yourself?**
    Use only positive ones. Be ready to illustrate each with a specific example of something you've done.

13. **What is your greatest strength?**
    Employers ask this question to give you a chance to sell yourself and to learn something about your values. Pick a strength related to work, school, or activities: "I'm good at working with people." "I really can sell things." "I'm good at solving

Instant Replay

What Successful Interviewees Do

Successful applicants

- Know what they want to do
- Have researched the company in advance
- Use the company name in the interview
- Support skills and knowledge claims with specifics
- Use industry language
- Ask specific questions
- Talk more of the time

Site *to* See

Go to
http://www.job-interview.net/
http://www.job-interview.net/interviewgen.htm

These job interview research sites cover how to respond to difficult and illegal questions.

Figure 29.2

Poor Responses to Behavioural Interview Questions

GORE-TEXT

Carolyn Murray (cmurray@wlgore.com), 37, a savvy recruiter at W.L. Gore & Associates, developers of Gore-Tex, pays little attention to a candidate's carefully scripted responses to her admittedly softball questions. Instead, she listens for a throwaway line that reveals the reality behind an otherwise benign reply. Herewith, Murray delivers a post-game analysis of how three job candidates whiffed during their interviews.

the PITCH	the SWING	the MISS
"Give me an example of a time when you had a conflict with a team member."	" 'Our leader asked me to handle all of the FedExing for our team. I did it, but I thought that FedExing was a waste of my time.' "	"At Gore, we work from a team concept. Her answer shows that she won't exactly jump when one of her team-mates needs help."
"Tell me how you solved a problem that was impeding your project."	" 'One of the engineers on my team wasn't pulling his weight, and we were closing in on a deadline. So I took on some of his work. ' "	"The candidate may have resolved the issue for this particular deadline, but he did nothing to prevent the prob-lem from happening again."
"What's the one thing that you would change about your current position?"	" 'My job as a salesman has become mundane. Now I want the responsibility of managing people.' "	"He's not maximizing his cur-rent position. Selling is never mundane if you go about it in the right way."

Source: Fast Company, January 1999, 156.

Site *to* See

Go to
ivillage.com/work/ job/get/articles/0,10 109,196965_192749, 00.html

The interview cheat sheet gives good and bad answers to interview questions.

problems." "I learn quickly." "I'm reliable. When I say I'll do something, I do it." Be ready to illustrate each with a specific example of something you've done.

14. **What is your greatest weakness?**
   Use a work-related negative, even if something in your personal life really is your greatest weakness. Interviewers won't let you get away with a "weakness" like being a workaholic or just not having any experience yet. Instead, use one of the following three strategies:

a. Discuss a weakness that is not related to the job you're being considered for and which will not be needed even when you're promoted. End your answer with a positive that is related to the job:
   [For a creative job in advertising:] I don't like accounting. I know it's important, but I don't like it. I even hire someone to do my taxes. I'm much more interest-ed in being creative and working with people, which is why I find this position interesting.
   [For a job in administration:] I don't like selling products. I hated selling cookies when I was a Girl Scout. I'd much rather work with ideas—and I really like sell-ing the ideas that I believe in.

b. Discuss a weakness that you are working to improve:
   In the past, I wasn't a good writer. But last term I took a course in business writ-ing that taught me how to organize my ideas and how to revise. I may never win a Pulitzer Prize, but now I'm a lot more confident that I can write effective reports and memos.

FOOL'S TOOL

Figure 29.3
**Good Responses
to Interview
Questions**

As CEO of Motley Fool, a wildly popular investment Web site, **Erik Rydholm** (erikr@fool.com), 31, has little time for fooling around with undesirable job candidates. To streamline the interview process, he's come up with three questions that quickly separate the fools from the Fools.

FOOLISH question	WISE answer	FOOL'S take-away
" 'What does Foolishness mean to you?' That's a great first question, one that separates those who get it from those who are clueless."	"One guy emphasized that we give people the power to gather investing information from many sources by visiting a single Web site."	"He understood that we're trying to revolutionize the way people lead their financial lives—by putting a lot of power at their disposal."
" 'Should the Motley Fool consider putting its name on mutual funds and selling a line of financial services?' "	"He encouraged us to consider whether branding a fund would undercut our integrity and whether it even related to our core competencies."	"He understood that there's integrity to the Motley Fool brand, and he recognized the risk of undercutting that integrity."
" 'How does the Motley Fool succeed?' That gets to the heart of how we can continue to capitalize on our current market share."	"One candidate argued that the Motley Fool is not a source—it's a service: We guide people through their investment decisions."	"He understood the difference between a 'source' and a 'service'—which made me confident that he could think distinctively for us."

Source: Fast Company, January 1999, 157.

c. Discuss a work-related weakness:
   Sometimes I procrastinate. Fortunately, I work well under pressure, but a couple of times I've really put myself in a bind.

15. Why are you looking for another job?
   Stress what you're looking for in a new job, not why you want to get away from your old one.
   If you were fired, say so. There are four acceptable ways to explain why you were fired:
a. You lost your job, along with many others, when the company downsized due to economic reasons.
b. It wasn't a good match. Add what you now know you need in a job, and ask what the employer can offer in this area.
c. You and your supervisor had a personality conflict. Make sure you show that this was an isolated incident, and that you normally get along well with people.
d. You made mistakes, but you've learned from them and are now ready to work well. Be ready to offer a specific anecdote proving that you have indeed changed.

16. What questions do you have?
   This gives you a chance to cover things the interviewer hasn't brought up; it also gives the interviewer a sense of your priorities and values. Don't focus on salary or fringe benefits. Instead ask

- What would I be doing on a day-to-day basis?
- What kind of training program do you have? If, as I'm rotating among departments, I find that I prefer one area, can I specialize in it when the training program is over?

- How do you evaluate employees? How often do you review them? Where would you expect a new trainee (banker, staff accountant) to be three years from now?
- What happened to the last person who had this job?
- How are interest rates (a new product from competitors, imports, demographic trends, government regulation, etc.) affecting your company?
- How would you describe the company's culture?
- This sounds like a great job. What are the drawbacks?

Benefits, working conditions, and the work itself are just as important as salary in evaluating job offers

Source: © Danny Shanahan/Riley Illustration

Increasingly, candidates are asking about work-life balance and about the control they'll have over their own work:

- Do people who work for you have a life off the job?
- If my job requires too much travel, can I change without doing serious damage to my career?
- What support can you offer my significant other?
- Do you offer flextime?
- How much pressure do you have to achieve your projects? How much freedom is there to extend a deadline?[8]

You won't be able to anticipate every question you may get. (One interviewer asked applicants, "What vegetable would you like to be?" Another asked, "If you were a cookie, what kind of cookie would you be?"[9]) Check with other people who have interviewed recently to find out what questions are being asked in your field.

How can I prepare for behavioural and situational interviews?

> Think about skills you've used that could transfer to other jobs.

Learn as much as you can about the culture of the company you hope to join.

Many companies are now using behavioural or situational interviews. **Behavioural interviews** ask the applicant to describe actual behaviours, rather than plans or general principles. Thus, instead of asking, "How would you motivate people?" the interviewer might ask, "Tell me what happened the last time you wanted to get other people to do something." Follow-up questions might include, "What exactly did you do to handle the situation? How did you feel about the results?

Negotiating Salary and Benefits

The best time to negotiate for salary and benefits is after you have the job offer. Try to delay discussing salary early in the interview process, when you're still competing against other applicants.

Prepare for salary negotiations by finding out what the going rate is for the kind of work you hope to do. Cultivate friends who are now in the workforce to find out what they're making. If your campus has a placement office, ask what last year's graduates got. Check Web sites and trade journals for salaries, often segmented into entry-level, median, and high salaries and even by city. Specialized books can also help (◁|▷ Module 22, Figure 22.3) such as the annual *Direct Marketing and Telemarketing Guide or the Robert Half and Accountemps Salary Guide.*

If the interviewer asks you about your salary requirements before a job offer has been made, try this response: "I'm sure your firm can pay me what I'm worth." Then either ask about pay ranges or go back to your qualifications for the job. If the interviewer demands a response, give a range using specific increments based on your research: "I'd expect to make between $37,300 and $41,900." As you say this, *watch the interviewer.* If he or she has that blank look we use to hide dismay, you may have asked for much more than the company was planning to offer. Quickly continue, ". . . depending, of course, on fringe benefits and how quickly I could be promoted. However, salary isn't the most important criterion for me in choosing a job, and I won't necessarily accept the highest offer I get. I'm interested in going somewhere where I can get good experience and use my talents to make a real contribution."

The best way to get more money is to convince the employer that you're worth it. During the interview process, show what you can do that the competition can't. Work to redefine the position in the employer's eyes from a low-level, anybody-could-do-it job to a complex combination of duties that only someone with your particular mix of talents could do.

After you have the offer, begin negotiating salary and benefits. You're in the strongest position when (1) you've done your homework and know what the usual salary and benefits are and (2) you can walk away from this offer if it doesn't meet your needs. Again, avoid naming a specific salary. Don't say you can't accept less. Instead, Kate Wendleton suggests, say you "would find it difficult to accept the offer" under the terms first offered.

Remember that you're negotiating a package, not just a starting salary. A company that truly can't pay any more money now might be able to review you for promotion sooner than usual, or pay your moving costs, or give you a better job title. Some companies offer fringe benefits that may compensate for lower taxable income: use of a company car, reimbursements for education, child care or eldercare subsidies, or help in finding a job for your spouse or partner. And think about your career, not just the initial salary. Sometimes a low-paying job at a company that will provide superb experience will do more for your career (and your long-term earning prospects) than a high salary now with no room to grow.

Work toward a win-win solution. You want the employer to be happy that you're coming on board and to feel that you've behaved maturely and professionally.

Sources: Kate Wendleton, *Through the Brick Wall: How to Job-Hunt in a Tight Market* (New York: Villard Books, 1992), 278; and Jack Griffin, *How to Say It at Work: Putting Yourself Across with Power Words, Body Language, and Communication Secrets,* (Priamus, NJ: Prentice Hall, 1998), 69.

How did the other people feel? How did your superior feel about the results?" Since behavioural questions require applicants to tell what they actually did—rather than to say what ought to be done—interviewers feel they offer better insight into how someone will actually function as an employee. Problem 29.14 on page 618 lists common behavioural questions.

Situational interviews put you in a situation that allows the interviewer to see whether you have the qualities the company is seeking. For example, Southwest Airlines found that 95 percent of the complaints it received were provoked by only 5 percent of its personnel. When managers explored further, they found that these 5 percent of employees were self-centred. To weed out self-centred applicants, Southwest now puts several candidates into a room and asks each to give a five-minute speech on "Why I Want to Work with Southwest Airlines." But the interviewers watch the audience to hire the people who are pulling for other speakers to do well, as opposed to those who are only thinking about their own performance.[10]

Situational interviews may also be conducted using traditional questions but evaluating behaviours other than the answers. Greyhound hired applicants for its customer-assistance centre who made eye contact with the interviewer and smiled at least five times during a 15-minute interview.[11]

Site *to* **See**

Go to esl.about.com/library /weekly/aa120797. htm

Essential Job Interview English II has good advice for everyone.

How can I prepare for phone or video interviews?

Practice short answers. Retape until you look good.

Try to schedule phone interviews for home, not work, and for a time when things will be quiet. If a company wants to interview you on the spot, accept only if the timing is good. If it isn't, say so: "We just sat down to dinner. Could you call back in 30 minutes?" Then get your information about the company, ask the kids to be quiet, and get your thoughts in order.

To prepare for a phone interview,

- Tape yourself so you can make any adjustments in pronunciation and voice qualities.
- Practice short answers to questions. After giving a short answer in the interview, say, "Would you like more information?" Without a visual channel, you can't see the body language that tells you someone else wants to speak.

Two kinds of video interviews exist. The first kind is a live interview using video-conferencing equipment. For this kind of interview, use the same guidelines for a phone interview. In the second kind, the company sends a list of questions, asking the applicant to tape the responses

If you're asked to prepare a videotape,

- Practice your answers
- Tape the interview as many times as necessary to get a tape that presents you at your best
- Be specific. Since the employer can't ask follow-up questions, you need to be detailed about how your credentials could help the employer

Employability Skills 2000+ Checklist for Job Interviews

In this module, the key skills from The Conference Board of Canada's Employability Skills 2000+ are:

Communicate

✔ read and understand information presented in a variety of forms (e.g. words, graphs , charts, diagrams)
✔ write and speak so others pay attention and understand
✔ share information using a range of information and communications technologies (e.g. voice, email, computers)
✔ use relevant scientific, technological, and mathematical knowledge and skills to explain or clarify ideas

Manage Information

✔ locate, gather, and organize information using appropriate technology and information systems
✔ access, analyze, and apply knowledge and skills from a variety of disciplines (e.g. the arts, languages, science, technology, mathematics, social sciences, and the humanities)

Think & Solve Problems

✔ assess situations and identify problems
✔ recognize the human, interpersonal, technical, scientific, and mathematical dimensions of a problem
✔ readily use science, technology, and mathematics as ways to think, gain and share knowledge, solve problems, and make decisions
✔ check to see if a solution works, and act on opportunities for improvement

Participate in Projects & Tasks

✔ develop a plan, seek feedback, test, revise, and implement

Review of Key Points

- Develop an overall strategy based on your answers to these three questions:
  1. What two to five facts about yourself do you want the interviewer to know?
  2. What disadvantages or weaknesses do you need to overcome or minimize?
  3. What do you need to know about the job and the organization to decide whether or not you want to accept this job if it is offered to you?
- Wear a conservative business suit to the interview.

- Bring an extra copy of your résumé, something to write on and write with, and copies of your work to the interview.

- Record the name of the interviewer, what the interviewer liked about you, any negative points that came up, answers to your questions about the company, and when you'll hear from the company.

- Rehearse in advance everything you can. Ask a friend to interview you. If your campus has videotaping facilities, watch yourself on tape so that you can evaluate and modify your interview behaviour.

- Be your best self at the interview.

- Successful applicants know what they want to do, use the company name in the interview, have researched the company in advance, back up claims with specifics, use technical jargon, ask specific questions, and talk more of the time.

- As you practice answers to questions you may be asked, choose answers that fit your qualifications and your interview strategy.

- **Behavioural interviews** ask the applicant to describe actual behaviours, rather than plans or general principles. **Situational interviews** put you in a situation that allows the interviewer to see whether you have the qualities the company is seeking.

- For a phone interview, give short answers. Then ask, "Would you like more information?"

- If you answer questions on videotape, retape as many times as necessary to show your best self.

Learning Applications

Questions for Comprehension

29.1 What three questions should form the basis for an interview strategy?

29.2 How do you use your interview strategy during an interview?

29.3 How do successful interviewees communicate?

Questions for Critical Thinking

29.4 What are your greatest strengths? How can you demonstrate them during an interview?

29.5 What are your weaknesses? How will you deal with them if they come up during an interview?

29.6 What are your options if you are asked what you believe is an illegal interview question? Which option seems best to you? Why?

29.7 Is it unethical to practice answering interview questions, so that you come across as very poised at an interview?

Questions for Building Skills

29.8 What skills have you read about in this module?

29.9 What skills are you practising in the assignments you're doing for this module?

29.10 How could you further develop the skills you're working on?

Exercises and Problems

29.11   Interviewing Job Hunters

Talk to students at your school who are interviewing for jobs this term. Possible questions to ask them include

- What field are you in? How good is the job market in that field this year?

- What questions have you been asked at job interviews? Were you asked any stress or sexist questions? Any really oddball questions?

- What answers seemed to go over well? What answers bombed?

- Were you asked to take any tests (skills, physical, drugs)?

- How long did you have to wait after a first interview to learn whether you were being invited for an office visit? How long after an office visit did it take to learn whether you were being offered a job? How much time did the company give you to decide?

- What advice would you have for someone who will be interviewing next term or next year?

As Your Instructor Directs,

a. Summarize your findings in a memo to your instructor

b. Report your findings orally to the class

c. Join with a small group of students to write a group report describing the results of your survey

29.12   Interviewing an Interviewer

Talk to someone who regularly interviews candidates for entry-level jobs. Possible questions to ask include the following:

- How long have you been interviewing for your organization? Does everyone on the management ladder at your company do some interviewing, or do people specialize in it?

- Do you follow a set structure for interviews? What are some of the standard questions you ask?

- What are you looking for? How important are (1) good grades, (2) leadership roles in extracurricular groups, or (3) relevant work experience? What advice would you give to someone who doesn't have one or more of these?

- What are the things you see students do that create a poor impression? Think about the worst candidate you've interviewed. What did he or she do (or not do) to create such a negative impression?

- What are the things that make a good impression? Recall the best student you've ever interviewed. Why did he or she impress you so much?

- How does your employer evaluate and reward your success as an interviewer?

- What advice would you have for someone who still has a year or so before the job hunt begins?

As Your Instructor Directs,

a. Summarize your findings in a memo to your instructor

b. Report your findings orally to the class

c. Join with a small group of students to write a group report describing the results of your survey

d. Write to the interviewer thanking him or her for taking the time to talk to you

29.13 Preparing an Interview Strategy

Based on your analysis for Problems 27.11 and 27.12, prepare an interview strategy.

1. List two to five things about yourself that you want the interviewer to know before you leave the interview

2. Identify any weaknesses or apparent weaknesses in your record and plan ways to explain them or minimize them

3. List the points you need to learn about an employer to decide whether to accept an office visit or plant trip

As Your Instructor Directs,

a. Share your strategy with a small group of other students

b. Describe your strategy in a memo to your instructor

c. Present your strategy orally to the class

29.14 Preparing Answers to Behavioural Interview Questions

Tell about a time when you

1. Worked effectively under pressure

2. Handled a difficult situation with a co-worker

3. Made an unpopular decision

4. Tolerated an opinion that differed from yours

5. Were unable to complete a project on time

6. Overcame a major obstacle

7. Adapted to a difficult situation

As Your Instructor Directs,

a. Share your answers with a small group of other students

b. Present your answers in a memo to your instructor, and explain why you've chosen the examples you describe

c. Present your answers orally to the class

29.15 Preparing Questions to Ask Employers

Prepare a list of questions to ask at job interviews.

1. Prepare a list of three to five general questions that apply to most employers in your field

2. Prepare two to five specific questions for each of the three companies you are most interested in

As Your Instructor Directs,

a. Share the questions with a small group of other students

b. List the questions in a memo to your instructor

c. Present your questions orally to the class

Polishing Your Prose

Matters on Which Experts Disagree

Any living language changes. New usages appear first in speaking. Here are five issues on which experts currently disagree:

1. Plural pronouns to refer to *everybody*, *everyone*, and *each*. Standard grammar says these words require singular pronouns: *his* or *her* rather than *their*.
2. Split infinitives. An infinitive is the form of a verb that contains to: to understand. An infinitive is **split** when another word separates the *to* from the rest of an infinitive: *to easily understand, to boldly go*. The most recent edition of the *Oxford English Dictionary* allows split infinitives. Purists disagree.
3. *Hopefully* to mean *I hope that*. *Hopefully* means "in a hopeful manner." However, a speaker who says "Hopefully, the rain will stop" is talking about the speaker's hope, not the rain's.
4. *Verbal* to mean *oral*. *Verbal* means "using words." Therefore, both writing and speaking are verbal communication. Non-verbal communication (for example, body language) does not use words.
5. Comma before *and* ("the serial comma"). In a series of three or more items, some experts require a comma after the next to last item (the item before the *and*); others don't.

Ask your instructor and your boss whether they are willing to accept the less formal usage. When you write to someone you don't know, use standard grammar and usage.

Exercises

Each of the following sentences illustrates informal usage. (a) Which would your instructor or your boss accept? (b) Rewrite each of the sentences using standard grammar and usage.

1. Everyone should bring their laptops to the sales meeting.
2. The schedule includes new product information, role plays with common selling situations and awards to the top sales people.
3. To really take advantage of the meeting, you need to bring all of your new product info.
4. Prepare to make a brief verbal report on a challenging sales situation.
5. Think of a time when it was hard to even get in the door to see a potential customer.
6. Hopefully, we will have time to work through many of these situations in our role plays.
7. Awards include best rookie sales representative, the most improved region, everyone who beat their quota and sales representative of the year.
8. We'll feature verbal quotes from customers in our radio ads.
9. Our Web page will let people listen to each customer summarizing verbally what they like best about our products.
10. Hopefully, the Web page will be live so that we can access it during the meeting.

Check your answers to the odd-numbered exercises on page 635.

Module 30

After the Interview: Follow-Up Letters and Calls, and Job Offers

Topics

- **What do I say in a follow-up phone call or letter?**

- **How do I decide which offer to accept?**

- **What do I do if my first offer isn't the one I most want?**

Review of Key Points

Learning Applications

Polishing Your Prose: Using Standard English

Learning Focus

After reading and applying the information in Module 30, you'll be able to demonstrate

Knowledge of

- The attitudes and behaviours employers seek

Skills to

- Make a good impression in follow-up letters and phone calls
- Choose a job that will give you what you want
- Express your enthusiasm to employers

"Thank you letters allow you to open the door one more time to reach a prospective employer."

"Clients have to demonstrate they can add value to the company they are applying to. They must articulate their uniqueness in such a way that the employer has a reason to hire them. Thank you letters can give you the edge you need," says Ronald Manchen, senior career advisor in the London, Ontario, office of Bernard Haldane Associates.

Haldane Associates, founded in 1947 is the oldest career counselling agency in the world, and with offices all across the United States, Canada, and the United Kingdom, it is generally regarded as the world's largest agency of its type. Haldane Associates offers a mentoring program for clients so that they can learn to help themselves.

Ronald's background is not that of the usual career counsellor. He holds degrees in Commerce and is a C.M.A, but states that he was hired because of his "street smarts." Ronald has worked in many different areas of business including customer relations, which, he believes, prepared him for this position.

Half of Haldane's clientele are people searching for a career, and the other half are currently working in jobs but wish to change careers. The process begins with psychometric testing, psychological profiling, and with focussing on past achievements, which do not have to be job related. "It is amazing what you know when you think about it," says Ronald.

The process at Haldane can take up to three years. The focus is not about just finding a job but on career development. The process involves learning how to assess one's strengths, how to transfer skills from one area to another, and how to approach prospective employers. Mock interviews, which are videotaped, are an interesting feature of the process. The client can then observe how he or she is seen by others.

A basic tenet of Haldane philosophy is that most jobs are not advertised, but found through the networking process. A large part of a clients's time at Haldane is spent learning how to network, how to approach prospective employers, and how to follow up on those initial visits.

Thank you letters are an important aspect of interview follow-up. Ronald says that such letters serve three purposes. The first purpose is to show courtesy to someone who has met with you. The second is that if the person who was hired does not work out, you will be the one that will be remembered. And the third reason for writing a thank you letter is that it allows you to write a focus piece that updates your interview and shows that now you have the necessary qualities to fill the job.

Ronald states that a job is a problem-solving process. And so is job hunting. What the job searcher must do is convince the employer that he or she can solve the problems that are presented by the job.

When asked to give his clients advice, Ronald emphasizes the importance of thank you letters. "Thank you letters allow you to open the door one more time to reach a prospective employer."

http://www.jobhunting.com
Bernard Haldane Associates

What you do after the interview may determine whether you get the job. One woman wanted to switch from banking, where she was working in corporate relations, to advertising. The ad agency interviewer expressed doubts about her qualifications. Immediately after leaving the agency, she tracked down a particular book the interviewer had mentioned he was looking for but had been unable to find. She presented it to him—and was hired.[1]

Xerox expects applicants for sales and repair positions to follow up within 10 days. If they don't, the company assumes that the person wouldn't follow up with clients.[2]

If the employer sends you an email query, answer it promptly. You're being judged not only on what you say but also on how quickly you respond.

What should I say in a follow-up phone call or letter?

> Reinforce positives and overcome any negatives.

After a first interview, make follow-up phone calls to reinforce positives from the first interview, to overcome any negatives, and to get information you can use to persuade the interviewer to hire you. Career coach Kate Weldon suggests asking the following questions:

- "What additional information can I give you?"
- "I've been giving a lot of thought to your project and have some new ideas. Can we meet to go over them?"
- "Where do I stand? How does my work compare with the work others presented?"[3]

A letter after an office visit is essential to thank your hosts for their hospitality. A well-written letter can be the deciding factor that gets you the job.[4] The letter should

- Thank the interviewer for his or her time and hospitality
- Reinforce the interviewer's positive impressions
- Counter any negative impressions that may have come up at the interview
- Use the jargon of the company and refer to specific things you learned during your interview or saw during your visit
- Be enthusiastic
- Refer to the next step: whether you'll wait to hear from the employer or whether you want to call to learn about the status of your application

Be sure that the letter is well written and error-free. One employer reports,

> I often interviewed people whom I liked, . . . but their follow-up letters were filled with misspelled words and names and other inaccuracies. They blew their chance with the follow-up letter.[5]

Use your PAIBOC analysis (see Figure 30.1) to compose your office visit follow-up message:

Being Enthusiastic

Every employer wants employees who are enthusiastic about their work. Enthusiastic, "can-do" people seem more energetic than others; they're more fun to be around. In fact, North American culture values and rewards enthusiastic individuals. The more enthusiasm you show, therefore, the better you'll do in job interviews and on the job itself.

It's easiest to show enthusiasm when you really feel it. Don't settle for "just a paycheque." In addition to meeting your financial needs, in the ideal job you would

- Use the skills you want to use
- Work with the kind of people you want to be around
- Work with a product, service, or idea that interests you
- Have the level of responsibility you want
- Build knowledge and skills so that you'll be even more employable in the future
- Achieve goals that matter

While you may not get all of these factors in a single job offer, you probably can get the ones that matter most to you—if you know what they are.

Seeming enthusiastic is easy for some outgoing people. If you're naturally shy or reserved, showing your enthusiasm may feel like "acting" at first. If you're reserved,

- Smile
- Lean forward as you talk
- Put lots of energy into your voice. Vary pace, tone, and volume.
- Use energy in body movements. Gesture while you sit still. Walk quickly.
- Listen actively. Comment to show your interest. Prove that you've done your homework. Volunteer to work on issues. Talk to people about issues informally and in meetings.
- Participate fully in games and activities designed to energize workers. Think of ways to showcase your talents to help energize others.

Dear Delmarie Land:

Thank you for your hospitality during my interview last Thursday. After visiting Wilson International and speaking with you, I am convinced that a career in logistics is the right choice for me.

Seeing Kelly, Gene, and Leah working together to co-ordinate an international client's shipment gave me some sense of the tight deadlines you have to meet, and the level of collaboration required for success. As we discussed, I've learned to meet deadlines and work collaboratively while working summers at Crowley Logistics. Moreover, as I mentioned to you, when I worked with three other Crowley employees to implement a just-in-time computerized system, our team idea saved the company over $30,000 in inventory costs annually. I welcome the opportunity to make similar contributions the Wilson team.

I look forward to a career in transportation planning and to hearing from you soon.

Site *to* **See**

Go to
http://www.quintcareers.com/job_interview_follow-up.html
This site explores the art of follow up after the interview.

Site *to* **See**

Go to
http://www.quintcareers.com/job_interviewing_quiz.html
See how you score on the job interview quiz.

How do I decide which offer to accept?

Use a forced choice.

The problem with choosing among job offers is that you're comparing apples and oranges. The job with the most interesting work pays peanuts. The job that pays best is in a city where you really don't want to live. It's your life. The secret of pro-

FYI

In their search for information technology talent, American companies will increase the value of their work outsourcing from $5.5 billion (U.S.) in 2000 to $18 billion by 2005. Countries expected to profit from the outsourcing demand include India, Canada, Ireland, and South Africa.[5]

Source: Agence France-Press, quoted in "U.S. outsourcing expected to soar," *The Globe and Mail,* March 2, 2001

fessional happiness is taking a job where the positives are things you want, and the negatives are things that don't matter much to you.

To choose among job offers, make a list of *everything you'd like in your ideal job.* Then, to see which points are really important to you, do a forced choice. In a **forced choice,** you compare each item against every other one. Number the items in the order in which they happened to occur to you. Then, using the table of fractions in Figure 30.2 on page 625, rank each pair. For "1/2" compare item 1 and item 2. If you could have only one of the two, which would you prefer? Circle that number. For "1/3," compare item 1 with item 3. Again, circle the item that's more important. Repeat until you've made a choice between each of the possible pairs. Then count the number of times you've chosen each item. The things you've chosen most often are the ones that matter: They're the ones you should look for in your job.

Figure 30.2 is the list that one man produced. The items are numbered in the order in which they occurred to him. To find out what's truly important and what's nice but not necessary, Mohammed can do a forced choice. If he had to choose between a high income and having time for his family, which would he prefer? Counting the number of times he chooses each factor will tell him what he really wants.

The secret of success

What do I do if my first offer isn't the one I most want?

Phone your first-choice employer to find out where you are on that list.

Some employers offer jobs at the end of the office visit. In other cases, you may wait for weeks or even months to hear. Employers almost always offer jobs orally. You must say something in response immediately, so plan some strategies.

If your first offer is not from your first choice, express your pleasure at being offered the job, but do not accept it on the phone. "That's great! I assume I have two weeks to let you know?" Some companies offer "exploding" job offers that expire in one week or less,[6] but most firms will give you two weeks.

Then *call* the other companies you're interested in. Explain, "I've just got a job offer, but I'd rather work for you. Can you tell me what the status of my application is?" Nobody will put that information in writing, but almost everyone will tell you over the phone. With this information, you're in a better position to decide whether to accept the original offer.

Figure 30.2
Forced Choice Chart

When you're not sure which job to accept, use this table of fractions. See instructions on page 624.

1/2	1/3	1/4	1/5	1/6	1/7	1/8	1/9	1/10	1/11	1/12	1/13	1/14	1/15	1/16	1/17	1/18	1/19	1/20
2/3	2/4	2/5	2/6	2/7	2/8	2/9	2/10	2/11	2/12	2/13	2/14	2/15	2/16	2/17	2/18	2/19	2/20	
3/4	3/5	3/6	3/7	3/8	3/9	3/10	3/11	3/12	3/13	3/14	3/15	3/16	3/17	3/18	3/19	3/20		
4/5	4/6	4/7	4/8	4/9	4/10	4/11	4/12	4/13	4/14	4/15	4/16	4/17	4/18	4/19	4/20			
5/6	5/7	5/8	5/9	5/10	5/11	5/12	5/13	5/14	5/15	5/16	5/17	5/18	5/19	5/20				
6/7	6/8	6/9	6/10	6/11	6/12	6/13	6/14	6/15	6/16	6/17	6/18	6/19	6/20					
7/8	7/9	7/10	7/11	7/12	7/13	7/14	7/15	7/16	7/17	7/18	7/19	7/20						
8/9	8/10	8/11	8/12	8/13	8/14	8/15	8/16	8/17	8/18	8/19	8/20							
9/10	9/11	9/12	9/13	9/14	9/15	9/16	9/17	9/18	9/19	9/20								
10/11	10/12	10/13	10/14	10/15	10/16	10/17	10/18	10/19	10/20									
11/12	11/13	11/14	11/15	11/16	11/17	11/18	11/19	11/20										
12/13	12/14	12/15	12/16	12/17	12/18	12/19	12/20											
13/14	13/15	13/16	13/17	13/18	13/19	13/20												
14/15	14/16	14/17	14/18	14/19	14/20													
15/16	15/17	15/18	15/19	15/20														
16/17	16/18	16/19	16/20															
17/18	17/19	17/20																
18/19	18/20																	
19/20																		

Number of times I've chosen

1 ________	5 ________	9 ________	13 ________	17 ________
2 ________	6 ________	10 ________	14 ________	18 ________
3 ________	7 ________	11 ________	15 ________	19 ________
4 ________	8 ________	12 ________	16 ________	20 ________

Some applicants have been successful in getting two weeks extended to several weeks or even months. Certainly if you cannot decide by the deadline, it is worth asking for more time: The worst the company can do is say *no*. If you do try to keep a company hanging, be prepared for weekly phone calls asking you if you've decided yet.

Make your acceptance contingent upon a written job offer confirming the terms. That letter should spell out not only salary but also fringe benefits and any special provisions you have negotiated. If something is missing, call the interviewer for clarification: "We agreed that I'd be reviewed for a promotion and higher salary in six months, but don't see that in the letter." You have more power to resolve misunderstandings now than you will after six months or a year on the job.

Site to See

Go to
http://www.careercity.com/content/interview/
This site offers excellent sample follow-up letters.

Follow-Up Phone Calls

After a first interview, make follow-up phone calls to reinforce positives from the first interview, to overcome any negatives, and to get information you can use to persuade the interviewer to hire you.

When you've accepted one job, let the other places you visited know that you're no longer interested. Then they can go to their second choices. If you're second on someone else's list, you'll appreciate other candidates' removing themselves so the way is clear for you. Because the world is a small place, because everyone is the customer and because you may someday want to work for the company you're currently turning down, follow the **KISS** formula: **keep it short and sweet**:

Dear Jackson Phillips:

Thank you for offering me the sales position in your electronics division. Allied Signal enjoys an international reputation for innovative quality products; I'm pleased to be considered part of the Allied team.

After a great deal of thought, however, I have decided to look for employment opportunities closer to home while investigating courses for an advanced degree. I must, therefore, decline your offer.

Again, thank you for your consideration.

Sincerely,

Site to See

Go to http://content.monster.com/resume/samples/thankyou/

For a selection of sample thank you letters.

Figure 30.3

Mohammed's List for a Forced Choice

You can list more items or fewer, in any order. Then use the Forced Choice Chart to see which really matter to you.

1. Competitive salary
2. Time to spend with my family
3. Near skiing
4. Job opportunities for Karishma
5. Opportunity for advancement
6. Equal employment opportunity employer
7. Company with other Middle Easterners in leadership roles
8. Socially responsible company
9. Lots of open land near by
10. Challenging work
11. Minimal travel as part of job
12. Good college or pro sports teams in town
13. Cost of living not too high
14. Good schools
15. Ethnically diverse community
16. Town with parks, civic services
17. Lots of interaction with other people
18. Company that will encourage me to get a master's degree and even pay for it
19. Company with good fringe benefits
20. No weekend work

Follow-Up Letters

A letter after an office visit should

• Remind the interviewer of what he or she liked in you
• Counter any negative impressions
• Use the jargon of the company and refer to specifics from the visit
• Be enthusiastic
• Refer to the next move

Employability Skills 2000+ Checklist
for Follow-Up Letters and Calls, and Job Offers

In this module, the key skills from The Conference Board of Canada's Employability Skills 2000+ are:

Communicate
✔ write and speak so others pay attention and understand

Manage Information
✔ locate, gather, and organize information using appropriate technology and information systems
✔ access, analyze, and apply knowledge and skills from a variety of disciplines (e.g. the arts, languages, science, technology, mathematics, social sciences, and the humanities)

Think & Solve Problems
✔ assess situations and identify problems
✔ seek different points of view and evaluate them based on facts
✔ recognize the human, interpersonal, technical, scientific, and mathematical dimensions of a problem
✔ readily use science, technology, and mathematics as ways to think, gain and share knowledge, solve problems, and make decisions
✔ check to see if a solution works, and act on opportunities for improvement

Demonstrate Positive Attitudes & Behaviours
✔ feel good about yourself and be confident
✔ recognize your own and other people's good efforts

Be Adaptable
✔ be innovative and resourceful: identify and suggest alternative ways to achieve goals and get the job done
✔ learn from your mistakes and accept feedback
✔ cope with uncertainty

Learn Continuously
✔ be willing to continuously learn and grow
✔ assess personal strengths and areas for development
✔ identify and access learning sources and opportunities

Work with Others
✔ accept and provide feedback in a constructive and considerate manner

Review of Key Points

- Use follow-up phone calls to reinforce positives from the first interview, to overcome any negatives, and to get information you can use to persuade the interviewer to hire you.
- A follow-up letter should
  - Remind the interviewer of what he or she liked in you
  - Counter any negative impressions that may have come up at the interview

- Use the jargon of the company and refer to specific things you learned during your interview or saw during your visit
- Be enthusiastic
- Refer to the next move you'll make
- In a **forced choice**, you compare each item against every other one to learn which points are most important to you.
- If your first offer isn't from your first choice, call the other companies you're interested in to ask the status of your application.

Assignments for Module 30

Questions for Comprehension

30.1 What should you do in a follow-up phone call?

30.2 What should you do in a follow-up letter?

30.3 What should you do if the first offer you get isn't from your first-choice employer?

30.4 Why should you phone rather than write or email your first-choice employer after you've received another job offer?

Questions for Critical Thinking

30.5 Is it ethical for a quiet, reserved person to try to seem more enthusiastic?

30.6 Why is it important to get a job offer in writing before you accept it officially?

30.7 How helpful did you find doing a forced choice? Why do you think it was or wasn't helpful?

Questions for Building Skills

30.8 What skills have you read about in this module?

30.9 What skills are you practising in the assignments you're doing for this module?

30.10 How could you further develop the skills you're working on?

Exercises and Problems

30.11   Making a Forced Choice

On another sheet of paper, list the criteria you'd like in a job. Number each item. Then compare each pair.

If you have 20 items or fewer, you can use the Forced Choice Chart in Figure 30.2 to record your preferences. If you have more than 20 items, make a new chart so that each number will be compared with every other number.

On the chart, mark the number in each pair that corresponds with the item you'd choose if you could have only one of them. Then count how many times you've marked *1*, how many times you've marked *2*, etc. The items that you mark most often are the features you should try to find in a job.

As Your Instructor Directs,

a. Share your answers with a small group of other students

b. Summarize your answers in a memo to your instructor

c. Present your answers orally to the class

30.12   Writing a Follow-Up Letter after an Office Visit or Plant Trip

Write a follow-up email message or letter after an office visit or plant trip. Thank your hosts for their hospitality; relate your strong points to things you learned about the company during the visit; overcome any negatives that may remain; be enthusiastic about the company; and submit receipts for your expenses so you can be reimbursed.

30.13   Clarifying the Terms of a Job Offer

Last week, you got a job offer from your first-choice company, and you accepted it over the phone. Today, the written confirmation arrived. The letter specifies the starting salary and fringe benefits you had negotiated. However, during the office visit, you were promised a 5 percent raise after six months on the job. The job offer says nothing about the raise. You do want the job, but you want it on the terms you thought you had negotiated.

Write to your contact at the company, Damon Winters.

Polishing Your Prose

Using Standard English

Many speakers use a dialect of English. Dialects are logical and clear to the group that developed and uses the dialect. Often, dialects illustrate considerable creativity. However, in Canadian business, it's easier to get hired and promoted if you use standard edited English.

Most speakers learn that they're speaking (and perhaps writing) a dialect only when someone else tells them that their words don't sound "right." Dialects are distinguished from each other first by pronunciation. (Does *pick* rhyme with *creek*?) In addition, some dialects use different idioms than does standard English; some handle verbs or negation differently. Many assign different meanings to words than does standard English.

Dialect: I thought youse was going.

Standard: I thought you were going.

Dialect: Don't give us no dead computers.

Standard: Don't give us any computers that don't work.

or: Give us only computers that work.

Dialect: I be takin' night classes to get my degree.

Standard: I am taking night classes to get my degree.

Dialect: This Web site is bad!

Standard: This Web site is good.

Exercises

Revise the following sentences to create standard English.

1. Did youse get the equipment?

2. I will ax her if she be surfing the Web.

3. Don't gimme no excuses, eh?

4. Them than can't use no computer ain't gonna get ahead.

5. Me, I think we oughtta reconsider.

6. So I'm like, where we gonna find workers? You know?

7. He don't know how good he's got it.

8. I got to go to a dépanneur for a gum.

9. I asked what the problem is and she goes, "Nothin!"

10. If I would have seen the report I would would have faxed it right away.

Check your answers to the odd-numbered exercises on page 635.

 **Video Case**

Go to www.mcgrawhill.ca/college/locker for "Résumés", an online CBC Video Case featuring advice from experts on how to put your résumé together. What comes first? What do you include? These questions and more are answered.

Credits

Figures

Figure 1.1: Reprinted with permission of the author.

Figure 1.6: Employability Skills 2000+ reproduced by permission of the Conference Board of Canada. Subsequent figures through the text containing excerpts from the Employability Skills 2000+ list also reproduced with permission.

Figure 2.6: Based on Isabel Briggs Myers "Effects of each Preference in Work Situations," *Introduction to Type*, Consulting Psychologists Press, 1962, 1980.

Figure 3.1: Adapted from table 5.1, p. 148 of *International Business Communication* by David A. Victor. Copyright 1992 by HarperCollins Publishers Inc. Reprinted by permission of Addison-Wesley Educational Publishers, Inc.

Figure 3.3: Reproduced by permission. From *Multicultural Management 2000*. Copyright © 1998, Gulf Publishing Company, Houston, Texas, 800-231-6275. All rights reserved.

Figure 3.4: Reproduced by permission. From *Multicultural Management 2000*. Copyright © 1998, Gulf Publishing Company, Houston, Texas, 800-231-6275. All rights reserved.

Figure 3.5: Reproduced by permission. From *Multicultural Management 2000*. Copyright © 1998, Gulf Publishing Company, Houston, Texas, 800-231-6275. All rights reserved.

Exercise 5.1: Reprinted from PC Magazine, October 13, 1987 with permission. Copyright © 1987, Ziff Davis Media Inc. All rights reserved.

Figure Reprinted with permission of General Electric, Fairfield, CT.

Figure Reprinted from copyrighted material by permission of the author.

Leading by Listening Excerpt: Reprinted from the April 1999 issue of *Fast Company* magazine. All rights reserved. To subscribe, please call (800) 688-1545.

Figure 18.1: Republished with permission of *Inc. Magazine*, from "The Color-Coded Priority Setter," June 1995; permission conveyed through Copyright Clearance Center, Inc.

Figure 20.1: Courtesy Michael Goldman and *The training report*.

Figure 25.1: *Maclean's*, May 21, 2001, 73. Reprinted with permission.

Figure 25.4 Mouse Power: Copyright © 1998 Time, Inc. Reprinted by permission.

Assignment 25.13.2: *Maclean's*, May 14, 2001, 21. Reprinted with permission.

Assignment 25.13.5: Copyright © 1999 by Selling Power. Reprinted by permission of the publisher.

Assignment 25.14.1: Statistics Canada Internet Site, <www.statcan.ca>, http://www.statcan.ca/english/Pgdb/People/Culture/arts23.htm, extracted June 22, 2001.

Assignment 25.14.2 Statistics Canada Internet Site, <www.statcan.ca>, http://www.statcan.ca/english/Pgdb/People/Culture/arts51.htm, extracted June 22, 2001.

Assignment 25.14.3: Reprinted from *American Demographics* magazine. Courtesy of Intertec Publishing Corporation, Stanford, Connecticut.

Figure 29.2: Reprinted from the January 1999 issue of *Fast Company* magazine. All rights reserved. To subscribe, please call (800)688-1545 or visit www.fastcompany.com.

Figure 29.3: Reprinted from the January 1999 issue of *Fast Company* magazine. All rights reserved. To subscribe, please call (800)688-1545 or visit www.fastcompany.com.

Photos

1-1: Courtesy Peter Snow
1-2: 30-1: © 2000 Dan Cohen
1-3: © Pablo Bartholomew/Liaison Agency
2-1: Courtesy Sarah Marshall
2-2 a&b: Courtesy Christine Liddell, Manager , Human Resources, White Rose
2-3 a&b: Courtesy Lifecode® Bob Greenspon
3-1: Courtesy Kristiina and Timmun Alariqaq
3-2: PhotoDisc
3-3: AP/Wide World
4-1: Courtesy Simone Graham
5-1: Courtesy Katie FitzRandolph
6-1: Courtesy Robin Honey
7-1: Courtesy Scott May
7-2: Courtesy Southwest Airlines
8-1: Courtesy Elaine Kergoat
8-2: Courtesy Floyd Hurt of the Rousing Creativity Group www.rousingcreativity.com
8-3: Courtesy Michael Turczyniak
9-1: Courtesy Ed Herr
10-1: Courtesy Kim Spirou
10-2: Copyright © Stone 2000
11-1: Courtesy Jan Graves
12-1: Courtesy Helen Connell
12-2: Courtesy Surrey Metro Savings Credit Union. Hans Sipma, photo.
12-3: Courtesy Robin McLeod, Evergreen
12-4: Courtesy Molson Canada; still provided by Thornley Fallis Communications
13-1: Courtesy Jeff Tandy
13-2: © Lucent Technologies and Telegeography, Inc., 1999. www.peacockmap.com
14-1: Courtesy Otte Rosenkrantz
15-1: Courtesy May Lee-Jarvis
16-1: Courtesy Melissa Hardy-Trevenna
18-1: Courtesy Sandi Ellis
18-2: © 2000 Mark Richards
19-1: Courtesy Sharon Bartosek
19-2: Courtesy Eagle's Flight
20-1: Courtesy Janet Maaten
20-2 Ingrid Bens, Participative Dynamics USA
21-1: Courtesy Richard Zelinka
22-1: Courtesy Bruce Lundgren
22-2: © 2000 Michael Mertz
23-1: Courtesy Tom Haight
24-1: Courtesy Paige Cantle
24-2: Courtesy MedFlight of Ohio
25-1: Courtesy Cecilia Hageman
26-1: Courtesy Kimberley Chresney
28-1: Courtesy Nancy Brown
29-1: Courtesy Chris Bocchini
29-2: © Sandy Nicholson Photography 2001
30-1: Courtesy Ronald Manchen

Polishing Your Prose

Shown here in blue are possible solutions to the odd-numbered exercises. Check with your instructor on any other solutions you propose.

Module 1: Sentence Fragments

1. Our retail sales division posted record sales for November.
3. Ms. Baumgartner began the meeting a few minutes late because the computer crashed.
5. Although the car ran fine, we were late to the meeting because of traffic.
7. Terrell announced a plan to introduce our latest computer model to retail electronics stores.
9. The Accounting Department recently received several awards for excellence.

Module 2: Comma Splices

1. The conference call came at 1 P.M., and we took it immediately.
3. Janelle drafted her problem-solving report and sent a copy to each of the committee members for review.
5. When Katya called the hotel in Montréal for a reservation, the desk staff booked a room for her immediately.
7. I'll have Tina call the main office; you ask Brian to set up an appointment for the four of us tomorrow.
9. I like to make oral presentations because they're fun.

Module 3: Using Idioms

1. Race the clock = Work quickly to meet a deadline.
3. Juggle a schedule = Make significant changes to a busy schedule.
5. Punch the clock = Begin or end the work day.
7. Cold call a customer = Make an unsolicited telephone sales call.
9. Open up new markets = Increase sales in a new market.

Module 4: Commas in Lists

1. Please send the "fruit of the month" in April, May, June, and July. (Last comma is optional).
3. The special parts division is opening offices in Brampton, Ontario; Frederickton, New Brunswick; and Big Salmon, Yukon.
5. I need to telephone Mary, Frank, and Paul, to finish my report, and mail copies of it to Ted, Sam, and Latanya. (While semi-colons could be used after Paul and report, commas are acceptable because the groupings of listed items are understandable with commas.)
7. The weather affects our offices in Montréal, New York City, and Philadelphia.
9. Elizabeth, Tyrone, Mark, and Sara presented the team's recommendations.

Module 5: Active and Passive Voice

1. Unless the context of the sentence is negative, change to active voice. The vice president of finance signed the contract.
3. The visitors' arrival is more important than who is expecting them. Therefore, use passive voice.
5. Changing this sentence to active voice would cast blame. Therefore, use passive voice.
7. The human resources administrator returned phone calls.
9. Return phone calls within 24 hours.

Module 6: It's/Its

1. It's too bad that the team hasn't finished its presentation.
3. It's going to require overtime because the data center needs its reports quickly.
5. The company will announce its new name at a press conference.
7. It's a good idea to keep your travel receipts in a separate file.
9. The Saskatoon office will share its findings with the other branch offices.

Module 7: Singular and Plural Possessives

1. We design products based on our customers' needs.
3. Canadians' views of the economy reflect their confidence in the stock market.
5. We meet the local, provincial, and federal governments' standards for quality control.
7. The committee's duties will be completed after it announces its decision.
9. We'll decide whether to have more computer training sessions based on employees' feedback.
10. The company's benefit plan is excellent.

Module 8: Plurals and Possessives

1. Canadian companies are competing effectively in the global market.
3. The manager's ability to listen is just as important as his or her technical knowledge.
5. Social workers should tell clients about services available in the community.
7. Information about the new community makes the family's move easier.
9. Memos are sent to other workers in the same organization.

Module 9: Making Subjects and Verbs Agree

1. Each of us is entitled to company health care benefits.
3. The price of our stocks is increasing.
5. We order a dozen new toner cartridges each month.
7. Ms. Schiff and her assistant are attending the conference in Halifax.
9. Professor Beauparlant, Mr. Kincaid, and Ms. Carolla are on the guest list and plan to sit at the same table.

Module 10: Dangling Modifiers

1. After working a year, you will be covered by dental insurance.
3. I bought my daughter her first share of stock when she was 10.
5. By calling ahead of time, you can make reservations efficiently.
7. As I told you on the phone, your order was shipped on April 1.
9. If you share files with our legal department, our attorneys can work better with you.

Module 11: Parallel Structure

1. Last week, Alain and Rochelle flew to Toronto, Montréal, Québec City, and Lansing.
3. To ship a package:
   1. Fill out an address form.
   2. Specify on the form how the package should be sent.
   3. Have your supervisor initial the appropriate box on the address form if you want the package shipped by overnight mail.
5. Appointments can be scheduled in 5-minute, 10-minute, 15-minute, or 20-minute intervals.
7. This report discusses
   Why We Should Upgrade Capital Equipment
   Why We Should Increase Staff by 25 percent
   Why We Should Decrease Employee Turnover
   Why We Should Identify New Product Markets
9. Use the telephone to answer customer questions, email to send order confirmations, and our Web page to take orders.

Module 12: Narrative Voice

1. This voice sounds authoritative, perhaps even threatening due to the constant use of will commands and all caps in no exception.
3. Phrases like superlative and most relevant and the wordiness make this voice overly contrived–some people might say old-fashioned.
5. Teenagers often interrupt speech with like and you know and end what should be declarative statements with questions. This statement sounds like a classic Valley Girl/Boy.
7. Most readers would find this voice acceptable in business.
9. Because of the large amount of jargon, this voice sounds cold and technical.

Module 13: Making Nouns and Pronouns Agree

1. Correct.
3. The company announces its quarterly profits today.
5. A CEO's pay is often based on the performance of his or her company.
7. In my first month of work, I learned to check my email at least three times a day.
9. Correct.

Module 14: Using Spell and Grammar Checkers

1. Their product is sitting over there.
3. It's not really a good idea to have lunch before the flight.
5. Martika is happy with her purchase; she'll order online again. (Online is generally not hyphenated.)
7. Les says, "Less is more."
9. The Internet is a powerful research tool—so what? (Internet is a proper term; most word processors will automatically make two hyphens into a dash, though two hyphens are acceptable.)

Module 15: Run-On Sentences

1. The marketing department ordered new, four-colour brochures. They are really nice.
3. Let's schedule a meeting next week. We'll talk about your promotion so you can transition easily into the new job.
5. Employees may request benefits changes during the annual enrollment period. Supervisors should pass out the required forms, and employees should have them completed by the deadline on the form.
7. Mohammed should make sure he specifies 20- rather than 15-pound paper stock, Jenna should call the print shop and ask if the employees need anything, and Bruce should tell Ms. Winans we appreciate her letting us know we originally ordered the wrong stock.
9. A few customers are concerned about the shipping date, but the mailroom is sure we can ship overnight. I think there's no reason to be concerned.

Module 16: End Punctuation

1. Where is the file on the Richman proposal?
3. Ms. Amarotti will arrive by plane tomorrow.
5. Take a moment to read the instructions before completing the form.
7. Congratulations on your recent promotion to line manager. (If you know this person well or the message is informal, then using an exclamation point may also be acceptable.)
9. Remember, when we turn on the breakroom lights, everyone is to yell, "Happy Birthday, Susharita!"

Module 17: Combining Sentences

1. To get promoted quickly at our company, be organized, be on time, and meet deadlines.
3. Changing the toner cartridge on the photocopier is simple. To begin, open the front panel. Find the green tabs and depress them with your thumbs. Next, pull the black toner cartridge out and put it in the recycling box. Slide a new toner cartridge into the compartment until the green tabs snap back into place. Finally, close the panel.
5. The tornado plan for our building has five parts: first, listen for the tornado alert siren; second, go to your designated shelter area in the basement of the building; third, be sure to take the stairs and not the elevator; fourth, sit down on the floor; fifth, cover your head with your arms.

Module 18: Hyphens and Dashes

1. Our biggest competitors—including those in the Asian and European markets—introduced more product models during the fourth quarter.
3. Please pick up three 2-by-4 posts at the lumber yard.
5. Painters from the building services department plan to give Tarik's office two coats of paint.
7. The latest weather reports suggest that travel over South and Latin America may be interrupted by storms.
9. You can email the results to my office in the early morning.

Module 19: Delivering Criticism

1. We need to make this report meet our company's standards.
3. This assignment must have library resources.
5. The information in this brochure is terrific. Let's work on making the design match the content.
7. Our instructor said that we have to use at least five sources.
9. Would you help me to better understand this proposal?

Module 20: Choosing Levels of Formality

1. On Monday, I inspected our inventory.
3. Though the representative was firm, we eventually negotiated a settlement.
5. The manager postponed making a decision.
7. In my last job, I worked as a go-fer for the Marketing manager.
9. This report has problems.

Module 21: Who/Whom and I/Me

1. Karen and I visited Shawnee Community College last week.
3. Dr. Jacobsen, who serves on the Board of Directors, is retiring.
5. Who is the most experienced person on your staff?
7. My supervisor told me the committee will decide who gets the promotion.
9. Three people at the firm who can speak a second language are Phillip, Stacy, and I.

Module 22: Mixing Verb Tenses

1. I went to the garage yesterday and got my tires changed.
3. Our vice president of consumer affairs resigned last week but came into the office yesterday to clean out her desk.
5. I will go to college when I graduate from high school.
7. Before we drove to the sales meeting, we got gasoline for the car.
9. The warranty provides service or replacement of defective parts for the next five years.

Module 23: Being Concise

1. Please return the order form ASAP.
3. The blue car is the Legal Affairs Director's.
5. Call to confirm your order.
7. The enclosed references can discuss my job qualifications further.
9. Let me start by sharing stories about our guest of honor.

Module 24: Improving Paragraphs

1. My experience in the secretarial field makes me an ideal candidate for a position as senior administrative assistant with Graham, Chang, and Associates. As a receptionist at McCandless Realty, I typed, answered phones, and handled payroll. Then, as a secretary at Dufresne Plastics, I took training courses in data entry and Microsoft Word and learned to type 70 WPM with no mistakes.

Module 25: Writing Subject Lines and Headings

1. An Introduction from the New Customer Service Department Supervisor. (Better with actual name.)
3. Your donation of blood on Tuesday can save a life.
5. Insurance Rates Will Increase July 31.
7. Research; Logistics; Profit
9. Clemente Research Group's Five-Year Goals; Clemente Research Group's Ten-Year Goals; Clemente Research Group's Fifteen-Year Goals

Module 26: Using Details

1. I am the Webmaster for the Jessica London Company.
3. In June, I plan to graduate from Seneca Community College and start my career in respiratory therapy at St. Ann's Hospital.
5. Fortified with antioxidants and Vitamins D and K, EnVigorate Power Drink will make you feel healthy and energetic all day long.
7. The new Mark VII pool filter is 33 percent more energy efficient than competitors' and features a 10-year warranty, the best on the market.
9. More than 17 years of experience and $7.9 million in real estate sales help make me the ideal candidate for district sales manager.

Module 27: Proofreading

1. Ours is a company worth doing business with. You can count on our promise to provide not only the best service but also the finest in materials, fit, and finish. All of our products are made to exacting specifications, meaning that you receive the best product for the best prices. If you aren't satisfied for any reason, simply call the toll-free hotline at 1-800-555-1212 to get a prompt refund. Or you can write us at The John Doe Company, 123 Main Street, Anytown, Canada M6V 2B4. Remember, our motto is "The customer is always right."

Module 28: Using You and I

1. Our team created a class Web page. I was responsible for much of the initial design and some of the HTML coding. Four of us tested the page to see how easily we could navigate it. We presented the page to a committee of local business people.
3. Team members should resolve any conflicts they have created with other team members.
5. Please distribute an agenda before the meeting.
7. Make the Web page accessible to users with impaired vision.

9. During my internship, I observed department meetings, sat in on client meetings, designed PowerPoint slides for client presentations, participated in strategy sessions, and drafted brochures.

Module 29: Matters on Which Experts Disagree

1. Everyone should bring his or her laptop to the sales meeting.
3. To take advantage of the meeting fully, you need to bring all of your new product information.
5. Think of a time when it was hard even to get in the door to see a potential customer.
7. Awards include best rookie sales representative, the most improved region, everyone who beat his or her sales quota, and sales representative of the year.
9. Our Web page will let people listen to each customer summarizing orally what he or she likes best about our products.

Module 30: Using Standard English

1. Did you get the equipment?
3. Don't give me any excuses.
5. I think we ought to reconsider.
7. He doesn't know how good he has it.
9. I asked her what the problem was and she answered, "Nothing!"

Notes

Module 1

1. "Technical Training Ain't All it's Cracked Up to Be," *The Training Report*, January/February 2000, 8.
2. Anne Fisher, "Ask Annie," *Fortune*, March 1, 1999, 244.
3. Henry Mintzberg, *The Nature of Managerial Work* (New York: Harper & Row, 1973), 32, 65.
4. Frederick K. Moss, "Perceptions of Communication in the Corporate Community," *Journal of Business and Technical Communication 9*, no. 1 (January 1995): 67.
5. Elaine Vets, "Voice Mail Converts Boss into a Secretary," The *Columbus Dispatch*, August 10, 1995, 3E; Rochelle Sharpe, "Work Week," *The Wall Street Journal*, September 26, 1995, A1.
6. "1996 Cost of a Business Letter" (Chicago: Dartnell/ From 9 to 5, September 30, 1996),1.
7. Dianne Booher, *Cutting Paperwork in the Corporate Culture* (New York: Facts on File, 1986), 24.
8. Claudia MonPere McIsaac and Mary Ann Aschauer, "Proposal Writing at Atherton Jordan, Inc.: An Ethnographic Study," *Management Communication Quarterly* 3 (1990): 535.
9. Elizabeth Allen, "Excellence in Public Relations & Communication Management," IABC/Dayton Awards Banquet, Dayton, OH, July 12, 1990.

Module 2

1. Audiences 1, 3, and 4 are based on J.C. Mathes and Dwight Stevenson, *Designing Technical Reports: Writing for Audiences in Organizations*, 2nd ed. (New York: Macmillan, 1991), 40. The fifth audience is suggested by Vincent J. Brown, "Facing Multiple Audiences in Engineering and R&D Writing: The Social Context of a Technical Report," *Journal of Technical Writing and Communication* 24, no. 1 (1994): 67–75.
2. Isabel Briggs Myers, "Introduction to Type" (Palo Alto, CA: Consulting Psychologists Press, 1980). The material in this section follows Myers's paper.
3. Isabel Briggs Myers and Mary H. McCaulley, *Manual: A Guide to the Development and Use of the Myers-Briggs Type Indicator* (Palo Alta, CA: Consulting Psychologists Press, 1985), 251, 248, respectively.
4. Alan W. H. Grant and Leonard A. Schlesinger, "Realize Your Customers' Full Profit Potential," *Harvard Business Review*, September–October 1995, 65–66.
5. Anne Fisher, "Internet Buyers Are Not What You Think," *Fortune*, January 10, 2000, 190.
6. "Ford's model E, " *Forbes.com*, July 2000, 30–34.
7. Daniel Pearl, "UPS Takes on Air-Express Competition," *The Wall Street Journal*, December 20, 1990, A4.
8. Matt Siegel, "The Perils of Culture Conflict," *Fortune*, November 9, 1998, 258.
9. Linda Driskill, "Negotiating Differences among Readers and Writers," presented at the Conference on College Composition and Communication, San Diego, CA, March 31–April 3, 1993.

Module 3

1. Citizenship and Immigration Canada, "Forging our Legacy, Canadian Citizenship and Immigration, 1900–1977," July 12, 2000; visited Web site October 1, 2001; www.cic.gc.ca/english/about/legacy/chap-1.html. Asia Pacific Foundation of Canada, "Proportion of Total Population," June 2001; visited Web site October 1, 2001; asiapacific.ca/data/people/demographics_dataset2_byprov.cfm.
2. "Amazing Numbers," *Selling Power*, September 1996, 28.
3. Poppy Lauretta McLeod, Sharon Alisa Lobel, and Taylor H. Cox, Jr., "Ethnic Diversity and Creativity in Small Groups," *Small Group Research 27*, no. 2 (May 1996): 248–64.
4. David A. Victor, *International Business Communication* (New York: HarperCollins, 1992), 148–60.
5. John Webb and Michael Keene, "The Impact of Discourse Communities on International Professional Communication," in *Exploring the Rhetoric of International Professional Communication: An Agenda for Teachers and Researchers*, ed. Carl R. Lovitt with Dixie Coswami (Amityville, NY: Baywood, 1999), 81–109.
6. Christina Haas and Jeffrey L. Funk, "'Shared Information': Some Observations of Communication in Japanese Technical Settings," *Technical Communication 36*, no. 4 (November 1989): 365.
7. Laray M. Barna, "Stumbling Blocks in Intercultural Communication," in *Intercultural Communication*, ed. Larry A. Samovar and Richard E. Porter (Belmont, CA: Wadsworth, 1985), 331.
8. Marjorie Fink Vargas, *Louder than Words* (Ames: Iowa State University Press, 1986), 47.
9. Michael Argyle, *Bodily Communication* (New York: International University Press, 1975), 89.
10. Jerrold J. Merchant, "Korean Interpersonal Patterns: Implications for Korean/American Intercultural Communication," *Communication 9* (October 1980): 65.
11. Ray L. Birdwhistell, *Kinesics and Context: Essays on Body Motion Communication* (Philadelphia: University of Philadelphia Press, 1970), 81.
12. Paul Ekman, Wallace V. Friesen, and John Bear, "The International Language of Gestures," *Psychology Today* 18, no. 5 (May 1984): 64.
13. Carmen Judith Nine-Curt, "Hispanic-Anglo Conflicts in Nonverbal Communication," in *Perspectivas Pedagogicas*, ed. I. Abino et al. (San Juan: Universidad de Puerto Rico, 1983), 235.
14. Baxter, 1970, reported in Marianne LaFrance, "Gender Gestures: Sex, Sex-Role, and Nonverbal Communication," in *Gender and Nonverbal Behavior*, ed. Clara Mayo and Nancy M. Henley (New York: Springer-Verlag, 1981), 130.
15. Nine-Curt, "Hispanic-Anglo Conflicts," 238.
16. Brenda Major, "Gender Patterns in Touching Behavior," in *Gender and Nonverbal Behavior*, ed. Clara Mayo and Nancy M. Henley (New York: Springer-Verlag, 1981), 26, 28.

17. "Minor Memos," *The Wall Street Journal*, February 12, 1988,1.

18. Natalie Porter and Florence Gies, "Women and Nonverbal Leadership Cues: When Seeing Is Not Believing," in *Gender and Nonverbal Behavior*, ed. Clara Mayo and Nancy M. Henley (New York: Springer-Verlag, 1981), 48–49.

19. Robert C. Christopher, *Second to None: American Companies in Japan* (New York: Crown, 1986), 102–103.

20. John Cordon and Keisuke Kurata, *In Search of What's Japanese about Japan* (Toyko: Shufunotomo Company, 1974), 77.

21. Lawrence B. Nadler, Marjorie Keeshan Nadler, and Benjamin J. Broome, "Culture and the Management of Conflict Situations," in *Communication, Culture, and Organizational Processes*, ed. William B. Gudykunst, Lea P. Stewart, and Stella Ting-Toomey (Beverly Hills, CA: Sage, 1985), 103.

22. Argyle, *Bodily Communication*, 90.

23. Mary Ritchie Key, *Paralanguage and Kinesics* (Metuchen, NJ: Scarecrow, 1975), 23.

24. Fred Hitzhusen, conversation with Kitty Locker, January 31, 1998.

25. Lisa Davis, "The Height Report: A Look at Stature and Status," The *Columbus Dispatch*, January 19, 1988, E1, New York Times Special Features.

26. Deborah Tannen, *That's Not What I Meant!* (New York: William Morrow, 1986).

27. Karen Ritchie, "Marketing to Generation X," *American Demographics*, April 1995, 34–36.

28. Thomas Kochman, *Black and White Styles in Conflict* (Chicago: University of Chicago Press, 1981), 103.

29. Daniel N. Maltz and Ruth A. Borker, "A cultural approach to male-female miscommunication," in *Language and Social Identity*, ed. John J. Gumperz (Cambridge: Cambridge University Press, 1982), 202.

30. Vincent O'Neill, "Training the Multi-Cultural Manager," Sixth Annual EMU Conference on Languages and Communication for World Business and the Professions, Ann Arbor, MI, May 7–9, 1987.

31. Akihisa Kumayama, comment during discussion, Sixth Annual EMU Conference on Languages and Communication for World Business and the Professions, Ann Arbor, MI, May 7–9, 1987.

32. Muriel Saville-Troike, "An Integrated Theory of Communication," in *Perspectives on Silence*, ed. Deborah Tannen and Muriel Saville-Troike (Norwood, NJ: Ablex, 1985), 10–11.

33. Lisa Tyler, "Communicating about People with Disablilties: Does the Language We Use Make a Difference?" *The Bulletin of the Association for Business Communications* 53, no. 3 (September 1990): 65.

34. Marilyn A. Dryrud, "An Exploration of Gender Bias in Computer Clip Art," *Business Communication Quarterly* 60, no. 4 (December 1997): 30–51.

Module 4

1. See especially Linda Flower and John R. Hayes, "The Cognition of Discovery: Defining a Rhetorical Problem," *College Composition and Communication* 31 (February 1980): 21–32; and the essays in two collections: Charles R. Cooper and Lee Odell, *Research on Composing: Points of Departure* (Urbana, IL: National Council of Teachers of English, 1978), and Mike Rose, ed., *When a Writer Can't Write: Studies in Writer's Block and Other Composing-Process Problems* (New York: Guilford Press, 1985).

2. Rebecca E. Burnett, "Content and Commas: How Attitudes Shape a Communication-Across-the-Curriculum Program," Association for Business Communication Convention, Orlando, FL, November 1–4, 1995.

3. Peter Elbow, *Writing with Power: Techniques for Mastering the Writing Process* (New York: Oxford University Press, 1981), 15–20.

4. See Gabriela Lusser Rico, *Writing the Natural Way* (Los Angeles: J.P. Tarcher, 1983), 10.

5. Rachel Spilka, "Orality and Literacy in the Workplace: Process- and Text-based Strategies for Multiple Audience Adaptation," *Journal of Business and Technical Communication* 4, no. 1 (January 1990): 44–67.

6. Fred Reynolds, "What Adult Work-World Writers Have Taught Me About Adult Work-World Writing," *Professional Writing in Context: Lessons from Teaching and Consulting in Worlds of Work*, (Hillsdale, NJ: Lawrence Erlbaum Associates, 1995), 18–21.

7. Raymond W. Beswick, "Communicating in the Automated Office," American Business Communication Association International Convention, New Orleans, LA, October 20, 1982.

8. Dianna Booher, *Cutting Paperwork in the Corporate Culture* (New York: Facts on File Publications, 1986), 23.

9. Susan D. Kleimann, "The Complexity of Workplace Review," *Technical Communication* 38, no. 4 (1991): 520–26.

10. This three-step process is modelled on the one suggested by Barbara L. Shwom and Penny L. Hirsch, "Managing the Drafting Process: Creating a New Model for the Workplace," *The Bulletin of the Association for Business Communication* 57, no. 2 (June 1994): 10.

11. Glenn J. Broadhead and Richard C. Freed, *The Variables of Composition: Process and Product in a Business Setting*, Conference on College Composition and Communication Studies in Writing and Rhetoric (Carbondale, IL: Southern Illinois University Press, 1986), 57.

12. Robert Boice, "Writing Blocks and Tacit Knowledge," *Journal of Higher Education* 64, no. 1 (January/February, 1993), 41–43.

Module 5

1. Linda Reynolds, "The Legibility of Printed Scientific and Technical Information," *Information Design*, ed. Ronald Easterby and Harm Zwaga (New York: Wiley, 1984), 187–208.

2. Once we know how to read English, the brain first looks to see whether an array of letters follows the rules of spelling. If it does, the brain then treats the array as a word (even if it isn't one, such as *tweal*). The shape is processed in individual letters only when the shape is not enough to suggest meaning. Jerry E. Bishop, "Word

Processing: Research on Stroke Victims Yields Clues to the Brain's Capacity to Create Language," *The Wall Street Journal*, October 12, 1993, A6.
3. Jakob Neilsen, "Top Ten Mistakes in Web Design," May 1996, http://222.useit.com/alertbox/9605.html.

Module 7

1. Charles Burck, "Learning from a Master," *Fortune*, December 27, 1993, 144; Kathy Casto, "Assumptions about Audience in Negative Messages," Association for Business Communication Midwest Conference, Kansas City, MO, April 30–May 2, 1987; and John P. Wanous and A. Colella, "Future Directions in Organizational Entry Research," *Research in Personnel/Human Resource Management*, ed. Kenneth Rowland and G. Ferris (Greenwich, CT: JAI Press, 1990).
2. Annette N. Shelby and N. Lamar Reinsch, Jr. "Positive Emphasis and You-Attitude: An Empirical Study, *Journal of Business Communication* 32, no. 4 (October 1995): 303–327.
3. Alan Farnham, "Are You Smart Enough to Keep Your Job?" *Fortune*, January 15, 1996, 42.
4. Mark A. Sherman, "Adjectival Negation and the Comprehension of Multiply Negated Sentences," *Journal of Verbal Learning and Verbal Behavior* 15 (1976): 143–57.
5. Margaret Baker Graham and Carol David, "Power and Politeness: Administrative Writing in an 'Organized Anarchy,'" *Journal of Business and Technical Communication* 10.1 (January 1996): 5–27.
6. John Hagge and Charles Kostelnick, "Linguistic Politeness in Professional Prose: A Discourse Analysis of Auditors' Suggestion Letters, with Implications for Business Communication Pedagogy," *Written Communication* 6, no. 3 (July 1989): 312–39.

Module 8

1. See Tove Helland Hammer and H. Peter Dachler, "A Test of Some Assumptions Underlying the Path-Goal Model of Supervision: Some Suggested Conceptual Modifications," *Organizational Behavior and Human Performance* 14 (1975): 73.
2. Edward E. Lawler, lll, *Motivation in Work Organizations* (Monterey, CA: Brooks/Cole, 1973), 59. Lawler also notes a third obstacle: people may settle for performance and rewards that are just OK. Offering reader benefits, however, does nothing to affect this obstacle.
3. Abraham H. Maslow, *Motivation and Personality* (New York: Harper & Row, 1954).
4. John J. Weger reports Herzberg's research in *Motivating Supervisors* (New York: American Management Association, 1971), 53–54.
5. Barrie McKenna, "Canadians among most disloyal workers in world: U.S. Study," Technology Search Associates, (The Hudson Institute: September 22, 2000); visited Web site June 28, 2001; http://www.hirethebest.net/canadians.htm.
6. Diane L. Coutu, "Human Resources: The Wages of Stress," *Harvard Business Review*, November-December

1998, 21–24; and Charles Fishman, "Sanity, Inc.," *Fast Company*, January 1999, 85–99.
7. Susan Greco, "Hire the Best," *Inc.*, June 1999, 32–52.
8. Kevin Leo, "Effective Copy and Graphics," DADM/DMEF Direct Marketing Institute for Professors, Northbrook, IL, May 31–June 3, 1983.

Module 10

1. In a study of 483 subject lines written by managers and M.B.A. students, Priscilla S. Rogers found that the average subject line was five words; only 10 percent of the subject lines used 10 or more words ("A Taxonomy for Memorandum Subject Lines," *Journal of Business and Technical Communication* 4, no. 2 [September 1990]: 28-29).
2. Richard C. Whitely, *The Customer-Driven Company* (Reading, MA: Addison-Wesley, 1991), 39–40.
3. Deborah Tannen, *That's Not What I Meant: How Conversational Style Makes or Breaks Your Relations with Others* (New York: Morrow, 1986), 108.
4. An earlier version of this problem, the sample solutions, and the discussion appeared in Francis W. Weeks and Kitty O. Locker, *Business Writing Cases and Problems* (Champaign, IL: Stipes, 1980) 40–44.

Module 11

1. Jack W. Brehm, *A Theory of Psychological Reactance* (New York: Academic Press, 1966).
2. Allan Sloan, "The Hit Men," *Newsweek*, February 26, 1996, 48.
3. John D. Pettit, "An Analysis of the Effects of Various Message Presentations on Communicatee Responses," Ph.D. dissertation, Louisiana State University, 1969; and Jack D. Eure, "Applicability of American Written Business Communication Principles Across Cultural Boundaries in Mexico," *The Journal of Business Communication* 14 (1976): 51–63.
4. Lillian H. Chaney and Jeanette S. Martin, *Intercultural Business Communication* (Englewood Cliffs, NJ: Prentice Hall Career and Technology, 1995), 185; and Larry A. Samovar and Richard E. Porter, *Communication Between Cultures* (Belmont, CA: Wadsworth Publishing, 1990), 234–44.
5. Gabriella Stern, "Companies Discover That Some Firings Backfire into Costly Defamation Suits," *The Wall Street Journal*, May 5, 1993, B1.
6. An earlier version of this problem, the sample solutions, and the discussion appeared in Francis W. Weeks and Kitty O. Locker, *Business Writing Cases and Problems* (Champaign, IL: Stipes, 1980), 40–44.

Module 12

1. For a discussion of sales and fund-raising letters, see Kitty O. Locker, *Business and Administrative Communication*, 5th ed. (Burr Ridge: Irwin/McGraw-Hill, 2000), 276–301.
2. Priscilla S. Rogers, "A Taxonomy for the Composition of Memorandum Subject Lines: Facilitating Writer Choice in Managerial Contexts," *Journal of Business and Technical Communication* 4, no. 2 (September 1994): 210–35.

3. Karen Lowry Miller and David Woodruff, "The Man Who's Selling Japan on Jeeps," *Business Week,* July 19, 1993, 56–57.

4. Min-Sun Kim and Steven R. Wilson, "A Cross-Cultural Comparison of Implicit Theories of Requesting," *Communicating Monographics* 61, no. 3 (September 1994): 210–35.

5. J.C. Mathes and Dwight W. Stevenson, *Designing Technical Reports: Writing for Audiences in Organizations* (Indianapolis: Bobbs-Merrill, 1979), 18–19.

6. Daniel J. O'Keefe, Persuasion (Newbury Park, CA: Sage, 1990), 168: Joanne Martin and Melanie E. Powers, "Truth or Corporate Propaganda," *Organizational Symbolism*, ed. Louis R. Pondy, Thomas C. Dandridge, Gareth Morgan, and Peter J. Frost (Greenwich, CT: JAI Press 1983) 97–107; and Dean C. Kazoleas, "A Comparison of the Persuasive Effectiveness of Qualitative versus Quantitative Evidence: A Test of Explanatory Hypotheses," *Communication Quarterly* 41, no. 1 (Winter 1993): 40–50.

7. "Phoning Slow Payers Pays Off," *Inc.,* July 1996, 95.

8. An earlier draft of this problem and analysis appeared in Francis W. Weeks and Kitty O. Locker, *Business Writing Problems and Cases* (Champaign, IL: Stipes, 1980), 78–81.

Module 13

1. Sara Kiesler, Jane Siegel, and Timothy W. McGuire, "Social Psychological Aspects of Computer-Mediated Communication," *American Psychologist* 39, no.10 (October 1984): 1129. People still find it easier to be negative in email than on paper or person; see John Affleck, "You've Got Bad News," Associated Press, June 19, 1999.

2. Bettina A. Bair, "Teaching Technology," email to Kitty Locker, October 22, 1999.

Module 15

1. Caleb Solomon, "Clearing the Air: EPA-Amoco Study of Refinery Finds Pollution Rules Focusing on Wrong Part of It," *The Wall Street Journal*, March 29, 1993, A6.

2. Philip B. Crosby, *Quality Is Free: The Art of Making Quality Certain* (New York: New American Library, 1979), 79–84.

3. *News-Gazette*, Champaign-Urbana, IL, January 16, 1979, C-8.

4. Richard C. Anderson, "Concretization and Sentence Learning," *Journal of Educational Psychology* 66, no. 2 (1974): 179–83.

5. Based on Lynn Ashby, "7, 8 Facilitate," *Houston Post*, February 17, 1978.

6. "Diversity in our Urban Centres: Canada's Ethnicities," Canada Heritage Multiculturalism, visited Web site August 6, 2001; http://www.pch.gc.ca/multi/reports/ann98-99/ethnicities_e.shtml.

Module 16

1. Robert L. Brown, Jr., and Carl G. Herndl, "An Ethnographic Study of Corporal Writing: Job Status as Reflected in Written Text," *Functional Approaches to Writing: A Research Perspective*, ed. Barbara Couture (Norwood, NJ: Ablex, 1986), 16–19, 22–23.

2. Linda Flower, *Problem-Solving Strategies for Writing* (New York: Harcourt Brace Jovanovich, 1981), 39.

3. Harris B. Savin and Ellen Perchonock, "Grammatical Structure and the Immediate Recall of English Sentences," *Journal of Verbal Learning and Verbal Behavior* 4 (1965): 348–53; Pamela Layton and Adrian J. Simpson, "Deep Structure in Sentence Comprehension," *Journal of Verbal Learning and Verbal Behavior* 14 (1975): 658–64.

4. Arn Tibbetts, "Ten Rules for Writing Readably," *The Journal of Business Communcation* 18, no. 4 (Fall 1981): 55–59.

5. Thomas N. Huckin, "A Cognitive Approach to Readability," *New Essays in Technical and Scientific Communication: Research, Theory, Practice*, ed. Paul V. Anderson, R. John Brockmann, and Carolyn R. Miller (Farmingdale, NY: Baywood, 1983), 93–98.

6. James Suchan and Ronald Dulek, "A Reassessment of Clarity in Written Managerial Communications," *Management Communication Quarterly* 4, no. 1 (August 1990): 93-97.

Module 17

1. For a full account of the accident, see Andrew D. Wolvin and Caroline Gwynn Coakely, *Listening*, 2nd ed. (Dubuque, IA: William C. Brown, 1985), 6.

2. "Listen Up and Sell," *Selling Power*, July/August 1999, 34.

3. Thomas Gordon with Judith Gordon Sands, *P.E.T. in Action* (New York: Wyden, 1976), 83.

Module 18

1. "Urban Canadian Office Workers Say That Sharing Information and Collaboration At Work is Becoming More Important," Ipsos Reid Press Release, May 31, 2001; visited Web site June 1, 2001; http://www.angusreid.com/media/content/displayerpr.cfm?id_to_view=1238.

2. Cathy Olofson, "So Many Meetings, So Little Time," *Fast Company*, January/February 2000, 48; Cheryl Dahle, "Sneak Previews Make Good Project Reviews," *Fast Company*, July/August 1999, 66; and Cathy Olofson, "Thank God It's First Friday," *Fast Company*, April 2000, 74.

3. Andrea Williams, "The Rhetoric of Corporate Communications: A Case Study of a Canadian Employee Communications Program in a Global Financial Services Organization," Ph.D. dissertation, The Ohio State University, 2000, Chapter 5.

4. Michael Schrage, "Meetings Don't Have to be Dull," *The Wall Street Journal*, April 29, 1996, A12.

5. Eric Matson, "The Seven Deadly Sins of Meetings," *Fast Company Handbook of the Business Revolution*, 1997, 29.

6. Matson, 30.

7. H. Lloyd Goodall, Jr., *Small Group Communications in Organizations* (Dubuque, IA: William C. Brown, 1985), 39–40.

8. Roger K. Mosvick and Robert B. Nelson, *We've Got to Start Meeting Like This: A Guide to Successful Meeting Management*, rev. ed. (Indianapolis: Park Avenue, 1996), 177.

9. Cynthia Crossen, "Spotting Value Takes Smarts, Not Sight, Laura Sloate Shows," *The Wall Street Journal*, December 10,1987, A1, A14; and Joan E. Rigdon, "Managing Your Career," *The Wall Street Journal*, December 1, 1993, B1.
10. Gina Imperator, "You Have to Start Meeting Like This," *Fast Company*, April 1999, 204–10.
11. Natalie Southworth, "Cyberspace Meetings a Virtual Flop," *The Globe and Mail*, March 1, 2001, T5.

Module 19

1. "Best Employee Traits," Canadian Federation of Independent Business, quoted in *The Globe and Mail*, February 26, 2001, M1.
2. For a fuller listing of roles in groups, see David W. Johnson and Frank P. Johnson, *Joining Together: Group Theory and Group Skills* (Englewood Cliffs, NJ: Prentice Hall, 1975) 26–27.
3. Beatrice Schultz, "Argumentativeness: Its Effects in Group Decision-Making and Its Role in Leadership Perception," *Communication Quarterly* 30, no. 4 (Fall 1982): 374–75; Dennis S. Gouran and B. Aubrey Fisher, "The Functions of Human Communication in the Formation, Maintenance, and Performance of Small Groups," in *Handbook of Rhetorical and Communication Theory*, ed. Carroll C. Arnold and John Waite Bowers (Boston: Allyn and Bacon, 1984), 640; and Curt Bechler and Scott D. Johnson, "Leadership and Listening: A Study of Member Perceptions," *Small Group Research* 26, no. 1 (February 1995): 77–85.
4. Nance L. Harper and Lawrence R. Askling, "Group Communication and Quality of Task Solution in a Media Production Organization," *Communication Monographs* 47, no. 2 (June 1980): 77–100.
5. Rebecca E. Burnett, "Conflict in Collaborative Decision-Making," in *Professional Communication: The Social Perspective*, ed. Nancy Roundy Blyler and Charlotte Thralls (Newbury Park, CA: Sage, 1993), 144–62.
6. Kimberly A. Freeman, "Attitudes Toward Work in Project Groups as Predictors of Academic Performance," *Small Group Research* 27, no. 2 (May 1996): 265–82.
7. Nancy Schullery and Beth Hoger, "Business Advocacy for Students in Small Groups," Association for Business Communication Annual Convention, San Antonia, TX, November 9–11, 1998.
8. Lisa Ede and Andrea Lunsford, *Singular Texts/Plural Authors: Perspectives on Collaborative Writing* (Carbondale, IL: Southern Illinois Press, 1990), 60.
9. Rebecca Burnett, "Characterizing Conflict in Collaborative Relationships: The Nature of Decision-Making During Coauthoring," Ph.D. dissertation, Carnegie-Mellon University, Pittsburgh, PA, 1991.
10. Kitty O. Locker, "What Makes a Collaborative Writing Team Successful? A Case Study of Lawyers and Social Service Workers in a State Agency," in *New Visions in Collaborative Writing*, ed. Janis Forman (Portsmouth, NJ: Boynton, 1991), 37–52.
11. Ede and Lunsford, 66.

12. Meg Morgan, Nancy Allen, Teresa Moore, Dianne Atkinson, and Craig Snow, "Collaborative Writing in the Classroom," *The Bulletin of the Association for Business Communication* 50.3 (September 1987): 22.

Module 20

1. Carol Hymowitz, "When You Tell the Boss, Plain Talk Counts," *The Wall Street Journal*, June 16, 1989, B1.
2. Linda Driskill, "How the Language of Presentations Can Encourage or Discourage Audience Participation," paper presented at the Conference on College Composition and Communication, Cincinnati, OH, March 18–21, 1992.
3. "A Study of the Effects of the Use of Overhead Transparencies on Business Meetings," Wharton Applied Research Center, reported in Martha Jewett and Rita Margolies, eds., *How to Run Better Business Meetings: A Reference Guide for Managers* (New York: McGraw-Hill, 1987), 109–110, 115.
4. Tad Simons, "Multimedia or Bust?" *Presentations*, February 2000, 44, 49–50.
5. Stephen E. Lucas, *The Art of Public Speaking*, 2nd ed. (New York: Random House, 1986), 248.
6. John Case, "A Company of Businesspeople," *Inc.*, April 1993, 90.
7. Edward J. Hegarty, *Humor and Eloquence in Public Speaking* (West Nyack, NY: Packer, 1976), 204.
8. Ray Alexander, Power Speech: *Why It's Vital to You* (New York: AMACOM, 1986), 156.
9. Robert S. Mills, conversation with Kitty O. Locker, March 10, 1988.
10. Phil Thiebert, "Speechwriters of the World, Get Lost!" *The Wall Street Journal*, August 2, 1993, A10.
11. Some studies have shown that previews and reviews increase comprehension; other studies have found no effect. For a summary of the research see Kenneth D. Frandsen and Donald R. Clement, "The Functions of Human Communication in Informing: Communicating and Processing Information," *Handbook of Rhetorical and Communication Theory*, ed. Carroll C. Arnold and John Waite Bowers (Boston: Allyn and Bacon, 1984), 340–41.
12. S.A. Beebe, "Eye Contact: A Nonverbal Determinant of Speaker Credibility," *Speech Teacher* 23 (1974): 21–25; cited in Marjorie Fink Vargas, *Louder than Words* (Ames, IA: Iowa State University Press, 1986), 61–62.
13. J. Wills, "An Empirical Study of the Behavioral Characteristics of Sincere and Insincere Speakers" Ph.D. dissertation, University of Southern California, 1961; cited in Marjorie Fink Vargas, *Louder than Words* (Ames, IA: Iowa State University Press, 1986), 62.

Module 21

1. For a useful taxonomy of proposals, see Richard C. Freed and David D. Roberts, "The Nature, Classification, and Generic Structure of Proposals," *Journal of Technical Writing and Communication* 19, no. 4 (1989): 317–51.
2. Christine Peterson Barabas, *Technical Writing in a Corporate Culture: A Study of the Nature of Information* (Norwood, NJ: Ablex Publishing, 1990), 327.

Module 22

1. Janice M. Lauer and J. William Asher, *Composition Research: Empirical Designs* (New York: Oxford University Press, 1986), 66.
2. Frederick F. Reichheld, "Learning from Customer Defects," *Harvard Business Review*, March–April 1996, 56–69.
3. Cynthia Crossen, "Margin of Error: Studies Galore Support Products and Positions, But Are They Reliable?" *The Wall Street Journal*, November 14, 1991, A1, A7.
4. Cynthia Crossen, "Diaper Debate: A Case Study of Tactical Research," *The Wall Street Journal*, May 27, 1994, B8.
5. "Whirlpool: How to Listen to Consumers," *Fortune*, January 11, 1993, 77.
6. Peter Lynch with John Rothchild, *One Up on Wall Street: How to Use What You Already Know to Make Money in the Market* (New York: Simon and Schuster, 1989), 187.
7. Patricia Sullivan, "Reporting Negative Research Results," and Kitty O. Locker to Pat Sullivan, June 8, 1990.

Module 23

1. Stephanie Nolan, "Dot-com this!" *The Globe and Mail*, August 28, 2000, R1.
2. Michael L. Keene to Kitty Locker, May 17, 1988.
3. Susan D. Kleimann, "The Need to Test Forms in the Real World," Association for Business Communication Annual Convention, Orlando FL, November 1-4, 1995.

Module 25

1. Gene Zelazny, *Say It with Charts: The Executive's Guide to Successful Presentations*, 2nd ed. (Burr Ridge, IL: IPRO, 1981), 52.
2. Most of these guidelines are given by Zelazny, *Say It with Charts: The Executive's Guide to Successful Presentations*.
3. W. S. Cleveland and R. McGill, "Graphical Perception: Theory, Experiments, and Application to the Development of Graphic Methods," *Journal of the American Statistical Association* 79, no. 3 & 7 (1984): 531–53; cited in Jeffry K. Cochran, Sheri A. Albrecht, and Yvonne A. Greene, "Guidelines for Evaluating Graphical Designs: A Framework Based on Human Perception Skills," *Technical Communication* 36, no. 1 (February 1989): 27.
4. L.G. Thorell and W. J. Smith, *Using Computer Color Effectively: An Illustrated Reference* (Englewood Cliffs, NJ: Prentice Hall, 1990), 12–13; William Horton, "The Almost Universal Language: Graphics for International Documents," *Technical Communication* 40, no. 4 (1993): 687; and Thyra Rauch, "IBM Visual Interface Design," *The STC Usability PIC Newsletter*, January 1996, 3.
5. Thorell and Smith, p.13.
6. Ibid., 49–51, 214–15.
7. Edward R. Tufte, *The Visual Display of Quantitative Information* (Cheshire, CT: Graphics Press, 1983), 113.
8. Thophilus Addo, "The Effects of Dimensionality in Computer Graphics," *Journal of Business Communication* 31, no. 4 (October 1994): 253–65.

Module 26

Module 27

1. Timothy D. Schellhardt, "Managing Pitfalls to Avoid in Drafting a Résumé," *The Wall Street Journal*, November 28, 1990, B1; Elizabeth Brockman and Kelly Belanger, "A National Study of CPA Recruiters' Preferences for Résumé Length," *The Journal of Business Communication*, January 2001.
2. Beverly H. Nelson, William P. Gallé, and Donna W. Luse, "Electronic Job Search and Placement," Association for Business Communication Convention, Orlando FL, November 1–4, 1995.
3. Rebecca Smith, *Electronic Résumés & Online Networking: How to Use the Internet to Do a Better Job Search, Including a Complete, Up-to-Date Resource Guide* (Franklin Lakes, NJ: Career Press, 1999), 191–96.
4. Taunee Besson, *The Wall Street Journal National Employment Business Weekly: Resumes* (New York: John Wiley and Sons, 1994), 245.

Module 28

1. Michael Van Aelst as quoted by Bertin Oliver, "Sleeman brew balance of risk and caution," *The Globe and Mail*, June 20, 2001, M1.

Module 29

1. Thomas Petzinger, Jr., "Lewis Roland's Knack for Finding Truckers Keeps Firm Rolling," *The Wall Street Journal*, December 1, 1995, B1.
2. Claud Dotson, comment, Association for Business Communication Western Regional Conference, Boise, ID, April 13, 1996; and Julie Amparano Lopez, "Choosy Firms Force Jobs Seekers to Jump Through Many Hoops," *The Wall Street Journal*, October 6, 1993, B4.
3. Judith A. Swartley to Kitty Locker, March 20, 1989.
4. Sherri Eng, "Company Culture Dictates Attire for Interviews," The *Columbus Dispatch*, August 25, 1996, 33J.
5. The Catalyst Staff, *Marketing Yourself* (New York: G. P. Putnam's Sons, 1980), 179.
6. Richard C. Rose and Echo Montgomery Garrett, "Guerrilla Interviewing," *Inc.* December, 1992, 145–47.
7. Julie Amparano Lopez, "Firms Force Job Seekers to Jump through Hoops," *The Wall Street Journal*, October 6, 1993, B1.
8. Sue Shellenbarger, "New Job Hunters Ask Recruiters, 'Is There Life After Work?'" *The Wall Street Journal*, January 29, 1996, B1; and Sue Shellenbarger, "What Job Candidates Really Want to Know: Will I Have a Life?" *The Wall Street Journal*, November 17, 1999, B1.
9. Donna Stine Kienzler, letter to Ann Granacki, April 6, 1988.
10. Joel Bowman, "Using NLP to Improve Classroom Communication," Association for Business Communication Regional Conference, Lexington, KY, April 9–11, 1992.
11. Christopher Conte, "Labor Letter," *The Wall Street Journal*, October 19, 1993, A1.

Module 30

1. The Catalyst Staff, *Marketing Yourself* (New York: G. P. Putnam's Sons, 1980), 101.
2. Claud Dotson, comment at the Association for Business Communication Western Regional Conference, Boise, ID, April 13, 1996.
3. Kate Weldon, *Through the Brick Wall: How to Job-Hunt in a Tight Market* (New York: Villard Books, 1992), 244.
4. Carol A. Hacker, *Job Hunting in the 21st Century: Exploding the Myths, Exploring the Realities*, (Boca Raton: St. Lucie Press, 1999), 154.
5. Ray Robinson, quoted by Dick Friedman, "The Interview as Mating Ritual," *Working Woman*, April 1987, 107.
6. Albert R. Karr, "Work Week," *The Wall Street Journal*, November 16, 1999, A1.

Index

A

Abdurhman, Ilias, 57
academic writing, *vs.* business
    communication, 7–8
Accoutemps, 491
accurate messages, 13
acknowledgement responses, 367
active
    listening, 362, 364–365, 367
    verbs, 343–345
    voice, 118
Adams, Michael, 257, 461
adjectives, 548
adjustments, 199–200
adverbs, 548
Advertising Age magazine, 249, 327
African American culture, 64
ageism, 69–70
agendas, 378, 381
Alariaq, Kristiina, 53
Alariaq, Timmun, 53
Allen, Robert, 4
Alliance of Canadian Manufacturers and
    Exporters, 541
alternatives, 226–228
alternatives, elimination of, 473
although, 24
American spelling, 301
Amiskwaciy Academy, 57
analytical reports, 433, 476–477
annual reports, 488
APA format, 462–464
apologies, 142–143
apostrophe, 308–309
Arbeláez, Brenda, 66
arrogant tone, 257
asianconnections.com, 54
assessment, 82
Association for Canadian Studies, 58
assumptions, 363–364
Atlantic Progress magazine survey, 581
attachments, and viruses, 289
audience
    analysis, use of, 40–42
    business communication, 7
    and business messages, 31–32
    and communication process, 28–31
    critical thinking, 33
    demographic factors, 34
    different needs, 41–42
    empathy, 33
    external, 9, 12
    gatekeeper, 28
    as group members, 33–34
    identification of, 15, 28
    importance of, 28
    as individuals, 33–34
    initial, 28
    internal, 9, 12
    international. *See* international audience
    knowledge of, 32–33
    large, 43
    letters, 168
    memos, 168
    PAIBOC questions, 31–32
    past behaviour, 37
    personality, 35
    primary, 28
    prior knowledge, 34

psychographic characteristics, 35–36
    questions from, 423–424
    reaching your audience, 42–43
    reaction, analysis of`, 37
    reader benefits, matching, 158
    remember your, 151
    secondary, 28
    talking to, as planning, 86–87
    testing designs, 109–110
    watchdog, 28

B

background, 492
bad news messages. *See* negative messages
bar chart, 518, 520–521
Battered Women's Advocacy Clinic, 361
because, 24
behavioural interviews, 612–614
behavioural styles, assessment of, 63
beliefs, 35–36, 56–58
Bell Canada, 42
benefits to readers. *See* reader benefits
Bernard Haldane Associates, 621
better writing, benefits of, 13–14
bias-free language
    definition, 66–67
    negative terms, 70
    nonagist language, 69–70
    nonracist language, 69–70
    nonsexist language, 67–69
black Canadians, 57
blind copies, 176
block format, 168, 172, 179
blocking responses, 365
blueprints, 478
Bocchini, Chris, 601
body language, 59–60
Boice, Jacklyn, 419
Boice, Robert, 93
boilerplate, 93
Bolles, Richard, 534
Bolt, Kathryn, 258
Booher, Dianna, 91
Boyd, Marion, 361
brainstorm, 84, 152
Brehm, Jack W., 226, 228
Broker, Ruth A., 64
Brown, Nancy, 579
budgets, 442
buffer, 221–224
Buffett, Warren, 341, 342
bullets, 102
Burnett, Rebecca, 395
business communication
    vs. academic writing, 7
    analysis of situations, 14–16
    audience, 7
    and culture, 56
    definition of, 7–8
    information, 7
    intercultural. *See* culture; diversity
    layout, 8
    organization, 7
    purpose, 7, 9, 12
    style, 8
    visuals, 8
    Web sites, 84
business jargon, 330
business plan Web sites, 442

business slang, 330
business travellers Web site, 326
Business Writer's Free Library, 231
businessese, 330
buying time, 400
bypassing, 326

C

Cameco Corporation, 151
Canada Post Web site, 171
Canada's Vehicle Information Centre Web
    site, 460
Canadian Association for Labour Media
    (2000), 101
Canadian Biotechnology Company Directory, 542
Canadian Centre for Mediation, 471
Canadian Charter of Rights and Freedoms, 54
Canadian government bidding
    opportunities, 442
Canadian government organizations
    Web site, 490
Canadian identity, 54–55
Canadian Labour Congress, 375
Canadian linguistic and cultural diversity
    study, 61
Canadian provinces, postal abbreviations, 177
Canadian spelling, 301
Canadian values, 54, 56
CANDIDATECH Placing Firm Inc., 542
Cantle, Paige, 487
Cantle Communications, 487
Cape Dorset Print Gallery, 53
Capelli, Paul, 38
career achievements, 566–567
Career Lab's Cover Letter Library, 581
career objective, 566
Caribbean and African Canadian Chamber of
    Commerce, 57
case, 302–303
Casselman, Cindy, 158
causation, 462
CD-ROM databases, 454
cellphone use, 433
Center for the Study of Work Teams, 394
Centre of Forensic Sciences (Ontario), 515
Cerner Corporation, 28
chair's role in meetings, 380
channel
    communication process, 30
    large audiences, 43
    multiple, 42–43
    overload, 30
chartjunk, 522
Chatman, Jennifer, 39
Chesney, Kimberley, 533
choice
    of details, 42
    forced, 623–624, 625
    of information, 30
choppy prose, 371
Christopher, Robert, 61
chronological
    oral presentations, 420
    progress reports, 444–445
    résumés, 554, 555, 560–561
    short report, 474
Cigna, 570
citation, 463